T0220780

Lecture Notes
in Business Information Processing   **387**

Series Editors

Wil van der Aalst ⓘ
  RWTH Aachen University, Aachen, Germany
John Mylopoulos ⓘ
  University of Trento, Trento, Italy
Michael Rosemann ⓘ
  Queensland University of Technology, Brisbane, QLD, Australia
Michael J. Shaw
  University of Illinois, Urbana-Champaign, IL, USA
Clemens Szyperski
  Microsoft Research, Redmond, WA, USA

Selmin Nurcan · Iris Reinhartz-Berger ·
Pnina Soffer · Jelena Zdravkovic (Eds.)

Enterprise, Business-Process and Information Systems Modeling

21st International Conference, BPMDS 2020
25th International Conference, EMMSAD 2020
Held at CAiSE 2020, Grenoble, France, June 8–9, 2020
Proceedings

 Springer

Editors
Selmin Nurcan 🆔
University Paris 1
Paris, France

Pnina Soffer 🆔
University of Haifa
Haifa, Israel

Iris Reinhartz-Berger 🆔
University of Haifa
Haifa, Israel

Jelena Zdravkovic 🆔
Stockholm University
Kista, Sweden

ISSN 1865-1348   ISSN 1865-1356   (electronic)
Lecture Notes in Business Information Processing
ISBN 978-3-030-49417-9   ISBN 978-3-030-49418-6   (eBook)
https://doi.org/10.1007/978-3-030-49418-6

This Springer imprint is published by the registered company Springer Nature Switzerland AG
The registered company address is: Gewerbestrasse 11, 6330 Cham, Switzerland

Preface

This book contains the proceedings of two long-running events held along with the CAiSE conference relating to the areas of enterprise, business-process and information systems modeling: the 21st International Conference on Business Process Modeling, Development and Support (BPMDS 2020) and the 25th International Conference on Exploring Modeling Methods for Systems Analysis and Development (EMMSAD 2020). The two working conferences had a joint keynote on "Automated Process Improvement: Status, Challenges, and Perspectives" given by Marlon Dumas, Professor of Information Systems at Institute of Computer Science, University of Tartu. More information on the individual events and their selection processes can be found below.

BPMDS 2020

BPMDS has been held as a series of workshops devoted to business process modeling, development, and support since 1998. During this period, business process analysis and design has been recognized as a central issue in the area of information systems (IS) engineering. The continued interest in these topics on behalf of the IS community is reflected by the success of the last BPMDS events and the recent emergence of new conferences and workshops devoted to the theme. In 2011, BPMDS became a two-day working conference attached to CAiSE (Conference on Advanced Information Systems Engineering). The goals, format, and history of BPMDS can be found on the website http://www.bpmds.org/.

In 2020, BPMDS took place virtually as an online event, keeping the general spirit and principles of BPMDS.

The intention of BPMDS is to solicit papers related to business process modeling, development, and support (BPMDS) in general, using quality as a main selection criterion. As a working conference, we aim to attract papers describing mature research, but we still give place to industrial reports and visionary idea papers. To encourage new and emerging challenges and research directions in the area of business process modeling, development, and support, we have a unique focus theme every year. Papers submitted as idea papers are required to be of relevance to the focus theme, thus providing a mass of new ideas around a relatively narrow but emerging research area. Full research papers and experience reports do not necessarily need to be directly connected to this theme (they still needed to be explicitly relevant to BPMDS though).

The focus theme for BPMDS 2020 idea papers was "BPM meets data." For the 21st edition of the BPMDS conference, we invited the interested authors to address, through their idea papers and the online discussions held during the two days of BPMDS 2020, issues related to the intersection between business processes and data. These relations can be viewed along the business process life-cycle:

- Designing and modeling data-aware processes
- Integrating and incorporating different kinds and sources of data in process execution environments (IoT, blockchain, network traffic)
- Monitoring, assessing performance and conformance, and predicting the outcomes of running processes using the data they generate
- Creating process models from various sources of data through process discovery

BPMDS 2020 received 30 submissions from 19 countries (Australia, Austria, Brazil, Canada, Estonia, France, Germany, Iraq, Italy, Paraguay, Portugal, Slovenia, South Africa, Spain, Switzerland, Tunisia, Ukraine, Uruguay, and the USA). The management of paper submission and reviews was supported by the EasyChair conference system. Each paper received at least three reviews. Eventually, 13 high-quality full papers and 1 short paper were selected. These include two idea papers and one experience report.

The accepted papers cover a wide spectrum of issues related to business process modeling, development, and support. They are organized under the following section headings:

- Business process execution and monitoring
- BPM applications in industry and practice
- Planning and scheduling in business processes
- Process mining
- Process models and visualizations

We wish to thank all the people who submitted papers to BPMDS 2020 for having shared their work with us, as well as the members of the BPMDS 2020 Program Committee, who made a remarkable effort in reviewing submissions.

We also thank the organizers of CAiSE 2020 for their help with the organization of the event, particularly adjusting to the changing circumstances during the global crisis and facilitating the transformation to a virtual event. We also thank IFIP WG8.1 for the support, and Springer and OCS for their kind assistance for the production of the proceedings.

April 2020

Selmin Nurcan
Pnina Soffer

EMMSAD 2020

The objective of the EMMSAD conference series is to provide a forum for researchers and practitioners interested in modeling methods for Systems Analysis and Development (SA&D) to meet and exchange research ideas and results. The conference aims to provide home for a rich heritage of modeling paradigms, including software modeling, business process modeling, enterprise modeling, capability modeling, ontology modeling, and domain-specific modeling. These important paradigms, and specific methods following them, continue to be enriched with extensions, refinements, and even new languages, to address new challenges. Even with some attempts to standardize, new modeling methods are constantly being introduced, especially in order to deal with emerging trends and challenges. Ongoing changes significantly impact the way systems are being analyzed and designed in practice. Moreover, they challenge the empirical and analytical evaluation of the modeling methods, which aims to contribute to the knowledge and understanding of their strengths and weaknesses. This knowledge may guide researchers towards the development of the next generation of modeling methods and help practitioners select the modeling methods most appropriate to their needs.

This year, EMMSAD 2020 took a virtual form. We continued with the five tracks which emphasize the variety of EMMSAD topics:

1. Foundations of modeling & method engineering – chaired by Jolita Ralyté and Janis Stirna
2. Enterprise, business process & capability modeling – chaired by Jānis Grabis and Paul Grefen
3. Information systems & requirements modeling – chaired by Oscar Pastor and Marcela Ruiz
4. Domain-specific & ontology modeling – chaired by Dimitris Karagiannis and Arnon Sturm
5. Evaluation of modeling approaches – chaired by Agnes Koschmider and Geert Poels

More details can be found at http://www.emmsad.org/.

29 submissions were received from 20 countries (Algeria, Austria, Bosnia and Herzegovina, Brazil, Canada, China, Estonia, France, Israel, Germany, Latvia, The Netherlands, Pakistan, Portugal, South Africa, Spain, Sweden, Switzerland, Turkey, and the USA). The division of submissions among tracks was as follows (a single paper could be categorized into multi tracks): 5 submissions related to foundations of modeling & method engineering; 10 to enterprise, business process & capability modeling; 15 to information systems & requirements modeling; to domain-specific & ontology modeling; and 5 to evaluation of modeling approaches. After a rigorous review process, which included 3 or 4 reviews per submission, 15 high-quality (11 long and 4 short) papers were selected. They were divided into 5 sections as follows:

1. Requirements & method engineering:

   - Onat Ege Adali, Oktay Turetken, Baris Ozkan, Rick Gilsing, and Paul Grefen: "A Multi-Concern Method for Identifying Business Services: A Situational Method Engineering Study"
   - Prince Singh, Luuk Veelenturf, and Tom van Woensel: "Modeling Complex Business Environments for Context Aware Systems"
   - Sara Perez-Soler, Gwendal Daniel, Jordi Cabot, Esther Guerra, and Juan De Lara: "Towards Automating the Synthesis of Chatbots for Conversational Model Query" (short paper)

2. Enterprise & business modeling:

   - Georgios Koutsopoulos, Martin Henkel, and Janis Stirna: "Conceptualizing Capability Change"
   - Kurt Sandkuhl and Janis Stirna: "Supporting Early Phases of Digital Twin Development with Enterprise Modeling and Capability Management: Requirements from Two Industrial Cases"
   - Jānis Grabis: "Integrated On-demand Modeling for Configuration of Trusted ICT Supply Chains" (short paper)

3. Software-related modeling:

   - Florian Rademacher, Sabine Sachweh, and Albert Zündorf: "A Modeling Method for Systematic Architecture Reconstruction of Microservice-Based Software Systems"
   - Marcela Ruiz and Björn Hasselman: "Can We Design Software as We Talk?" (short paper)
   - Luiz Marcio Cysneiros and Julio Cesar Leite: "Non-Functional Requirements Orienting the Development of Socially Responsible Software" (short paper)

4. Domain-specific modeling:

   - Roman Lukyanenko: "A journey to BSO: Evaluating Earlier and More Recent Ideas of Mario Bunge as a Foundation for Information and Software Development"
   - Thomas Gray, Dominik Bork, and Marne De Vries: "A New DEMO Modelling Tool that Facilitates Model Transformations"
   - Sabine Molenaar, Laura Schiphorst, Metehan Doyran, Albert Salah, Fabiano Dalpiaz, and Sjaak Brinkkemper: "Reference Method for the Development of Domain Action Recognition Classifiers: the Case of Medical Consultations"

5. Evaluation-related research:

   - Ben Roelens and Dominik Bork: "An Evaluation of the Intuitiveness of the PGA Modeling Language Notation"
   - Mouaad Hafsi and Said Assar: "Does Enterprise Architecture support Customer Experience Improvement? Towards a Conceptualization in Digital Transformation Context"

- Rick Gilsing, Anna Wilbik, Paul Grefen, Oktay Turetken, and Baris Ozkan: "A Formal Basis for Business Model Evaluation with Linguistic Summaries"

We wish to thank EMMSAD 2020 authors for having shared their work with us, as well as the members of EMMSAD 2020 Program Committee for their valuable reviews in the difficult times of COVID-19 epidemic. Special thanks go to the track chairs for their help in EMMSAD advertising and submission attraction. Finally, we thank the organizers of CAiSE 2020 for their help with the organization of the event, IFIP WG8.1 for its support, and Springer staff (especially Ralf Gerstner, Christine Reiss, and OCS support).

April 2020   Iris Reinhartz-Berger
                                              Jelena Zdravkovic

BPMDS 2020 Organization

Program Chairs

Selmin Nurcan   Université Paris 1 Panthéon Sorbonne, France
Pnina Soffer   University of Haifa, Israel

Steering Committee

Ilia Bider   Stockholm University, IbisSoft, Sweden
Selmin Nurcan   Université Paris 1 Panthéon Sorbonne, France
Rainer Schmidt   Munich University of Applied Sciences, Germany
Pnina Soffer   University of Haifa, Israel

Industrial Advisory Board

Ilia Bider   Stockholm University, IbisSoft, Sweden
Pascal Negros   Arch4IE, France
Gil Regev   EPFL, Itecor, Switzerland

Program Committee

João Paulo A. Almeida   Federal University of Espírito Santo, Brazil
Eric Andonoff   Université Toulouse 1, France
Saïd Assar   Institut-Mines, Télécom Business School, France
Judith Barrios Albornoz   University de Los Andes, Venezuela
Ilia Bider   Stockholm University, IbisSoft, Sweden
Karsten Boehm   FH KufsteinTirol, Austria
Cristina Cabanillas   Vienna University of Economics and Business, Austria
Claudio di Ciccio   Vienna University of Economics and Business, Austria
Dirk Fahland   Eindhoven University of Technology, The Netherlands
Claude Godard   Université de Lorraine, France
Renata Guizzardi   Federal University of Espírito Santo, Brazil
Jens Gulden   Utrecht University, The Netherlands
Amin Jalali   Stockholm University, Sweden
Marite Kirikova   Riga Technical University, Latvia
Agnes Koschmider   Kiel University, Germany
Henrik Leopold   Kühne Logistics University, Germany
Jan Mendling   Vienna University of Economics and Business, Austria
Michael Möhring   Munich University of Applied Sciences, Germany
Pascal Negros   Arch4IE, France
Oscar Pastor   Universitat Polytechnica de Valencia, Spain
Gil Regev   EPFL, Itecor, Switzerland

Manfred Reichert   Ulm University, Germany
Hajo Reijers   Utrecht University, The Netherlands
Iris Reinhartz-Berger   University of Haifa, Israel
Colette Rolland   Université Paris 1 Panthéon-Sorbonne, France
Michael Rosemann   Queensland University of Technology, Australia
Marcella Ruiz   Zurich University of Applied Sciences, Switzerland
Rainer Schmidt   Munich University of Applied Sciences, Germany
Stefan Schönig   University of Bayreuth, Germany
Samira Si-Said Cherfi   CNAM, France
Irene Vanderfeesten   Eindhoven University, The Netherlands
Han van der Aa   Humboldt University of Berlin, Germany
Barbara Weber   Technical University of Denmark, Denmark
Jelena Zdravkovic   Stockholm University, Sweden
Alfred Zimmermann   Reutlingen University, Germany

Additional Reviewers

Inge van de Weerd   Utrecht University, The Netherlands
Jan Martijn van der Werf   Utrecht University, The Netherlands
Dominik Janssen   Kiel University, Germany
Sebastian Steinau   Ulm University, Germany

EMMSAD 2020 Organization

Program Chairs

Iris Reinhartz-Berger   University of Haifa, Israel
Jelena Zdravkovic   Stockholm University, Sweden

Track Chairs

Janis Grabis   Riga Technical University, Latvia
Paul Grefen   Eindhoven University of Technology, The Netherlands
Dimitris Karagiannis   University of Vienna, Austria
Agnes Koschmider   Kiel University, Germany
Oscar Pastor Lopez   Universitat Politècnica de València, Spain
Geert Poels   Ghent University, Belgium
Jolita Ralyté   University of Geneva, Switzerland
Marcela Ruiz   Zurich University of Applied Sciences, Switzerland
Janis Stirna   Stockholm University, Sweden
Arnon Sturm   Ben-Gurion University, Israel

Program Committee

Giuseppe Berio   Université de Bretagne Sud, France
Ghassan Beydoun   University of Technology Sydney, Australia
Dominik Bork   University of Vienna, Austria
Drazen Brdjanin   University of Banja Luka, Bosnia and Herzegovina
Tony Clark   Aston University, UK
Nelly Condori-Fernández   Universidade da Coruña, Spain
Sergio de Cesare   University of Westminster, UK
Mahdi Fahmideh   University of Wollongong, Australia
Michael Fellmann   University of Rostock, Germany
Christophe Feltus   Luxembourg Institute of Science and Technology, Luxembourg
Peter Fettke   Saarland University, Germany
Hans-Georg Fill   University of Fribourg, France
Ulrich Frank   Universität Duisburg-Essen, Germany
Frederik Gailly   Ghent University, Belgium
Mohamad Gharib   University of Florence, Italy
Asif Qumer Gill   University of Technology Sydney, Australia
Cesar Gonzalez-Perez   Spanish National Research Council, Spain
Sérgio Guerreiro   University of Lisbon, Portugal
Renata Guizzardi   Universidade Federal do Espirito Santo, Brazil
Martin Henkel   Stockholm University, Sweden

Jennifer Horkoff	Chalmers and the University of Gothenburg, Sweden
Ivan Jureta	University of Namur, Belgium
Jānis Kampars	Riga Technical University, Latvia
Evangelia Kavakli	University of the Aegean, Greece
Marite Kirikova	Riga Technical University, Latvia
Dimitris Kiritsis	EPFL, Switzerland
Elena Kornyshova	CNAM, France
Thomas Kuehne	Victoria University of Wellington, New Zealand
Birger Lantow	University of Rostock, Germany
Tong Li	Beijing University of Technology, China
Raimundas Matulevicius	University of Tartu, Estonia
John Mylopoulos	University of Toronto, Canada
Andreas L. Opdahl	University of Bergen, Norway
Elda Paja	IT University of Copenhagen, Denmark
Klaus Pohl	Paluno, University of Duisburg-Essen, Germany
Irina Rychkova	University of Paris 1 Pantheon-Sorbonne, France
Mattia Salnitri	Politecnico di Milano, Italy
Kurt Sandkuhl	University of Rostock, Germany
Monique Snoeck	Katholieke Universiteit Leuven, Belgium
Steven van Kervel	Formetis BV, The Netherlands
Yves Wautelet	Katholieke Universiteit Leuven, Belgium
Hans Weigand	Tilburg University, The Netherlands
Carson Woo	The University of British Columbia, Canada
Anna Zamansky	University of Haifa, Israel
Didar Zowghi	University of Technology Sydney, Australia

Additional Reviewers

Michael Poppe	University of Rostock, Germany
Fabienne Lambusch	University of Rostock, Germany
Felix Härer	University of Fribourg, France
Florian Johannsen	University of Regensburg, Germany

Automated Process Improvement: Status, Challenges, and Perspectives (Keynote Abstract)

Marlon Dumas

University of Tartu, Estonia
marlon.dumas@ut.ee

Business processes are the operational backbone of modern organizations. Their continuous management and improvement is key to the achievement of business objectives. Accordingly, a common task for managers and analysts is to discover, assess, and exploit process improvement opportunities. Current approaches to discover process improvement opportunities are expert-driven. In these approaches, data are used to assess opportunities derived from experience and intuition rather than to discover them in the first place. Moreover, as the assessment of opportunities is manual, analysts can only explore a fraction of the overall space of improvement opportunities.

Recent advances in machine learning and artificial intelligence are making it possible to move from manual to automated (or semi-automated) approaches to business process improvement. This talk will present a vision for the emerging field of AI-driven automated process improvement. The talk will focus on three families of methods: (1) predictive process monitoring; (2) robotic process mining; and (3) search-based process optimization.

Predictive process monitoring methods allow us to analyze ongoing executions of a process in order to predict future states and undesirable outcomes at runtime. These predictions can be used to trigger interventions in order to maximize a given reward function, for example by generating alerts or making recommendations to process workers. The talk will provide a taxonomy of the state of the art in this field, as well as open questions and possible research directions.

Robotic process mining seeks to analyze logs generated by user interactions in order to discover repetitive routines (e.g. clerical routines) that are fully deterministic and can therefore be automated via Robotic Process Automation (RPA) scripts. These scripts are executed by software bots, with minimal user supervision, thus relieving workers from tedious and error-prone work. The talk will present initial results in the field of robotic process mining and discuss challenges and opportunities.

Finally, the talk will introduce a gestating family of methods for search-based process optimization. These techniques rely on multi-objective optimization algorithms in conjunction with data-driven process simulation, in order to discover sets of changes to one or more business processes, which maximize one or more performance measures. The talk will present a framework for search-based process optimization and will sketch approaches that could be explored to realize the vision of a recommender system for process improvement.

Short Bio of the Speaker

Marlon Dumas is Professor of Information Systems at University of Tartu, Estonia and Co-Founder of Apromore Pty Ltd - a company dedicated to developing and commercialising an open-source process mining solution. He is recipient of an Advanced Grant from the European Research Council with the mission of developing algorithms for automated discovery of business process improvement opportunities. His research in the field of business process management and process mining has led to over 300 research publications, 10 best paper awards, 10 US/EU patents, and a textbook (Fundamentals of Business Process Management) used in close to 300 universities worldwide.

Contents

Process Models and Visualizations (BPMDS 2020)

Requirements and Method Engineering (EMMSAD 2020)

Enterprise and Business Modeling (EMMSAD 2020)

Software-Related Modeling (EMMSAD 2020)

Domain-Specific Modeling (EMMSAD 2020)

Evaluation-Related Research (EMMSAD 2020)

Business Process Execution and Monitoring (BPMDS 2020)

Dynamically Switching Execution Context in Data-Centric BPM Approaches

Kevin Andrews[✉], Sebastian Steinau, and Manfred Reichert

Institute of Databases and Information Systems, Ulm University, Ulm, Germany
{kevin.andrews,sebastian.steinau,manfred.reichert}@uni-ulm.de

Abstract. In contemporary business process management software, the context in which a process is executed is largely static. While the execution of the process itself may be flexible, on-the-fly changes to the context, i.e., physical or logical surroundings, are either limited or impossible. This paper presents concepts for enabling context switching at runtime for the object-aware process management paradigm. Such context switches are enabled at various granularity levels, such as shifting entire process instances to different systems, or migrating sub-processes between different parent processes. We further contribute the algorithms employed in our proof-of-concept implementation and discuss use cases in which context switching capabilities can be utilized. Implementing these advanced concepts helps showcase the maturity of data-centric BPM.

Keywords: Object-aware processes · BPM · Process context switching

1 Introduction

The context in which a process is executed determines essential factors at runtime. These range from trivial ones, e.g. whether or not a process may be executed, to complex factors, such as the selection of sub-process variants at runtime. Making business process management systems (BPMS) *context-aware* increases the flexibility of processes they execute by supporting business rules that are enforced based on the context [1]. Informally, process context is defined as "the minimum set of variables containing all relevant information that impacts the design and execution of a business process" [2], which emphasizes the importance of context for process execution. However, contemporary BPMS do not allow changing the execution context of running process instances, even though this would increase flexibility. Consider a recruitment process from the HR domain, in which applicants apply for a job offer, as an example in which flexibility could be increased by allowing for process context switches at runtime. More specifically, the context of a job application process corresponds to the job offer an applicant applies to, as well as meta information such as the department the respective job is allocated to. Furthermore, consider an unsolicited application.

© Springer Nature Switzerland AG 2020
S. Nurcan et al. (Eds.): BPMDS 2020/EMMSAD 2020, LNBIP 387, pp. 3–19, 2020.
https://doi.org/10.1007/978-3-030-49418-6_1

In the first case, while the context of the application process seems to be clear at the beginning, during the course of a job interview, it might be decided that the applicant would better fit a different job at another department. In the second case, parts of the context, such as a concrete job offer, are missing entirely and can only be determined after the process starts. Although both cases can be partially handled in an activity-centric BPMS by adding gateways and loops into the process model, this would make the process model unnecessarily complex. Therefore, most companies handle cases like these by forcing applicants to resubmit their application to a different job offer, which, in future, might cause confusion due to multiple applications from the same person.

This paper presents solutions to these issues for object-aware BPM, a data-centric process management paradigm, by enabling dynamic process context switches without requiring process model changes. The paper builds upon previous work that led to the development of the PHILharmonicFlows process engine and contributes fundamental research into the notion of process context in data-centric BPM paradigms. The fundamentals of object-aware BPM are explained in Sect. 2. The notion of process context in object-aware processes is examined in Sect. 3. The concepts and algorithms for enabling context switching are presented in Sect. 4. An overview of our prototype implementation is given in Sect. 5. Section 6 discusses related work and Sect. 7 summarizes the paper.

2   Backgrounds

The PHILharmonicFlows implementation of object-aware BPM, a data-centric BPM paradigm, has been under development for many years and serves as a testbed for the concepts presented in this paper [3,4]. PHILharmonicFlows takes the idea of a data-driven BPMS and enhances it with the concept of *objects*. An *object* describes the structure of its contained data and process logic at design-time whereas an *object instance* holds concrete data values and executes the process logic at runtime. This may be compared to the concept of a table and its rows in a relational database. For each business object present in a real-world business process one such object exists. We further examine the concept of objects utilizing an *Application* object from the HR domain. As can be seen in Fig. 1, the object consists of data, in the form of *attributes*, and a state-based process model describing the data-driven *object lifecycle*.

As object-aware BPM is *data-driven*, the lifecycle execution of an instance of the *Application* object is as follows: The initial state is *Created*. Once an *Applicant* has entered data for attributes *Job Offer*, *Applicant*, and *CV*, he or she may trigger the transition to the *Sent* state. This causes the *Application* to change its state to *Sent*, in which it waits until the reviewing period is over,

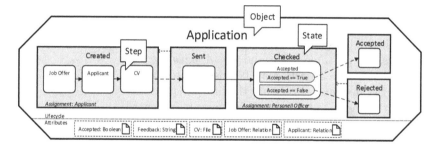

Fig. 1. Example object including lifecycle process (Application)

after which it automatically enters state *Checked*. As *Checked* is assigned to a *Personnel Officer*, a user with that role must input data for the *Accepted* attribute. Based on the value of *Accepted*, the state either changes to *Accepted* or *Rejected*.

This fine-grained approach to modeling the processing of a single business object increases complexity compared to the activity-centric paradigm, where the minimum granularity of a user action corresponds to one atomic "black box" activity, instead of an individual data attribute. However, as one of the major benefits, the object-aware approach allows for *automated form generation* at runtime. This is facilitated by the lifecycle process of an object, which dictates the attributes to be filled out before the object may switch states. This information is combined with permissions, resulting in a personalized form with interaction logic. An example of such a form, derived from the *Application* object from Fig. 1, is shown in Fig. 2.

Fig. 2. Form

Note that a single object and its resulting forms are only part of a complete business process. To allow for more complex business processes, many different objects and users may have to be involved [3]. It is noteworthy that *users* are simply special objects in the object-aware paradigm. The entire set of objects present in a PHILharmonicFlows process is the *data model*, an example of which can be seen in Fig. 3, with objects representing users, e.g. *Employee*, marked in green.

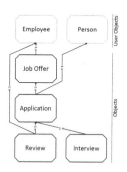

Fig. 3. Data model (Color figure online)

In addition to the objects and users, the data model
contains information about the *relations* existing between
them. A relation constitutes a logical association between
two objects, e.g., a *Job Offer* and an *Application*. At
runtime, each of the objects may be instantiated many
times as *object instances*. Note that the lifecycle processes
present in the various object instances may be executed
concurrently at runtime, thereby improving overall system performance. Relations may also be instantiated at
runtime, e.g., between an instance of a *Review* and an
Application, thereby associating the two object instances
with each other. The resulting meta information, expressing that the *Review* in question belongs to the *Application*,
can be used to coordinate the processing of the two object
instances with each other at runtime [3]. Figure 4 shows
an example of a *data model instance* at runtime.

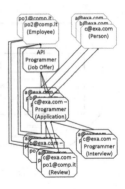

Fig. 4. Data model
instance

The coordination of object instances is necessary as business processes often
consist of hundreds or thousands of interacting business objects [5], whose concurrent processing needs to be synchronized at certain states. As object instances
publicly advertise their state information, the current state of an object instance
(e.g. *Sent* or *Check*ed) can be used for coordinating its processing (i.e., execution) with other object instances corresponding to the same business process
through a set of constraints and rules, defined in a separate *coordination process*
[3]. As an example, consider a simple subset of constraints stating the following:

1. An *Application* must be in state *Sent* for *Reviews* to be *Prepared* for it.
2. An *Application* may only be *Checked* once its corresponding *Reviews* are
   either in state *Reject Proposed* or *Invite Proposed*.

A coordination process with these constraints is shown in Fig. 5. The transitions describe the kind of relation that exists between the objects referenced
by the steps on either side. For example, between steps *Review - Reject Proposed* and *Application - Checked*, a *bottom-up* coordination exists, as there is a
bottom-up many-to-one relation between *Review* and *Application* in the data
model (cf. Fig. 3). This enables advanced coordinations, based on the information delivered by relations at runtime, e.g. that at least 5 *Reviews* must be either
in states *Reject Proposed* or *Invite Proposed* for an *Application* to enter state
Checked [3].

3   Determining Object-Aware Process Context

This section examines the concepts we developed for enabling *process context
switching*. To reiterate, an object-aware process instance consists of a data
model instance that comprises many object instances. Further, there are relation
instances between associated object instances. Finally, the coordination process

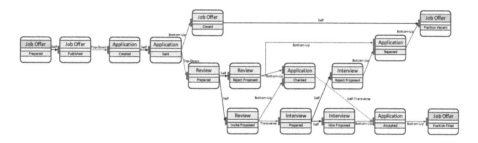

Fig. 5. Coordination process (Recruitment - Job Offer)

instance monitors the object instances and coordinates their execution. Consequently, in an object-aware process instance, many different processes, such as lifecycle processes and the coordination process, are executed concurrently. As one can not simply determine a *single* process context for this collection of largely independent processes, this section presents four points of view, or *scopes*, one may use to examine the combined process context.

3.1 Process Context in the Scope of a Lifecycle Process

When examining process context, the notion of *scope* becomes important. In the scope of a lifecycle process, the context is the object instance the lifecycle process is executed in, or, more specifically, the set containing all current attribute values present in the object instance. This complies with the definition in [2]. As an object-aware lifecycle process is entirely data-driven, the process context, i.e., the object instance, contains all necessary execution information, i.e., the attribute values. As an example, take the lifecycle process instance shown in Fig. 6.

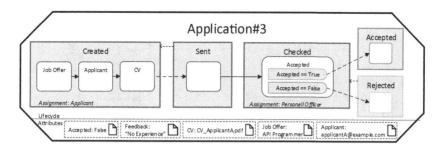

Fig. 6. Lifecycle process of an Application object instance

The lifecycle process is currently in state *Rejected*, as all attribute values from the previous states have already been written. This includes attribute *Accepted* with its value *False*, which forced the corresponding decision step in *Checked* to trigger the transition to *Rejected*. In turn, this led to the current state of the object instance being *Rejected*. Note that these attribute values always lead to the same state if the lifecycle process is re-executed. In summary, if the scope of the process context is limited to a lifecycle process, the context will solely consist of attribute values. However, this scope is too limited for most purposes.

3.2 Process Context in the Scope of a Single Object Instance

The value of the *Accepted* attribute of *Application#3*, shown in Fig. 6, is set to *False*. While a personnel officer may immediately accept or reject an applicant, it is more realistic that the application is first reviewed and applicants are invited for an interview before making a decision. In the data model of the recruitment example (cf. Fig. 3), these reviews and interviews are represented by objects, *Review* and *Interview*, with their own lifecycle processes. Note that *Review* and *Interview* constitute so-called *lower-level objects* of *Application*, as level-wise they are below *Application* in the data model due to the layouting of the graph that is based on incoming and outgoing relations. This layout makes the parent/child relations between objects evident, e.g., it becomes obvious from Fig. 3 that *Reviews* belong to *Applications*. These relations, together with the notion of scope, are crucial when determining process context.

As stated before, the smallest scope is given by a single lifecycle process, for which the process context is the object it is associated with. The next larger scope is the scope of an object instance, e.g., one instance of a *Review* object. Clearly, a *Review* is always conducted by an *Employee* for a specific *Application*, which can be deduced by examining the relations to the higher-level objects of *Review* (cf. Fig. 3). Therefore, the process context of a *Review* object instance is given by the *Employee* and *Application* object instances it is related to, i.e., all higher-level object instances of the *Review*. Taking the example from Fig. 4, the process context of one of the *Reviews* is shown in Fig. 7a.

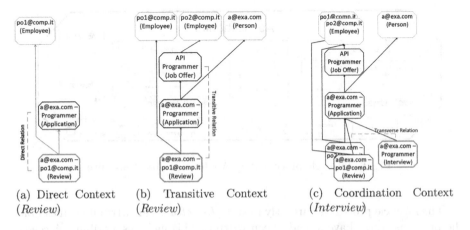

(a) Direct Context (*Review*)   (b) Transitive Context (*Review*)   (c) Coordination Context (*Interview*)

Fig. 7. Process contexts

Note that Fig. 7a is captioned "Direct Context", as opposed to the "Transitive Context" shown in Fig. 7b. The difference between these notions is that the transitive context includes *all* object instances that are higher-level object instances of the review object instance, not just those that are directly related. Note that even the *transitive context* of an object instance does not cover the complete process context in the scope of a single object instance, as not all object instances are contained that can have an impact on the execution of the object instance in question.

Specifically, the coordination process, which determines the interactions between object instances at runtime, provides additional context for object instances. (cf. Fig. 5). In particular, the coordination process allows process modelers to define constraints, such as that an *Interview* may only be *Prepared* if there are *Reviews* in state *Invite Proposed*, which are *transversely* related to them, i.e., via the same *Application* (cf. Fig. 5). The existence of such a constraint means that the execution of an *Interview* object instance may be impacted by a *Review* object instance, which is not be part of the transitive context of the *Interview*, as *Review* is not a higher-level object of *Interview*. Therefore, the coordination context is the most complete context in the scope of an object instance, as it contains all other object instances that may impact this instance. Figure 7c shows an example of the coordination context of an *Interview* object instance.

3.3   Process Context in the Scope of Multiple Object Instances

This section examines process context in the scope of multiple related objects. Note, for instance, that the process context of, e.g., an instance of the *Application* object, would be comprised of (1) the higher-level object instances it is related to (e.g., a *Job Offer*) as well as (2) other objects that may impact the execution of the *Application*, as defined in the coordination process (e.g., *Reviews*). However, when switching this process context to a completely different one, we need to consider that an *Application* is not an independent entity in a data model instance. Simply deleting all relation instances from an *Application* object instance, e.g. *Application#3*, and attaching it to a different *Job Offer* object instance, e.g. from *Job Offer API Programmer* to *Job Offer UI Programmer*, would leave all the *Review* and *Interview* object instances as orphans in the current data model instance. Therefore, concepts for switching the process context of object instances must always consider the context of all dependent object instances as well.

The set of dependent object instances can be defined as all transitively related lower-level object instances. Note that this is an inversion of the logic for finding transitive process context (cf. Fig. 7b). As an example, the aggregation of the dependent object instances of an *Application* object instance may be algorithmically determined by recursively evaluating incoming relations from lower-level object instances, the result of which is shown in Fig. 8.

Fig. 8.   Dependent object instances

In summary, the process context of an individual object must always include its dependent object instances, as switching the context of an individual object instance with lower-level instances attached to it would lead to orphaned object instances. In essence, this means recursively calling the functions that determine the dependent object instances and the coordination process context of all identified instances, which, in most cases, leads to the entire data model instance (cf. Fig. 4) being identified as the process context of an object instance. Consequently, we must examine the notion of process context in the scope of a data model instance.

3.4 Process Context in the Scope of the Data Model Instance

In contrast to the concept of a "process instance" from the realm of activity-centric BPMSs, an object-aware data model instance does not have any input parameters or meta information it holds at runtime, apart from the object instances, relation instances, and coordination process instances it comprises. Consequently, as opposed to an activity-centric process instance, whose context would include the input parameters provided to the process instance upon its creation, a data model instance possesses no process context information. Returning to the recruitment management process example, there might be multiple instances of the recruitment data model running at the same time across different departments in a company. The context in which they are executed, such as the department, is not captured in the data model. However, this also means that there is no conceptual challenge in changing the context of a data model instance. Specifically, moving the data model instance from one server to another is merely an administrative challenge.

4 Enabling Dynamic Process Context Switching

In Sect. 3, we presented the scopes one has to consider when determining what constitutes process context in an object-aware process. There is no simple way of taking a single object instance or other conceptual element and determining its process context in a general fashion, as, when including all constraints and relations, the process context of a single object instance consists of all object instances present in a data model instance. Without additional concepts, there is no way to remove an object instance from its process context and re-insert

---

Algorithm 1. Re-Execute Lifecycle with altered Attribute Values

---

Require: $oi, newAttributes[]$ ▷ object instance, new attribute values
1: $o \leftarrow$ **getObject**(oi) ▷ get underlying object of oi
2: $oi_{temp} \leftarrow$ **instantiate**(o) ▷ create an empty instance of o
3: **for all** a in $oi.attributes[]$ **do**   ▷ copy O by change log replay
4:    **if** a **not in** $newAttributes[]$ **then**   ▷ if a is not being replaced
5:       $newAttributes[] \leftarrow a$ ▷ append attribute values from oi
6:    **end if**
7: **end for**
8: $c \leftarrow$ **getCoordinationProcess**(oi)
9: **for all** a in $newAttributes[]$ **do**   ▷ insert attribute values from O
10:    $oi_{temp}.changeAttributeValue(a)$ ▷ each value advances the lifecycle, re-executing it step by step
11:    $c.update(oi)$ ▷ notify coord. process if state changes
12: **end for**
13: $delete(oi)$
14: $oi \leftarrow oi_{temp}$ ▷ replace all pointers to original instance

---

it into another, as this would also change the context of other object instances, causing inconsistencies. This section presents concepts to enable changing or switching only parts of the process context of one or more object instances. We facilitate this with (a) the help of algorithms that perform the actual context changes, and (b) the inherent execution flexibility of object-aware BPM, which allows fixing inconsistent processes at runtime with dynamically generated forms.

4.1   Enabling Changes to the Context of a Lifecycle Process

The basic building block for enabling process context changes in object-aware process management is to enable context changes at the smallest scope possible, i.e., the process context of a lifecycle process (cf. Sect. 3.1). To reiterate, the process context of the lifecycle process being executed in an object instance corresponds to the supplied attribute values. As the lifecycle process is data-driven, its execution is advanced when certain data becomes available. The context of a lifecycle process, therefore, changes continuously, which drives process execution. This data-driven approach allows for the re-execution of a lifecycle process instance based on a *replay algorithm*. To be more precise, the data-driven nature of lifecycle processes ensures that the lifecycle process is re-executed in an identical fashion if the attribute values, i.e., the process context, remains unchanged. However, as we *want* to be able to change attribute values and then re-execute the lifecycle process, we extended the algorithm for re-executing a lifecycle process instance with the ability to alter attribute values (cf. Algorithm 1).

Note that it is not necessary to allow users to trigger this kind of process context change, as it is merely considered a building block for the higher-level user-facing context changes. Algorithm 1 is essential as it allows the lifecycle process to be re-executed when the object instance it belongs to switches its process context.

4.2   Enabling Changes to the Context of an Object Instance

The context of an object instance can be considered to be the data model instance itself. However, it is possible to alter only specific parts of the process context identified in Sect. 3.2, i.e., *direct context*, *transitive context*, and *coordination context*. Starting with the *direct context*, we developed a concept for enabling the exchange of directly related higher-level object instances, thereby altering or even entirely switching process context. As an example consider an *Application* related to a *Job Offer*. During a job interview, it turns out that *Applicant a@exa.com* is better qualified for a different *Job Offer*, e.g. *UI Programmer*. The personnel officer *po2@comp.it* may want to switch the context of the *Application* object instance from *API Programmer* to *UI Programmer* as shown in Fig. 9.

The changes necessary for switching the direct process context of the *Application* object instance shown in Fig. 9 are (a) removing the relation between the *Application* object instance and the *API Programmer Job Offer* object instance and (b) adding a new relation between the orphaned *Application* object instance and the *UI Programmer* object instance.

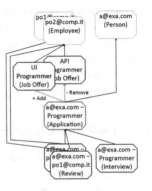

Fig. 9. Direct process context switch

These changes are inherently supported by object-aware processes. However, an impact analysis becomes necessary to determine which steps are required to restore consistency. As, up until now, we only take the direct context of the single object instance into account, the analysis must merely check that the new relation to *UI Programmer* is instantiatable, adhering to any cardinality or coordination constraints the data model may impose. An example of a cardinality constraint could be that each *Job Offer* object instance may have at most five *Application* object instances attached to it. Furthermore, a coordination constraint preventing the creation of the new relation could be that the *UI Programmer* object instance is not in state *Published* yet, which is necessary for *Applications* to be attached to it, according to the coordination process shown in Fig. 5. If none of these constraints is violated by the new relation, it may be created, causing the direct context of the *Application* to be switched to the *UI Programmer* object instance.

Algorithm 2 ensures that the context switch adheres to the constraints imposed on relations between, e.g., *Job Offers* and *Applications*, i.e., the object instances affecting the direct context of the *Application* object instance. Although Algorithm 2 is not overly complex, it is an important foundation that ensures that the direct context may be switched, thereby ensuring consistency of the data model instance after the process context change. If the algorithm finds a violation, the process context of the *Application* must not be switched.

Algorithm 2. Check Direct Context Constraints

Require: oi_s, oi_t ▷ source and target of new relation
1: $o_s \leftarrow$ **getObject**(oi_s) ▷ get underlying object of oi_s
2: $o_t \leftarrow$ **getObject**(oi_t) ▷ get underlying object of oi_t
3: $r \leftarrow$ **getRelation**(o_s, o_t) ▷ get relation between o_s and o_t
4: **if** **count**$(oi_t.incomingRelations) >= r.maxCard$ **then**
5:     **return** false   ▷ violated relation cardinality
6: **end if**
7: $c \leftarrow$ **getCoordinationProcess**(oi_t)
8: **for all** s in $c.steps$ **do**
9:     **if** $s.object = o_s$ and $s.state = oi_s.currState$ **then**
10:         **if** **constraintPreventsRelation**(s, oi_s, oi_t) **then**
11:             **return** false   ▷ violated coordination constraint
12:         **end if**
13:     **end if**
14: **end for**
15: **return** true   ▷ allow relation instance between oi_s and oi_t

Fig. 10. Coordination process (cf. Fig. 5)

The direct process context change shown in Fig. 9 may be also viewed from a different angle. The change clearly impacts the context of the *Application* object instance, but it impacts the coordination context of both *Job Offer* instances as well. Assuming that the lifecycle process of the *Application* object instance is in state *Accepted* when the context switch occurs, the excerpt of the coordination process shown in Fig. 10 would force changes to the *Job Offers UI Programmer* and *API* Programmer. The new context, i.e., *Job Offer UI Programmer*, then has a lower-level *Application* object instance in state *Accepted*, which allows it to transition to state *Position Filled* as shown in the coordination process excerpt in Fig. 10. This causes the coordination process to inform the *UI Programmer* object instance that it may advance to state *Position Filled* as soon as the context change creating the new relation instance occurs.

Conversely, the old context, i.e., *Job Offer API Programmer*, no longer has an *Application* in state *Accepted* related to it. Therefore, if it is already in state *Position Filled*, this switch would introduce an inconsistency that needs to be resolved. This can be facilitated by re-executing the lifecycle process instance of the *API Programmer* object instance. As shown in Algorithm 1, a lifecycle process instance must always notify the coordination process when a state change occurs. This is, however, just part of the regular execution of a lifecycle process. Furthermore, this is explicitly done when re-executing a lifecycle process as part of a coordination context change, to ensure that state transitions, which were allowed in the old coordination context, are still valid in the new one. To be more precise, for the example of the *Accepted Application* being removed from *Job Offer API Programmer*, the re-execution of the *Job Offer* would be blocked in a state before *Position Filled*, as the coordination process no longer has knowledge of an *Accepted Application* attached to *Job Offer API Programmer*. Once the coordination process has been notified and all affected object instances were advanced or reverted into the appropriate states according to the process context changes, they were impacted by, process consistency is restored. Note that a change to the context of one object instance might have a cascading impact on others, requiring a re-execution or lifecycle advancement to restore consistency.

4.3   Enabling Context Changes to Multiple Object Instances

The final, and most complete, case of process context change is switching the process context of multiple object instances at the same time. We re-use the example of moving an *Application* object instance from one *Job Offer* to another. However, this time we assume that the new process context for the *Application* is a *Job Offer* in a different data model instance, albeit instantiated from the same data model. Furthermore, we employ the concept of dependent object instances presented in Sect. 3.3 to move the applicant, i.e. *Person a@exa.com*, his *Application*, and all other dependent object instances (*Reviews, Interviews*) in one atomic operation. Figure 11 shows the concrete example of moving *a@exa.com* to a different data model instance containing *Job Offer C++ Programmer*.

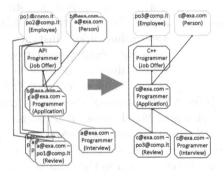

Fig. 11. Switching context of multiple object instances

While the process context changes in the previous examples were rather small in scope, e.g., consisting of the replacement of a single relation to a parent object instance by another, the above change is conducted in the scope of multiple object instances at the same time. Ensuring consistency before the change would require the user to determine replacement relations for all relation instances to objects not existing in the new data model instance. As an example, consider the relation between one of the *Review* object instances and the *Employee* assigned as a reviewer, e.g. *po2@comp.it* (cf. Fig. 11). In the new data model instance (i.e. the other department), *po2@comp.it* does not exist, causing the relation instance between the *Review* and the *Employee* to be deleted. One way to solve this is to require the determination of replacement relations for each deleted relation, as previously suggested. Instead, once again, we leverage the flexible (re-)execution supported by object-aware lifecycle processes to elegantly solve this problem.

To be precise, we delete the relations to all objects not present in the new data model instance. Furthermore, we delete the attribute values referencing the relations, e.g. the *Job Offer* attribute in the *Application* object (cf. Fig. 6). Moreover, due to the presence of the *Job Offer* relation attribute as a step in the lifecycle process, an instance of the *Application* object must not progress past state *Created* without a value for *Job Offer* being provided. Coincidentally, a value for an attribute with the data type "relation" is provided by creating a relation to another object and vice versa. However, deleting the value of an attribute, once execution has progressed past the state it is required in, causes a lifecycle inconsistency. For example this happens when the *Applications* and *Reviews* are moved between the two data model instances, causing the relations to the no longer existing *Employees* and *Job Offers* to be deleted. If we trigger a re-execution of the lifecycle process instance of all object instances with now deleted relation instances (cf. Algorithm 1), the data-driven lifecycle process reacts by executing, for example, the *Application* object instance until the end of the *Created* state, and then waiting for user input.

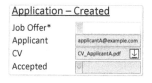

Fig. 12. *Application* after context switch

Here, the dynamic form generation capabilities (cf. Sect. 2) are utilized. After changing the process context, the *Application* is missing a *Job Offer*. The form shown in Fig. 12 is generated and added to the worklist of a personnel officer, allowing him to select the *C++ Programmer*. Once the *Job Offer* is selected, the data-driven lifecycle execution advances the *Application* object to its previous state. Similar forms are generated for both *Reviews*, and once all three forms are completed, process consistency is restored.

5 Prototypical Implementation and Real-World Use-Cases

In the PHILharmonicFlows implementation of object-aware process management, the higher level conceptual elements are implemented as microservices. For each object instance, relation instance, or coordination process instance, one microservice instance is created at runtime, turning the implementation into a fully distributed object-aware process management system.

Note that all the information from the various microservices can be utilized at runtime to generate an entire user interface, complete with navigation and form elements for a specific data model – a goal of the object-aware process management paradigm from the very beginning. A screenshot of the current user interface for end-users (with demo data) is shown in Fig. 13. The engine and user interface are currently evaluated in a large scale real-world deployment in the context of a course with hundreds of students, utilizing an object-aware process representing an e-learning platform called PHoodle (**PH**ILharmonicFlows **Moodle**)[1].

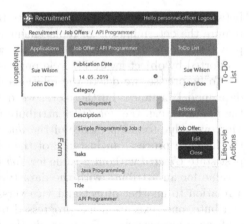

Fig. 13. PHILharmonicFlows UI

This study enables us to evaluate scalability, usability, and advanced concepts such as dynamic context switching. While, for the sake of brevity, we solely offered examples in the context of the recruitment data model, there are numerous scenarios from different domains in which the concepts from object-aware process management can be useful. We found multiple use-cases in our various data models, such as the re-assignment of a transport job from a robot to a human worker in our logistics research[2], or a student assigned to the wrong lecture in PHoodle, both powered by the PHILharmonicFlows engine.

In the context of the real-world PHoodle deployment, we had cases of students wishing to switch their tutorials, while retaining access to completed worksheet submissions. As we had not thought of this possibility at design-time, it is a perfect use-case for context switching, as it may be employed to move an *Attendance* (representing a student), with all related *Submissions*, from one *Tutorial* to another. Our experience has shown that supporting this additional dimension of flexibility empowers users by offering them additional actions without increasing model complexity. For example, in PHoodle, we hide the complexity of reassigning a *Student* from one *Tutorial* to another by offering an *Employee* viewing object instance representing the *Student* a simple drop-down menu generated by the PHILharmonicFlows form logic for selecting a different *Tutorial*. When a *Tutorial* is selected, PHILharmonicFlows completes the process context change on all dependent object instances, deleting and creating relations, re-executing lifecycle processes, and updating the coordination process, in a single click.

---

[1] Feel free to log in to the live instance at https://phoodle.dbis.info
Username: *edoc.demo@uni-ulm*.de Password: *edoc.demo*.

[2] https://www.youtube.com/watch?v=oGKjK7K76Ck.

6   Related Work

LateVa [6], enables automated late selection of process fragments based on process context. In essence, a process model does not define all possible variations but contains variation points that are replaced with process fragments at runtime depending on the process context. The actual replacement is done by the "fragment recommender", based on data mined from historical process instances.

The inclusion of "pockets of flexibility" into workflow models is proposed in [7]. Each pocket contains multiple individual process fragments that can be rearranged at runtime according to the needs of the process context, allowing for greater flexibility at certain points. CaPI (context-aware process injection) [8] analyses process context and allows injecting process fragments into extension areas. These fragments and the context in which they may be injected are determined at design-time using a sophisticated modeling tool.

The approaches presented in [6–8] follow a similar approach, limiting process context flexibility to predefined regions of a process model. Our approach aims to remove this limitation through relaxation. Instead of defining regions in which flexibility is possible, we allow for context changes except for in some situations.

Controlled evolution of process choreographies are examined in [9]. A process choreography describes the interactions of business processes with partner processes in a cross-organizational setting. [9] examines ways to gauge the impact of changes to processes with respect to their partner processes. This is a similar problem to the one examined in this paper, determining how to understand the impact that process context changes have on other object instances that are part of the same data model instance.

The concept of batch regions is introduced in [10]. A batch region is a part of a process model that may be executed in a single batch if there are other process instances available corresponding to the same context. Similar capabilities may be introduced to object-aware process management by extending the context switching concepts detailed in this paper to aggregate different object instances with similar contexts and executing them in batches.

Finally, [11] presents the context-oriented programming (COP) paradigm, which introduces a number of interesting aspects that could be incorporated into our future research. Combining our contribution with COP, which allows for objects in a programming language to behave differently depending on the context they are executed in, would be an interesting research direction. COP introduces *layering* for grouping behavioral variants of code with selectors that choose the correct variant after a context switch occurs at runtime. Similar notions could be used to extend the research presented in this paper.

7   Summary and Outlook

This paper used the running example of a recruitment data model to examine how process context can be freely switched and changed in object-aware processes. We presented a detailed examination of the notion of process context in object-aware processes, as well as the concepts and algorithms we developed to enable process context changes in our proof-of-concept implementation of an object-aware process management system – PHILharmonicFlows. In essence, we leverage the highly flexible execution provided by the object-aware process management paradigm to adapt running process instances to incurred process context changes. Some issues are still open, such as finding a generic solution for cases in which external services (e.g. payment services or e-mails) are used. Nonetheless, the presented concept constitutes an advancement for data-centric BPM. Together with our work on ad-hoc changes [4], the presented research brings us a step closer to a fully fledged data-centric process engine with which we can demonstrate the many flexibility advantages that data-centric processes have, thereby increasing the perceived maturity of data-centric BPM.

Acknowledgments. This work is part of the ZAFH Intralogistik, funded by the European Regional Development Fund and the Ministry of Science, Research and the Arts of Baden-Wuerttemberg, Germany (F.No. 32-7545.24-17/3/1).

References

1. Saidani, O., Nurcan, S.: Context-awareness for business process modelling. In: 3rd International Conference on Research Challenges in Information Science, pp. 177–186. IEEE (2009)
2. Rosemann, M., Recker, J.C.: Context-aware process design. In: 18th International Conference on Advanced Information Systems Engineering (CAiSE) Workshops, pp. 149–158 (2006)
3. Steinau, S., Andrews, K., Reichert, M.: The relational process structure. In: Krogstie, J., Reijers, H.A. (eds.) CAiSE 2018. LNCS, vol. 10816, pp. 53–67. Springer, Cham (2018). https://doi.org/10.1007/978-3-319-91563-0_4
4. Andrews, K., Steinau, S., Reichert, M.: Enabling runtime flexibility in data-centric and data-driven process execution engines. Inf. Syst. (2019)
5. Müller, D., Reichert, M., Herbst, J.: Flexibility of data-driven process structures. In: Eder, J., Dustdar, S. (eds.) BPM 2006. LNCS, vol. 4103, pp. 181–192. Springer, Heidelberg (2006). https://doi.org/10.1007/11837862_19
6. Murguzur, A., Sagardui, G., Intxausti, K., Trujillo, S.: Process variability through automated late selection of fragments. In: Franch, X., Soffer, P. (eds.) CAiSE 2013. LNBIP, vol. 148, pp. 371–385. Springer, Heidelberg (2013). https://doi.org/10.1007/978-3-642-38490-5_35
7. Sadiq, S., Sadiq, W., Orlowska, M.: Pockets of flexibility in workflow specification. In: S.Kunii, H., Jajodia, S., Sølvberg, A. (eds.) ER 2001. LNCS, vol. 2224, pp. 513–526. Springer, Heidelberg (2001). https://doi.org/10.1007/3-540-45581-7_38
8. Mundbrod, N., Grambow, G., Kolb, J., Reichert, M.: Context-aware process injection. In: Debruyne, C., et al. (eds.) OTM 2015. LNCS, vol. 9415, pp. 127–145. Springer, Cham (2015). https://doi.org/10.1007/978-3-319-26148-5_8

9. Rinderle, S., Wombacher, A., Reichert, M.: On the controlled evolution of process choreographies. In: 22nd International Conference on Data Engineering, ICDE 2006, p. 124. IEEE (2006)
10. Pufahl, L., Meyer, A., Weske, M.: Batch regions: process instance synchronization based on data. In: 18th International Enterprise Distributed Object Computing Conference, pp. 150–159. IEEE (2014)
11. Hirschfeld, R., Costanza, P., Nierstrasz, O.M.: Context-oriented programming. J. Object Technol. **7**(3), 125–151 (2008)

Exception Handling in the Context of Fragment-Based Case Management

Kerstin Andree[1](✉), Sven Ihde[1], and Luise Pufahl[2]

[1] Hasso Plattner Institute, University of Potsdam, 14482 Potsdam, Germany
kerstin.andree@student.hpi.de, sven.ihde@hpi.de
[2] Software and Business Engineering, Technische Universitaet Berlin,
Berlin, Germany
luise.pufahl@tu-berlin.de

Abstract. Case Management supports knowledge workers in defining, executing, and monitoring the handling of their cases, e.g. in healthcare or logistics. Fragment-based case management (fCM) allows to define a case model with the help of several process fragments, which can be flexible combined at run-time based on case characteristics and the case worker's intuition. Cases are often influenced by unknown exception, e.g., the sudden change of patient condition's or a storm delaying transports. So far, fCM only reacts to known circumstances. In this paper, we want to extend fCM by an exception handling approach. Thereby, existing exception patterns for workflow systems are used and extended by the fragment-level for handling unknown events. In order to enable direct integration and avoid a duplication of semantics, precise rules are specified in order to clarify how to extend which pattern in detail. The applicability of the developed exception handling technique is exemplified on a last mile delivery for parcels.

Keywords: Case management · Exception handling · Business process modeling · Flexible process automation

1 Introduction

Business Process Management (BPM) enables companies to optimize their processes in such a way that an overall business goal is achieved. The main artifact of BPM are business process models [3]. Traditional control-flow oriented process models represent all possible execution paths of a business process and provide a complete description of possible alternatives.

The discrepancy of a business process between the planned flow and the reality is called an exception [12]. For a successful process execution, exceptions occurring during run-time (e.g., weather changes, missing data) need to be handled. Standard process modeling languages, such as Business Process Model and Notation (BPMN) [17], offers concepts to capture and handle exception. However, they often lead to difficulties to read complex process models [6].

© Springer Nature Switzerland AG 2020
S. Nurcan et al. (Eds.): BPMDS 2020/EMMSAD 2020, LNBIP 387, pp. 20–35, 2020.
https://doi.org/10.1007/978-3-030-49418-6_2

A structured overview on the capabilities of event handling in existing business process management systems (BPMSs) was offered by Russell et al. [20].

Another more flexible approach for process execution is Case Management, in which so-called *knowledge workers* determine the exact process path by their decisions at run-time and enable a non-deterministic process execution [10,14]. It supports variant-rich business processes, such as healthcare or logistic processes, and should by its nature already support known exceptions. Motahari-Nezhad and Swenson [16] distinguish between adaptive and production case management; whereas the first one assumes that knowledge workers work very independently based on their knowledge which can quickly change, in the latter certain structure in the work exists which can be also defined at design time. *Fragment-based Case Management* (fCM) offers one way of implementing the Case Management approach as a hybrid variant between the two paradigms [8,9]. Nevertheless, it keeps the control-flow-based approach of process models in parts to ensure that certain processes are executed correctly. A *case* of a fCM application consists of several smaller processes, the so-called fragments, which are designed in advance. Only within these fragments, the sequential flow of individual activities is relevant. Knowledge workers can then flexibly combine those during case execution in the fCM engine[1] and thereby determine the concrete process path. So, it is not predictable how the process will look like in detail at run-time and this can lead to unexpected behaviour during execution.

Already today, exceptions can be handled by adding new fragments [9], however, a structured Exception Handling approach, such as the exception patterns for BPMSs [20] does not yet exist for the fCM engine. There are no instructions or support to which knowledge workers can refer back when unexpected or even unknown events occur. A delay during the handling of cases due to incorrect data or missing information leads to unnecessary costs for organizations. That makes a good Exception Handling very important for business processes. This work provides a structured approach for handling exceptions in a fCM application which can be used to implement an user interface (UI) for supporting knowledge workers to react fast and structured to an unexpected event. Based on the exception pattern of Russell et al. [20] which fits very well for workflow systems, it provides a suitable extension of those to make them applicable to fCM.

For better understanding, the explained approach is illustrated by an application example from the last mile delivery, an alternative delivery approach of parcels with a pickup place infrastructure researched in the SMile[2] project. In the remainder, this example is used to explain the concepts of fCM and further motivation in Sect. 2. The background on exception handling as well as used abbreviations of Russell et al. [20] are summarized in Sect. 3. The fourth section of this paper explains the concept of exception handling approach for fCM at run-time. Finally, we provide an application of the explained concept to the last mile scenario and give an example of a possible UI.

---

[1] https://github.com/bptlab/chimera.
[2] http://smile-project.de/smile-projekt/.

2   Fragment-Based Case Management and Motivation

To better understand the concept of fCM as well as its advantages and disadvantages in the context of exception handling, the last mile delivery scenario researched in SMile project [18] is explained briefly in this section by using a simplified fCM model. fCM reuses a subset of BPMN modeling concepts [17].

SMile tackles the problem of the last mile delivery which is defined as the movement of parcels from a high-capacity freight station or port to their final destination. The last mile takes up to 28% of the total delivery costs [19] because recipients are often not at home during delivery time, such that increased delivery tries or additional storage of deliveries are necessary. With a pick-up place infrastructure near to recipients, where parcels are delivered first, SMiles explores the last mile for parcels more efficient and user friendly [18]. Either, recipients can collect their parcels themselves or use the service of parcel delivery at a desired time frame by a local carrier, whereby the focus of the project is the latter one.

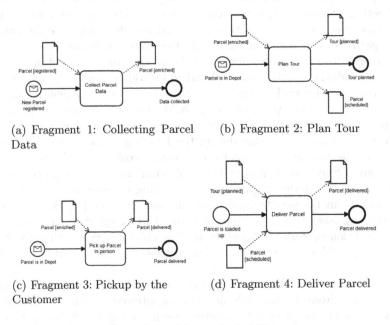

(a) Fragment 1: Collecting Parcel Data

(b) Fragment 2: Plan Tour

(c) Fragment 3: Pickup by the Customer

(d) Fragment 4: Deliver Parcel

Fig. 1. Simplified fCM model of SMile use case

Fragment-based case management consists of four basic concepts [6,8]: process fragments describing the flow of a case, the goal state describing when a case is finished, a data class diagram describing relevant data for a case and their structure, and finally, the object-life cycles for each data type describing the allowed changes on them.

In Fig. 1(a), we have visualized four fragments, in which the last mile process is split. The fragments are either triggered by external events (shown as message events) or by certain available data. The first fragment is triggered by an event called *New Parcel registered*, which is sent by the sender of the parcel. For registered parcels, the recipients are notified and asked when they want to receive their parcel. This is what happens in the activity *Collect Parcel Data*, which transfers the data object *Parcel* from its state *registered* to *enriched*. As soon as the information is received that the parcel has arrived at the depot (i.e. the pick-up place, e.g., a gas station or a greengrocer just around the corner), the parcel can be planned (cf. Fig. 1(b)), if it is *enriched*, into a delivery tour for a local carrier. The activity *Plan Tour* calls a complex planning service. This service collects at a certain point in time all parcels requesting a planning with the same postal code and looks for a suitable carrier who delivers in this area. It plans a route which ensures that each parcel will be delivered in its specific time slot. If a planned tour is allocated to a carrier, the parcel can be collected at the depot by the carrier. Alternatively, recipients can pick up their parcel in person as soon as the parcel has arrived at the depot but was not yet planned for a tour. Then, the third fragment Fig. 1(c) is executed instead of fragment 2 and 4. The process ends when the parcel is in state *delivered* (Fig. 1(d)), the goal state of this case model.

In fCM, not all of the fragments have to be used for the execution of a certain case to achieve the defined goal of the parcel delivery. Because fCM is both data-driven and event-driven, it is very important to have a valid *Object-Lifecycle (OLC)* which is consistent with the modeled fragments [8]. It describes the state transitions of each data object as shown in Fig. 2.

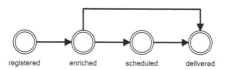

Fig. 2. OLC of data object *Parcel*

Predictable situations at design time, e.g., recipients get parcel in person, can be easily captured by designing fragments to cope with them. Unknown exceptions can be also solved, e.g. for misreadings of the recipient's address on the parcel by the scanner. The fCM engine allows knowledge workers to add fragments at runtime. So far, knowledge workers have to solve exceptions without any structured support in fCM and this is what we want to change. Given that the process fragments in fCM are small workflows, we want to reuse the exception handling patterns by Russell et al. [20] originally designed for workflow systems.

3   Background on Exception Handling

After introducing fCM, we provide in this section the background on exception handling. First, a precise definition of the term exception is given by classifying it into different exception types, each illustrated with an example of the introduced use case. Related work is discussed afterwards and the remaining text introduces the work of Russell et al. [20] as a fundamental basis for this paper.

3.1   Exceptions

Usually, we describe a discrepancy of a business process between the planned flow and the reality as an *exception*. Nevertheless, a discrepancy does not always have to be an exception. Therefore, Lohmeyer [12] distinguishes between in success and failure regarding the goal of a business process. If the goal is achieved although there is a deviation, we talk about a special variation which is already known by the process and pre-defined. However, if a deviation leads to failure, Lohmeyer talks about a real exception. It is a deviation which is unknown by the process.

The difference between *known* and *unknown* exceptions traces back to Luo et al. [13]: A deviation is unknown if it cannot be resolved with the rules of a

Table 1. Exception types according to [20]

Type	Explanation	Example from last mile delivery
Activity failure	Activity is not able to continue its execution [20]	Due to an ambiguous address, the activity *Plan Tour* (Fig. 1(b)) fails because the system cannot include it into the tour
Resource allocation		
a) Non-availability	Non-availability of resources causes non-execution of corresponding activity	No carrier can be found for a specific zip code In this context the carrier is the resource to which a parcel is allocated
b) Depleted capacity	Due to exhausted capacity of the resource during execution, the activity cannot be completed successfully	Parcel volume is bigger than space of transport vehicle, e.g. a cargo bike. Fragment 4 (Fig. 1(d)) can not be executed anymore
c) Wrong allocation	Resource is identified as incorrect after successful assignment	Scanner misreads the address. This causes wrong linking of parcel to recipient
External Trigger	Required information to start a fragment is missing	Database is not reachable. The activity *Plan Tour* does not start because of missing information (Fig. 1(b))

system that have been defined in advance. This means there is no alternative path in the process model. Moreover, an unknown and therefore unexpected exception cannot be handled according to [13].

Russell et al. [20] specify, additional to the distinction into known and unknown exceptions, different exception types. This paper is based on this grouping and works with exceptions as a clearly identifiable event which occurs at *run-time* of a business process. Three of those five types are exemplified in Table 1.

3.2   Related Work

Many authors have addressed the need of flexibility in business processes to enable reliability and support of static and dynamic changes [1,2,20]. Whereas adaptability is a key factor in the context of exception handling, it is also still a major challenge in Case Management [7]. Pattern like Rollback which are mentioned by [20] often address just an instance of a case and this does not suffice for all types of exceptions. Needed changes concerning the structure of a whole case are not covered [21].

Kurz et al. [11] differentiates between three types of exceptions: (1) routine, (2) minor, and (3) major exceptions. Whereas, routine ones can be handled with standard BPM techniques, such as boundary events in BPMN, the handling minor (predictable) and major (not predictable) needs flexibility to handle them at run-time. For handling the minor exceptions, Kurz et al. [11] propose a template-based strategy with best practices and guidelines to handle them, but unpredictable are handled outside of the case management system. Similarly, Fahland and Woith [5] proposes a flexible process execution system based on small Petrinets fragments similar to fCM – called Oclets –, which can be dynamically combined at runtime, and additional Oclets can be defined to handle predictable exceptions. Furthermore, unpredictable exceptions can be handled by adapting the case model while running, which are also verified [4]. A systematization is not given.

For predictable exceptions for which a handling can be defined in advance, there are lots of strategies of handling these. All of them are based on a systematization "in form of exception handling patterns" [15]. We use a similar concept in this paper and show how to adapt known workflow-based handling strategies for handling unpredictable exceptions in a fCM applications.

3.3   Pattern for Exception Handling in Workflow Systems

This section explains the pattern of Russell et al. [20] on which this paper is based on. After introducing the life cycle of an activity, an example of the pattern is used to explain the general structure of the exception handling strategies.

Business process activities can adopt different states, from the initial offering until final termination. To capture these states, life cycles as shown in Fig. 3 are useful for a detailed analysis of an activity during process execution. States are illustrated by boxes. Their abbreviations which are used in this paper are shown in brackets. Each activity can change its state via state transitions, which are

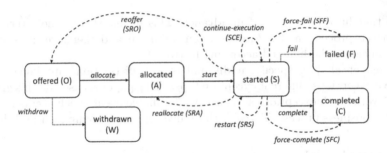

Fig. 3. Simplified life cycle of an activity according to [20]

represented as solid arrows. This is the case, for example, when an exception is triggered in state *started*. As a consequence, the activity changes into its state *failed*. The difference to the dashed arrows, which also represent state transitions, is that the transition is executed automatically whereas the transition using the dashed arrows is deliberately enforced from the outside. A state of an activity can change from *started* to *failed* by two different ways, the natural one or the enforced one. In this paper, we concentrate on activities which are already in state *started*[3]. Therefore Fig. 3 only shows the possible handling strategies for activities which are halted due to an exception.

Like the example pattern *SFF-CWC-COM*, each pattern of Russel et al. [20] is divided into three parts, each marked by an abbreviation which represents one of the three main aspects of exception handling in workflow systems which are defined as follows:

1. Handling of the activity which provoked the exception;
2. Handling of the following activities of the whole case; and
3. Recovery measures which are needed to remove the effects.

The handling of the activity which provoked the exception is summarized by the first part of the pattern. In the example this corresponds to the abbreviation *SFF*. The first three letters of each pattern has to be read separately, i.e. **S**tarted **F**orce-**F**ail, because the first letter explains in which state an activity is (cf. Fig. 3) when an unknown exception occurred and an automatic state transition can not be executed. The other two letters describe the status to which the activity is manually transferred. So *SFF* = **S**tarted **F**orce-**F**ail means that an activity is halted in state *started* and transferred to state *failed*.

Whereas the first part of a 3-tuple pattern handles one activity, the second part deals with the best strategy for handling on case-level, i.e. all of the following activities after the one which provoked the exception. This is necessary because the occurred exception could affect some or all following activities. The abbreviation by three letters describes one out of three possibilities for it:

1. *Continue Current Case (CWC)* - Every activity following will be executed without any interruptions, the workflow still exists.

---

[3] An overview of all possible state transitions can be found in [20].

2. *Remove Current Case (RCC)* - Either a selection or all of the activities are deleted.
3. *Remove All Cases (RAC)* - All cases of the same process model are deleted.

The last part of each pattern deals with recovery. Recovery describes the action performed in order to remove any aftereffects of an exception to ensure the possibility of still achieving the business goal. Three methods which are presented in [20] can be used:

1. *Do nothing (NIL)*
2. *Rollback (RBK)* - The effects of the exception are reversed, i.e. the state of the case is reset shortly before the time at which the exception occurred.
3. *Compensate (COM)* - The damage caused by the exception that has occurred will be compensated.

The introductory example pattern *SFF-CWC-COM* can therefore be interpreted as a strategy that transfers the activity, of which the exception occurred, into the status *failed* (SFF). The case as well as the following activities are continued in execution without making any special changes (CWC). Any damage that the exception caused is compensated (COM).

4   Exception Handling for fCM

Because an exception is not only linked to a single activity and/or case but also to a fragment, it is no longer sufficient to handle exceptions only on the activity- and case-level. Therefore, a new level of abstraction is needed: the fragment-level.

There are two possible consequences when an exception occurs in a fragment. Either it leads to an inability of a fragment to start or it impedes the successful execution of the fragment. As a direct effect of the latter, needed state transitions, which are trigger for further fragments, cannot be fulfilled.

Since there is no predefined order how fragments are going to be executed, it does not suffice to just look at subsequent activities as we do in the patterns for workflow systems. In the fCM approach, all case fragments have to be considered. Their handling goes hand in hand with the handling of the case (second part of the 3-tuple explained in Sect. 3.3). Nevertheless, an extension of the workflow pattern is needed to cover the fragment-level. This section explains how this can be done by adding a fourth tuple element to the existing pattern of Russell et al. [20]. Whereas the first part discusses the possibilities of recovery measures on fragment-level, the second part focuses on the concrete extension by defining a notation and specific rules. The last section suggests how an integration of the provided exception handling pattern could look like.

4.1   Compensation and Rollback

The main component of a good exception handling is the compensation and rollback of effects. A fCM application offers knowledge workers the opportunity to actively intervene the process by manipulating data and modeling new fragments. So there are different varieties to handle a fragment in which an exception has occurred. On the one hand, knowledge workers can start fragments manually and on the other hand, they can terminate them on purpose. It is up to the knowledge worker whether the termination condition is evaluated as successful or failed. Moreover, it is very important that the rules given by the model are strictly adhered to. This means, a knowledge worker has the obligation to compensate or withdraw the effects of an exception to ensure a correct execution to achieve the business process goal. There are four options to do so:

1. *Create new fragments*
   Creating new fragments can be helpful if an exception occurs and there is no alternative path in the process model, an extra fragment can be modeled. Nevertheless, it is important to check all of the following fragments to make sure everything can be executed afterwards e.g. through a compliance check explained in [10].
2. *Delete existing fragments*
   If a selection of fragments may no longer be executed, they can be removed by the knowledge worker. Note that a fragment is only removed in the current case so that it is not lost across the whole instance.
3. *Manipulation of states*
   There is a correlation between manipulation and the first two options. For both, adding a new fragment and remove one, state transitions have to be consistent. That is the reason why a continuous verification of the object live cycle is necessary. Therefore, it is important that knowledge workers have the right to put a data object in every state which is defined in the OLC. This means they can also adapt the OLC itself. Moreover, this option is important if you want to set back the execution of a fragment because you have to make sure that the data objects have the right state.
4. *Do nothing*
   This option should be chosen carefully and only if the effects of an exception have no influence on other fragments.

A strict differentiation in compensation and rollback as proposed in traditional exception handling is not possible anymore. Knowledge workers have to react situational. They have to decide for each exception individually if a rollback does make sense or not. So, the success of achieving a business goal lies with the knowledge workers. Due to the complexity of a fCM business process model, knowledge workers have to be more qualified in modeling skills than a ACM-User and has to have more rights than a PCM-User to be able to add new fragments or change states of data objects.

4.2   Notation

Exception handling on fragment-level is directly connected with the handling of the activity which has provoked the exception and the handling on case-level. That is the reason why an extension of the existent pattern for workflow systems is best suitable for a good exception handling in the context of fCM. These pattern already suggest a strategy on how to handle an activity and the following ones.

Our idea is to modify the given notation of Russell et al. [20] by adding a fourth tuple element to the existing 3-tuple pattern. Amongst handling the activity which triggers the exception, the case-level and the concrete recovery measures, the notation is extended by exception handling on fragment-level. This section explains the extension by defining specific rules because not every extended pattern leads to meaningful exception handling strategies.

Like the first part of the given notation (i.e. the activity handling), the fourth part is also an abbreviation consisting of three letters which have to be read separately. The first letter specifies the further execution of the fragment in which the exception has occurred. Suggested recovery measures are covered by the last two letters. While the first aspect correlates directly with the handling of the activity (first tuple element), the second topic is connected to the recovery component which is the third part of the strategy tuple. This relation to the first and third element of the tuple is the general rule of how to extend an existing workflow pattern to fCM.

Whenever an exception occurs, it is important to decide whether a fragment should be continued (C) or terminated (T) in its execution. This decision relates to the handling of the activity which has provoked the exception. If the activity is forced to state *failed* (e.g. SFF = Started Force-Fail), the fragment has to be terminated manually by knowledge workers. Any further execution would endanger a correct execution path regarding OLCs because any failed activity do not trigger following activities within the same fragment. In contrast to that, there are methods which still allow a continuation of the fragment. For example, SCE (Started Continue-Execution) does not terminate any activity because there is not state transition to *failed* (cf. Fig. 3) as an effect of the exception. Following activities can therefore still be triggered. Table 2 shows this correlation of handling an activity and a fragment for exceptions which has occurred in activity state *started*.

Table 2. Correlation of handling an activity and a fragment

Termination (terminate T)	Continuation (continue C)
SFF (force failing)	SCE (continue execution)
	SRS (restart)
	SRA (reallocate)
	SFC (force completion)
	SRO (reoffer)

There are different ways to implement the presented recovery measures of compensation, rollback and faineance on fragment-level. Each method has an abbreviation by two letters which is used for the second part of the extension:

- NE - Adding a **new** fragment
- DE - **D**elete an existing fragment
- MA - **Ma**nipulation of states
- NT - Do **not**hing

This results in eight possible combinations (cf. Table 3). However, the notation of a pattern is always interpreted in the overall context. That means, a free combination of the presented possibilities with the patterns of Russell et al. [20] is not wise, but it is dedicated to some rules. Here comes the direct correlation of the handling of an activity and the recovery measures into play.

Table 3. Possibilities of handling exceptions on fragment-level

State of fragment	Recovery measures			
	Add	Remove	Manipulate	Do nothing
Terminate (T)	TNE	TDE	TMA	TNT
Continue (C)	CNE	CDE	CMA	CNT

For recovery measures, Fig. 4 gives an overview of the different rules. It is assumed that the compensation (COM) presented by Russell et al. [20] implies a manipulation of object states. This means that a pattern that relies on compensation as a recovery measure cannot contain state manipulation (MA) as the fourth tuple element. For the option of a rollback (RBK), i.e. the return of the process for a new execution, it is assumed that the object state must be manipulated too. If knowledge workers re-execute a fragment with different parameters, they have to ensure that the data conditions are consistent with the process model. For this reason, a rollback only specifies whether a change was made to the process model or whether the fragment is executed again without an active intervention by knowledge workers. If the exception does not have any serious consequences, in most cases no recovery action is needed (NIL). Knowledge workers can now consider whether to keep the process model as it is or whether it makes sense to add a fragment (NE) or remove an existing one (DE) for future executions of the process.

In combination with the rules specified for the first letter of the extension, each pattern of Russell et al. [20] can be extended by looking at the first and third element of the tuple. For example, the pattern *SFF-CWC-COM* can be extended to *SFF-CWC-COM-TNE* because the considered activity was forced to state *failed* due to SFF = Started Force-Fail. Therefore, the fragment has to be terminated (first letter of fourth element is T). As a compensation method (third element COM) the strategy pattern suggests the creation of a new fragment (last two letters of fourth element are NE).

There is more than one possibility to extend a pattern for workflow systems to make it suitable for fCM. The pattern *SFF-CWC-COM* from above has another extended version which is *SFF-CWC-COM-TDE* because a deletion of existing

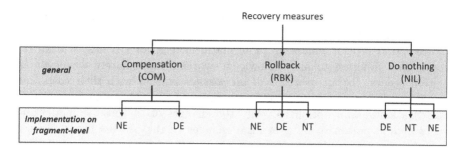

Fig. 4. Possibilities for implementing recovery measures

Table 4. Extension of exception patterns for workflow systems

Workflow system	fCM application
SFF-CWC-COM	SFF-CWC-COM-TNE
	SFF-CWC-COM-TDE
SRS-CWC-RBK	SRS-CWC-RBK-CNE
	SRS-CWC-RBK-CDE
	SRS-CWC-RBK-CNT
SRA-CWC-NIL	SRA-CWC-NIL-CNE
	SRA-CWC-NIL-CDE
	SRA-CWC-NIL-CNT
SFF-RCC-COM	SFF-RCC-COM-TNE
	SFF-RCC-COM-TDE
SCE-CWC-NIL	SCE-CWC-NIL-CNE
	SCE-CWC-NIL-CDE
	SCE-CWC-NIL-CNT

fragments can also be considered as a compensation method. Table 4 illustrates this aspect for the workflow pattern where the activity was in state *started* when an exception occurred.

4.3   Integration into a fCM Application

Knowledge workers often have to design own fragments or modify existing ones to implement the presented pattern. This has a huge implications on their process modeling knowledge, but also on the verification of fCM at run-time. They have to be adept in the area of the certain process to choose the best suitable pattern for handling an exception if there are more than one possible strategies. These enormously high demands on knowledge workers require a tool support to enable the feasibility of the presented concept of exception handling in fCM.

For implementation, the listing of possible pattern has to be automated. This can be done by analysing in which activity state an exception occurs and what exception type it relates to. The platform, e.g. an UI, has to have (a) a *notification function* to alert knowledge workers immediately whenever an exception occurs, (b) an *overview of all possible pattern* with their costs and consequences, (c) a *modeling space* to design new fragments or modify existing ones, (d) a *simulation* option to verify the changes of the process model and (e) a *compiling* option to integrate the changes to the process model. In the next chapter, we are going to show how a possible implementation, following our criteria, could look like on the example of an use case.

5   Application to Use Case

The concepts for exception handling in fCM described in the previous section are exemplified in this section with the help of the last mile delivery fCM model introduced in Sect. 2 as well as the exceptions described in Sect. 3.1.

First of all, the handling for the failure of an activity is discussed. This may be the case when a recipient's address does not exist. The algorithm for optimizing the delivery tour cannot be executed because it cannot identify the stop on a map. The activity *Plan tour* (Fig. 1(b)) is set to state *failed* and while the case continues in execution the fragment which includes the failed activity is terminated manually. Because there is no handling on the part of the process model, knowledge workers would be notified. The mock-up in Fig. 5 shows how this could look like. The interface provides an overview of what exception occurred and how it can be handled. Here, it is important that the case itself continues in executing to ensure a successful delivery of all other parcels. The parcel with the non existent address has to be scanned again or transferred to a human who can then correct the address in the system. This strategy conforms to the pattern *SFF-CWC-RBK-TNT* and *SFF-CWC-COM-TNE*. Both ensure the continuation of the case, but while the first one suggests a rollback by terminating the fragment and restart it, the second one recommends compensation by creating a new fragment e.g. for manual input of the address.

Secondly, an exception of type *Resource not available* is discussed: the case that no carrier can be found to deliver a given parcel. The third fragment can not terminate successfully because the allocation of the planned tour failed. In this case, the concept explained above suggests the pattern *SFF-CWC-COM-TNE*. The case has to continue (CWC) because the parcel has to be delivered to achieve the process goal. So, the best strategy to handle the situation is to compensate the effects (COM), e.g. through modeling new fragments which allow parking of parcels until a carrier is available. As an alternative, a new carrier could be employed. Although this handling would work, the strategy is expensive because ensuring a delivery within a two hour time slot can cost very much.

If the database is not reachable temporarily and does not receive any requests, many fragments will not be triggered. For handling, the patterns *SRS-CWC-RBK-CNT* and *SRS-CWC-RBK-CNE* are both possible. It is very useful, to

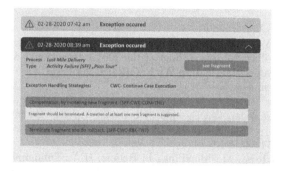

Fig. 5. Mock-up of UI showing occurrence of activity failure

restart the activity once it failed and moreover, there is no reason to stop the case. A rollback is necessary to ensure the correct state of the needed data objects, but on fragment-level a knowledge worker can either do nothing or add a new fragment notifying an engineer to fix the problem.

6   Conclusion

The topic of exception handling in context of fragment-based Case Management (fCM) during run-time is complex and requires a deep understanding of both, the technical context and advanced skills in process modeling. This paper explains a concept of how the strategies of Russell et al. [20] can be used for exception handling in fCM by introducing the fragment-level. Due to an extension of the notation by a fourth element, the handling of the fragment in which the exception occurred can be defined as well as the handling of subsequent fragments can be defined within one pattern. Each handling method for fCM can be mapped as a quadruple. Special rules avoid duplication of semantics of the patterns [20] and ensure direct integration into them. For each original exception handling strategy, there are at least two extensions that can be used in a fCM application. That is why exception handling in fCM is more powerful than in a control-flow based system.

This paper provides a foundation that knowledge workers and developers of an fCM application can use and build on to ensure efficient exception handling. In the future, we want evaluate the usability of our approach by checking the given requirements (see Sect. 4.3) with knowledge workers, as this is essential to guarantee the effectiveness of our future implementation.

Acknowledgement. The research leading to these results has been partly funded by the BMWi under grant agreement 01MD18012C, Project SMile. http://smile-project. de.

References

1. van der Aalst, W.M.P., Berens, P.J.S.: Beyond workflow management: product-driven case handling. In: Proceedings of the 2001 International ACM SIGGROUP Conference on Supporting Group Work, GROUP 2001, pp. 42–51. Association for Computing Machinery, New York (2001)
2. Agostini, A., De Michelis, G.: Improving flexibility of workflow management systems. In: van der Aalst, W., Desel, J., Oberweis, A. (eds.) Business Process Management. LNCS, vol. 1806, pp. 218–234. Springer, Heidelberg (2000). https://doi.org/10.1007/3-540-45594-9_14
3. Dumas, M., La Rosa, M., Mendling, J., Reijers, H.A.: Fundamentals of Business Process Management. Springer, Heidelberg (2018). https://doi.org/10.1007/978-3-662-56509-4
4. Fahland, D.: From scenarios to components. Ph.D. thesis, Humboldt University of Berlin (2010)
5. Fahland, D., Woith, H.: Towards process models for disaster response. In: Ardagna, D., Mecella, M., Yang, J. (eds.) BPM 2008. LNBIP, vol. 17, pp. 254–265. Springer, Heidelberg (2009). https://doi.org/10.1007/978-3-642-00328-8_25
6. Gonzalez-Lopez, F., Pufahl, L.: A landscape for case models. In: Reinhartz-Berger, I., Zdravkovic, J., Gulden, J., Schmidt, R. (eds.) BPMDS/EMMSAD -2019. LNBIP, vol. 352, pp. 87–102. Springer, Cham (2019). https://doi.org/10.1007/978-3-030-20618-5_6
7. Hauder, M., Pigat, S., Matthes, F.: Research challenges in adaptive case management: a literature review. In: 2014 IEEE 18th International Enterprise Distributed Object Computing Conference Workshops and Demonstrations, pp. 98–107, September 2014
8. Hewelt, M., Pufahl, L., Mandal, S., Wolff, F., Weske, M.: Toward a methodology for case modeling. Softw. Syst. Model. **2019**, 1–27 (2019). https://doi.org/10.1007/s10270-019-00766-5
9. Hewelt, M., Weske, M.: A hybrid approach for flexible case modeling and execution. In: La Rosa, M., Loos, P., Pastor, O. (eds.) BPM 2016. LNBIP, vol. 260, pp. 38–54. Springer, Cham (2016). https://doi.org/10.1007/978-3-319-45468-9_3
10. Holfter, A., Haarmann, S., Pufahl, L., Weske, M.: Checking compliance in data-driven case management. In: Di Francescomarino, C., Dijkman, R., Zdun, U. (eds.) BPM 2019. LNBIP, vol. 362, pp. 400–411. Springer, Cham (2019). https://doi.org/10.1007/978-3-030-37453-2_33
11. Kurz, M., Fleischmann, A., Lederer, M., Huber, S.: Planning for the unexpected: exception handling and BPM. In: Fischer, H., Schneeberger, J. (eds.) S-BPM ONE 2013. CCIS, vol. 360, pp. 123–149. Springer, Heidelberg (2013). https://doi.org/10.1007/978-3-642-36754-0_8
12. Lohmeyer, B.: Writing Use Cases: Exception or Alternate Flow? Lohmeyer Business UX (2013). https://www.lohmy.de/2013/03/06/writing-use-cases-exception-or-alternate-flow/. Accessed 28 Feb 2020
13. Luo, Z., Sheth, A., Kochut, K., Miller, J.: Exception handling in workflow systems. Appl. Intell. **13**, 125–147 (2000). https://doi.org/10.1023/A:1008388412284
14. de Man, H.: Case management: a review of modeling approaches. Technical report, BPTrends (2009)
15. Marin, M.A., Hauder, M., Matthes, F.: Case management: an evaluation of existing approaches for knowledge-intensive processes. In: Reichert, M., Reijers, H.A. (eds.) BPM 2015. LNBIP, vol. 256, pp. 5–16. Springer, Cham (2016). https://doi.org/10.1007/978-3-319-42887-1_1

16. Motahari-Nezhad, H.R., Swenson, K.D.: Adaptive case management: overview and research challenges. In: 2013 IEEE 15th Conference on Business Informatics (CBI), pp. 264–269. IEEE (2013)
17. OMG: Notation BPMN Version 2.0. OMG Specification, Object Management Group, pp. 22–31 (2011)
18. Pufahl, L., Ihde, S., Glöckner, M., Franczyk, B., Paulus, B., Weske, M.: Countering congestion: a white-label platform for the last mile parcel delivery. In: Business Information Systems 2020. Springer, Cham (to be published)
19. Ranieri, L., Digiesi, S., Silvestri, B., Roccotelli, M.: A review of last mile logistics innovations in an externalities cost reduction vision. Sustainability **10**(3), 782 (2018)
20. Russell, N., van der Aast, W., ter Hofstede, A.: Exception handling patterns in process-aware information systems. Technical report. Queensland University of Technology/Eindhoven University of Technology(2006)
21. Weber, B., Reichert, M., Rinderle-Ma, S.: Change patterns and change support features - enhancing flexibility in process-aware information systems. Data Knowl. Eng. **66**(3), 438–466 (2008)

Business Process Monitoring
on Blockchains: Potentials and Challenges

Claudio Di Ciccio[1], Giovanni Meroni[2]([✉]), and Pierluigi Plebani[2]

[1] Sapienza University of Rome, Rome, Italy
diciccio@di.uniroma1.it
[2] Politecnico di Milano, Milan, Italy
{giovanni.meroni,pierluigi.plebani}@polimi.it

Abstract. The ability to enable a tamper-proof distribution of immutable data has boosted the studies around the adoption of blockchains also in Business Process Management. In this direction, current research work primarily focuses on blockchain-based business process design, or on execution engines able to enact processes through smart contracts. Although very relevant, less studies have been devoted so far on how the adoption of blockchains can be beneficial to business process monitoring. This work goes into this direction by providing an insightful analysis to understand the benefits as well as the hurdles of blockchain-enabled business process monitoring. In particular, this work considers the adoption of programmable blockchain platforms to manage the generation, distribution, and analysis of business process monitoring data.

Keywords: Blockchain · Business process monitoring · Business Process Management

1 Introduction

Blockchains are gaining momentum in Business Process Management (BPM) research as the infrastructural platform of choice on which collaborative, multi-party business processes are conducted [12]. Thanks to their guarantee of persistence and immutability of the recorded transactions, not only can they operate as a solid backbone for the storage of data and actions, but they are also promising aids for the monitoring of processes that run atop [16].

Research towards the adoption of blockchains for the monitoring of processes is, however, still at its early stages. Thus far, most of the attempts have focused on the generation of readily usable data for the application of existing process mining techniques [5,8,14] and the creation of networks highlighting the most common patterns of exchange of information and assets among peers [6,7,16]. A comprehensive analysis of the aspects of blockchains that may favour or encumber the monitoring of processes is, to the best of our knowledge, still missing.

© Springer Nature Switzerland AG 2020
S. Nurcan et al. (Eds.): BPMDS 2020/EMMSAD 2020, LNBIP 387, pp. 36–51, 2020.
https://doi.org/10.1007/978-3-030-49418-6_3

The goal of this paper is to clarify to what extent a blockchain can be beneficial for business process monitoring. On this basis, the paper identifies a set of research challenges that are worth to be addressed by the research community for the design and realization of blockchain-based process monitoring platforms.

The remainder of this paper is as follows. Section 2 describes the fundamental elements of process monitoring. Section 3 describes the concepts on which blockchain platforms are based and illustrates the main research conducted so far for the process-oriented analysis of blockchain data. Section 4 examines the challenges and opportunities we envision for a blockchain-based process monitoring architecture. Finally, Sect. 5 concludes the paper.

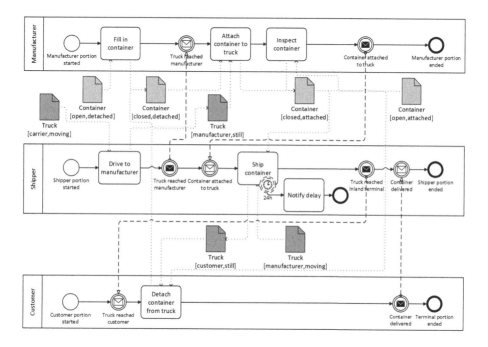

Fig. 1. Motivating example.

2 Business Process Monitoring

Business process monitoring aims at identifying how well running processes are performing with respect to performance measures and objectives. Depending on the available tools and data, a business process platform can report on the running processes, from the sole tracking of the running instances to the checking of deviations with respect to the expected behaviour and the identification of other anomalies. This section briefly introduces the main characteristics of business process monitoring platforms in terms of the possible objectives of the monitoring (i.e., the why), the available techniques (i.e., the how), and the subject of monitoring (i.e., the what).

To better explain these aspects, we use an example taken from the logistics domain. Figure 1 shows the Business Process Model and Notation (BPMN) model of a shipment process in particular. The example involves a manufacturer, M, who receives an order from one of its customers, C, and a shipper, S, on whom M relies for the delivery of the goods to C. At first, M starts filling a shipping container with the goods requested by C. Meanwhile, S starts driving one of its trucks to M's production facility. Once the truck arrives, M firstly attaches the container to the truck, then inspects the container to verify if all the goods requested by C are present. Such an inspection should be performed only at this stage, and the container should not be opened again until it reaches the premises of C. Once the inspection completes, S ships the container to C, which detaches it from the truck. In case the shipping activity takes longer that 24 h, S must justify the delay.

Why to Monitor. There are several reasons why a monitoring platform should be introduced. As a general need, the process owner and the recipients are interested in verifying and demonstrating that the process is behaving correctly. A monitoring platform can be a passive element that merely records the performed actions, or it can actively contribute to handle the occurring deviations.

Moreover, the objectives of a business process monitoring platform can be various: to determine if activities take longer than expected to complete, if there are bottlenecks in the process, if resources are under- or over-utilized, and if there are violations in the process execution, among other things. Depending on the needs of the process owner, all – or a subset – of these aspects can be considered.

How to Monitor. According to the classification proposed by [1] and [17], process monitoring techniques can be classified in five main groups: event data logging, Business Activity Monitoring, runtime performance analysis, conformance checking, and compliance checking.

Event data logging is the generation of sequences of events related to a specific process instance being executed. Events can provide notifications on the activities being executed, or on the artifacts (i.e., the physical or virtual objects manipulated by the process) and the resources (i.e., the human operators or software components responsible for executing activities) participating in the process. Once collected, events are typically stored in so-called event logs. Since several other monitoring techniques require event data to work, this technique is often seen as a prerequisite for them.

Business Activity Monitoring (BAM) and Runtime Performance Analysis: Also known as "monitoring" [1], BAM analyzes real-time information on the activities being executed (e.g., response time and failure rate). With this technique it is possible to measure Key Performance Indicators (KPIs) relevant for the process, thus determining how well activities are performed. Given event data, BAM produces measurements for KPIs. Instead, runtime performance analysis focuses on the data analysis of performance information on the processes being executed to identify bottlenecks or resource allocation problems. Unlike BAM, which focuses on single activities, Runtime performance analysis focuses on process runs, thus accounting for dependencies among activities. Given a process model and event data, runtime performance analysis produces performance-related diagnostic information.

By resorting on BAM, and runtime performance analysis, it is possible to measure KPIs and identify other issues not directly related to the process structure. For instance, it is possible to determine if activity *Attach container to truck* is causing a bottleneck, or if *Drive to manufacturer* consumes too many resources (e.g., if M is located in a poorly connected area). Based on the agreements between organizations, these techniques may be confined only to activities belonging to each organization, or they may be applied to all the activities.

Conformance checking consists in the techniques that compare the modeled process behavior with the one evidenced by execution data. To this end, the gathered event data are replayed on the process model, so as to detect deviations from the expected behaviour. Given a process model and event data, Conformance checking produces conformance-related diagnostic information.

With conformance checking, the stakeholders can verify if the execution is in line with the process description. In particular, the nature of the model plays an important role in defining the degrees of freedom that are left to the process executors. A collaboration diagram (e.g., the complete collaboration diagram in Fig. 1) will force the whole process to strictly adhere to the specifications. A process diagram (e.g., only the portion of the process inside a specific pool) will force the process portion belonging to that stakeholder to adhere to the specifications. Finally, a choreography diagram will force only the interactions among stakeholders to adhere to the specifications, leaving the stakeholders free to alter their internal processes.

Compliance checking encompasses the techniques aimed at verifying that constraints representing regulations, guidelines, policies and laws, are fulfilled by the process. It differs from conformance checking because constraints focus on process rules, rather than on entire process runs.

Through compliance checking techniques, it is possible to define complex constraints on the process that predicate both on the structure and on non functional aspects. Instead of relying on a process model, compliance checking relies on compliance rules that describe only the elements of the process that are useful to assess the constraint. For instance, it is possible to monitor if the container is delivered to C within two days since when M finished preparing it. Likewise, it is possible to monitor if less than 1% of the shipments were carried out without inspecting the container. To this aim, according to [10], several compliance checking techniques and languages exist. Since constraints predicate on specific portions of the process, rather than on the process as a whole, it is much easier for stakeholders to agree on monitoring them. In fact, only activities required for the assessment of such constraints have to be disclosed, thus overcoming one of the issues of conformance checking.

What to Monitor. Depending on the monitoring technique and on the underlying representation of the process to monitor, different kinds of events have to be logged for the monitoring to be reliable. Conformance checking techniques typically require events notifying the start or termination of activities, or the transmission and receipt of messages among participants. BAM, runtime performance analysis and compliance checking techniques usually require more complex events, also indicating when artifacts were manipulated or who performed a task (e.g., starting an activity or modifying an artifact).

Typically, if the reference model adopted for process monitoring is a *process diagram*, only events belonging to the owner of the process are collected and analyzed. When the process consists only of either automated activities or form-based ones, obtaining events is a relatively easy task. In fact, event logs can be retrieved from the Business Process Management System (BPMS) in charge of executing the process. Also, since users are required to interact with the BPMS to perform business activities, event logs contain accurate information on who performed which task, when the task was performed, and which artifacts were involved during its execution. However, when the process also involves manual activities, that is, activities that are performed by users without interacting with the BPMS (e.g., shipping the container), collecting reliable event logs becomes challenging. In fact, users may forget to notify to the BPMS when they perform activities, they may incorrectly indicate in the notifications when the activities were performed, they may indicate that they performed an activity which was not done or which was done by another user. These issues can be partially solved with Internet of Things (IoT)-based solutions, such as artifact-driven monitoring [13] or Unicorn [2], which autonomously collect events from the artifacts being manipulated, to be then analyzed to infer which activity was executed.

If the process to monitor is represented as a *collaboration diagram*, events belonging to all the involved organizations have to be logged and shared among participants. This is a challenging task both from the organizational and technical standpoint. However, from an organizational viewpoint, the participants may be reluctant to share events on the activities being performed, as it may allow competitors to uncover their operations. In case of BAM and runtime performance analysis, sharing such events may even violate privacy regulations, such as the General Data Protection Regulation (GDPR), since information on the employees performing activities may be shared to the other organizations. Technical-wise, sharing events typically requires either individual information systems to be federated, or a centralized cross-organizational information system to be deployed and adopted by all the participants. To partially overcome these issues, organizations can autonomously monitor their own portions, and then share aggregated monitoring data to the other participants. However, this approach reintroduces the problem of trust between organizations, moving it from the execution to the monitoring of the processes. In fact, for this approach to hold, organizations are required to trust each other, assuming that monitoring data reflect the actual behavior of the process.

In case the process is represented as a *choreography diagram*, events related to the transmission and reception of messages between organizations have to be logged. From the technical standpoint, as long as the message exchanges are performed digitally (e.g., email, web service invocations), it is relatively easy to log and distribute events. In fact, it is sufficient to passively monitor the communication channels, generating events whenever communication activity is detected. On the other hand, if physical objects are exchanged, generating event logs is a more complex task. In fact, an active agent is required to observe the real world and produce an event whenever some physical object is either received or sent. Originally, this was done by relying on human operators, but it suffered from the same limitations as the ones outlined for manual activities. Therefore, IoT-based solutions to track physical objects are adopted as long as the contents of the messages are kept confidential, and only events relevant for the process being monitored are disclosed.

Finally, in case compliance rules have to be monitored, depending on the language and technique adopted, events related to messages, activities, or artifacts have to be logged. Consequently, compliance checking has the same technical limitations as all the conformance checking techniques. However, not every event related to the process has to be logged, but only the ones required for verifying the compliance rules. Therefore, monitoring has a much lower footprint on the organizations. Also, since organizations can selectively choose which events to be logged and made available to the other participants, they can agree on not to share information that discloses their know-how.

3 Monitoring with the Blockchain: State of the Art

In this section, we summarize the fundamental notions on which blockchain platforms are based and the research conducted thus far that aims at analysing blockchain data for process execution and analysis.

3.1 Elements of Blockchains

A blockchain is a protocol for the decentralized storage of a tamper-proof sequence of transactions, maintained and verified by the nodes participating in the network. A *ledger* is an append-only list of data units named *transactions*. Every transaction records a transfer of value (digital assets, cryptocurrencies, information bits, etc.) between two accounts. The sender cryptographically signs the transaction to provide evidence that it is not counterfeit. Blockchains such as Bitcoin [15] and Ethereum [21] collate transactions into so-called blocks. Blocks are thus used as the messages to be broadcast to every node. The order among blocks (and, a fortiori, the transactions therein) is kept by a hash-based backward linking: every block keeps the digest of a hashing function applied to the previous block. All together, the links generate a chain-like structure: hence the name blockchain. Locally to a node, transactions are subject to a total ordering relation: the evolution of the state of the parties' accounts depend on the sequence of operations recorded in the ledger. Blocks are, in fact, a measure of time as their addition to the chain determines the passage to the next global system state. To pay back the effort of nodes, an economic incentive is proposed that distributes so-called cryptocurrencies to the nodes that publish the accepted blocks. Nodes participating in the network guarantee that transactions and blocks are valid and thus prevent the data structure to be tampered with. Also, the replication of the ledger makes it possible to have the stored information always available locally to every node. However, the ledger may differ from node to node: the nodes reach *eventual consensus* on the correct sequence in the ledger. Temporary divergences between the local images of the ledger are called *forks*. The way in which access and right to write are granted, determine two main categorisations of the blockchain platform in use: *private* blockchains are accessible only to a restricted number of peers, as opposed to the *public* ones; if a selected number of participants only is allowed to decide on the next blocks, the blockchain is *permissioned*, otherwise it is *permissionless*. Natively, Bitcoin and Ethereum are natively public permissionless blockchain, although for the latter private networks can be created that operate within conortia, allowing only a subset of nodes to mine blocks. Hyperledger Fabric,[1] instead, is conceived as a consortium (private) permissioned blockchain.

Second-generation blockchains such as Ethereum and Hyperledger Fabric support the so-called *smart contracts* [18], that is, executable code expressing how business is to be conducted among contracting parties (e.g., transfer digital assets after a condition is fulfilled). In this paper, we will focus on this kind of blockchains operating as distributed programmable platforms. Smart contracts often require data from the world outside the blockchain sphere (e.g., financial data, weather-related information, random numbers, sensors from hardware devices). However, they cannot directly invoke external APIs. Therefore, smart contracts need software adaptors that play that interfacing role. Those artefacts are named *oracles* [22]. Oracles can be further classified as *software* or *hardware* oracles. Software oracles aim to extract information from programmed applications (e.g., web services), whereas hardware oracles extract data from the physical world (e.g., IoT devices).

3.2 Current Approaches

To date, preliminary attempts have been proposed that can be the basis to be built upon for process monitoring in the blockchain. Smart contracts allow for the codification of business process logic on the blockchain, as shown in the seminal work of Weber et al. [20]. Later, a similar approach has been applied within the Caterpillar [9] and Lorikeet [19] tools, as well as by Madsen et al.

---

[1] https://www.hyperledger.org/projects/fabric.

[11]. As several modern Business Process Management Systems (BPMSs) do, those approaches adopt a Model-Driven Engineering (MDE) paradigm to let the process analysts provide graphical representations of the process and turn it into executable code enacting it [4].

From the monitoring perspective, the efforts have been mostly devoted to event data logging thus far: the main rationale is to extract and process the payload of transactions to turn them into event logs that are readily available for process mining tools. The ordering of events is based upon the ordering of the transactions in the ledger, whereas the attributes of the event (activity name, timestamp, resource, and the like) are identified based on the signature of the invoked function on the smart contract [14], a user-defined descriptor (manifest) [8], or the change of the smart contract's attribute value [5]. Thereupon, process mining techniques (including conformance checking) are held to analyse the generated event logs.

Other approaches have been applied to analyse blockchain-mediated communications among peers, such as GraphSense [7]. Filtz et al. [6] studied the graph of addresses in Bitcoin and thereby examined the transaction behavior of users, taking into consideration exchange rates between virtual and fiat currencies. Prybila et al. [16] focus in particular on the transposition of handovers of tasks in a process to Bitcoin transactions. With their software prototype, they are thus able to verify the execution flow of a process by tracking the transactions exchanged among peers.

The research conducted thus far constitutes a clear advancement towards future architectures for business processes monitoring that are based on the blockchain. In the following section, we discuss challenges and opportunities that come along with their design and adoption.

4   Monitoring with Blockchain: Challenges and Opportunities

Due to its properties, a blockchain can be adopted as a distributed infrastructure on top of which a new type of business process monitoring platforms can be built. These platforms can exploit the properties of data immutability, trust among the parties, and data distribution offered by design by blockchains. Owing to their programmability, we focus in particular on second-generation blockchains in the remainder of this paper.

To properly describe the potentials of introducing blockchains to this end, Fig. 2 shows a reference architecture that couples the typical BPMS monitoring subsystem with a blockchain. Without focusing on one of the specific monitoring approaches discussed in Sect. 2, we can generalize the input of the monitoring platform with the status of the process instances and the ongoing activities (*process status*), and of the artifacts managed thereby (*artifact status*). Depending on the adopted technique, the logic implemented by the monitoring platform transforms this information about the status. The produced output, generally referred as *monitoring data*, can be a collection of event logs, or a transformation

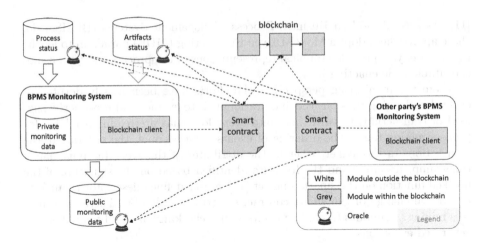

Fig. 2. Blockchain-enhanced BPMS monitoring reference architecture

of the obtained input data into aggregated information that is more meaningful to the analysis (e.g., at a higher level of abstraction than low-level events). A portion of this output can be kept private (*private monitoring data*) or made public (*public monitoring data*), to let other interested parties to check, for instance, the compliance of the process.

When enriching the monitoring platform with a blockchain, the monitoring logic may be encoded in one or more *smart contracts*. First of all, this requires that the monitoring system includes a *blockchain client* which enables the communication with the rest of the blockchain infrastructure. Secondly, as the output of a smart contract is published as a transaction payload on the blockchain, the resulting monitoring data produced by the smart contract is automatically available to anyone allowed to access the blockchain. This implies that the monitoring logic implemented as smart contract must be limited to the part producing public monitoring data. On the one hand, this opportunity increases the transparency of the monitoring and the possibility for external actors to evaluate the behaviour of the process, as the smart contract is immutable and executed on all the nodes in the blockchain network. On the other hand, since the publication of data on the blockchain has an impact in terms of cost and performance, it becomes of utmost importance to establish which monitoring data can be included in the blockchain (i.e., on-chain thus trusted by definition), and which one can be left off-chain as typical public monitoring data (i.e., only under the control of the party producing them).

The distinction between data on- and off-chain is relevant not only when considering the output of the monitoring platform, but also concerning the input of a smart contract as they can natively operate only on data published on the blockchain. To overcome this limitation, blockchains offer *oracles* to extend the smart contract accessibility to off-chain data. For this reason, it is required that any dataset to which a smart contract requires access for its computation, needs to be coupled with an oracle. Since coupling a dataset with an oracle means making those data visible to all the members of the blockchain, this implies that the data set should be properly partitioned into public (i.e., accessible through the oracle) and private parts.

Table 1. Challenges in monitoring with the blockchain

Aspect	Challenge	Perspective		
		Design rationale	Lack of capability	Trust management
Smart contracts	Monitoring transparency	X		X
	Observability	X		
	Lack of reactivity	X	X	
Oracles	Time management		X	X
	Reliability	X		X
	Flexibility	X	X	
Data management	Data quality		X	X
	Data size	X		
	Side effects		X	

In light of the above discussion, we observe that, to improve the business process monitoring via blockchain, a thorough blueprint is required in terms of the smart contracts (reflecting the monitoring capabilities), the oracles (identifying the data sources), and the monitoring data (balancing between on-chain and off-chain data). Table 1 illustrates the research challenges related to those three aspects and categorizes them according to three main perspectives: the need for a thorough *design rationale* behind the realisation of the monitoring infrastructure; the necessity to tackle the *lack of capabilities* that the infrastructural usage of the blockchain brings; the demand for a policy of *trust management* with information and actors. Each of the following subsections discusses in further detail those aspects and the related challenges, emphasizing the perspectives from which the issues are analyzed.

4.1   Challenges About Smart Contracts

Monitoring Transparency. To improve the transparency of compliance checking, especially in case of multi-party business processes, a smart contract holds a crucial role. In fact, based on the information that can be made accessible through oracles and the relevant transactions mined in the blockchain, a smart contract can analyse the current status of the process enactment and verify if the control flow – in the case of orchestrated processes – or the message exchange – in the case of a choreographed process – are behaving as expected. As the code composing the smart contract is immutably stored on the blockchain, and it is executed on all the blockchain clients to reach consensus, it is extremely hard for a single party to alter it in order to counterfeit the result. As a consequence, when a single party is involved in the business process, being the smart contract published on the blockchain, the logic that drives compliance becomes publicly available to all the parties interested in the soundness of the process, even if they are not directly involved in the enactment (e.g., auditors). Conversely, in multi-party business processes, information about the obligations involving the parties can be produced and observed with smart contracts. For example, by turning the process model in Fig. 1 into a smart contract, M, S and C agree on how the process should be carried out. As the constraints become public, none of them can complain that they expected the process to be executed differently.

If, on the one hand, such a transparency offered by smart contracts increases the trust in the process execution, on the other hand, it requires smart contracts to be properly *designed* in order to expose only the information that should be made available to external actors. Moreover, the ability for a smart contract to verify possible deviations in the process enactment is strictly related to the monitoring data that are available through the oracles. As a consequence, the availability of proper data sources that can be accessed by the smart contract is fundamental. With single-party business processes, this issue is not so critical as the party is responsible for designing the smart contract as well as for designing the oracles and choosing the data sources. Conversely, when talking about multi-party business processes, an agreement among parties must include also the possibility to make available some of the data about the process and artifact status to other parties. This opens an additional issue about the accessibility of those data. For instance, to determine if the process portion carried out by S is correctly performed, S must expose the information on the position and speed of its trucks.

In a blockchain, the transactions of mined blocks are available to all participants. Consequently, additional mechanisms must be implemented on top of the blockchain (e.g., based on encryption) to limit the visibility of this data only to the subset of clients that are actually allowed to see them, so as to enable *trust*. For example, S may agree on sharing information on its trucks with M, but may refuse to make this information publicly available, as competitors may exploit it (e.g., by finding areas that are not well covered by S).

Observability. Although both the smart contracts and the invocations of its methods are stored in the blockchain, and their execution can be performed and analyzed by any participant, most blockchains require smart contracts to explicitly define methods to retrieve their information. In other words, variables that are used by smart contracts are accessible only by the smart contract itself, unless methods to make their contents available are explicitly defined in the smart contracts *design*. As a consequence, before putting in place a blockchain-based monitoring platform, care should be taken defining which information can be retrieved from the smart contract. For example, suppose that, to monitor the process in Fig. 1, a smart contract is implemented that has an internal representation of the process and of the status of each activity. That smart contract may expose a function to check whether the process conforms to the model or not, without providing information on the activities. As a consequence, although the smart contract internally knows that, e.g., *Ship container* is running and *Attach container to truck* is complete, it would lack a way to communicate this information to other smart contracts or other participants, which cannot rely on it to determine the status of the process and its activities.

To mitigate this issue, one could "debug" a smart contract by tracing the execution of each transaction since when the deployment took place, thus identifying the variables and how they change over time, similarly to the approach of Duchmann and Koschmider [5]. However, if the discovered information is required by another smart contract, this information should be provided off-chain even though it originated on-chain, with consequent trust issues and the need, once again, to rely on an oracle.

Lack of Reactivity. A smart contract *lacks the capability* of independently making calls or invocations to endpoints outside the blockchain upon the verification of certain conditions. This is a limitation for business process monitoring, as in case of deviations, the process owner or the parties involved in the process wish they were informed in order to properly react. For example, if the smart contract monitoring the process in Fig. 1 detects that activity *Inspect container* was performed while the container was being shipped, it cannot autonomously contact *S* off-chain to request a justification for that action.

To solve this issue, a smart contract has to be *designed* so as to either expose public methods that can be periodically called by the interested parties to check if some deviations occurred, or emit events and require parties to constantly monitor the blockchain in order to catch them as soon as they fire. In both cases, e.g., it is *S*'s duty to constantly check for events notifying an anomaly in its own process and promptly react to them.

4.2 Challenges About Oracles

Time Management. Among the several aspects that are interesting to monitor about a business process, one of the most pivotal is checking if an activity, or a group of them, is performed on time. Nevertheless, implementing a smart contract able to verify this condition could be cumbersome as a blockchain *lacks a notion* of time aside from the coarse-grained block time [14]. More in detail, although a blockchain sorts the transactions, it cannot deal with timers. This is due to the fact that the expiration of a timer, or more simply a clock-ticking event, would be an action that originates from the smart contract itself. However, as a smart contract can only perform actions that are externally invoked, such actions cannot be performed without the help of an external entity. For example, suppose that a smart contract is adopted to check whether activity *Ship container* is executed on time. That smart contract cannot determine that activity *Ship container* took longer than 24 h until it receives a notification that the activity was completed, unless it is actively polled by an external entity.

For this reason, time must be managed externally to the blockchain by means of specific oracles which must be configured by the smart contract to send a trigger whenever a timeout expires. It is also important to consider that those oracles are external to the blockchain by definition, hence outside the chain of *trust* managed by the blockchain. For this reason, when designing a time oracle, the situation in which the oracle experiences a failure or produces fake data (e.g., it goes out of sync) must be taken into consideration. To mitigate this issue, oracles may integrate time synchronization protocols.

Reliability. The goal of an oracle is to allow the smart contracts to acquire information from the real world. Thus, oracles must guarantee the correctness of the data they emit. However, this may not occur for two reasons. Firstly, the oracle may deliver data that are intentionally wrong or – because of a man-in-the-middle attack – data are forged before being sent to the smart contract. Secondly, the oracle may not be reliable and the data produced could be accidentally wrong. For example, if the truck's GPS receiver is breached, the related oracle could send incorrect information on its location.

Both circumstances hamper the *trust* in the gathered data. The solution is to rely not on a single oracle to obtain information about a phenomenon occurring in the real world, but to have a set of oracles, possibly managed by different actors. With such a *design*, the effort to cheat on the smart contract becomes significant as it requires to forge several oracles. Moreover, the smart contract can query several oracles and – assuming that problems may occur only on a minority of them – compare the data being sent to determine which ones cannot be trusted. For instance, the smart contract may rely on information coming from the truck's GPS receiver, the truck driver's smartphone, and the highway tollbooths, to know the location of a truck. Although this approach could solve the problem, having a set of oracles for the same phenomena is not always feasible or affordable, especially when monitoring human-based activities.

A possible solution to the problem of trust is to certify the oracles. In this sense, approaches similar to the Public Key Infrastructure (PKI) can be adopted to introduce authentication and authorization mechanisms.

Flexibility. Adopting oracles to allow smart contracts to check the behaviour of a process implies that all the phenomena relevant for the monitoring should be exposed through oracles. Since the smart contract should know in advance which are the oracles providing the needed data, this could result in a *lack of flexibility*. In fact, adding new oracles after the monitoring has been designed could be useless, as there is no possibility to inform the smart contract about their existence. For example, suppose that the monitoring platform relied initially on manual notifications to determine when the container was filled in, and references to that oracle were hardcoded in the platform's smart contracts. If later on containers are equipped with scales to automatically infer if they are full or empty, it is not possible for the platform to rely on that information, unless smart contracts are redesigned and deployed anew.

Mechanisms for enabling late binding of oracles to smart contracts are thus desirable for a proper *design*. Notice that late binding would also tackle problems of reliability. Without that mechanism in place, an oracle that is no longer available cannot be replaced.

4.3   Challenges About Monitoring Data Management

Data Quality. In addition to the problems discussed in the previous section related to the possibility that the oracles are not able to provide reliable data, there is also the possibility that the data provider used by the oracle itself is *not trustworthy*. For instance, in the case of a manual activity, it might happen that the oracle is not connected to any sensor, as it is not possible to automatically get the information, but the change in the status of the activity is personally done by the operator. Consequently, the operator could cheat the system declaring, for instance, that an activity is concluded even though it is not the case. Although this is a well-known problem in business process monitoring, we are confident that also the adoption of blockchains may not be beneficial to solve it.

Furthermore, if erroneous data are stored in the blockchain, they can be amended only by appending the correct information, as the blockchain *does not allow* for the alteration of data in a mined block. Therefore, effective mechanisms to assess the quality of monitoring data during the consensus phase are key [3].

Data Size. In a blockchain, the larger the amount of stored data is, the more expensive the transaction gets. This simple rule has a significant impact on monitoring costs. Indeed, in the initial approaches [8,14], all the data that could be useful for monitoring were supposed to be stored on-chain. Nevertheless, to reduce these costs, care should be taken in the *design* of the smart contract to minimize the amount of on-chain information to the sole data that are required to perform monitoring [8]. To this aim, distributed file systems such as IPFS[2] can be adopted to store the entire monitoring data set. Then, the transaction only includes a link to externally stored data, and a hash value computed to guarantee immutability. However, as smart contracts cannot natively retrieve and process off-chain data, this could imply that oracle-mediated operations are required again.

Side Effects. Most blockchains are prone to soft forks, i.e., branches in the chain of blocks caused by two or more blocks pointing to the same predecessor. To solve ambiguities, blockchain clients consider as valid the longest chain, that is, the one having the highest number of subsequent blocks originating from the point of forking. From a monitoring standpoint, this *lack of information consistency* is an issue, since valid monitoring data may not be considered as the block containing them happen to lie on a discarded post-fork branch.

Aside from soft forks, public blockchains such as Ethereum are also prone to so-called hard forks. In case a change in the consensus protocol is made

---

[2] Interplanetary File System (IPFS), https://ipfs.io.

– for either technical or political reasons – some participants may not accept it. Unlike soft forks, hard forks cause a split in the blockchain network, which hampers interoperability. From the monitoring standpoint, hard forks may break the platform if some participants decide not to migrate to the new protocol.

5   Conclusion

Throughout this paper, we have discussed the advantages and challenges that come along the interplay between blockchain data and process analysis for monitoring. Despite the growing interest in the adoption of blockchain technologies for process execution environments, research in that direction is still at its early stages. Considering a reference architecture for the realisation of blockchain-based process monitoring, we have focused on the role that smart contracts, oracles and data management strategies play, in pursuit of a fruitful discussion in the community that drives the adoption of blockchain in process monitoring.

Acknowledgements. The work of Claudio Di Ciccio was partly supported by the MIUR under grant "Dipartimenti di eccellenza 2018–2022" of the Department of Computer Science at Sapienza University of Rome.

References

1. van der Aalst, W.M.P.: Business process management: a comprehensive survey. ISRN Softw. Eng. **2013**(507984), 37 (2013)
2. Beyer, J., Kuhn, P., Hewelt, M., Mandal, S., Weske, M.: Unicorn meets Chimera: integrating external events into case management. In: Proceedings of the BPM Demo Track, pp. 67–72 (2016)
3. Cappiello, C., Comuzzi, M., Daniel, F., Meroni, G.: Data quality control in blockchain applications. In: BPM (Blockchain and CEE Forum), pp. 166–181 (2019)
4. Di Ciccio, C., et al.: Blockchain support for collaborative business processes. Informatik Spektrum **42**, 182–190 (2019)
5. Duchmann, F., Koschmider, A.: Validation of smart contracts using process mining. In: ZEUS, pp. 13–16 (2019)
6. Filtz, E., Polleres, A., Karl, R., Haslhofer, B.: Evolution of the bitcoin address graph. In: Haber, P., Lampoltshammer, T., Mayr, M. (eds.) Data Science - Analytics and Applications, pp. 77–82. Springer, Wiesbaden (2017). https://doi.org/10.1007/978-3-658-19287-7_11
7. Haslhofer, B., Karl, R., Filtz, E.: O bitcoin where art thou? Insight into large-scale transaction graphs. In: SEMANTiCS (Posters, Demos) (2016)
8. Klinkmüller, C., Ponomarev, A., Tran, A.B., Weber, I., van der Aalst, W.: Mining blockchain processes: extracting process mining data from blockchain applications. In: BPM (Blockchain and CEE Forum), pp. 71–86 (2019)
9. López-Pintado, O., García-Bañuelos, L., Dumas, M., Weber, I., Ponomarev, A.: Caterpillar: a business process execution engine on the Ethereum blockchain. Sofw. Pract. Exp. **49**(7), 1162–1193 (2019)

10. Ly, L.T., Maggi, F.M., Montali, M., Rinderle-Ma, S., van der Aalst, W.M.P.: Compliance monitoring in business processes: functionalities, application, and tool-support. Inf. Syst. **54**, 209–234 (2015)
11. Madsen, M.F., Gaub, M., Høgnason, T., Kirkbro, M.E., Slaats, T., Debois, S.: Collaboration among adversaries: distributed workflow execution on a blockchain. In: FAB, pp. 8–15 (2018)
12. Mendling, J., et al.: Blockchains for business process management - challenges and opportunities. ACM Trans. Manag. Inf. Syst. **9**(1), 4:1–4:16 (2018)
13. Meroni, G., Baresi, L., Montali, M., Plebani, P.: Multi-party business process compliance monitoring through IoT-enabled artifacts. Inf. Syst. **73**, 61–78 (2018)
14. Mühlberger, R., Bachhofner, S., Di Ciccio, C., García-Bañuelos, L., López-Pintado, O.: Extracting event logs for process mining from data stored on the blockchain. In: Di Francescomarino, C., Dijkman, R., Zdun, U. (eds.) BPM 2019. LNBIP, vol. 362, pp. 690–703. Springer, Cham (2019). https://doi.org/10.1007/978-3-030-37453-2_55
15. Nakamoto, S.: Bitcoin: a peer-to-peer electronic cash system (2008). https://bitcoin.org/bitcoin.pdf
16. Prybila, C., Schulte, S., Hochreiner, C., Weber, I.: Runtime verification for business processes utilizing the bitcoin blockchain. In: FGCS (2017)
17. Reichert, M., Weber, B.: Enabling Flexibility in Process-Aware Information Systems - Challenges, Methods, Technologies. Springer, Heidelberg (2012). https://doi.org/10.1007/978-3-642-30409-5
18. Szabo, N.: Formalizing and securing relationships on public networks. First Monday **2**(9) (1997). https://firstmonday.org/ojs/index.php/fm/article/view/548
19. Tran, A.B., Lu, Q., Weber, I.: Lorikeet: a model-driven engineering tool for blockchain-based business process execution and asset management. In: BPM Demos, pp. 56–60 (2018)
20. Weber, I., Xu, X., Riveret, R., Governatori, G., Ponomarev, A., Mendling, J.: Untrusted business process monitoring and execution using blockchain. In: La Rosa, M., Loos, P., Pastor, O. (eds.) BPM 2016. LNCS, vol. 9850, pp. 329–347. Springer, Cham (2016). https://doi.org/10.1007/978-3-319-45348-4_19
21. Wood, G.: Ethereum: a secure decentralised generalised transaction ledger (2018). https://ethereum.github.io/yellowpaper/paper.pdf
22. Xu, X., Weber, I., Staples, M.: Architecture for Blockchain Applications. Springer, Cham (2019). https://doi.org/10.1007/978-3-030-03035-3

BPM Applications in Industry and Practice (BPMDS 2020)

Factors Impacting Successful BPMS Adoption and Use: A South African Financial Services Case Study

Ashley Koopman and Lisa F. Seymour(✉) ⓘ

University of Cape Town, Cape Town, South Africa
lisa.seymour@uct.ac.za

Abstract. Business Process Management Suites (BPMS) are being adopted in organisations to increase business process agility across a diverse application landscape. Yet many organisations struggle to achieve agile business processes when using a BPMS. This South African financial services case study explains factors found to negatively impact successful BPMS adoption and use. The Alter work system's framework and the Rosemann and vom Brocke core BPM elements were used as theoretical lenses to understand the case. The paper describes frustrations of an IT team trying to increase process agility with a BPMS in a large legacy application landscape. The main factors driving this frustration were the difficulty of integrating with other applications and staff bypassing design and code approval procedures. The impact of BPM strategy, culture and governance on BPM methods, resourcing and technology is explained. The paper presents an explanatory model which should be useful for practitioners wanting to adopt a BPMS. The BPM literature lacks empirical qualitative case studies and theoretical models and this paper aimed to contribute to both.

Keywords: Business Process Management · Business Process Management Suites · BPM adoption

1 Introduction

Business process (BP) agility is defined as the organisation's ability to swiftly alter their BPs in response to changes in the market [1], and is important for competitiveness. Yet, BP agility is challenged by rapidly evolving technologies and business environments [2, 3]. To achieve BP agility, BP management software, also referred to as BP Management Suites (BPMS) is often combined with various information technology (IT) architectures, such as service oriented architecture (SOA) [4, 5].

BPMS solutions, packaged as a single solution, are collections of software such as graphical modelling tools, process analysis tools, orchestration engines and integration platforms [6]. Software tools earlier described as workflow, business intelligence, rules engines, or enterprise application integration tools are now integrated into BPMS products. BPMS and SOA are seen as two sides of the same coin [7]. In 2012, Gartner defined the BPMS market as one of the most rapid growing markets within the IT industry [8].

© Springer Nature Switzerland AG 2020
S. Nurcan et al. (Eds.): BPMDS 2020/EMMSAD 2020, LNBIP 387, pp. 55–69, 2020.
https://doi.org/10.1007/978-3-030-49418-6_4

BPMS growth accelerated in 2018, attributed to cloud-native capabilities and robotic process automation [9].

Agile BPs have become important in financial services due to regulations relating to financial institutions being extremely dynamic [10], and lessons from the financial crisis of 2008. In this crisis many financial service organisations were unable to react swiftly [11]. Banks changed quickly from having sufficient cash reserves to being desperately in need of financial support from their governments [11].

While achieving BP agility is the primary goal of implementing and using a BPMS, achieving agile BPs is not guaranteed. In certain instances, organisations struggle to attain the level of agility they set out to achieve. It is for this reason that the adoption and use of BPMS needs to be better understood. Recker and Reijers at the BPM 2019 conference noted that there is a lack of empirical qualitative BP case studies and they stated that "we need to identify issues organizations are facing" [12]. The BPM literature has also been labelled as theoretically weak [13]. This study hoped to address these concerns and set out to answer the research question "How do organisational factors affect successful adoption and usage of a BPMS in a South African financial service organisation?" To answer the question, this paper first reviews the relevant literature on BPMS adoption and use. The case study research approach is described and the financial services organization and its BPMS project is then described. The factors which were found to affect successful BPMS adoption and use in the case are described and discussed, and an explanatory model is presented before the paper concludes.

2   Literature Review

Innovation adoption is defined as the decision of an individual or organization to use an innovation. Hence, organisational adoption of a technology, includes but is much broader than individual technology adoption [14]. Usage of the technology follows the adoption decision. There has been a call from researchers for a more holistic approach to studying adoption which is shown in the call for papers of the ECIS 2019 IS innovation and adoption track [15]. The predominant research approach focuses on variables that contribute to individual adoption and is said to distance researchers from practitioners [15]. A more holistic approach is the Alter systems theory of IT innovation, adoption and adaption [16], referred to as the work system approach.

A work system is seen as a natural unit of analyzing the adoption of socio-technical systems in organisations [15] and comprises four elements: processes and activities; participants; information; and technology. Furthermore, the work system needs to be considered in terms of the products and services it produces; the customers it serves; the organizational environment, strategies and infrastructure. Alter notes that often organizational IT is mandated, but there are post-adoption environments where employees might not comply with prescribed business processes and/or IT usage patterns. It is also noted that this area of research although highly relevant is under-researched. A systems approach sees the entity being adopted as not the technology but the information system or work system which comprises the people, processes and information, in addition to the technology [15, 16]. Hence when looking at successful BPMS adoption and use, one needs to look more broader, in terms of adoption and use of the relevant BP management (BPM) practices and processes that support adoption and use of the BPMS technology.

BPM is defined as management practice integrating technology and BP knowledge and harnessing BPs as exploitable assets [17]. BPM practice incorporates many prior approaches to BP change [7]. Earlier BPM research in South African financial services categorised the enablers of BPM as strategic, cultural, people, IT and methodological [18]. More recently, the six core elements of BPM have been identified as strategic alignment, governance, methods, IT, people, and culture [19].

Another relevant model in this context is the Lyytinen and Newman, socio-technical change model which is used to describe when a new technical system is designed, adopted and modified. The socio-technical model has four components: technology, which includes development tools and the technical platform; structure, which includes the project organization and institutional arrangements; actors, including users, managers and designers; and tasks [20]. The alignment of the elements from these three models is shown in Table 1. We chose the Core BPM element model as a classification framework for this study's findings. Firstly, as it is more comprehensive than the socio-technical change model, secondly, because we didn't believe information, products and services will dominate in BPMS adoption, and finally because it is specialized for the BPM context. Hence, we argue that the core BPM elements are important not only for BPM but also for BPMS adoption and use.

Table 1. Mapping Core BPM, work system framework and socio-technical change elements.

Core BPM elements	Socio-technical change elements	Work system framework elements
Strategic alignment		Strategies
Methods	Task	Processes and activities
		Information, products and services
IT	Technology	Technologies and infrastructure
People	Actors	Participants and customers
Governance and culture	Structure	Environment

The core BPM elements have been confirmed in some empirical studies. For example, one study noted that to achieve effective BPM solution implementation, the following needs to be achieved: the organisation should have adequate IT infrastructure to support a process orientated architecture; individuals within the organisation should have a comprehensive understanding of process orientated frameworks; and the organisation should have an effective change management process regarding software changes [21]. Successful BPM has been found to depend on employees' attitudes towards embracing BP change [22], people change management can be extremely challenging [23] and BPM projects frequently fail due to cultural issues [24]. It is also suggested that IT capabilities need to ensure BP efficiency as opposed to rudimentary BP automation [25]. Ensuring that the appropriate tools and IT infrastructure is in place for BPM has also been seen to be critical [17, 26]. While adopting a BPMS is intended to produce agile BPs, it needs to be acknowledged that IT can be both an enabler and a disabler for business agility [3].

Factors that contribute to inflexible IT solutions include: insufficient capacity and project priorities of IT staff members, traditional architectures and the complexity of integrating with legacy applications within the organization, and poor interfacing capabilities of legacy applications [3].

3   Research Method and Case Description

This study presents an interpretive descriptive case study. The unit of analysis was the adoption and usage of a BPMS by a BPM team within the IT cluster of a financial institution, which we will refer to as BigFin. The team is responsible for providing support for the BPMS and engaging in IT projects that involve enhancements to the tool. Prior to collecting data, organizational permission was secured as well as ethics approval from the University's ethics committee. One of the researchers was working for the BigFin IT cluster at the time of the study but not in the BPM team. The interview protocol developed asked open ended questions loosely based on the different elements of a work system, namely strategy, infrastructure, environment, processes, participants, information and technology.

Eight semi structured interviews, each approximately forty-five minutes long, were conducted, and three BigFin documents (D1–D3) were secured. A judgement sample strategy, where the most knowledgeable individuals that can add the most value are chosen to be interviewed [27], was employed. The interviewees were from the BPM IT team (coded as I1–I4) as well as IT architecture teams (coded as A1–A4). The interviews were transcribed, and then thematic analysis was performed on the documents and interview data using NVivo. Table 2 lists all 11 data sources. To ensure anonymity of BigFin and interviewees, the relevant codes are not listed in the table and the BPMS software is simply referred to as the BPMS.

Table 2.   List of interviews and documents analysed.

Data sources analysed	
Meeting Minutes – Design and Governance Walkthrough Session	
Project Retrospection Report – BPM Workflow Migration Project	
BPMS Positioning Document – IT Architecture	
Project Manager Interview	Business Architect Interview
Senior Business Analyst Interview	Solution Architect Interview
Solution Designer Interview	Enterprise IT Architect Interview
Development Manager Interview	Senior IT Architect Interview

Data was analysed using as soon as collected and prior to conducting further interviews. This allowed questions to be amended based on the themes that emerged. As data was iteratively analysed, new themes emerged. The Attride-Stirling [28] six step inductive method of thematic analysis was followed: 1) Coding the text; 2) Identifying themes;

3) Developing the thematic network; 4) Describing and exploring the network; 5) Summarising the network; 6) Interpreting patterns emerging from the data. The core BPM element framework was used during thematic analysis as a lens to classify the themes that emerged from the case study. The thematic network and themes are presented in the findings section.

BigFin is a well-established organisation operating in the investment and insurance industry, listed on various stock exchanges and a constituent of the Financial Times Stock Exchange (FTSE) 100 index. BigFin was selected as it has an established BPM IT team supporting a BPMS. As BigFin was established many decades ago it has a very large legacy IT estate. BigFin consists of various business units with their own strategies, budgets and visions and has multiple projects that run concurrently. The BPMS was first implemented during 2014 with the assistance of the vendor, and was implemented on Microsoft .NET and Microsoft SQL platforms using the native interfaces of the BPMS tool. This allows multiple integration points to other applications within BigFin via the SOA layer. An architectural review noted that the BPMS has the capabilities to be used as a strategic solution within BigFin to improve BP agility, scale their infrastructure and accommodate high user concurrency (D3). Management believed that the BPMS is a vital enabler for attaining a more client centric and process-oriented approach to business (D2). Improved reporting, segregation of duties and a clear audit trail were also cited benefits (D2). The main purpose of the BPMS was to model business processes, automate process steps, integrate with applications and manage workflow, mainly for enterprise wide processes (D3). The BPMS was also expected to improve BigFin's BPM maturity.

4   Findings and Discussion

The main aim of this research is to explain factors that affect the successful adoption and use of the BPMS by the IT team. As the intent of the BPMS implementation was to improve BP agility, we defined successful adoption and use as achieving BP agility. However, it became apparent that agile BPs were not achieved at BigFin. The relevant themes will now be discussed and this will be followed by the thematic network and explanatory model.

4.1   Strategic Alignment

Strategy can apply to the organisation, the department and the work system itself. The work system framework stresses the importance of these being aligned [29]. The work system strategies should support departmental strategies and ultimately organisational strategies. Three strategic alignment themes emerged.

BPM and Business as Usual are not Strategic Priorities. Strategic   priorities   of BigFin were impacting budget allocation. I1 highlighted that legislative requirements in BigFin take the highest priority, followed by strategic projects and then business as usual and other BPM IT projects. D1 and D2 noted that key resources are utilised by strategic projects, leaving few resources available for BPM migration projects. I4 noted that the current strategic priority is delivering a new product into the market which is at the expense of setting up a BPM centre of excellence that would govern processes implemented on the BPMS. I2 reiterated this as he stated, "One of the challenges is when we have these strategic initiatives the business as usual improvements and agility fall by the wayside."

Legacy System Strategy Misaligned with BPM Strategy. It was noted that the strategy for legacy systems was misaligned with the BPM strategy. A2 noted that the strategy clearly defines the core IT architectures that BigFin requires to become an agile enterprise. This entails defining where the enterprise is now, what the roadmap is to their desired strategy outcome and what the potential hurdles are from achieving the desired outcome. These hurdles come in the form of licences for software products the BPMS integrates with which have been bought for a defined period. As a result, decisions have been made by senior management to utilize these software products until the licences expire as they have already been paid for. This creates obstacles to achieving agility within business processes as alternative solutions cannot be implemented until software licences have expired.

Lack of BPM Strategic Vision. Lack of BPM strategic vision was identified by three of the interviewees as a factor contributing to the lack of BP agility. I3 noted that there was no central directive within BigFin regarding the BPM strategy although a BPM centre of excellence would assist in formalising the BPM vision within BigFin to provide efficient and effective BPM which would support BP agility. Organisations that implement a BPM centre of excellence offer consistent and cost-effective BPM services and can adopt a project portfolio management approach to BPM enabling IT teams to implement agile BPs [30].

4.2 Governance and Culture

Governance and Culture concerns impacting BPM include support obtained from top management, the culture that exists within the organisation and various complexities at different levels of management [31]. BPM Governance elements include BP standards, BP roles and responsibility, BP objectives, control methods, assessment methods, governance structures, architecture, and infrastructure [32] and BPM culture has been defined as collective values and beliefs that shape BP attitudes and behaviour to improve BPs [19]. Four governance and culture themes emerged.

Legacy and Standardization Decisions Made by Management. These   decisions refer to organisational decisions made by top management regarding the BPMS, two types of decisions were hampering the use of the BPMS; firstly, choosing to retain legacy applications, and secondly, choosing niche processes. Decisions regarding the decommissioning of legacy workflow applications by BigFin was found to impact the rate of change of BPM solutions as they had too many applications. I1 stated "This is the problem with this organisation, we don't decommission old legacy stuff and we keep incurring the respective costs." Literature notes that organisations are unclear regarding the correct time to implement a solution, modify it or stop using it altogether [33]. With respect to niche processes, A4 explained that one business unit had five different product lines but seventy-eight different implementations on the BPMS because every time a new line of business or a new type of customer came on board, they developed niche for that scenario. These decisions were seen to be driven by a lack of alignment between the BPM and legacy system strategies.

Misalignment Between Business and BPM IT Teams. The participants of the interview process addressed issues such as overdesign of solutions, silos within BigFin that operate in isolation and business units not willing to change the way they conduct their business processes. Alter highlights that all components within a work system should be aligned [29]. A1 noted that there was misalignment between the different development teams and business in terms of what they were expected to deliver. Change on the business unit side of the process resulted in IT staff having to work differently and think differently and, in this case, there was a lack of process thinking in the IT teams. I2 reiterated this by stating, "Arguably the biggest challenge is the business change in thinking. Don't just own your users' tasks, own a process end to end." Not having a BPM centre of excellence or process architects that govern process design and implementation was another factor that contributed to the misalignment between business teams and BPM IT teams. It seemed that this lack of alignment was being driven by the lack of a central BPM strategy and BPM not being a strategic priority.

Budget Allocation for BPM Business As Usual Initiatives. While BigFin appeared to support strategic projects well, it was noted that as soon as a project shifts from the build phase into the support or business as usual phase after implementation, the funding for that solution is no longer available. A2 note that, "The problem within BigFin is when a project is in a project phase there is money available but as soon as it flips over to the BAU phase there's no money. What that means is that just enough money is supplied to the project to keep it running. There is no additional funding supplied to grow it. So that is probably the single biggest challenge that we have." As no additional funding is sup
led for continuous process improvement, agility within business processes are sacrificed. Hence while the BPM IT team sees the potential benefits that solution changes will provide, they cannot implement them as no funds are available. The budget allocation was clearly being impacted by the lack of a central BPM strategy and BPM not being a strategic priority.

Business is Resistant to Change. A4 noted that a core impediment to BP agility is individuals' attitudes towards change. This can be summarised by the culture that exists within BigFin. D2 validated this by reporting that the lack of a change mind-set in business units is an inhibiting factor for process change. A4 further highlighted that as individuals become familiar with BPs, they become resistant to change within those processes. Resistance to change can be overcome strategically and an organisational culture can be developed to be supportive of BPM [34]. In the absence of a BPM strategic vision this culture of change resistance persisted.

4.3 Information Technology

Under IT impacts one dominant theme emerged and that was the lack of agility due to integrating with legacy and external software applications. Integration is the predominant theme that emerged as it was addressed by seven of the eight interviewees. Integration complexities range from interactions with legacy applications which can't be changed or have incomplete data, the tightly coupled nature of the legacy application integration and complexities regarding integration outside BigFin's secure network. Changes to applications or web services that are consumed by the BPMS impact the time to deliver a process implemented on the BPMS. D3 confirmed that the BPMS solution has multiple integration points via BigFin's web service integration layer. If a change is required for a web service that is consumed by several other applications, extensive impact analysis needs to be performed in order to determine if the required change for the BPM project poses a risk to the other applications. I4 referred to the increase in required analysis, design, governance and testing when altering processes integrated with other applications. A3 stated that a problem with integrating with legacy applications is that some of them do not have REST and SOAP capabilities. They only offer point to point tight integration which creates tightly coupled solutions. The literature confirms that with tightly coupled IT solutions that integrate business processes across various disparate software applications even the smallest of changes become time consuming with a degree of risk [35]. "Being so highly integrated sometimes I worry it is not necessarily enabling us to change quickly" (I4).

Integration is also impacted by data incompleteness and an inability to change legacy applications and security concerns with external applications. A1 highlighted that data governance was limited when many legacy applications were developed which impacts the accuracy and completeness of the data. This has agility implications if certain data validations need to be introduced within a process. I2 noted BigFin's resistance to invest funds in aging legacy applications which the BPMS integrated with impacted use of the BPMS and diminished process agility as legacy solutions will not be changed. A3 noted that when integrating with applications outside of BigFin's secure network, various considerations need to be made in terms of establishing secure communication channels and if an external party changes the application, the process of implementing secure integration channels needs to be repeated.

4.4 People

The BP people category refers to the individuals and groups that improve BPs [19]. The dominant theme was found to be resourcing constraints for BPM initiatives. Resourcing constraints in this study refers to the limited time that IT staff from application teams, the BPM IT team and architecture teams can spend on the BPM projects and the inability to staff the BPM IT team. This is an area of concern within BigFin as five out of the eight interviewees raised staff resourcing as a challenge for the BPM IT team.

The BigFin BPM IT team appeared to be constantly understaffed. I2 confirmed that finding high calibre resources that are technically capable and who possess the business understanding proved to be a challenge for the BPM IT team. A2 noted that developers do not find BPM development appealing as the skill is perceived to be a niche technology skill not broadly utilized. These developers would rather work on pure object orientated languages like java or C#.

Key resources within the BPM IT team face similar situations in terms of resource constraints. Training and on-boarding of new staff is fundamental to ensure knowledge sharing and continuity when key resources leave. I4 stated that senior staff members are responsible for all new staff on-boarding within the BPM IT team and are also responsible for all BPMS design documentation and their review. because of high staff turnover, they have very little time to maintain existing processes to ensure agility is retained.

A3 also indicated that it is extremely difficult to deliver BPM processes in an integrated environment without constant interaction with the various application teams. These interactions involve consulting with the various teams to ensure they are aware of how to integrate with the BPMS. These consultations are not just from a technical perspective but also relate to standards and governance. This is a further resource drain on the IT resources within the BPM IT team. The resource constraints of other teams ultimately affect delivery for the BPM IT team. I4 highlighted that project and hence resourcing priorities of the IT teams that support applications that integrate with the BPMS may not be aligned and therefore BP change cannot be implemented until resources are allocated.

People are known to be assigned to roles and project teams based on manager's experience of people, their availability and the required skills [36]. Often projects tend to draw on a common resource pool within the organisation [37]. As large organisations run multiple projects concurrently, obtaining time from the most valuable resources is challenging. A2 noted that he is often one of the resources whose time is debated over. He is allocated to BigFin's number one strategic project where he needs to provide input in terms of the overall program architecture. However, there are also other strategic projects that require his attention. As a result, he does not have much time to spend with the BPM IT team or on continuous process improvement hence BPMS usage suffers.

4.5 Methods

The BPM method category refers to methods specific to the BP lifecycle [19]. Two themes emerged under the method category.

Lengthy Project Initiation Processes. Five of the eight interviewees referred to lengthy project initiation procedures for BPM projects. A2 referred to business architecture and enterprise architecture documentation required prior to project sign-off and the involvement of business analysts and solution architects for requirements gathering and solution design. Project initiation documentation ensures that the BP change is appropriately scoped and that resource availability is considered. Literature highlights the importance of the project initiation phase to define the problem and opportunities and reduce the risk of project failure and acknowledges that this can be lengthy [38].

Bypassing Design and Code Approval Procedures. In addition to the pre-project initiation processes, approval is needed for the artefacts that are produced. It appeared that these approval procedures were being bypassed and this concern was referred to the most by interviewees (14 mentions). I1 stated that problems arise when developers or project managers try and rush projects into the production environments by trying to bypass sign-off procedures resulting in inflexible and niche BPs. It seemed that the desire for niche BPs in many cases was driven by the culture which was resistant to change. Sign-off processes could also have been implemented more efficiently if proper governance had been completed. Pre-production approval processes come in the form of security sign-off and code review sign-off and ensure that final approval is obtained from a design, technology, quality assurance, architecture, risk and security perspective. Although these processes are necessary for implementing efficient and agile BPs in the long term, the interviewees noted that these processes also hamper quick delivery of BP changes in the short term.

4.6 Model of Factors Impacting Successful BPMS Adoption and Use

This research aimed to identify factors that affect the successful adoption and use of the BPMS by the IT team and success was defined as achieving BP agility. While the BPMS was adopted and in use, agile BPs were not achieved at BigFin. Hence as the interviews progressed, it was noted that the major factors identified were all negatively impacting success. The eleven dominant factors are presented in Table 3 and the interlinked factors are shown in Fig. 1.

Table 3. BPM themes with Sources (S) and References (R).

Core BPM elements	Themes	S	R
Strategic alignment	BPM and business as usual are not strategic priorities	3	3
	Legacy system strategy misaligned with BPM strategy	2	2
	Lack of BPM strategic vision	5	10
Governance and culture	Business is resistant to change	2	2
	Legacy and standardization decisions made by management	5	11
	Misalignment between business and BPM IT teams	4	7
	Budget allocation for BPM business as usual initiatives	4	7
Methods	Lengthy project initiation processes	5	7
	Bypassing design and code approval procedures	7	14
IT	BPMS and legacy system integration implications	7	14
People	Resourcing constraints for BPM initiatives	7	12

The sources column represents the number of interviewees that made statements related to each theme and the references column represents the numbers of statements made by the interviewees. While the respondents referred to concerns with the BPMS work system itself (its methods, technology and participants), these concerns were being

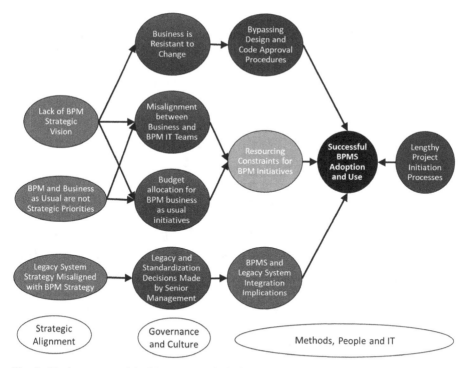

Fig. 1. Explanatory model of factors negatively impacting successful BPMS adoption and use.

driven by governance and cultural concerns and these in turn were driven by strategic alignment concerns. Together these factors negatively impacted successful BPMS adoption and use and BP agility.

While the organisation wanted to improve their BPM maturity, they did not have a BPM strategic vision and the "business as usual" nature of process improvement and BPM were not seen as strategic priorities. This resulted in misalignment between business and IT teams and insufficient budget allocation for BPM. Both factors drove resourcing constraints for BPM initiatives.

The organisation had a large legacy estate and this impacted the lack of agility because of technical integration implications and because of governance decisions made regarding changing legacy applications. These in turn were driven by their legacy system strategy being misaligned with the BPM strategy for agility. Software development methods had been put in place to ensure long term BP agility but these resulted in slowing software development in the short term. This and the reluctance of business to change and standardise resulted in bypassing some of these methods. Without a BPM strategic vision, the culture of the organisation could not be changed.

Considering the factors negatively impacting BPMS adoption and use at BigFin allowed us to propose a tentative explanatory model which the organisation could follow to improve BPMS adoption and use. This more generalisable model is presented as a framework in Fig. 2. While the Rosemann and vom Brocke core BPM model lists the components needed for BPM success this model provides an explanatory contribution to understanding improved BPMS success. The model notes that a clear BPM vision is needed and it needs to be aligned with the organisation's legacy application strategy. This is needed to enable better budget and resource alignment for BPM; a BPM culture [19]; appropriate BPM governance structures and BPM aligned legacy and standardization decisions. These four factors, in turn, will influence an improved BPMS work system.

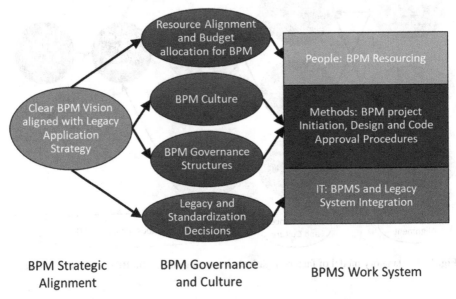

Fig. 2. Framework for successful BPMS adoption and use.

5   Conclusion

While organisations adopt BPMS and SOA technology primarily to achieve BP agility, in many cases this agility is not achieved. There has been a call by BP researchers for studies highlighting issues organisations are facing. Hence this research took a systems approach to looking at the adoption and use of a BPMS in a South African financial services organisation that was struggling to achieve BP agility. The systems approach to technology adoption sees technology adoption as a work system change. Hence a BPMS is seen as merely a technology in the BPMS work system trying to achieve agile business processes for the organisation's customers. Researchers Rosemann and vom Brocke have identified the six core elements of BPM and their framework was used as a lens in classifying the factors found impacting successful BPMS adoption and use in the organisation studied.

This case study described the frustrations the IT team was facing using the BPMS solution. While standalone applications can be implemented quickly, as soon as integration with other applications increases, the level of agility within those process was found to decrease. The inherent integrative nature of the BPMS solution and rigid nature of integration with legacy applications made changing applications very time consuming. Having insufficient resources and a user base that did not want to standardise or change processes increased their frustrations. A work system's view of the factors impacting this frustration is shown in Fig. 2 and these also pointed to a generic explanatory model. Implementing a BPMS without considering the strategic priorities and alignment as well as governance and culture will result in frustration and a lack of agility. Hence the usefulness of this framework to practitioners considering implementing a BPMS.

While this framework offers an explanatory model of how some factors negatively impact successful BPMS adoption and use, it does have limitations. Firstly, the model is not complete, interviewees were working in the IT function and a richer picture and more factors could have been obtained if employees from business functions were interviewed. Secondly, the study was cross sectional and a longitudinal study looking at the stages the organisation went through would be much richer. Thirdly, in terms of context generalisation, the case organisation was in financial services and therefore was risk averse and had a large legacy estate. Hence the framework has a focus on considering legacy applications and their strategy and a younger or more risk tolerant organisation with more modern applications will experience less frustration and hence parts of the model might not be relevant. Also, this model might not include factors important to an organisation which has other complexities or contextual factors.

Therefore, we note that this model is incomplete and contextual and further studies, particularly longitudinal studies, with other organisations and a broader user base will be able to further refine it. The framework could also be tested quantitatively to confirm the importance of the relevant factors.

References

1. Chen, Y., Wang, Y., Nevo, S., Jin, J.F., Wang, L.N., Chow, W.S.: IT capability and organizational performance: the roles of business process agility and environmental factors. Eur. J. Inf. Syst. **23**, 326–342 (2014). https://doi.org/10.1057/ejis.2013.4
2. Kryvinska, N.: Building consistent formal specification for the service enterprise agility foundation. J. Serv. Sci. Res. **4**, 235–269 (2012). https://doi.org/10.1007/s12927-012-0010-5
3. van Oosterhout, M., Waarts, E., van Hillegersberg, J.: Change factors requiring agility and implications for IT. Eur. J. Inf. Syst. **15**, 132–145 (2017). https://doi.org/10.1057/palgrave.ejis.3000601
4. Abramowicz, W., Filipowska, A., Kaczmarek, M., Kaczmarek, T.: Semantically Enhanced Business Process Modeling Notation: Semantic Technologies for Business and Information Systems Engineering, pp. 259–275. IGI Global, Hershey (2012)
5. Tallon, P.P.: Inside the adaptive enterprise: an information technology capabilities perspective on business process agility. Inf. Technol. Manage. **9**(1), 21–36 (2008)
6. Hill, J.B., Cantara, M., Kerremans, M., Plummer, B.C.: Magic Quadrant for Business Process Management Suites. Gartner RAS Core Research Note G152906 (2007)
7. Harmon, P.: The scope and evolution of business process management. In: Brocke, J., Rosemann, M. (eds.) Handbook on Business Process Management 1, pp. 37–80. Springer, Heidelberg (2015). https://doi.org/10.1007/978-3-642-00416-2_3
8. Heininger, R.: Requirements for business process management systems supporting business process agility. In: Oppl, S., Fleischmann, A. (eds.) S-BPM ONE 2012. CCIS, vol. 284, pp. 168–180. Springer, Heidelberg (2012). https://doi.org/10.1007/978-3-642-29294-1_12

9. Kerremans, M., Miers, D., Dunie, R., Wong, J., Iijima, K., Vincent, P.: Magic Quadrant for Business Process Management Suites. Gartner G00345694 (2019)
10. Kidwell, D.S., Blackwell, D.W., Sias, R.W., Whidbee, D.A.: Financial Institutions, Markets, and Money. Wiley, New Jersey (2016)
11. Nijssen, M., Paauwe, J.: HRM in turbulent times: how to achieve organizational agility? Int. J. Hum. Resour. Manage. **23**, 3315–3335 (2012). https://doi.org/10.1080/09585192.2012.689160
12. Di Francescomarino, C., Dijkman, R., Zdun, U. (eds.): BPM 2019. LNBIP, vol. 362, pp. VII–X. Springer, Cham (2019). https://doi.org/10.1007/978-3-030-37453-2
13. Trkman, P.: The critical success factors of business process management. Int. J. Inf. Manage. **30**, 125–134 (2010). https://doi.org/10.1016/j.ijinfomgt.2009.07.003
14. Frambach, R.T., Schillewaert, N.: Organizational innovation adoption: a multi-level framework of determinants and opportunities for future research. J. Bus. Res. **55**, 163–176 (2002). https://doi.org/10.1016/s0148-2963(00)00152-1
15. Davison, R.M.W., Louie, H.M., Alter, S., Ou, C.: Adopted globally but unusable locally: what workarounds reveal about adoption, resistance, compliance and non-compliance. Presented at the ECIS (2019). https://aisel.aisnet.org/ecis2019_rp/19/
16. Alter, S.: A systems theory of IT innovation, adoption, and adaptation. In: ECIS (2018). https://aisel.aisnet.org/ecis2018_rp/26
17. Niehaves, B., Poeppelbuss, J., Plattfaut, R., Becker, J.: BPM capability development – a matter of contingencies. Bus. Process Manag. J. **20**, 90–106 (2014). https://doi.org/10.1108/bpmj-07-2012-0068
18. Thompson, G., Seymour, L.F., O'Donovan, B.: Towards a BPM success model: an analysis in South African financial services organisations. In: Halpin, T., et al. (eds.) BPMDS/EMMSAD 2009. LNBIP, vol. 29, pp. 1–13. Springer, Heidelberg (2009). https://doi.org/10.1007/978-3-642-01862-6_1
19. Rosemann, M., vom Brocke, J.: The six core elements of business process management. In: vom Brocke, J., Rosemann, M. (eds.) Handbook on Business Process Management 1. IHIS, pp. 105–122. Springer, Heidelberg (2015). https://doi.org/10.1007/978-3-642-45100-3_5
20. Lyytinen, K., Newman, M.: Explaining information systems change: a punctuated sociotechnical change model. Eur. J. Inf. Syst. **17**, 589–613 (2017). https://doi.org/10.1057/ejis.2008.50
21. Imanipour, N., Talebi, K., Rezazadeh, S.: Obstacles in business process management (BPM) implementation and adoption in SMEs. SSRN Electron. J. (2012). https://doi.org/10.2139/ssrn.1990609
22. vom Brocke, J., Petry, M., Schmiedel, T., Sonnenberg, C.: How organizational culture facilitates a global BPM project: the case of Hilti. In: vom Brocke, J., Rosemann, M. (eds.) Handbook on Business Process Management. IHIS, pp. 693–713. Springer, Heidelberg (2015). https://doi.org/10.1007/978-3-642-45103-4_29
23. Kirchmer, M.: People enablement for process execution. In: High Performance Through Business Process Management, pp. 67–80. Springer, Cham (2017). https://doi.org/10.1007/978-3-319-51259-4_4
24. Schmiedel, T., vom Brocke, J., Recker, J.: Culture in business process management: how cultural values determine BPM success. In: vom Brocke, J., Rosemann, M. (eds.) Handbook on Business Process Management 2. IHIS, pp. 649–663. Springer, Heidelberg (2015). https://doi.org/10.1007/978-3-642-45103-4_27
25. Bandara, W., Alibabaei, A., Aghdasi, M.: Means of achieving business process management success factors. In: Proceedings of the 4th Mediterranean Conference on Information Systems. Athens University of Economics and Business, Athens (2009)
26. Von Rosing, M., von Scheel, J., Gill, A.Q.: Applying Agile Principles to BPM. The Complete Business Process Handbook. Morgan Kaufmann, Waltham (2015)

27. Marshall, M.N.: Sampling for qualitative research. Fam. Pract. **13**, 522–526 (1996). https://doi.org/10.1093/fampra/13.6.522

28. Attride-Stirling, J.: Thematic networks: an analytic tool for qualitative research. Qual. Res. **1**, 385–405 (2016). https://doi.org/10.1177/146879410100100307

29. Alter, S.: Work system theory: overview of core concepts, extensions, and challenges for the future. J. Assoc. Inf. Syst. **14**, 72–121 (2013). https://doi.org/10.17705/1jais.00323

30. Rosemann, M.: The service portfolio of a BPM center of excellence. In: vom Brocke, J., Rosemann, M. (eds.) Handbook on Business Process Management 2, pp. 381–398. Springer, Heidelberg (2010). https://doi.org/10.1007/978-3-642-01982-1_13

31. Awa, H.O., Ojiabo, O.U., Emecheta, B.C.: Integrating TAM, TPB and TOE frameworks and expanding their characteristic constructs for e-commerce adoption by SMEs. J. Sci. Technol. Policy **6**, 76–94 (2015). https://doi.org/10.1108/jstpm-04-2014-0012

32. Santana, A.F.L., Alves, C.F., Santos, H.R.M., de Lima Cavalcanti Felix, A.: BPM governance: an exploratory study in public organizations. In: Halpin, T., et al. (eds.) BPMDS/EMMSAD-2011. LNBIP, vol. 81, pp. 46–60. Springer, Heidelberg (2011). https://doi.org/10.1007/978-3-642-21759-3_4

33. Taudes, A., Feurstein, M., Mild, A.: Options analysis of software platform decisions: a case study. MIS Q. **24**, 227–243 (2000). https://doi.org/10.2307/3250937

34. Tumbas, S., Schmiedel, T.: Developing an organizational culture supportive of business process management. In: Wirtschaftsinformatik, p. 115 (2013)

35. Tanriverdi, H., Konana, P., Ge, L.: The choice of sourcing mechanisms for business processes. Inf. Syst. Res. **18**, 280–299 (2007). https://doi.org/10.1287/isre.1070.0129

36. Andre, M., Baldoquin, M.G., Acuna, S.T.: Formal model for assigning human resources to teams in software projects. Inform. Softw. Tech. **53**, 259–275 (2011). https://doi.org/10.1016/j.infsof.2010.11.011

37. Engwall, M., Jerbrant, A.: The resource allocation syndrome: the prime challenge of multi-project management? Int. J. Project Manage. **21**, 403–409 (2003). https://doi.org/10.1016/s0263-7863(02)00113-8

38. Westland, J.: The Project Management Life Cycle: A Complete Step-by-step Methodology for Initiating Planning Executing and Closing the Project. Kogan Page Publishers, London (2007)

Chatting About Processes in Digital Factories: A Model-Based Approach

Donya Rooein[1(✉)], Devis Bianchini[2], Francesco Leotta[3], Massimo Mecella[3],
Paolo Paolini[1], and Barbara Pernici[1]

[1] Politecnico di Milano, Milan, Italy
{donya.rooein,paolo.paolini,barbara.pernici}@polimi.it
[2] Università di Brescia, Brescia, Italy
devis.bianchini@unibs.it
[3] Sapienza Università di Roma, Rome, Italy
{leotta,mecella}@diag.uniroma1.it

Abstract. Using chatbots in digital factories, to interact with devices through instant messages and voice commands, can make the understanding of underlying manufacturing, logistic and business processes easier for workers. Intelligent chatbots can provide flexible conversations and tailor them to the specific users who are interacting. The iCHAT framework conceptually represents all the aspects related to a conversation, with different facets for the user, the conversation flow, and the conversation contents, and combining them to obtain a flexible interaction with the user. In digital factories, flexible production is driven by processes combining different services. In this paper, we present an original approach extending iCHAT to be able to chat about processes, aiming at instructing a worker about a process.

Keywords: Conversational user interface · Chatbot modelling · Digital factory · Industry 4.0

1 Introduction

Given the dynamic nature of today's business world, organizations should quickly respond to a wide range of possible changes in their environment. The changes can have either short-term effects, like disruptions in the supply or production chain, or long-term effects, like changes in one part of the production system that affect other subsystems and processes. Changes may also have an impact on controlling and monitoring essential parameters, that refer to the situation in which a production process is being executed. The introduction of data-driven solutions and enabling technologies, to transform collected data into actionable insights, has raised the complexity of monitoring and controlling activities. In addition, different roles, including business managers, data analysts, machine operators and designers, need to be informed on the processes and their changes to perform their job. These workers: (a) need tools to find the right information

© Springer Nature Switzerland AG 2020
S. Nurcan et al. (Eds.): BPMDS 2020/EMMSAD 2020, LNBIP 387, pp. 70–84, 2020.
https://doi.org/10.1007/978-3-030-49418-6_5

within a complex ecosystem of information, configurations, workflows, sensors and devices; (b) should be enabled to use their own language, that is far from the technical notation used to store and manage these kinds of information; (c) might have different levels of knowledge about the processes.

Conversational interfaces, such as the ones implemented by chatbots, might adapt to the new structure(s) and behavior(s) of the production processes. They may help workers, who have not exactly in mind what they are searching for or have partial knowledge about the process, to properly refine and focus questions, moving across many pathways in the production process. Using chatbots can mitigate the gap between a worker's language and formal notation used to model processes and data. Moreover, when the production is running, and some activities have already been carried out, a conversational interface like a chatbot may support a worker in learning the process, by making explicit for worker's the current context.

The goal of this paper is to present a flexible approach to generate conversations with a chatbot taking into account the structure of the process.

In this paper, we focus on the adoption of chatbots to *teach* a worker about the process structure. The present work is based on a conversational approach to generic education [3], proposing new general conversational structures for process teaching. The proposed approach is able to adapt to the context of the interaction and the context of the environment as it evolves during the process execution, going beyond the traditional question-answering mechanisms used for chatbots. The chatbot helps a learner in a possibly complex learning pathway for navigation over the process tasks. We aim to support the changing role of human beings in the digital factory landscape, according to the human-in-the-loop paradigm [8], where workers are expected to enjoy greater responsibility, to act as decision makers and to take on supervising tasks, while relying on chatbots for more operative levels (product quality control, process control and productivity, anomaly detection and health assessment). To make our contribution clear in the paper, we use an example of MyMuffin factory from [2], providing a conversational interface in a small factory to support the digital transformation.

The paper is structured as follows. In Sect. 2, we introduce challenges and motivations about using chatbots in digital factories. In Sect. 3, we introduce the iCHAT framework which is the basis for the rest of the paper and how the generic domain conversations by chatbots are managed, based on a data-driven approach. In Sect. 4 we discuss how different types of pathway structures about a process can be represented. In Sect. 5, we describe the process in MyMuffin factory and present an example of conversation showing how it can be dynamically generated by our data-driven approach. In Sect. 6, we discuss the state of the art in chatbots and in process- and service-based digital factories.

2 Challenges for Chatbots in Digital Factories

The introduction of a chatbot in digital factories aims to address the following challenges.

Adaptation to the Users' Language. Formal process modeling notation might not be suitable or understandable for all the users who are interested in learning about the business process. Chatbots using natural language, possibly adopting general-purpose and domain-specific terminology, may mitigate the gap between the business process notation and the users' language. The chatbot can also act as a mediator between raw data coming from sensors and the users, presenting information in such a way to ease the decision making about process instances.

Iterative Questions About the Process. The conversation style of the chatbot might enable a progressive refinement of the information to be provided to users, also proposing different options to users and relying on their choices to infer their skill about the business process. This also allows skipping undesired details and proposing dialogue pathways that are more suitable for users and their operating context.

Incomplete Knowledge About the Process. The level of user's knowledge about the business process might be unknown, nevertheless it is of paramount importance to focus the process exploration on the relevant activities, flows and data, also targeting the right level of detail. The conversational structure of chatbots and AI models behind them might enable to infer this information from the interactions with the users, thus improving the exploration experience.

Managing Data and Process Complexity. A human being is mainly unable to perceive and collect massive streaming data about processes and to create the best insights and actionable decisions. For example, considering the multiple configurations and product personalisation on the MyMuffin production process, how can users select the best solution with minimum cost? How do some data correlate to other data? In a digital factory based on digital twins [6], what is the cause-and-effect relating to the twin data differently from the real sensors data? According to the Human-In-the-Loop Data Analysis [8], experts must act as decision makers, while relying on chatbots for more repetitive and operative operations due to the data complexity and volume.

3   The iCHAT Framework

The iCHAT framework is our foundation for applying chatbots in digital factories. We first introduce the previous version of iCHAT, developed targeting educational chatbots (iChat-v1), then we illustrate the main extensions proposed in this paper (iCHAT-v2), that will be presented in detail in next sections.

3.1   Background: iChat-v1

The goal of iCHAT is to create "flexible and adaptive" conversational interfaces, capable of supporting complex tasks and going beyond Question Answering paradigms. Designing a conversation application in iCHAT (besides a more or less standard interface component) is committed to three separate main engines that are embedded inside a chatbot. These engines interact with each other to deliver an engaging conversation with the user via control tables. The engines are the *Conversation Engine*, the *Interpretation Engine*, and the *Transition Engine*, and all of them are table-driven, following a data-driven approach [3].

The *Conversation Engine* allows a user "to speak to" ("to be spoken by") an application, taking into account the user's profile to tailor the conversation. The role of the *Transition Engine* is to control the progress on a *pathway*, i.e., a sequence of content items for teaching. When a request is received, the Transition Engine takes care of the transitions across content items, i.e., determining which one is the most suitable "next item". It is driven by a database (storing the content items) and tables describing the "pathways" (defined by the author of the contents) that allow traversing the content. A conversational interface interacts with the user through different devices (e.g., mobile phone, tablet, Alexa device) through a variety of media (e.g., text and videos).

The *Interpretation Engine* is responsible to maintain a number of parameters describing the dynamic situation of the user (from cognitive, emotional, psychological points of view) and, more importantly, to interpret them properly. Using the parameters, in fact, the engine should "interpret" the situation and instruct the Transition Engine about what to do at the next step. The Interpretation Engine is controlled via a set of rules stored in "interpretation tables".

In addition, the *Interface Component* is responsible for technical jobs, like managing the various input/output devices, managing possible media conversions (e.g., text-to-speech, speech-to-text), transferring user turns to the conversation engine, transferring "content items" and chatbot turns to the user.

3.2   New Features Introduced in iCHAT for Digital Factories

In this paper, we propose a new architecture for iCHAT and a modified state transition machine for the chatbot, to develop it in the broader scope of processes in digital factories and tailor it to specific users who want to use a chatbot as an interaction interface to learn about a process. The overall architecture of this new version of iCHAT (iCHAT-v2) is shown in Fig. 1.

To re-design the Conversation Engine, it is crucial to separate chatbot's dialogues in two domains: the generic domain and the specific application domain. The generic domain is responsible for the chitchat of the chatbot to peruse the conversation in a natural way. Besides, this chatbot should be domain-specific to deliver those conversations which are tailored for the specific purpose. For instance, if the chatbot is used in the production process, it needs to support a specific conversation on each component in the production process. These two domains are managed by the dialog manager component in the conversation engine through controlling tables and configuration data. The dialogue manager is a "decision-maker" in the conversation engine. It can take one of the following decisions: i) the chatbot has to say something; ii) the chatbot must wait for the user to say something; iii) the learning process should move on based on the state machine. In case "i" it passes control (and parameters) to the chatbot controller to continue the general conversation; in case "ii" it passes control to

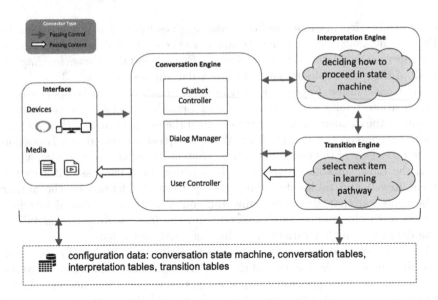

Fig. 1. The extended architecture of iCHAT.

the user controller to manage specific domain conversation; in case "iii" it passes control and parameters to the interpretation engine for any further actions on both state machine and learning path.

3.3 Generating Dialogues

Starting from the reference state diagram in iCHAT [3], we built a new state diagram in Fig. 2 to consider more situations in the conversation between a human and a chatbot. The state diagram allows controlling the utterances that the chatbot produces when reaching each state. This graph consists of a set of states and transitions between them. The transition from one state to the next depends on the user's utterance. The state diagram allows controlling the utterances that the chatbot produces when reaching each transition or a state.

This finite state machine is defined as a tuple, $(Q, \Sigma, \tau, q_0, F)$ consisting of a finite set of states Q, a finite set of input messages Σ, a transition function $\tau : Q \times \Sigma \rightarrow Q$, an initial state $q_0 \in Q$, and final states $F \subseteq Q$. The transition function here is a set of predefined data-driven rules in the conversation table (Fig. 3a[1]) that activate a message for the chatbot.

A conversation goes on as a sequence of "turns" by the chatbot and the user. According to the state machine in Fig. 2, a conversation can be *paused* (for a short break and later resumed), *suspended* (for a long break and later resumed), *stopped* (leaving the conversation), or *completed* (at the end of the pathway).

---

[1] '*' in message ID and '?' before the category name indicate enquiring from the user. For readability, states and related transitions are separated by lines.

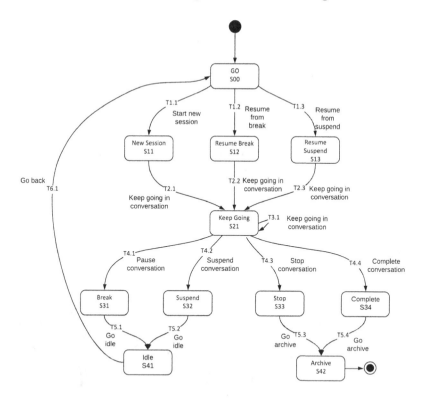

Fig. 2. The state transitions for the generic domain of conversation.

The number of consecutive turns and other chatbot's behaviours[2] are controlled by tables.

The dialogue of the chatbot is designed by a set of categories. For each state in Fig. 2, different sequences of categories are associated. There are some dialogues associated to each state and transition. The dialogues are generated by considering different categories regarding the situation. The sentence(s) for each turn belongs to one out of seven different categories: *'greetings, support, preview* (of content), *summary* (of what has been done), *forecast* (of what is needed to complete the pathway), *action* (asking the user for taking action), and *reinforcement* messages.

For example, in state "S00", the chatbot performs a dialog from "greetings" category; in transition "T3.1" the chatbot first says a "summary" message of what is done by user and a "forecast" message for what the user has to learn next. All information for generating the chatbot dialogues is derived from controlling tables.

---

[2] The behaviour can be customized on the basis of the user's profile or context information. The chatbot, for example, could take several turns or a few ones; the chatbot could take long verbose turns, or could speak very briskly; the chatbot could use different wording styles (e.g., "professional", "friendly", "soft").

In iCHAT-v2, an acceptable conversation to teach a production process, is the one leading the learner to complete a learning pathway in a proactive way. As it is illustrated in the following, beyond the state transition graph to manage a generic conversation, we introduce a new transition graph to handle the conversation on the different learning pathways defined to teach about processes. We develop a new structure for pathways beyond the sequential one originally used in iCHAT, to be able to deal with the complex structure of processes and, in addition, we develop conceptual models for transition graphs for teaching processes. The dialogue graph for this chatbot provides the structure for generating sentences, while the contents depends on the conversation tables. In Fig. 3b, we show part of a simulator for our chatbot to generate chatbot's messages in the states and transitions that are defined in Fig. 3a. This is a sustainable solution to empower the instruction designers to build an adaptive learning process and adaptive learning conversation via chatbot and It is important to depict that the workers in the process do not need any additional background more than what is required for online learners to get trained by this chatbot.

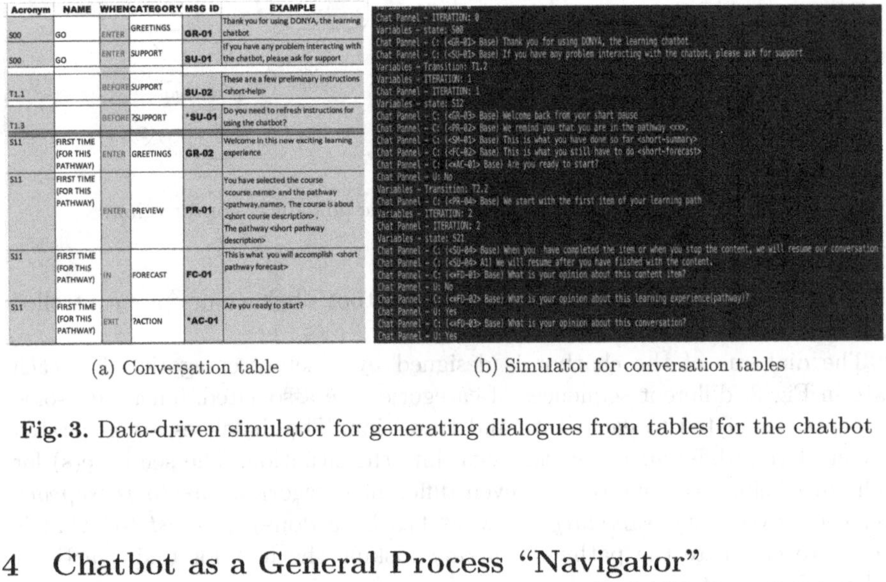

Acronym	NAME	WHEN	CATEGORY	MSG ID	EXAMPLE
S00	GO	ENTER	GREETINGS	GR-01	Thank you for using DONYA, the learning chatbot
S00	GO	ENTER	SUPPORT	SU-01	If you have any problem interacting with the chatbot, please ask for support
T1.1		BEFORE	SUPPORT	SU-02	These are a few preliminary instructions <short-help>
T1.3		BEFORE	?SUPPORT	*SU-01	Do you need to refresh instructions for using the chatbot?
S11	FIRST TIME (FOR THIS PATHWAY)	ENTER	GREETINGS	GR-02	Welcome in this new exciting learning experience
S11	FIRST TIME (FOR THIS PATHWAY)	ENTER	PREVIEW	PR-01	You have selected the course <course.name> and the pathway <pathway.name>. The course is about <short course description>. The pathway <short pathway description>
S11	FIRST TIME (FOR THIS PATHWAY)	IN	FORECAST	FC-01	This is what you will accomplish <short pathway forecast>
S11	FIRST TIME (FOR THIS PATHWAY)	EXIT	?ACTION	*AC-01	Are you ready to start?

(a) Conversation table   (b) Simulator for conversation tables

Fig. 3. Data-driven simulator for generating dialogues from tables for the chatbot

4   Chatbot as a General Process "Navigator"

A chatbot as a general process "navigator" is a finite state machine. It is driven by a graph, describing the current pathway. Given the "current position" it determines which is the most suitable next item for the learner. Nodes and arcs of the graph are enriched by colors and metadata to semantically recognize the characteristics of the items. Colors and metadata are basically used to "preview" what is coming or (more important) to help the user with "adaptivity in the small", i.e., skipping unwanted items of the pathway, or looking for specific ones. For instance, in order to demonstrate the adaptivity in the small, nodes in the pathway are labeled by colors (blue for mandatory items in the path, green for optional ones, and purple for additional materials). These content items are stored in table "Item DB" and organized in the learning pathways. Besides, users can select the pathway topology most suitable in a given context, which is called "adaptivity in the large".

4.1   Conversations for Teaching About a Process

To teach a process, three learning pathways structures have been defined:

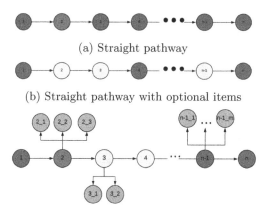

(a) Straight pathway

(b) Straight pathway with optional items

(c) Straight pathway with additional material

Fig. 4. Pathway structures

- **Quick overview**. The learner can go through the overview items of the process. The goal is to improve the quality time of an employee to perceive the outline of the production process. In this regard, just items with proper metadata and tags are used to create a conversation on the highest abstraction of the process. The learning topology regarding to this pathway can be expressed as a straight pathway as shown in Fig. 4a. A straight pathway contains a list of items that have the nodes with "Overview" flavor type and the role is "Core" that is demonstrated by blue color in the graph. The user can go next through items to complete the learning path. Jumping back through items is not possible in this pathway. The Transition Engine keeps a list of items for each pathway in the straight pathway.
- **Full learning**. The full learning pathway shows more details about the process by considering all optional nodes for each activity. Figure 4b is a straight pathway with optional items and users have control to select optional items or skip them. All blue items in the pathway are coming from "Core" role and they are mandatory for the user to follow. The optional items are depicted with green node color and the Transition Engine informs the chatbot if the next item is optional and the chatbot gives the user a choice to select the

optional item or not during her learning path. If the user takes the items, the Transition Engine marks that item "visited" otherwise "skipped".

- **Advanced learning**. Advanced learning pathways declare a straight pathway with core, optional and additional material items, which include all information (e.g., process, sub-processes, and variables related to each process). An example of this topology is shown in Fig. 4c. Additional material in item DB are tagged by "Recommended" and they are purple in the graph. If a user wants go deep on one item, this pathway structure is applicable. From the learning path viewpoint, these recommended materials are for an advanced learning experience. In a process, these additional materials can be inserted by the author which is designing the pathway to add information about the gateways, flow conditions, task data, and so on.

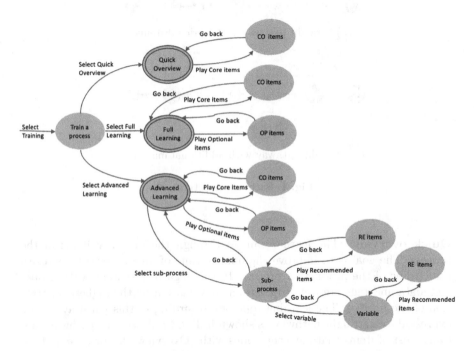

Fig. 5. State transitions for teaching on a process

4.2   State Transitions for Teaching a Process

Figure 5 displays the state diagram for accessing an item in teaching a process. When a user selects process training, the chatbot goes in the initial "Train a process" state. From this state, it is possible to go deep in one of the possible topologies. As it is shown, items are tagged in three different roles (Core: CO, Optional: OP, and Recommended: RE). From the "Quick Overview" state, the

Transition Engine derives core items from "Item DB". From the "Full Learning" state, going to core or optional items is achievable, based on the underlying structure of the pathway. From the "Advanced Learning" state, users can also go further to a component of the process to retrieve recommended information for available sub-processes and variables in a component.

5   The Chatbot in the MyMuffin Factory

It is important to consider two criteria for using iCHAT in your application scenario. Firstly, the content must be managable by "pathways" to be followed of some complexity. Secondly, the user should accept a "constrained" conversation within the limit of the application domain.

Now we describe how we proceed by using a chatbot in a teaching a process in a factory, as the key contribution of this work, based on an example of a production factory first described in [2]. The overall production process in MyMuffin is shown in Fig. 6. The client orders box(es) (each one containing 4 muffins) online, by choosing among different possible variants, such as: *(a)* chocolate chips vs. blueberry vs. apricot bits vs. carrot bits vs. nothing as additional ingredient; *(b)* butter cream vs. hazelnut cream vs. icing sugar vs. nothing as topping; *(c)* yogurt vs. honey vs. nothing in the dough. The client can also customize the colors of the baking paper (wrapping the single muffin) as well as the colors of the box. The MyMuffin factory collects orders and organizes batches of muffin dough for production. As an example, if a client asks for 3 boxes of carrot

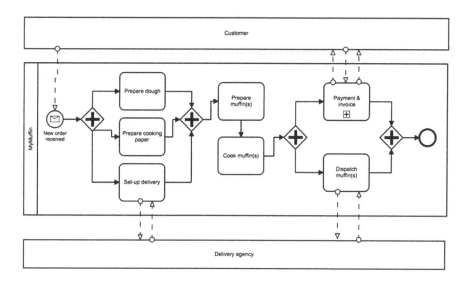

Fig. 6. The process at MyMuffin factory, BPMN diagram [2]

muffins with yogurt, icing sugar on top, pink baking paper, and another client for 2 boxes of carrot muffins with yogurt, nothing on top, yellow baking paper, the same dough can be used for both orders. Clearly, this scheduling service is based on the number of (and capacity of each) dough mixers, the stream of received orders, etc. The factory has a pool of dough mixers, of different capacity. The fact that the number of different combinations is finite guarantees that such a scheduling can be performed. When an order is received, in parallel to the dough preparation, the baking paper should be set up as well. In addition to prepare a set of the requested paper baking cases, a QR-code should be printed on each of them and used as a unique identifier of the specific order. The identification of the single muffin is crucial for customization. After the dough has been prepared, the muffins are placed in the baking paper cases and sent to the oven (connected to a QR code reader) for cooking. Muffins are cooked in batches of about 1,000 items and the length of this step is equal for all of them. After the baking has been performed, the cart is operated in order to route the different muffins to the right boxes, after putting the right topping, and then to the proper delivery station. Depending on the order, different delivery agents can be used.

The objective of introducing the chatbot here is to create a conversation to teach the process. As soon as a new employee arrives in the MyMuffin factory, the chatbot takes care of the initial orientation briefing about the company process components and all necessary information. Once the information regarding the initial training, operational knowledge, and other processes are handled by the chatbot, neither the employees and the trainer have to depend on each other. In the MyMuffin use case, the semantic tag related to each learning item is defined by four flavors ("Overview", "Definition", "Subdivision", and "FAQ") that are dependent to the specific process domain and three roles ("Core", "Optional", and "Recommended") which they are general for any learning content related to process navigation.

The conversation is driven by tables governing how the chatbot speaks and how it understands the user's utterances (Fig. 7). Below the tables a simple example of a conversation between chatbot and user is shown. As shown in Fig. 7, in state "S13" in the state machine, there are predefined categories for the chatbot turn when resuming a suspended conversation. Each sentence from the conversation table calls contents from "Item DB" table to create chatbot's dialogues, selecting items for the categories specified for the "S13" to create a complete dialogue.

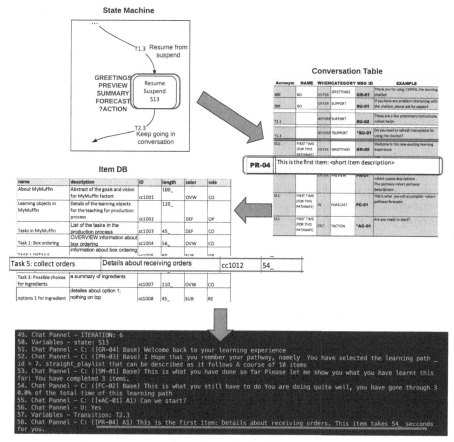

Fig. 7. Conversation simulation for the MyMuffin use case

6   Related Work

During the last years, some attempts were made to ease the creation of chatbots, aiming at querying data available in unstructured and structured formats.

Romero et al. [18] explored a set of application domains that can support human to supervise cyber-physical systems in digital factories. According to the authors in [16], these possible domains can be supported by using chatbots. They introduced many use case scenarios, where softbots can bring proactive insights over the production planners to optimize and support all operational demands. The authors mentioned that in smart supply network softbots provide monitoring (e.g., track and trace) to empower companies against any disruption in a supply network. In [7], a chatbot was developed to aid new hires through their onboarding process and reach related information needs as if it were a human assistant.

In [15], a chatbot was constructed on top of some open data. Here the first step is to extract plain text from documents stored as PDF files by employing an optical character recognition (OCR) software. At this point, a set of possible questions about the extracted contents were constructed using a "Overgenerating Transformations and Rankings" algorithm, which was implemented using the question generation framework presented in [9]. Finally, the matching patterns, essential to the chatbot's answering capability, are defined through Artificial Intelligence Markup Language (AIML).

OntBot [1] employs a mapping technique to transform an ontology into a relational database and then uses that knowledge to construct answers. The main drawback of traditional chatbots, implemented for example through AIML language, is the fact that the knowledge base has to be constructed ad-hoc by handwriting thousands of possible responses. Instead of providing answers by looking for a matching one inside a database, OntBot retrieves information from the database, which will be then used to build up the response. Therefore, likewise our solution, OntBot does not need to handwrite all the knowledge base that stands behind the system.

In [10] authors declare that chatbots are the proper solution to provide personalized learning in MOOCs (Massive Open Online Courses). iMOOC [5] is a novel methodology for designing customizable MOOCs that brings adaptivity into the learning experience. iMOOC supports that various users of MOOCs may have different purposes, some learners may want to get personalized content, not learning the entire material. Here a chatbot is introduced to support the learner in choosing the most appropriate path. In the TEL (Technology-Enhanced Learning) literature, since several years Intelligent Pedagogical Agents (IPAs) are proposed as embodied intelligent agents designed for pedagogical purposes to support learning. Chatbots as those ones proposed in this paper are basically a form of IPA, and here we demonstrate their applicability to learning manufacturing processes.

The dialogue management component of the chatbot is one of the key parts in designing a conversational interface. In [14], dialogue management design and management in industry is discussed. A dialogue manager for a goal-oriented chatbot to conduct a proper conversation with user is illustrated in [11]. In [17], a model based on a Finite-State Turn Taking Machine is introduced in order to select an action any time.

Our aim is to propose a framework to query and teach processes. The interest in the employment of chatbots in the context of Business Process Management (BPM) is quite recent. Authors in [12] propose a way to take a business process flow as input and to produce a Watson conversation model as output. Differently from our approach, here authors focus on the execution of the process instead of teaching or monitoring it. In [4] an approach is proposed to use chatbots to learn business processes from input data. Here the focus is not on process participants. Instead the final users are data analysts in charge of mining business processes. In [13] the use of chatbots to help a process actor via conversation to perform tasks of a process model is presented.

7   Concluding Remarks and Future Work

In this work, we have introduced a framework to represent conversations to support instruction about manufacturing/production processes.

In future work, we will develop further the idea of connecting a conversation with a service-based process in a factory, in order to be able to control flexible process executions, with the chatbot as an interface for monitoring and controlling a running process in a digital factory using the same structures we presented for teaching as a basis for controlling conversations.

A robust validation in industrial settings is also foreseen, to measure the acceptability of the approach by workers and its effectiveness over current production processes.

Acknowledgements. The work of Donya Rooein has been supported by EIT Digital and IBM. The work of Francesco Leotta and Massimo Mecella has been supported by the EU H2020-RISE project FIRST. The work of Devis Bianchini has been supported by Smart4CPPS Lombardy Region project. This work expresses the opinions of the authors and not necessarily those of the funding agencies and companies.

References

1. Al-Zubaide, H., Issa, A.A.: OntBot: ontology based chatbot. In: International Symposium on Innovations in Information and Communications Technology, pp. 7–12. IEEE (2011)
2. Bicocchi, N., Cabri, G., Mandreoli, F., Mecella, M.: Dynamic digital factories for agile supply chains: an architectural approach. J. Ind. Inf. Integr. **15**, 111–121 (2019)
3. Di Blas, N., Lodi, L., Paolini, P., Pernici, B., Renzi, F., Rooein, D.: A new approach to conversational applications. In: SEBD, Data Driven Chatbots (2019)
4. Burattin, A.: Integrated, ubiquitous and collaborative process mining with chat bots. In: 17th International Conference on Business Process Management, BPM Demo Track, Vienna, Austria, pp. 144–148. CEUR-WS (2019)
5. Casola, S., Di Blas, N., Paolini, P., Pelagatti, G.: Designing and delivering MOOCs that fit all sizes. In: Society for Information Technology & Teacher Education International Conference, pp. 110–117. (AACE) (2018)
6. Catarci, T., Firmani, D., Leotta, F., Mandreoli, F., Mecella, M., Sapio, F.: A conceptual architecture and model for smart manufacturing relying on service-based digital twins. In: IEEE International Conference on Web Services, ICWS, Milan, Italy, pp. 229–236 (2019)
7. Chandar, P., et al.: Leveraging conversational systems to assists new hires during onboarding. In: Bernhaupt, R., Dalvi, G., Joshi, A., Balkrishan, D.K., O'Neill, J., Winckler, M. (eds.) INTERACT 2017. LNCS, vol. 10514, pp. 381–391. Springer, Cham (2017). https://doi.org/10.1007/978-3-319-67684-5_23
8. Doan, A.: Human-in-the-loop data analysis: a personal perspective. In: ACM International Workshop on Human-In-the-Loop Data Analysis (HILDA 2018), pp. 1–6 (2018)
9. Heilman, M., Smith, N.A.: Question generation via overgenerating transformations and ranking. Technical report, Carnegie Mellon University Pittsburgh PA Language Technologies Institute (2009)

10. Holotescu, C.: MOOCbuddy: a chatbot for personalized learning with MOOCs. In: Iftene, A., Vanderdonckt, J. (eds.) RoCHI-International Conference on Human-Computer Interaction, pp. 91–94, Bucarest (2016)

11. Ilievski, V., Musat, C., Hossmann, A., Baeriswyl, M.: Goal-oriented chatbot dialog management bootstrapping with transfer learning. arXiv preprint arXiv:1802.00500 (2018)

12. Kalia, A.K., Telang, P.R., Xiao, J., Vukovic, M.: Quark: a methodology to transform people-driven processes to chatbot services. In: Maximilien, M., Vallecillo, A., Wang, J., Oriol, M. (eds.) ICSOC 2017. LNCS, vol. 10601, pp. 53–61. Springer, Cham (2017). https://doi.org/10.1007/978-3-319-69035-3_4

13. López, A., Sànchez-Ferreres, J., Carmona, J., Padró, L.: From process models to chatbots. In: Giorgini, P., Weber, B. (eds.) CAiSE 2019. LNCS, vol. 11483, pp. 383–398. Springer, Cham (2019). https://doi.org/10.1007/978-3-030-21290-2_24

14. Paek, T., Pieraccini, R.: Automating spoken dialogue management design using machine learning: an industry perspective. Speech Commun. **50**(8–9), 716–729 (2008)

15. Pichponreay, L., Kim, J.-H., Choi, C.-H., Lee, K.-H., Cho, W.-S.: Smart answering chatbot based on OCR and overgenerating transformations and ranking. In: 8th International Conference on Ubiquitous and Future Networks (ICUFN), pp. 1002–1005. IEEE (2016)

16. Rabelo, R.J., Romero, D., Zambiasi, S.P.: Softbots supporting the operator 4.0 at smart factory environments. In: Moon, I., Lee, G.M., Park, J., Kiritsis, D., von Cieminski, G. (eds.) APMS 2018. IAICT, vol. 536, pp. 456–464. Springer, Cham (2018). https://doi.org/10.1007/978-3-319-99707-0_57

17. Raux, A., Eskenazi, M.: A finite-state turn-taking model for spoken dialog systems. In: Proceedings of Human Language Technologies: The 2009 Annual Conference of the North American Chapter of the Association for Computational Linguistics, pp. 629–637 (2009)

18. Romero, D., et al.: Towards an operator 4.0 typology: a human-centric perspective on the fourth industrial revolution technologies. In: International Conference on Computers and Industrial Engineering (CIE46) (2016)

Enforcing a Cross-Organizational Workflow: An Experience Report

Susanne Stahnke[✉], Klym Shumaiev, Jorge Cuellar,
and Prabhakaran Kasinathan

Siemens AG - Corporate Technology, Otto-Hahn-Ring 6, 81739 Munich, Germany
{susanne.stahnke,klym.shumaiev,jorge.cuellar,
prabhakaran.kasinathan}@siemens.com

Abstract. Today business processes often exceed organizational boundaries and the participants may not fully trust each other. In the past, this trust was guaranteed solely through legal contracts. To digitally establish trust without requiring a trusted third party, Blockchain technology together with Smart Contracts is used to ensure that involved organizations can not break their agreements. This experience report introduces a workflow enforcement method for a particular use case, the certification of the construction of industrial plants. The method comprises the modelling of the workflow, the verification of the models and the translation into Smart Contracts.

Keywords: Business process modelling · Cross-organizational processes · Workflow enforcement · Blockchain · Smart Contracts · Experience report

1 Introduction

Globalization, novel technologies, fast-changing environments, the need for cost reduction, and the rapid evolution of information and communication technologies introduce challenges for enterprises, which are tackled by the cross-organizational collaboration between organizations, as stated in [9]. Establishing such cross-organizational collaboration requires the involved enterprises to specify the different interoperations and a common goal beforehand. This can be done by modelling these cooperative processes.

Already in 1998, before emergence of mature business process modelling standards, like BPMN, van der Aalst suggested how inter-organizational workflows could be modelled and verified. In [18], he describes the concept of loosely coupled workflow processes, which use asynchronous communication. A workflow consists of one or more processes, each one assigned to a given organization. The processes operate independently from each other but synchronize at specified points to ensure the correct execution of the whole workflow. However, in the same paper van der Aalst did not provide any details on how such an approach can be implemented in practice.

© Springer Nature Switzerland AG 2020
S. Nurcan et al. (Eds.): BPMDS 2020/EMMSAD 2020, LNBIP 387, pp. 85–98, 2020.
https://doi.org/10.1007/978-3-030-49418-6_6

Inter-organizational business processes require a certain level of trust between the participating organizations. This trust is traditionally guaranteed solely through legal contracts, which specify a collection of responsibilities and obligations agreed upon all participating parties. With emergence of Blockchain, Smart Contracts assure that involved organizations cannot break their agreements and therefore, serve as a machine enforceable and verifiable protocol for inter-organizational workflows. This establishes trust between the participating parties without requiring a trusted third party.

This experience report demonstrates how to digitalize a cross-organizational business process on the basis of the use case "Certification of the Construction of Industrial Plants". Coloured Petri Net modelling notation is used to capture and verify inter-organizational business processes. It serves as a base for the implementation of Smart Contracts running in the *Hyperledger Fabric* environment. Petri Nets are easy to understand and use, and offer formal semantics and analysis techniques. Therefore, different behavioural properties can be analysed and verified. Implementing the business process as Smart Contracts on a Blockchain enforces all involved parties to execute the workflow correctly. Since we require that the identity of the participants is known and secured, a private permissioned Blockchain is used to implement the use case. In this experience report we discuss an approach on how to enforce cross-organizational business processes, and we present the lessons learned to be considered by the practitioners in the future.

The report is structured as follows. In Sect. 2, the use case is described. Section 3 presents the background to this work: we compare different Workflow Modelling Languages and introduce private permissioned Blockchain networks. The workflow enforcement method, comprising the modelling of the use case, the verification of the models, the translation into Smart Contracts and the evaluation of the Smart Contracts, is described in Sect. 4. In Sect. 5, encountered problems and best practices are discussed. Related work is presented in Sect. 6 and conclusions drawn from this experience report and an outlook to future work are described in Sect. 7.

2   Use Case: Certification of the Construction of Industrial Plants

Particular industrial plants, designed and built under the global supervision of a company called the *EPC* (abbreviation for Engineering, Procurement and Construction), require a certification by a governmental entity. In this report we take a detailed look at the certification process for a power plant, which is also valid in other types of industrial construction. The certification process requires the governmental body to issue approvals throughout the different stages of the power plant functional safety life cycle (consisting of design, fabrication, mounting, commissioning and test approval). In Fig. 1 we illustrate high-level phases of the life cycle.

In each step of the process, multiple documents are sent to the governmental body, that checks the documents, if needed asks for revisions and eventually

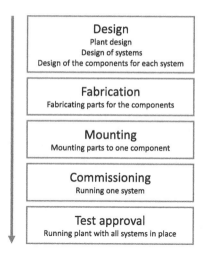

Fig. 1. High-level phases of the industrial plant functional safety life cycle

issues a certificate with its statement. This process includes different parties with different goals. Therefore, various steps of the process should be secured, to assure to all parties that the others execute the workflow correctly, and therefore, certain invariants (safety properties in the sense of temporal logic) hold. In case one of those invariants does not hold, all parties should be able to ascertain the responsible entity. Digitalizing this certification process results in an acceleration of the overall certification process, a secure management of all versions of the published documents, an easy search through the documents, a clear overview of all requirements and tasks during the entire plant life cycle, and finally, a paperwork reduction.

The following stakeholders are involved in the certification process. The *Owner* issues the plant, checks that the participating parties proceed correctly, and gives its approval throughout the entire life cycle. *EPC*[1] represents the service provider, which designs and builds the industrial plant. In our case, the *EPC* was represented by Siemens AG. *NOBO*, short for *Notified Body*, is a governmental agency responsible for examining and eventually approving the result of different stages of the construction of the industrial plant throughout the overall plant life cycle. In our case, the participating *NOBO* was TÜV Rheinland. *Manufacturer* produces parts of a component and delivers them to EPC. The certification process, described in this experience report, is an industrial standard.

---

[1] https://www.marquard-bahls.com/de/news-info/glossar/detail/term/epc-engineer ing-procurement-and-construction.html.

3 Background

3.1 Modelling Inter-organizational Workflows

A *workflow* can be defined as a set of activities or tasks, which is executed by certain entities, see [8]. The participating entities execute the workflow according to a defined set of rules to achieve, or contribute to an overall goal, as described in [6]. If the workflow is constructed to achieve business goals, it is also called business process. An *inter-organizational business process* is a workflow which involves multiple different, untrusted parties. To define such a business process Workflow Modelling Languages (WML) can be used. WMLs give the opportunity to not only define a workflow, but verify its *correctness*. A workflow is called correct, when it achieves its pre-defined goals by executing the defined partially ordered set of activities.

YAWL, BPMN, UML activity diagrams and Petri Nets are four WMLs, which are evaluated in this section. *YAWL*[2] (Yet Another Workflow Language, see [16]), inspired by Petri Nets, offers various workflow patterns, like basic control flow patterns, advanced branching and synchronization patterns, structural patterns and cancellation patterns. Since YAWL does not support PNML (Petri Net Markup Language), the possibility to export and import nets from/into different tools is very restricted. Since *BPMN*[3] (Business Process Modelling Notation) and UML activity diagrams lack a complete formal semantics and analysis techniques, the papers [3,12,13] suggest mapping workflow modelling languages, which lack rigorous semantics, to Petri Nets.

An ordinary *Petri Net* (P/T-Net) is a directed graph, in which the nodes are places or transitions, and the arcs connect places to transitions or vice versa. Informally, places can be seen as local states and transitions as local activities. Additionally, tokens mark the current state of the Net. A *Coloured Petri Net (CPN)* is a combination of a Petri Net and a programming language, called Standard ML. Petri Nets allow the definition of concurrency, control structures, synchronization and communication. The addition of Standard ML extends this definition with the ability to specify colour sets (data types) and markings, arc expressions and guards. For further definition and a concrete example see [7]. Petri Nets are easy to understand and use, and offer formal semantics and analysis techniques. Therefore, different behavioural properties can be analysed and verified. That is the main reason why Petri Nets are preferred to other modelling languages. Petri Nets are general, easy and abstract models, but on the same time very clean semantics.

3.2 Private Permissioned Blockchain Networks

Distributed Ledger Technologies (DLTs) enable a verifiable and transparent way to enforce an inter-organizational business process. It implements a decentralized

---

[2] http://yawlfoundation.org/.

[3] http://yoann.nogues.free.fr/IMG/pdf/07-04_WP_Intro_to_BPMN_-_White-2.pdf.

record of transactions. Blockchain is a particular type of DLTs. A blockchain is a replicated and distributed data structure, called ledger, that verifies and stores transactions occurring in a peer-to-peer network, as defined in [14]. The ledger is a timestamped list of blocks. Each block contains multiple transactions, is identified by its cryptographic hash and has a reference to the previous block's hash. This results in a linear, chronological chain of blocks. Each change on a block results in a change of the block's hash. This results in an immutable ledger, which allows the storage of transactions/assets in a tamper-proof way. Since each node holds a copy of the ledger, all nodes are able to verify all prior transactions. This decentralization grants transparency about every transaction for all participants of the network. Private permissioned Blockchain technologies, which restrict the participation in the network and the access to assets within the network, enforce access control. This enables a trustless network, conceding a transaction between parties, who do not trust each other, described in [2].

4   Workflow Enforcement Method

In order to digitalize the certification process for the construction of power plants, the following steps are performed (Fig. 2). First, the use case is modelled using a Workflow Modelling Language. In the second step, the derived models are translated into one coherent model to verify its correctness. Third, the model is translated into Smart Contracts in Hyperledger Fabric, and in the fourth and last step, the Smart Contract functionality is validated in regard to the model, which was verified in the second step.

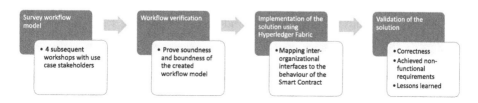

Fig. 2. Overview of our method

4.1   Modelling of the Workflow

The first step for the digitalization of the certification process was modelling the workflow. Four workshops each with three representatives from the involved organizations are performed; two domain experts from the company, in charge of the design and construction of the power plant, and one expert from a governmental authority. We, as researchers and facilitators, analysed several aspects of the process together with the domain experts: the different stages of the safety life cycle, the involved parties, the documents to be certified by the governmental entity, and the overall workflow. Since this initial modelling phase required participation of domain experts, who are not IT experts, ordinary P/T-Nets were used to make sure the models are easy to understand and adapt.

Dealing with an inter-organizational business process, van der Aalst's method was used for modelling and verifying this type of workflows; the concept of loosely coupled processes, which use asynchronous communication. This method is described in [18], and explained in more detail in [5]. Using this concept, shared places were introduced to the P/T-Nets. This can be seen as an assumption-commitment specification of a contract, which defines the interfaces between the participating parties. In the later implementation only those interfaces are known by everyone, internal business logic stays secret. Therefore, the confidentiality of internal states and processes by all participants is guaranteed, but nevertheless there is an understanding that a certain activity has been done but not how it has been done. Additionally, special operators (i.e. XOR-Joins/Splits) were added to enable decision-making in the Net.

Since the tasks of the certification process of a power plant are bound to documents, only the publication of the so-called documentation packages were modelled. The tool *WoPeD* was used to model the different stages of the certification process in ordinary P/T-Nets with special operators and shared places extension. After two workshops with the domain experts two meta-models emerged. Those meta-models were applied to all models of the different stages of the life cycle. This resulted in 7 models (Plant Design, System Design, Component Design, Fabrication, Mounting, Commissioning, Test Approval), 200 places and 83 transitions. Since a plant consists of multiple systems, which consist of multiple components, and each component is composed of several parts, an overall model was introduced to represent the parallel execution of designing the systems and components, manufacturing the different parts of a component, mounting the components, running each system, and finally combining the systems and running the whole plant.

4.2 Workflow Verification

Extending the ordinary P/T-Nets with shared places and special operators, the Petri Nets could not be verified by the tool *WoPeD*. Therefore, the Petri Nets, resulting from the initial modelling process, were translated to Coloured Petri Nets and verified in *CPN Tools* supporting these two extensions (special operators and shared places). During the translation from P/T-Nets to a CPN, the Net was verified for its behavioural correctness through the token game (simulation), which already eliminated several errors. To verify the resulted CPN, the state space (reachability graph) of the Net was calculated in CPN Tools. A report was generated from the calculated state space in CPN Tools and analysed in regard to the following properties:

1. Termination: The report contains at least one dead marking, which is also a home marking. (A marking is called dead if it does not enable any transition in the Net. A home marking is reachable from each marking of the reachability graph.)

2. Deadlock-freeness: The overall state space is finite.
3. Boundness and Safeness: The upper bound of each place is 1.
4. Soundness: The report contains only one dead marking.

The first state space, calculated from the finished CPN, was infinite and therefore, only the partial state space was presented in the first report (Fig. 4). The state space was calculated for ten minutes, which resulted in a state space with almost 300000 nodes. Four unbound places (Fig. 3) and over 500 dead-markings existed.

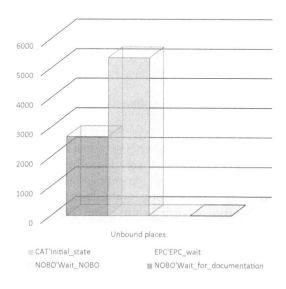

Fig. 3. Statistics about unbound places

Fixing the discovered unbound places, resulted in a finite state space with 186 nodes, 225 arcs and two dead markings (*final report* in Fig. 4). Analyzing the generated state space for the before defined properties resulted in the following: the CPN model terminates, is deadlock-free, holds no unbound places, and is therefore bound. The Net is not sound, since the state space contains two dead markings. Since both markings are valid end states, only distinguished by the placement of tokens in the final places, no further adjustments were made to the model.

4.3   Implementation of the Solution Using Hyperledger Fabric

Cross-organizational business processes require a certain level of trust between the involved organizations. This trust, traditionally guaranteed solely through legal contracts, can be established through the use of Blockchain, together with Smart Contracts. Smart Contracts assure that involved organizations cannot

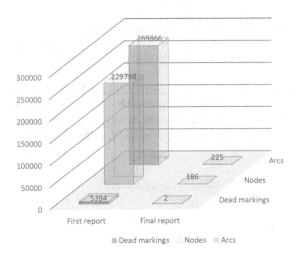

Fig. 4. Statistics about first and final report

break their agreements and therefore, serve as a machine enforceable and verifiable protocol for inter-organizational workflows. Implementing the business process as Smart Contracts on a Blockchain enforces all involved parties to execute the workflow correctly and therefore, establishes trust between all workflow participants without requiring a trusted third party. The following requirements were considered in the choice of a suitable Blockchain platform. All participants of the network must be identifiable at any time. Unauthorized access of non-involved organizations must be prevented. Privacy and confidentiality of transactions and data must be guaranteed at all times. The private permissioned Blockchain platform *Hyperledger Fabric* supports all before mentioned requirements, and is therefore used to implement the use case.

The CPN model was manually translated into Chaincode using *Golang* and the *IBM Blockchain Platform*[4] extension in *Visual Studio Code*. Interfaces, involving the publication of documents, were extracted from the CPN model and the surrounding transitions were examined. Internal places and transitions, framing the interfaces, were merged to one transition. Figure 5 displays the original part of the CPN model covering the publication of the Plant Design documentation package by EPC.

The internal places and transitions (creating, processing and publishing the documentation package) were merged to one atomic transition (Fig. 6). This transition is only representing the publication of the documentation package itself. This ensures that the internal processes and states of each participant in the workflow, and later in the Blockchain, are kept secret. The transition is surrounded by incoming/outgoing places, constituting the before extracted interfaces. The incoming places are named preconditions, whereas the outgoing

---

[4] https://marketplace.visualstudio.com/items?itemName=IBMBlockchain.ibm-block chain-platform.

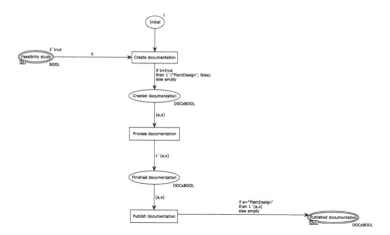

Fig. 5. Part of the CPN model covering the publication of the plant design

places are postconditions, see Fig. 6. All pre- and postconditions are represented as interfaces in the CPN model. In the end, all interfaces constituting published documents were represented in the Smart Contracts, which determined a sequence of tasks.

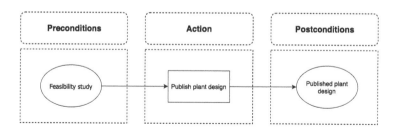

Fig. 6. Simplification of the publication of the plant design

For simplicity, *LevelDB*, a simple key-value store, was used. Additional to LevelDB, composite keys were created to be able to improve the search through the database. Only a *Document* structure was stored in the ledger; the actual documentation packages were stored off-chain, in a separate database. The Document structure contained a hash of the published documentation package, as well as a link to the actual documents.

The *IBM Blockchain Platform* extension provides a fast way to write, debug and test Chaincode in Hyperledger Fabric without the requirement of an elaborate network setup.

4.4 Validation of the Solution

To evaluate that the Smart Contracts implement the workflow correctly, the token game was run on the model, which resulted in a set of executed tasks, together with their initial and current, local markings. These tuples were put into logical orders:

- **Prerequisites:**
  $publish(FeasibilityStudy) \rightarrow SUCCESS$
- **Positive test case:**
  $published(FeasibilityStudy),$
  $publish(PlantDesign) \rightarrow SUCCESS$
- **Negative test case:**
  $\neg published(FeasibilityStudy),$
  $publish(PlantDesign) \rightarrow ERROR$

The resulting orders were manually translated into unit tests, which were run against the Smart Contracts. The partial state of the Net should be equal to the current state of the ledger.

Formulating unit tests from the extracted logic resulted in 87 tests with a test coverage of 44.4%. To cover also simple checks for wrongly inserted (number of) arguments, additional unit tests were formulated. A regression test was written to cover the overall execution. The written tests cover 56.6% of all statements. Certain error cases (i.e. JSON encoding/decoding failures, errors while getting/putting Document structures from/on the ledger) were not considered in the unit tests, which explains the low test coverage.

5 Results and Discussion

The introduced method is a new approach of digitalizing cross-organizational business processes, displayed in Fig. 7. In the first step of digitalizing the "Certification of the Construction of Industrial Plants", the workflow of the certification of a power plant was modelled as a simple P/T-Net with extensions that are required for this process. This first modelling process included domain experts from multiple participating organizations. Using ordinary P/T-nets, together with the tool *WoPeD*, during the initial modelling phase was well-received by all participating entities. With their simplicity on the one hand and formal semantics on the other, Petri Nets were accepted from all involved stakeholders. We explained the semantics of Petri Nets to the domain experts while running the token game. Consequently, the domain experts described Petri Nets as "easy to understand and adjust".

In the second step, the resulting P/T-Nets were translated to CPN and verified in CPN Tools. During the process of translating the simple P/T-Nets into a CPN, the model was verified by simulation (token game) and calculation of the partial state space (reachability graph). The finished Net was then verified by calculating and analysing the whole state space. Behavioural properties

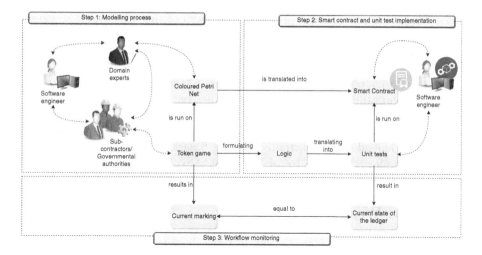

Fig. 7. Suggested development approach

(i.e. termination, deadlock-freeness, boundness and soundness), which should be fulfilled by the Net, were specified beforehand. Since the specified properties were not fulfilled, the CPN was adapted accordingly. Using Petri Nets as a modelling language for cross-organizational business processes, enables a formal verification of the workflow from early stages of the modelling process on.

In this experience report, application specific properties for the models were not considered in the verification process. This should be done in future work to guarantee not only behavioural properties, but make sure that the business process is modelled in the intended way. In our case, an application specific property would look like the following: "the system design phase can only be entered after the plant design is finished and accepted by NOBO".

After the Net fulfilled all properties, a suitable Blockchain platform was chosen and the CPN model was translated into Smart Contracts. To evaluate that the Smart Contracts implement the workflow correctly, the token game was run on the model and the resulted current markings were translated into logical orders, which were then translated into unit tests. These unit tests were run against the Smart Contracts. It was checked that the partial state of the Net was equal to the current state of the ledger. Translating the extracted logic into unit tests and running them against the Smart Contracts, resulted in a low test coverage, since edge and error cases are not considered in the calculated state space. Therefore, additional unit and regression tests were formulated.

Running the resulted Smart Contracts on Hyperledger Fabric ensures that all participating stakeholders execute the workflow correctly and therefore, establishes trust between the participants.

Although this method, including the elaborate modelling process takes time and contains multiple revisions, the method, introduced in this report, supports a correct implementation of the cross-organizational business process. Unfortunately, a model often cannot represent every detail of the workflow. Therefore, information that is not captured by the model has to be recorded in textual form, can not be verified and has to be considered in the implementation and testing phase additionally.

In case of a change in the model, the Smart Contracts are easily adaptable. Backwards compatibility is not guaranteed. Also, once the Smart Contracts are running, they can't be updated, since in our case keys to get earlier performed transactions from the ledger are saved locally by each node in the Blockchain network and depend on the currently running Smart Contracts. This approach does not force all participants to use the same SDK, but gives each stakeholder the flexibility to use any technology they want behind the API.

6   Related Work

In [4], the authors demonstrate the use of Blockchain technology in the context of inter-organizational business processes for the use case of a documentary letter of credit. Unfortunately, no method was introduced to specify a workflow. Since we are dealing with a large workflow, a method to specify the workflow and translate this specification into Smart Contracts is necessary. Routis investigates the use of Case Management Modelling and Notation for collaborative processes [15]. A method on how to translate the defined processes in Smart Contracts is not given. The authors in [11] introduce the notion of Enforceable Business Processes (EBP), a cooperative stable process, managed by multiple mutually independent organizations with a common goal. Challenges regarding running EBPs as Smart Contracts are analysed. A method on how to map such processes onto Smart Contracts is not introduced.

Caterpillar [10] and Lorikeet [17] translate BPMN to Solidity. Caterpillar is an open-source Business Process Management System running on Ethereum. Models in BPMN are translated to Solidity with the compilation tools provided by Caterpillar. Furthermore, the execution engine enables the deployment of the generated Smart Contract by the compilation tools, as stated in [10]. Lorikeet is a model-driven engineering tool to implement business processes on a Blockchain, described in [17]. The tools create Solidity Smart Contract code from BPMN specifications, which is demonstrated by an industrial use case. These tools restrict the modelling of the business process to BPMN. Since we use Petri Nets to model our use case, because of the above mentioned advantages, those systems are not applicable.

Nakamura presents in [1] a similar approach to ours. Defining the cross-organizational business processes in statecharts, applying statechart reduction algorithms to optimize the size of the statechart and generating software artifacts, Smart Contracts, running on Blockchain. Since we are dealing with an inter-organizational business process that comprises obligations which are agreed upon by all parties beforehand, a reduction of the size of the specified workflow, and therefore, a possible loss of information, is not permitted. Furthermore, statecharts lack formal semantics and therefore, can not be formally verified. The proposed solution in [1] does not include a verification of the statecharts.

7 Conclusion

Today business processes often exceed organizational boundaries and therefore, trust between the organizations that participate in this process has to be established. In the past, this trust was guaranteed solely through legal contracts. To digitally establish trust without requiring a trust third party, Blockchain technology together with Smart Contracts is used to ensure that involved organizations can not break their agreements. Smart Contracts can serve as a machine enforceable and verifiable protocol for inter-organizational workflows. This experience report introduced a solution on how to model, verify and implement an enforcement of cross-organizational business processes. This was done on the basis of the use case "Certification of the Construction of Industrial Plants". Using different types of Petri Nets and verifying the resulted models in CPN Tools, assured the correct representation of the workflow. The verified models were then translated into Smart Contracts, which were evaluated based on the simulation and reachability graph of the models.

To enhance the outcome of this report, the following points could be considered in the future. Building a generator that generates Smart Contracts from Petri Nets, Coloured Petri Nets in particular, could improve the cost for the method introduced in this report. Furthermore, versioning and updating the Smart Contracts have to be improved, and the admissibility of the ledger and the published documents as evidence in a court of law should be researched.

Acknowledgement. - This research work has been partially funded by the European Union's H2020 Programme under the Grant Agreement No. 830929 (Cyber-Sec4Europe). Also, we would like to thank our colleagues from Siemens and TÜV who were involved.

References

1. B, S.M.G., Yakhchi, S., Beheshti, A.: Inter-organizational Business Processes Managed by Blockchain, pp. 161–177 (2018). https://doi.org/10.1007/978-3-030-02922-7, https://doi.org/10.1007/978-3-030-02922-7_11
2. Christidis, K., Devetsikiotis, M.: Blockchains and smart contracts for the Internet of Things. IEEE Access **4**, 2292–2303 (2016). https://doi.org/10.1109/ACCESS.2016.2566339
3. Dijkman, R.M., Dumas, M., Ouyang, C.: Formal semantics and analysis of BPMN process models using petri nets. Technical Report, Prepr. 7115, 1–30 (2007). http://eprints.qut.edu.au/7115/
4. Fridgen, G., Radszuwill, S., Urbach, N., Utz, L.: Cross-organizational workflow management using blockchain technology - towards applicability, auditability, and automation. In: Proceedings of 51st Hawaii International Conference System Science, vol. 4801 (2018). https://doi.org/10.24251/hicss.2018.444
5. Heckel, R.: Open petri nets as semantic model for workflow integration. In: Ehrig, H., Reisig, W., Rozenberg, G., Weber, H. (eds.) Petri Net Technology for Communication-Based Systems. LNCS, vol. 2472, pp. 281–294. Springer, Heidelberg (2003). https://doi.org/10.1007/978-3-540-40022-6_14

6. Hollingsworth, D.: Workflow management coalition: the workflow reference model. Work. Manag. Coalit. **59**(10), 904–913 (1993). https://doi.org/10.1007/s00101-010-1752-4

7. Jensen, K., Kristensen, L.M., Wells, L.: Coloured Petri Nets and CPN tools for modelling and validation of concurrent systems. Int. J. Softw. Tools Technol. Transf. **9**(3–4), 213–254 (2007). https://doi.org/10.1007/s10009-007-0038-x

8. Kasinathan, P., Cuellar, J.: Securing the integrity of workflows in IoT. In: International Conference on Embedded Wireless Systems and Networks, pp. 252–257 (2018)

9. Leal, G., Guédria, W., Panetto, H., Proper, E.: Towards a meta-model for networked enterprise. In: Schmidt, R., Guédria, W., Bider, I., Guerreiro, S. (eds.) BPMDS/EMMSAD -2016. LNBIP, vol. 248, pp. 417–431. Springer, Cham (2016). https://doi.org/10.1007/978-3-319-39429-9_26

10. López-Pintado, O., García-Bañuelos, L., Dumas, M., Weber, I.: Caterpillar: a blockchain-based business process management system. In: CEUR Workshop Proceedings, vol. 1920, pp. 1–5 (2017)

11. Migliorini, S., Gambini, M., Combi, C., La Rosa, M.: The rise of enforceable business processes from the hashes of blockchain-based smart contracts. In: Reinhartz-Berger, I., Zdravkovic, J., Gulden, J., Schmidt, R. (eds.) BPMDS/EMMSAD -2019. LNBIP, vol. 352, pp. 130–138. Springer, Cham (2019). https://doi.org/10.1007/978-3-030-20618-5_9

12. Raedts, I., Petković, M., Usenko, Y.S., Van Der Werf, J.M., Groote, J.F., Somers, L.: Transformation of BPMN models for behaviour analysis. In: Proceedings of 5th International Workshop on Modeling Simulation, Verification and Validation Enterprise Information Systems - MSVVEIS 2007; Conjunction with ICEIS 2007, pp. 126–137 (2007)

13. Ramadan, M., Elmongui; H., Hassan, R.: BPMN formalisation using Coloured Petri Nets. In: Proceedings of the 2nd GSTF Annual International Conference on Software Engineering and Application (2011)

14. Rimba, P., Tran, A.B., Weber, I., Staples, M., Ponomarev, A., Xu, X.: Comparing blockchain and cloud services for business process execution. In: Proceedings of 2017 IEEE International Conference on Software Architecture ICSA 2017 (Section III), pp. 257–260 (2017). https://doi.org/10.1109/ICSA.2017.44

15. Routis, I., Nikolaidou, M., Anagnostopoulos, D.: Modeling collaborative processes with CMMN: success or failure? An experience report. In: Gulden, J., Reinhartz-Berger, I., Schmidt, R., Guerreiro, S., Guédria, W., Bera, P. (eds.) BPMDS/EMMSAD -2018. LNBIP, vol. 318, pp. 199–210. Springer, Cham (2018). https://doi.org/10.1007/978-3-319-91704-7_13

16. Ter Hofstede, A., van der Aalst, W.M.P.: YAWL: yet another workflow language. Inf. Syst. **30**(4), 245–275 (2005)

17. Tran, A.B., Lu, Q., Weber, I.: Lorikeet: a model-driven engineering tool for blockchain-based business process execution and asset management. In: CEUR Workshop Proceedings, vol. 2196, pp. 56–60 (2018)

18. Van Der Aalst, W.: Loosely coupled interorganizational workflows: modeling and analyzing workflows crossing organizational boundaries. Inf. Manag. **37**(2), 67–75 (2000). https://doi.org/10.1016/S0378-7206(99)00038-5

Planning and Scheduling in Business Processes (BPMDS 2020)

Automated Planning for Supporting Knowledge-Intensive Processes

Sheila Katherine Venero[1(✉)], Bradley Schmerl[2], Leonardo Montecchi[1],
Julio Cesar dos Reis[1], and Cecília Mary Fischer Rubira[1]

[1] University of Campinas, Campinas, SP, Brazil
[2] Carnegie Mellon University, Pittsburgh, PA, USA

Abstract. Knowledge-intensive Processes (KiPs) are processes characterized by high levels of unpredictability and dynamism. Their process structure may not be known before their execution. One way to cope with this uncertainty is to defer decisions regarding the process structure until run time. In this paper, we consider the definition of the process structure as a planning problem. Our approach uses automated planning techniques to generate plans that define process models according to the current context. The generated plan model relies on a metamodel called METAKIP that represents the basic elements of KiPs. Our solution explores Markov Decision Processes (MDP) to generate plan models. This technique allows uncertainty representation by defining state transition probabilities, which gives us more flexibility than traditional approaches. We construct an MDP model and solve it with the help of the PRISM model-checker. The solution is evaluated by means of a proof of concept in the medical domain which reveals the feasibility of our approach.

Keywords: Knowledge-intensive process · Business process modeling · Case management · Automated planning · Markov Decision Process · Business process management systems

1 Introduction

In the last decades, the business process management (BPM) community has established approaches and tools to design, enact, control, and analyze business processes. Most process management systems follow predefined process models that capture different ways to coordinate their tasks to achieve their business goals. However, not all types of processes can be predefined at design time—some of them can only be specified at run time because of their high degree of uncertainty [18]. This is the case with *Knowledge-intensive Processes (KiPs)*.

This work is partially supported by CAPES and CNPq scholarships, by the Mobility Program of the Santander Bank, and by the São Paulo Research Foundation (FAPESP) with grants #2017/21773-9 and #2019/02144-6. The opinions expressed in this work do not necessarily reflect those of the funding agencies.

© Springer Nature Switzerland AG 2020
S. Nurcan et al. (Eds.): BPMDS 2020/EMMSAD 2020, LNBIP 387, pp. 101–116, 2020.
https://doi.org/10.1007/978-3-030-49418-6_7

KiPs are business processes with critical decision-making tasks that involve domain-specific knowledge, information, and data [4]. KiPs can be found in domains like healthcare, emergency management, project coordination, and case management, among others. KiP structure depends on the current situation and new emergent events that are unpredictable and vary in every process instance [4]. Thus, a KiP's structure is defined step by step as the process executes, by a series of decisions made by process participants considering the current specific situations and contexts [13]. In this sense, it is not possible to entirely define beforehand which activities will execute or their ordering and, indeed, it is necessary to refine them as soon as new information becomes available or whenever new goals are set.

These kinds of processes heavily rely on highly qualified and trained professionals called *knowledge workers*. Knowledge workers use their own experience and expertise to make complex decisions to model the process and achieve business goals [3]. Despite their expertise, it is often the case that knowledge workers become overwhelmed with the number of cases, the differences between cases, rapidly changing contexts, and the need to integrate new information. They therefore require computer-aided support to help them manage these difficult and error-prone tasks.

In this paper, we explore how to provide this support by considering the process modeling problem as an automated planning problem. Automated planning, a branch of artificial intelligence, investigates how to search through a space of possible actions and environment conditions to produce a sequence of actions to achieve some goal over time [10]. Our work investigates an automated way to generate process models for KiPs by mapping an artifact-centric case model into a planning model at run time. To encode the planning domain and planning problem, we use a case model defined according to the METAKIP metamodel [20] that encloses data and process logic into domain artifacts. It defines data-driven activities in the form of tactic templates. Each tactic aims to achieve a goal and the planning model is derived from it.

In our approach, we use Markov decision processes (MDP) because they allow us to model dynamic systems under uncertainty [7], although our definition of the planning problem model enables using different planning algorithms and techniques. MDP finds optimal solutions to sequential and stochastic decision problems. As the system model evolves probabilistically, an action is taken based on the observed condition or state and a reward or cost is gained [7,10]. Thus, an MDP model allows us to identify decision alternatives for structuring KiPs at run time. We use PRISM [11], a probabilistic model checker, to implement the solution for the MDP model.

We present a proof of concept by applying our method in a medical treatment scenario, which is a typical example of a non-deterministic process. Medical treatments can be seen as sequential decisions in an uncertain environment. Medical decisions not only depend on the current state of the patient, but they are affected by the evolution of the states as well. The evolution of the patient state is unpredictable, since it depends on factors such as preexisting patient illnesses or patient-specific characteristics of the diseases. In addition, medical treatment decisions involve complex trade-offs between the risks and benefits of various treatment options.

We show that it is possible to generate different optimal treatment plans according to the current patient state and a target goal state, assuming that we have enough data to accurately estimate the transition probabilities to the next patient state. The resulting process models could help knowledge workers to make complex decisions and structure execution paths at run time with more probability of success and optimizing constraints, such as cost and time.

The remainder of this paper is organized as follows: Sect. 2 presents a motivating medical scenario. Section 3 introduces the theoretical and methodological background. Section 4 describes the proposed method to encode a case model as a planning model. Section 5 reports on the application of the methodology in a scenario. Section 6 discusses the obtained findings and related work. Finally, Sect. 7 wraps up the paper with the concluding remarks.

2 Motivating Example

This section presents a motivating medical case scenario. Suppose we have the following medical scenario in the oncology department stored in the Electronic Medical Record (EMR).

Mary, 58 years old, married, two children. She was diagnosed with a lymphoma non-Hodgkin admitted on 20/07/2019 and is receiving R-ICE Chemotherapy. R-ICE is named after the initials of the drugs used: rituximab, ifosfamide, carboplatin, etoposide. R-ICE is applied as a course of several sessions (cycles) of treatment over a few months. On 02/10/2019, Mary is supposed to receive the second cycle of R-ICE. However, on admission, she is febrile at 38 °C and presents severe nausea (Level 4).

In order to receive the second cycle of R-ICE, it is necessary to stabilize Mary's health status as soon as possible. Thus, at this time the goal is to decrease her body temperature to $36.5\,°C \leq Temp \leq 37.2\,°C$ and reduce the level of nausea to zero $LN = 0$. For that, physicians need to choose from vast treatment strategies to decide which procedures are the best for Mary, in her specific current context.

Assume that we have statistical data about two possible tactics for achieving the desired goal: fever (FVR) and nausea (NAUSEA) management, shown in Table 1 adapted from [2]. Each of these tactics can be fulfilled through multiple activities that have different interactions and constraints with each other, as well as to the specifics of the patient being treated. For example, (a) treating nausea with a particular drug may affect the fever, (b) administration of the drug may depend on the drugs that the patient is taking, (c) drug effectiveness may depend on the patient history with the drug, or (d) giving the drug may depend on whether the drug has already been administered and how much time has elapsed since the last dose. These issues make manual combination of even this simple case challenging, and it becomes much harder for more complex treatments and patient histories. Support is therefore needed that can take into account patient data, constraints, dependencies, and patient/doctor preferences to help advise the doctor on viable and effective courses of treatment.

Table 1. Tactics templates for fever (FVR) and nausea (NAUSEA) management

Tactic: Fever Management (FVR)	**Tactic:** Nausea Management (NAUSEA)
Definition: Management of a patient with hyperpyrexia caused by non-environmental factors	**Definition:** Prevention and alleviation of nausea
Goal: Thermoregulation $(36.5\,^{\circ}\text{C} \leq Temp \leq 37.2\,^{\circ}\text{C})$	**Goal:** Stop Nausea (LoN = 0)
Metric: Temperature (Temp)	**Metric:** Level of Nausea (LoN)
Preconditions: $Temp > 37.2\,^{\circ}\text{C}$	**Preconditions:** LoN > 0
Activities:	**Activities:**
A1. Administer ORAL antipyretic medication,as appropriate **A2.** Administer INTRAVENOUS antipyretic medication, as appropriate **A3.** Administer medications to treat the cause of fever, as appropriate **A4.**Encourage increased intake of oral fluids, as appropriate **A5.** Administer oxygen, as appropriate	**B1.** Ensure that effective antiemetic drugs are given to prevent nausea when possible (except for nausea related to pregnancy) **B2.** Control environmental factors that may evoke nausea (e.g., aversive smells, sound and unpleasant visual stimulation **B3.** Give cold, clear liquid and odorless and colorless food, as appropriate

3   Background

This section presents the underlying concepts in our proposal. Section 3.1 provides an overview of the METAKIP metamodel; Sect. 3.2 introduces basic concepts of automated planning; Sect. 3.3 explains Markov decision process (MDP). Section 3.4 describes the PRISM tool and language.

3.1   METAKIP: A Metamodel for KiPs Definition

Our previous work proposed an artifact-centric metamodel [20] for the definition of KiPs, aiming to support knowledge workers during the decision-making process. The metamodel supports data-centric process management, which is based on the availability and values of data rather than completion of activities.

In data-centric processes, data values drive decisions and decisions dynamically drive the course of the process [18]. The metamodel is divided into four major packages: case, control-flow, knowledge, and decision, in such a way that there is an explicit integration of the data, domain, and organizational knowledge, rules, goals, and activities.

The Case Package defines the base structure of the metamodel, a *Case*. A case model definition represents an integrated view of the context and environment data of a case, following the artifact-centric paradigm. This package is composed of a set of interconnected artifacts representing the logical structure of the business process. An *artifact* is a data object composed of a set of items, attributes, and data values, defined at run time.

The Knowledge Package captures explicit organizational knowledge, which is encoded through *tactic templates, goals*, and *metrics* that are directly influenced by business rules. Tactics templates represent best practices and guidelines. Usually, they have semi-structured sequences of activities or unstructured loose alternative activities pursuing a goal.

The Control-flow Package defines the *behavior* of a case. It is composed of a set of data-driven activities to handle different cases. Activity definitions are made in a declarative way and have *pre-* and *post-conditions*. The metamodel refines the granularity of an *activity* that could be a step or a task. A *task* is logically divided into *steps*, which allows better management of data entry on the artifacts. Step definitions are associated with a single attribute of an artifact, a resource, and a role type at most. This definition gives us a tight integration between data, steps and resources.

These packages are used to model alternative plans to answer emergent circumstances, reflecting environmental changes or unexpected outcomes during the execution of a KiP. The Decision Package represents the structure of a collaborative decision-making process performed by knowledge workers. We proposed a representation of how decisions can be made by using the principles of strategic management, such as, looking towards goals and objectives and embracing uncertainty by formulating strategies for the future and correct them if necessary. The strategic plan is structured at run time by goals, objectives, metrics and tactic templates.

3.2   Automated Planning

Planning is the explicit and rational deliberation of actions to be performed to achieve a goal [7]. The process of deliberation consists of choosing and organizing actions considering their expected outcomes in the best possible way. Usually, planning is required when an activity involves new or less familiar situations, complex tasks and objectives, or when the adaptation of actions is constrained by critical factors such as high risk. Automated planning studies the deliberation process computationally [7].

A conceptual model for planning can be represented by a state-transition system, which formally is a 4-tuple $\Sigma = (S, A, E, \gamma)$, where $S = \{s_1, s_2, ...\}$ is a finite or recursively enumerable set of states; $A = \{a_1, a_2, ...\}$ is a finite or recursively enumerable set of actions; $E = \{e_1, e_2, ...\}$ is a finite or recursively enumerable set of events; and $\gamma : S \times A \times E \rightarrow 2^S$ is a state-transition function.

Actions are transitions controlled by a plan executor. Events are unforeseen transitions that correspond to the internal dynamics of the system and cannot be controlled by the plan executor. Both events and actions contribute to the evolution of the system. Given a state transition system Σ, the purpose of planning is to deliberate which actions to apply into which states to achieve some goal from a given state. A plan is a structure that gives the appropriate actions.

3.3 Markov Decision Process (MDP)

A Markov decision process (MDP) is a discrete-time stochastic control process. It is a popular framework designed to make decisions under uncertainty, dealing with nondeterminism, probabilities, partial observability, and extended goals [7].

In MDPs, an agent chooses action a based on observing state s and receives a reward r for that action [10]. The state evolves probabilistically based on the current state and the action taken by the agent.

Figure 1(a) presents a decision network [10], used to represent a MDP. The state transition function $T(s'|s, a)$ represents the probability of transitioning from state s to s' after executing action a. The reward function $R(s, a)$ represents the expected reward received when executing action a from state s. We assume that the reward function is a deterministic function of s and a.

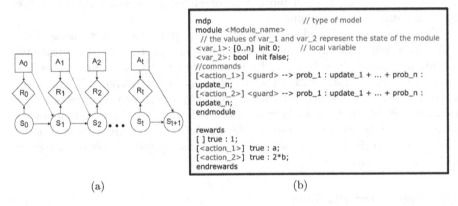

(a)   (b)

Fig. 1. (a) MDP representation [10] and (b) Example syntax of *mdp* PRISM [11] module and rewards

An MDP treats planning as an optimization problem in which an agent needs to plan a sequence of actions that maximizes the chances of reaching the goal. Action outcomes are modeled with a probability distribution function. Goals are represented as utility functions that can express preferences on the entire execution path of a plan, rather than just desired final states. For example, finding the optimal choice of treatment optimizing the life expectancy of the patient or optimizing cost and resources.

3.4 PRISM

PRISM [11] is a probabilistic model checker that allows the modeling and analysis of systems that exhibit probabilistic behavior. The PRISM tool provides support for modeling and construction of many types of probabilistic models: discrete-time Markov chains (DTMCs), continuous-time Markov chains (CTMCs), Markov decision processes (MDPs), and probabilistic timed automata (PTAs). The tool supports statistical model checking, confidence-level approximation, and acceptance sampling with its discrete-event simulator. For non-deterministic models it can generate an optimal adversary/strategy to reach a certain state.

Models are described using the PRISM language, a simple, state-based language based on the reactive modules formalism [1]. Figure 1(b) presents an example of the syntax of a PRISM module and rewards. The fundamental components of the PRISM language are modules. A module has two parts: variables and commands. Variables describe the possible states that the module can be in at a given time. Commands describe the behavior of a module, how the state changes over time. A command comprises a guard and one or more updates. The guard is a predicate over all the variables in the model. Each update describes a transition that the module can take if the guard is true. A transition is specified by giving the new values of the variables in the module. Each update has a probability which will be assigned to the corresponding transition. Commands can be labeled with actions. These actions are used for synchronization between modules. Cost and rewards are expressed as real values associated with certain states or transitions of the model.

4 Dynamic Plan Generation for KiPs Execution

In our approach, plans are fragments of process models that are frequently created and modified during process execution. Plans may change as new information arrives and/or when a new goal is set. We advocate the creation of a planner to structure process models at run time based on a knowledge base. The planner synthesizes plans on-the-fly according to ongoing circumstances. The generated plans should be revised and re-planned as soon as new information becomes available. Thereby, it involves both computer agents and knowledge workers in a constant interleaving of planning, execution (configuration and enactment), plan supervision, plan revision, and re-planning. An interactive software tool might assist human experts during planning. This tool should allow defining planning goals and verifying emerging events, states, availability of activities and resources, as well as preferences.

4.1 Model Formulation

The run-time generation of planning models according to a specific situation in a case instance requires the definition of the planning domain and then the planning problem itself.

Definition 1. *Let the case model be represented according to the METAKIP metamodel. The planning domain is derived from the case model that can be described using a state-transition system defined as a 5-tuple $\Sigma = (S, A, E, \gamma, C)$ such as that: S is the set of possible case states. A is the set of actions that are represented by activities inside tactics that an actor may perform. E is the set of events in the context or in the environment. $\gamma : S \times A \times E \rightarrow 2^S$, is the state-transition function, so the system evolves according to the actions and events that it receives. $C : S \times A \rightarrow [0, \infty)$ is the cost function that may represent monetary cost, time, risk or something that can be minimized or maximized.*

The state of a case is the set of values (available data) of the attributes contained in artifacts of the *context* and the *environment*. However, since the number of attributes of the artifacts is very large, it is necessary to limit the number of attributes to only the most relevant ones, which determines the current state of the case at a given time t.

Definition 2. *A state s_t is the set of values corresponding to a set of relevant attributes $\{v_1, v_2, \ldots v_r\}$, with $r \geq 1$, contained in the business artifacts at a given time t.*

Actions in the METAKIP metamodel are represented by the activities within a tactic. Tactics represent best practices and guidelines used by the knowledge workers to make decisions. In METAKIP, they serve as tactic templates to be instantiated to deal with some situations during the execution of a case instance. Tactics are composed of a finite set of activities pursuing a goal. A tactic can be structured or unstructured. A tactic is a 4-tuple $T = (G, PC, M, A)$, where: G is a set of variables representing the pursuing goal state, PC is a finite set of preconditions representing a state required for applying the tactic, M is a set of metrics to track and assess the pursuing goal state, and A is a finite set of activities.

In METAKIP, an activity could be a single step or a set of steps (called a task). An activity has some preconditions and post-conditions (effects). We map activities into executable actions. An executable action is an activity in which their effects can modify the values of the attributes inside business artifacts. These effects can be deterministic or non-deterministic.

Definition 3. *An action is a 4-tuple $a = (Pr, Eff, Pb, c)$ where: Pr is a finite set of preconditions. Eff is a finite set of effects. Pb is a probability distribution on the effects, such that, $P_{ef}(i)$ is the probability of effect $ef \in Eff$ and $\sum_{ef \in Eff} P_{ef}(i) = 1$. c is the number which represents the cost (monetary, time, etc.) of performing a.*

As the state-transition function γ is too large to be explicitly specified, it is necessary to represent it in a generative way. For that, we use the planning operators from which it is possible to compute γ. Thus, γ can be specified through a set of planning operators O. A planning operator is instantiated by an action.

Definition 4. *A planning operator O is a pair (id, a) where a is an action and id is a unique identifier of action a.*

At this point, we are able to define the planning problem to generate a plan as a process model.

Definition 5. *The planning problem for generating a process model at a given time t is defined as a triple $P = (OS_t, GS_t, RO_t)$, where: OS_t is the observable situation of a case state at time t. GS_t is the goal state at time t, a set of attributes with expected output values. RO_t represents a subset of the O that represents only available and relevant actions for a specific situation during the execution of a case instance at a given time t.*

Definition 6. *The observable situation of a case instance C state at a given time t is a set of attributes $OS_t = \{v_1, v_2, \ldots, v_m\}$, with $m \geq 1$, such that $v_i \in S_t \cup I_t$ for each $1 \leq i \leq m$, where the state of C is S_t and the set issues in the situation of C is I_t.*

Definition 7. *The goal state of an observable situation of case instance C at a given time t is the set of attributes $GS_t = \{v_1, v_2, \ldots, v_m\}$, with $m \geq 1$, such that, for $1 \leq i \leq m$, v_i is an attribute with an expected output value, v_i belongs to an artifact of C. These attributes are selected by the knowledge workers. Some metrics required to asses some goals inside tactics can be added to the goal. GS_t represents the expected reality of C.*

GS_t serves as an input for searching an execution path for a specific situation. Different goal states can be defined over time.

Definition 8. *Let $P = (OS_t, GS_t, RO_t)$ be the planning problem. A plan π is a solution for P. The state produced by applying π to a state OS_t in the order given is the state GS_t. A plan is any sequence of actions $\pi = (a_1, \ldots, a_k)$, where $k \geq 1$. The plan π represents the process model.*

Our problem definition enables the use of different planning algorithms and the application of automatic planning tools to generate alternatives plans. As we are interested in KiPs, which are highly unpredictable processes, we use Markov Decision Processes for formulating the model for the planner. MDPs allows us to represent uncertainty with a probability distribution. MDP makes sequential decision making and reasons about the future sequence of actions and obstructions, which provides us with high levels of flexibility in the process models. In the following, we show how to derive an MDP model expressed in the PRISM language from a METAKIP model automatically.

4.2   PRISM Model Composition

Algorithm 1 shows the procedure to automatically generate the MDP model for the PRISM tool, where the input parameters are: OS_t, GS_t, set of domain

Tactics, t is the given time, PP minimum percentage of preconditions satisfaction, and PG minimum percentage of goal satisfaction, both PP and PG are according to the rules of the domain. As described in Sect. 3.4, a module is composed of variables and commands. Variables of the module are the set of attributes from the case artifacts that belong to $OS_t \cup GS_t$. Commands are represented for the relevant planning operators RO_t. The name of the command is the identifier of the action, the guards are the preconditions PC and the effects *Eff* are the updates with associated probabilities. Rewards are represented by the cost of actions c and are outside of the module of PRISM.

Algorithm 1. PRISM Model Generator

Require: OS_t, GS_t, *Tactics*, t, PP, PG
  $V \leftarrow OS_t \cup GS_t$ ▷ Attributes of OS_t and GS_t correspond to PRISM variables
  for all $T \in$ *Tactics* **do**   ▷ For each tactic
    $p_1 \leftarrow |T.PC \cap OS_t|/|T.PC|$ ▷ Percentage of satisfied preconditions
    $p_2 \leftarrow |GS_t \cap T.G|/|GS_t|$ ▷ Percentage of achievable target goal
    if $p_1 \geq PP$ and $p_2 \geq PG$ **then**   ▷ If percentages are acceptable
      $ST \leftarrow ST \cup T$ ▷ Add to the set of selected tactics
    end if
  end for
  $RT \leftarrow SelectRevevantTactics(ST)$ ▷ Relevant tactics for the current situation OS_t
  $A_t \leftarrow CheckAvailableActivities(RT, t)$ ▷ Select available activities at time t
  $RO_t \leftarrow CreatePlanningOperators(A_t)$
  $C \leftarrow CreateCommands(RO_t)$
  $R \leftarrow CreateRewards(RO_t)$
  $V \leftarrow V \cup \{T.M : T \in RT\}$ ▷ Add necessary metrics to evaluate
  $CreatePRISMModel(V, C, R)$

For finding the set of relevant planning operators RO_t, first, we select tactics whose preconditions must be satisfied by the current situation OS_t and whose goal is related to the target state GS_t. This can be done by calculating the percentages of both the satisfied preconditions and achievable goals. If these percentages are within an acceptable range according to the rules of the domain, the tactics are selected. Second, this first set of tactics is shown to the knowledge workers who select the most relevant tactics. The set of the selected relevant tactics is denoted as RT. From this set of tactics, we verify which activities inside the tactics are available at time t. Thus, the set of available actions at time t is denoted by $A_t = a_1, a_2, \ldots, a_n$. Finally, the relevant planning operators, RO_t, are created by means of A_t.

4.3 Plan Generation

To generate plans in PRISM, it is necessary to define a property file that contains properties that define goals as utility functions. PRISM evaluates properties over an MDP model and generates all possible resolutions of non-determinism in the model, state graphs, and gives us the optimal state graph. The state graph describes a series of possible states that can occur while choosing actions aiming to achieve a goal state. It maximizes the probability to reach the goal state taking into consideration rewards computed, that is maximizing or minimizing rewards and costs.

In our context, a property represents the goal state GS_t to be achieved while trying to optimize some criteria. Then, PRISM calculates how desirable an executing path is according to one criterion. Thus, plans can be customized according to knowledge workers' preferences (costs and rewards). To generate a plan, we need to evaluate a property. The generated plan is a state graph that represents a process model to be executed at time t. The generated process model shows case states as nodes and states transitions as arcs labeled with actions which outcomes follow probability distribution function. According to this state graph, the knowledge worker could choose which action to execute in a particular state. This helps knowledge workers to make decisions during KiPs execution.

5 Proof of Concept

This section formulates a patient-specific MDP model in PRISM for the medical scenario presented in Sect. 2. In the area of health care, medical decisions can be modeled with Markov Decisions Processes (MDP) [5,17]. Although MDP is more suitable for certain types of problems involving complex decisions, such as liver transplants, HIV, diabetes, and others, almost every medical decision can be modeled as an MDP [5]. We generate the PRISM model by defining the observable situation OS_t, Goal state GS_t, and the set of relevant planning operators RO_t.

Table 2. Activity modeling

Activity A1: Administer Oral antipyretic medication, as appropriate	Activity B1: Ensure that effective antiemetic drugs are given to prevent nausea when possible
Pre-condition: ((Temp > 37.2) and (LN = 0 or LN = 1)) and (allergic = false) and (conflict with current medications = false) and (medication is available = true)	**Pre-condition:** Pregnancy(FALSE) and (LN > 2) and (allergic = false) and (conflict with current medications = false)
Effects:	**Effects:**
E1: p = 0.6 Respond to treatment (Temp = 37)	**E1:** p = 0.7 Respond to treatment (LN = 0)
E2: p = 0.3 Partial Respond to treatment (Temp = Temp − 0.5)	**E2:** p = 0.2 Partially respond to treatment (LN = LN −1)
E3: p = 0.1 Not Responding to treatment (Temp = Temp + 0.5)	**E3:** p = 0.1 Not Responding to treatment (LN = LN +1))
Task execution time : 5 min	**Task execution time :** 5 min
Cost: 0.08	**Cost: 0.08**

Taking in consideration the medical scenario, the observable situation is $OS_0 = \{Temp_0 = 38°, LN_0 = 4\}$ and the goal state is $GS_0 = \{36°C \leq Temp \leq 37.2°C, LN = 0\}$ where: Temp is the temperature of the patient and LN is the level of nausea, both attributes of the *Health Status* artifact. We assume that the set of relevant tactics RT according to the current health status of the patient are fever and nausea management, presented in Sect. 2.

Table 2 shows the specification of one activity of each tactic, showing their preconditions, effects with their probability, time, and cost of execution. We modeled the activity effects with probabilities related to the probability of the patient to respond to the treatment. For example, the possible effects of applying the activity *Administer ORAL antipyretic medication* are: (E1) the patient successfully responds to treatment, occurring with a probability 0.6; (E2) 30% of the time the patient partially responds to treatment where their temperature decreases by 0.5° or more fails to reach the goal level; and (E3) the patient does not respond at all to treatment or gets worse (occurring with a probability of 0.1). The other activities are similarly modeled according to the response of the patient. Assuming that all activities from both tactics are available, the set of executable actions is $A_t = \{A1, A2, A3, A4, A5, B1, B2, B3\}$. Then, it is possible to model the set of relevant planning operators RO_t. Having OS_t, GS_t and RO_t, it is possible to generate the MDP model in the language PRISM.

Once we created the MDP model, the following utility functions were evaluated: minimize time and cost while reaching the target state. The optimal plan to achieve the goal state GS_t while minimizing the cost shows that reachability is eight iterations. The resulting model has 13 states, 35 transitions, and 13 choices. The time for the model construction was 0.056 s.

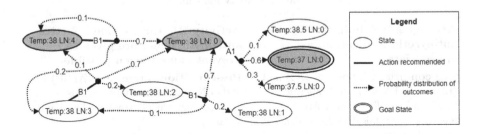

Fig. 2. Plan for reaching the goal state optimizing the cost

Figure 2 presents only a fragment of the model generated, highlighting the most probable path from the initial state to the goal state. The first suggested action is $B1$ (labeled arc) with possible outcome states with their probabilities. If the most probable next state is achieved, the next action to perform is $A1$ which has a probability of 0.6 to reach the goal state. Knowledge workers can use this generated plan to decide which is the next activity they should perform in a particular state. To make the plan readable to knowledge workers, they could be presented with only the most probable path, and this could be updated according to the state actually reached after activity execution. Further studies are necessary to help guiding knowledge workers in interpreting and following the model.

6   Discussion and Related Work

In the last decades, there has been a growing interest in highly dynamic process management, with different types of approaches that deal with the variability, flexibility, and customization of processes at design time and at run time. Most approaches start from the premise that there is a process model to which different changes have to be made, such as adding or deleting fragments according to a domain model or to generate an alternative sequence of activities due to some customization option. A few approaches use automated planning for synthesizing execution plans. Laurent *et al.* [12] explored a declarative modeling language called Alloy to create the planning model and generate the plans. This approach seems to be very promising for activity-centric processes, but not effective enough for data-centric processes, as data is not well-enough treated to be the driver of the process as required in KiPs.

SmartPM [16] investigated the problem of coordinating heterogeneous components inside cyber-physical systems. They used a PDDL (Planning Domain Definition Language) planner that evaluates the physical reality and the expected reality, and synthesize a recovery process. Similarly, Marrella and Lespérance proposed an approach [15] to dynamically generate process templates from a representation of the contextual domain described in PDDL, an initial state, and a goal condition. However, for the generation of the process templates, it is assumed that tasks are black boxes with just deterministic effects. On the other hand, Henneberger *et al.* [8] explored an ontology for generating process models. The generated process models are action state graphs (ASG). Although this work uses a very interesting semantic approach, they did not consider important aspects such as resources and cost for the planning model.

There has been an increasing interest in introducing cognitive techniques for supporting the business process cycle. Ferreira *et. al.* [6] proposed a new life cycle for workflow management based on continuous learning and planning. It uses a planner to generate a process model as a sequence of actions that comply with activity rules and achieve the intended goal. Hull and Nezhad [9] proposed a new cycle Plan-Act-Learn for cognitively-enabled processes that can be carried out by humans and machines, where plans and decisions define actions, and it is possible to learn from it. Recently, Marrella [14] showed how automatic planning techniques can improve different research challenges in the BPM area. This approach explored a set of steps for encoding a concrete problem as a PDDL planning problem with deterministics effects.

In this paper we introduced the notion of the state of a case regarding data-values in the artifacts of a case instance. From this state, we can plan different trajectories towards a goal state using automated planning techniques. Our solution generates action plans considering the non-deterministic effects of the actions, new emerging goals and information, which provides high levels of flexibility and adaptation. As we describe a generic planning model, it is possible to use different planning algorithms or combine other planning models, such as the classical planning model or the hierarchical task network (HTN), according to the structuring level of the processes at different moments. Thereby, we could apply this methodology to other types of processes, from well-structured processes to loosely or unstructured processes.

Our approach relies on MDP, which requires defining transition probabilities, which in some situations can be very difficult and expensive to get. Nowadays a huge amount of data is produced by many sensors, machines, software systems, etc, which might facilitate the acquisition of data to estimate these transition probabilities. In the medical domain, the increasing use of electronic medical record systems shall provide the medical data from thousands of patients, which can be exploited to derive these probabilities. A limitation in MDPs refers to the size of the problem because the size of the state-space explodes, and it becomes more difficult to solve. In this context, several techniques for finding approximate solutions to MDPs can be applied in addition to taking advantage of the rapid increase of processing power in the last years.

Flexible processes could be easily designed if we replan after an activity execution. In fact, our approach suggests a system that has a constant interleaving of planning, execution, and monitoring. In this way, it will help knowledge workers during the decision-making process.

7   Conclusion

Process modeling is usually conducted by process designers in a manual way. They define the activities to be executed to accomplish business goals. This task is very difficult and prone to human errors. In some cases (*e.g.*, for KiPs), it is impossible due to uncertainty, context-dependency, and specificity. In this paper, we devised an approach to continually generate run-time process models for a case instance using an artifact-centric case model, data-driven activities, and automatic planning techniques, even for such loosely-structured processes as KiPs.

Our approach defined how to synthesize a planning model from an artifact-oriented case model defined according to the METAKIP metamodel. The formulation of the planning domain and the planning problem rely on the current state of a case instance, context and environment, target goals, and tactic templates from which we can represent actions, states, and goals. As our focus is KiPs management, we chose to use the MDP framework that allows representing uncertainty, which is one of KiPs essential characteristics. To automatically generate the action plan, we used the tool PRISM, which solves the MDP model and provides optimal solutions.

Future work involve devising a user-friendly software application for knowledge workers to interact with the planner and improve the presentation of plans in such a way that it is more understandable to them. Our goal is to develop a planner which combines different types of planning algorithms to satisfy different requirements in business processes, especially regarding the structuring level. This planner will be incorporated into a fully infrastructure for managing Knowledge-intensive processes that will be based on the DW-SAArch reference architecture [19].

References

1. Alur, R., Henzinger, T.A.: Reactive modules. Form. Methods Syst. Des. **15**(1), 7–48 (1999)
2. Butcher, H.K., Bulechek, G.M., Dochterman, J.M.M., Wagner, C.: Nursing Interventions classification (NIC)-E-Book. Elsevier Health Sciences (2018)
3. Davenport, T.: Thinking for a Living. How to Get Better Performance and Results. Harvard Business School Press, Boston (2005)
4. Di Ciccio, C., Marrella, A., Russo, A.: Knowledge-intensive processes: characteristics, requirements and analysis of contemporary approaches. J. Data Semant. **4**(1), 29–57 (2015)
5. Díez, F., Palacios, M., Arias, M.: MDPs in medicine: opportunities and challenges. In: Decision Making in Partially Observable, Uncertain Worlds: Exploring Insights from Multiple Communities (IJCAI Workshop), vol. 9, p. 14 (2011)
6. Ferreira, H.M., Ferreira, D.R.: An integrated life cycle for workflow management based on learning and planning. Int. J. Cooper. Inf. Syst. **15**(04), 485–505 (2006)
7. Ghallab, M., Nau, D., Traverso, P.: Automated Planning: Theory and Practice. Elsevier (2004)
8. Henneberger, M., Heinrich, B., Lautenbacher, F., Bauer, B.: Semantic-based planning of process models. In: Multikonferenz Wirtschaftsinformatik (MKWI). GITO-Verlag (2008)
9. Hull, R., Motahari Nezhad, H.R.: Rethinking BPM in a cognitive world: transforming how we learn and perform business processes. In: La Rosa, M., Loos, P., Pastor, O. (eds.) BPM 2016. LNCS, vol. 9850, pp. 3–19. Springer, Cham (2016). https://doi.org/10.1007/978-3-319-45348-4_1
10. Kochenderfer, M.J.: Decision Making Under Uncertainty: Theory and Application. MIT press, Cambridge (2015)
11. Kwiatkowska, M., Norman, G., Parker, D.: PRISM 4.0: verification of probabilistic real-time systems. In: Gopalakrishnan, G., Qadeer, S. (eds.) CAV 2011. LNCS, vol. 6806, pp. 585–591. Springer, Heidelberg (2011). https://doi.org/10.1007/978-3-642-22110-1_47
12. Laurent, Y., Bendraou, R., Baarir, S., Gervais, M.P.: Planning for declarative processes. In: Proceedings of the 29th Annual ACM Symposium on Applied Computing, pp. 1126–1133. ACM (2014)
13. Marjanovic, O.: Towards is supported coordination in emergent business processes. Bus. Process Manag. J. **11**(5), 476–487 (2005)
14. Marrella, A.: Automated planning for business process management. J. Data Seman. **8**(2), 79–98 (2019)
15. Marrella, A., Lespérance, Y.: A planning approach to the automated synthesis of template-based process models. SOCA **11**(4), 367–392 (2017)
16. Marrella, A., Mecella, M., Sardina, S.: SmartPM: an adaptive process management system through situation calculus, IndiGolog, and classical planning. In: Proceedings of the Fourteenth International Conference on Principles of Knowledge Representation and Reasoning (KR 2014), pp. 518–527 (2014)

17. Mattila, R., Siika, A., Roy, J., Wahlberg, B.: A Markov decision process model to guide treatment of abdominal aortic aneurysms. In: 2016 IEEE Conference on Control Applications (CCA), pp. 436–441. IEEE (2016)
18. Reichert, M., Weber, B.: Enabling Flexibility in Process-Aware Information Systems: Challenges, Methods Technologies. Springer, Heidelberg (2012)
19. Venero, S.K.: DW-SAAArch: a reference architecture for dynamic self-adaptation in workflows. Master's Thesis, UNICAMP, Campinas, Brazil (2015)
20. Venero, S.K., Dos Reis, J.C., Montecchi, L., Rubira, C.M.F.: Towards a metamodel for supporting decisions in knowledge-intensive processes. In: Proceedings of the 34th ACM/SIGAPP Symposium on Applied Computing, pp. 75–84. ACM (2019)

Scheduling Processes Without Sudden Termination

Johann Eder$^{(\boxtimes)}$ ⓘ, Marco Franceschetti ⓘ, and Josef Lubas ⓘ

Department of Informatics-Systems, Universität Klagenfurt, Klagenfurt, Austria
{johann.eder,marco.franceschetti,josef.lubas}@aau.at

Abstract. Dynamic controllability is the most general criterion to guarantee that a process can be executed without time failures. However, it admits schedules with an undesirable property: starting an activity without knowing its deadline. We analyze the specific constellations of temporal constraints causing such a sudden termination. Consequently, we introduce the somewhat stricter notion of semi-dynamic controllability, and present necessary and sufficient conditions to guarantee that a process can be executed without time failures and without sudden termination. A sound and complete algorithm for checking whether a process is semi-dynamically controllable complements the approach.

Keywords: Process scheduling · Contingent durations · Sudden termination · Controllability

1 Introduction

Modeling and verification of the temporal aspects of a business process are crucial for process management. Modeling temporal aspects includes defining deadlines, durations, and other temporal constraints [5]. Verification of the temporal qualities aims at determining, whether a given process model meets certain quality criteria, in particular, whether time failures can be avoided by defining adequate schedules for the dispatching of activities.

In recent years, there has been increasing awareness on the distinction between activities whose duration is under the control of an agent, and activities whose duration cannot be controlled, but merely observed at run time [22]. These uncontrollable durations are called *contingent*. A good example for activities with contingent durations is bank money transfers within the EU, which are guaranteed to take between 1 and 4 working days, but the client cannot control the actual duration. In a similar way, a service contract might covenant a visit by a technician within 24 hours but it is not controllable by the client when the technician will actually appear.

The existence of contingent activities in processes led to the formulation of *dynamic controllability* [7,19,22] as preferred criterion for temporal correctness of processes. Dynamic controllability requires the existence of a dynamic schedule

© Springer Nature Switzerland AG 2020
S. Nurcan et al. (Eds.): BPMDS 2020/EMMSAD 2020, LNBIP 387, pp. 117–132, 2020.
https://doi.org/10.1007/978-3-030-49418-6_8

(execution strategy), which assigns timestamps for starting and finishing activities in a reactive manner in response to the observation of the actual durations of contingent activities at run time. Dynamic controllability is the most relaxed notion for guaranteeing that a process controller is able to steer the execution satisfying all temporal constraints. Consequently, several techniques have been developed to check the dynamic controllability of a process [3,19].

Nevertheless, dynamic controllability might admit processes where each admissible dynamic schedule requires some activities to start, without knowing yet, when they need to complete. This leads to the subsequent *sudden termination* scheduling of their end-event. In Sect. 2 we give a precise demonstration and an example of this phenomenon. While for some activities this poses no problem (e.g. for waiting tasks), for other non-contingent activities a sudden termination is highly undesirable, unacceptable, or even impossible, in particular, for activities involving human actors or invoking uninterruptible external services [10,12]. We call such activities *semi-contingent*, i.e. their duration between minimum and maximum duration can be chosen by the process controller but only until the activity starts. In Sect. 2 we give some examples for semi-contingent activities and the sudden termination problem.

The research question we address here is: *how to determine, whether a given process can be scheduled without the risk of a sudden termination of a task?*

Here we show that sudden termination can be identified by the presence of specific constraint patterns, and propose a technique to check, whether it is possible to (dynamically) schedule a process with the guarantee that no sudden termination will be forced at run time.

The contributions of this paper are the following:

- The discovery and characterization of the problem of sudden termination, which might arise in dynamically controllable processes
- The introduction of the notion of semi-contingent activities to model relevant temporal characteristics of activities
- The identification and characterization of patterns of temporal constraints and conditions, which are sufficient and necessary for the problem of sudden termination
- The definition of semi-dynamic controllability, which specializes the traditional notion of dynamic controllability to address semi-contingent activities and sudden termination
- A procedure to check semi-dynamic controllability

These results contribute to the development of a comprehensive framework to support the design, modeling, and analysis of business processes at design time and to monitor the time-aware execution of business processes at run-time.

The reminder of this paper is structured as follows: in Sect. 2 we illustrate the problem with the help of examples. In Sect. 3 we introduce a lean process model which allows the formulation of the problem, show how a specific pattern can induce the problem, and show how to solve it. In Sect. 4 we provide an implementation of a checking procedure. In Sect. 5 we discuss related works, and in Sect. 6 we draw conclusions.

2 Semi-contingent Activities and the Sudden Termination Problem

Dynamic controllability of processes distinguishes two kinds of activities: contingent and non-contingent activities. A process controller striving to meet all temporal constraints can control the duration of non-contingent activities but can only observe and not influence the duration of contingent activities. Dynamic controllability implicitly assumes that a non-contingent activity can be terminated spontaneously at any time (between minimum and maximum duration) without any earlier notice. We nickname this phenomenon as *sudden termination*. Such a behavior may be undesirable, unacceptable, or even impossible. Frequently, one can control the duration of an activity only until this activity starts. We call such activities *semi-contingent*. For an example, we could deliver a talk on temporal constraints for any time between 10 min and 2 hours. But we need to know beforehand for how long we can talk otherwise we would have to stop maybe right after the introduction. Other examples include:

- Ship products with express delivery or regular delivery
- Prepare a meal: from quick lunch to 4 course gourmet dinner
- Apply an expensive quick test or a budget slow test
- Assign more or less people to finish a task earlier or later
- etc. etc.

We explain the sudden termination problem with a small example. Figure 1 shows a simplified procurement process. The controller may choose the duration of semi-contingent task A for arranging shipment of goods between 5 and 7 days. A is bound to a contingent task R of receiving payment which lasts between 3 and 5 days. A lower-bound constraint demands that the end of A is at least 3 days after the end of R to allow a customer to cancel the order. The upper-bound constraint states that A has to finish within 4 days after R to guarantee timely delivery. Now, lets assume R should start at time point 10 and hence ends anytime between 13 and 15. Is there a choice for the start time and duration of A satisfying the constraints? After some trials you see: no! A might e.g. start at 12 and end between 17 and 19, but 19 is too late, if R ends at 13, and 17 is too early, if R ends at 15. And at 12 the end of R is unknown.

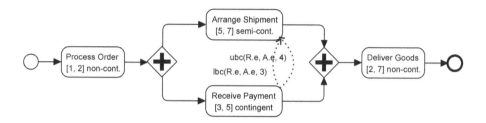

Fig. 1. Example process with a sudden termination problem

It is easy to see that it is not possible to determine a duration for A such that for all possible durations of R the constraints are satisfied. The end of the ongoing activity A can only be scheduled, when the end of R has been observed.

How should we treat semi-contingent activities for checking dynamic controllability? If we treat them as non-contingent activities, we risk sudden termination. If we treat them as contingent activities, we are unnecessarily strict and reject processes, which could be scheduled without sudden termination. Therefore, we introduce the notions of *semi-contingent activities* and *semi-dynamic controllability* to adequately deal with such activities.

3   Process Model and Semi-dynamic Controllability

3.1   Process Model with Temporal Constraints

For most general applicability, here we introduce a minimal process model, which is sufficient to capture the patterns for which sudden termination may occur.

We consider the most common control flow patterns: sequence, inclusive and disjunctive splits, and the corresponding joins. To avoid design flaws, and according to the current state-of-the-art in this field, we assume that processes are acyclic and block-structured [6].

We consider activity durations, process deadline, and upper- and lower-bound constraints between events (start and end of activities). We measure time in *chronons*, representing, e.g., hours, days, ..., which have domain the set of natural numbers and are on an increasing time axis starting at *zero*. A duration is defined as the distance between two time points on the time axis.

Finally, we distinguish between non-contingent, semi-contingent, and contingent activities. The duration of contingent activities, by their nature, cannot be controlled, thus it cannot be known, when they will actually terminate. The process controller may however control the duration of non-contingent activities at any time. This means in particular, that they are allowed to start with no knowledge about the time when they have to end, thus conceding to be suddenly terminated. Semi-contingent activities, in contrast, require to know, at their start time, when they must terminate: this means the process controller can set their duration until the activity starts.

Definition 1 (Process Model). *A process P is a tuple (N, E, C, Ω), where:*

- *N is a set of nodes n with $n.type \in \{start, activity, xor - split, xor - join, par - split, par - join, end\}$. Each $n \in N$ is associated with $n.s$ and $n.e$, the start and end event of n. From N we derive $N^e = \bigcup \{n.s, n.e | n \in N\}$.*
- *E is a set of edges $e = (n1, n2)$ defining precedence constraints.*
- *C is a set of temporal constraints:*
  - *duration constraints $d(n, n_{min}, n_{max}, dur) \, \forall n \in N$, where $n_{min}, n_{max} \in \mathbb{N}$, $dur \in \{c, sc, nc\}$, stating that n takes some time in $[n_{min}, n_{max}]$. n can be contingent ($dur = c$), semi-contingent ($dur = sc$), non-contingent ($dur = nc$);*

- upper-bound constraints $ubc(a, b, \delta)$, where $a, b \in N^e$, $\delta \in \mathbb{N}$, requiring that $b \leq a + \delta$;
- lower-bound constraints $lbc(a, b, \delta)$, where $a, b \in N^e$, $\delta \in \mathbb{N}$, requiring that $b \geq a + \delta$.
  - $\Omega \in \mathbb{N}$ is the process deadline.

We now define the temporal semantics of the process model.

3.2   Temporal Semantics

We define the temporal semantics of temporally constrained process definitions by defining which scenarios are valid. A scenario is a run of the process (a process instance) with timestamps, when each event (starting and ending of process steps) occurred. A scenario is *valid*, if it satisfies all temporal constraints.

Definition 2 (Valid Scenario). *Let $P(N, E, C, \Omega)$ be a process model. Let σ be a scenario for P, assigning to each time point t a timestamp $\bar{t}$. σ is a valid scenario for P iff:*

1. $\forall (n1, n2) \in E$, $\overline{n1.e} \leq \overline{n2.s}$;
2. $\forall d(n, n_{min}, n_{max}, [c|sc|nc]) \in C$, $\overline{n.s} + n_{min} \leq \overline{n.e} \leq \overline{n.s} + n_{max}$;
3. $\forall ubc(a, b, \delta) \in C$, $\bar{b} \leq \bar{a} + \delta$;
4. $\forall lbc(a, b, \delta) \in C$, $\bar{a} + \delta \leq \bar{b}$;
5. $\overline{end.e} \leq \overline{start.s} + \Omega$.

A schedule for a process states when each activity should be started and terminated. If a schedule exists, we call the process controllable. Controllability is often considered too strict, as it would not admit situations where, e.g. the time-point for the start of an activity depends on the observed duration of preceding contingent activities.

Dynamic controllability requires the existence of a dynamic schedule (or dynamic execution strategy), where the decision about starting and ending activities can be made based on the timestamp of all earlier events.

There are several techniques for checking the dynamic controllability of processes. We use here the technique of mapping a process model to a Simple Temporal Network with Uncertainty (STNU) and apply constraint propagation techniques which are proven to be sound and complete for checking dynamic controllability [3]. We present this technique in Sect. 4.

In Sect. 2 we gave an example of a process which is dynamically controllable, but suffers from the problem of sudden termination of a semi-contingent activity.

In the next section we explore a pattern of constraints, which may lead to the sudden termination of an activity. We use this pattern to formulate a new notion of controllability, which is somewhat stricter than dynamic controllability, and introduce a technique to verify a process model for such a notion.

3.3 Constellations for a Sudden Termination Problem

For the following considerations we assume, that a process is dynamically controllable, i.e. there is a dynamic schedule, such that no constraint is violated. We use the term *condition* or *constraint* in a process model P in the sense that such a constraint is either explicitly stated in P or that it can be derived from the constraints in P (see Sect. 4 for techniques to derive implicit constraints). We use Φ as the set of all implicit and explicit constraints valid in P.

We now characterize precisely what constitutes a sudden termination problem for a semi-contingent activity, and observe which conditions have to be satisfied, such that a sudden termination problem might occur. We distinguish between a sudden termination constellation (STC) and a sudden termination pattern (STP). In a STP, constraints can only be satisfied with sudden termination, while in the more general STC, it might depend on the controller, whether a sudden termination actually occurs. In a STP, sudden termination needs to happen, while in a STC which is not a STP sudden termination is avoidable.

A STC requires (at least) 2 constraints. So let us consider two activities, one contingent (C) and one semi-contingent (S). A sudden termination means that the admissible times for ending S depend on the observation of the end of C and this is not known, when S starts. This requires that there is a constraint between the end events of C and S.

A sudden termination only occurs, if C and S have to be executed concurrently, i.e. it is not possible that they are executed sequentially. This requires an additional constraint. When $S.e$ can always be executed before $C.e$, it cannot depend on the observed duration of C. In a similar way, if S can always start after C has ended, the duration of C is already known at the start of S.

Definition 3 (Sudden Termination Constellation and Pattern). *Let P be a dynamically controllable process. Let S and C be activities in P, with the duration constraints $d(S, S.d_{min}, S.d_{max}, sc)$ and $d(C, C.d_{min}, C.d_{max}, c)$. Let Φ be the set of constraints in P.*

*S and C are in a **sudden termination constellation (STC)** iff*
$$\forall C.s \exists S.s \ \forall S.d_{min} \leq S.d \leq S.d_{max} \ \exists C.d_{min} \leq C.d \leq C.d_{max} : \ \neg \Phi$$
*S and C are in a **sudden termination pattern (STP)** iff*
$$\forall S.s, C.s \ \forall S.d_{min} \leq S.d \leq S.d_{max} \ \exists C.d_{min} \leq C.d \leq C.d_{max} : \ \neg \Phi$$
We use the notation $STC_{S,C}$ to indicate that S and C are in a sudden termination constellation, and $STP_{S,C}$ for a sudden termination pattern.

If there is a STP in a process, sudden termination cannot be avoided, without changing the process. If there is a STC but not an STP, the execution of a process can be (dynamically) scheduled in a way to both observe all constraints and avoid sudden termination. We are now interested, whether it is possible for a process controller to schedule without sudden termination, i.e. whether it is possible to avoid that a STC becomes a STP.

3.4 Semi-dynamic Controllability

The constellation of constraints which renders two activities in a sudden termination pattern is compatible with the dynamic controllability of a process, i.e. there exist processes which are dc but have a pair of activities in a STP. So dynamic controllability is not strict enough, in the sense that it allows semi-contingent activities to start without knowing when to end. We define a specialization of dynamic controllability which recognizes the need to know the required end time for a semi-contingent activity at its start time.

Definition 4 (Semi-dynamic Controllability). *Let P be a process. P is semi-dynamically controllable (sdc) iff P is dc, and $\nexists\ S,C \in P.N$: $STP_{S,C}$.*

Semi-dynamic controllability is stricter than dynamic controllability, but not as strict as controllability. With semi-dynamic controllability we require a process to be dynamically controllable, and no semi-contingent activity is involved in a sudden termination pattern.

3.5 Basic Sudden Termination Pattern

First we consider and discuss the most fundamental constellation for a sudden termination problem: the end events of a contingent activity C and and a semi-contingent activity S are connected with one upper- and one lower-bound constraint: $ubc(C.e, S.e, w)$, and $lbc(C.e, S.e, v)$.

In this constellation, there is only one uncertainty, which cannot be controlled: the actual duration of C. The constraint $ubc(C.e, S.e, w)$ requires that $S.e \leq C.e + w$. For actual durations $S.d$, resp. $C.d$, this requires that $S.s + S.d \leq C.s + C.d + w$. The constraint $lbc(C.e, S.e, v)$ requires that $C.e + v \leq S.e$.

A *Sudden Termination Pattern 1 (STP-1)* is defined as follows: A contingent activity C and a semi-contingent activity S, with constraints $ubc(C.e, S.e, w)$ and $lbc(C.e, S.e, v)$ as above are in a STP-1, iff there is no way to schedule the start of S and the start of C, such that the value for the end of S can be fixed, when S starts.

Definition 5 (Sudden Termination Pattern: STP-1). *Let P be a dynamically controllable process. Let S and C be activities in P, with the duration constraints $d(S, S.d_{min}, S.d_{max}, sc)$ and $d(C, C.d_{min}, C.d_{max}, c)$.*
Let $ubc(C.e, S.e, w)$ and $lbc(C.e, S.e, v)$ be constraints in P.
  S and C are in STP-1, iff
$\forall S.s, C.s\ \forall S.d_{min} \leq S.d \leq S.d_{max}\ \exists C.d_{min} \leq C.d \leq C.d_{max}$:
$S.s + S.d > C.s + C.d + w$, or $S.s + S.d < C.s + C.d + v$.

3.6 Characterization of STP

In the following, we derive conditions to check, whether a STP might occur for a given pair of activities S and C.

General preconditions for the existence of a sudden termination problem is that the following constraints do not hold in P: $S.s > C.e, C.s > S.e$.

Theorem 1. *Let P be a dynamically controllable process. Let S be a semi-contingent activity, and C be a contingent activity in P, with duration constraints $d(S, S.d_{min}, S.d_{max}, sc)$ and $d(C, C.d_{min}, C.d_{max}, c)$. Let $ubc(C.e, S.e, w)$ and $lbc(C.e, S.e, v)$ be constraints in P.*

A sudden termination of S cannot occur, iff
$C.d_{max} + v \leq S.e - C.s \leq C.d_{min} + w$ holds in P.

Proof. We show that $C.d_{max} + v < S.e - C.s \leq C.d_{min} + w$ is a necessary and sufficient condition that the activities S and C are not in a STP.

Necessary condition: we show that if the condition does not hold, a sudden termination might occur. If the condition does not hold then $\nexists S.s, S.d, C.s$ with $C.d_{max} + v < S.e - C.s \leq C.d_{min} + w$. This is only possible, if $C.d_{max} + v > C.d_{min} + w$.

We now assume that C and S are in a STP. This means that $\forall C.s, S.s$ there is no $S.d$ such that $\forall C.d$ the constraints hold: $S.s + S.d \leq C.s + C.d + w$ and $S.s + S.d \geq C.s + C.d + v$. Hence $\nexists S.d$ such that $\forall C.d: C.d + v \leq S.s + S.d - C.s \leq C.d + w$. Which requires in particular, that $\nexists S.d$ to satisfy $C.d_{max} + v \leq S.e - C.s \leq C.d_{min} + w$.

Sufficient condition: We show that if the inequality holds, sudden termination does not occur. We show that $\exists C.s, S.s, S.d$ such that $\forall C.d_{min} \leq C.d \leq C.d_{max}$ the constraints are satisfied, i.e. $C.s + C.d + v \leq S.s + S.d \leq C.s + C.d + w$, which holds since $\forall C.d_{min} \leq C.d \leq C.d_{max}: C.d + v \leq C.d_{max} + v \leq S.s + S.d - C.s \leq C.d_{min} + w \leq C.d + w$.   □

This theorem can now be used to establish conditions that a process model has to fulfill, such that it is dynamically controllable and a STP cannot occur. In particular, we can show that a STP cannot occur, when the process model includes a particular lower-bound constraint resp. upper-bound constraint between the start of S and the start of C.

Theorem 2. *Let P be a process. Let S be a semi-contingent activity, and C be a contingent activity in P with duration constraints $d(S, S.d_{min}, S.d_{max}, sc)$ and $d(C, C.d_{min}, C.d_{max}, c)$. Let $ubc(C.e, S.e, w)$ be a constraint in P.*

A sudden termination of S cannot occur, iff constraints $lbc(C.s, S.e, C.d_{max} + v)$ and $ubc(C.s, S.e, C.d_{min} + w)$ hold in P.

Proof. The constraints express exactly the condition in Theorem 1. Hence in a process model P including these constraints S and C cannot be in a STP.   □

This theorem helps us to develop a procedure to check whether a process is semi-dynamically controllable, resp. transforming a process with a STC such that it avoids a STP.

3.7   Checking Semi-dynamic Controllability

We are now ready to apply this result for checking, whether a sudden termination problem can be avoided in the execution of a process. For each ST-constellation in a process P (a semi-contingent activity S, and a contingent activity C with duration constraints $d(S, S.d_{min}, S.d_{max}, sc)$ and $d(C, C.d_{min}, C.d_{max}, c)$, and the constraints $ubc(C.e, S.e, w)$ and $lbc(C.e, S.e, v)$) we include 2 additional constraints: $lbc(C.s, S.e, C.d_{max} + v)$ and $ubc(C.s, S.e, C.d_{min} + w)$. Then we check the resulting process for dynamic controllability. If it is dynamically controllable, then (with Theorem 2) it is also semi-dynamically controllable.

3.8   Further STP Constellations

After a detailed characterization of the basic constellation, we enumerate in Table 1 all possible constellations between a contingent and a semi-contingent activity which could cause a sudden termination problem.

The first column shows the constraints specifying the constellation, the second column states the necessary and sufficient condition which has to be fulfilled such that a sudden termination does not occur, and the third column the constraints to add for checking the process for semi-dynamic controllability. The proofs for these conditions and constraints follow the structure of the proofs for the basic constellation but for space reasons they cannot be repeated here.

Table 1. Sudden termination constellations, with conditions to avoid sudden termination, and constraints to add to check for semi-dynamic controllability.

Constraints	Condition to avoid sudden termination	Constraints to add
$ubc(C.e, S.e, w)$ $lbc(C.e, S.e, v)$	$C.d_{max} + v \leq S.e - C.s \leq C.d_{min} + w$	$lbc(C.s, S.e, C.d_{max} + v)$ $ubc(C.s, S.e, C.d_{min} + w)$
$ubc(C.e, S.e, w)$ $lbc(C.s, S.e, v)$	$v < S.e - C.s \leq C.d_{min} + w$	$lbc(C.s, S.e, v)$ $ubc(C.s, S.e, C.d_{min} + w)$
$ubc(C.s, S.e, w)$ $lbc(C.e, S.e, v)$	$C.d_{max} + v < S.e - C.s \leq w$	$lbc(C.s, S.e, C.d_{max} + v)$
$ubc(C.e, S.e, w)$ $lbc(C.s, S.s, v)$	$S.d_{min} + v < S.e - C.s \leq C.d_{min} + w$	$lbc(C.s, S.s, S.d_{min} + v)$ $ubc(C.s, S.e, C.d_{min} + w)$
$ubc(C.e, S.e, w)$ $ubc(S.s, C.e, v)$	$C.d_{max} + S.d_{min} - v < S.e - C.s \leq C.d_{min} + w$	$lbc(C.s, S.e, C.d_{max} + S.d_{min} - v)$ $ubc(C.s, S.e, C.d_{min} + w)$
$ubc(C.e, S.e, w)$ $ubc(S.s, C.s, v)$	$S.d_{min} - v < S.e - C.s \leq C.d_{min} + w$	$lbc(C.s, S.e, S.d_{min} - v)$ $ubc(C.s, S.e, C.d_{min} + w)$

4   Checking Semi-dynamic Controllability with STNUs

In this section we show how we can kill two birds with one stone, and meet the two requirements of (1) deriving all implicit constraints, and (2) checking whether a process is semi-dynamically controllable, by mapping process models into temporal networks.

(1) The temporal constraints causing a STC or STP need not necessarily to be explicitly stated in the process model, but may be implicitly induced by the explicit temporal constraints in the process model. Therefore, we need to compute the set of all (implicit) constraints for identifying all possible STCs.

(2) Checking whether a process model is semi-dynamically controllable, requires applying some dynamic controllability checking procedure, as per Theorem 2 and Sect. 3.7.

4.1   Mapping to STNUs

In previous works [9] we showed how to check whether a process model, such as the process in Fig. 1, is dynamically controllable by mapping it into a equivalent STNU (Simple Temporal Network with Uncertainty) [19].

In a nutshell, a STNU is a directed graph, in which nodes represent time points and edges represent constraints between time points. A special time point *zero* marks the reference in time, after which all other time points occur. Edges can be non-contingent or contingent. Non-contingent edges represent constraints which can be enforced by the execution environment by assigning appropriate values to the time points. Contingent edges (also called links) represent constraints which are guaranteed to hold, but the corresponding time point assignments cannot be controlled, only observed.

We use the notation (A, B, δ) for non-contingent edges from A to B with weight δ, which require that $B \leq A + \delta$; and (A^C, l, u, C) for contingent links between A^C and C, which state that C occurs some time between l and u after A^C. For a detailed formalization on STNUs, we refer to [19].

Figure 2 shows the STNU derived by mapping the process model of Fig. 1. Note that in Fig. 2 we adopted the usual STNU notation with contingent edges dashed, inverted w.r.t. non-contingent edges, and labeled with the contingent time point name. For a more compact presentation, in the figure we did not include nodes resulting from the mapping of the par-split and par-join.

4.2   Checking Dynamic Controllability

Several techniques have been developed to check the dynamic controllability of STNUs. Most of these techniques, such as [3], build on deriving implicit constraints from the existing ones. In particular, they work by propagating the existing constraints based on certain sets of propagation rules.

Constraint propagation can be applied until: (1) no new implicit edges can be derived, or (2) a negative cycle (in the usual sense of graph theory) is found. If constraint propagation stops in case (1), then the STNU, hence its originating process, is dynamically controllable. In case (2), instead, a constellation of contradicting constraints exists, and the STNU is not dynamically controllable. As an example, one can verify, by applying constraint propagation, that the STNU in Fig. 2 is dynamically controllable, since no negative cycle can be derived.

The effect of applying a constraint propagation procedure is twofold. First, the procedure derives all implicit constraints which hold if the explict constraints hold. Second, it determines whether a STNU is dynamically controllable. We use these results, in combination with the results of Sect. 3, to design a procedure for checking, whether a given process model is semi-dynamically controllable.

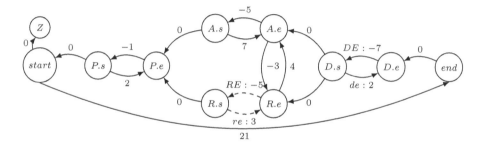

Fig. 2. STNU derived from the example process shown in Fig. 1.

4.3   Checking Semi-dynamic Controllability

Algorithm 1 shows the procedure we propose for checking the semi-dynamic controllability. A process model P is mapped into a STNU T. Additionally, we keep a data structure S_T containing STNU nodes representing semi-contingent activities, which is needed for identifying sudden termination patterns.

First, T is checked for dynamic controllability by applying a constraint propagation procedure $check\_dc(T)$, which as a side effect computes the closure of the set of constraints. If the procedure returns True, the process is dc. Then $find\_stp(T, S_T)$ searches and returns all STPs. Then there is a loop (repeated as long as the network is dc and there are unresolved STPs) with three steps: (i) For each STP p found, edges corresponding to the constraints to resolve p to avoid a sudden termination problem are added to T. (ii) check for dynamic controllability and derive additional implicit constraints. (iii) search for unresolved STPs. If at the end of the iteration T remains dc, then it is also sdc and True is returned. One can verify (see the negative cycle introduced in Fig. 3 between $R.s$ and $A.e$) that the process of the running example is not sdc.

The correctness of the procedure trivially follows from the correctness of the existing constraint propagation procedures, and from the Theorems of Sect. 3.

5   Implementation and Evaluation

We implemented Algorithm 1, and performed experiments to evaluate its scalability.

We ran our experiments on a Windows 10 machine with an i7 CPU and 16GB of RAM. For the experiments we randomly generated a set 30 processes of different sizes in terms of number of process steps. We structured the test set into 5 subsets of processes: one for processes of size 10, one for 20, one for 30, one for 40, and one for 50. Each subset contained 10 processes. The smallest process contained 10 activities and 2 constraints, resulting in a STNU with 20 nodes. The largest process contained 50 activities and 10 constraints, resulting in a STNU with 100 nodes. We regard the range of process sizes used for the experiments as representative of most of the cases found in practical applications.

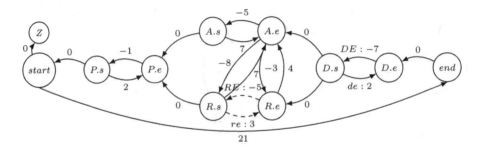

Fig. 3. STNU resulting from the application of Algorithm 1 to the process of Fig. 1.

We report the average measured execution times for the various process sizes in Fig. 4. On average, executing Algorithm 1 for a process of size 10 required 0.13s; for size 20, 0.83s; for size 30, 6.29s; for size 40, 18.94s; for size 50, 41.00s.

Our experiments showed that, despite the addition of new constraints to solve the STP, and the repeated execution of the dynamic controllability checking procedure, the required computation times are still acceptable for a design time check. Thus, we regard the proposed approach applicable for most practical applications which require design time checking for semi-dynamic controllability.

Algorithm 1. Check semi-dynamic controllability

1: **Input:** Process P
2: $T := map\_to\_STNU(P)$
3: $S_T := get\_semicontingent\_nodes(P, T)$
4: **if** $(\neg check\_dc(T))$ **then**
5:     **return** $False$
6: **else**
7:     $STP := find\_stp(T, S_T)$
8:     **while** $(STP \neq \emptyset)$ **do**
9:         $p := extract\_first(STP)$
10:         $T := T \cup compute\_resolving\_constraints(p)$
11:         **if** $(\neg check\_dc(T))$ **then**
12:             **return** $False$
13:         **else**
14:             $STP := STP \cup find\_stp(T, S_T)$
15:         **end if**
16:     **end while**
17: **end if**
18: **return** $True$

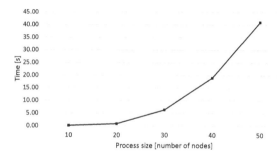

Fig. 4. Results of the evaluation.

6   Related Work

To the best of our knowledge, semi-contingent activities and hence semi-dynamic controllability have never been studied before. Related work, therefore, comprises of (a) formulation of temporal constraints in process models and (b) checking consistency and controllability of temporally constrained process models and (c) scheduling and monitoring of process execution.

General overviews of time management for business processes are provided in [5,8,11]. [16] presents a formalization of time patterns and their semantics, based on the analysis of recurring temporal constraints in process models, however, without considering semi-contingent activities.

Verification of deadlines and temporal constraints was subject of several previous works, such as [1,4,13,18]. Similarly to our proposed approach based on STNUs, these approaches are based on network analysis, scheduling, and constraint networks. None of these works, however, addressed the problem of induced sudden termination of tasks.

More recent works combine the temporal aspects of a process definition with other constraining dimensions such as resource availability [23,24]. While with our work we currently focus only on the temporal dimension, these works offer interesting possibilities to further investigate the problem of sudden termination with a holistic view on process models.

While we address the design time verification of process qualities here, considerable research (e.g., [14,17,20]) explored the pro-active monitoring of the compliance of process instances to their process model. However, to the best of our knowledge, all approaches to monitoring and compliance checking address the notion of satisfiability rather than dynamic controllability and do not consider the problem of sudden termination.

In contrast to all these approaches, process mining techniques [21] rely on the existence of a large number of cases (process logs) before they are able to provide scheduling and monitoring information. Thus they are not adequate for new or frequently changing processes, or processes with small number of instances [2].

For the implementation of our approach we map process definitions to Simple Temporal Networks with Uncertainty (STNUs) [19]. Considerable research efforts have been devoted in the last decades both to developing different notions of controllability for temporal constraint networks, and to developing more expressive network models [15,19,22,25]. With this work, we contribute to this field of research introducing a specialization of dynamic controllability to avoid a class of unwanted behaviors.

7   Conclusions

The presence of activities with uncontrollable duration requires a dynamic schedule to ensure that all temporal constraints are met. Dynamic scheduling, however, may entail not knowing, at activity start time, when an activity has to terminate. This leads to the sudden termination of an activity. Such a behavior is undesirable for a large number of activities.

With this paper we proposed semi-dynamic controllability as a new notion for temporal correctness. It requires a process to be dynamically controllable, and that the end time of activities, which cannot be interrupted, is known at their start time. We have shown how to verify whether a process is semi-dynamically controllable, based on patterns of temporal constraints. Our implementation of a verification procedure demonstrated that semi-dynamic controllability can be efficiently checked at design time. We regard semi-dynamic controllability as a desirable quality for process models, which process designers may easily check.

The results of the research reported here contribute to the development of a comprehensive set of tools supporting the design of business processes by checking relevant properties of process models at design time. The notions and techniques also provide the basis for monitoring of temporal properties of the process execution at run-time, enabling pro-active avoidance of time failures.

References

1. Bettini, C., Wang, X., Jajodia, S.: Temporal reasoning in workflow systems. Distrib. Parallel Databases 11(3), 269–306 (2002)
2. Breu, R., et al.: Towards living inter-organizational processes. In: 15th IEEE Conference on Business Informatics, pp. 363–366. IEEE (2013)
3. Cairo, M., Rizzi, R.: Dynamic controllability made simple. In: 24th International Symposium on Temporal Representation and Reasoning (TIME 2017), vol. 90 of LIPIcs, pp. 8:1–8:16 (2017)
4. Cardoso, J., Sheth, A., Miller, J., Arnold, J., Kochut, K.: Quality of service for workflows and web service processes. J. Web Semant. 1(3), 281–308 (2004)
5. Cheikhrouhou, S., Kallel, S., Guermouche, N., Jmaiel, M.: The temporal perspective in business process modeling: a survey and research challenges. SOCA 9(1), 75–85 (2014). https://doi.org/10.1007/s11761-014-0170-x
6. Combi, C., Gambini, M.: Flaws in the flow: the weakness of unstructured business process modeling languages dealing with data. In: Meersman, R., Dillon, T., Herrero, P. (eds.) OTM 2009. LNCS, vol. 5870, pp. 42–59. Springer, Heidelberg (2009). https://doi.org/10.1007/978-3-642-05148-7_6

7. Combi, C., Posenato, R.: Controllability in temporal conceptual workflow schemata. In: Dayal, U., Eder, J., Koehler, J., Reijers, H.A. (eds.) BPM 2009. LNCS, vol. 5701, pp. 64–79. Springer, Heidelberg (2009). https://doi.org/10.1007/978-3-642-03848-8_6

8. Combi, C., Pozzi, G.: Temporal conceptual modelling of workflows. In: Song, I.-Y., Liddle, S.W., Ling, T.-W., Scheuermann, P. (eds.) ER 2003. LNCS, vol. 2813, pp. 59–76. Springer, Heidelberg (2003). https://doi.org/10.1007/978-3-540-39648-2_8

9. Eder, J., Franceschetti, M., Köpke, J.: Controllability of business processes with temporal variables. In: Proceedings of the 34th ACM/SIGAPP Symposium on Applied Computing, pp. 40–47. ACM (2019)

10. Eder, J., Liebhart, W.: Workflow transactions. In: Workflow Handbook 1997, pp. 195–202. Wiley (1997)

11. Eder, J., Panagos, E., Rabinovich, M.: Workflow time management revisited. Seminal Contributions to Information Systems Engineering, pp. 207–213. Springer, Heidelberg (2013). https://doi.org/10.1007/978-3-642-36926-1_16

12. Franceschetti, M., Eder, J.: Dynamic service binding for time-aware service compositions. In: 2019 IEEE 23rd International Enterprise Distributed Object Computing Workshop (EDOCW), pp. 146–151. IEEE (2019)

13. Guermouche, N., Godart, C.: Timed model checking based approach for web services analysis. In: ICWS 2009. IEEE International Conference on Web Services, pp. 213–221. IEEE (2009)

14. Hashmi, M., Governatori, G., Lam, H.-P., Wynn, M.T.: Are we done with business process compliance: state of the art and challenges ahead. Knowl. Inf. Syst. **57**, 1–55 (2018). https://doi.org/10.1007/s10115-017-1142-1

15. Lanz, A., Posenato, R., Combi, C., Reichert, M.: Controlling time-awareness in modularized processes. In: Schmidt, R., Guédria, W., Bider, I., Guerreiro, S. (eds.) BPMDS/EMMSAD -2016. LNBIP, vol. 248, pp. 157–172. Springer, Cham (2016). https://doi.org/10.1007/978-3-319-39429-9_11

16. Lanz, A., Reichert, M., Weber, B.: Process time patterns: a formal foundation. Inf. Syst. **57**, 38–68 (2016)

17. Ly, L.T., Maggi, F.M., Montali, M., Rinderle-Ma, S., van der Aalst, W.M.: Compliance monitoring in business processes: functionalities, application, and toolsupport. Inf. Syst. **54**, 209–234 (2015)

18. Marjanovic, O., Orlowska, M.E.: On modeling and verification of temporal constraints in production workflows. Knowl. Inf. Syst. **1**(2), 157–192 (1999). https://doi.org/10.1007/BF03325097

19. Morris, P.H., Muscettola, N.: Temporal dynamic controllability revisited. In: Proceedings of AAAI, pp. 1193–1198 (2005)

20. Pichler, H., Wenger, M., Eder, J.: Composing time-aware web service orchestrations. In: van Eck, P., Gordijn, J., Wieringa, R. (eds.) CAiSE 2009. LNCS, vol. 5565, pp. 349–363. Springer, Heidelberg (2009). https://doi.org/10.1007/978-3-642-02144-2_29

21. van der Aalst, W.M., Schonenberg, M., Song, M.: Time prediction based on process mining. Inf. Syst. **36**(2), 450–475 (2011)

22. Vidal, T.: Handling contingency in temporal constraint networks: from consistency to controllabilities. J. Exp. Theor. Artif. Intell. **11**(1), 23–45 (1999)

23. Watahiki, K., Ishikawa, F., Hiraishi, K.: Formal verification of business processes with temporal and resource constraints. In: 2011 IEEE International Conference on Systems, Man, and Cybernetics (SMC), pp. 1173–1180. IEEE (2011)

24. Zavatteri, M., Combi, C., Viganò, L.: Resource controllability of workflows under conditional uncertainty. In: Di Francescomarino, C., Dijkman, R., Zdun, U. (eds.) BPM 2019. LNBIP, vol. 362, pp. 68–80. Springer, Cham (2019). https://doi.org/10.1007/978-3-030-37453-2_7
25. Zavatteri, M., Viganò, L.: Conditional simple temporal networks with uncertainty and decisions. Theoret. Comput. Sci. **797**, 77–101 (2019)

Process Mining (BPMDS 2020)

Cherry-Picking from Spaghetti: Multi-range Filtering of Event Logs

Maxim Vidgof[(✉)], Djordje Djurica, Saimir Bala, and Jan Mendling

Institute for Information Business, Vienna University of Economics
and Business (WU), Vienna, Austria
`maxim.vidgof@wu.ac.at`

Abstract. Mining real-life event logs results into process models which provide little value to the process analyst without support for handling complexity. Filtering techniques are specifically helpful to tackle this problem. These techniques have been focusing on leaving out infrequent aspects of the process which are considered outliers. However, it is exactly in these outliers where it is possible to gather important insights on the process. This paper addresses this problem by defining multi-range filtering. Our technique not only allows to combine both frequent and non-frequent aspects of the process but it supports any user-defined intervals of frequency of activities and variants. We evaluate our approach through a prototype based on the PM4Py library and show the benefits in comparison to existing filtering techniques.

Keywords: Multi-range filter · Filtering event logs · Infrequent behavior · Process mining

1 Introduction

The goal of process mining is extracting actionable process knowledge using event logs of IT systems that are available in the organizations [1]. Process discovery is one of the areas of interest of process mining that is concerned with the extracting the process models from logs. With the development of process mining, a number of automated process discovery algorithms that address this problem has appeared.

The problem with automated process discovery of process models from event logs is that despite the variety of different algorithms, automated process discovery methods all suffer from joint deficiencies when used for real-life event logs [1]: they produce large spaghetti-like models and they produce models with either low level of fitness to the event log, or have low precision or generalization. Managing to correct these shortcomings proved to be a difficult task. Research by Augusto et al. [2] states that for complex event logs it is highly recommended to use filtering of the logs before automated process discovery techniques and that without this type of filtering precision of the resulting models is close to

© Springer Nature Switzerland AG 2020
S. Nurcan et al. (Eds.): BPMDS 2020/EMMSAD 2020, LNBIP 387, pp. 135–149, 2020.
https://doi.org/10.1007/978-3-030-49418-6_9

zero. The authors also highlight a research gap that is necessary to be closed suggesting the need to develop a filter which will can be tuned at will to deal with complex logs.

Therefore, the purpose of our study was to rectify this research gap by implementing a new filter, able to capture both most frequent behavior and the rare one. We created a prototype based on the PM4Py, process mining toolkit for Python [3]. Our prototype is fully customizable in which the user define an arbitrary number of ranges for both activities and variants of the process that user wants to analyze. In this research, we demonstrate how our technique helps to unveil new insights into the process using an illustrative example from the real-world event log.

This paper is structured as follows. Section 2 describes the problem setting and discusses common process mining techniques that rely on filtering of the logs in order to simplify models. Further, we present different types of filters and compare them. Finally, we derive requirements for new filter type. Section 3 presents a conceptual description of our filter with the formal definitions, while Sect. 4 presents an example that emphasizes the benefits of this technique. Section 5 shows the benefits of our technique against existing process mining tools. Section 6 concludes the paper and discusses future work.

2   Theoretical Background

This section describes the problem and provides an overview on related literature before deriving three requirements for a filtering technique.

2.1   Motivation and Problem Description

Data analysis plays a fundamental part in Business Process Management (BPM) and allows to improve processes based on facts. Process mining is the main technique to analyze processes using data which stem from event logs. These event logs keep track of the history of the various runs of the business process execute over time. Real world event logs typically contain a high number of cases, which may or may not differ from one another in the way they were handled. Mining such event logs usually results in models which contain an overwhelming amount of behavior (i.e., process variants). These models are also referred to as *Spaghetti* models as they make it hard to identify specific paths in their chaotic layout.

Spaghetti models provide little value as they are hard to understand. Literature has defined several techniques to overcome this problem, such as reducing complexity on a log level [11] and reducing complexity on a model level [6]. A main technique for reducing complexity offered by many of the process mining techniques is *filtering*. Usually process mining techniques show their results in visual interfaces which offer sliders to set up custom parameters for filtering. By moving these sliders the user are able to focus on specific aspects of the process.

What makes spaghetti models so complex is the fact that they show all possible behaviour, including paths that were seldom taken in the process. Therefore, the focus of existing techniques from both academia and practice has been on filtering out this infrequent behaviour. We argue that in some cases, it is the infrequent behaviour that gives us better important insights on problems in the process, thus helping improvement. Indeed, existing tools such as ProM[1], Disco[2] and Celonis[3] are able to filter for specific behaviour. However, there is no way to set these filters in such a way that multiple variants or activities are shown together. This way of filtering leaves out important information, which might be seen for instance by a combination of the most and the least frequent cases.

Let us illustrate the problem through a running example. Figure 1 shows a simple complaint handling process adapted from [5]. The process works as follows. After a client files a complaint, (s)he immediately receives an automated confirmation message. Next, an employee brings the application to a meeting with colleagues in order to discuss a solution. The same employee is in charge of contacting back the customer with an apology and proposes a solution. The solution may be accepted or rejected by the client. In case of acceptance, the solution is executed right away. In case of rejection, the employee contacts the client to investigate on alternatives. As long as a reasonable alternative is found, the employee has a new meeting with colleagues to discuss the solution and proceed as usual. If no alternative solutions can be found, the complaint is brought to court and the process fails.

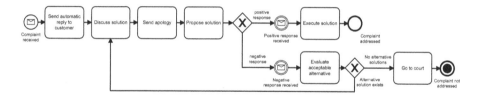

Fig. 1. Running example (adapted from [5])

There are several ways in which instances of the process may traverse the depicted process model. The *sunny case* scenario, is the one in which an agreement with the client is found right away. In a good process this case should occur frequently. On the opposite, the *rainy case* scenario consists of the cases which result in no agreement and the company is brought to court. In this case, the costs sustained from the company may be much higher than settling for a solution. An intermediate scenario is the one in which a customer does not accept the first proposed solution, but some iterations are done.

In order to improve the process, the company is interested to compare the sunny case scenario in order to understand which were the decisions and the proposed solutions that lead to the respective outcomes. Table 1a lists the activities involved in the process as well as their short labels for better readability.

---

[1] www.promtools.org.

[2] fluxicon.com/disco.

[3] www.celonis.com.

Typical process mining techniques retrieve variants as shows in Table 1b (i.e., sorted by frequency). Each variant represents one path in the output process model. In order to simplify the model, filtering must be used. However, if we filter out the least frequent behavior, we lose the information on the rainy case, which is the one that bears higher costs for the company. Some process mining tools like Celonis, would allow to select exactly the variant corresponding to the *rainy case* scenario. Unfortunately, this would leave out the *sunny case* scenario, which is also of interest of the company as this is the scenario in which the best decisions were taken.

Table 1. Process activities and variants

Activity or Event	Label
Complaint received	A
Send automatic reply to customer	B
Discuss solution	C
Send apology	D
Propose solution	E
Positive response received	F
Execute solution	G
Complaint addressed	H
Negative response received	I
Evaluate acceptable alternative	J
Go to court	K
Complaint not addressed	L

(a) Activities of the process

Variant	Count
⟨A,B,C,D,E,F,G,H ⟩	807
⟨A,B,C,D,E,I,J,C,D,E,F,G,H ⟩	132
⟨A,B,C,D,E,I,J,K,L ⟩	30
⟨A,B,C,D,E,I,J,C,D,E,I,J,C,D,E,F,G,H ⟩	21
⟨A,B,C,D,E,I,J,C,D,E,I,K,L ⟩	6
⟨A,B,C,D,E,I,J,C,D,E,I,J,C,D,E,I,J,C,D,E,F,G,H ⟩	2
⟨A,B,C,D,E,I,J,C,D,E,I,J,C,D,E,I,J,K,L ⟩	2

(b) Process variants ordered by trace frequency

The same consideration also holds for events and activities. Indeed, the company might be interested in activities or events which occur within a specific range of frequencies. For instance, the top 10 most frequent and the top 10 most infrequent activities can play a role into guiding process redesign. In other words, frequency of traces and activities do not necessarily reflect importance. There may be extremely infrequent variants or activities which have a very high impact on the process (e.g., Black Swans [10]). Hence, it is crucial that filtering does not compromise this information.

2.2   Filtering Techniques

According to Dumas et al. [5], process mining tools use two approaches to simplify event logs: *abstraction* and *event log filtering*. Abstraction is used to remove the subset of the nodes from the process map, producing a smaller dependency graph of the given event log. This way of simplifying process models is often beneficial because it enables model viewers to aggregate paths or activities of a given Spaghetti model and provides them with a better understanding about how the process functions on a macro level. However, while abstraction can visualize large event logs, it lacks the efficiency of coping with the full complexity of real-life event logs [6].

Consequently, process mining offers another type of event log simplification called event log filtering. Filtering an event log can be achieved with the use of three types of filters that remove a subset of the traces, events, or event pairs intending to produce a simpler log. *Event filters* allow users to remove or to keep all the events that satisfy a predefined condition set by the user. They allow users to focus only on a particular activity. *Event pair filter*, allow users to remove or keep all the pairs of events that fulfill a specific condition. This type of event log filtering is used to show a relation between two events and gather more insight into, for instance, situations where event A is followed by event B. Finally, using *trace filters* enables users to remove or retain all the traces from the log that fit the defined criteria. This filter can be used to, for example, show all the traces that occur with a defined level of frequency, or all traces that have a specific duration of cycle time [6].

In their paper on filtering out infrequent behaviour from event logs, Conforti et al. [4] mention more types of event filters mainly used in process mining tool ProM. First such filter is *Filter Log by Attribute* which removes all the events where the value of the attribute is not equal to the value defined by the user. It can also remove all the events that do not contain a certain selected attribute. Next, *Filter on Timeframe* serves to filter out all the events which fall into the desired timeframe. Some filters serve to filter out infrequent behaviour. One such instance is a *Filter Log using Simple Heuristics* which can remove all the traces that do not start and/or end with a particular event. It also can remove all the events related to the specific process task by calculating frequencies of event occurrence. Another example of the infrequent behaviour filter is *Filter Log using Prefix-Close Language*. This filter eliminates all the traces that are not a prefix of another prefix in the log by using a frequency threshold defined by the user.

While both abstraction and event log filtering techniques work well with structured processes but have problems visualizing and discovering less structured ones, recently, new techniques have been emerging that try to bridge this gap [9,12]. *Trace clustering* is a technique where the event log is divided into homogeneous subsets which are then used to create separate process models. This approach is able to cope with real flexible environments and improve process mining results. However, trace clustering is shown to suffer from a significant difference between clustering and the evaluation biases. The technique that tackles this problem, and manages to bridge this difference is *Active Trace Clustering* [12] inspired by principles of active learning. This approach borrows elements from machine learning and utilizes selective sampling strategy which enables an active learner to decide which instances to select based on their informativeness. Most frequently used informativeness measure is the frequency of the trace.

Several process discovery algorithms deal with noise in the logs are developed. The most well-known ones are *Heuristics Miner* [13], *Inductive Miner* [7], and *Fuzzy Miner* [6]. Heuristics miner deals with noise by introducing frequency-based metrics, while Inductive Miner uses two types of filters that accomplish this. The first filter applies a similar approach to Heuristics Miner and removes all the edges from the directly-follows graphs. In contrast, the second filter removes edges that the first filter did not remove by using eventually-follows graphs. However, process models mined using Inductive miner are often oversimplified. A different approach to the previous two is Fuzzy Miner. This algorithm filters noise directly on the discovered model using the desired level of significance and correlation thresholds defined by users.

As we can see, there are numerous techniques and algorithms which can be used to simplify event logs and models to help users understand the core process better. However, all of them are achieving this by filtering out infrequent behaviour, considering it to be the noise in the event logs [1]. We argue that this is a substantial limitation that needs to be addressed since infrequent behaviour can carry important information which is lost by filtering it out of the log. For example, having an insight into rare cases can help companies detect errors in the process or even detect fraud. Furthermore, none of the presented techniques considers that users might want to observe a process model that comprises both the most frequent and infrequent traces of the process.

2.3 Requirements for a Filtering Technique

Against this background, we derive the following requirements for a filtering technique.

RQ1. (Select variants). A filtering technique must allow the user to *slice* the log. That is, it must offer a way of selecting process variants relevant to the user.

RQ2. (Select activities). A filtering technique must be able to *dice* the log. That is, it must offer a way of selecting the most relevant activities for the user.

RQ3. (Multi-range filtering). A filtering technique must be able to *slice* and *dice* on multiple ranges. That is, it must offer a way of selecting relevant information form several frequency intervals.

3 Technique for Multi-range Filtering

In this section we describe our filtering technique that allows to learn process models without ruling out infrequent behaviour. We show an overview of the technique, provide the necessary definitions and then describe the technique in detail.

3.1 Overview of the Technique

Our technique is summarized in Fig. 2. It takes as input an event log and two user defined multi-ranges. A multi-range is a set of intervals of frequencies. As we use frequencies, interval boundaries are from 0 to 1, where [0,0] means that we get the least frequent variant or activity, and [0,1] means that that we consider all possible behavior. The aforementioned multi-ranges are used respectively by two filter types: *i)* variants filter; and *ii)* activities filter. These two filters can be used independently or consecutively. In the latter case, their application must follow the order: variants filter first. The output of each filter is a simplified event log, complying with filtering criteria. This event log can be used by any process mining technique to generate a process model which allows the user to analyze the data.

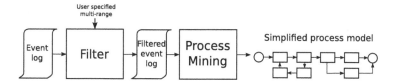

Fig. 2. Overview of the approach

3.2 Preliminaries

Definition 1 (Event, activity). *Let $\mathcal{A}$ be the universe of events. Each event has attributes. Let AN be the set of attribute names. For any event $e \in \mathcal{A}$ and name $n \in AN$, $\#_n(e)$ is the value of the attribute n for event e. An activity is a specific attribute of an event, i.e., $\#_{activity}(e)$ is the activity associated to the event.*

For example, $\#_{activity}(e) = $ 'Discuss solution'.

Definition 2 (Trace, variant, event log). *A trace $t = \langle e_1, \ldots, e_n \rangle$ is a finite sequence of events. An event log $L \subseteq \{t\}^*$ is a multi-set of traces, i.e. A process variant is a subset of traces $V \subseteq L$. Variants group together traces which have similarities to one another and differences to traces in other variants.*

An example of trace is $t = \langle a, b, c, d, e, f, g, h \rangle$. An example of log is $L = [\langle a, b, c, d, e, f, g, h \rangle^{20}, \langle a, b, c, d, e, i, j, k, l \rangle^5]$. In this event log, the first trace occurs 20 times whereas the second one occurs 5 times.

Definition 3 (Variant frequency, Activity frequency). *Variant frequency $vf(V)$ is defined as the frequency occurrence of its constituting traces $t \in V$. Activity frequency $af(a)$ is defined as the sum of the number of times activity a in the event log L.*

For example, given $L = [\langle a, b, c, d, e, f, g, h \rangle^{20}, \langle a, b, c, d, e, i, j, k, l \rangle^5]$, then $vf(\langle a, b, c, d, e, f, g, h \rangle) = 20$ and $af(a) = 25$.

A filtering technique is a function $f : L \rightarrow L'$ which transforms an event log L into a simpler event log L'. Next, we use the given definitions to describe the algorithms used by our technique.

3.3 Implementation

Our implementation provides two filters: the variants filter and the activities filter. These two filters are composable but their application is not commutative, i.e. it has to be performed in strictly defined order. Namely, first the variants filter is applied and then the activities filter is applied on the results of the variants filter. In case the former one filtered out some variants, only the activities present in the remaining variants can be used in the latter one.

We are interested in filtering at multiple ranges in the event log. These ranges represent frequencies expressed by the user in the form of sets of intervals. That is, $R = \{[min_0, max_0], [min_1, max_1], \dots [min_n, max_n]\}$ with $min_i <= max_i$, $i = 1, \dots, n$ signifies that the user want to retain from the log an amount of information that falls into either of the intervals $[min_0, max_0], \dots, [min_n, max_n]$. Ranges can be applied to both filtering on the variants level - referred to as R_v - and filtering on the activities level - R_a. Since the range boundaries are specified as frequency percentages, the minimum value of min_i is 0, and the maximum value of max_i is 1. We also establish that $[min, max]$ means that the boundaries of the interval are included and (min, max) means the boundaries are excluded. With this definition we can express the non-overlaps condition on the ranges specified by the user as $\forall i, j \in [0...n] \Rightarrow [min_i, max_i] \cap [min_j, max_j] = \varnothing$. This is a precondition for applying both the activity and the variants filters. In other words, ranges may share boundaries but they must not overlap.

Our implementation consists of three main blocks. First, the ranges specified by the user for each of the applied filters are checked for overlaps. If the ranges are incorrect, an error is produced and the filtering is not applied.

Second, if the ranges are correct, the variants filter can be applied. The variants are filtered according to Algorithm 1.

Third, we can apply Algorithm 2 on the resulting log. First, it builds a list of activities sorted by their frequency, analogous to Algorithm 1. Then, a range filter is applied in the same manner. Finally, we iterate over all traces in the input log and rebuild them in such a way that only filtered activities remain in the trace. The new trace is appended to the output log only in case it is not empty, i.e. it contains at least one of the activities that should remain.

Algorithm 1. Filter variants

Input: Event log L. Ranges $V = \{(min_0, max_0) \dots (min_m, max_m)\}$, $m \in \mathbb{N}_0$
Result: A new event log $L' \subseteq L$

1 $variants \leftarrow \forall$ variants $\in L$;
2 $variants \leftarrow$ **sort** $variants$ **by** $vf_L(variant)$;
3 $nr\_variants \leftarrow |variants|$;
4 $indices \leftarrow \bigcup\limits_{i=0}^{m} \{n \in \mathbb{N}_0 | n \in$
   $[round(min_i \times nr\_variants), round(max_i \times nr\_variants)]\}$;
5 $filtered\_variants \leftarrow \bigcup\limits_{i \in indices} variants_i$;
6 $L' \leftarrow \forall trace \in L \cap filtered\_variants$;

Algorithm 2. Filter activities

Input: Event log L'. Ranges $A = \{(min_0, max_0), \ldots, (min_p, max_p)\}$,
        $p \in \mathbb{N}_0$
Result: A new event log $L'' \subseteq L'$

1 $activities \leftarrow dict(key = activity, value = af_L(activity))$;
2 **forall** $variant \in L'$ **do**
3   **forall** $activity \in variant$ **do**
4   **if** $activity \notin activities$ **then**
5           $activities = activities \cup \{activity\}$;
6           $af_L(activity) \leftarrow vf_L(variant)$;
7   **else**
8           $af_L(activity) \leftarrow af_L(activity) + vf_L(variant)$
9   **end**
10   **end**
11 **end**
12 $activities \leftarrow$ **sort** $activities$ **by** $af_L(activity)$;
13 $nr\_activities \leftarrow |activities|$;
14 $indices \leftarrow \bigcup_{i=0}^{p} \{n \in \mathbb{N}_0 | n \in$
   $[round(min_i \times nr\_activities), round(max_i \times nr\_activities)]\}$;
15 $filtered\_activities \leftarrow \bigcup_{i \in indices} activities_i$;
16 $L'' \leftarrow []$;
17 **forall** $trace \in L'$ **do**
18    $new\_trace \leftarrow []$;
19   **forall** $activity \in trace$ **do**
20   **if** $activity \in filtered\_activities$ **then**
21          $new\_trace = new\_trace \cup \{activity\}$;
22   **end**
23   **end**
24   **if** $new\_trace \neq \varnothing$ **then**
25       $L'' \leftarrow L'' \cup \{new\_trace\}$;
26   **end**
27 **end**

---

4 Results

Next, we built a prototype to evaluate our technique. This section presents the results. First, we describe the experimental setup. Then we demonstrate that our technique addresses all the requirements by applying our technique to the running example we provided in Sect. 2.1. Last, we show the usefulness of our technique in a real-life log.

4.1   Experimental Setup

We implemented our technique as a prototype. We built our prototype using the PM4Py [3] library. It is a library for process mining implemented in the Python programming language. We used Jupyter notebook for our implementation. We tested on a laptop with Intel®Core ™ i7-8565U CPU @ 4.60 GHz x 4 machine with 16 GB of DDR4 RAM and Linux kernel 4.15.0-88-generic 64-bit version.

By default, our tool takes an event log in XES format as input but it can be also configured to accept event log in CSV format. The output is a filtered log, again, in XES or CSV format. The output of our tool can be used with any other process process mining tool. Apart from mining the resulting log in PM4Py, the user can export it and work on it with other tools like ProM, Disco, Celonis, etc. We used PM4Py and ProM in our evaluation. Our prototype is publicly available as open source software on GitHub[4].

4.2   Results on Artificial Log

We generated a log of our example process in Fig. 1 using BIMP[5]. The log contains 1000 cases and was built with the following rules: *i)* positive response is received with 80% probability; *ii)* negative response is received with 20% probability; *iii)* alternative solution exists with 80% probability; *iv)* no alternative solutions exist with 20% probability.

In order to evaluate our technique, let us apply our prototype on this artificial log. As already mentioned, the two filters can be used both separately and combined. First, we can use the variants filter to keep process behaviour that is of interest to us. Let us say, we are interested in the most frequent and the least frequent variants. To do that, we apply Algorithm 1 and specify two ranges for the filter: $R_v = \{[0, 0.15], [0.9, 1]\}$. It means we want to keep the 15% least frequent paths as well as 10% most frequent ones. It is very important to interpret these ranges correctly: by saying we take 15% most infrequent paths we do not mean taking 15% of the cases. Instead, we mean here paths that are between the 0th and the 15th percentile in a list of all variants in the input log sorted by their frequency.

We do not want to filter out any activities at this point, thus we specify one range $R_a = [0, 1]$ for the activities filter, meaning we want to keep 100% of activities. This gives us a filtered log L' that we can use further either in PM4Py or in any other tool. Figure 3 shows a Petri net resulting from applying Heuristics miner in ProM on the filtered log and adapted for better readability.

However, we may also want to filter activities at this point. Note that as we already applied the first filter on our log, only the activities present in the selected variants will be available for us to pick from. Let us say, we want to see the least frequent activities as well as the ones of medium frequency but not the most frequent ones. In order to do that, we can set multiple ranges for

---

[4] https://github.com/MaxVidgof/cherry-picker.

[5] http://bimp.cs.ut.ee.

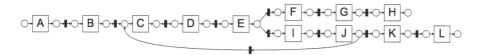

Fig. 3. Model from the artificial log in Table 1 with variants ranges R_v = $\{[0, 0.15], [0.9, 1]\}$ produced by heuristics miner and transformed into a Petri net.

the activities filter: $R_a = \{[0, 0.1], [0.1, 0.3], [0.4, 0.6]\}$. You can also see that the range boundaries are allowed to be the same but an overlap between ranges is not allowed.

Figure 4 shows the resulting model, again, adapted to improve readability. As we can see, it only includes the activities that are in the specified range: 40% least frequent activities and some activities with medium frequency. However, the new model does not contain the most frequent activities as they are outside of the specified range. This allows the user to concentrate on the less frequent and presumably more interesting activities.

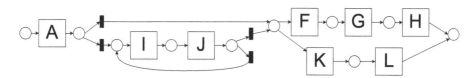

Fig. 4. Model from the artificial log in Table 1 with variants ranges R_v = $\{[0, 0.15], [0.9, 1]\}$ and activities ranges $R_a = \{[0, 0.1], [0.1, 0.3], [0.4, 0.6]\}$ produced by heuristics miner and transformed into a Petri net.

In conclusion, the proposed technique fulfills the requirements for an information-preserving filtering technique. More specifically, the requirements identified in Sect. 2.3 are addressed as follows.

RQ1. (Select variants) is addressed as the resulting model only shows the least frequent behaviour and the most frequent one.

RQ2. (Select activities) is addressed by the activities filter. Here the less frequent activities such as *Evaluate acceptable alternative* (J), *Go to court* (K) as well as the ones with medium frequency like *Complaint received* are present whereas the most frequent ones like *Discuss solution* (C) and *Send apology* (D) are filtered out.

RQ3. (Multi-range filtering) is addressed by our novel range specification approach. Instead of only selecting one threshold or manually picking some variants, the user can now specify multiple non-overlapping frequency ranges, and the union of sets of entities (variants or activities, depending on the filter) is written to the filtered log. The models above not only contain the least frequent traces like ⟨A,B,C,D,E,I,J,C,D,E,I,J,C,D,E,I,J,K,L⟩ but also the most frequent one such as ⟨A,B,C,D,E,F,G,H⟩. However, the traces with medium frequency are not included in the filtered log L'.

4.3   Results on Real-Life Logs

Next, we applied our technique on a real-life event log of sepsis cases [8]. This is a publicly available log containing more than 1000 traces and 15000 events, each trace corresponding to a pathway through the hospital.

By exploring the log, we can find out that there are 846 different variants, the most frequent of which includes only 35 cases that corresponds to slightly more than 3% of all traces in the log. There are also 784 variants having only a single conforming trace in the log. This means that the term frequent variant is not applicable to this log. Thus, it makes little sense to apply the variants filter on the log so we can set the range of the first filter to [0,1].

What is really of interest to us is the activities filter. While the filters of the traditional process mining tools only allow to keep the most frequent activities, which we will discuss in more detail in Sect. 5, our filter gives us more opportunities. Fir instance, we can decide to take a deeper look only into the least frequent activities. For this, we would set the activities filter to a range of [0, 0.25]. But we can also add additional ranges to these filter. Let us say, apart from the least frequent activities we are also interested in the one activity lying at the 65th percentile of frequency. This is also possible, for this we just set the second range to [0.65,0.65].

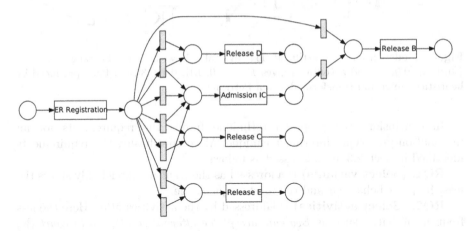

Fig. 5. Model from the real-life log with activities ranges [0,0.25] and [0.65,0.65] produced by heuristics miner and transformed into a Petri net

Now, if we apply the Heuristics miner on the filtered log and convert it to a Petri net, we will get a model in Fig. 5. Again, here we only see the activities that are in the specified range of frequency, and this picture cannot be achieved by any other process mining tool.

5   Discussion

Process mining allows the users to turn event logs into process models. However, real-life behaviour captured in these event logs of the process may be complex and exhibit notable variability. This leads to so-called spaghetti models (Fig. 6a) that are difficult to comprehend. Filtering reduces the complexity of such models by limiting the number of traces used to produce the model or the number of activities shown in the resulting model.

However, the users have little options to decide what information stays in the model and what can be left out for the moment, since existing process mining tools treat frequency as an ultimate measure of importance of a variant or an activity. Due to this, they only offer the user to keep the most frequent activities or paths. We claim, however, that a process can contain activities that are still very important despite infrequency but the tools provide virtually no possibility to include them and reduce complexity at the same time. Some of the tools provide the option to focus on any single path - also possibly an infrequent one - but then the big picture is lost and the process analyst has to manually incorporate this path in the model in case it is important. Moreover, no tool offers an option to focus on infrequent activities.

Our novel technique increases the utility of filtering event logs for the process analysts by allowing to set multiple ranges of frequency both for filtering variants and activities. Let us provide an illustrative example. Figure 6b shows a model produced by PM4Py heuristics miner from the real-life log about sepsis cases that we used in the previous section. Here, we used single-range filtering with $R_v = [0.65, 1]$ for the variants filter and $R_a = [0.6, 1]$ for the activities filter. Figure 6c is generated from a log where multi-range filtering was applied. In fact, only a slight modification was done to the activities filter: $R_a = \{[0.3, 0.3], [0.6, 1]\}$. This modification leads to the new activity *Return ER* - the patient returning to the hospital - appearing in the model. This activity, judging from the name, may be extremely important for the domain expert, although it does not happen frequently.

As this example shows, our filtering technique fills the gap that other techniques cannot fill. It does so by allowing the user to set multiple frequency ranges for both variants and activities, which in turn makes it possible to focus on previously disregarded behaviour and gain insights about the process behaviour that no other tool can provide. This can be beneficial in scenarios like monitoring of safety-critical processes, or controlling for possible fraudulent behaviour in companies. In such cases, it is of utmost importance that a filtering technique does not leave out information about potentially harmful cases.

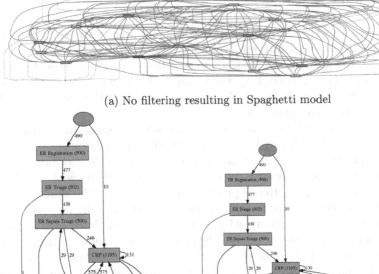

(a) No filtering resulting in Spaghetti model

(b) single-range filtering   (c) multi-range filtering

Fig. 6. Impact of filtering on the resulting process models

6   Conclusion

In this paper we provide a novel filtering technique which sacrifices infrequent occurrence neither of process variants nor of process activities. We leveraged the PM4Py libraries to build a prototype which can work with multiple event logs formats. As well, the result of our technique can be input to several process mining algorithms. We tested our technique both on a synthetic log generated from a well known process model as well as with real-world event logs. Our evaluation shows that we can obtain new insights which were either too hard to implement or not offered by existing process mining tools.

Our work has limitations. At current stage, intervals are defined as lists of tuples in Jupyter notebooks. This does not target end users with limited programming skills. In future work, we plan to implement a user-friendly interface. Furthermore, we plan to apply our technique in real-world scenarios, such as auditing, in which multi-range filtering may unveil possible pattern of fraud or non-compliance. Finally, we plan to extend state of the art techniques by enriching them with multi-range capabilities.

References

1. van der Aalst, W.M.P.: Process Mining - Data Science in Action, 2nd edn. Springer, Heidelberg (2016). https://doi.org/10.1007/978-3-662-49851-4
2. Augusto, A., et al.: Automated discovery of process models from event logs: review and benchmark. IEEE Trans. Knowl. Data Eng. **31**(4), 686–705 (2019)
3. Berti, A., van Zelst, S.J., van der Aalst, W.M.P.: Process mining for python (PM4PY): bridging the gap between process - and data science. CoRR abs/1905.06169 (2019)
4. Conforti, R., La Rosa, M., ter Hofstede, A.H.M.: Filtering out infrequent behavior from business process event logs. IEEE Trans. Knowl. Data Eng. **29**(2), 300–314 (2017)
5. Dumas, M., La Rosa, M., Mendling, J., Reijers, H.A.: Fundamentals of Business Process Management, 2nd edn. Springer, Heidelberg (2018). https://doi.org/10.1007/978-3-642-33143-5
6. Günther, C.W., van der Aalst, W.M.P.: Fuzzy mining – adaptive process simplification based on multi-perspective metrics. In: Alonso, G., Dadam, P., Rosemann, M. (eds.) BPM 2007. LNCS, vol. 4714, pp. 328–343. Springer, Heidelberg (2007). https://doi.org/10.1007/978-3-540-75183-0_24
7. Leemans, S.J.J., Fahland, D., van der Aalst, W.M.P.: Discovering block-structured process models from event logs - a constructive approach. In: Colom, J.-M., Desel, J. (eds.) PETRI NETS 2013. LNCS, vol. 7927, pp. 311–329. Springer, Heidelberg (2013). https://doi.org/10.1007/978-3-642-38697-8_17
8. Mannhardt, F.: Eindhoven University of Technology. Dataset. Sepsis Cases - Event Log (2016). https://doi.org/10.4121/uuid:915d2bfb-7e84-49ad-a286-dc35f063a460
9. Song, M., Günther, C.W., van der Aalst, W.M.P.: Trace clustering in process mining. In: Ardagna, D., Mecella, M., Yang, J. (eds.) BPM 2008. LNBIP, vol. 17, pp. 109–120. Springer, Heidelberg (2009). https://doi.org/10.1007/978-3-642-00328-8_11
10. Taleb, N.N.: The Black Swan: The Impact of the Highly Improbable, vol. 2. Random house, New York (2007)
11. Veiga, G.M., Ferreira, D.R.: Understanding spaghetti models with sequence clustering for ProM. In: Rinderle-Ma, S., Sadiq, S., Leymann, F. (eds.) BPM 2009. LNBIP, vol. 43, pp. 92–103. Springer, Heidelberg (2010). https://doi.org/10.1007/978-3-642-12186-9_10
12. Weerdt, J.D., vanden Broucke, S.K.L.M., Vanthienen, J., Baesens, B.: Active trace clustering for improved process discovery. IEEE Trans. Knowl. Data Eng. **25**(12), 2708–2720 (2013)
13. Weijters, A.J.M.M., Ribeiro, J.T.S.: Flexible Heuristics Miner (FHM). In: CIDM, pp. 310–317. IEEE (2011)

Truncated Trace Classifier. Removal of Incomplete Traces from Event Logs

Gaël Bernard[1(✉)] and Periklis Andritsos[2]

[1] Faculty of Business and Economics (HEC), University of Lausanne, Lausanne, Switzerland
gael.bernard@unil.ch
[2] Faculty of Information, University of Toronto, Toronto, Canada
periklis.andritsos@utoronto.ca

Abstract. We consider truncated traces, which are incomplete sequences of events. This typically happens when dealing with streaming data or when the event log extraction process cuts the end of the trace. The existence of truncated traces in event logs and their negative impacts on process mining outcomes have been widely acknowledged in the literature. Still, there is a lack of research on algorithms to detect them. We propose the Truncated Trace Classifier (TTC), an algorithm that distinguishes truncated traces from the ones that are not truncated. We benchmark 5 TTC implementations that use either LSTM or XGBOOST on 13 real-life event logs. Accurate TTCs have great potential. In fact, filtering truncated traces before applying a process discovery algorithm greatly improves the precision of the discovered process models, by 9.1%. Moreover, we show that TTCs increase the accuracy of a next event prediction algorithm by up to 7.5%.

Keywords: Process mining · Predictive process monitoring · Predictive analytics · Truncated trace classifier

1 Introduction

The execution of a business process often leaves trails in information systems called event logs. Using these event logs, process mining techniques can extract data-driven insights about business processes. For example, it is possible to discover process models from event logs [1], to predict the next event [2,3], or to assess whether an ongoing process will fulfill a time constraint [4].

A truncated trace is a trace where the last events are missing. In fact, these events happened or will happen, but they are not available at the time of the analysis. The presence of truncated traces in event logs is acknowledged by researchers [5–8]. Interestingly, organizers of the latest edition of the Process Discovery Contest [9]–a contest where participants have to infer process models from event logs–have included truncated traces to make the synthetic event logs more realistic.

© Springer Nature Switzerland AG 2020
S. Nurcan et al. (Eds.): BPMDS 2020/EMMSAD 2020, LNBIP 387, pp. 150–165, 2020.
https://doi.org/10.1007/978-3-030-49418-6_10

We propose a Truncated Trace Classifier (TTC) that distinguishes truncated traces from the ones that are not truncated. We refer to the latter as the 'complete trace'. We foresee three benefits of using a TTC. First, a TTC can filter truncated traces. This is important because the success of process mining depends on the quality of the input event logs [10–13]. Second, a TTC helps to increase operational efficiency. For instance, a ticket in a call center might stay open for several days because an agent forgot to close it or because the customer did not follow up on a requested action. Using a TTC, we could avoid the manual task of closing them by doing it in an automated manner. Third, a TTC has potential that goes beyond filtering techniques. For instance, we show in this work that a TTC can improve the accuracy of predicting the next event.

It is not uncommon to read that truncated traces can be filtered out by looking at the very last event [5–8]. For example, a ticket is complete only when the activity 'closing the ticket' happens. However, such a closing event might not exist. Instead, a recurring one might occur [14]. For instance, the event 'delivering package' might be a good indicator to predict that an order is fulfilled, but it might reoccur if some items are being shipped separately. In such a case, relying on the very last event will result in a poorly performing TTC. This observation is in line with the conclusion drawn by Conforti et al. that existing techniques to filter traces are often simplistic [11].

To the best of our knowledge, we are the first work focusing on building an accurate TTC. Our contributions are the following: (1) We propose five machine learning-based TTC implementations. (2) We benchmark these five implementations and a baseline approach using 13 event logs. (3) We highlight the benefit of using a TTC for two process mining tasks, that of process discovery and next event prediction.

The rest of this paper is organized as follows. In Sect. 2, we provide an overview of process mining and define truncated traces. In Sect. 3, we propose several approaches to building a TTC, which we benchmark in Sect. 4. Sections 5 and 6 demonstrate the value of a TTC by showing how it can increase the process model precision and next event prediction, respectively. In Sect. 7, we discuss related work and we conclude the paper in Sect. 8.

2   Preliminaries

In this section, we briefly introduce the process mining discipline. Then, we define truncated traces.

2.1   Process Mining

Process mining brings data science and business process management closer together [6]. As stated in the process mining manifesto, the starting point of process mining is an event log [12]. An event log contains traces, which are sequences of events. Event logs often contain additional information such as a timestamp or the resource. We will use the simple event log definition introduced in [6]. A simple trace σ is a sequence of events. A simple event log L is a multi-set of traces. For example, $L = [\langle abc \rangle^3, \langle ab \rangle^2]$ is an event log containing 5 traces and 13 events. Taking an event log as input, several process mining techniques are available. Typically, a process discovery algorithm such as the inductive miner, [15], can infer the most likely business process model behind an event log. To ensure that process mining works well, event logs need to be noise-free [10–12]. Truncation is one type of noise [16], which we introduce in the next section.

2.2   Truncated Traces

A truncated trace is an ongoing trace where the end of the process is missing. Truncated traces are sometimes referred to as 'incomplete cases' [7,8], 'incomplete traces' [5], or 'missing heads' [10]. We favor the term truncated over the term incomplete as the latter is often used for the concept of 'event log incompleteness', referring to the fact that an event log will most likely not contain all the combinations of behaviors that are possible because there are too many of them [12]. For instance, when there is a loop in the process model, the number of unique combinations is infinite. Event logs will most likely be incomplete while they may not contain truncated traces.

There are several reasons to explain the existence of incomplete traces. They might exist because of a flawed event log extraction process that cuts the traces at a fixed date, leaving the traces that finish after truncated. This issue–named 'the snapshots challenge'–has been identified by van der Aalst as one of the five challenges that occurs when extracting event logs [6, chapter 5.3]. This type of truncated trace could be avoided by extracting only the traces where no event happens after the extraction date. However, once the data is extracted, we cannot know which traces are truncated. As another example, incomplete traces can exist because the events have not happened yet. This is especially relevant when working with streaming data. Finally, truncated traces can result from a wrong execution (e.g., the ticket was supposed to be closed but the agent forgot to do it) or when the information system fails. In the next section, we introduce a classifier to automatically detect truncated traces.

3   Truncated Trace Classifier

A TTC inputs the current execution of a trace and predicts whether it is truncated. As shown in Table 1, we generate one input sample and one target for each prefix length of each trace. The input sample represents the current state of the process on which we apply a TTC. The target is a binary label that is 'true' when the trace is truncated or 'false' otherwise.

This setting implies that 'real' truncated traces that we would like to identify as such using the TTC would be labeled as complete. However, our intuition is that the model will also learn from similar complete traces where the truncated parts will be labeled as 'truncated'. For illustration purposes, let us define the following event logs: $\langle abc^3, ab \rangle$. During the training phase, the sequence ab

appears three times as 'truncated' and once as 'complete'. Hence, during the prediction phase, the sequence ab would most likely be predicted as 'truncated'.

Trace	#	Input Sample	Target: (Truncated?)
\<abc\>	1	a	true
	2	ab	true
	3	abc	false
\<acadd\>	4	a	true
	5	ac	true
	6	aca	true
	7	acad	true
	8	acadd	false

Fig. 1. The traces $\langle abc \rangle$ and $\langle acadd \rangle$ result in eight samples.

To build a classifier, we need to map the input sample to a feature space. There are several options to do so, covered in depth in [8,17–19]. We provide non-exhaustive examples that are illustrated in Fig. 2.

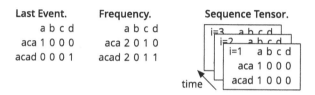

Fig. 2. Illustration of the feature spaces for the input samples $\langle aca \rangle$ and $\langle acad \rangle$.

Last Event. Relying only on the last event to predict that a trace is truncated is one option often mentioned in the literature [5–8]. For example, the input for sample #3 from Fig. 1 would be 'c'.

Frequency. The 'frequency' feature space counts the occurrences of each event. As shown in Fig. 2, $\langle aca \rangle$ becomes {a:2,b:0,c:1,d:0}. This feature space does not record the order in which the events appear.

Sequence Tensor. A sequence tensor contains an extra 'timestep' dimension. Each timestep is a matrix similar to the 'last event'; i.e., it describes which event happens. The extra dimension allows to describe the full sequence of timesteps in a lossless way. The number of timesteps is equal to the longest sequence in the event logs.

Once the input samples have been mapped into a feature space, it can be fed together with the target to a classifier. We propose five TTC implementations depicted in Fig. 3. As can be seen in Fig. 3, We also add a few base features: (1) the number of activities in the prefix, (2) the number of seconds since the first event in the trace, and (3) the number of seconds since the previous event in

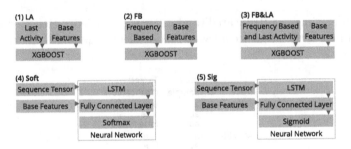

Fig. 3. Five implemented TTCs.

the trace. Such extra features were also added in the predictive business process monitoring proposed by Tax et al. [3]. The five TTCs are described below.

1 LA (Last Activity). This TTC relies on the last activity to predict that the trace is truncated.

2 FB (Frequency Based). This TTC uses the 'frequency' feature space described in Sect. 3.

3 FB&LA. This TTC concatenates the TTCs '1 LA' and '2 FB' because they both convey complementary information.

4 Soft (Softmax). This TTC corresponds to a next event prediction algorithm. In fact, the implementation is similar to the predictive business process monitoring from Tax et al. [3]. Predicting which event will occur is a multi-class prediction problem. Thus, we rely on the Softmax function because it transforms the output to a probability distribution. The end of the process is treated as any other event. If the latter is predicted as the most likely next event, we predict that the trace is complete. If not, we predict that the trace is truncated.

5 Sig (Sigmoid). The TTC '5 Sig' turns the multi-class problem into a binary one by using a one-vs-all strategy with the special 'end' event. We implemented both TTCs to compare the accuracy when the neural network is specially trained to recognize truncated traces ('5 Sig') or when the task is to predict the next event ('4 Soft').

TTCs 1 to 3 use XGBoost[1] [20], which stands for eXtreme Gradient Boosting. It relies on an ensemble of decision trees to predict the target. This technique is widely used among the winning solutions in machine learning challenges [20]. For the main settings, we set the number of trees to 200 and the maximum depth of the trees to 8. The last two TTCs rely on a neural network implemented in Keras [21]. As shown in Fig. 3, the architecture has two inputs. First, the sequence tensor is passed to a Long Short-Term Memory (LSTM) network. LSTM is a special type of Recurrent Neural Network (RNN) introduced in [22]. Compared to RNN, LSTM possesses a more advanced memory cell that gives LSTM powerful modeling capabilities for long-term dependencies [3]. The output of the LSTM network and the base features are provided to a fully connected

---

[1] Available at https://github.com/dmlc/xgboost/tree/master/python-package.

layer. Both the LSTM network and the fully connected layer have 16 cells. We use Adam [23] as an optimizer and we set the number of epochs to 100.

4   Benchmark

In this section, we benchmark the five TTCs described in the previous section, in addition to a baseline approach.

4.1   Datasets

We used 13 event logs[2] well known in the process mining literature. The event logs come from "real-life" systems, offering the advantage of containing complex traces and a wide range of characteristics visible in Table 1.

To the best of our knowledge, these event logs do not contain truncated traces. However, this is difficult to confirm. For instance, exceptional events might happen several months after the event log extraction date. In general, without having a deep expertise of the domain under analysis and direct access to the person in charge of the dataset extraction, it is not possible to guarantee that all traces are complete. We use the term 'false complete' to refer to traces that we wrongly consider complete during the training phase but that are in fact truncated because more events will happen. We claim that a TTC should be resilient to 'false complete'. In other words, a TTC should not overfit on a single 'false complete' and wrongly classify all similar traces as complete.

To test the resilience of the TTCs, we generated 0%, 10%, and 20% of 'false complete' traces by randomly cutting them. The setting with 0% of 'false complete' reflects how the TTC should be used with a real dataset, i.e., considering all the traces as complete. For the two other settings, we kept track of the traces that are truncated and refer to them as 'ground truth'. To benchmark the various TTCs, we use the ground truth. For instance, let us define that $\langle abc \rangle$ is a complete trace that we randomly cut to become the following 'false complete': $\langle ab \rangle$. During the training phase, we train the classifier to consider $\langle ab \rangle$ as a complete trace, while during the evaluation $\langle ab \rangle$ should be classified as truncated to be well classified.

4.2   Baseline: Decreasing Factor

Standard process mining tools and libraries such as the plugin 'Filter Log using Simple Heuristics' in ProM[3], the software Disco[4] or the Python library PM4Py [24] offer some options to remove truncated traces. Typically, a set of ending activities is selected by the end-user and the traces that do terminate with the ending activities are considered truncated and removed. It is also possible to automatically determine the set of ending activities. Let S be the set of

---

[3] http://www.promtools.org.

[4] https://fluxicon.com/disco/.

Table 1. Characteristics of the 13 datasets.

Dataset	#σ	# activities	Unique activities	Max length (σ)	Min length (σ)	Mean length (σ)
BPI_12	13.1K	164.5k	23	96	3	12.6
BPI_13_CP	1.5K	6.7K	7	35	1	4.5
BPI_13_i	7.6K	65.5k	13	123	1	8.7
BPI_15_1	1.2K	52.2K	398	101	2	43.6
BPI_15_2	0.8K	44.4K	410	132	1	53.3
BPI_15_3	1.4K	59.7K	383	124	3	42.4
BPI_15_4	1.1K	47.3K	356	116	1	44.9
BPI_15_5	1.2K	59.1K	389	154	5	51.1
BPI_17	31.5K	561.7K	26	61	8	17.8
BPI_18	2.0K	123.3K	129	680	35	61.9
BPI_19	251.7K	1.6M	42	990	1	6.3
Env_permit	0.9K	38.9K	381	95	2	41.6
Helpdesk	3.8K	13.7K	9	14	1	3.6

ending activities that we will use to filter the truncated traces. As a baseline, we use the method implemented in PM4Py which works as follows: First, the number of occurrences of each activity as a last activity is counted. Let C_i be the count of the ith most frequent end activity. We start by adding the most frequent end activity, C_1, to S. Then, we calculate the decreasing factor of the next most frequent activity using the following formula: C_i/C_{i-1}. If the decreasing factor is above a defined threshold we add C_i to S and move to next most frequent activity. If the threshold is not met, we stop the process. We tried the following thresholds: 0.40, 0.45, 0.50, 0.55, 0.60, 0.65, and 0.70. We report the results obtained using a threshold of 0.60 as it is the one that yields the best accuracy to detect truncated traces. Interestingly, it is also the default value in PM4Py.

4.3   Evaluation

The first 80% of the traces were used to train the model, and the evaluation was done on the remaining 20%. Out of the 80% of training data, 20% was used to validate the parameters. To compare the ground truth with the output of the TTC, we used the Matthews Correlation Coefficient (MCC) [25]. The MCC has the nice property of using all the quantities of the confusion matrix, i.e., True Positive (TP), True Negative (TN), False Positive (FP), and False Negative (FN). Its value lies between −1 and 1, where 0 represents a random prediction, 1 a perfect score, and −1 an inverse prediction. It is defined as:

$$MCC(\sigma) = \frac{TP \cdot TN - FP \cdot FN}{\sqrt{(TP+FN)(FP+FN)(TN+FP)(TN+FN)}}$$

Figure 4 aggregates the results per TTC, while Fig. 5 contains the detailed results. In Fig. 5, we can see a large MCC score gap per dataset. This gap highlights the various levels of complexity involved in detecting truncated traces. Also, none of the techniques always outperforms the others. This is in line with a similar conclusion that was drawn from large predictive business process monitoring experiments [26]. Nonetheless, when looking at Fig. 4, we observe that the TTC '3 FB&LA' has the highest median MCC score. Interestingly, the performance of the baseline is comparable to the best implementations for the following five datasets: BPI_13_CP, BPI_13_i, BPI_18, Env_permit, Helpdesk (see Fig. 5). For the other eight datasets, there is a clear drop in performance between the baseline and more sophisticated methods. Looking at Table 1, we do not see any clear dataset characteristics to explain the performance gap. We conclude that looking at the last activity might work well, but for some datasets it is better to use a more sophisticated TTC.

We also tested the null hypothesis that the results from different TTCs come from the same distribution. To do this, we ran a permutation test with 100,000 random permutations and a p-value of 0.05. The results are visible in Fig. 6. As can be seen, '3 FB&LA' outperforms the baseline approach with strong statistical significance. We also observe that transforming a multi-class problem into a binary classifier–using the '4 Soft' instead of the '5 Sig'–does not seem to improve the ability of the TTC to detect truncated traces, as the MCC scores of Fig. 4 are comparable.

Figure 7 compares the execution time per TTC. The baseline takes in the order of milliseconds to run. TTCs that are based on XGboost take in the order of seconds or minutes to run, while approaches that rely on neural networks take from minutes to hours to run. In fact, the '4 Soft' and '5 Sig' are on average 112 times slower than the other TTCs that rely on XGBoost.

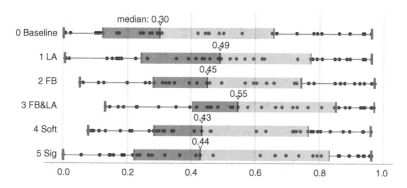

Fig. 4. Boxplot showing the MCC scores per technique. Each dot depicts an individual value. The median is written on top.

	Noise: 0						Noise: 0.1						Noise: 0.2					
	0 Baseline	1 LA	2 FB	3 FB&LA	4 Soft	5 Sig	0 Baseline	1 LA	2 FB	3 FB&LA	4 Soft	5 Sig	0 Baseline	1 LA	2 FB	3 FB&LA	4 Soft	5 Sig
BPI_12	.28	.89	.97	.97	.88	.92	.27	.85	.93	.93	.72	.86	.25	.78	.85	.85	.77	.78
BPI_13_CP	.96	.96	.13	.96	.96	.96	.94	.94	.13	.94	.94	.94	.87	.87	.13	.87	.84	.87
BPI_13_i	.80	.52	.33	.53	.80	.81	.78	.62	.61	.62	.78	.79	.73	.57	.57	.58	.73	.74
BPI_15_1	.22	.49	.45	.46	.22	.00	.09	.23	.35	.46	.13	.15	.13	.27	.31	.40	.11	.06
BPI_15_2	.26	.49	.72	.72	.28	.32	.25	.41	.63	.69	.30	.15	.21	.35	.60	.55	.21	.18
BPI_15_3	.12	.15	.11	.19	.09	.22	.12	.18	.06	.23	.10	.16	.11	.14	.05	.23	.08	.12
BPI_15_4	.00	.01	.28	.15	.46	.28	.00	.01	.27	.13	.35	.27	.00	.02	.26	.15	.27	.19
BPI_15_5	.13	.19	.29	.30	.34	.23	.13	.17	.20	.18	.32	.23	.12	.17	.32	.36	.32	.19
BPI_17	.68	.79	.97	.97	.78	.96	.67	.77	.94	.94	.72	.92	.64	.73	.88	.88	.74	.86
BPI_18	.50	.50	.50	.52	.18	.23	.49	.49	.45	.49	.47	.24	.46	.39	.46	.47	.34	.37
BPI_19	.32	.63	.77	.77	.61	.70	.31	.60	.73	.73	.64	.66	.30	.54	.66	.67	.41	.62
Env_permit	.45	.46	.42	.46	.34	.43	.44	.44	.45	.45	.44	.47	.42	.44	.40	.42	.29	.41
Helpdesk	.94	.94	.91	.94	.94	.94	.90	.90	.87	.90	.90	.90	.81	.81	.78	.81	.81	.81

Fig. 5. Detailed MCC score.

	0 Baseline	1 LA	2 FB	3 LA&FB	4 Sig	5 Soft
0 Baseline		.147	.141	.008	.146	.151
1 LA	.147		.986	.204	.929	.974
2 FB	.141	.986		.206	.941	.959
3 LA&FB	.008	.204	.206		.268	.188
4 Sig	.146	.929	.941	.268		.906
5 Soft	.151	.974	.959	.188	.906	

Fig. 6. P-values of the permutation tests between the MCC scores per techniques.

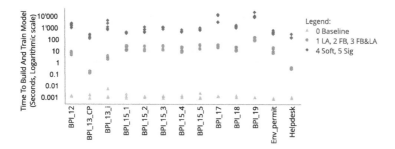

Fig. 7. Execution time for the five TTCs. The vertical axis uses a logarithmic scale.

The full benchmark implementations, the parameters, and the event logs, as well as the results are available online[5]. The machine used for the experiment has 61GB of RAM, 4 CPUs, and a GPU that speeds up the neural network training phase.

5   Improving Discovered Process Models with a TTC

A process discovery algorithm discovers a process model from an event log [6]. Because the discovered process model is based on event logs, it offers the advantage of being a data-driven approach that shows how the process is really executed. However, discovering a process model from an event log is a challenging task. Typically, process discovery algorithms are sensitive to noise [10–13]. Applying process mining techniques on traces that must supposedly be complete but are instead truncated is no exception. The quality of a process model is commonly measured using four competing metrics [12]: (1) The *precision* measures to what extent behaviors that were not observed can be replayed on the process model. (2) The *fitness* measures to what extent the traces from the event logs can be replayed on the model. (3) The *generalization* ensures that the model does not overfit. Finally, (4) the *simplicity* measures the complexity involved to read the process model. When facing truncated traces, a process discovery algorithm will wrongly infer that the process can be stopped in the middle. This will negatively impact the precision of the discovered process model. To solve this issue, researchers advocate removing truncated traces [5,6,8]. As highlighted by Conforti et al., "[t]he presence of noise tends to lower precision as this noise introduces spurious connections between event labels" [11].

We ran an experiment to measure the impact of removing truncated traces on the quality of the process models using PM4Py [24], a process mining library in Python. We used the default metrics in PM4Py which are described in the following papers: precision [27], fitness [6, p. 250], generalization [28], and simplicity [29]. To start, we randomly generated 100 process models with the PM4py

---

[5] https://github.com/gaelbernard/truncated-trace-classifier.

implementation of PTandLogGenerator [30], using the default parameters[6]. For each process model, we produced an event log containing 1,000 traces. We produced 20 variations of each event log with a level of noise ranging from 0 to 1, where 0 means that no traces were truncated and 0.05 means that 5% of the traces were truncated, and so on. Altogether, this process produced 20,000 event logs. For each of the 20,000 event logs, we ran the following experiment: (1) We applied the Inductive Miner [15] on the event logs to discover a process model, and (2) then we replayed the original event log–that did not contain the truncated traces–on the process model to measure the quality of the discovered process models. This was the experiment without a TTC. For the experiment with a TTC, we applied the exact same steps, but, beforehand, we automatically removed the truncated traces with the TTC '3 FB&LA' described in Sect. 3.

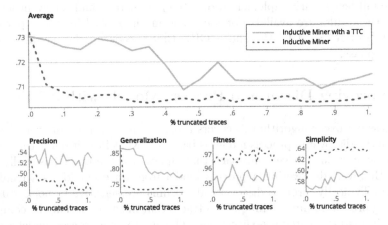

Fig. 8. Impact of the truncated traces on the process model qualities.

In Fig. 8, the results are averaged. As can be seen, the precision and the generalization metrics are greatly improved, while the simplicity and the fitness dimensions are negatively impacted. Table 2 shows that the average process quality is improved by 1.7%. Figure 8 shows the link

Table 2. Mean process quality of the discovered process models with and without the TTC.

	Without ttc	With ttc	Increase
Precision	0.4829	0.5267	9.10%
Generalization	0.7413	0.8112	9.40%
Fitness	0.9687	0.9523	−1.70%
Simplicity	0.6328	0.5833	−7.80%
Average	**0.7064**	**0.7184**	**1.70%**

between the ratio of truncated traces in the event logs and the quality of the resulting process models. The average process quality visible at the top of Fig. 8 shows that when there are some truncated traces in the event logs, applying the TTC is always beneficial. In the next section, we show that a TTC can also increase the prediction of the next events.

---

[6] Visible at: https://pm4py.fit.fraunhofer.de/documentation#process-tree-generation.

6   Improving Next Event Prediction with a TTC

The goal of a next event algorithm is to predict the most likely event that will follow a truncated trace. As shown with the '4 Soft' TTC, we can turn a next event algorithm into a TTC. Looking at the benchmark in Fig. 4, we show that the TTC '3 FB&LA' outperforms the TTC '4 Soft'. We have the intuition that combining the best TTC with a next event algorithm will increase the prediction accuracy. The rationale is that we will more accurately predict the end of the process with a TTC because it has been trained for this purpose. Hence, we first rely on the TTC to predict if more events are expected. If not, we do not need to call the next event algorithm. Overall, we should improve the results as we avoid predicting a next event when the trace is not truncated. The goal of this section is to validate this hypothesis.

As it is initially a next event prediction algorithm, we use the TTC '4 Soft' for the prediction of the next event. In the setting without a TTC, it is the only algorithm involved. In the version with a TTC, we complement the architecture with the TTC '3 FB&LA' in the following way. First, we assess if the trace is truncated using the TTC. If the trace is truncated, we predict the next event. Conversely, if the trace is already complete, we do not need to predict the next event. The results are visible in Table 3. Including a TTC improves the accuracy by up to 7.5% and on average by 1.4%. In the experiment, building the TTC took an extra 2.4% of duration. We claim that including a TTC is beneficial for the accuracy while having a limited negative execution time impact. A TTC solves one problem noted by Tax et al.: "We found that LSTMs have problems [...] to predict overly long sequences of the same activity, resulting in predicted suffixes that are much longer than the ground truth suffixes" [3].

7   Related Work

To the best of our knowledge we are the first to focus on the task of distinguishing truncated from complete traces. Still, existing works—especially in the area of predictive process monitoring—are relevant to uncover truncated traces.

Predictive process monitoring anticipates whether a running process instance will comply with a predicate [4]. For instance, a predicate might be about the process execution time, the execution of a specific event, or the total amount of sales. As highlighted by Verenich et al., techniques in this space differ according to their object of prediction [18]. A TTC is a specific type of predictive process monitoring task where the predicate is whether we will observe more events. In [31], Maggi et al. propose a generic predictive process monitoring approach. Once the predicate is set, the most similar prefixes are selected based on the edit distance. Finally, a classifier is used to correlate the goal with the data associated with the process execution. Insights are then provided to the end-user to optimize the fulfillment of the goal while the process is being executed. It was later extended with a clustering step to decrease the prediction time [4]. Tax et al. propose a neural network that leverages LSTM that could serve as

Table 3. Comparing the accuracy of predicting the next event and the execution time, without and with a TTC.

Dataset	Accuracy			Execution time (in seconds)		
	Without ttc	With ttc	Increase	Without ttc	With ttc	Increase
BPI_12	0.6899	0.6896	–	1060	1066	0.6%
BPI_13_CP	0.5559	0.5559	–	172	172	–
BPI_13_i	0.6478	0.6486	0.1%	519	521	0.4%
BPI_15_1	0.0851	0.0915	7.5%	324	347	6.6%
BPI_15_2	0.1509	0.1584	5.0%	606	628	3.5%
BPI_15_3	0.1364	0.1364	–	851	873	2.5%
BPI_15_4	0.1385	0.1394	0.6%	366	383	4.4%
BPI_15_5	0.0873	0.0884	1.3%	634	663	4.4%
BPI_17	0.7642	0.7689	0.6%	2318	2342	1.0%
BPI_18	0.6277	0.6323	0.7%	786	804	2.2%
BPI_19	0.4755	0.4855	2.1%	8674	8797	1.4%
Env_permit	0.2325	0.2324	–	373	388	3.9%
Helpdesk	0.8226	0.8226	–	116	116	–

another generic predictive process monitoring algorithm capable of fitting different predicates [3]. In our work, we use the approach from Tax et al. as a baseline (i.e., TTC '4 Soft'). Despite the advantage of being generic, we show that a tailor-made algorithm to detect a TTC outperforms such an approach.

The goal of a business process deviance mining algorithm is to assign a binary class–normal or deviant–to a trace. In this sense, it shares similarities with predictive process monitoring. This is especially true because of their overlapping inputs and feature extraction methods [32]. However, deviance mining works on completed instances and focuses on the why [32].

Finally, Bertoli et al. propose a reasoning-based approach to recover missing information from event logs [33]. Ultimately, it would allow us to turn a truncated trace into a complete one. To work, this technique requires a reference process model as input. Therefore, it is not applicable if the task at hand is to discover a process model.

8   Conclusion

Event logs are often noisy, which makes the application of process mining sometimes difficult in a real setting [13]. Typically, the existence of truncated traces is known. Still, there is a research gap in systematically detecting them. In this work, we treat the identification of truncated traces as a predictive process monitoring task and we benchmark several TTCs using 13 complex event logs. We show that building a TTC that consistently achieves high accuracy is challenging. This finding highlights the importance of conducting further research to build an efficient TTC. Typically, for some event logs, using a baseline approach that relies solely on the last activity works well. Still, we show that the TTC '3 FB&LA' outperforms such baseline approach with strong statistical significance.

We also measure the process model quality impact when a process discovery algorithm is run on event logs that contain truncated traces. We show that only a few truncated traces can greatly decrease the process model quality and that a TTC can alleviate this problem by automatically removing truncated traces. Finally, we highlight the unexplored potential of a TTC to increase the accuracy of predicting the next event. We expect that more benefits of TTCs are yet to be discovered, especially in the predictive business process monitoring area.

In this work, we use the sequence of activities as well as some timing information. Using more information such as the name of the resource, the day of the week or any other event attributes could further improve the accuracy of the TTCs. Higher accuracy could also be achieved by using different classifiers, trying new neural network architecture, or implementing alternative feature spaces. This is an area for future research where our work can serve as a baseline.

References

1. Leemans, S.J.J., Fahland, D., van der Aalst, W.M.P.: Discovering block-structured process models from incomplete event logs. In: Ciardo, G., Kindler, E. (eds.) PETRI NETS 2014. LNCS, vol. 8489, pp. 91–110. Springer, Cham (2014). https://doi.org/10.1007/978-3-319-07734-5_6
2. Bernard, G., Andritsos, P.: Accurate and transparent path prediction using process mining. In: Welzer, T., Eder, J., Podgorelec, V., Kamišalić Latifić, A. (eds.) ADBIS 2019. LNCS, vol. 11695, pp. 235–250. Springer, Cham (2019). https://doi.org/10.1007/978-3-030-28730-6_15
3. Tax, N., Verenich, I., La Rosa, M., Dumas, M.: Predictive business process monitoring with LSTM neural networks. In: Dubois, E., Pohl, K. (eds.) CAiSE 2017. LNCS, vol. 10253, pp. 477–492. Springer, Cham (2017). https://doi.org/10.1007/978-3-319-59536-8_30
4. Di Francescomarino, C., Dumas, M., Maggi, F.M., Teinemaa, I.: Clustering-based predictive process monitoring. IEEE Trans. Serv. Comput. **12**, 896–909 (2016)
5. Bezerra, F., Wainer, J., van der Aalst, W.M.P.: Anomaly detection using process mining. In: Halpin, T., Krogstie, J., Nurcan, S., Proper, E., Schmidt, R., Soffer, P., Ukor, R. (eds.) BPMDS/EMMSAD -2009. LNBIP, vol. 29, pp. 149–161. Springer, Heidelberg (2009). https://doi.org/10.1007/978-3-642-01862-6_13
6. Aalst, W.: Data science in action. Process Mining, pp. 3–23. Springer, Heidelberg (2016). https://doi.org/10.1007/978-3-662-49851-4_1
7. Fluxicon: Deal with incomplete cases, process mining in practice, disco 2.1 documentation. http://processminingbook.com/incompletecases.html
8. Verenich, I.: Explainable predictive monitoring of temporal measures of business processes. Ph.D. thesis, Queensland University of Technology (2018)
9. Carmona, J., de Leoni, M., Depaire, B.: Process discovery contest. In: International Conference on Process Mining 2019 (2019)
10. Suriadi, S., Andrews, R., ter Hofstede, A.H., Wynn, M.T.: Event log imperfection patterns for process mining: towards a systematic approach to cleaning event logs. Inf. Syst. **64**, 132–150 (2017)

11. Conforti, R., La Rosa, M., ter Hofstede, A.H.: Filtering out infrequent behavior from business process event logs. IEEE Trans. Knowl. Data Eng. **29**(2), 300–314 (2016)
12. van der Aalst, W., et al.: Process mining manifesto. In: Daniel, F., Barkaoui, K., Dustdar, S. (eds.) BPM 2011. LNBIP, vol. 99, pp. 169–194. Springer, Heidelberg (2012). https://doi.org/10.1007/978-3-642-28108-2_19
13. Bose, R.J.C., Mans, R.S., van der Aalst, W.M.: Wanna improve process mining results? In: 2013 IEEE Symposium on Computational Intelligence and Data Mining (CIDM), pp. 127–134. IEEE (2013)
14. Selig, H.: Continuous event log extraction for process mining (2017)
15. Leemans, S.J.J., Fahland, D., van der Aalst, W.M.P.: Discovering block-structured process models from event logs containing infrequent behaviour. In: Lohmann, N., Song, M., Wohed, P. (eds.) BPM 2013. LNBIP, vol. 171, pp. 66–78. Springer, Cham (2014). https://doi.org/10.1007/978-3-319-06257-0_6
16. de Medeiros, A.K.A., Weijters, A.J., van der Aalst, W.M.: Genetic process mining: an experimental evaluation. Data Min. Knowl. Disc. **14**(2), 245–304 (2007). https://doi.org/10.1007/s10618-006-0061-7
17. Verenich, I., Dumas, M., La Rosa, M., Maggi, F.M., Di Francescomarino, C.: Complex symbolic sequence clustering and multiple classifiers for predictive process monitoring. In: Reichert, M., Reijers, H.A. (eds.) BPM 2015. LNBIP, vol. 256, pp. 218–229. Springer, Cham (2016). https://doi.org/10.1007/978-3-319-42887-1_18
18. Verenich, I., Dumas, M., La Rosa, M., Maggi, F.M., Chasovskyi, D., Rozumnyi, A.: Tell me what's ahead? Predicting remaining activity sequences of business process instances (2016)
19. Leontjeva, A., Conforti, R., Di Francescomarino, C., Dumas, M., Maggi, F.M.: Complex symbolic sequence encodings for predictive monitoring of business processes. In: Motahari-Nezhad, H.R., Recker, J., Weidlich, M. (eds.) BPM 2015. LNCS, vol. 9253, pp. 297–313. Springer, Cham (2015). https://doi.org/10.1007/978-3-319-23063-4_21
20. Chen, T., Guestrin, C.: Xgboost: a scalable tree boosting system. In: Proceedings of the 22nd ACM SIGKDD International Conference on Knowledge Discovery and Data Mining, pp. 785–794. ACM (2016)
21. Chollet, F.: Keras (2015). https://github.com/fchollet/keras
22. Hochreiter, S., Schmidhuber, J.: Long short-term memory. Neural Comput. **9**(8), 1735–1780 (1997)
23. Kingma, D.P., Ba, J.: Adam: a method for stochastic optimization. arXiv preprint arXiv:1412.6980 (2014)
24. Berti, A., van Zelst, S.J., van der Aalst, W.: Process mining for python (PM4PY): bridging the gap between process-and data science. arXiv preprint arXiv:1905.06169 (2019)
25. Matthews, B.W.: Comparison of the predicted and observed secondary structure of t4 phage lysozyme. Biochimica et Biophysica (BBA)-Acta Protein Struct. **405**(2), 442–451 (1975)
26. Di Francescomarino, C., et al.: Genetic algorithms for hyperparameter optimization in predictive business process monitoring. Inf. Syst. **74**, 67–83 (2018)
27. Muñoz-Gama, J., Carmona, J.: A fresh look at precision in process conformance. In: Hull, R., Mendling, J., Tai, S. (eds.) BPM 2010. LNCS, vol. 6336, pp. 211–226. Springer, Heidelberg (2010). https://doi.org/10.1007/978-3-642-15618-2_16
28. Buijs, J.C., van Dongen, B.F., van der Aalst, W.M.: Quality dimensions in process discovery: the importance of fitness, precision, generalization and simplicity. Int. J. Coop. Inf. Syst. **23**(01), 1440001 (2014)

29. Blum, F.: Metrics in process discovery. Technical report, TR/DCC. 1–21 (2015)
30. Jouck, T., Depaire, B.: Ptandloggenerator: a generator for artificial event data (2016)
31. Maggi, F.M., Di Francescomarino, C., Dumas, M., Ghidini, C.: Predictive monitoring of business processes. In: Jarke, M., et al. (eds.) CAiSE 2014. LNCS, vol. 8484, pp. 457–472. Springer, Cham (2014). https://doi.org/10.1007/978-3-319-07881-6_31
32. Nguyen, H., Dumas, M., La Rosa, M., Maggi, F.M., Suriadi, S.: Business process deviance mining: review and evaluation. arXiv preprint arXiv:1608.08252 (2016)
33. Bertoli, P., Di Francescomarino, C., Dragoni, M., Ghidini, C.: Reasoning-based techniques for dealing with incomplete business process execution traces. In: Baldoni, M., Baroglio, C., Boella, G., Micalizio, R. (eds.) AI*IA 2013. LNCS (LNAI), vol. 8249, pp. 469–480. Springer, Cham (2013). https://doi.org/10.1007/978-3-319-03524-6_40

Secure Multi-party Computation for Inter-organizational Process Mining

Gamal Elkoumy[1], Stephan A. Fahrenkrog-Petersen[2], Marlon Dumas[1(✉)],
Peeter Laud[3], Alisa Pankova[3], and Matthias Weidlich[2]

[1] University of Tartu, Tartu, Estonia
{gamal.elkoumy,marlon.dumas}@ut.ee
[2] Humboldt-Universität zu Berlin, Berlin, Germany
{fahrenks,weidlima}@hu-berlin.de
[3] Cybernetica, Tartu, Estonia
{peeter.laud,alisa.pankova}@cyber.ee

Abstract. Process mining is a family of techniques for analyzing business processes based on event logs extracted from information systems. Mainstream process mining tools are designed for intra-organizational settings, insofar as they assume that an event log is available for processing as a whole. The use of such tools for inter-organizational process analysis is hampered by the fact that such processes involve independent parties who are unwilling to, or sometimes legally prevented from, sharing detailed event logs with each other. In this setting, this paper proposes an approach for constructing and querying a common artifact used for process mining, namely the frequency and time-annotated Directly-Follows Graph (DFG), over multiple event logs belonging to different parties, in such a way that the parties do not share the event logs with each other. The proposal leverages an existing platform for secure multi-party computation, namely Sharemind. Since a direct implementation of DFG construction in Sharemind suffers from scalability issues, we propose to rely on vectorization of event logs and to employ a divide-and-conquer scheme for parallel processing of sub-logs. The paper reports on experiments that evaluate the scalability of the approach on real-life logs.

Keywords: Process mining · Privacy · Secure multi-party computation

1 Introduction

Contemporary process mining techniques enable users to analyze business processes based on event logs extracted from information systems [1]. The outputs of process mining techniques can be used, for example, to identify performance bottlenecks, waste, or compliance violations. Existing process mining techniques require access to the entire event log of a business process. Usually, this requirement can be fulfilled when the event log is collected from one

© Springer Nature Switzerland AG 2020
S. Nurcan et al. (Eds.): BPMDS 2020/EMMSAD 2020, LNBIP 387, pp. 166–181, 2020.
https://doi.org/10.1007/978-3-030-49418-6_11

or multiple systems within the same organization. In practice, though, many business processes involve multiple independent organizations. We call such processes *inter-organizational business processes*. An example of such process is the process for ground handling of an aircraft, as illustrated in Fig. 1. This process involves two parties: the airline and the ground handler (called "airport" in the model).

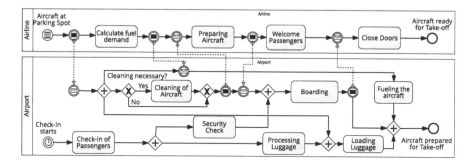

Fig. 1. Aircraft ground handling process.

Due to confidentiality concerns as well as privacy regulations, such as GDPR[1] and HIPAA[2], it is not always possible for organizations to share process execution data with each other. Exchanging execution data may reveal personal information of customers or it may expose business secrets. As a result, common techniques for process mining cannot be employed for inter-organizational business processes. Yet, analyzing these processes is often crucial for improving operational performance. With reference to the above scenario, the effective coordination of ground handling activities is crucial for both involved parties. It determines the number of flights an airport can operate and the number of flights an airline can offer. At the same time, each of the parties needs to protect their confidential data.

In this paper, we focus on the question of how to enable process mining for inter-organizational business processes without requiring the involved parties to share their private event logs or trust a third party. To this end, we propose an architecture for process mining based on *secure multi-party computation* (MPC) [25]. In essence, MPC aims at the realization of some computation over data from multiple parties, while exposing only the result of the computation, but keeping the input data private. We consider the setting of an MPC platform where the involved parties upload their event logs to a network of compute nodes. Before the upload, secret sharing algorithms locally split each single data value into different parts (i.e., shares) that are then stored at different nodes. Since each share does not provide any information about the original

---

[1] https://eur-lex.europa.eu/eli/reg/2016/679/oj.
[2] https://www.hhs.gov/hipaa/.

data, the uploaded event log is encrypted and exposed neither to the platform operator nor other involved parties. Nonetheless, the MPC platform enables the computation over the encrypted data through protocols for result sharing among the nodes.

We realize the above architecture to answer analysis queries that are common in process mining. Specifically, we show how to construct a frequency and time-annotated Directly-Follows Graph (DFG), which is a starting point for process discovery algorithms and performance analysis. While keeping the computed DFG private, we are revealing only the output of performance analysis queries such as finding the top-k bottlenecks (i.e. activities with longer cycle time) or the top-k most frequent hand-offs. We implement our proposed architecture using the Sharemind platform [7]. In order to tackle scalability issues that would be imposed by a naive implementation, we employ vectorization of event logs and propose a divide-and-conquer scheme for parallel processing of sub-logs. We test the effectiveness of these optimizations in experiments with real-world event logs.

The remainder of the paper is structured as follows. Section 2 lays out related work and the background for this work. Section 3 introduces our architecture for privacy-preserving inter-organizational process mining along with the optimizations needed for efficient implementation. An experimental evaluation is presented in Sect. 4, before Sect. 5 concludes the paper.

2   Background and Related Work

In this section, we review work on privacy-preserving process mining, inter-organizational process mining, and secure multi-party computation.

2.1   Privacy-Preserving Process Mining

The necessity of privacy-preserving process mining, due to legal developments such as the GDPR, was recently discussed in [18,19]. In general, two approaches have been established [11]: (i) anonymizing the event data to apply standard techniques to it, and (ii) directly incorporating privacy considerations in process mining techniques. The anonymization of event logs from one organization may be done using algorithms, like *PRETSA* [12], that provide privacy guarantees such as k-anonymity [23]. These notions, based on data similarity, are widely adopted and offer protection against certain attacks like the disclosure of the identity of individuals involved in the dataset. Approaches based on cryptography [10,20] have also been proposed. Following the idea to incorporate privacy guarantees directly in process mining techniques, algorithms for privacy-preserving process discovery [17,24] have been proposed. Recently, techniques for privacy-preserving process mining, following either of the aforementioned paradigms, have been made available for a large audience with the tool ELPaaS [5].

All of the above techniques, with the exception of [24], concern process mining for a single organization and have not yet been adopted or evaluated for an inter-organizational setting. While the focus of [24] is on an inter-organizational setting, the approach targets solely the creation of a process model, while we aim at answering a wide range of analysis queries about business processes.

2.2 Inter-organizational Process Mining

The problem of automated discovery of process models in an inter-organizational setting has been considered in [21, 26]. However, these approaches do not address privacy concerns. Similarly, another line of related research proposes techniques to compare executions of the same process across multiple organizations [2, 9], but without considering privacy requirements.

The problem of ensuring privacy in inter-organizational process mining has been addressed by Liu et al. [16]. They provide a process mining framework based on the assumption that the parties in the process are willing to share confidential information with a third (trusted) party. This assumption is unrealistic in many situations. In this paper, we address the problem of inter-organizational process mining in the context where the parties in the process are unwilling to share any execution data with each other or with a third party. In one of the embodiments of our proposal, a third party is involved for computation purposes, but this third party does not get access to any information during this computation.

2.3 Secure Multi-party Computation

Secure Multi-party Computation (MPC) [13] is a cryptographic functionality that allows n parties to cooperatively evaluate $(y_1, \ldots, y_n) = f(x_1, \ldots, x_n)$ for some function f, with the i-th party contributing the input x_i and learning the output y_i, and no party or an allowed coalition of parties learning nothing besides their own inputs and outputs. There exist a few approaches for constructing MPC protocols. Homomorphic secret sharing [22] is a common basis for MPC protocols. In such protocols, the arithmetic or Boolean circuit representing f is evaluated gate-by-gate, constructing secret-shared outputs of gates from their secret-shared inputs. Each evaluation requires some communication between parties (except for addition gates), hence the depth of the circuit determines the round complexity of the protocol. On the other hand, there exist protocols with low communication complexity [3], allowing the secure computation of quite complex functions f, as long as the circuit implementing it has a low multiplicative depth.

The complexity of MPC protocols is dependent on the number of parties jointly performing the computations. Hence the typical deployment of MPC has a small number of compute nodes, also known as *computation parties*, which execute the protocols for evaluating gates, while an unbounded number of parties may contribute the inputs and/or receive the outputs of the computation. Several frameworks support such deployments of MPC and provide APIs to simplify the development of privacy-preserving applications [4]. One of such frameworks is Sharemind [7], whose main protocol set is based on secret-sharing among three computing parties. In this paper, we build on top of Sharemind, but our techniques are also applicable to other secret sharing-based MPC systems.

In Sharemind, a party can play different roles: an input party, a computation party, and/or an output party. In the case where only two parties are involved in an inter-organizational process, these two parties play the role of input parties and also that of computing parties. To fulfill the requirements of Sharemind, they need to enroll a third computing node, which merely performs computations using secret shares from which it can infer no information.[3]

The Sharemind framework provides its own programming language, namely the SecreC language [6], for programming privacy-preserving applications. SecreC allows us to abstract away certain details of cryptographic protocols.

3   Multi-party Computation Based Process Mining

This section introduces our techniques for process mining based on secure multi-party computation. Section 3.1 first clarifies our model for inter-organizational process mining including the required input data and the obtained analysis results. We then introduce our architecture for realizing the respective analysis using secure multi-party computation in Sect. 3.2. In Sect. 3.3, we elaborate on vectorization and parallelization to improve the efficiency of our approach.

3.1   Model for Inter-organizational Process Mining

We consider a model in which an event log $L = \{e_1, \ldots, e_n\}$ is defined as a set of events $e = (i, a, ts)$, each capturing a single execution of an activity a at time ts, as part of a single instance i of the business process. Grouping events by the latter and ordering them according to their timestamp enables the construction of traces $t = \langle e_1, \ldots, e_m \rangle$, i.e., single executions of the process, so that we refer to i also as the trace identifier.

For an inter-organizational business process, an event log that records the process execution from start to end is commonly not available. Rather, different parties record sub-logs, built of events that denote activity executions at the respective party. To keep the notation concise, we consider a setting in which two parties, I_a and I_b, execute an inter-organizational process, e.g., the airport and the airline in our motivating example. Then, each of the two parties records an event log, denoted by L_a and L_b. Each of these logs is the projection of L on the events that denote activity executions at the respective parties I_a and I_b. We assume that each activity can only be executed by one of the parties, so that this projection is defined unambiguously.

For the above setting, we consider the scenario that the parties I_a and I_b want to answer some analysis queries Q over the inter-organizational event log L, yet *without* sharing their logs L_a and L_b with each other. More specifically, we focus on analysis queries that can be answered on a frequency or time-annotated

---

[3] When three or more parties are involved in a process, no external party is required.

DFG of the inter-organizational process. The basic DFG captures the frequencies with which the executions of two activities have been observed to directly follow each other in a trace. Moreover, we consider temporal annotations of the directly-follows dependencies in terms of time between the respective activity executions. Queries over the frequency and time-annotated DFGs allow us to analyze the main paths of the process, the rarely executed paths, as well as the activities that most contribute to delays in a process. Note though that only query answers are to be revealed whereas the actual DFG shall be kept private.

Formally, the time-annotated DFG is captured by an $|A| \times |A|$ matrix, where A is the set of all possible activities of the process. Each cell contains a tuple (c, Δ). The counter c represents the frequency with which a directly-follows dependency has been observed in L, i.e., for the cell (a_1, a_2) it is the number of times that two events $e_1 = (i_1, a_1, ts_1)$ and $e_2 = (i_2, a_2, ts_2)$ follow each other directly in some trace (i.e., $i_1 = i_2$) of L. Also, Δ is the total sum of the time passed by between all occurrences of the respective events, i.e., $ts_2 - ts_1$ for the above events.

In inter-organizational process mining, the above time-annotated DFG cannot be computed directly, as this would require the parties to share their sub-logs.

3.2 MPC Architecture for Process Mining

To enable inter-organizational process mining *without* requiring parties to share their event logs with each other, we propose an architecture based on secure multi-party computation (MPC). As outlined in Fig. 2, we rely on a platform for MPC (in our case Sharemind [7]) that takes the event logs of the participating parties, i.e., L_a and L_b, as secret-shared input. Inside the MPC platform, the respective data is processed in a privacy-preserving way in order to answer analysis queries over the time-annotated DFG computed from that data. In Fig. 3, we present a running example of the processing steps of the system.

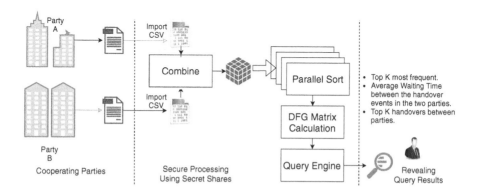

Fig. 2. Overview of the proposed approach

Below we summarize the functionality enbodied in the proposed MPC platform for inter-organizational process mining.

Preprocessing. Each party performs the preparation of its log at its own site. The parties share the number of unique activities and the maximum number of events per trace. In Fig. 3a, we show an example with two traces. In the preprocessing step, all traces are padded to the same length, as illustrated with the blue event in Fig. 3a. The activities are transformed into a one-hot encoding that is used for masking at the DFG calculation step, as will be explained later. The logs are sorted by traces.

Combination. The parties upload their event logs L_a and L_b to the MPC platform in a secret-shared manner. That is, the values (i, a, ts) of each event (encoded as integers) are split into shares, which do not provide any information on the original values and are stored at different nodes of the platform. This way, each party can only see the total number of records uploaded by each party, but not the particular data. Subsequently, the logs are unified, creating a single log of events L. The combination is performed in a manner to divide the logs into processing chunks. As long as we are making the number of events per trace is fixed, that is possible by dividing the index by the number of traces for each event and assigning data from the same trace to the same chunk. In Fig. 3a, the system processes one trace with its own chunk.

Sorting. To calculate the annotated DFG, we have to determine which events follow each other in a trace by grouping the events by their trace identifier and ordering them by their timestamp. Since the trace identifier is secret-shared, we cannot group events directly. Instead, we use a privacy-preserving quicksort algorithm [14] as implemented in Sharemind to sort the events by their trace identifier. Applying the same algorithm also to the secret-shared timestamps ensures that the events of the same trace follow each other in the order of their timestamps, which is illustrated as the last step in Fig. 3a.

DFG Matrix Calculation. Next, we construct the DFG matrix inside the MPC platform, keeping it secret. Since the information on the activity of an event is secret-shared, we cannot simply process the events of traces sequentially as the matrix cell to update would not be known. Hence, we adopt a one-hot encoding for activities, so that each possible activity is represented by a binary vector of length $|A|$. To mask the actual number of possible activities, the set over which the vector is defined may further include some padding, i.e., the vector length can be chosen to be larger than $|A|$. Now, if we compute the *outer product* of such vectors for activities a_1 and a_2, we get a mask matrix M such that $M[a_1, a_2] = 1$, while all other entries are 0. An example of such masks is given in Fig. 3b. The first mask represents the directly-follows dependency from activity A to B of our running example. The second mask encodes the directly-follows dependency from activity A to C. For all sequential pairs of events in the sorted log, we sum up these matrices to get the frequency count c of the directly-follows dependency

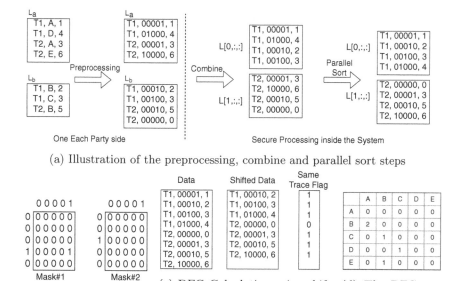

(a) Illustration of the preprocessing, combine and parallel sort steps

(b) Example of two masks

(c) DFG Calculation using shift and a flag

(d) The DFG matrix with counts

Fig. 3. Example of two event logs and their processing steps inside the system

for (a_1, a_2). Multiplying M by the duration between two events further enables us to derive the total sum duration passed, i.e., Δ, of the directly-follows-relation. The duration operation is performed between every two consecutive events of the same trace. We can perform the duration calculation by using an element-wise vector subtraction by duplicating the dataset and then shifting its events by one as in Fig. 3c. Technically, the outer product is a function that is realized as a protocol over secret-shared data in Sharemind, and its runtime complexity is linear in $|A|$ [15].

However, the above approach could mix up events of different traces. We therefore also compute a flag b that is 1, if the trace identifiers of two events are equivalent, and 0 otherwise, which is illustrated as the "Same Trace Flag" column in Fig. 3c. Then, we multiply the mask matrix M by b, so that the values of M are ignored, if $b = 0$. Again, the functionality for comparison and multiplication can be traced back to predefined protocols in Sharemind. We show the DFG matrix with counts of our running example in Fig. 3d.

Algorithm 1 summarizes the computation of the annotated DFG from the sorted, combined log L, where $\llbracket \cdot \rrbracket$ denotes a secret-shared data value.

Query Answering. A query Q defines a subset S of the annotated DFG, which is generated by the MPC platform and revealed to the participating parties. Through sharing the S solely, but not the complete annotated DFG, we are able to limit the amount of information each party can learn about the process. As an example, consider the query to derive the average waiting time between the

---

Algorithm 1. Calculating the combined, annotated DFG($[\![L]\!]$)

INPUT: The sorted, combined event log $[\![L]\!]$ of length n.
OUTPUT: Annotated DFG comprising a count matrix $[\![G]\!]$ and a time matrix $[\![W]\!]$.

1: Initialize $[\![G]\!] = 0$, $[\![W]\!] = 0$
2: **for all** $j \in \{1, \ldots, n-1\}$ **do**
3:     $[\![b]\!] \leftarrow ([\![L[j-1].i]\!] = [\![L[j].i]\!]);$ //compute the flag for traces
4:     $[\![M]\!] \leftarrow [\![b]\!] \cdot ([\![L[j-1].a]\!] \otimes [\![L[j].a]\!]);$ //compute the outer product
5:     $[\![G]\!] \leftarrow [\![G]\!] + [\![M]\!];$ //incorporate the current dependency
6:     $[\![W]\!] \leftarrow [\![W]\!] + [\![M]\!] \cdot ([\![L[j].ts]\!] - [\![L[j-1].ts]\!]);$ //Incorporate the time lag
7: **return** $[\![G]\!], [\![W]\!]$

---

handover events between the two parties. Based on the secret-shared DFG, the respective activities may be identified through grouping and sorting the events, similar to the procedure outlined above, which is again based on the predefined protocols of an MPC platform such as Sharemind.

3.3 Performance Optimizations

Inter-organizational process mining using the above general architecture might suffer from scalability issues. The reason is that privacy-preserving computation through protocols over secret-shared data is inevitably less efficient than plain computation. Hence, even for functions that have a generally low runtime complexity ($\mathcal{O}(n)$ for the combination, $\mathcal{O}(n \log(n))$ for the sorting, $\mathcal{O}(nm^2)$ for the calculation of the annotated DFG, where n is the log length and m is the number of activities), there is a non-negligible overhead induced by MPC. For instance, a naive realization of the quicksort algorithm to sort events would require $\mathcal{O}(n \log(n))$ rounds of communication between the nodes and $\mathcal{O}(n \log(n))$ value comparisons per round [14]. We therefore consider two angles to improve the efficiency of the analysis, namely vectorization and parallelization.

Vectorization. A computation that adopts a single-instruction multiple-data (SIMD) approach is highly recommended in MPC applications. Since MPC assumes continuous interaction between distributed nodes, the number of communication rounds shall be reduced as much as possible. For instance, while computing n multiplications sequentially would result in n rounds of communication, one may alternatively multiply element-wise two vectors of length n, for which one round of network communication is sufficient. Sharemind offers efficient protocols for such vector-based functions [15].

Parallelization. Further runtime improvements are obtained by parallelizing the algorithm itself. Again, our goal is to reduce the number of rounds of communication among the nodes of the MPC platform. We, therefore, split the input data into *chunks*, such that all chunks can be processed independently from each other. In our scenario, this is done by grouping the party logs by trace, or by a group of traces, generating an annotated DFG per group, and finally integrating the different DFGs. Since events of the same trace will never occur in different chunks, instead of sorting one log of length n, we will need to sort c chunks of length n/c each. Since the communication complexity of a privacy-preserving quicksort is $O(n \cdot \log n)$ [14], this improves efficiency.

The above approach raises the question of determining the size of the chunks. Separating each trace reveals the total number of events of that trace provided by a party, which may be critical from a privacy perspective. On the other hand, a small chunk size reduces the overhead of sorting. This leads to a trade-off between runtime performance and privacy considerations.

However, in our current implementation, all chunks must have the same length, as Sharemind allows parallel sorting only for equal-length vectors. Therefore, we apply padding to the traces in the log, adding dummy events (for which an empty vector in the one-hot encoding represents the activity so that the events are ignored for the DFG calculation) until the number of events of the longest trace is reached. Such padding may be employed locally, by each party, and also has the benefit that the length of individual traces is not revealed.

4   Evaluation

We implemented the proposed approach on top of the Sharemind multi-party computation platform.[4] The source code of our implementation is available at https://github.com/Elkoumy/shareprom. The implementation is written using the SecreC programming language supported by Sharemind.

Using this implementation, we conducted feasibility and scalability experiments, specifically to address the following research questions:

RQ1: How do the characteristics of the input event logs influence the performance of the secure multi-party computation of the DFG?

RQ2: What is the effect of increasing the number of parallel chunks on the performance of the multi-party computation of the DFG?

4.1   Datasets

The proposed approach is designed to compute the DFG of an inter-organizational process where the event log is distributed across multiple parties, and each party is responsible for executing a subset of the activities (i.e. *event types*) of the process. We are not aware of publicly available real-life datasets with this property. We identified a collection of synthetic inter-organizational business process event logs [8]. However, these logs are too small to allow us to conduct performance experiments (a few dozen traces per log). On the other hand, there is a collection of real-life event logs of intra-organizational processes comprising logs of varying sizes and characteristics[5]. From this collection, we selected three logs with different size and complexity (cf. Table 1):

---

[4] https://sharemind-sdk.github.io.
[5] https://data.4tu.nl/repository/collection:event_logs_real.

BPIC 2013 This event log captures incident and problem management process at an IT department of a car production company.

Credit Requirement This event log comes from a process for background checking for the purpose of granting credit at a Dutch bank. It has a simple control-flow structure: All traces follow the same sequence of activities.

Traffic Fines This event log comes from a process to collect payment of fines from traffic law violations at a local police office in Italy.

Table 1. Event logs for evaluation

Event Log	# Events	# Cases	# Activities	# Events in Case		
				Avg	Max	Min
BPIC 2013	6,660	1,432	6	4.478	35	1
Credit Requirement	50,525	10,034	8	15	15	15
Traffic Fines	561,470	150,370	11	3.73	20	2

To simulate an inter-organizational setting, we use a round-robin approach to assign each event type (activity) in the log to one of two parties. Hence, each party executes half of the event types.

4.2 Experimental Setup

To answer the above questions, we use the following performance measures:

o **Runtime.** We define runtime as the amount of time needed to transform the event logs of the two parties securely into an annotated DFG. We also report the throughput, the number of events processed by the system per second, to provide a complementary perspective.

o **Communication Overhead.** We define the communication overhead as the amount of data transferred between the computing parties during the multi-party computation. We measure this overhead as the volume of the data sent and received. The communication overhead gives insights into how much the performance of the multi-party computation would degrade if the computing nodes of the parties were distributed across a wide-area network.

We performed five runs per dataset per experiment. We report the average maximum values for latency and the average value for both throughput and communication overhead, across the five runs. We used *Nethogs*[6] to measure the communication overhead, and we report the average value per compute node. The experiments were run in an environment with three physical servers as compute nodes with Sharemind installed on them. Each server has an AMD Processor 6276 and 192 GB RAM. The servers are connected using a 1GB Ethernet switch.

---

[6] https://github.com/raboof/nethogs.

The experiments focus on the time needed to construct the annotated DFG, since it is the most sophisticated and time-consuming portion of the proposed analysis pipeline, due to the communication required between the compute nodes. Once the annotated DFG is available, stored in a secret-shared manner, the calculation of the actual queries has a lower complexity.

4.3   Results

Runtime Experiment. In Fig. 4a, we illustrate the observed execution time when varying the number of chunks used in the parallelization. We plot a bar for each chunk size. Each bar represents the runtime of the parallel sort in blue and the run time of the DFG calculation in orange. From Fig. 4a, we conclude that the runtime decreases with an increasing number of chunks, due to the parallel sorting of chunks. We also note that the runtime for the DFG calculation stays constant. In Fig. 4b, we report the number of processed events per second when varying the number of chunks. We find a consistent improvement for the throughput across all event logs.

Regarding RQ1, we summarise that the proportion of runtime between sorting and DFG calculation differs based on the event log characteristics. For the log with the largest number of event types, the DFG calculation makes up the most substantial proportion of the total runtime. In contrast, the proportion is significantly lower for the logs with a smaller number of event types. A possible explanation for this finding is the increasing size of the vectors required to represent each activity due to our bit-vector representation. Such increase results in more computational heavy calculations. Regarding RQ2, we conclude that the runtime decreases for event logs with an increasing number of chunks.

Communication Overhead. In Fig. 4c, we present the amount of data transferred to each server, again also varying the number of chunks. We observe that the communication overhead decreases with an increase in the number of chunks. These findings confirm our earlier findings regarding RQ2. In summary, a higher number of chunks leads to improved performance across all three measures.

Threats to Validity. The evaluation reported above has two limitations. First, the event logs used in the evaluation, while coming from real-life systems, are intra-organizational event logs, which we have split into separate logs to simulate an inter-organizational setting. It is possible that these logs do not capture the communication patterns found in inter-organizational processes. Second, the number of event logs is reduced, which limits the generalizability of the conclusions. The results suggest that the proposed technique can handle small-to-medium-sized logs, with relatively short traces, but there may be other characteristics of event logs that affect the performance of the proposed approach.

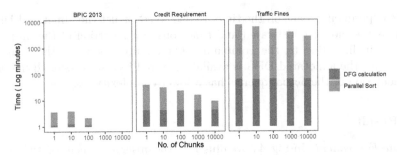

(a) Runtime Experiment: Execution Time (Log) vs no. of Chunks.

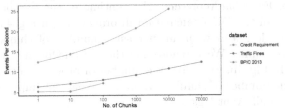

(b) Throughput Experiment: Events per Second vs no. of Chunks.

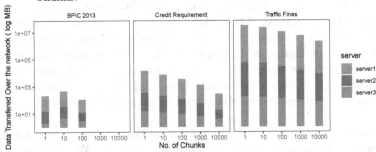

(c) Communication Overhead Experiment: Data Transferred (Log) vs no. of Chunks.

Fig. 4. Experimental evaluation of the proposed approach

5   Conclusion

This paper introduced a framework for inter-organizational process mining based on secure multi-party computation. The framework enables two or more parties to perform basic process mining operations over the partial logs of an inter-organizational process held by each party, without any information being shared besides: (i) the output of the queries that the parties opt to disclose; and (ii) three high-level log statistics: the number of traces per log, the number of event types, and the maximum trace length. The paper specifically focuses on the computation of the DFG, annotated with frequency and temporal information. This is a basic structure used by process mining tools to perform various operations, including automated process discovery and various performance analysis queries (e.g. top-k bottlenecks and least-frequent and most-frequent flow dependencies).

To mitigate the high-performance overhead commonly observed for secure multi-party computation, we introduced two optimizations over the basic DFG computation algorithm: one based on vectorization of the event log and the other based on a divide-and-conquer strategy, where the log is processed in chunks.

An evaluation using real world event logs shows that with these optimizations, it is possible to compute the DFG of real-life logs with execution times that make this technique usable in practice. The divide-and-conquer approach provides opportunities to scale up the proposed technique by using a map-reduce execution-style, however not to a sufficient level to enable interactive process mining (which requires execution times in the order of seconds). Also, the approach is not able to handle logs with thousands of traces.

In future work, we will explore further optimizations to address these limitations, for example, by taking into account metadata about the event types in the event log where hand-offs occur between participants. Usually, such event types are known as they correspond to message exchange. Therefore, it becomes possible to split the logs into a "private" part and a "public" part (the latter being the points where hand-offs occur), and to process them separately using different approaches.

Another avenue for future work is to combine the proposed approach with approaches that provide complementary guarantees such as differential privacy techniques. The latter techniques allow us to noisify the DFG or the outputs from the queries of the DFG to limit the information leaked by these outputs.

Acknowledgments. This research is partly funded by ERDF via the Estonian Centre of Excellence in ICT (EXCITE) and the IT Academy programme.

References

1. van der Aalst, W.M.P.: Process Mining - Data Science in Action, Second edn. Springer, Heidelberg (2016). https://doi.org/10.1007/978-3-662-49851-4
2. Aksu, Ü., Schunselaar, D.M., Reijers, H.A.: A cross-organizational process mining framework for obtaining insights from software products: accurate comparison challenges. In: 2016 IEEE 18th Conference on Business Informatics (CBI), vol. 1, pp. 153–162. IEEE (2016)
3. Araki, T., Furukawa, J., Lindell, Y., Nof, A., Ohara, K.: High-throughput semi-honest secure three-party computation with an honest majority. In: Proceedings of the 2016 ACM SIGSAC Conference on Computer and Communications Security, Vienna, Austria, 24–28 October 2016, pp. 805–817 (2016)
4. Archer, D.W., et al.: From keys to databases—real-world applications of secure multi-party computation. Comput. J. **61**(12), 1749–1771 (2018)
5. Bauer, M., Fahrenkrog-Petersen, S.A., Koschmider, A., Mannhardt, F., van der Aa, H., Weidlich, M.: Elpaas: event log privacy as a service. In: Proceedings of the Dissertation Award, Doctoral Consortium, and Demonstration Track at BPM 2019 co-located with 17th International Conference on Business Process Management, BPM 2019, Vienna, Austria, 1–6 September 2019, pp. 159–163 (2019)

6. Bogdanov, D., Laud, P., Randmets, J.: Domain-polymorphic programming of privacy-preserving applications. In: Proceedings of the Ninth Workshop on Programming Languages and Analysis for Security, p. 53. ACM (2014)
7. Bogdanov, D., Laur, S., Willemson, J.: Sharemind: a framework for fast privacy-preserving computations. In: Jajodia, S., Lopez, J. (eds.) ESORICS 2008. LNCS, vol. 5283, pp. 192–206. Springer, Heidelberg (2008). https://doi.org/10.1007/978-3-540-88313-5_13
8. Borkowski, M., Fdhila, W., Nardelli, M., Rinderle-Ma, S., Schulte, S.: Event-based failure prediction in distributed business processes. Inf. Syst. (2017)
9. Buijs, J.C., van Dongen, B.F., van der Aalst, W.M.: Towards cross-organizational process mining in collections of process models and their executions. In: Daniel, F., Barkaoui, K., Dustdar, S. (eds.) International Conference on Business Process Management, pp. 2–13. Springer, Heidelberg (2011). https://doi.org/10.1007/978-3-642-28115-0_2
10. Burattin, A., Conti, M., Turato, D.: Toward an anonymous process mining. In: 2015 3rd International Conference on Future Internet of Things and Cloud, pp. 58–63. IEEE (2015)
11. Fahrenkrog-Petersen, S.A.: Providing privacy guarantees in process mining. In: (CAiSE Doctoral Consortium 2019), Rome, Italy, 3–7 June 2019, pp. 23–30 (2019)
12. Fahrenkrog-Petersen, S.A., van der Aa, H., Weidlich, M.: PRETSA: event log sanitization for privacy-aware process discovery. In: International Conference on Process Mining, ICPM 2019, Aachen, Germany, 24–26 June 2019, pp. 1–8 (2019)
13. Goldreich, O., Micali, S., Wigderson, A.: How to play any mental game or a completeness theorem for protocols with honest majority. In: Aho, A.V. (ed.) Proceedings of the 19th Annual ACM Symposium on Theory of Computing, pp. 218–229. ACM (1987)
14. Hamada, K., Kikuchi, R., Ikarashi, D., Chida, K., Takahashi, K.: Practically efficient multi-party sorting protocols from comparison sort algorithms. In: Kwon, T., Lee, M.-K., Kwon, D. (eds.) ICISC 2012. LNCS, vol. 7839, pp. 202–216. Springer, Heidelberg (2013). https://doi.org/10.1007/978-3-642-37682-5_15
15. Laud, P., Pankova, A.: Privacy-preserving frequent itemset mining for sparse and dense data. In: Lipmaa, H., Mitrokotsa, A., Matulevičius, R. (eds.) NordSec 2017. LNCS, vol. 10674, pp. 139–155. Springer, Cham (2017). https://doi.org/10.1007/978-3-319-70290-2_9
16. Liu, C., Duan, H., Zeng, Q., Zhou, M., Lu, F., Cheng, J.: Towards comprehensive support for privacy preservation cross-organization business process mining. IEEE Trans. Serv. Comput. 12(4), 639–653 (2019)
17. Mannhardt, F., Koschmider, A., Baracaldo, N., Weidlich, M., Michael, J.: Privacy-preserving process mining - differential privacy for event logs. Bus. Inf. Syst. Eng. 61(5), 595–614 (2019)
18. Mannhardt, F., Petersen, S.A., Oliveira, M.F.: Privacy challenges for process mining in human-centered industrial environments. In: 2018 14th International Conference on Intelligent Environments (IE), pp. 64–71. IEEE (2018)
19. Pika, A., Wynn, M.T., Budiono, S., ter Hofstede, A.H., van der Aalst, W.M., Reijers, H.A.: Towards privacy-preserving process mining in healthcare. In: Proceedings of the Workshop on Process-Oriented Data Science in Healthcare (PODS4H) (2019)
20. Rafiei, M., von Waldthausen, L., van der Aalst, W.M.P.: Ensuring confidentiality in process mining. In: Proceedings of the 8th International Symposium on Data-driven Process Discovery and Analysis (SIMPDA 2018), Seville, Spain, 13–14 December 2018, pp. 3–17 (2018)

21. Schulz, K.A., Orlowska, M.E.: Facilitating cross-organisational workflows with a workflow view approach. Data Knowl. Eng. **51**(1), 109–147 (2004)
22. Shamir, A.: How to share a secret. Commun. ACM **22**(11), 612–613 (1979)
23. Sweeney, L.: k-anonymity: a model for protecting privacy. Int. J. Uncertainty Fuzziness Knowl.-Based Syst. **10**(05), 557–570 (2002)
24. Tillem, G., Erkin, Z., Lagendijk, R.L.: Mining encrypted software logs using alpha algorithm. In: SECRYPT, pp. 267–274 (2017)
25. Yao, A.C.: Protocols for secure computations. In: 23rd Annual Symposium on Foundations of Computer Science (SFCS 1982), pp. 160–164. IEEE (1982)
26. Zeng, Q., Sun, S.X., Duan, H., Liu, C., Wang, H.: Cross-organizational collaborative workflow mining from a multi-source log. Decis. Support Syst. **54**(3), 1280–1301 (2013)

Process Models and Visualizations
(BPMDS 2020)

Visualizing Business Process Evolution

Anton Yeshchenko[(✉)] [iD], Dina Bayomie [iD], Steven Gross, and Jan Mendling [iD]

Vienna University of Economics and Business, Vienna, Austria
{anton.yeshchenko,dina.sayed.bayomie.sobh,steven.gross,
jan.mendling}@wu.ac.at

Abstract. Literature in business process research has recognized that process execution adjusts dynamically to the environment, both intentionally and unintentionally. This dynamic change of frequently followed actions is called process drift. Existing process drift approaches focus to a great extent on drift point detection, i.e., on points in time when a process execution changes significantly. What is largely neglected by process drift approaches is the identification of temporal dynamics of different clusters of process execution, how they interrelate, and how they change in dominance over time. In this paper, we introduce process evolution analysis (PEA) as a technique that aims to support the exploration of process cluster interrelations over time. This approach builds on and synthesizes existing approaches from the process drift, trace clustering, and process visualization literature. Based on the process evolution analysis, we visualize the interrelation of trace clusters over time for descriptive and prescriptive purposes.

Keywords: Process drift · Process change · Process evolution · Process trace clustering

1 Introduction

Business process management (BPM) has long researched business processes through a prescriptive lens. This perspective emphasizes the static nature of processes, their design, and their execution. The descriptive perspective, on the other hand, acknowledges the dynamic nature of processes and their intentional and unintentional adjustment over time due to changes in the environment, technological capabilities, seasonal differences, and other factors [1, 2]. Similarly, literature in routine research has increasingly recognized the dynamic change of routine executions over time [3, 4].

To address this dynamism, recent research aims to identify changes in processes over time. Most prominently, process drift uses event logs to detect points in time when changes take place [1, 5]. While process drift offers insights into when changes in the process happen, it does not provide information on how different executions of the same process interrelate with each other, in particular, when and how similar process executions occur and dominate. Thus, the meaningful interpretation of process evolution over time, i.e., the changes in the process execution over time, remains a research challenge. Evolution is defined as a recurring variation, selection, and retention among entities of a designated population [6]. We build on this concept by declaring all traces

© Springer Nature Switzerland AG 2020
S. Nurcan et al. (Eds.): BPMDS 2020/EMMSAD 2020, LNBIP 387, pp. 185–192, 2020.
https://doi.org/10.1007/978-3-030-49418-6_12

generated during the execution of a process as the designated population, while the variation, selection, and retention (i.e. the appearance, disappearance, and change) happens among sub-groups of these traces. This is due to scarce environmental resources [6] which correspond to the organizational resources available for the execution of the process.

In order to advance our understanding of business process evolution, this research aims to answer the following research question: *How can temporal dynamics of different process executions be analyzed?* To approach this question, we propose a process evolution analysis (PEA) method that uses process execution clustering and time-series line plots to study the evolution of the process execution clusters over time. PEA thereby aims to show insights on how clusters of process executions are interrelated overtime on a process evolution graph.

This paper proceeds as follows. Section two discusses the main concepts. Section three describes our research method. Section four presents the results of applying PEA. Section five concludes with a discussion of the results, limitations of the approach, and future research directions.

2 Background

In this section, we describe the main concepts used in this paper. First, we describe and emphasize the difference in our approach to process drift. Next, we outline the process mining method to find trace clustering. It is used to reduce the complexity of process mining problems by grouping the process instances based on their similarity, i.e., trace fitness, execution time, etc. Lastly, we summarize the state of the art of different visualization techniques that influenced our technique.

2.1 Process Drift

Process drift refers to a change in processes executions and is known as a key challenge in process mining [7]. Process drift is extensively studied in the process mining literature [1, 5, 8, 9] with a focus on drift points, drift types [1, 8], and drift visualizations [5, 9]. Seeliger et al. [10] define process drift as a significant behavioral change during the execution of a process that has occurred over time. A drift in a process, according to their definition, occurs when almost all traces are influenced by that drift [10]. Similarly, Maaradji et al. [1] focus on the detection of process drifts by identifying statistically significant differences between the observed process behavior of different intervals in time. Yeshchenko et al. [5] focus on the detection of separate behavioral drifts within a process that are simultaneously present in the event log.

Most existing process drift research interprets process change as a change of the underlying control flow (implicit process model change). However, changes in the process can also be viewed through various process performance measures that are important for the analysis of the process executions [11]. These measures show how the process characteristics (such as cycle time, cost per instance, etc.) change over time. Existing process drift approaches thereby focus on the discovery of behavioral change within the event log, ignoring the impact on process measures. That creates a process overview where the analyst might be incapable of inferring what change in the process is important enough to manage. Our method allows for tracking the process KPIs with correspondence to the change.

2.2 Trace Clustering

Trace clustering techniques aim to reduce the complexity of process mining problems [12–15]. These techniques simplify an event log by creating groups of traces based on some trace similarity metric. The clustering procedure ensures that the clusters have minimal in-cluster distance between traces based on that metric. The metrics used in trace clustering range from the structural similarity between traces (i.e., based on fitness [12]) and performance-related, such as the cost per instance and the cycle time [15].

One use case of trace clustering algorithms is to simplify the problem of process discovery on sparse event logs to provide more accurate and comprehensive results [12]. Process mining literature emphasizes the use of trace clustering for the discovery of models which are based on the clusters. Instead, our approach directly explores the interrelations of different clusters using visualization techniques.

2.3 Visualization of Change

Process mining research focuses on discovering precise process models rather than exploring the change in processes. On the other hand, the visualization field is rich with approaches to analyze such data [16]. The canonical example of visualizing change is line plotting, where the x-axis corresponds to a time, and the y-axis displays the selected measure. More recently, developments on these types of graphs are visualization of opinion change in social media [17–22]. These approaches are built upon the plots that emphasize the change of variables with time and include line plots [18, 20, 21], theme river [19, 21], and Sankey diagram [17–20] representations. Our approach is influenced by the ideas from the field to represents the change of several time-series.

3 Process Evolution Analysis Technique

Figure 1 shows an overview of our proposed process evolution analysis (PEA) technique, which visualizes the change of the process execution behavior over time. PEA takes an event log as input and produces a time series line chart as output. PEA has three steps to generate the required visualization. The first step is using trace clustering to partitioning the log, then compute some process metric over the clusters (e.g., the number of cases for each cluster). Finally, PEA visualizes the clusters and their process metric values to show the process evolved.

Trace clustering – an event log is clustered into several clusters in order to find distinct regions in the process behavior. There are different techniques used to cluster an event log [14]. A simple cluster technique is partitioning the log based on time window interval. For instance, cases that occurred in the first quarter of the year are in the same cluster. Although, cases that occurred in the last quarter are in another cluster. One established clustering technique is based on trace similarity to achieve high fitness

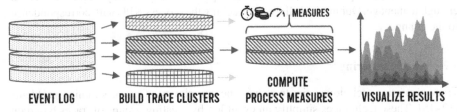

Fig. 1. Overview of the proposed approach

between the cases within the same cluster [12, 13]. Another technique to cluster the log is using the cycle time to distribute the cases over the clusters [15]. Thus, all the cases that have a long cycle time are in the same cluster, while cases with a short cycle time are in another cluster.

Process evolution graphs – We use the time-series line plot [18, 20, 21] and theme river [19, 22] visualization in order to analyze the change in the behavior between the different clusters. The graph shows the change of a process metric over time for each trace cluster. Different process execution characteristics can be measured; for instance, the number of executed cases per day, the average cycle time of cases per month, or the average resource workload per day.

By combining trace clustering with the computation of process metrics and visualizing the result on a time-series plot, behavioral changes in the process execution can be made visible.

4   Findings

Experiment setup – We conduct two experiments on two datasets and visualize process evolution using different trace clustering techniques. The first experiment uses the log from the help desk of an Italian software company[1]. The traces are clustered based on the cycle time per trace with the python script, made available on GitHub[2]. The clusters are used to visualize process evolution using a theme-rivers chart. Each generated cluster represents a different cycle time behavior. The second experiment uses the traffic logs from BPIC[3]. We applied a trace clustering based on trace fitness using ActiTrace ProM plugin [12] with the following settings: target ICS fitness 0.9, the maximal number of clusters is 6, and add the remaining traces to other clusters. Each generated cluster represents a different process behavior. Moreover, we visualize process evolution using a time-series line chart.

For the first experiment, Fig. 2 shows the number of cases for each cluster over 50 months. The x-axis depicts the months within this timespan, while the y-axis represents the number of active cases. As has been described before, the traces were clustered according to the cycle time of each case. The 25% of cases with the slowest cycle time

---

[1] https://data.4tu.nl/repository/uuid:0c60edf1-6f83-4e75-9367-4c63b3e9d5bb.

[2] https://github.com/yesanton/Visualizing-Business-Process-Evolution.

[3] https://data.4tu.nl/repository/uuid:270fd440-1057-4fb9-89a9-b699b47990f5.

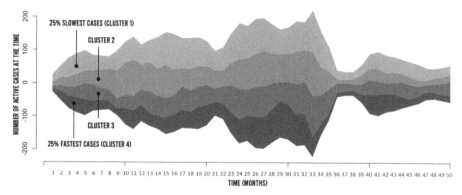

Fig. 2. Number of cases for each cluster over time for *help desk* event log

are in Cluster 1. Cluster 2 and 3 follow to cluster 1 in steps of 25%. Cluster 4 contains 25% of cases, which were the fastest.

The graph can be analyzed in several ways. First, the *cluster containing the most active cases at a certain point in time* can be identified. For instance, cluster 1 (25% slowest cases in the process) contains the most active cases in the first five months. In the sixth month, however, cluster 2 is dominating the other clusters, until most cases can be found in cluster 1 from month 15 to 26. Second, the *discrepancy in case distributions* between the different clusters can be observed. One example is the timespan from the 7th to 20th month, in which there is a substantial discrepancy of active cases for the clusters (i.e., the number of cases in each cluster differ considerably) compared to the timespan between the 24th and 28th month (i.e., the clusters contain a similar amount of cases). Third, it can be seen whether the number of cases for the *clusters correlates over time*. For instance, all clusters in the timespan between the 33rd and 36th month decrease similarly in number. However, between the 27th and 32nd month, cluster 3 and cluster 4 negatively correlate. Fourth, *quick changes in a cluster* can be spotted. For instance, cluster 2 is more than doubled its active cases within a quarter of a year from month 7 onwards.

For the second experiment, Fig. 3 shows the number of cases for each cluster over 56 months. Differently to the previous experiment, the clusters were not generated by grouping traces with similar cycle time but based on their trace fitness (ICS-fitness). Six clusters were generated. It can be seen that cluster 1 dominated all other clusters in terms of active cases until month 41. From this point in time, the cluster does not contain enough active cases to be visible on the graphical representation. Until the 41st month, cluster 1 also seems to correlate with cluster 2, while the magnitude of changes for cluster 1 is much bigger. Sudden changes are also visible. In month and 28, cluster 1 increases substantially in the number of active cases within one month by the factor 3 to 4. Clusters 3, 4, 5, and 6 are having fewer cases than 250 for most of the time; thus, they are not paying a significant role during the execution of the process.

Cluster 3 is dominating clusters 4, 5, and 6 in the period between the 1st to 7th and 53rd to 55th. Aside from that period, no clear dominance can be found within these four clusters. Cluster 5 seems to be inactive for most of the time.

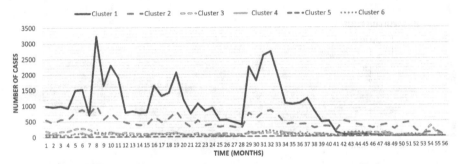

Fig. 3. Number of cases for each cluster overtime for *traffic fines* event log

5 Discussion and Conclusion

In this paper, we described the process evolution analysis (PEA) method, which visual-izes different clusters of process executions and their interrelation over time. PEA builds on the concepts of trace clustering, process drift, and process visualization.

PEA has several practical and theoretical implications. From a practical viewpoint, PEA can be used as a technique to analyze process executions and to identify undesired behaviors that emerge. For instance, if the clusters are generated by categorizing cases based on their cycling time, a rise of cases with a long cycling time can be identified, and take the required actions. Thereby, PEA can be used for real-time analysis of process execution to intervene directly, or as a retrospect, analysis to identify recurring patterns of undesired process behaviors. The same applies to clusters, which were generated by their trace fitness. The underlying process models from these clusters can be generated through process discovery (e.g., by the use of a process mining tool) and thereby unwanted process executions discovered. The evolution of these clusters can again be made explicit through PEA.

From a theoretical point, this is a first step towards synthesizing research on trace clustering, process drift, and process visualization into one technique. By doing so, we enabled the identification and analysis of changes within the different clusters of traces over time. While process drift focuses mainly on points in time in which the general process behavior changes [10], PEA shows how these underlying behavioral changes interrelate over time. It also extends existing research on process clustering, which has mainly focused on discovering the underlying process models of these clusters for further analysis.

We recommend conducting future research in the following directions. First, alterna-tive forms of visualization could be investigated. One such promising visualization is the stacked graphs, which is designed to facilitate the identification of patterns, trends, and unexpected occurrences [23]. Future research should investigate which forms of visu-alization for PEA are useful, taking into consideration different application scenarios. Second, different information besides the number of active cases within a cluster could be plotted on the graph. For instance, the y-axis could depict the average cycle time for active cases, which start at a specific time. Third, other forms of clustering the traces could be explored. In this paper, we clustered the traces according to their trace fitness and the cycle time of the cases. One alternative could be to cluster the traces according to the costs or revenue of the cases to investigate the evolution of these clusters.

References

1. Maaradji, A., Dumas, M., La Rosa, M., Ostovar, A.: Fast and Accurate Business Process Drift Detection. Springer, Cham (2015). https://doi.org/10.1007/978-3-319-23063-4
2. Pentland, B., Recker, J., Kim, I.: Capturing reality in flight? Empirical tools for strong process theory. In: Thirty Eighth International Conference on Information Systems, pp. 1–12, Seoul (2017)
3. Feldman, M.S., Pentland, B.T.: Reconceptualizing organizational routines as a source of flexibility and change. Adm. Sci. Q. **48**, 94 (2003). https://doi.org/10.2307/3556620
4. Pentland, B.T., Feldman, M.S., Becker, M.C., Liu, P.: Dynamics of organizational routines: a generative model. J. Manag. Stud. **49**, 1484–1508 (2012). https://doi.org/10.1111/j.1467-6486.2012.01064.x
5. Yeshchenko, A., Di Ciccio, C., Mendling, J., Polyvyanyy, A.: Comprehensive process drift detection with visual analytics. In: Laender, A.H.F., Pernici, B., Lim, E.-P., de Oliveira, J.P.M. (eds.) ER 2019. LNCS, vol. 11788, pp. 119–135. Springer, Cham (2019). https://doi.org/10.1007/978-3-030-33223-5_11
6. van de Ven, A.H., Poole, M.S.: Explaining development and change in organizations. Acad. Manag. Rev. **20**, 510–540 (1995). https://doi.org/10.2307/258786
7. van der Aalst, W., et al.: Process mining manifesto. In: Daniel, F., Barkaoui, K., Dustdar, S. (eds.) BPM 2011. LNBIP, vol. 99, pp. 169–194. Springer, Heidelberg (2012). https://doi.org/10.1007/978-3-642-28108-2_19
8. Maaradji, A., Dumas, M., Rosa, M.La, Ostovar, A.: Detecting sudden and gradual drifts in business processes from execution traces. IEEE Trans. Knowl. Data Eng. **29**, 2140–2154 (2017). https://doi.org/10.1109/TKDE.2017.2720601
9. Denisov, V., Belkina, E., Fahland, D., Van Der Aalst, W.M.P.: The performance spectrum miner: visual analytics for fine-grained performance analysis of processes. In: CEUR Workshop Proceedings, vol. 2196, pp. 96–100 (2018)
10. Seeliger, A., Nolle, T., Mühlhäuser, M.: Detecting concept drift in processes using graph metrics on process graphs. In: ACM International Conference Proceeding Series Part F1271 (2017). https://doi.org/10.1145/3040565.3040566
11. Dumas, M., La Rosa, M., Mendling, J., Reijers, H.A.: Fundamentals of Business Process Management. Springer, Heidelberg (2018). https://doi.org/10.1007/978-3-642-33143-5
12. De Weerdt, J., Vanden Broucke, S., Vanthienen, J., Baesens, B.: Active trace clustering for improved process discovery. IEEE Trans. Knowl. Data Eng. **25**, 2708–2720 (2013). https://doi.org/10.1109/TKDE.2013.64
13. De Leoni, M., Van Der Aalst, W.M.P., Dees, M.: A general process mining framework for correlating, predicting and clustering dynamic behavior based on event logs. Inf. Syst. **56**, 235–257 (2016). https://doi.org/10.1016/j.is.2015.07.003
14. Song, M., Günther, C.W., van der Aalst, W.M.P.: Trace clustering in process mining. In: Ardagna, D., Mecella, M., Yang, J. (eds.) BPM 2008. LNBIP, vol. 17, pp. 109–120. Springer, Heidelberg (2009). https://doi.org/10.1007/978-3-642-00328-8_11
15. Bose, R.P.J.C., van der Aalst, W.M.P.: Trace clustering based on conserved patterns: towards achieving better process models. In: Rinderle-Ma, S., Sadiq, S., Leymann, F. (eds.) BPM 2009. LNBIP, vol. 43, pp. 170–181. Springer, Heidelberg (2010). https://doi.org/10.1007/978-3-642-12186-9_16

16. Aigner, W., Miksch, S., Schumann, H., Tominski, C.: Visualization of Time-Oriented Data. Springer, London (2011). https://doi.org/10.1007/978-0-85729-079-3
17. Liu, S., Wu, Y., Wei, E., Liu, M., Liu, Y.: StoryFlow: tracking the evolution of stories. IEEE Trans. Vis. Comput. Graph. **19**, 2436–2445 (2013). https://doi.org/10.1109/TVCG.2013.196
18. Cui, W., Liu, S., Wu, Z., Wei, H.: How hierarchical topics evolve in large text corpora. IEEE Trans. Vis. Comput. Graph. **20**, 2281–2290 (2014). https://doi.org/10.1109/TVCG.2014.2346433
19. Sung, C.Y., Huang, X.Y., Shen, Y., Cherng, F.Y., Lin, W.C., Wang, H.C.: Exploring online learners' interactive dynamics by visually analyzing their time-anchored comments. Comput. Graph. Forum. **36**, 145–155 (2017). https://doi.org/10.1111/cgf.13280
20. Liu, S., Yin, J., Wang, X., Cui, W., Cao, K., Pei, J.: Online visual analytics of text streams. IEEE Trans. Vis. Comput. Graph. **22**, 2451–2466 (2016). https://doi.org/10.1109/TVCG.2015.2509990
21. Wu, Y., Liu, S., Yan, K., Liu, M., Wu, F.: OpinionFlow: visual analysis of opinion diffusion on social media. IEEE Trans. Vis. Comput. Graph. **20**, 1763–1772 (2014). https://doi.org/10.1109/TVCG.2014.2346920
22. Havre, S., Hetzler, B., Nowell, L.: ThemeRiver: visualizing theme changes over time. In: Proceedings of IEEE Symposium on Information Visualization, pp. 115–123 (2000). https://doi.org/10.1109/infvis.2000.885098
23. Byron, L., Wattenberg, M.: Stacked graphs – geometry & aesthetics. IEEE Trans. Vis. Comput. Graph. **14**, 1245–1252 (2008). https://doi.org/10.1109/TVCG.2008.166

Mining BPMN Processes on GitHub for Tool Validation and Development

Thomas S. Heinze[1](✉), Viktor Stefanko[2], and Wolfram Amme[2]

[1] Institute of Data Science, German Aerospace Center (DLR), Jena, Germany
thomas.heinze@dlr.de
[2] Institute of Computer Science, Friedrich Schiller University Jena, Jena, Germany
{viktor.stefanko,wolfram.amme}@uni-jena.de

Abstract. Today, business process designers can choose from an increasing number of analysis tools to check their process model with respect to defects or flaws, before, e.g., deploying the model in a process engine. Answering questions about the tools' effectiveness though is difficult, as their validation often lacks empirical evidence. In particular, for a modeling language like BPMN, where the process is the product, tools are validated by means of case studies or even artificial process examples. We here advocate instead an approach to systematically mine software repositories on GitHub.com for a large corpus of BPMN business process models and discuss how it can be used for tool validation and guiding tool development, using the example of the linting tool BPMNspector.

1 Introduction

Mining software repositories, i.e., the systematic retrieval, processing and analysis of data about software artifacts and software development from software forges and repositories, has drawn considerable attention in recent years. On the one hand, the increasing popularity and usage of platforms like GitLab.com, Bitbucket.org, SourceForge.net or GitHub.com for collaborative software development provide a tremendous source of data, encompassing software from a rich and heterogeneous spectrum of domains. On the other hand, the data mining techniques available today have made it possible to start to seize this treasure, and thus allow to answer research questions and empirically validate hypotheses on the development and usage of IT and software systems based upon real-world data. While the research field is mainly focused on source code of conventional programming languages, mining software repositories can as well help to understand more about the use of other artifacts in software development [12].

In particular the area of modeling languages, such as the *Unified Modeling Language (UML)* or the *Business Process Model and Notation* (BPMN) [4], can benefit from a data-driven approach like mining software repositories. There is a common lack of larger datasets with real-world models, which hinders empirical research in this area [20,28,30]. Retrieving systematically a corpus of models by mining software repositories promises to overcome this lack. For instance,

S. Nurcan et al. (Eds.): BPMDS 2020/EMMSAD 2020, LNBIP 387, pp. 193–208, 2020.
https://doi.org/10.1007/978-3-030-49418-6_13

research questions on how modeling languages are used in practice can be investigated based on the mined corpus, in order to distinguish the more frequently used and important parts of a language from unimportant parts and thus guide language and tool development. Analyzing the different modeling styles in the corpus allows for identifying best practices and guidelines to help model designers. Furthermore, best practices and tools proposed by academic research or by industry can be validated in a more realistic manner. Currently, there are often case studies, including only a small and homogeneous set of models, or artificial examples used when evaluating new tools and methods, with consequences for an evaluation's validity. Instead using a large set of real-world models as retrieved by mining software repositories allows for increasing validity. In this respect, the prior work on the creation of the *Lindholmen dataset* with UML models mined from software repositories on `GitHub.com` was an inspiration for this paper [12,28].

Empirical research is limited by the access to primary sources. Especially in case of modeling languages used for business processes, like BPMN, where the model is usually the product and thus subject to strict nondisclosure restrictions [30], this can pose an insurmountable challenge. Previous empirical studies on business process modeling and BPMN were using methods like experiments, surveys or case studies, each implying limitations to their generalizability [23]. In an experiment, a certain aspect, e.g., a modeling practice, is typically researched by differentiating two groups based on the aspect. The need to provide a large population and to strictly control the experiment's environment for all other variables, however, restricts the applicability of this method to narrow research problems. Surveys allow for more general problems, but are subject to bias, introduced, e.g., by the selection of survey participants or by inaccurate responses from the participants. Case studies are frequently used and in particular allow for insights into real-world practices and constraints. Compared to experiments, there is though no control of environment and influencing variables. Furthermore, reproducibility and comparability is usually not given. Due to the often homogeneous origin of business process models included in case studies, their findings also need to be validated by other research to increase generalizability [20,23]. Most of the empirical research focused on conceptual process models and omitted implemented and executable process models [23]. This also applies to community efforts to assemble collections of business process models like the *BPM Academic Initiative* [20], which mostly covers educational process models. Mining software repositories for business process models, as introduced in the following can be seen as another empirical approach, complementing established methods.

In this paper, we present our efforts to create a corpus of BPMN process models by mining software repositories hosted on `GitHub.com`. Due to the sheer amount of repositories and the bottleneck caused by the *GitHub API*'s rate limit, we limited our search to a random subset of 6,163,217 repositories, or 10% of all repositories on `GitHub.com` in November 2018. As a result, we were able to identify 1,251 repositories with at least one potential BPMN artifact and overall 21,306 potential artifacts. We thereby discovered a wide range of file formats, indicating the various uses of BPMN, e.g., modeling conceptual process models or implementing executable processes. Further narrowing our search to business process models in the BPMN 2.0 XML serialization format and removing duplicates, we eventually gained a corpus of 8,904 distinct BPMN process models, conjoined with corresponding repository metadata. Based on this data, we studied descriptive questions on the usage of BPMN on `GitHub.com`. We also ran the analysis tool *BPMNspector* [10] for all the collected business process models to exemplify the use of the corpus for tool validation. Notably, the tool reported at least one violation of BPMN's syntax and semantic rules for 7,365 business process models or 83% of our corpus, which indicates the need for linting tools like *BPMNspector*. In summary, our contributions are:

– To the authors' knowledge, we provide the first corpus of BPMN, comprising 8,904 unique business process models in the BPMN 2.0 serialization format, which is retrieved by mining software repositories on `GitHub.com`.
– In doing so, we confirm the feasibility of the mining software repositories approach for BPMN, which can therefore also be used by others to complement their empirical research on business process models.
– We confirm results on the frequency of violations of BPMN's syntax and semantic rules, which have already been reported for a case study in [10], and thus demonstrate the usefulness of linting tools like *BPMNspector*.

The rest of the paper is structured as follows: We first provide a brief overview of BPMN and available analysis tools in Sect. 2. Our methodology, i.e., the systematic retrieval and analysis of BPMN process models on `GitHub.com` is described in Sect. 3. In Sect. 4, we present our findings with respect to the usage of BPMN on `GitHub.com` and the effectiveness of the analysis tool *BPMNspector*. Section 5 contains a discussion of related work. We conclude the paper in Sect. 6.

2   BPMN and Static Process Analysis

In the following, we shortly sketch the use of the BPMN process modeling language for business processes and provide a brief overview of the several static analysis tools, which are available for helping process designers in identifying modeling flaws and errors prior to process deployment and execution.

The *Business Process Model and Notation (BPMN)* [4] defines a industrial standard for the IT support of business processes and business process management. The language in its current version 2.0 provides a notation for defining the central artifact of a business process lifecycle [8], i.e., the process model, supporting process modeling on a conceptual level as conduced by domain experts as well as the fully-automated deployment and execution of implemented business process models in process engines like *Activiti*[1], *Camunda*[2], or *jBPM*[3]. To this

---

[1] https://www.activiti.org.
[2] https://camunda.com.
[3] https://www.jbpm.org.

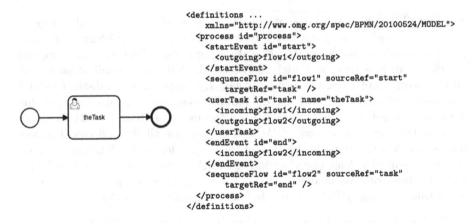

```
<definitions ...
    xmlns="http://www.omg.org/spec/BPMN/20100524/MODEL">
  <process id="process">
    <startEvent id="start">
      <outgoing>flow1</outgoing>
    </startEvent>
    <sequenceFlow id="flow1" sourceRef="start"
        targetRef="task" />
    <userTask id="task" name="theTask">
      <incoming>flow1</incoming>
      <outgoing>flow2</outgoing>
    </userTask>
    <endEvent id="end">
      <incoming>flow2</incoming>
    </endEvent>
    <sequenceFlow id="flow2" sourceRef="task"
        targetRef="end" />
  </process>
</definitions>
```

Fig. 1. Graphical modeling notation and process interchange format of BPMN.

end, the BPMN standard not only includes a graphical modeling notation, but also a machine-processable serialization format for process model interchange and the natural language definition of an execution semantics. In Fig. 1, a simple sample BPMN process model, consisting of a single human task, is shown in its graphical modeling notation as well as in the XML-based interchange format.

Process modeling with BPMN is known to be error-prone, in particular when it comes to executable business processes [9,10,22]. This is due to deliberate decisions on the language's design, e.g., unstructured vs structured process modeling and implied control flow errors, and to the complexity of applications and underlying technologies [29]. To illustrate the latter, consider an executable process package deployed on a process engine like *Camunda*, which not only includes the BPMN process model, but also XML schema files, Groovy or JavaScript code snippets, Java classes, and various configuration scripts. Accordingly, there exists a large body of work on process analysis tools, both from industry and academic research, to help process designers to detect modeling errors as early as possible.

Proposed tools span the whole spectrum of static analysis, i.e., automated rule-based inspection of process models for finding modeling errors or flaws. Linting tools, like *bpmnlint*[4] or *BPMNspector* [10] can be used to check business process models for suspicious and non-portable modeling styles, mostly on the syntactical level. More elaborate tools allow for checking conformance to best practices, e.g., *Signavio*[5], or identifying control and data flow anomalies, e.g., deadlocks [31], processing of undefined data [29], and support even more specific analysis problems like data leak detection [13,16]. Eventually, full-fledged model checking and verification tools can prove the compliance of a process model to certain desirable properties, e.g., proper termination known as soundness [9], by mapping the process model to a formalism like Petri nets [7,14]. Recapitulating

---

[4] https://github.com/bpmn-io/bpmnlint.

[5] https://www.signavio.com.

the tool evaluations in the literature, we observe the frequent use of case studies, where the most thorough evaluation in [9] comprises 735 process models.

3 Mining Software Repositories for BPMN

In this section, we introduce the approach of mining software repositories and discuss the several ways for retrieving software artifacts and metadata from software repositories hosted on `GitHub.com`. Based upon this, we present our implemented mining process for creating a corpus of BPMN processes models.

Systematically mining software repositories can be seen as a traditional data mining task, including steps for defining a research objective, selecting and extracting data, data preparation and cleansing, data analysis and eventually interpreting the analysis results. The most important data sources for repository mining are public software forges, where in particular `GitHub.com` plays a prominent role due to the sheer number of its hosted repositories. There are several ways for extracting data from software repositories on `GitHub.com`:

GitHub API. `GitHub.com` provides the public REST-based *GitHub API v3*[6], which allows for extracting repository metadata, e.g., specific commits, number of repository contributors or main programming language, as well as information on the repository structure and the repository contents. The API can be accessed without or with authentication, supporting up to 60 or 5.000 queries per hour, respectively. Repository mining using the API is therefore often implemented using authenticated access with a smaller or larger set of different user credentials [11,12]. Note that there also exists the *GitHub API v4*[7], which allows for queries based on the GraphQL language. There apply similar rate limits.

GHTorrent. The *GHTorrent*[8] project provides an alternative way for extracting repository data from `GitHub.com`, thereby avoiding any rate limits. It basically consists of two databases, one for mirroring the stream of events (push events, pull requests, etc.) for software repositories on `GitHub.com` and one for repository metadata, populated by interlinking and analyzing the events' contents [11]. The resulting databases can be accessed via web services or by using the provided dumps to set up local database instances. However, as only repository metadata and events are included, neither the repository structure nor the repository contents can be directly accessed. As a project similar in nature, *GHArchive*[9] provides a database with the repositories raw event data only.

Google BigQuery. In recent years, several datasets containing data on `GitHub.com` software repositories are provided via Google's *BigQuery*[10] service,

---

[6] https://developer.github.com/v3.
[7] https://developer.github.com/v4.
[8] http://ghtorrent.org.
[9] http://gharchive.org.
[10] https://cloud.google.com/bigquery.

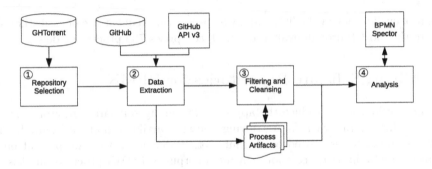

Fig. 2. Schematic illustration of the mining process.

including *GHTorrent* and *GHArchive*. There is as well a dedicated dataset[11] for GitHub.com including repository contents for a significant fraction of its repositories, though not all. Using the BigQuery service allows for querying massive datasets like the above-mentioned with SQL queries in a scalable manner. However, as in case of *GitHub API v3*, rate limits apply. Notably, 1TB per month can be accessed freely, which is instantly consumed when querying on tables with repository contents.

Web Scraping and Git. Since GitHub.com implements a web interface for managing and accessing hosted software repositories, conventional web scraping can also be used for extracting repository data out of the websites' HTML code. Eventually, knowing the URL of a software repository allows for cloning the repository using the standard git tooling. However, as cloning a repository is time-consuming due to downloading its complete history and all its contents, this may not scale in the presence of thousands or even millions of repositories.

Our approach of mining software repositories for BPMN 2.0 process models uses a combination of the methods discussed above, inspired by previous work on the creation of the *Lindholmen dataset* with UML models from GitHub.com [12, 28]. The approach consists of four steps, which we conducted in the beginning of 2019, see also Fig. 2: (1) Get a list of repositories hosted on GitHub.com and select a proper subset thereof, (2) Find and extract potential BPMN process model artifacts as well as associated metadata, (3) Examine the artifacts to identify BPMN 2.0 process models and clean up the resulting data, (4) Analyze the resulting set of process models for answering our research questions:

Repository Selection. In the first step, we used the *GHTorrent* database to get a list of all software repositories on GitHub.com. To this end, a local copy of the MySQL database was setup downloading the most recent database dump (*mysql-2018-11-01*, 85GB). Querying table *projects* allowed for randomly

---

[11] https://cloud.google.com/bigquery/public-data (table *github_repos.contents*).

selecting a set of 6,163,217 repositories, which comprises 10% of all non-forked and non-deleted repositories on GitHub.com in November 2018.

Data Extraction. All 6,163,217 repositories have been examined for BPMN process model artifacts, using three steps for each repository. Similar to [12], the default branch of the repository (master in most cases, though not always) and its latest commit is identified first, using up to three queries to the *GitHub API*. Afterwards, the repository structure is accessed for this commit, in order to generate the list of files for the repository, again querying the *GitHub API*. We reused and adapted the Python scripts[12] from [12,28] for implementing this step. Note that alone this step would require more than 100 days for our repository subset using the credentials of a single user due to the rate limit imposed by the *GitHub API*. In order to increase throughput, we therefore conducted data extraction using several user credentials, which were donated, in parallel. However, this step was still the bottleneck of our approach and lasted 31 days.

Based on the resulting lists, we then scanned for potential BPMN process model artifacts. Having tried several heuristics, we opted for simply including all files with the term "bpmn" in their name or file extension. As a result, we found 1,251 repositories with at least one potential artifact and overall 21,306 potential artifacts. Each of the identified repositories was then cloned locally with the standard git tooling. Metadata was extracted from the downloaded repositories using *Code Maat*[13]. Information about the repository, its metadata and the identified artifacts were stored in a relational database for later analysis.

Filtering and Cleansing. We expect to find a wide range of file formats, including images with graphical process models and source code of various programming languages as included in process packages deployed on process engines. Nonetheless, BPMN defines a standard XML-based interchange format, and most tools support to import and export using this format. For our corpus of BPMN process models, we focused on this format and filtered for XML files containing a schema reference matching the BPMN 2.0 serialization standard [4], i.e., http://www.omg.org/spec/BPMN/20100524/MODEL. Furthermore, we looked for duplicates using the tooling *Duplicate Files Finder*[14] and only kept distinct files in the resulting corpus of 8,904 BPMN process models.

Analysis. In the final step, we analyzed the retrieved metadata and the identified BPMN process models. The former analysis was mainly implemented by querying a relational database. For the latter analysis, we processed the models and ran the tool *BPMNspector*[15] [10] for them. The tool's reports were fed back into the database and afterwards analyzed and aggregated using SQL queries.

---

[12] https://github.com/LibreSoftTeam/2016-uml-miner.
[13] https://github.com/adamtornhill/code-maat.
[14] http://doubles.sourceforge.net.
[15] https://github.com/uniba-dsg/BPMNspector.

4   Results and Discussion

The results of our mining process are presented and discussed in this section. In general, the generated corpus of BPMN process models allows for addressing a multitude of research questions and for validating various hypotheses. Due to space constraints, we here focus on the following research questions:

Research Question 1: *Are there projects which use BPMN on* GitHub.com*?*
    This first questions is used to study the feasibility of the mining repositories approach. Obviously, if there are no BPMN models on GitHub.com, the approach can not be used for empirical studies on BPMN. An answer to this question also helps in understanding BPMN's state of practice on GitHub.com.

Research Question 2: *How diverse is the corpus of BPMN process models?*
    As mentioned in Sect. 1, the generalizability of an empirical study is influenced by the availability of heterogeneous and comprehensive data. We here do not address this question directly. Instead, we analyze indicators as the number of original models, the geographical origin of repositories, the models' age, size, and frequency of changes. Deeper analysis is prospect to future work.

Research Question 3: *How common are violations of BPMN's syntax and semantic rules as identified by BPMNspector?*
    With this question, we want to understand, if there is the need for tools like *BPMNspector* with respect to the compliance of process models to the BPMN standard. An answer to this question could guide the development of process modeling tools, e.g., through the integration of respective linting tools, or help in classifying certain rules of the BPMN language as obsolete.

The corpus of BPMN process models and more information, including the list of identified repositories and their metadata, is available online [15][16]. The scripts used to implement the mining process can be obtained from the same source.

4.1   Usage of BPMN on GitHub.com

We have found 21,306 potential BPMN process model artifacts, included in 1,251 repositories on GitHub.com, which represents a 0.02% share of the overall 6,163,217 analyzed software repositories. Filtering for file formats, we identified serialized BPMN 2.0 process models to be the largest fraction among all the artifacts, counting for more than two thirds as shown in the following table:

File format	XML (BPMN 2.0)	XML (other)	Images (*.png, *.jpg, etc.)	Other (*.jar, *js, etc.)
Number of artifacts	16,907 (79.3%)	384 (1.8%)	1,635 (7.7%)	2,380 (11.2%)

When just considering the serialized BPMN 2.0 process models, the identified artifacts where distributed over 928 software repositories.

---

[16] https://github.com/ViktorStefanko/BPMN_Crawler.

While we apparently used a very simple heuristic for identifying BPMN process models and therefore may have missed many BPMN models hosted on GitHub.com, we nevertheless found a substantial number of artifacts and also of serialized BPMN 2.0 files. The resulting number of BPMN process models clearly exceeds the numbers used in case studies (compare with Sect. 2), but is smaller than the numbers reported for UML models (21,316 in [12] and 93,596 in [28]). The share of 0.02% of repositories with at least one potential BPMN process model artifact is also smaller than the share of 2.8% reported for UML in [12]. The results can be well explained by UML being a family of general-purpose modeling languages, while BPMN is a domain-specific modeling language. Note that UML is also older than BPMN. The reports on UML also present a larger fraction of images among the identified UML models (51.7% in [12] and 61.8% in [28]), which may be reasoned by their more permissive heuristic to consider files with terms like "diagram" or "design" in their name as UML models.

> **Answer to Research Question 1: There have been 1,251 repositories with at least one potential BPMN process model artifact, containing 21,306 potential artifacts and 16,907 serialized BPMN 2.0 models.**

4.2   Properties of Identified BPMN Artifacts

The next question concerns the diversity of identified BPMN process models. A first hint for an answer is given by the different types of files. As already noted above, found file formats range from XML, over image formats, to source code of programming languages. Assuming that images are used for conceptual models and source code may indicate executable process models, the formats reflect the different uses of BPMN along the business process lifecycle.

Age. We also looked at the age of the identified potential BPMN process model artifacts, i.e., the time passed since their last modification in a repository. Unsurprisingly, most artifacts are recent. More than each third artifact was modified in the last year at the time of conducting the study in the beginning of 2019:

Age in years	< 1	1	2	3	4	> 4	n.a.
Number of	7,656	5,154	3,291	2,344	712	2,079	70
artifacts	(36.0%)	(24.2%)	(15.4%)	(11.0%)	(3.3%)	(9.8%)	(0.3%)

We though sporadically found artifacts older than 8 years, which thus do not reference the BPMN 2.0 standard. The results can be well explained by the exponential growth of the number of software repositories on GitHub.com.

Updates. The number of updates, i.e., commits implying changes on a given artifact, excluding artifact creation, was also analyzed. We found that 16,285 or over two third of the potential BPMN process model artifacts are never updated. For the remaining artifacts, the number of updates is low, such that only 7.6% of the artifacts are updated more than once, as shown in the following table:

Number of updates	0	1	2	3	> 3	n.a.
Number of artifacts	16,285 (76.4%)	3,378 (15.9%)	620 (2.9%)	572 (2.7%)	427 (2.0%)	24 (0.1%)

BPMN process models thus seem to be rather static contents of software repositories on GitHub.com. These results are in line with the findings for UML in [12], where they found that only 26% of the UML models are updated at least once.

Geographical Location. Information on the geographical distribution of potential BPMN process model artifacts was investigated using location information for contributors to a software repository, if available. Unfortunately, we were only able to retrieve the locations of 627 contributors for 395 repositories, or 31.6% of all analyzed 1,251 repositories. Furthermore, a contributor of a repository may not necessary contribute to a process model. However, our findings, as shown below, at least indicate that the artifacts originate from several regions:

Location	China	Germany	USA	Switzerland	France	Other
Number of contributors	92 (14.7%)	90 (14.4%)	90 (14.4%)	24 (3.8%)	22 (3.5%)	309 (49.2%)

Duplicates. Furthermore, we analyzed whether the identified potential BPMN process model artifacts are distinct or if there are any duplicates. We found surprisingly many duplicates, almost one half of all artifacts are duplicates of other artifacts, either in the same or in another repository, lowering the number of distinct artifacts to 10,707 or 50.3%. In the following table, we show how often duplicates occur among the identified BPMN process model artifacts:

Number of occurences	1	2	3	4	5	6	7	8	> 8
Number of artifacts	8,030	852	571	193	110	219	272	342	118

As can be seen, all duplicates can be traced back to 2,677 unique artifacts or 12.6% of all artifacts. In the majority of cases, there are no more than 5 duplicates of a unique artifact, though we also found artifacts with up to 89 duplicates. Just considering serialized BPMN 2.0 process models, we made the same observation, with 8,904 distinct process models and 8,003 duplicates thereof. Why there are so many duplicates is an open question. Possible reasons may be found in the reuse of process models, which are part of platforms like the *Camunda* process engine, in several software repositories, or repositories that are manually derived from other software repositories avoiding GitHub.com's forking mechanism [12].

Size. Analyzing process model size was conducted for the 8,904 distinct process models in the BPMN 2.0 serialization format. The XML-based format includes the XML node <process>, which defines a process' logical structure [4]. To get a simple measure for the size of a model, we thus simply counted the number of children elements for the <process> node. As can be seen in the following table, the corpus of BPMN 2.0 process models includes a range of different model sizes:

Number of nodes	$1-10$	$11-20$	$21-50$	$51-100$	>100	n.a.
Number of artifacts	1,881 (21.1%)	2,714 (30.5%)	2,346 (26.3%)	978 (11.0%)	878 (9.9%)	107 (1.2%)

While half of the process models are small and contain no more than 20 XML element nodes, we find a substantial share of medium-sized models. There are also larger models in the corpus. Notably, 57 process models contain more than 1,000 nodes. The largest model even contains 4,096 nodes. In [20], they report similar results for BPMN process models collected by the *BPM Academic Initiative*. The average number of nodes there is 16 and the largest model contains 156 nodes. Note that the numbers can though not be directly compared, since we count element nodes in the XML serialization format of a process, which is larger than the sum of its activities and gateways reported in [20].

> **Answer to Research Question 2: While the majority of identified artifacts are static and recent contents of a software repository, we also found artifacts which are older than 8 years, updated more than once and come from different geographical regions. At least half of the potential BPMN process model artifacts and half of the serialized process models are distinct, yielding a corpus of 8,904 unique BPMN 2.0 process models. The corpus contains models of various sizes.**

4.3 *BPMNspector* Analysis Results

The third research question concerns the frequency of violations against BPMN's syntax and semantic rules, as reported when applying the linter *BPMNspector* to the 8,904 BPMN 2.0 process models. *BPMNspector* has been designed to check models for compliance with the BPMN standard [4]. Checks include BPMN's schema validation, referential integrity, and more sophisticated constraints [10]. Violations against the rules imposed by the standard, on the one hand, impede the portability of process models between different tools and vendors and, on the other hand, can cause unexpected behavior when process models are executed [21].

Results of the analysis revealed issues for almost all the process models. While we were not able to run the analysis for 57 process models, we identified only 1,471 process models or 16.5% of all 8,904 models to be compliant with respect to the standard. All other 7,376 models, a share of 82,8%, were analyzed to have at least one violation of rules of the BPMN standard. Overall, *BPMNspector* reported 150,168 rule violations for our corpus of BPMN 2.0 process models. We also took a closer look into the reported issues and found a large fraction to be violations of rules EXT.023, EXT.101 and EXT.107, as can be seen in the following tables, showing the Top-5 rule violations with respect to the number of models with at least one violation and the absolute number of violations:

Rule	EXT.101	EXT.023	EXT.107	EXT.150	EXT.151
Models with violation	5,299 (59.5%)	5,206 (58.5%)	5,112 (57.4%)	1,846 (20.7%)	1,796 (20.2%)

Rule	EXT.023	XSDCHECK	EXT.107	EXT.092	EXT.101
Absolute	58,015	43,516	7,398	6,788	6,699
Number	(38.6%)	(29.0%)	(4.9%)	(4.5%)	(4.5%)

Rules EXT.023, EXT.101, EXT.107 refer to the non-compliant definition of sequence flows in the BPMN 2.0 serialization format[17]. According to the standard, a sequence flow must be redundantly defined using a node `<sequenceFlow>` and nodes `<incoming>` and `<outgoing>` for the flow's source and target nodes, respectively (also compare with Fig. 1). If one is missing, *BPMNspector* reports an issue. The other shown rules denote violations of BPMN's XML schema (XSDCHECK), missing or ambiguous sources of data associations (EXT.092), or missing incoming sequence flow (EXT.150) and missing outgoing sequence flow (EXT.151). We additionally repaired violations of rules EXT.023, EXT.101, EXT.107 in the process models using a tool[18] provided alongside with *BPMN-spector*. As a result, the number of models with at least one rule violation shrank to 4,106, still constituting a share of 46.1%, and the absolute number of violations to 64,652.

The authors of *BPMNspector* found similar results when evaluating their tool using a case study of 66 BPMN process models. Though, they reported only a share of 42 models or 63.6% to be non-compliant to the standard's rules. They also identified the largest fraction of violations referring to the wrong use of sequence flows. The high frequency of rule violations can be reasoned by missing tool support, as discussed in [21]. However, as most process engines tolerate the violations reported by *BPMNspector*, the results may also indicate that at least some rules of the BPMN standard are obsolete [10]. In summary, our corpus of BPMN process models confirmed the results of the case study in [10] and therefore provided further empirical evidence for the usefulness of *BPMNspector*.

Answer to Research Question 3: Violations of BPMN's syntax and semantic rules as reported by *BPMNspector* are frequent in the corpus of BPMN process models, affecting 82,8% of the models.

---

5   Related Work

Most related to our work is the creation and research on the *Lindholmen dataset*[19], which was also the inspiration for our approach. The creators of the dataset describe the used mining software repositories approach [12], introduce the dataset [28], and report on insights gained about the use of UML on GitHub.com by analyzing the dataset, e.g., in [5,18]. Their main research question was though on the usage of UML in conventional software development, while we were mainly interested in using our corpus to validate analysis tools for

---

[17] http://bpmnspector.org/ConstraintList_EXT.html.

[18] https://github.com/matthiasgeiger/BPMNspector-fixSeqFlow.

[19] http://oss.models-db.com/.

BPMN process modeling. The *Lindholmen dataset* is considerably larger than our corpus, currently counting 93,596 UML models [28]. Note again, that UML is a family of general-purpose modeling languages while BPMN is one domain-specific modeling language. They also put more effort into the identification of graphical models, using machine learning in order to identify images which contain UML. Due to our research objective, we were more interested in BPMN's XML-based serialization format. The authors are not aware of any other work, which systematically mines software repositories to create a corpus of BPMN business process models. There though exists approaches in BPM research, which mine software repositories for other purposes. The authors in [3] argue to use repository metadata to mine software development processes. According to their approach, metadata can be for example used to create GANTT charts based on the contributors activities [2] or to classify repository contributors into roles, e.g., developers or testers [1].

As mentioned in Sect. 1, most empirical research on BPMN is based on experiments, surveys or case studies. Notable tool evaluations, going beyond the usual number of included process models, are [9] with 735 customized UML process models and [22] with 585 BPMN models. There have also been several community efforts to create open model collections [17]. For business process modeling, the *BPM Academic Initiative* provides a platform to create and share process models for academic teaching. The authors report on 1,903 different process models in [20], including BPMN, created by 4,500 users and spanning different model size and complexity. The recent number of models is 29,285, but data collection has stopped and the focus is on conceptual business process models [17]. Also note the need for executable process models and their difference to conceptual models [23]. A similar platform was presented by the name *RePROSitory* [6], currently including 174 business process models. Another initiative is the *BenchFlow* project [30], where process models were collected from industrial partners and used for process engine benchmarking. The authors claim to have collected 8,363 models, with a share of 64% of BPMN [30]. Unfortunately, the collection is not public.

Another line of empirical research focuses on the quality of business process models and modeling practices [24]. In [25], process metrics like modularity or complexity are used for predicting modeling errors based on the analysis of a collection of 2000 conceptual models. Experiments where used in [26,27] to investigate on modeling styles in order to better understand and support process designers. More recent work investigated on best practices for BPMN modeling by inspecting practices in industrial process models [22]. Analyzing similarities and differences of these analyses and our corpus is a prospect of future work.

6   Conclusion

In this paper, we describe our efforts to systematically extract a corpus of BPMN business process models from software repositories hosted on `GitHub.com`. Mining 10% of all repositories yielded 21,306 potential BPMN process model artifacts, originating from 1,251 repositories, which after further filtering and cleansing constituted a corpus of 8,904 distinct serialized BPMN 2.0 process models. The corpus can be used to answer various empirical research questions on the use of business process models. We here demonstrate, how to complement an existing case study for the linting tool *BPMNspector* with an evaluation on a much larger scale. Doing so, we can confirm results on the frequency of violations of the BPMN standard, thus showing the need for analysis tools like *BPMNspector*.

Threats to Validity. There are a number of threats that affect the validity of our approach. For a general discussion on the threats of mining software repositories, we refer the reader to [19]. Process modeling in software repositories may not resemble industrial practice and our results may thus not generalize beyond open software development and academia [19,23]. This is a common threat to external validity, which we also find for other studies, e.g. [20]. Analyzing the transferability of empirical results about software repositories and academia to an industrial context is an open research question. We therefore advocate the complimentary use of our approach with other empirical research methods. Furthermore, we just mined `GitHub.com` and did not consider other software forges. Since `GitHub.com` counts the largest number of hosted repositories, we though believe that our results apply for most open software development. Due to the heuristics used for the identification of BPMN models, we also have missed process models and thus may underestimate certain effects [12], e.g., model duplication or the frequency of graphical process models. We therefore only provide a descriptive analysis of the use of BPMN on `GitHub.com` and do not use our corpus for inferential statistics and prediction. Finally, due to `GitHub.com` being a dynamic environment, repositories may change or be removed over time.

References

1. Agrawal, K., Aschauer, M., Thonhofer, T., Bala, S., Rogge-Solti, A., Tomsich, N.: Resource classification from version control system logs. In: EDOC Workshops 2016, pp. 1–10. IEEE (2016)
2. Bala, S., Cabanillas, C., Mendling, J., Rogge-Solti, A., Polleres, A.: Mining project-oriented business processes. In: Motahari-Nezhad, H.R., Recker, J., Weidlich, M. (eds.) BPM 2015. LNCS, vol. 9253, pp. 425–440. Springer, Cham (2015). https://doi.org/10.1007/978-3-319-23063-4_28
3. Bala, S., Mendling, J.: Monitoring the software development process with process mining. In: Shishkov, B. (ed.) BMSD 2018. LNBIP, vol. 319, pp. 432–442. Springer, Cham (2018). https://doi.org/10.1007/978-3-319-94214-8_34
4. Business Process Model and Notation (BPMN), Version 2.0. Object Management Group (OMG) Standard (2011). https://www.omg.org/spec/BPMN/2.0/PDF
5. Chaudron, M.R.V., Fernandes-Saez, A., Hebig, R., Ho-Quang, T., Jolak, R.: Diversity in UML modeling explained: observations, classifications and theorizations. In: Tjoa, A.M., Bellatreche, L., Biffl, S., van Leeuwen, J., Wiedermann, J. (eds.) SOFSEM 2018. LNCS, vol. 10706, pp. 47–66. Springer, Cham (2018). https://doi.org/10.1007/978-3-319-73117-9_4

6. Corradini, F., Fornari, F., Polini, A., Re, B., Tiezzi, F.: RePROSitory: a repository platform for sharing business PROcess modelS. In: BPM PhD/Demos 2019, pp. 149–153. CEUR (2019)
7. Dijkman, R.M., Dumas, M., Ouyang, C.: Semantics and analysis of business process models in BPMN. Inf. Softw. Techn. **50**(12), 1281–1294 (2008)
8. Dumas, M., Rosa, M.L., Mendling, J., Reijers, H.A.: Fundamentals of Business Process Management, 2 edn. Springer, Heidelberg (2018)
9. Fahland, D., Favre, C., Jobstmann, B., Koehler, J., Lohmann, N., Völzer, H., Wolf, K.: Instantaneous soundness checking of industrial business process models. In: Dayal, U., Eder, J., Koehler, J., Reijers, H.A. (eds.) BPM 2009. LNCS, vol. 5701, pp. 278–293. Springer, Heidelberg (2009). https://doi.org/10.1007/978-3-642-03848-8_19
10. Geiger, M., Neugebauer, P., Vorndran, A.: Automatic standard compliance assessment of BPMN 2.0 process models. In: ZEUS 2017, pp. 4–10. CEUR (2017)
11. Gousios, G.: The GHTorent dataset and tool suite. In: MSR 2013, pp. 233–236. IEEE (2013)
12. Hebig, R., Quang, T.H., Chaudron, M., Robles, G., Fernandez, M.A.: The quest for open source projects that use UML: mining GitHub. In: MODELS 2016, pp. 173–183. ACM (2016)
13. Heinze, T.S., Amme, W., Moser, S.: Process restructuring in the presence of message-dependent variables. In: Maximilien, E.M., Rossi, G., Yuan, S.-T., Ludwig, H., Fantinato, M. (eds.) ICSOC 2010. LNCS, vol. 6568, pp. 121–132. Springer, Heidelberg (2011). https://doi.org/10.1007/978-3-642-19394-1_13
14. Heinze, T.S., Amme, W., Moser, S.: Static analysis and process model transformation for an advanced business process to Petri net mapping. Softw.: Pract. Exp. **48**(1), 161–195 (2018)
15. Heinze, T.S., Stefanko, V., Amme, W.: Mining von BPMN-Prozessartefakten auf GitHub. In: KPS 2019, pp. 111–120 (2019). https://www.hb.dhbw-stuttgart.de/kps2019/kps2019_Tagungsband.pdf
16. Heinze, T.S., Türker, J.: Certified information flow analysis of service implementations. In: SOCA 2018, pp. 177–184. IEEE (2018)
17. Ho-Quang, T., Chaudron, M.R.V., Robles, G., Herwanto, G.B.: Towards an infrastructure for empirical research into software architecture: challenges and directions. In: ECASE@ICSE 2019, pp. 34–41. IEEE (2019)
18. Ho-Quang, T., Hebig, R., Robles, G., Chaudron, M.R.V., Fernandez, M.A.: Practices and perceptions of UML use in open source projects. In: ICSE-SEIP 2017, pp. 203–212. IEEE (2017)
19. Kalliamvakou, E., Gousios, G., Blincoe, K., Singer, L., German, D.M., Damian, D.E.: The promises and perils of mining GitHub. In: MSR 2014, pp. 92–101. ACM (2014)
20. Kunze, M., Luebbe, A., Weidlich, M., Weske, M.: Towards understanding process modeling – the case of the BPM academic initiative. In: Dijkman, R., Hofstetter, J., Koehler, J. (eds.) BPMN 2011. LNBIP, vol. 95, pp. 44–58. Springer, Heidelberg (2011). https://doi.org/10.1007/978-3-642-25160-3_4
21. Lenhard, J., Ferme, V., Harrer, S., Geiger, M., Pautasso, C.: Lessons learned from evaluating workflow management systems. In: Braubach, L., et al. (eds.) ICSOC 2017. LNCS, vol. 10797, pp. 215–227. Springer, Cham (2018). https://doi.org/10.1007/978-3-319-91764-1_17
22. Leopold, H., Mendling, J., Günther, O.: Learning from quality issues of BPMN models from industry. IEEE Softw. **33**(4), 26–33 (2016)

23. Lübke, D., Pautasso, C.: Empirical research in executable process models. Empirical Studies on the Development of Executable Business Processes, pp. 3–12. Springer, Cham (2019). https://doi.org/10.1007/978-3-030-17666-2_1

24. Mendling, J.: Empirical studies in process model verification. In: Jensen, K., van der Aalst, W.M.P. (eds.) Transactions on Petri Nets and Other Models of Concurrency II. LNCS, vol. 5460, pp. 208–224. Springer, Heidelberg (2009). https://doi.org/10.1007/978-3-642-00899-3_12

25. Mendling, J., Sánchez-González, L., García, F., Rosa, M.L.: Thresholds for error probability measures of business process models. J. Syst. Softw. **85**(5), 1188–1197 (2012)

26. Pinggera, J., et al.: Styles in business process modeling: an exploration and a model. Softw. Syst. Model. **14**(3), 1055–1080 (2013). https://doi.org/10.1007/s10270-013-0349-1

27. Pinggera, J., et al.: Tracing the process of process modeling with modeling phase diagrams. In: Daniel, F., Barkaoui, K., Dustdar, S. (eds.) BPM 2011. LNBIP, vol. 99, pp. 370–382. Springer, Heidelberg (2012). https://doi.org/10.1007/978-3-642-28108-2_36

28. Robles, G., Ho-Quang, T., Hebig, R., Chaudron, M., Fernandez, M.A.: An extensive dataset of UML models in GitHub. In: MSR 2017, pp. 519–522. IEEE (2017)

29. Schneid, K., Usener, C.A., Thöne, S., Kuchen, H., Tophinke, C.: Static analysis of BPMN-based process-driven applications. In: SAC 2019, pp. 66–74. ACM (2019)

30. Skouradaki, M., Roller, D., Leymann, F., Ferme, V., Pautasso, C.: On the road to benchmarking BPMN 2.0 workflow engines. In: ICPE 2015, pp. 301–304. ACM (2015)

31. Vanhatalo, J., Völzer, H., Leymann, F.: Faster and more focused control-flow analysis for business process models through SESE decomposition. In: Krämer, B.J., Lin, K.-J., Narasimhan, P. (eds.) ICSOC 2007. LNCS, vol. 4749, pp. 43–55. Springer, Heidelberg (2007). https://doi.org/10.1007/978-3-540-74974-5_4

An Empirical Investigation of the Intuitiveness of Process Landscape Designs

Gregor Polančič[1]([⊠]), Pavlo Brin[2], Lucineia Heloisa Thom[3], Encarna Sosa[4], and Mateja Kocbek Bule[1]

[1] Faculty of Electrical Engineering and Computer Science,
University of Maribor, Koroška cesta 46, 2000 Maribor, Slovenia
{gregor.polancic,mateja.kocbek}@um.si
[2] National Technical University "Kharkiv Polytechnic Institute",
2 Kirpicheva Street, Kharkiv 61002, Ukraine
pavelbrin@ukr.net
[3] Federal University of Rio Grande do Sul, Av. Bento Gonçalves, 9500,
Porto Alegre, RS 91501-970, Brazil
lucineia@inf.ufrgs.br
[4] Universidad de Extremadura, Cáceres, Spain
esosa@unex.es

Abstract. Process landscapes define the scope and relationships between an organization's business processes and are therefore essential for their management. However, in contrast to business process diagrams, where nowadays BPMN prevails, process landscape diagrams lack standardization, which results in numerous process landscape designs. Accordingly, our goal was to investigate how intuitive are current landscape designs to users with low expertise, as well as users having expertise in BPMN and landscape modeling. A total of 302 subjects participated in the research showing that previous expertise impacts the interpretation of landscape elements and designs whereas, in the case of having contextual information, subjects responded more consistently. The results also show that the basic relationships between processes are intuitive to users, also in the case when only proximity between shapes is facilitated. Our findings may imply future designs of languages for process landscapes. They also may be useful for those who actually model process landscape diagrams and search for suitable notations.

Keywords: Process landscape · Diagram · Semantic transparency · BPMN

1 Introduction

A process landscape diagram represents the top-level part of a process architecture, which stands for *"an organized overview of business processes that specifies their relations, which can be accompanied by guidelines that determine how these processes must be organized"* [1]. The specification of a process landscape model is the most important challenge for the establishment of a process architecture [2]. For example, a high amount of organizations' services requires an efficient representation of the entire

© Springer Nature Switzerland AG 2020
S. Nurcan et al. (Eds.): BPMDS 2020/EMMSAD 2020, LNBIP 387, pp. 209–223, 2020.
https://doi.org/10.1007/978-3-030-49418-6_14

process landscape in order to measure the overall organization's potential [3]. A process landscape represents processes as 'black-boxes' and so focuses on interrelationships between processes and external participants. In this manner, a process landscape enables an organization to maintain an overview of processes, which simplifies process-related communication and may represent a starting point for process discovery.

Accordingly, a process landscape model has to be comprehensible by all major stakeholders of an organization [2, 3]. This implies the usage of a common, compact, and intuitive language for the creation of process landscape diagrams. However, no standardized languages for creating process landscapes exist [4], whereas BPMN 2.0 does not cover the wide landscapes and complexities that exist in the process-modeling domain [5, 6]. Consequently, organizations, as well as process modeling tool vendors (e.g., ARIS Express, Visual Paradigm, Vizi Modeler and Signavio), define their own 'overviews of processes' most commonly by imitating 'value chain' diagrams.

As a result, landscape diagrams differ from each other, and while there is no common landscape modeling language, an inexperienced user could infer a different meaning from the appearance of a language element, which could negatively impact the comprehension of a diagram and the corresponding decisions made. And while the graphical representation significantly impacts the cognitive effectiveness of a diagram [7–9], it is important to specify a common palette of comprehensible symbols fitting with the process landscapes domain.

According to these challenges, the main goal of our work was to investigate the intuitiveness of the representations of process landscape designs as found in academia and industry, i.e., to test if representations of landscape concepts are intuitive (i.e. semantically transparent, clear) to people with 'near-to-zero' knowledge of a process landscape design. In this light, we defined the following research questions which could be tested empirically:

– *RQ1: Are common landscape designs semantically transparent to 'novice users'?*
– *RQ2: How does the previous knowledge impacts the comprehension of process landscape designs?*

Accordingly, the paper is organized as follows. The introduction chapter already identified the problem and motivation for the research, whereas the second chapter contains background on process landscapes, semiotics, and semantic transparency. The third chapter introduces empirical research, which was applied to provide answers to the stated research questions. The fourth chapter presents and discusses the results of our research. The last chapter brings conclusions and limitations of our approach as well as implications and future research directions.

2   Research Background

2.1   Process Landscapes

A high-level model of an organization that represents an overall structure of business processes and their relationships, emerged as a tool to aid process-oriented companies in managing large business process collections [10]. With roots in the early 1980s, when Porter [11] introduced the value chain model, the concept is commonly specified as a 'process landscape' and represents a set of interconnected processes within an organizational system. Alternative terms in use are 'process overview' [12], and 'process map'. However, according to the findings of Poels et al. [13], the term 'process map' may either represent a model of a business process architecture or an entry-level model of a business process model architecture.

A process landscape model (Fig. 1) shows the structure, grouping, modularity, functionality, and technology of chain processes, business processes, and working processes. In contrast to business process models, processes on the landscape level are modeled as 'black-boxes' whose internal complexity is hidden for the sake of simplicity and clarity.

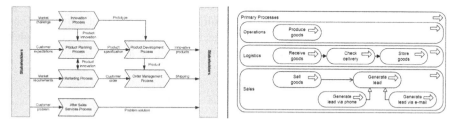

Fig. 1. Examples of process landscape diagrams [15, 16]

Process landscape diagrams may be used in numerous ways, addressing the concerns of business-oriented users as well as technically-oriented ones [12]. While being specified on the macro level, they provide a comprehensive understanding and highlight different types of relationships or dependencies with other processes and artifacts [14]. Process landscape diagrams help process owners, quality managers, and other process-related stakeholders to ease the maintenance of their processes by offering a quick overview of processes. Afterward, in detailed process diagrams, individual business processes may be decomposed into finer levels of detail (i.e., sub-processes and tasks). In summary, like modeling individual processes is a starting point for any process improvement effort, modeling the architecture of an organization's collection of business processes is required for any analysis, design or improvement effort that transcends the level of individual processes [13].

Figure 1 represents two common process landscape diagrams, with processes depicted as chevron arrows (left) or rectangles (right), whereas arrows represent between-process relationships. The left diagram in Fig. 1 additionally connects organizational processes with the environment by specifying connections to external participants (i.e., stakeholders).

2.2 Modeling Process Landscapes with BPMN 2.0

The evidence from academia and practice show that BPMN is used for modeling of process landscapes in an informal way [17, 18]. In our previous work [18], three different BPMN-based approaches for modeling of process landscaped have been investigated: (1) use of black-box Pools and Message flows for modeling of BPMN Collaboration diagrams with hidden details; (2) use of BPMN Collaboration diagrams and (3) use of Enterprise-wide BPMN Process diagrams.

An analysis performed in [18] demonstrates that none of the BPMN approaches results in diagrams with a graphical similarity to common landscape diagrams (e.g., value chains). Analytically, this was confirmed by Malinova et al. [19], who performed a semantical mapping between BPMN and 'Process maps'. Their results show that BPMN in its current form is not appropriate for process landscape design.

2.3 Semiotics

The theoretical foundation on how a visual vocabulary of a notation is defined can be explained by semiotics [20], i.e. a study of signs, an investigation into how the meaning is created and communicated. According to semiotics, a sign consists of a signifier (i.e. any material thing that is signified, be it an object, words on a page, or an image) and signified (i.e. the concept which the signifier refers to) (Fig. 2, left).

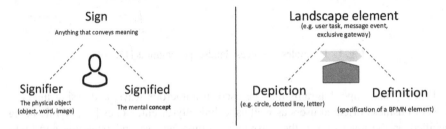

Fig. 2. Main concepts as specified in semiotics (left) and OMG's namespace (right)

Based on the relation between the signifier and signified, semiotics defines three types of signs: (1) icon, where a signifier physically resembles the signified (i.e. person sign on Fig. 2); (2) symbol, where the signifier presents the signified with an arbitrary or conventional relation; and (3) index, where the signifier is related to the signified by an associative relation (i.e. Fig. 2, right – the darker symbol supports the lighter one (from below), which is analogous to common real-life situations). In the process languages' space (e.g. BPMN, CMMN, DMN), a sign is commonly referred to as an element, whereas the signifier is commonly referred to as a depiction of an element [21]. The definition of a process element has an equal meaning as a 'signified' in semiotics, meaning the specification of a language concept. Since the focus of our investigation is on process languages, we will use the terms according to the process languages namespace, i.e. a *'process element consists of its definition and depiction'*.

2.4 Semantic Transparency

Caire et al. [22] stated that *"The key to designing visual notations that are understandable to naïve users is a property called semantic transparency"*, which means that the meaning (semantics) of a sign is clear (i.e. intuitive, transparent) from its appearance alone (as in the case of onomatopoeia in spoken languages). Therefore, addressing semantic transparency is recognized as one of the most powerful approaches for improving the understandability, especially for novice users [22].

Semantic transparency of a sign is a continuous function with two endpoints. On the positive side, a sign may be semantic transparent, which means that a novice reader could accurately deduce the meaning of a sign from its appearance (e.g., a drawn tree representing a tree). Semantically transparent signs tend to be defined either by similarity or an associative relationship (index). In contrast, semantic perversity means that a novice reader would likely deduct an incorrect meaning from the sign's appearance (e.g., an arrow directed in an opposite way to an actual flow). On the midpoint, a sign may be defined as semantically opaque, which means that it is defined by a convention [22]. Semantically transparent signs reduce cognitive load because they have built-in mnemonics: as a result, their meaning can be either perceived directly or easily learned [23]. Such representations speed up recognition and improve intelligibility to naïve users [24, 25]. Indeed, one of the main challenges of modeling languages is to model the diagram in a precise and user-friendly way, where each applied graphical element should be intuitive for users [26], which positively implies the acceptance of a modeling technique [27].

3   Empirical Research

3.1   Research Model and Process

In respect to *RQ1*, we identified two independent variables, namely 'depiction of a landscape concept' and 'contextual information'. In the case of the former, we searched for the levels of the independent variable among the various sources of process landscape diagrams whereas the visual vocabularies of the corresponding notations have been identified (i.e. levels represented common landscape symbols). The 'contextual information' variable was additionally introduced, since the meaning of an individual element may be more precisely identified when putting it into the context (element level and diagram level). The dependent variable was defined as 'semantic transparency', which represents the extent to which the meaning of a symbol can be inferred from its appearance. We operationalized the 'semantic transparency' as the number of correctly identified meanings of the investigated elements, i.e. comprehension. Higher values were preferred, representing semantic immediate symbols (i.e. a novice reader can infer the meaning from its appearance alone).

In respect to *RQ2*, two types of previous knowledge (i.e. expertise) have been considered as independent variables: 'BPMN expertise' and 'Landscape modeling expertise'. 'BPMN expertise' was considered since BPMN represents ISO and the de-facto standard for process modeling, where some attempts in academia and practice actually apply BPMN for landscape modeling [28]. Accordingly, we presume that BPMN expertise may impact the subjects on how they perceive landscape elements. In a similar manner, 'Landscape modeling expertise' may impact the subjects' answers. In both cases, the 'expertise' was investigated on a 7-point Likert scale from highest to lowest degree of disagreement, with items adapted from Recker [29].

To provide answers to the stated research questions, we performed empirical research as follows. To test to what extent 'novice users' would be likely to infer the correct meaning for the common landscape designs, subjects were introduced with different landscape elements and (partial) diagrams, where their task was to identify the meaning for the provided depictions. The applied research protocol may correspond to pre-experimental designs, more specifically 'one group posttest only design' [30]. In our case, the treatments were associated with the instructions, provided to subjects, whereas the observations are associated with the subject's responses.

3.2 Subjects and Sampling

Since we investigated intuitiveness, the ideal candidate for the research would be an individual who (1) understands the meaning of the concepts, which are used in land-scape modeling, yet has (2) no experiences with the corresponding landscape modeling notations. According to this, IT and business students of the same degree were selected as suitable candidates for the research.

3.3 Research Instrument

The focal research instrument was an online questionnaire, which was categorized into the following parts. In the first part, subjects were asked to provide basic demographic information (age, gender), and their experiences in BPMN as well as in landscape modeling (both measured on a 7-point Likert scale from lowest to the highest degree of experience, and self-reported number of modeled diagrams). In the second part, subjects were introduced by alternative depictions of common landscape elements (i.e. landscape elements as used in academia and industry, including BPMN and Archimate), where they were asked to associate the most appropriate meaning to them (including the 'undecided' answer). In addition, partial diagrams were presented to subjects to test if they would more effectively infer the meaning if using a diagram's contextual information. To minimize learning effects, the individual items as well the answers were randomized. In the third part of the questionnaire, a "two-treatments" alike design was applied to test the alternative notations used in landscaped modeling. Due to the paper's length limitations, this part was excluded from this paper. The instrument was prepared in Slovenian and English version and was completely anonymized. The actual research was performed in January 2019. In total, 588 subjects were invited to participate, 347 subjects actually opened the questionnaire or partially completed it, whereas 302 subjects successfully completed the questionnaire. Out of them, 65% of the subject came from Slovenia, whereas 35% came from Ukraine.

4 Results

The results were collected and partially analyzed in 1KA (https://www.1ka.si/d/en), an advanced open-source application that enables services for online surveys. Afterward, the data was exported into MS Excel as well as SPSS, to perform additional analysis.

4.1 Descriptive Statistics

As previously mentioned, 302 subjects successfully completed the questionnaire, 161 of them male (53%) and 141 female (47%). In average subjects were 21.3 years old when completing the questionnaire. 197 subjects (65%) come from Slovenia, whereas 105 subjects (35%) came from Ukraine and so completed the survey in the English language. On average, it took eight minutes and four seconds to complete the questionnaire. Based on subjects' expertise with BPMN and landscapes modeling, subjects were classified into the following levels of expertise (Table 1): (1) inexperienced - the subjects who partially or fully disagreed on having any experience in BPMN or landscapes modeling (in all Likert items); (2) BPMN experts - subjects who partially to fully agreed on having expertise in BPMN (in all Likert items); (3) landscape modeling experts - subjects who partially to fully agreed on having expertise in landscape modeling (in all Likert items).

Table 1. Descriptive statistics with respect to subjects' expertise

Expertise	Male	Female	Slovenia	Ukraine	Total	T. [%]
Inexperienced	80	68	102	46	148	49%
BPMN expertise	34	18	44	8	52	17%
Landscape modeling expertise	7	9	10	6	16	5%
All	161	141	197	105	302	100%

As evident from Table 1, the sum of all levels of expertise does not match all subjects, since those subjects who specified 'undecided' on their level of expertise were not classified into any level of expertise.

4.2 Comprehension of Process Landscape Elements

In order to investigate the comprehension of the depictions of common landscape elements, subjects were asked to associate the correct meaning to the stated symbols, where they had an additional 'undecided' option to answer. In total 291 subjects completely answered this question, choosing 'undecided' at an average of 25% of the answers. Table 2 summarizes these results by showing the percentage of answers associated with individual definitions. We bolded the highest (preferred) values for individual depictions and highlighted (in the gray background) the correct definitions (i.e. as specified or use d in praxis). As evident from Table 2, subjects associated the symbols to the correct definitions, consistently and at all levels of expertise in the cases of all process elements (depictions D1, D2, D3, and D5) as well in the cases of 'data elements' (depictions D8, and D9). In the remaining cases, the associations of definitions of the stated symbols depend on the level of expertise as follows. The rectangle (D4) was recognized either as a process or as a participant, which may have roots in BPMN's specification of the concept of a Pool. A BPMN Pool may either be treated as a participant or as a process in case it references one.

Table 2. Comprehension of landscape elements

D	Process landscape element depiction	Expertise	Process	Participant	Supp. pro.	Mng. Proc.	Datastore	Document	Proc. collect.	Triggering r.	Inf. flow	Cond. trigger	Gen.-spec. r.	Undecided	Valid a.
1		I	29%	3%	1%	6%	3%	0%	3%	5%	7%	4%	4%	34%	146
		B	39%	4%	2%	10%	0%	0%	6%	2%	8%	2%	0%	27%	51
		L	31%	0%	6%	19%	0%	0%	6%	6%	6%	0%	0%	25%	16
		A	32%	4%	3%	8%	2%	0%	3%	4%	8%	3%	3%	31%	291
2		I	18%	6%	8%	10%	3%	1%	4%	2%	3%	5%	5%	35%	146
		B	25%	4%	8%	8%	2%	0%	2%	0%	2%	8%	4%	37%	51
		L	25%	6%	19%	0%	0%	0%	0%	0%	0%	0%	6%	44%	16
		A	16%	5%	8%	10%	4%	1%	3%	2%	4%	8%	4%	35%	291
3		I	5%	11%	12%	10%	3%	1%	3%	1%	3%	4%	2%	44%	146
		B	4%	4%	29%	10%	0%	2%	0%	0%	2%	0%	0%	49%	51
		L	6%	6%	19%	6%	0%	0%	0%	0%	0%	6%	6%	50%	16
		A	5%	11%	17%	9%	4%	2%	2%	1%	2%	5%	2%	40%	291
4		I	9%	27%	1%	1%	12%	6%	1%	0%	1%	2%	1%	38%	146
		B	41%	20%	2%	6%	2%	2%	0%	0%	0%	0%	2%	25%	51
		L	44%	19%	0%	13%	0%	6%	0%	6%	0%	0%	6%	6%	16
		A	19%	24%	1%	3%	10%	5%	1%	0%	1%	2%	2%	32%	291
5		I	3%	8%	12%	12%	2%	3%	2%	3%	3%	5%	1%	45%	146
		B	2%	0%	18%	25%	0%	2%	0%	2%	2%	2%	2%	45%	51
		L	0%	0%	13%	25%	6%	0%	0%	6%	6%	0%	6%	38%	16
		A	3%	6%	12%	14%	3%	3%	3%	5%	3%	3%	2%	42%	291
6		I	8%	7%	18%	5%	3%	1%	5%	3%	3%	6%	5%	34%	146
		B	8%	0%	16%	12%	0%	0%	22%	0%	2%	8%	6%	27%	51
		L	0%	0%	25%	6%	6%	0%	13%	0%	6%	6%	6%	31%	16
		A	7%	4%	18%	6%	3%	1%	9%	3%	3%	7%	6%	32%	291
7		I	3%	5%	1%	1%	59%	1%	8%	3%	1%	2%	1%	16%	146
		B	2%	2%	0%	0%	88%	0%	2%	0%	0%	0%	0%	6%	51
		L	0%	6%	0%	0%	69%	0%	19%	0%	0%	0%	0%	6%	16
		A	2%	7%	1%	1%	58%	1%	9%	2%	1%	2%	1%	16%	291
8		I	1%	1%	1%	1%	2%	85%	1%	0%	1%	1%	0%	6%	146
		B	0%	0%	0%	2%	6%	92%	0%	0%	0%	0%	0%	0%	51
		L	0%	0%	0%	0%	13%	88%	0%	0%	0%	0%	0%	0%	16
		A	1%	0%	0%	1%	3%	88%	1%	0%	1%	0%	0%	5%	291
9		I	18%	0%	3%	5%	1%	1%	1%	14%	32%	3%	6%	17%	146
		B	4%	2%	0%	0%	2%	0%	2%	55%	25%	4%	2%	4%	51
		L	0%	6%	6%	0%	0%	0%	6%	31%	31%	0%	0%	19%	16
		A	15%	1%	2%	5%	1%	1%	1%	22%	30%	3%	7%	14%	291
10		I	6%	1%	3%	4%	0%	0%	4%	13%	15%	10%	16%	27%	146
		B	6%	0%	4%	2%	0%	0%	2%	10%	4%	31%	24%	18%	51
		L	6%	0%	0%	6%	0%	0%	0%	19%	25%	25%	6%	13%	16
		A	7%	1%	4%	4%	1%	0%	3%	12%	13%	14%	17%	24%	291

Expertise: I=inexperienced; B= BPMN expert; L= landscapes modeling expert; A= all subjects.

The symbol for the collapsed processes collection (D6) was correctly identified by BPMN experts, which may have roots in an analogous representation of a collapsed BPMN subprocess. Expanded collections of processes (D9 and D10) haven't been identified correctly. However, this may have roots in the research instrument since subjects focused on the relationships between processes present on the collection instead of the collection itself.

Individual landscape elements, as well as the relationships between them, were additionally investigated by considering contextual information, i.e. by putting elements into (partial diagrams). Initially, subjects were asked to identify the type of process by providing them a simple value chain-based landscape diagram (Fig. 3).

Fig. 3. Common depictions of process types in a value chain model

In this case, subjects recognized the core process correctly in 73%, whereas the supporting process was recognized correctly by 68% of subjects. This is a significant increase when compared to the individually investigated symbols (17%, Table 2, D3). In the case of the management process, the success rate was 59%, whereas in the individual investigation it was 14% (Table 2, D5).

4.3 Comprehension of Between-Processes Relationships

The explicit relationships between processes in a process landscape diagram were investigated individually and by providing subjects the following two diagrams (Fig. 4).

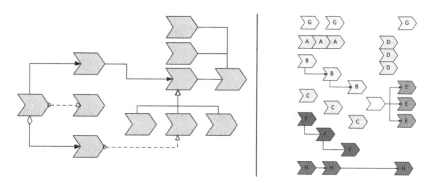

Fig. 4. Investigation of relationships between processes (part 1, left; part 2, right)

The focus of the left diagram in Fig. 4 was to investigate the relationships between processes as specified by Eid Sabbagh et al. [31], namely composition, specialization, trigger, and information flow, with the last two being specified as behavioral ones (Table 3, the highest values are bolded). While two symbols may share the same meaning in praxis which stands for 'symbol overload' (e.g. solid line and arrow, different types of arrows), we did specify any correct definitions in this case.

Table 3. Comprehension of explicit relationships

D	Depiction of a between-process relationship	Expertise L.	Information flow	Sequential flow (trigger)	Conditional sequential f.	Gen.- spec. process	Undecided	Valid a.
11		I	21%	**23%**	**23%**	19%	14%	145
		B	6%	12%	**49%**	25%	8%	51
		L	0%	25%	**50%**	19%	6%	16
		A	17%	20%	**29%**	21%	13%	289
12		I	14%	17%	**38%**	20%	10%	145
		B	**51%**	8%	35%	0%	6%	51
		L	**50%**	0%	31%	0%	19%	16
		A	24%	16%	**35%**	13%	11%	289
13		I	17%	**34%**	21%	17%	11%	145
		B	14%	20%	18%	**43%**	6%	51
		L	6%	31%	13%	**38%**	13%	16
		A	19%	**28%**	21%	21%	11%	289
14		I	**36%**	33%	6%	10%	15%	145
		B	27%	**57%**	2%	14%	0%	51
		L	**31%**	**31%**	13%	25%	0%	16
		A	34%	**36%**	7%	13%	11%	289
15		I	26%	8%	6%	**31%**	29%	145
		B	**27%**	18%	6%	18%	31%	51
		L	25%	**38%**	0%	19%	19%	16
		A	24%	10%	6%	**29%**	31%	289

Expertise: I=inexperienced; B= BPMN expert; L= landscapes modeling expert; A= all subjects.

Table 3 reveals that subjects responded the most consistently (in respect to different levels of expertise) in the case of a conditional trigger relationship (D11), which may be associated with the intuitiveness of a diamond shape symbol, commonly representing a decision-point. Information flow (D12) was correctly recognized by experts, which may be related to the fact that the depiction is equal to BPMN's message flow. In a similar manner, the 'generic-specific' relationship (D13) was correctly identified by the experts, who may have the knowledge either of UML class diagrams or Archimate. The sequential relationship (D14) was not correctly recognized by inexperienced users, whereas all other expertise levels including all answers inferred the correct meaning. The answers were also inconsistent in the case of a solid line, whereas the majority of subjects reported as being a 'generic-specific' relationship (i.e. as common in organizational charts).

The focus of the right diagram in Fig. 4 was to investigate the implicit relationships between processes, which commonly occur on a landscape diagram, especially value-chain based. In this manner, subjects were asked to specify the relationships between the processes sharing the same letter and color (Table 4).

Table 4. Comprehension of explicit and implicit relationships

Element set		Sequentially	Parallel	Independent	Undecided	Valid	Element set	Sequentially	Parallel	Independent	Undecided	Valid
A	I	**72%**	17%	1%	9%	144	E	9%	**61%**	16%	14%	144
	B	**82%**	16%	2%	0%	51		8%	**75%**	14%	4%	51
	L	**69%**	31%	0%	0%	16		6%	**63%**	19%	13%	16
	A	**72%**	20%	2%	6%	288		10%	**63%**	17%	11%	288
B	I	**78%**	6%	6%	10%	144	F	**65%**	12%	10%	13%	144
	B	**82%**	10%	6%	2%	51		**82%**	8%	4%	6%	51
	L	**75%**	13%	6%	6%	16		**88%**	6%	0%	6%	16
	A	**75%**	11%	6%	9%	288		**66%**	13%	9%	11%	288
C	I	5%	4%	**80%**	11%	144	G	11%	4%	**69%**	16%	144
	B	2%	4%	**92%**	2%	51		14%	2%	**80%**	4%	51
	L	6%	6%	**88%**	0%	16		19%	6%	**75%**	0%	16
	A	5%	5%	**81%**	9%	288		11%	5%	**72%**	12%	288
D	I	8%	**67%**	13%	11%	144	H	**77%**	3%	2%	17%	144
	B	6%	**76%**	16%	2%	51		**94%**	0%	4%	2%	51
	L	0%	**94%**	6%	0%	16		**81%**	0%	13%	6%	16
	A	7%	**73%**	12%	8%	288		**79%**	4%	4%	13%	288

Expertise: I=inexperienced; B= BPMN expert; L= landscapes modeling expert; A= all subjects.

As evident from Table 4, subjects responded completely consistently in all sets of related processes (Fig. 4, right) and in all expertise levels. So, we can conclude that they have no problems identifying sequentially, parallel or independent processes either connected explicitly with arrows or implicitly by using the mechanism of proximity.

5   Conclusions

Based on the results which were presented and discussed in the previous chapter, we may provide the answers to the stated research questions as follows.

RQ1: Are common landscape designs semantically transparent to 'novice users'?
When observing the subgroup of subjects, who did not report any level of expertise in
BPMN and landscapes modeling (Table 1, 'inexperienced'), we may conclude that they
were able to successfully associate the stated depictions of process landscape elements to
the meanings they share in the diagrams (Table 2), especially in the cases, where symbols
share the same meaning over different notations (e.g. D7 and D8 in Table 2). They also
successfully recognized all process symbols, especially when considering them in the
context, as summarized in Table 5.

Table 5. Process depictions as recognized by inexperienced users

Symbol	⬠	⬡	⬡
Individual element level	12%	29%	12%
Diagram level (context)	58%	72%	67%

When comparing the results of alternative process representations (e.g. D1 and D2 in
Table 2), subjects reported better in the case of the chevron symbol (D1) despite the fact
D2 is used in a formal specification (ArchiMate). In respect to between-process connections, the 'inexperienced' subgroup of subjects failed to associate the stated depictions
to the proper meanings as used in landscape diagrams (Table 3), despite the fact that
the investigated depictions were put into the context (Fig. 4, left). However, the same
subjects reported consistently with experienced users when identifying sequentially, parallel or independent processes either connected explicitly with arrows or implicitly by
facilitating the mechanism of proximity between the elements.

*RQ2: How does the previous knowledge impacts the comprehension of process landscape
designs?*
Two types of previous knowledge were investigated in our research: experiences with
BPMN and experience with landscape modeling (Table 1). The results of our investigation show that by considering previous knowledge subjects responded differently in
several cases when compared to 'inexperienced' subgroup of subjects. These were most
evident in the cases of a rectangle (Table 2, D4) and chevron arrow with a plus sign
(Table 2, D6). Table 6 summarizes these by comparing the comprehension of process
landscape elements by considering their definitions as specified or used in praxis.

Besides, the connection elements, which depictions are mainly specified in a conventional way (they do not have any 'built-in mnemonics') have reported different comprehension levels, when considering different levels of expertise. E.g. in the case of BPMN
experts a dotted arrow was successfully associated with an information flow (in BPMN
it represents a Message flow), whereas they successfully associated solid arrow with a
triggering relationship (in BPMN it represents a Message flow).

Table 6. Comprehension of landscape elements in respect to levels of expertise

Expertise	Process (chevron)	Process (ArchiMate)	Support process	Participant	Mngm. process	Process collection	Database	Document	Collection (chevron)	Collection (ArchiMate)	Average "undecided"
I	29%	18%	12%	27%	12%	5%	59%	85%	1%	4%	27%
L	39%	25%	29%	20%	25%	22%	88%	92%	2%	2%	21%
B	31%	25%	19%	19%	25%	13%	69%	88%	6%	0%	21%

Expertise: I=inexperienced; B= BPMN expert; L= landscapes modeling expert;

5.1 Implications

We foresee several implications of our investigation. First, experts involved in developing and evolving process landscape languages may consider our research results to select and/or specify the depictions of elements which are intuitive to modelers. Secondly, the selection of visual elements for process landscape design should consider related notations (e.g. BPMN), where elements depictions may already have standardized meanings and therefore should not be overridden. Our research may also be of use for researchers who investigate and propose simplifications of complex process languages, as well as for the ones who extend existing visual languages.

5.2 Research Limitations and Future Work

The results of this research should be considered with the following internal and external limitations in mind. With respect to the external validity, there is a certain degree of risk of generalizing results above the research sample. While students reported as not being skilled in BPMN and landscape modeling languages, another group of subjects could provide different results (e.g. subjects from another environment could be impacted by other signs in their everyday life). Besides, the sample of subjects experienced in landscape design was rather small (16 subjects). Secondly, there is also a certain degree of risk associated with the instrument, where the subject may not be able to correctly interpret the depictions as well the semantics of the symbols out of the instructions (e.g. as in the case of expanded process collections).

Our future work will be focused on specifying a modified landscape modeling notation, based on these results and test if the resulting diagrams are more cognitively effective when compared to existing ones. Besides, we may extend the research to other regions to test on how cultural differences may impact the intuitiveness of symbols.

Acknowledgment. The authors (Gregor Polančič) acknowledge the financial support from the Slovenian Research Agency (research core funding No. P2-0057).

References

1. Dijkman, R., Vanderfeesten, I., Reijers, H.A.: Business process architectures: overview, comparison and framework. Enterp. Inf. Syst. **10**, 129–158 (2016). https://doi.org/10.1080/17517575.2014.928951
2. Dumas, M., Rosa, M.L., Mendling, J., Reijers, H.: Fundamentals of Business Process Management. Springer, Heidelberg (2018). https://doi.org/10.1007/978-3-662-56509-4
3. Becker, J., Pfeiffer, D., Räckers, M., Fuchs, P.: Business process management in public administrations-the PICTRUE approach. In: PACIS 2007 Proceedings, p. 142 (2007)
4. Malinova, M., Leopold, H., Mendling, J.: An explorative study for process map design. In: Nurcan, S., Pimenidis, E. (eds.) CAiSE Forum 2014. LNBIP, vol. 204, pp. 36–51. Springer, Cham (2015). https://doi.org/10.1007/978-3-319-19270-3_3
5. Van Nuffel, D., De Backer, M.: Multi-abstraction layered business process modeling. Comput. Ind. **63**, 131–147 (2012). https://doi.org/10.1016/j.compind.2011.12.001
6. von Rosing, M., von Scheel, H., Scheer, A.-W.: The Complete Business Process Handbook: Body of Knowledge from Process Modeling to BPM, Volume I: Body of Knowledge from Process Modeling to BPM, vol. 1. Morgan Kaufmann, Waltham (2014)
7. Larkin, J.H., Simon, H.A.: Why a diagram is (sometimes) worth ten thousand words. Cogn. Sci. **11**, 65–100 (1987)
8. Siau, K.: Informational and computational equivalence in comparing information modeling methods. JDM **15**, 73–86 (2004). https://doi.org/10.4018/jdm.2004010103
9. Zhang, J., Norman, D.: Representations in distributed cognitive tasks. Cogn. Sci. **18**, 87–122 (1994)
10. Gonzalez-Lopez, F., Bustos, G.: Business process architecture design methodologies – a literature review. Bus. Process Manag. J. (2019). https://doi.org/10.1108/BPMJ-09-2017-0258
11. Porter, M.E.: Competitive Advantage: Creating and Sustaining Superior Performance. Free Press; Collier Macmillan, New York, London (1985)
12. Gonzalez-Lopez, F., Pufahl, L.: A landscape for case models. In: Reinhartz-Berger, I., Zdravkovic, J., Gulden, J., Schmidt, R. (eds.) BPMDS/EMMSAD -2019. LNBIP, vol. 352, pp. 87–102. Springer, Cham (2019). https://doi.org/10.1007/978-3-030-20618-5_6
13. Poels, G., García, F., Ruiz, F., Piattini, M.: Architecting business process maps. Comput. Sci. Inf. Systems. (2019). https://doi.org/10.2298/csis181118018p
14. Stefanov, V., List, B., Schiefer, J.: Bridging the gap between data warehouses and business processes: a business intelligence perspective for event-driven process chains. In: Ninth IEEE International EDOC Enterprise Computing Conference, EDOC 2005, pp. 3–14. IEEE (2005)
15. Weske, M.: Business Process Management: Concepts, Languages, Architectures. Springer, Heidelberg (2019)
16. Dijkman, R., Vanderfeesten, I., Reijers, H.A.: The Road to a Business Process Architecture: An Overview of Approaches and Their Use. Einhoven University of Technology, The Netherlands (2011)
17. Muehlen, M.Z., Ho, D.T.: Service process innovation: a case study of BPMN in practice. In: Hawaii International Conference on System Sciences, Proceedings of the 41st Annual. p. 372 (2008). https://doi.org/10.1109/HICSS.2008.388
18. Polančič, G., Huber, J., Tabares, M.S.: An analysis of BPMN-based approaches for process landscape design [Elektronski vir]. Presented at the Gregor Polančič, Jernej Huber, Marta S. Tabares (2017)
19. Malinova, M., Mendling, J.: Why is BPMN not appropriate for Process Maps? In: ICIS 2015 Proceedings. (2015)
20. Chandler, D.: Semiotics: The Basics. Routledge, London; New York (2007)

21. OMG: Business Process Model and Notation version 2.0, http://www.omg.org/spec/BPMN/2.0/. Accessed 15 Mar 2011
22. Caire, P., Genon, N., Heymans, P., Moody, D.L.: Visual notation design 2.0: towards user comprehensible requirements engineering notations. In: 2013 21st IEEE International Requirements Engineering Conference (RE), pp. 115–124 (2013). https://doi.org/10.1109/RE.2013.6636711
23. Petre, M.: Why looking isn't always seeing: readership skills and graphical programming. Commun. ACM **38**, 33–44 (1995). https://doi.org/10.1145/203241.203251
24. Britton, C., Jones, S.: The untrained eye: how languages for software specification support understanding in untrained users. Hum.-Comput. Interact. **14**, 191–244 (1999). https://doi.org/10.1080/07370024.1999.9667269
25. Britton, C., Jones, S., Kutar, M., Loomes, M., Robinson, B.: Evaluating the intelligibility of diagrammatic languages used in the specification of software. In: Anderson, M., Cheng, P., Haarslev, V. (eds.) Diagrams 2000. LNCS (LNAI), vol. 1889, pp. 376–391. Springer, Heidelberg (2000). https://doi.org/10.1007/3-540-44590-0_32
26. Hruby, P.: Structuring specification of business systems with UML (with an emphasis on workflow management systems). In: Patel, D., Sutherland, J., Miller, J. (eds.) Business Object Design and Implementation II, pp. 77–89. Springer, London (1998). https://doi.org/10.1007/978-1-4471-1286-0_9
27. Neiger, D., Churilov, L., Flitman, A.: Business process modelling with EPCs. In: Neiger, D., Churilov, L., Flitman, A. (eds.) Value-Focused Business Process Engineering: A Systems Approach. ISIS, vol. 14, pp. 1–31. Springer, Boston (2009). https://doi.org/10.1007/978-0-387-09521-9_5
28. Polančič, G., Šumak, B., Pušnik, M.: A case-based analysis of process modeling for public administration system design. Inf. Model. Knowl. Bases XXXI **321**, 92 (2020)
29. Recker, J.: Continued use of process modeling grammars: the impact of individual difference factors. Eur. J. Inf. Syst. **19**, 76–92 (2010)
30. Christensen, L.B., Johnson, B., Turner, L.A., Christensen, L.B.: Research methods, design, and analysis (2011)
31. Eid-Sabbagh, R.-H., Dijkman, R., Weske, M.: Business process architecture: use and correctness. In: Barros, A., Gal, A., Kindler, E. (eds.) BPM 2012. LNCS, vol. 7481, pp. 65–81. Springer, Heidelberg (2012). https://doi.org/10.1007/978-3-642-32885-5_5

Requirements and Method Engineering (EMMSAD 2020)

A Multi-concern Method for Identifying Business Services: A Situational Method Engineering Study

O. Ege Adali$^{(\boxtimes)}$, Oktay Türetken, Baris Ozkan, Rick Gilsing, and Paul Grefen

Eindhoven University of Technology, De Zaale, 5612 AR Eindhoven, The Netherlands
{o.e.adali,o.turetken,b.ozkan,r.a.m.gilsing,
p.w.p.j.grefen}@tue.nl

Abstract. Business services are offerings that enable organizations to achieve their strategic objectives by making their functionality accessible to their customers and business partners. Thus, organizations pay significant attention to and invest in the explicit identification and definition of their business services. This is, however, not a trivial endeavor as multiple concerns that are intrinsic to the concept of business service should be taken into consideration in identifying services. Existing business service identification methods used in isolation do not offer adequate coverage for these concerns. Addressing this issue, we propose a novel method assembled by situational method engineering from a set of existing service identification methods, taking the best aspects from each of them. In this paper, we present an instantiation of the situational method engineering approach alongside the details of the constructed method. We also provide a demonstration of the method with an illustrative scenario based on a real-life business case.

Keywords: Service identification · Method · Situational method engineering

1 Introduction

The most recent business approaches are increasingly shifting their focus away from goods-thinking to services-thinking [1]. Driven by the influence of digitalization, increased connectivity, and global economy, the concept of service has become central to value-creation [2]. As a result, many organizations are providing services as first-class standalone offerings in their value propositions, whereas many others are enhancing their offerings by transforming their products into services through servitization [3].

In this context, one major challenge for such organizations is the identification of their service offerings. When identifying service offerings, organizations have to deal with various service provisioning issues, such as determining what can be offered to which existing and potential customers and business partners [4–8], alignment of service offerings with the long-term strategic interests of the organization [9], and identification of business capabilities to provide a specific service offering [10–12]. To address this broad range of concerns, scholars have proposed the concept of 'business service', and relevant business service identification methods (BSIMs).

© Springer Nature Switzerland AG 2020
S. Nurcan et al. (Eds.): BPMDS 2020/EMMSAD 2020, LNBIP 387, pp. 227–241, 2020.
https://doi.org/10.1007/978-3-030-49418-6_15

The business service concept is a powerful abstraction that incorporates a number of *design concerns* to address service provisioning issues. At the meta-level, BSIMs provide *procedures* specifically designed to identify business services while addressing a number of these design concerns. BSIM procedures focus on a key business artifact (e.g., a business process, goal, business function, feature) and include a set of activities that employ this artifact in business service identification [13].

The literature reviews on BSIMs put forward a wide array of design concerns and investigate the BSIMs that they identified from various perspectives, each emphasizing a subset of such design concerns [13]. However, a thorough investigation of these reviews reveals that, while each BSIM addresses certain design concerns, a BSIM that is driven by a complete and refined set of reported design concerns is still lacking. Furthermore, existing BSIMs do not recognize contemporary perspective of markets reflected as the Service-Dominant (S-D) logic [2]. Therefore, a BSIM driven by both a complete and refined set of business service concerns and the contemporary business perspective can help organizations to identify business services that can enable them to better leverage this concept in addressing service provisioning issues.

In this paper we address this gap by developing a *multi-concern business service identification method* –MCBSIM- that covers a wider and more comprehensive selection of business service design concerns. In developing the MCBSIM, we followed the situational method engineering (SME) approach as it enables the construction of a method by assembling existing and reusable method fragments stored in a method base [14, 15]. In this regard, first, we have defined requirements for the MCBSIM based on the concerns related to business services and identified and analyzed 47 existing BSIMs to investigate the extent to which they meet these requirements. Next, we have identified and integrated carefully selected parts of a number of BISMs into a coherent method that meets the requirements set-forth. This paper presents the MCBSIM and demonstrates it by going through a real-life business scenario.

The rest of this paper is organized as follows: Sect. 2 introduces the related work on business services and BSIMs. Section 3 presents the research design for the development of the MCBSIM. We describe the MCBSIM and demonstrate its use in the business case in Sects. 4 and 5, respectively. Finally, Sect. 6 concludes with limitations and future research directions.

2 Background and Related Work

In this section, we first provide related work on business services and concerns related to the concept of business service and then, on BSIMs and their shortcomings.

2.1 Business Services

Business services are engineering artifacts designed by service providers with the purpose of achieving their strategic goals [4–6]. In that sense, the design of a business service involves bringing specificity to resources which have the potential to be acquired by specific customers or customer segments [16]. All in all, business services represent different types of value propositions in the form of offerings that service providers expose to advertise and manage their resources and interactive processes [11]. As is the case with the parent term service, the literature provides many different definitions of the term business service. Each definition caters to a set of *design concerns* intrinsic to the context in which the term is used. As a result, this creates an ambiguity surrounding the term and this ambiguity represents a challenge to the investigation of how business services are identified and defined. Therefore, as a first step in the purpose of designing a BSIM, we have studied the definitions of the concept of business service in the scholarly literature. These definitions bring together various *design concerns* related to the concept.

To discover these associated *design concerns* -which we will refer to as *business service concerns* from this point on-, we conducted a literature review by performing searches on established scientific databases (Ebsco, ScienceDirect, Scopus Springer-Link, Web of Science, and Wiley) using the search string "business service". This resulted in an initial set of 104 studies. Next, we applied backward snowballing on these studies [17]. The main inclusion criterion for selecting studies from the start set was that the study should propose a definition for the term 'business service'. We conducted two iterations and our final list of studies included a total of 16 studies. The references of these studies can be found in Table 1 below. We extracted each definition introduced by the aforementioned 16 studies and applied a grounded theory approach [18] to extract and refine a complete set of business service concerns. Accordingly, we first coded the business service concerns that each definition adheres to and then translated these into overarching themes by applying axial coding [19]. The resulting themes with the sources of definitions is presented in Table 1.

Table 1. Business service concerns

#	Business service concern	Source(s)
C1	A business service is connected to business goals and objectives	[4, 20–24]
C2	A business service offers a business capability	[4–7, 10, 11, 25]
C3	A business service encapsulates combinations of basic intangible and tangible resources	[6, 7, 26]
C4	A business service is customer-facing - external	[4–8, 27]
C5	A business service is composed of infrastructure services	[5, 7]
C6	A business service has a well-defined interface that explicates to the service customer how to interact with the business service	[25, 26]
C7	A business service has mechanisms that realize its delivery	[7]
C8	A business service shall have a service owner	[4–7, 25]
C9	A business service is connected to one or more value propositions	[7, 22]
C10	A business service's temporal and logical dependencies to other business services is explicitly defined	[5, 7, 28]
C11	All the information regarding a business service is stored in a service catalogue	[9, 29]

2.2 Business Service Identification Methods (BSIMs)

The aim of Business service identification is to identify and define candidate business services on the basis of business service concept [9]. Since the concept of business service involves multiple concerns, service identification involves the consideration of these concerns as well. This requires a systematic method that supports the examination of organizations from multiple perspectives [13]. In order to address this need, scholars and practitioners proposed several BSIMs. These methods use different *techniques* that involve procedures focusing on a key business artifact (e.g., business processes, goals, business functions, features) and a set of activities that employ this artifact in identifying business services [13]. However, reviews conducted on these BSIMs conclude that, while BSIMs recognize the business service concerns to a certain degree, there is no consensus on how to deal with multiple business service concerns in a systematic way [13]. Comparing the previous work on BSIMs, we identified 47 unique BSIMs[1] which populate our method base.

3 Research Design

In the development of MCBSIM, we employed an SME approach [14, 30]. Accordingly, every SME process includes two main tasks: setting the method engineering goal and constructing a method that meets this goal [14]. Below we elaborate on each task.

3.1 Setting the Method Engineering Goal

Aligned with the most contemporary perspective to marketing S-D logic [2] we define the context of our project as "identification of business services for a service provider making a value proposition to a business network to co-create value with other actors in the same network". Furthermore, the service provider's major concern is to leverage the business service concept to the fullest in terms of addressing 11 business service concerns. In the light of this context information, an analysis of our method base revealed that the present methods provided method chunks to perform certain aspects of business service identification aligned with our context such as consideration of network or value propositions during identification. Additionally, we observed the existence of at least one method that adheres to a specific business service concern. Therefore, we decided to follow a method driven strategy and set our method engineering goal as "assembling a new method by re-using the method chunks of existing BSIMs".

3.2 Construction of the Method

In line with our goal, we followed an *assembly-based method engineering strategy* described in [30]. The process for this strategy consists of three steps: specification of method requirements, selection of method chunks, and assembly of method chunks. Below we elaborate on each step.

---

[1] Please visit the following link for the method base: https://sites.google.com/view/bsimbase/.

Specification of Method Requirements

For this stage we followed the *process driven strategy* as our goal was to construct a new method [30]. Accordingly, we first determined our method engineering intentions (MEIs) as shown in Table 2. These intentions were directly elicited from the characteristics of the method context described in Sect. 3.1.

Table 2. Method engineering intentions

#	Method intention
MEI1	The method should identify business service(s) that comply with 11 business service concerns
MEI2	The method should target a focal business unit (FBU) to specify business service(s)
MEI3	The method should identify business services based on a value proposition of the FBU
MEI4	The method should be applied in a business network consisting of actors defined in the value proposition

To realize our MEIs, we developed a strategy driven requirements map (Fig. 1) as described in [30]. This map was based on the most comprehensive BSIM [31] in our method base. Each meta-step (MS) of the map and the business service concern it complies with are shown in Fig. 1 as well. The meta-steps MS3 and MS5 were already present in the BSIM and were directly carried over to the map. To comply with C9, we added MS1 which simply involves selecting a value proposition. Furthermore, we added MS2 to comply with C4 and C8 and MS4 to comply with C1 and C10. The arrows in the map represent strategies, each satisfying the objective of the MS connected to the arrowheads. Accordingly, the initial strategy: "Value proposition driven strategy" simply involves selecting a value proposition and the terminating strategy "Completeness strategy" involves identification of all business services for the selected value proposition. The remaining strategies (S1-4) represent placeholders for specific method chunks. What S1–S4 entail and how method chunks were selected for them are explained in the next step.

Selection of Method Chunks

As indicated in Fig. 1, our method selection was targeted at finding suitable method chunks for strategies S1-4. For selecting the chunks, we extensively used the MEIs and based on them we developed the following queries for each strategy:

- **S1:** Application domain = 'Information Systems' & Design activity = 'Model the Value Co-Creation Context' & Situation = 'Business Services' & Intention = 'Identify goal dependencies between actors'
- **S2:** Application domain = 'Information Systems' & Design activity = 'Capture the Core Business' & Situation = 'Business Services' & Intention = 'Map business capabilities of the focal business unit'
- **S3:** Application domain = 'Information Systems' & Design activity = 'Relate the Core Business to the Value Creation Context' & Situation = 'Business Services' &

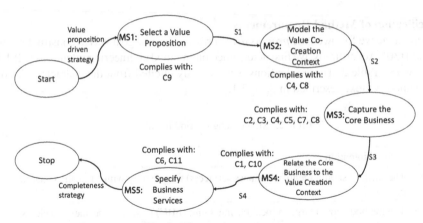

Fig. 1. The requirements map

Intention = 'Map business capabilities of the focal business unit to goals of the value creation actors'

- **S4:** Application domain = 'Information Systems' & Design activity = 'Design Service Specifications' & Situation = 'Business Services' & Intention = 'Create service specifications'

Each BSIM residing in our method base is labeled with specific tags indicating its domains, design activity, situation and intention. Therefore, we utilized these tags for querying the method chunks meeting the requirements of each strategy. Our queries resulted in selection of a total of 13 method chunks (MCs). The resulting set of MCs for each query is given in Table 3.

Assembly of Method Chunks

We followed the *association strategy* at this stage as our selected method chunks each corresponded to a different functionality [30]. Accordingly, we looked for method chunks which can be bridged together through their input and output products. This means, the output product of the first chunk in line should be the input product of the following chunk and so on. The input and output products of each method chunk are given in Table 3. Apart from the match between input and output products the assembled set of methods should also comply with all of the strategies S1-4.

In terms of complying with strategies, S3 demands *MC3: Capability Modeling* method chunk. Considering the fact that MC3 is a *must-have* method chunk, the method chunks that are both covering S1 and compatible with MC3 are *MC1: i* Strategic Dependency Modelling* and *MC11: Goal and Scenario Modelling*. In terms of covering S1 and being compatible with MC3, *MC8: Business Service Specification* stands out from the crowd as the only option (as MC2: P2S' input product does not match with MC3's output product). Overall, our final assembly consists of method chunks MC1, MC3 and MC8 and explained in the next section.

Table 3. Selected method chunks

MC #	Method chunk	Input	Output	S1	S2	S3	S4
MC1	i* Strategic Dependency Modelling [32–35]	Stakeholders and Their Objectives	Goal Model including Goals and Means (Tasks)	x	x		
MC2	P2S (from process to services) [36]	Business Process Models	Service Specifications				x
MC3	Capability Modeling [31, 35]	Business Tasks	Capability Model/Map		x	x	
MC4	Enterprise Business Modeling (Input Process and Entity Models) [37]	Business Process Models	Service Model (Object diagram)	x	x		
MC5	Intention – Strategy Map [38]	Business Goals	Intention – Strategy Model	x			
MC6	Business Process Decomposition with Activity clustering [39]	Business Use Cases	Activity Clusters		x		
MC7	Functional Decomposition with Visibility and Takeover [40]	Business Process Models	Activity Clusters with Associated Actors	x	x		
MC8	Business Service specification [31]	Capability Model/Map	Business Service Specification				x
MC9	Enterprise modeling with financial network modeling [41]	Business Process Models	Activity Clusters	x	x		
MC10	Feature and Feature Binding analyses [42]	Features	Feature Model		x		
MC11	Goal and Scenario Methodology [43, 44]	Business Goals	Goal and Task Model	x			
MC12	A Service Model Design Based on Use Case [45]	Business Use Cases	Activity Clusters		x		
MC13	Inter-Enterprise Business Process Modeling [46]	Business Process Models	Inter- Enterprise Business Process Models	x			

4   MCBSIM

The method, which consists of four main steps as presented in Fig. 2, has been designed to be used in a context where a focal business unit (FBU) makes a value proposition to co-create value with the actors (including customers and other stakeholders) in a certain context. Accordingly, the initial input for the method is a value proposition that the FBU aims to make in a certain value co-creation context.

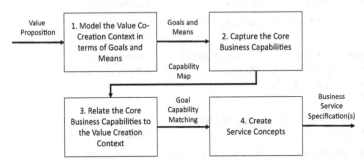

Fig. 2. MCBSIM

In Step 1, the objective is to model the value co-creation context in terms of determining goals and means dependencies between the value co-creation actors. The chosen method chunk for carrying out this step MC1: i* Strategic Dependency Model [47] that supports four main modelling concepts:

- *Actor:* A business role (e.g., organization and customer) that carries out actions to achieve goals by exercising its knowhow. We refer to an actor as a *Value Co-creation Actor* in this body of work.
- *Goal:* A desirable business state an actor aims to reach or sustain.
- *Means:* A concrete course of action (task) taken to accomplish goals. The realization of a means is under the control of the actor who proposes (owns) the means.
- *Dependency:* A link between two actors indicating that one actor (depender) depends on the other (dependee) for something in order that the former may attain some goal. Two types of dependencies are considered:
- – *Goal Dependency:* The depender depends on the dependee to bring about a certain state in the world. The dependee is given the freedom to choose how to do it.
- – *Means or Task-dependency:* The depender depends on the dependee to carry out an activity. A task dependency specifies how the task is to be performed, but not why.

The output of this step is a set of goal models: a generic model of the whole context, and goal models focusing on one-to-one goals and means dependencies between the FBU and each party in the context. It should be noted that the goal models are relative to the value co-creation context.

In Step 2, the main objective is to focus on the FBU and determine the business capabilities of the FBU, which contribute in making the selected value proposition.

Various definitions of capabilities exist in the literature [48], however, we adopted the definition provided in [49] as it is a synthesis of the definitions provided in the literature. Accordingly, a capability (1) is possessed by a resource or resource groups of resources (tangible and intangible), (2) is the potential for action via a process, and (3) produces a value for a customer (internal/external).

To capture such capabilities, we used the template given in Fig. 5 which was adapted from [49]. The method chunk for carrying out this step MC8: Capability Modeling [31] captures capabilities by defining service domains and identifying capabilities that exist in a specific service domain [31]. A service domain is described as a sphere of control that contains a collection of service operations to achieve related goals [31]. The service operations are the activities that are carried out within the service domain to interact with other service domains [50].

In Step 3, the main objective is to determine the capabilities that enable the achievement of identified goals and means. As described in MC8: Capability Modeling [31], the focus of the determination activity is to match the delivered business outcome of each capability with one or more goals and processes (or activities in the processes) to the means. After the matching, the capabilities that are necessary to make the value proposition are identified. These capabilities are the main output of this stage.

In Step 4, the achieved outputs are combined and processed for specification of the business services as described in MC8: Business Service Specification [31]. For specification, we used the template given in Fig. 7 which was designed in accordance with 11 business service concerns. As depicted in template, a business service specification involves a set of business service attributes, such as the capability, owner, service operations, used resources, etc.

5 Demonstration

In this section, we demonstrate the utility of our method by applying it in an illustrative scenario that is based on a real-life business case. The scenario depicts the case for a new urban bike sharing business model. We omit the names of the organizations in the scenario to keep their anonymity. In the selected business model, there are four actors: traveler (e.g., tourists, students, employees), bike sharing service provider, bike maintenance provider, and the local municipality. The co-created value proposed for the traveler is *flexible and comfortable travelling experience* via cycling around the city. Thus, the value to be co-created with the business model encapsulates high availability and widespread coverage of bicycles within the city. This should allow traveler, whenever s/he desires, to take a bicycle and travel around the city. The traveler is not concerned with managing or maintaining the bicycle and can store the bicycle at any available slot at a parking station. As such, flexibility and comfort should be granted to the travelers. How each actor contributes to the value co-creation is described below:

Traveler-being the customer-contributes to the value co-creation through providing data on the usage of the service. Therefore, the value proposition of the traveler is profile data and data about service-use. *Bike Sharing Service Provider* contributes to the value co-creation by providing the facilities for bike sharing. As such, it is responsible for establishing the infrastructure for the bicycles, the software system to operate and use the bicycles, as well as the IT system to interact with users. Bike Sharing Service Provider is the focal business unit (FBU) of the business case. *Bike Maintenance Provider* contributes to the value co-creation by ensuring that bikes are in good conditions and *available* for travelers wherever and whenever they desire. *Local Municipality* contributes to the value co-creation by providing either the legal, financial or operational support.

In step 1, we regarded the value co-creation contribution of each actor (except the customer) as that actor's motivations and interests [47] and iteratively dissected these contributions into goals and means. On the other hand, the goal(s) and the single mean of the customer were defined by dissecting the main characteristic of the co-created value which is *flexible* travel. For space considerations, we only provide the goal model (Fig. 3) that depicts the goals and means dependencies between the FBU (service provider) and customer (traveler).

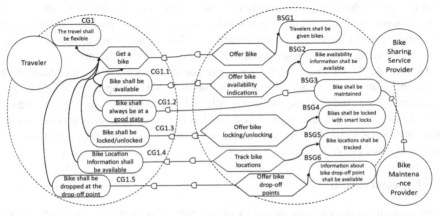

Fig. 3. i* goal model for value co-creation context (between service provider and traveler)

In step 2, we determined the service domains and service operations of the FBU based on the means of the FBU defined in goal models. Then, we matched these service operations to an already existing list of business capabilities of the FBU which are shown in Fig. 4. Furthermore, we re-defined each capability in detail according to our template. Figure 5 presents an example that depicts a specification for the capability "bike lending".

In step 3, we explicitly linked the capabilities that enable the FBU to achieve the goals defined in Step 1. Then, we examined the linked capabilities against 11 business service concerns to identify capabilities that can be business service candidates. This resulted in selection of the set of capabilities: *Bike Lending* and *Traveler Guidance* (as depicted in Fig. 6). The capability: *Service Platform Management* is an enabling capability for the other capabilities, and it is not provided to the value co-creation context (i.e. does not comply with concern C4), therefore, is not a candidate business service. Furthermore, the capabilities *Bike Maintenance* and *Accident Handling* are partner capabilities that do not belong to the FBU.

Service Operations		Capabilities

Service Domains		Service Operations	Capabilities
	Bike Pick-up	Unlock Bike	Bike Lending
		Start Session	
	Bike Commute	Track Travel	
		Handle Bike Failure	Bike Maintenance
		Handle Accident	Accident Handling
	Bike Drop-off	Lock Bike	Bike Lending
		End Session	
	Traveler Guidance	Suggest Station	Traveler Guidance
		Share Avail. Information	
	Bike Availability	Maintain Bikes (Predictive)	Bike Maintenance
	Platform Management	Manage Data	Service Platform Management
		Secure Platform	
		Analyze Data	
		Provide Analytics	

Fig. 4. Service domains and business capabilities

Business Capability:	Primary Capability 1: Bike Lending	
Business Purpose:	Enable travelers to get bikes.	
Capability Type:	Primary Capability	
Capability Owner:	Bike Sharing Service Provider	
Strategic Goals Addressed:	Travelers shall be given bikes Bikes shall be locked with smart locks Bike locations shall be tracked	
Dependencies to Other Capabilities:	Enabling Capability: Service Platform Management	
Process	Tangible Resources	Intangible Resources
Unlock Bike	Bike Lock, Bike	
Start Session	Bike, Bike Station	Mobile App
Track Commute	Bike	Mobile App
Lock Bike	Bike Lock, Bike	
End Session	Bike, Bike Station	Mobile App

Fig. 5. Business capability specification for bike lending

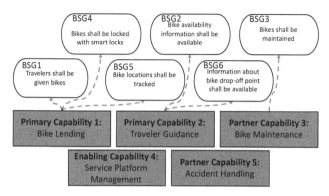

Fig. 6. Relationship between capabilities and goals

In step 4, we specified two business services for 2 FBU capabilities: *Bike Lending* and *Traveler Guidance* by bringing together all the entities and properties of a business service as defined by our 11 business service concerns. A specification for the Bike Lending business service is presented in Fig. 7.

Business Service:	Bike Lending Service
Connected Value Proposition:	Flexible Urban Travel via Bike
Connected Business Capability:	Bike Lending
Customer Goals Addressed:	The travel shall be flexible
Strategic Goals Addressed:	Travelers shall be given bikes Bikes shall be locked with smart locks Bike locations shall be tracked
Business Service Owner:	Bike Sharing Service Provider
Business Service Operations:	Unlock Bike Start Session Track Travel Lock Bike End Session
Related Processes:	Unlock Bike Start Session Track Travel Lock Bike End Session
Used Resources:	Bike Lock, Bike, Bike Station, Mobile App
Required Business Services:	Traveler Guidance, Bike Maintenance, Accident Handling

Fig. 7. Business service specification for bike lending

6   Conclusion, Limitations and Future Work

In this paper, we present a method for the identification of business services. The main objective of the proposed method is to cover the concerns that relate to the design of business services during their identification. To achieve this objective, we identified the business service concerns and followed an SME approach to develop the method. In terms of the followed SME approach, we transformed business service concerns into method building objectives, identified method chunks realizing these objectives from a method-base of 47 methods, and assembled the identified method chunks into a procedural method. Furthermore, we demonstrated the method with an illustrative scenario based on a real-life business case.

Business service concept is a powerful abstraction to determine the service offerings of organizations. However, fully leveraging this abstraction requires recognition of the concerns affiliated with it. In comparison, the proposed method recognizes and leverages the business service concept better than previously proposed methods. It yields business services that are true to their intended form and purpose by building on carefully selected method chunks each adhering to a specific concern affiliated to the business service concept. Furthermore, previously proposed methods are disconnected from the contemporary perspective of markets that is conceptualized as the Service-Dominant (S-D) logic [2]. The proposed method takes the central theme of S-D logic -value co-creation- as its context to better align with the views of modern business.

This study is subject to potential limitations mainly due to the strategy used to demonstrate the utility of the proposed method. A demonstration with an illustrative scenario is usually tailored to an ideal context and thus, is highly prone to hinder the discovery of issues that might result from the use of the artifact at hand in a real setting or context [51]. Since the proposed method and particularly its steps are highly rooted in academic literature –mainly in the form of business service concerns and existing BSIMs-, its effects on a real-world situation are yet to be discovered. Therefore, as future work, the method can be applied in a number of real-life scenarios in the form of case studies, and its utility and validity can be further evaluated using qualitative research methods that involve the practitioners as users of the method. Accordingly, the method can be improved and finetuned to address any potential shortcomings discovered in these evaluations.

References

1. Plugge, A., Janssen, M.: Exploring determinants influencing a service-oriented enterprise strategy: an executive management view BT - digital services and platforms. Considerations for Sourcing, pp. 35–55 (2019)
2. Vargo, S.L., Lusch, R.F.: Evolving to a new dominant logic for marketing. J. Mark. **68**(1), 1–17 (2004)
3. Wolfson, A., Dominguez-Ramos, A., Irabien, A.: From goods to services: the life cycle assessment perspective. J. Serv. Sci. Res. **11**(1), 17–45 (2019)
4. Cherbakov, L., Galambos, G., Harishankar, R., Kalyana, S., Rackham, G.: Impact of service orientation at the business level. IBM Syst. J. **44**(4), 653–668 (2005)
5. Sanz, J., Nayak, N., Becker, V.: Business services as a modeling approach for smart business networks (2006)
6. Tohidi, H.: Modelling of business services in service oriented enterprises. Procedia Comput. Sci. **3**, 1147–1156 (2011)
7. Flaxer, D., Nigam, A.: Realizing business components, business operations and business services. In: IEEE International Conference on E-Commerce Technology for Dynamic E-Business, pp. 328–332 (2004)
8. Brocke, H., Uebernickel, F., Brenner, W.: A methodical procedure for designing consumer oriented on-demand IT service propositions. Inf. Syst. E-bus. Manag. **9**(2), 283–302 (2011)
9. Arsanjani, A., Ghosh, S., Allam, A., Abdollah, T., Ganapathy, S., Holley, K.: SOMA: a method for developing service-oriented solutions. IBM Syst. J. **47**(3), 377–396 (2008)
10. Lusch, R.F., Nambisan, S.: Service innovation in the digital age service innovation: a service-dominant logic perspective. MIS Q. **39**(1), 155–176 (2015)
11. Turetken, O., Grefen, P., Gilsing, R., Adali, O.E.: Service-dominant business model design for digital innovation in smart mobility. Bus. Inf. Syst. Eng. **61**(1), 9–29 (2019)
12. Suratno, B., Ozkan, B., Turetken, O., Grefen, P.: A method for operationalizing service-dominant business models into conceptual process models. In: Shishkov, B. (ed.) BMSD 2018. LNBIP, vol. 319, pp. 133–148. Springer, Heidelberg (2018). https://doi.org/10.1007/978-3-319-94214-8_9
13. Huergo, R.S., Pires, P.F., Delicato, F.C., Costa, B., Cavalcante, E., Batista, T.: A systematic survey of service identification methods. Serv. Oriented Comput. Appl. **8**(3), 199–219 (2014)
14. Ralyte, J., Deneckere, R., Rolland, C.: Towards a generic model for situational method engineering. In: Eder, J., Missikoff, M. (eds.) CAiSE 2003. LNCS, vol. 2681, pp. 95–110. Springer, Heidelberg (2003). https://doi.org/10.1007/3-540-45017-3_9

15. Iacovelli, A., Souveyet, C., Rolland, C.: Method as a Service (MaaS). In: 2008 Second International Conference on Research Challenges in Information Science, pp. 371–380 (2008)
16. Arnould, E.J.: Service-dominant logic and resource theory. J. Acad. Mark. Sci. 36(1), 21–24 (2008)
17. Wohlin, C.: Guidelines for snowballing in systematic literature studies and a replication in software engineering. In: Proceedings of the 18th International Conference on Evaluation and Assessment in Software Engineering, pp. 38:1–38:10 (2014)
18. Corbin, J., Strauss, A.: Basics of Qualitative Research: Techniques and Procedures for Developing Grounded Theory, 3rd edn. Thousand Oaks, California (2008)
19. Charmaz, K.: The search for meanings - grounded theory. In: Rethinking Methods in Psychology, pp. 27–49. Sage Publications, London (1996)
20. Estrada, H.: A service-oriented approach for the i* framework. Universidad Politecnica de Valencia (2008)
21. Flaxer, D., Nigam, A., Vergo, J.: Using component business modeling to facilitate business enterprise architecture and business services at the US Department of Defense. In: IEEE International Conference on e-Business Engineering (ICEBE 2005), pp. 755–760 (2005)
22. Nayak, N., Nigam, A., Sanz, J., Marston, D., Flaxer, D.: Concepts for service-oriented business thinking. In: Proceedings - 2006 IEEE International Conference on Services Computing, SCC 2006, pp. 357–364 (2006)
23. Tians, C., Ding, W., Cao, R., Lee, J.: Business componentization: a guidance to application service design. In: Min Tjoa, A., Xu, L., Chaudhry, S.S. (eds.) Research and Practical Issues of Enterprise Information Systems, pp. 97–107. Springer US, Boston (2006). https://doi.org/10.1007/0-387-34456-x_10
24. Sanz, J., et al.: Business services and business componentization: new gaps between business and IT. In: IEEE International Conference on Service-Oriented Computing and Applications (SOCA 2007), pp. 271–278 (2007)
25. Estrada, H., Martínez, A., Santilí An, L.C., Erez, J.: A new service-based approach for enterprise modeling (2013)
26. Karakostas, B., Zorgios, Y., Alevizos, C.C.: The semantics of business service orchestration. In: Eder, J., Dustdar, S. (eds.) BPM 2006. LNCS, vol. 4103, pp. 435–446. Springer, Heidelberg (2006). https://doi.org/10.1007/11837862_41
27. Cartlidge, A., Hanna, A., Rudd, C., Macfarlane, I., Windebank, J., Rance, S.: An introductory overview of ITIL V3 (2007)
28. Böttcher, M., Klingner, S.: Providing a method for composing modular B2B services. J. Bus. Ind. Mark. 26(5), 320–331 (2011)
29. Kohlborn, T., Fielt, E., Korthaus, A., Rosemann, M.: Towards a service portfolio management framework. In: Proceedings of 20th Australasian Conference on Information Systems, pp. 1–12 (2009)
30. Ralyté, J., Rolland, C.: An assembly process model for method engineering. In: Dittrich, K.R., Geppert, A., Norrie, M.C. (eds.) CAiSE 2001. LNCS, vol. 2068, pp. 267–283. Springer, Heidelberg (2001). https://doi.org/10.1007/3-540-45341-5_18
31. Kohlborn, T., Korthaus, A., Chan, T., Rosemann, M.: Identification and analysis of business and software services-a consolidated approach. IEEE Trans. Serv. Comput. 2(1), 50–64 (2009)
32. Andersson, B., Johannesson, P., Zdravkovic, J.: Aligning goals and services through goal and business modelling. Inf. Syst. E-bus. Manag. 7(2), 143–169 (2009)
33. Ramel, S., Grandry, E., Dubois, E.: Towards a design method supporting the alignment between business and services software. In: Proceedings - International Computer Software and Applications Conference, vol. 1, pp. 349–354 (2009)
34. Lo, A., Yu, E.: From business models to service-oriented design: a reference catalog approach. In: Parent, C., Schewe, K.D., Storey, V.C., Thalheim, B. (eds.) ER 2007, vol. 4801, pp. 87–101. Springer, Heidelberg (2007). https://doi.org/10.1007/978-3-540-75563-0_8

35. Grandry, E., Dubois, E., Picard, M., Rifaut, A.: Managing the alignment between business and software services requirements from a capability model perspective. In: Mähönen, P., Pohl, K., Priol, T. (eds.) ServiceWave 2008. LNCS, vol. 5377, pp. 171–182. Springer, Heidelberg (2008). https://doi.org/10.1007/978-3-540-89897-9_15

36. Bianchini, D., Cappiello, C., De Antonellis, V., Pernici, B.: P2S: a methodology to enable inter-organizational process design through web services. In: van Eck, P., Gordijn, J., Wieringa, R. (eds.) CAiSE 2009. LNCS, vol. 5565. LNCS, pp. 334–348. Springer, Heidelberg (2009). https://doi.org/10.1007/978-3-642-02144-2_28

37. Jamshidi, P., Sharifi, M., Mansour, S.: To establish enterprise service model from enterprise business model. In: Proceedings of 2008 IEEE International Conference on Services Computing, SCC 2008, vol. 1, pp. 93–100 (2008)

38. Kaabi, R.S., Souveyet, C., Rolland, C.: Eliciting service composition in a goal driven manner. In: Proceedings of the 2nd International Conference on Service Oriented Computing - ICSOC 2004, p. 308 (2004)

39. Kim, Y., Doh, K.: The service modeling process based on use case refactoring. In: Abramowicz, W. (eds.) BIS 2007. LNCS, vol. 4439, pp. 108–120. Springer, Heidelberg (2007). https://doi.org/10.1007/978-3-540-72035-5_9

40. Klose, K., Knackstedt, R., Beverungen, D.: Identification of services - a stakeholder-based approach to SOA development and its application in the area of production planning. In: ECIS, no. 2007, pp. 1802–1814 (2007)

41. Kohlmann, F., Alt, R.: Business-driven service modeling - a methodological approach from the finance industry. In: Sabre 2007, pp. 1–14 (2007)

42. Lee, J., Muthig, D., Naab, M.: An approach for developing service oriented product lines. In: 2008 12th International Software Product Line Conference, pp. 275–284 (2008)

43. Lee, J., Sugumaran, V., Park, S., Sansi, D.: An approach for service identification using value co-creation and IT convergence. In: Proceedings of 1st ACIS/JNU International Conference on Computers, Networks, Systems, and Industrial Engineering, CNSI 2011, pp. 441–446 (2011)

44. Suntae, K., Minseong, K., Sooyong, P.: Service identification using goal and scenario in service oriented architecture. Neonatal. Paediatr. Child Heal. Nurs. 419–426 (2008)

45. Si, H., Ni, Y., Yu, L., Chen, Z.: A service-oriented analysis and modeling using use case approach. In: Proceedings of 2009 International Conference Computational Intelligent Software Engineering, CiSE 2009, no. 60773163 (2009)

46. Wang, Z., Xu, X., Zhan, D.: Normal forms and normalized design method for business service. In: IEEE International Conference on e-Business Engineering (ICEBE 2005), pp. 79–86 (2005)

47. Yu, E.: Modelling strategic relationships for process reengineering (1995)

48. Offerman, T., Stettina, C.J., Plaat, A.: Business capabilities: a systematic literature review and a research agenda. In: 2017 International Conference on Engineering, Technology and Innovation (ICE/ITMC) (2017)

49. Michell, V.: A Focused Approach to Business Capability, no. Bmsd, pp. 105–113 (2013)

50. Grefen, P., Turetken, O., Traganos, K., den Hollander, A., Eshuis, R.: Creating agility in traffic management by collaborative service-dominant business engineering. In: Camarinha-Matos, L., Bénaben, F., Picard, W. (eds.) PRO-VE 2015, IFIP Advances in Information and Communication Technology, vol. 463, pp. 100–109. Springer, Heidelberg (2015). https://doi.org/10.1007/978-3-319-24141-8_9

51. Peffers, K., Rothenberger, M., Tuunanen, T., Vaezi, R.: Design science research evaluation. In: Design Science Research in Information Systems. Advances in Theory and Practice, pp. 398–410 (2012)

Modeling Complex Business Environments for Context Aware Systems

P. M. Singh[✉], L. P. Veelenturf, and T. van Woensel

OPAC Research Group, Department of IE&IS,
Eindhoven University of Technology,
Eindhoven, The Netherlands
{p.m.singh,l.p.veelenturf,t.v.woensel}@tue.nl

Abstract. Context awareness in complex business environments has been recognized as a major challenge for enterprise information systems. Although, the development of a context aware system in different application domains is convincingly documented in current literature, the design of such systems requires greater attention. Particularly, investigating the context of a context aware system. In this paper, we present a step-wise method to model a complex business environment. The method provides an approach for investigating a context and using the investigation results in subsequent design steps.

Keywords: Context aware · Business environment · System design · Complexity

1 Introduction

Advances in Information Technology (IT) have changed the nature of business environments. Today, business entities exist and work in an environment where they are interdependent and co-create value [1]. Some characteristics of such a business environment are, intricate value exchanges, a dynamic market, innovative products/services and loose customer loyalties.

By leveraging the advances in IT and computing capabilities, business entities adapt and customize their products/services to better align with customers' needs. In other words, they strive to provide *context-aware* products/services. Providing context aware services is no trivial task, particularly in today's business environments. Consequently, *"How to offer contextual capabilities in complex business environments?"*, is one of the four major challenges for Information Systems researchers highlighted by Kadiri et al. in [2]. In the same article, as a suggestion for future research, Kadiri et al. noted that *"Context models for complex enterprise applications.... are not being addressed in the research community so far"*. Similar observations have been made by Hong et al. in [3].

Contextual data is necessary to provide context aware products/services. However, the extraction of (relevant) contextual data in complex business environments require proper understanding of the environment [4]. In this paper, we

© Springer Nature Switzerland AG 2020
S. Nurcan et al. (Eds.): BPMDS 2020/EMMSAD 2020, LNBIP 387, pp. 242–256, 2020.
https://doi.org/10.1007/978-3-030-49418-6_16

present a step-wise method to model complex business environments. Thus, our method will help system designers in the design of context aware systems.

In Sect. 2, Background, we clarify our understanding of a complex business environment. We also highlight the challenges presented by complex business environments for context aware services/products. Thereafter, in Sect. 3, we present our method which is divided in three phases, Motivation Modeling, Use Case Modeling and Situation Modeling. Section 4, illustrates our method using the case of Janssen Transport b.v, a transport company. The company desires dynamic routing of its trucks to provide context aware transportation services. Section 5 is the discussion section which provides a reflection over our proposed method. Finally, Sect. 6 concludes the paper and highlights the main takeaways.

2   Background

2.1   Context-Aware Systems

Context aware systems gather and analyze (relevant) contextual data, thereby aiding a business entity to provide context aware services [4]. Using such systems the business entity can adapt, modify, update or even change its products/services & underlying processes. Context aware systems are being developed and used in various application domains including; health-care [5], disaster management [6] and smart cities [7].

2.2   Complex Business Environments

According to Chen et al. [8] complexity in an industry, corresponds to the number, multiplicity and distribution of external factors. Thus, it refers to the heterogeneity and concentration of businesses within an industry. Based on their study of 746 business entities, they concluded that as the complexity of a business environment increases, it becomes increasingly difficult for managers to make strategic decisions. Saleh and Watson [9] in their study of VUCA[1] business environments, define complexity as, the interconnected parts, networks and procedures within the organization and within the external business environment. Both studies discussed above, approach business complexity from a rather, wide perspective. While Chen et al. discuss complexity of industries as a whole, e.g., the air conditioning (manufacturing) industry, steel industry; Saleh & Watson discuss complexity w.r.t long term strategic decision making.

Our understanding of business complexity, relevant for context aware services, is complexity at the *operational*, business process level. It is aligned to Vaconselos and Ramirez's [10] concept of *natural complexity*. According to them there are two types of complexities;

1. algorithmic complexity - the difficulty in solving a given, well-defined, problem.

---

[1] volatile, uncertain, complex and ambiguous.

2. natural complexity - characterized by no unique solution since the solution depends on the interpretation of the problem.

An example of algorithmic complexity is, to find all words in a dictionary which start with 'q' and end with 't'. An example of a natural complexity is, say, to find all words in a dictionary which a child can easily read. The correct answer to the first example is unique, a fixed list of words, irrespective of who searches for the words. However, there is no one correct answer for the second example. The list of words, in this case, depends on interpretations like, who is a *child*? *what* does *easily read* mean? For distinction between the two complexities, Vascocelos & Ramirez call algorithmic complexity as *complication* and natural complexity as *complexity*.

From the perspective of context aware services, a complex business environment is one where interpreting the system's context, is a complex problem and cannot be achieved with certainty. Moreover, determining/computing the appropriate response based on contextual event(s) might involve high complication. The above discussion leads us to divide business environments into four broad categories as shown in Fig. 1. By proposing a method in this paper, our goal is to aid system designers in the interpretation of Category II and IV environments.

Increasing complication →

Increasing complexity ↓

Category I	Category III
Interpretation is not complex. Computation of correct response is not complicated	Interpretation is not complex. Computation of correct response is complicated
Category II	Category IV
Interpretation is complex. Computation of correct response is not complicated	Interpretation is complex. Computation of correct response is complicated

Fig. 1. Different business environments along with context interpretation and response computation in each of them. Text in blue indicates the focus of this paper. (Color figure online)

3   Method

This section presents our method for modeling complex business environments. Using our method, situation of interest for a context aware system can be interpreted and modeled. The method has three sequential phases, i.e., Motivation Modeling, Use-case Modeling and Situation Modeling. With each phase the level of detail about the system's context increases, thereby enabling its interpretation. We have designed the method based on our experiences in different research projects aimed at designing context aware systems.

3.1   Phase I Motivation Modeling

Phase I, motivation modeling, provides a high level view of the current and desired scenario. Modeling them clarifies the motivation behind providing context aware services. The output of Phase I is a motivation model, linking the current scenario, to-be-provided services and the desired scenario.

Besides obvious value exchanges like money, products and services, business entities in a business environment also exchange intangible assets, e.g., knowledge, data, expertise and information. To correctly model all value exchanges in a complex business environment, a formal yet simple modeling technique is needed. Previous research, e.g. [1], shows that e-3 value modelling is an useful modeling tool for that purpose. It enables identification, modeling and analysis of all value exchanges between business entities in a complex business environment [1]. An e-3 value model consists of actors, value offerings and value transfers (Table 1).

Table 1. Text vs e-3 value model

Text	e-3 value model
Business entities	Actors
Users/customer	Actors
Products, services, knowledge, etc.	Value objects
Transactions between entities	Value transfers

- Activity 1: Model the current scenario of the complex business environment using an e-3 value model.
  Rationale. To identify all relevant business entities in the environment and their value exchanges.
- Activity 2: Model the desired scenario of the complex business environment using an e-3 value model. Add new *value objects* representing new services to be provided in the desired scenario.
  Rationale. To identify *(a)* what is the additional value provided by context aware service, *(b)* who is the beneficiary *(c)* who (possibly more than one business entity) provides the new services and *(d)* which additional activities are needed to provide these services.
  A link between the two scenarios is needed to specify, which concerns in the current scenario are addressed by introduction of context aware services in the desired scenario. Although, such relationships can be (textually) deduced from the two e-3 models, however, their deduction may not be straight forward and explicit. Therefore, a modeling tool may be used which links the motivation (current scenario) and the goal (desired scenario). A motivation-goal modeling language, like ArchiMate 3.0 [11] is one such modeling tool.

- Activity 3: Make a motivation model linking the concerns in the current scenario to the goals of the desired scenario, using a motivation-goal modeling approach, e.g. Motivation Extension (ArchiMate 3.0) or Business Motivation Model (OMG) [12]
  Rationale: Specifying the motivation to provide context aware services. By creating the motivation model, the intended value from context aware services in the desired scenario is better understood.

3.2 Phase II Use-Case Modeling

In Phase II, use-case modeling, results from Phase I are used to create a domain model and use case diagrams. A domain model includes both physical and abstract objects, thereby facilitating a clearer understanding of the context. It is derived from the motivation model and thus restricts domain modeling to relevant entities only. The use case diagrams build upon the domain model and the motivation model to further dissect (new) services. They provide the designer a concrete view of the interactions between the user, the system and the context.

- Activity 4: Create a domain model showing relevant entities, intrinsic and relational entities in the environment. An *Entity* is an object capable of independent existence. An *Intrinsic Entity* is a property of the entity and a *Relational Entity* is an entity which models the relationships between two entities.
  Rationale: To document and model all relevant entities, their properties and relationships.
- Activity 5: Use the motivation model and domain model to create use case diagrams. Typical questions to be asked during this activity are *(a)* who uses the (new-context aware) services? *(b)* when are these services used? *(c)* do these services re-use existing services?
  Rationale: A use case diagram clarifies the user-system interaction. It is a first attempt by the designer to understand the situations in which the system should provide its services.

3.3 Phase III Situation Modeling

In Phase III, situation modeling, results from Phase II are used to create situation models. Here, a situation refers to a *state of the environment* in which the user uses the context aware service.

- Activity 6: Using the use case diagrams write the situations in which the user, uses the services provided by the system.
  Rationale: Documenting situations of interest.
- Activity 7: If Activity 6 produces new entities, add them to the domain model.
  Rationale: A more comprehensive representation of the context. All entities in the domain model can together represent all situation in which the user uses the services.

- Activity 8: Based on the domain model, formalize the situations from Activity 6. Represent them using pseudo code or graphical situation models [13]. **Rationale:** To give a formal representation of the situation of interest in the business environment. Pseudo code or situation models are then converted to executable code.

At the end of Phase III, the designer has modeled situations of interest in the business environment. They are represented in terms of entities and their properties. It is these situations which a context aware systems should detect and interpret. By employing the above steps the system designer has a methodical approach for modeling a complex business environment. The following section illustrates the method using the case of Janssen Transport b.v., a transport company desiring dynamic routing of its trucks.

4 Illustrative Case Study - Janssen Transport b.v.

4.1 Current Scenario

Janssen Transport b.v. (JT) is a transport company in The Netherlands. It owns trucks and provides transportation services to retail stores and laundry businesses. Frank Cleaners (FC), a laundry business, is a client of JT. FC washes laundry from hotels, restaurants, vacation parks and dry cleaning stores. The collection of dirty laundry is outsourced by FC to JT. All Hotels[2] to be visited by JT, have been divided into five *sectors* by JT's management based on their proximity to each other. Every day one truck is assigned to a sector. The truck driver collects dirty laundry from all hotels in that sector and brings it to FC's Cleaning Unit. The sequence in which a truck visits the hotels in a sector, i.e., a sector's route, is fixed and is decided by JT's management. Hotels farthest to the cleaning unit are visited first.

The quantity of dirty laundry to be picked at a hotel, is not known in advance and varies considerably per day. Frequently, during their routes, trucks become full, while some hotels still need to be visited by them. The trucks then go to the FC cleaning unit, off-load the dirty laundry and continue further to visit the remaining hotels. Traffic conditions affect the arrival time of trucks at hotels. If a truck is delayed en-route to a hotel, often it is delayed to all subsequent hotels on the route, i.e., a *domino effect*. Hotels have a fixed time window (08:00 h–14:00 h), during which they allow their laundry to be picked up by the trucks.

4.2 Desired Scenario

JT has the following concerns over its client FC.

1. Numerous instances of unpicked laundry from hotels, a direct monetary loss for JT.

---

[2] further on we will use the term Hotels to refer to all collection points for laundry.

2. Late arrival of trucks at the hotels, i.e., beyond the time window. Delays are primarily due to traffic conditions. Due to delays, the same hotels, those visited last in each route, get affected. In the desired scenario JT wants to adopt a pro-active approach of routing its trucks based on historical travel time data and real time traffic data.
3. While some trucks, at the end of their route, return to FC Cleaning Unit half empty (unused free capacity); others offload laundry and have to resume on their routes. In the desired scenario JT wants to predict the daily demands of each hotel and optimize the truck routes. Demand prediction will be based on historic demand data.

To address above concerns, JT requires a context aware routing system. The system should dynamically route trucks, optimize truck capacities and minimize delayed arrival of trucks.

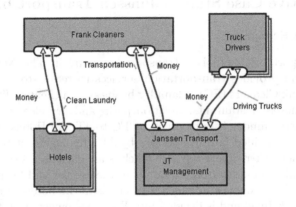

Fig. 2. Janssen transport current scenario

4.3   Phase I: Motivation Modeling

- Activity 1: Fig. 2 shows the e-3 value model for JT's current scenario. It models the business entities in the environment and the services they offer.
- Activity 2: Fig. 3 shows the e-3 value model for JT's desired scenario. In it, JT provides better transportation services to FC. Instances of unpicked dirty laundry decrease and trucks arrive at hotels on time. These are achieved via the new value activity, Context aware dynamic routing. Beside driving, truck drivers now provide their location and amount of laundry picked up at each hotel to JT. Data providers furnish real time traffic information to JT used for ETA calculation of its trucks.
- Activity 3: Fig. 4 show the Motivation Model based on Activity 1, 2 and textual descriptions. In the model *(a)* Assessment elements model problems/concerns of JT based on the current scenario. *(b)* Driver elements model

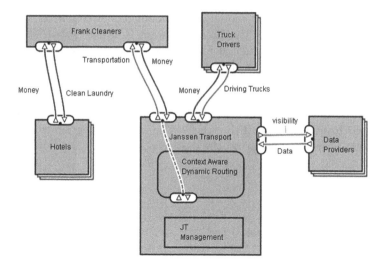

Fig. 3. Janssen transport desired scenario

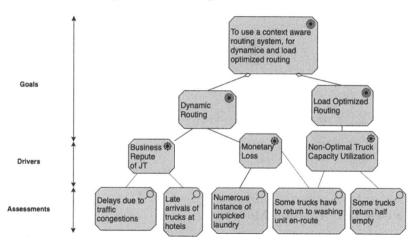

Fig. 4. Motivation model using ArchiMate 3.0 motivation elements (assessment, drivers and goals)

the relevance and effect of each problem/concern. *(c)* Goal elements model the new/improved service provided in the desired scenario. Each goal caters to at least one driver or a lower level goal.

4.4   Phase II. Use-Case Modeling

- Activity 4: The motivation model enables us to design a simple domain model (Fig. 5). Entities are in **Bold**, intrinsic entities in blue and relational entities in red.

- Activity 5: The motivation model and domain model enable us to make a simple use-case diagram of the Context Aware Routing System (Fig. 6). To determine a truck's delay, the truck's location is provided by the truck driver after logging in the system. The location is used for dynamically routing the truck (Goal). When the truck arrives at a hotel, the driver enters the arrival time and the picked up laundry in the system. The total capacity of the truck and cumulative load of laundry picked up is required for Load Optimized Routing (Goal) of the trucks. The use-case diagram thus connects the system's services to goals in the desired scenario.

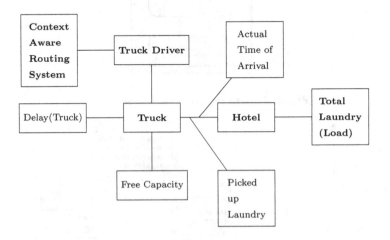

Fig. 5. Domain model (Color figure online)

4.5   Phase III. Situation Modeling

- Activity 6: The following three situation in the business environment have to be detected by the context aware routing system.
  - **Situation 1.** A truck's route in a sector is not the fastest route and remaining hotels can be visited earlier via a different route. To determine this situation, historical travel time data and real time traffic data is required.
  - **Situation 2.** A truck might have to return to the cleaning unit during its route. In other words, the current free capacity of the truck is less than the predicted load of the remaining hotels. A different truck should pick up the load from such hotels. In Fig. 7, (top) Truck 1 becomes full after loading laundry from Hotel C, and still has to visit Hotel D. The subsequent route for Truck 1 in the current situation is shown highlighted using red arrow. In the desired scenario (bottom) when Truck 1 becomes full, Truck 2 from an adjacent sector visits Hotel D.

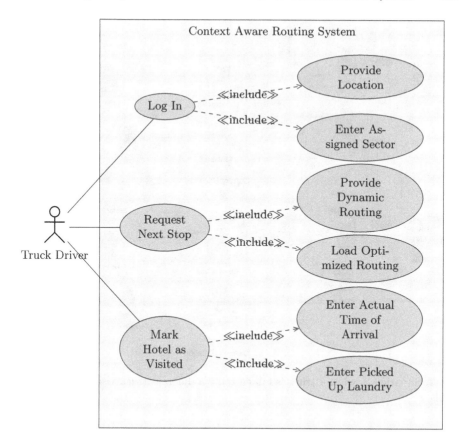

Fig. 6. Use case diagram

- **Situation 3.** A truck can not arrive at hotel(s) within the time window. It should be possible for another truck to pick-up laundry from such hotel(s). In Fig. 8 (top) Truck 2 is en-route between Hotel E and Hotel F. The road has traffic congestion, thus traffic movement is slow. Though Truck 2 can reach Hotel F on time it will not be able to do so for Hotel G. In the current scenario, dirty laundry from Hotel G would be left uncollected. In the desired scenario another truck picks up dirty laundry from Hotel G, as shown in Fig. 8 (bottom).
- Activity 7: After describing Situations 1–3 in textual form, new entities were discovered and have been added in the domain model (Fig. 9).
- Activity 8: The three situations from Activity 6 are formalized (pseudo code) using entities from the updated domain model.
  - **Situation 1.** At time t, elements of the set $RemainingHotels_{Truck}(t)\{\}$ are all hotels still to be visited by a truck. It is equal to all hotels in the sector assigned to the truck minus $VisitedHotels$. Thus, when a truck, say Truck B, leaves JT in the morning, $RemainingHotels_{TruckB}\{\}$

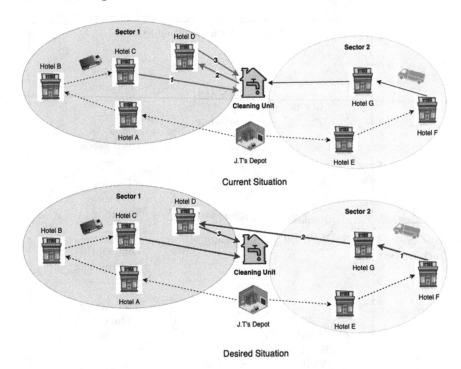

Fig. 7. Situation 2, when a truck is full en-route a different truck visits the remaining hotels

consists all hotels in the assigned sector. The route of a truck, at any given time, is represented by the sequence of hotels in the set $RemainingHotels_{Truck}(t)\{\}$. When the set $RemainingHotels_{Truck}(t)\{\}$ is empty, the truck goes to Cleaning Unit.

Given a route, at t, $Route_{Truck}(t)$; a faster route, $RouteFaster_{Truck}(t)$, exist, if the ETA for $RemainingHotels_{Truck}$ via $RouteFaster_{Truck}(t)$ is earlier than via $Route_{Truck}(t)$. Situation 1 is thus formulated as:

$$\exists Route_{Truck} \textbf{ such that}$$
$$ETA(Route_{Truck}) < ETA(Route_{Current})$$

At any time t, there may be multiple routes such that the ETA for hotels is earlier than the current route. We may call the set of all faster routes at any given time t as $FasterRoutes_{Truck}(t)\{\}$. The system selects the fastest route, $Route_{Fastest}$, from the set $FasterRoutes_{Trucks}(t)\{\}$.

- **Situation 2.** In this situation, $FreeCapacity_{Truck}(t)$ is less than the total $PredictedLoad$ for $RemainingHotels_{Truck}(t)\{\}$.

  Figure 7, shows a special case of Situation 2, where the $FreeCapacity = 0$ and Hotel D still needs to be visited, i.e., $RemainingHotels_{Truck}(t) = \{HotelD\}$. At any time (t), Situation 2 can be formulated as follows:

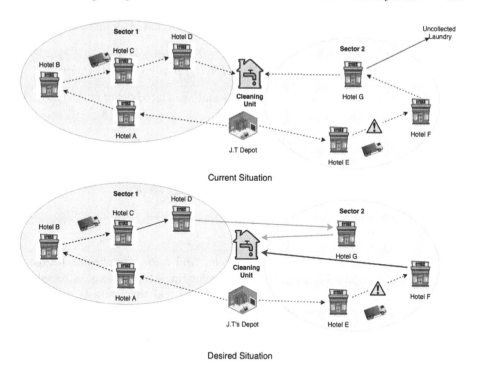

Current Situation

Desired Situation

Fig. 8. Situation 3, when a truck cannot arrive at a hotel on time, a different truck visits the remaining hotels

$$FreeCapacity_{Truck}(t) < PLoad(RemainingHotels_{Truck}(t), day) \wedge$$
$$RemainingHotels_{Truck}(t) \neq empty$$
$$where$$

$$RemainingHotel_{Truck}(t) = \{HotelM, HotelN, ...\}$$
$$and$$
$$PLoad(RemainingHotels_{Truck}(t), day) = PLoad(HotelM, day) +$$
$$PLoad(HotelN, day) + \quad (1)$$
$$PLoad(HotelP, day) +$$
$$.....$$

If the above situation is detected, the system assigns truck(s) to collect laundry from the remaining hotels of the truck with limited capacity. The assignment of trucks is non-trivial and will depend on various conditions, including; cost, distance of the truck and its free capacity etc.

- **Situation 3.** In situation 3, the ETA of some trucks at remaining hotels is beyond the time window. In this situation, to optimize capacity utilization, the routing system assigns trucks to collect laundry from those hotels. At time t, Situation 3 can thus be formulated as follows:

$$\exists Hotel_i \in RemainingHotels_{Truck}\{\} ::$$
$$ETA_{Truck}((Location(Truck(t)), Hotel_i)) \text{ beyond } TimeWindow \quad (2)$$

For calculation of ETA, traffic events and associated delay related to each event is needed.

After Activity 8, we have modeled situations of interest in terms of contextual data from JT environment. The system designer can use these in the subsequent design steps. The contextual data is in turn, itself derived from the domain, use-case and motivation models from previous design steps.

5   Discussion

JT's business environment is a *more complex* and *more complicated* business environment (Category IV, Fig. 1). The identification of situations, is based on historic data (e.g., travel times, pick up load) and real time data (e.g., traffic, truck capacity). However, such an identification cannot be done with certainty as travel times and pick up load are stochastic, not deterministic. The context aware routing system would constantly monitor the context for detecting the situations. Furthermore, the situations are difficult to identify via manual monitoring of the context, thereby making it a complex environment. The following points make the desired scenario *more complicated*, i.e., the computation of the correct system response, difficult:

1. Computation of the fastest route for each truck, using historic travel time data and real time traffic information.
2. Calculation of the monetary loss owing to unpicked dirty laundry from a hotel.
3. The ETA of a truck at a hotel can not be determined with certainty.
4. Selection of a truck among all trucks, such that extra costs associated with visiting additional hotels (e.g. fuel, driver compensation, etc.) is less than the loss incurred by unpicked laundry.

In Sect. 1, Introduction, we used the article by Kadiri et al. [2] to motivate our research. In the same article the authors had presented a generic model showcasing four layers of a context processing life cycle, i.e., Acquisition, Modeling, Processing and Dissemination. Table 2 compares these layers vis-à-vis the phases in our method. Phase III maps to the Processing Layer partially, since only Activity 8 delivers *codes* and *situation models* suitable for processing by development tools. Our method doesn't prescribe how situations of interest be communicated to the actors/business entities in the context. Consequently, there is no apparent mapping between the Dissemination layer and a phase in our method. Further study is needed to assess the above comparison and it is an area for future research. Additionally, future researchers should investigate the domain specific modifications needed for the method.

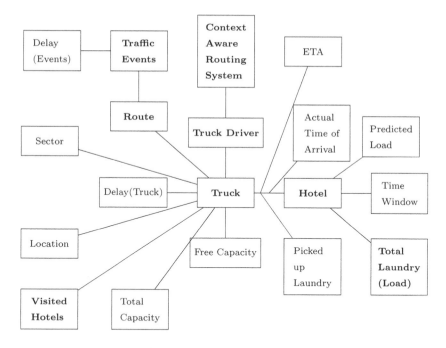

Fig. 9. Updated domain model

Table 2. Context processing lifecycle in [2] vs. Phases of the method

Layers [2]	Description in [2]	Phases in the method
Acquisition	Data and process contributing to context instance definition	Phase I
Modeling	Context representation in structured form	Phase II & III
Processing	Fusion of data and modeling with processing and reasoning mechanism	Phase III (partially)
Dissemination	Distributing the processed high-level context to context-consuming actors	No apparent mapping

Our method will enable system designers to avoid two pitfalls during context aware system design; (a) considering significant amount of contextual information during the initial design steps which later proves to be less relevant and (b) not including relevant contextual data in system design. Using our method, the designer is not overwhelmed with the complexity of business environments, thus avoiding the above pitfalls.

The proposed method is based on our experiences in system design and development. We did not follow a specific design methodology for designing the method. This a limitation of our research as design choices made by us may not be explicit.

6   Conclusion

Complex business environments pose unique challenges for the design of context aware systems. In this paper we presented a step-wise method to model a complex business environment. Via our method we, (a) provide a direction for investigating the context and (b) highlight the use of investigation results in subsequent design steps. System designers will find our method useful for the design of context aware systems in complex business environments. Future researchers should apply the method in varied application domains which would lead to further improvement of the method.

References

1. Wieringa, R., Engelsman, W., Gordijn, J., Ionita, D.: A business ecosystem architecture modeling framework. Paper presented at the 21st IEEE Conference on Business Informatics (CBI) 2019, Moscow, Russia (2019)
2. Kadiri, S.E., et al.: Current trends on ICT technologies for enterprise information systems. Comput. Ind. **79**, 14–33 (2016)
3. Hong, J., Suh, E., Kim, S.-J.: Context-aware systems: a literature review and classification. Expert Syst. Appl. **36**(4), 8509–8522 (2009)
4. van Engelenburg, S., Janssen, M., Klievink, B.: Designing context aware systems: a method for understanding and analysing context in practice. J. Logical Algebraic Methods Program. **103**, 79–104 (2019)
5. Trinugroho, Y.P.D., Reichert, F., Fensli, R.: An ontology enhanced SOA-based home integration platform for the well being of inhabitants. Paper presented at the 4th IADIS International Conference on e-Health 2012, Lisbon, Portugal (2012)
6. Fleischer, J., et al.: An integration platform for heterogeneous sensor systems in GITEWS - Tsunami Service Bus. Nat. Hazards Earth Syst. Sci. **10**, 1239–1252 (2010)
7. Auger, A., Exposito, E., Lochin, E.: iQAS: an integration platform for QoI assessment as a service for smart cities. Paper presented at 3rd World Forum on IoT 2016, Reston, USA (2016)
8. Chen, H., Zeng, S., Lin, H., Ma, H.: Munificence, dynamism, and complexity: how industry context drives corporate sustainability. Bus. Strategy Environ. **25**, 125–141 (2017)
9. Saleh, A., Watson, R.: Business excellence in a volatile, uncertain, complex and ambiguous environment (BEVUCA). TQM J. **29**(5), 705–724 (2017)
10. Vasconcelos, F.C., Ramirez, R.: Complexity in business environments. J. Bus. Res. **64**, 236–241 (2011)
11. ArchiMate 3.0.1 Specification. https://pubs.opengroup.org/architecture/archimate3-doc/chap06.html
12. OMG Business Motivation Model v1.3. https://www.omg.org/spec/BMM/1.3/PDF
13. Costa, P.D., Mielke, I.T., Pereira, I., Almeida, J.P.A.: A model-driven approach to situations: situation modeling and rule-based situation detection. Paper presented at the IEEE 16st International EDOC Conference 2012, Beijing, China (2012)

Towards Automating the Synthesis of Chatbots for Conversational Model Query

Sara Pérez-Soler[1], Gwendal Daniel[2], Jordi Cabot[2,3], Esther Guerra[1(✉)], and Juan de Lara[1]

[1] Universidad Autónoma de Madrid, Madrid, Spain
{Sara.PerezS,Esther.Guerra,Juan.deLara}@uam.es
[2] Universitat Oberta de Catalunya, Barcelona, Spain
gdaniel@uoc.edu
[3] ICREA, Barcelona, Spain
jordi.cabot@icrea.cat

Abstract. Conversational interfaces (also called chatbots) are being increasingly adopted in various domains such as e-commerce or customer service, as a direct communication channel between companies and end-users. Their advantage is that they can be embedded within social networks, and provide a natural language (NL) interface that enables their use by non-technical users. While there are many emerging platforms for building chatbots, their construction remains a highly technical, challenging task.

In this paper, we propose the use of chatbots to facilitate querying domain-specific models. This way, instead of relying on technical query languages (e.g., OCL), models are queried using NL as this can be more suitable for non-technical users. To avoid manual programming, our solution is based on the automatic synthesis of the model query chatbots from a domain meta-model. These chatbots communicate with an EMF-based modelling backend using the Xatkit framework.

Keywords: Model-driven engineering · Model query · Automatic chatbot synthesis

1 Introduction

Instant messaging platforms have been widely adopted as one of the main technologies to communicate and exchange information. Most of them provide built-in support for integrating *chatbot applications*, which are automated conversational agents capable of interacting with users of the platform [10]. Chatbots have proven useful in various contexts to automate tasks and improve the user experience, such as automated customer services [23], education [9] and e-commerce [21]. However, despite many platforms have recently emerged for creating chatbots (e.g., DialogFlow [6], IBM Watson [7], Amazon Lex [1]), their construction and deployment remains a highly technical task.

© Springer Nature Switzerland AG 2020
S. Nurcan et al. (Eds.): BPMDS 2020/EMMSAD 2020, LNBIP 387, pp. 257–265, 2020.
https://doi.org/10.1007/978-3-030-49418-6_17

Chatbots are also increasingly used to facilitate software engineering activities [5,12] like automating deployment tasks, assigning software bugs and issues, repairing build failures, scheduling tasks like sending reminders, integrating communication channels, or for customer support. In this context, we explored the use of chatbots for domain modelling in previous work [16,17]. Modelling chatbots can be embedded within social networks to support collaboration between different stakeholders in a natural way, and enable the active participation of non-technical stakeholders in model creation.

In the present work, we extend the previous ideas to support natural language (NL) conversational queries over the models. This is a more accessible and user-friendly way to query models than the use of technical languages like OCL (Object Constraint Language [15]). Moreover, we avoid the manual programming of the model query chatbots by their automatic synthesis. For this purpose, our solution is based on (i) the availability of a meta-model describing the structure of the models, (ii) its configuration with NL information (class name synonyms, names for reverse associations, etc.), and (iii) the automatic generation of a chatbot supporting queries over instances of the given meta-model. This approach is implemented on top of the Xatkit model-based chatbot development platform [4], which interprets the generated chatbot model and interacts with an EMF (Eclipse Modeling Framework) backend.

The rest of the paper is structured as follows. First, Sect. 2 provides motivation using a running example, and introduces background about chatbot design. Then, Sect. 3 explains our approach, and Sect. 4 describes the prototype tool support. Finally, Sect. 5 compares with related works, and Sect. 6 concludes.

2 Motivation and Background

In this section, we first provide a motivating example, and then introduce the main concepts behind chatbots.

2.1 Motivation

As a motivating example, assume a city hall would like to provide open access to its real-time traffic information system. Given the growth of the open data movement, this is a common scenario in many cities, like Barcelona[1] or Madrid[2].

We assume that the data provided includes a static part made of the different districts and their streets, with information on the speed limits. In addition, a dynamic part updated in real-time decorates the streets and their segments with traffic intensity values and incidents (road works, street closings, accidents or bottlenecks). Figure 1 shows a meta-model capturing the structure of the provided information.

In this scenario, citizens would benefit from user-friendly ways to query those traffic models. However, instead of relying on the construction of dedicated frontends with fixed queries, or on the use of complex model query languages like

---

[1] https://opendata-ajuntament.barcelona.cat/.

[2] https://datos.madrid.es.

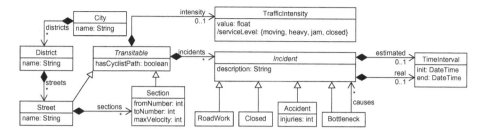

Fig. 1. A meta-model for real-time traffic information.

OCL, our proposal is the use of conversational queries based on NL via chatbots. Chatbots can be used from widely used social networks, like Telegram or Twitter, facilitating their use by citizens. Hence, citizens would be able to issue simple queries like *"give me all accidents with more than one injury"*; and also conversational queries like *"what are the incidents in Castellana Street now?"*, and upon the chatbot reply, focus on a subset of the results with *"select those that are accidents"*. Finally, for the case of dynamic models, reactive queries like *"ping me when Castellana Street closes"* would be possible.

Our proposal consists in the generation of a dedicated query chatbot given the domain meta-model. But, before introducing our approach, the next subsection explains the main concepts involved in chatbot design.

2.2 Designing a Chatbot

The widespread interest and demand for chatbot applications has emphasized the need to quickly build complex chatbots supporting NL processing (NLP) [8], custom knowledge base definition [18], and complex action responses including external service composition. However, the development of chatbots is challenging as it requires expertise in several technical domains, ranging from NLP to a deep understanding of the API of the targeted instant messaging platforms and third-party services to be integrated. To alleviate this situation, many chatbot creation frameworks have emerged, like DialogFlow [6], IBM Watson [7] or Amazon Lex [1].

Figure 2 shows a simplification of the typical working scheme of chatbots. Chatbots are often designed on the basis of *intents*, where each intent represents some user's aim (e.g., booking a ticket). The chatbot waits for NL inputs from the user (label 1 in the figure); then, it tries to match the phrase with some intent (label 2), optionally calling an external service (label 3) for intent recognition or additional data collection; finally, it produces

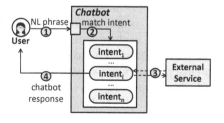

Fig. 2. Chatbot working scheme.

a response, which is often a NL sentence among a predefined set (label 4).

Intents are defined via training phrases. These phrases may include parameters of a certain type (e.g., numbers, days of the week, countries). The parameter types are called *entities*. Most platforms come with predefined sets of entities and permit defining new ones. Some platforms permit structuring the conversation as an expected flow of intents. For this purpose, a common mechanism is providing intents with a *context* that stores information gathered from phrase parameters, and whose values are required to trigger the intent. In addition, there is normally the possibility to have a *fallback* intent, to be used when the bot does not understand the user input.

3   Approach

Figure 3 shows the scheme of our approach. First, the chatbot designer needs to provide a domain meta-model (like the one in Fig. 1) defining the structure of the models to be queried, and complemented with NL hints on how to refer to its classes

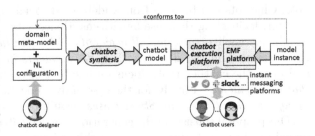

Fig. 3. Scheme of our approach.

and features (synonyms). From this information, an executable chatbot model that can be used to query model instances is generated. The next subsections explain these two steps.

3.1   Chatbot Generation: Intents and Entities Model

The chatbot designer has to provide a domain meta-model and optionally, a NL configuration model. The latter is used to optionally annotate classes, attributes and features with synonyms, and the source of references with a name to refer to its backward navigation. From this information, we generate the chatbot intents and entities.

Table(a) of Fig. 4 captures the generation of intents. We create an intent per query type, plus an additional intent called loadModel to select the model to be queried. The second row of the table shows the intent allInstances, which returns all objects of a given class. The intent is populated with training phrases that contain the class name as parameter. The possible class names are defined via an entity Class (see Table(b)). This intent would be selected on user utterances such as *"give me all cities"* or *"show every incident"*. The intent requires having a loaded model, which the table indicates as the intent requiring a model as context.

In the same table, intent filteredAllInstances returns all instances that satisfy a given condition. The intent is populated with training phrases that combine a class name and a condition made of one or more filters joined via logical

a) Intents

name	description	training phrases	provided context	required context
loadModel	loads working model from the backend	load the model {MODEL} open model {MODEL}...	MODEL type text	-
allInstances	returns all instances of a given class	give me all the {CLASSNAME} show me the {CLASSNAME}...	CLASSNAME type Class	MODEL
filtered AllInstances	returns all instances of a given class and satisfying a condition	select the {CLASSNAME} with {FILTER1} display the {CLASSNAME} with {FILTER1} {CONJ} {FILTER2}...	CLASSNAME type Class FILTER1 and FILTER2 type Condition CONJ type Conjunction	MODEL

b) Class entity

entries	synonyms
city	metropolis, town
...	...
bottleneck	traffic jam, congestion

c) StringAttribute entity

entries	synonyms
name	title, designation
description	summary

d) NumericAttribute entity

entries	synonyms
from number	from, starts
to number	to, ends
max velocity	velocity limit
value	amount of traffic
injuries	harm

e) NumericOperator entity

entries	synonyms
greater than	bigger, more than
smaller than	less than
equals	is same as

f) Condition composite entity

type	entries
StringCondition	StringAttribute + StringOperator + text
	StringAttribute + StringOperator + StringAttribute
NumericCondition	NumericAttribute + NumericOperator + number
	NumericAttribute + NumericOperator + NumericAttribute

g) Conjunction entity

entries
and
or

h) StringOperator entity

entries	synonyms
starts with	begins with
ends with	finishes with, end is
equals	is same as
contains	has

Fig. 4. Intents and entities generated for the running example chatbot.

connectives. We provide an entity Condition for the filters, explained below. This intent would be selected upon receiving phrases like *"give me all accidents with more than one injury"* (please note the singular variation w.r.t. the attribute name injuries).

In addition to intents, we create several entities based on the domain meta-model and the NL configuration. Specifically, we create an entity named Class (Table(b)) with an entry for each meta-model class name. These entries may have synonyms, as provided by the NL configuration, to refer to the classes in a more flexible way. Likewise, we create an entity for each attribute name attending to their type: String (Table(c)), Numeric (Table(d)), Boolean and Date (omitted for space constraints). For example, the StringAttribute entity (Table(c)) has an entry for all String attributes called name. Just like classes, these entries may have synonyms if provided in the NL configuration.

The Condition entity (Table(f)) is a composite one, i.e., its entries are made of one or more entities. This entity permits defining filter conditions in queries, such as *"name starts with Ma"* or *"injuries greater than one"*.

Regarding the complexity of the chatbot, the number of intents is fixed, and it depends on the primitives of the underlying query language that the chatbot exposes. Figure 4 exposes two primitives of OCL: allInstances, and allInstances()→select(cond). Other query types can be added similarly, which would require defining further intents. The number of generated entities is also fixed, while the number of entries in each entity depends on the meta-model size and the synonyms defined in the NL configuration.

3.2   Chatbot Generation: Execution Model

The generated chatbot also contains actions, required to perform the query on a modelling backend, which we call the *execution model*. This execution model contains a set of *execution rules* that bind user intentions to response actions as part of the chatbot behaviour definition (cf. label 4 in Fig. 2). For each intent in the *Intent* model, we generate the corresponding execution rule in the execution model using an event-based language that receives as input the recognized intent together with the set of parameter values matched by the NL engine during the analysis and classification of the user utterance.

All the execution rules follow the same process: the matched intent and the parameters are used to build an OCL-like query to collect the set of objects the user wants to retrieve. The intent determines the type of query to perform (e.g., allInstances, select, etc.), while the parameters identify the query parameters, predicates, and their composition. The query computation is delegated to the underlying modelling platform (see next section), and the returned model elements are processed to build a human-readable message that is finally posted to the user by the bot engine.

As an example, Listing 1 shows the execution rule that handles an allInstances operation. The class to obtain the instances of is retrieved from the context variable (available in every execution rule) and passed to our EMF Platform, which performs the query. Next, the instances variable holding the results is processed to produce a readable string (in this case a list of names), and the Chat Platform is called to reply to the user.

```
1  on intent GetAllInstances do
2    val Map<String, Object> collectionContext = context.get("collection")
3    val instances = EMFPlatform.GetAllInstances( collectionContext.get("class") as String )
4    val resultString = instances.map[name].join(", ")
5    ChatPlatform.Reply("I found the following results" + resultString)
```

Listing 1. Execution rule example

4   Proof of Concept

As a proof of concept, we have created a prototype that produces Xatkit-based chatbots [4], following the two phases depicted in Fig. 3. Xatkit is a model-driven solution to define and execute chatbots, which offers DSLs to define the bot intents, entities and actions. The execution of such chatbots relies on the Xatkit *runtime* engine. At its core, the engine is a Java library that implements all the execution logic available in the chatbot DSLs. Besides, a connector with Google's DialogFlow engine [6] takes care of matching the user utterances, and a number of platform components enable the communication between Xatkit and other external services.

In the context of this paper, we have developed a new EMF Platform that allows Xatkit to query EMF models in response to matched intents. The first version of our prototype platform[3] provides actions to retrieve all the instances of a given class, and filter them based on a composition of boolean predicates on the object's attributes or references. These predicates are retrieved from the context parameter defined in the intents (see Sect. 3.1), and mapped

---

[3] https://github.com/xatkit-bot-platform/xatkit-emf-platform.

to Java operations (e.g., the StringComparison "contains" is translated into ((String)value).contains(otherValue). The query result is returned as a list of EObjects, which is processed using the bot expression language to produce the response message. Listing 1 showed an example of the use of this EMF Platform.

We have also developed a web application, where domain meta-models (in .ecore format) can be uploaded, and then (optionally) configured with synonyms. Once the configuration is finished, the application synthesizes a Xatkit chatbot model, which then can be executed using the Xatkit runtime engine.

Figure 5(a) shows the web application on the left, where the running example meta-model (cf. Fig. 2) is being configured. Figure 5(b) shows a moment in the execution of the generated Xatkit chatbot, and the result returned by the bot when processing the example utterance *"show all accidents with more than one injury"*.

(a)   (b)

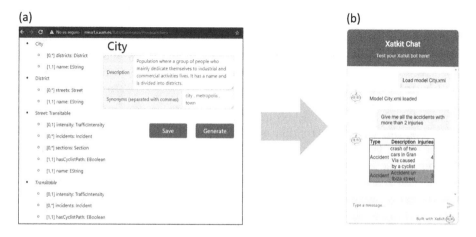

Fig. 5. (a) Web application to configure the chatbot. (b) A query in the generated chatbot.

5   Related Work

Next, we review approaches to the synthesis of chatbots for modelling or data query.

Our work relies on NL as a kind of concrete syntax for DSLs [17]. NLP has been used within Software Engineering to derive UML diagrams/domain models from text [2,11]. However, the opposite direction (i.e., generating chatbots from domain models) is largely unexplored. Almost no chatbot platform supports automatic chatbot generation from external data sources. A relevant exception is Microsoft QnA Maker [14], which generates bots for the Azure platform from FAQs and other well-structured textual information.

Closest approaches to ours are tools like ModelByVoice [13] and VoiceTo-Model [20], which offer some predefined commands to create model elements for specific types of models. In contrast, our framework targets model queries and not model creation, which was pursued in our previous work [17]. None of those two approaches support queries. Castaldo and collaborators [3] propose generating chatbots for data exploration in relational databases, but requiring an annotated schema as starting point, while in our case providing synonyms is an optional step. Similarly, [19] integrates chatbots to service systems by annotating and linking the chatbot definition to the service models. In both cases, annotations and links must be manually created by the chatbot designer to generate the conversational elements. In contrast, our approach is fully automatic. In [22], chatbots are generated from OpenAPI specifications but the goal of such chatbots is helping the user in identifying the right API Endpoint, not answering user queries.

Altogether, to our knowledge there are no automatic approaches to the generation of flexible chatbots with model query capabilities. We believe that applying classical concepts from CRUD-like generators to the chatbot domain is a highly novel solution to add a conversational interface to any modelling language.

6   Conclusion

Conversational interfaces are becoming increasingly popular to access all kind of services, but their construction is challenging. To remedy this situation, we have proposed the automatic synthesis of chatbots able to query the instances of a domain meta-model.

In the future, we aim to support more complex queries, including the conversational and reactive ones mentioned in Sect. 2.1. Our approach could be used to query other types of data sources (e.g., databases or APIs) via an initial reverse engineering step to build their internal data model and translate the NL query into the query language of the platform. Finally, we would like to add access control on top of the bot definition to ensure users cannot explore parts of the model/system unless they have permission.

Acknowledgments. Work funded by the Spanish Ministry of Science (RTI2018-095255-B-I00 and TIN2016-75944-R) and the R&D programme of Madrid (P2018/TCS-4314).

References

1. Amazon: Amazon Lex (2019). https://aws.amazon.com/lex/
2. Arora, C., Sabetzadeh, M., Briand, L.C., Zimmer, F.: Extracting domain models from natural-language requirements: approach and industrial evaluation. In: Proceedings of the MoDELS, pp. 250–260. ACM (2016)
3. Castaldo, N., Daniel, F., Matera, M., Zaccaria, V.: Conversational data exploration. In: Bakaev, M., Frasincar, F., Ko, I.-Y. (eds.) ICWE 2019. LNCS, vol. 11496, pp. 490–497. Springer, Cham (2019). https://doi.org/10.1007/978-3-030-19274-7_34

4. Daniel, G., Cabot, J., Deruelle, L., Derras, M.: Xatkit: a multimodal low-code chatbot development framework. IEEE Access **8**, 15332–15346 (2020)
5. Erlenhov, L., de Oliveira Neto, F.G., Scandariato, R., Leitner, P.: Current and future bots in software development. In: Proceedings of the BotSE@ICSE, pp. 7–11. IEEE/ACM (2019)
6. Google: DialogFlow (2019). https://dialogflow.com/
7. IBM Watson Assistant (2019). https://www.ibm.com/cloud/watson-assistant/
8. Jackson, P., Moulinier, I.: Natural Language Processing for Online Applications: Text Retrieval, Extraction and Categorization, vol. 5. John Benjamins Publishing, Amsterdam (2007)
9. Kerlyl, A., Hall, P., Bull, S.: Bringing chatbots into education: towards natural language negotiation of open learner models. In: Ellis, R., Allen, T., Tuson, A. (eds.) SGAI 2006, pp. 179–192. Springer, London (2007). https://doi.org/10.1007/978-1-84628-666-7_14
10. Klopfenstein, L., Delpriori, S., Malatini, S., Bogliolo, A.: The rise of bots: a survey of conversational interfaces, patterns, and paradigms. In: Proceedings of the DIS, pp. 555–565. ACM (2017)
11. Landhäußer, M., Körner, S.J., Tichy, W.F.: From requirements to UML models and back: how automatic processing of text can support requirements engineering. Softw. Qual. J. **22**(1), 121–149 (2014)
12. Lebeuf, C., Storey, M.D., Zagalsky, A.: Software bots. IEEE Softw. **35**(1), 18–23 (2018)
13. Lopes, J., Cambeiro, J., Amaral, V.: ModelByVoice - towards a general purpose model editor for blind people. In: Proceedings of the MODELS Workshops. CEUR Workshop Proceedings, vol. 2245, pp. 762–769. CEUR-WS.org (2018)
14. Microsoft: QnA Maker (2019). https://www.qnamaker.ai/
15. OCL (2014). http://www.omg.org/spec/OCL/
16. Pérez-Soler, S., Guerra, E., de Lara, J.: Collaborative modeling and group decision making using chatbots in social networks. IEEE Softw. **35**(6), 48–54 (2018)
17. Pérez-Soler, S., González-Jiménez, M., Guerra, E., de Lara, J.: Towards conversational syntax for domain-specific languages using chatbots. JOT **18**(2), 5:1–21 (2019)
18. Shawar, A., Atwell, E., Roberts, A.: FAQchat as in information retrieval system. In: Proceedings of the LTC, pp. 274–278. Wydawnictwo Poznańskie, Poznań (2005)
19. Sindhgatta, R., Barros, A., Nili, A.: Modeling conversational agents for service systems. In: Panetto, H., Debruyne, C., Hepp, M., Lewis, D., Ardagna, C.A., Meersman, R. (eds.) OTM 2019. LNCS, vol. 11877, pp. 552–560. Springer, Cham (2019). https://doi.org/10.1007/978-3-030-33246-4_34
20. Soares, F., Araújo, J., Wanderley, F.: VoiceToModel: an approach to generate requirements models from speech recognition mechanisms. In: Proceedings of the SAC, pp. 1350–1357. ACM (2015)
21. Thomas, N.: An e-business chatbot using AIML and LSA. In: Proceedings of the ICACCI, pp. 2740–2742. IEEE (2016)
22. Vaziri, M., Mandel, L., Shinnar, A., Siméon, J., Hirzel, M.: Generating chat bots from web API specifications. In: Proceedings of the ACM SIGPLAN Onward!, pp. 44–57 (2017)
23. Xu, A., Liu, Z., Guo, Y., Sinha, V., Akkiraju, R.: A new chatbot for customer service on social media. In: Proceedings of the CHI, pp. 3506–3510. ACM (2017)

Enterprise and Business Modeling
(EMMSAD 2020)

Conceptualizing Capability Change

Georgios Koutsopoulos[(⊠)], Martin Henkel, and Janis Stirna

Department of Computer and Systems Sciences, Stockholm University, Stockholm, Sweden
{georgios,martinh,js}@dsv.su.se

Abstract. Organizations are operating within dynamic environments that present changes, opportunities and threats to which they need to respond by adapting their capabilities. Organizational capabilities can be supported by Information Systems during their design and run-time phases, which often requires the capabilities' adaptation. Currently, enterprise modeling and capability modeling facilitate the design and analysis of capabilities but improvements regarding capability change can be made. This design science research study introduces a capability change meta-model that will serve as the basis for the development of a method and a supporting tool for capability change. The meta-model is applied to a case study at a Swedish public healthcare organization. This application provides insight on possible opportunities to improve the meta-model in future iterations.

Keywords: Capability · Enterprise Modeling · Change · Adaptation · Transformation

1   Introduction

Organizations are dynamic systems, constantly being in a state of change and evolution [1]. This state is driven by the dynamism existing in the organization's environment, both internally and externally. In the face of environmental opportunities and threats, organizations need to change to improve their effectiveness at achieving their goals [2], or ensure survival [3]. The changes occurring in an organization's environment are characterized by speed and direction which are often difficult to anticipate [3]. In addition, the environment's pace of change is higher that the organization's [4], and the speed is further increased by factors like the digital transformation of the society [5] and emerging technologies and strategies [3]. The concepts of change and strategy are not only linked to each other, but also to the concept of capability [6].

The notion of capability bears significance because it depicts an organizational viewpoint that encompasses several notions significant to organizational change. For example, goal, decision, context, process and service [7, 8] have been used, especially in the management literature, not only to describe an organization's value-generating elements, but have also been used as the core concepts of Enterprise Modeling (EM) approaches [8, 9].

EM, as a discipline, captures relevant knowledge and provides motivation and input for designing Information Systems (IS) to support the organization [10]. ISs are significant for every organization since they help in simplifying the organization's activities and processes and have gradually become integrated with almost every aspect of the

© Springer Nature Switzerland AG 2020
S. Nurcan et al. (Eds.): BPMDS 2020/EMMSAD 2020, LNBIP 387, pp. 269–283, 2020.
https://doi.org/10.1007/978-3-030-49418-6_18

business [11], to the level where business and IT have been "fused" into one [5]. This integration has raised several challenges for EM, especially regarding the organizations that are in motion, changing and evolving. Due to a high rate of change in modern enterprises, the maintenance of models that are sufficiently capturing the architecture from the perspective of involved stakeholders does not seem to be feasible. One of the main challenges for EM is how to capture the motion of an organization, that is, its current and desired affairs [5]. Capability modeling, as a specialization of EM, also needs to tackle this challenge. This can be achieved by optimizing existing approaches or developing specific modeling approaches for depicting capability change.

The objective of this study is *to propose a meta-model for depicting capability change*. It belongs to a research project that aims to provide methodological and tool support for organizations that are undergoing changes or need to. The project is elaborated following the principles of Design Science Research (DSR) [12, 13]. Following the exploration of the field [14], the elicitation of requirements for the artifact [15], and the introduction of a typology for changing capabilities [16], the present study belongs to the project step that concerns the initial development of a meta-model. This is a design artifact that will serve as a basis for a capability modeling method. In addition, the meta-model is demonstrated by applying it to an existing case, in particular, a public healthcare organization in Sweden which is undergoing changes.

The rest of the paper is structured as follows. Section 2 provides a brief presentation of the background and research related to this study. Section 3 describes the methods employed in this study. Section 4 introduces and describes the capability change meta-model and its components. Section 5 presents an example application of the meta-model on a case study. Section 6 discusses the meta-model and its application. Section 7 provides concluding remarks.

2   Background and Related Research

This section presents a brief overview of the existing capability modeling research and the topics relevant to the development of the meta-model.

2.1   Organizational Change

Organizations are social goal-directed systems which maintain boundaries that reflect their goals [3]. Changing organizations have been widely researched. There are several terms describing the phenomenon with different terms, for example change, transformation, adaptation [3]. These terms are sometimes used interchangeably or used to reflect different scopes of undergoing changes [17]. The terms business, organization and enterprise are often used interchangeably as well, however, there are also cases where they are distinguished, like for example [1], where an enterprise is defined as a collection of organizations that share a common set of goals.

Regarding the drivers of organizational change, there are several perspectives and associated theories. Zimmermann [3] has provided a detailed analysis of these perspectives. One of the main perspectives is based on the assumption of human rationality and utility maximization, which results in assuming that entire organizations are rationally adapting to the environment [3]. These theories that consider the environment as the factor setting the point of time and the direction of change are called deterministic, in comparison to the voluntaristic theories that build on the importance of the consideration of strategic choice. This perspective emphasizes on strategic choice of the organization's decision-makers and their role in shaping the organization [3].

However, there are also theories that reconcile these perspectives to facilitate understanding of change as a combination of environmental and managerial forces taking also organizational inertia into consideration. For example, the cognitive approach aims to understand the processes of an organization that lead both to prosperity and decline, and also to failure to change. This is preceded by the definition of cognition as the process that involves the perception and interpretation of the environment and the translation of this information into strategic choice [3]. Including the negative aspect of change is in line with our earlier work [16].

A noteworthy point is that the diverse drivers of change do not provide any indication between causes and consequences. The causality of change and the causal relationships among the factors driving change, which have often been neglected, should be implemented in research methods aiming to capture the complexity of change [3].

2.2 Enterprise Modeling

The process of creating a model capturing all the aspects of an enterprise that a modeling purpose requires, is called EM. Thus, the produced model consists of interconnected models, each of them being focused on one specific viewpoint of the modeled enterprise, for example, processes, goals, concepts and business rules [18]. Any organization or its part can benefit from the application of EM.

An enterprise model can help people in an organization to develop a deeper understanding of the system, in other words, how their work gets integrated in a bigger picture and, additionally, models can enable the users' understanding of the supporting information systems and its interplay with organizational action patterns [19].

Furthermore, since the meta-models specify modeling languages, they are valuable to (i) modelers, who are interested in understanding and applying the language, (ii) researchers, who have interest in evaluating and adapting a language, for example to a domain-specific version, and (iii) tool vendors, who have interest in developing tool for the language [20].

2.3 Capabilities

There is no consensus on the definition of capability in the literature. In this study, the notion of capability is defined as a set of resources, whose configuration bears the ability and capacity to create value by fulfilling a specific goal within a specific context. This definition is the result of combining two earlier definitions from [8, 21].

The concept of capability is often considered as the missing link in business/IT transformation [22]. Its growing popularity can be attributed to the fact that it enables business/IT transformations by (i) providing a common language to the business, (ii) enabling to-the-point investment focus, (iii) serving as a baseline for strategic planning, change management and impact analysis, and (iv) leading directly to business specification and design [22].

Capability Modeling

The capability modeling approaches that exist in the literature have been identified and their meta-models have been explored in our earlier work. In particular, 64 capability meta-models have been analyzed using a change function-related framework [14]. The change functions of the framework are observation, decision and delivery of capability change. It has been identified that the majority of the meta-models include concepts that address at least partially, all the above mentioned functions and have a scope combining business and IT. A set of change related-concepts has been elicited for inclusion in a capability change meta-model, so as to facilitate the development of a method.

Regarding the modeling of capabilities, [23] have suggested three strategies within the Capability-Driven Development (CDD) method. All three strategies consist of three steps, which are (i) Capability design, (ii) Capability evaluation, and (iii) Development of Capability delivery application. Steps two and three are common in all strategies. The second step concerns the evaluation of the design from both business and technical perspectives before the implementation of the capability. The third step involves packaging the indicators for monitoring and the algorithms for run-time adjustments as a support application. The differentiation among the three strategies lies only in the first step. It concerns the design of the capability using as a starting point: (i) goals, (ii) processes, or (iii) concepts [23].

3   Methodology

This section presents the methods employed for the development of the meta-model and the case study.

3.1   Design Science

The DSR project to which this study belongs follows the guidelines of [13]. According to this framework, a DSR project consists of five activities, namely (i) problem explication, (ii) outline artifact and define requirements, (iii) design and develop artifact, (iv) demonstrate artifact, and (v) evaluate artifact. The present study belongs to the third step which, creates an artefact fulfilling the requirements elicited during the previous activity, since it presents the first stage of the development of a method artifact, the creation of a meta-model. The process is iterative and incremental, which means that several rounds of development are needed to reach a final version of the artifact.

3.2   Meta-model Development

A meta-model is a part of a modeling language which consists of (i) notation, which is its graphical representation, (ii) syntax, that is the available language concepts, and (iii) semantics, the meaning of the language concepts [24]. Different meta-model specification techniques result to different meta-model types, i.e. slicing, referencing, generic, notation-aware, matrix and tabular meta-models. In this work, a generic meta-model is developed. The role of generic meta-models is to focus on understanding the structure of the meta-model by providing generic concepts [20]. In this study, the notation aspect is not being addressed.

Regarding the syntax of the developed meta-model itself, the principles of the Unified Modeling Language (UML) [25] have been followed. The common element types that existing in meta-models are (i) First Class concepts (classes), (ii) Relationships (of classes), (iii) attributes, (iv) inheritance and (v) others [26]. The element types have been used in the development of the proposed meta-model.

Regarding the semantics, we use as input our preceding research. In our earlier work, a plethora of existing capability modeling approaches has been explored and 64 meta-models have been identified and analyzed in terms of their inclusion of concepts relevant to change [14]. A framework has been used that identified the main functions of a capability oriented adaptive system. The three functions are *observation*, *decision* and *delivery*, which reflect capturing information from the organizational internal and external environment, deciding on a change based on analyzing the observed conditions and applying criteria based on intention elements and finally, delivering the change in the capability's configuration, taking into consideration the interrelation of existing capabilities. In this way, the adaptive characteristics of capability meta-models that have been explored in the literature, have been analyzed to identify the concepts that may be useful to include in a meta-model aiming to capture changing capabilities. Furthermore, the literature review, combined with a case study involving inter-organizational capabilities have resulted in a set of goals [15] for the meta-model under development. These goals are:

1. To manage capability change
2. To observe business context
3. To support decision on capability change
4. To manage capability delivery
5. To identify decision criteria
6. To identify capability alternatives
7. To analyze observed context data
8. To ensure that decision complies with intentions
9. To elicit internal and external business context
10. To manage transition delivery
11. To manage capability architecture
12. To observe external business context
13. To observe internal business context
14. To monitor political, economic, social, technological and legal context
15. To measure relevant properties
16. To establish KPIs
17. To manage introduction of a new capability
18. To manage retirement of a new capability
19. To manage modification of a new capability
20. To manage capability configuration
21. To allocate resources to capability

22. To specify capability ownership
23. To specify resource ownership
24. To manage internal resources
25. To identify external resources
26. To identify outsourced tasks
27. To support defining organizational boundaries
28. To identify collaborating organization

The manner in which these have driven the development of the meta-model is discussed below. In addition, the dimensions of capability and change have been researched and this resulted in introducing a state-based capability typology [16], where the possible states of capability change have been presented as a UML State Machine diagram. This earlier work serves as input for the development of the meta-model.

Finally, the constraints in [27] have been taken into consideration, which suggest that (i) the meta-model should be minimal, which means that no elements that are not motivated by the elicited information needs should be included, (ii) the design rationale for the included elements should be recorded and (iii) the semantics of the included elements should be clarified to avoid possible misunderstandings among different stakeholders.

3.3 Case Study

A regional public healthcare organization responsible for providing healthcare in a Swedish county is the object of the case study. We refer to the organization as Regional Healthcare (RH) to retain their anonymity along with the names of the organizations they collaborate with. The specific object of the study was the organization's capability to provide healthcare guidance via phone to its residents. The data collection process for the capability's undergoing change was iterative and consisted of:

- Unstructured group interviews, conducted within four meetings. Two RH experts were involved in the first one and one expert in the following three. The aim of these interviews was to explore the changing capability based on change requests the organization had received.
- Workshops, aiming to identify the main resources comprising the capability's configuration, along with the associations among the resources. Three workshops resulted in the creation of a value network model.
- Document studies, in order to explore the existing documentation concerning the changing capability.

For the analysis, the experts were asked to identify the potential impact of the change, which means that an experiential approach [28] was applied.

4   A Meta-model for Capability Change

The meta-model and its component elements are presented in this section.

4.1 The Meta-model

The meta-model is presented in Fig. 1 as a UML Class Diagram that includes all the relevant concepts. As can be seen, a central part is the three change functions: observation, decision, and delivery.

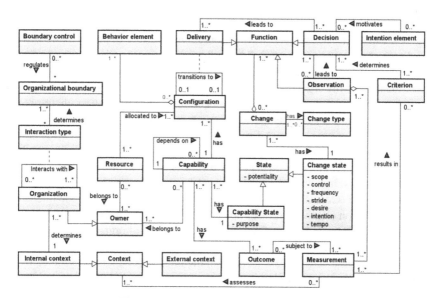

Fig. 1. The capability change meta-model.

4.2 Meta-model Elements

In this section, we present the components of the meta-model which are addressing the information needs elicited as goals for capability change in [15] and the capability and change states in [16]. The meta-model elements and the goals they are addressing are discussed below.

Capability (Goal 10, 11, 20, 22): The concept has been defined in Sect. 2. By definition, modeling capability change requires the inclusion of the concept of capability. A capability depends on one or more capabilities, has one or more configurations, has a state and one or more outcomes and belongs to an owner.

Context (Goal 7, 9, 12, 13, 14): The context of the organization refers to all the environmental factors that are relevant to the performance of the capability. Specialized context-modeling methods exist within the area of capability modeling [29]. Context may be assessed via measurements and has two specializations, internal and external context.

Internal context (Goal 13): These are the factors existing within the organization and are determined by at least one organization owning the capability.

External context (Goal 12): Refers to factors outside the organization, like political, economic, social, environmental, or technological factors.

Resource (Goal 21, 23, 24, 25): Employing resources and capabilities analysis explains how resources can deliver added value [30]. The concept includes capital, infrastructures, human resources etc. Apart from being one of the most popular concepts in capability meta-models, the concept has also been identified as an important factor for two of the change functions. A set of resources is what comprises a capability configuration and is involved not only in the delivery of change due to reallocations, but also in the decision function using reallocation and new resources as a means for identifying new capability alternatives [15]. Resource may belong to one or more owners, and is allocated to one or more capability configurations.

Organization (Goal 28): The concept refers to any public or private organization or organizational unit. Any organization can interact with one or more organizations. In this meta-model, the emphasis is not on the architecture of an organization, therefore, the organization element only depicts an organization as a capability owner. Additionally, the organization determines a capability's internal context.

Owner (Goal 22, 23, 24, 25): This concept determines the ownership of capabilities and resources. Any number of owners can own any number of capabilities and any number of resources. In the meta-model, it is used as a generalization of organization.

Interaction type (Goal 28): This association class element describes the interaction between organization elements, for example, collaboration or outsourcing.

Organizational boundary (Goal 26, 27): The importance of organizational boundary has been identified in our earlier work [15, 31]. It defines the limits of an organization's capabilities. As an association class element in the meta-model, it is determined by the interaction type, it determines at least one type of interaction and may be regulated by boundary control.

Boundary control (Goal 27): Initially explored as a modeling element in [31], the concept concerns any type of control between organizations, so as to regulate the interaction. It may refer to any level of control, from an informal agreement, to a detailed formal contract.

Configuration (Goal 4, 6, 10, 20, 21): The complete set of resources that comprise the capability along with the behavior elements that deliver it. A capability may have several different configurations but only one may be active at any given moment in time. In the meta-model, the actual change is captured as a transition between configurations. It partially consists of one or more behavior elements and has allocated resources, thus specifies a capability.

Change (Goal 1, 2, 3, 4): captures the change process as a whole. It has at least one change type and consists of at least one function. In addition, it is associated to one state.

Change Type (Goal 17, 18, 19): This element may describe change elements. Possible types of changes are introduction, modification or retirement [15].

Function (Goal 2, 3, 4): The function element refers to the specific change functions that have been identified in our earlier work [14]. More specifically, one or more functions comprise change and it is a generalization of observation, decision and delivery.

Observation (Goal 2, 7, 12, 13, 14): The observation function concerns monitoring a capability by capturing relevant external and internal data. The observation element in the meta-model is meant to depict the collecting sources of data valuable for evaluating a capability's performance. It is a change function, it consists of one or more measurements, and leads to one or more decisions.

Measurement (Goal 15, 16): It concerns the activity of assessing a factor relevant to the capability's performance. The element has a natural association to measurable indicators like KPIs. It is a part of observation, can be applied to outcomes, is assessing one or more context factors, and may result in the elaboration of decision criteria.

Outcome (Goal 15, 17, 18, 19): The outcome of a capability realization is used to provide insight on whether a capability change is required or not. It is the result of one or more capabilities and may be subjected to one or more measurements.

Decision (Goal 3, 5, 6, 7, 8): The decision activities are related to analyzing context data to make a decision on capability change, in association to whether an adjustment or transformation is required and which capability configuration is optimal for the adaptation. Therefore, decision is a change function, is determined by at least one criterion, may be motivated by one or more intention elements, leads to delivery and observation leads to it.

Intention element (Goal 8): This abstract meta-element includes all the concepts that refer to the intentions driving the change, i.e. concepts like goal, objective and desire. An intention element may motivate one or more decisions.

Criterion (Goal 5): Decision criteria provide the standards that will be used in order to make a decision. A criterion is often formulated through observation of the context. In the meta-model, one or more criteria determine a decision and may be determined by one or more measurements of the context.

Delivery (Goal 4, 10): Delivery of change refers to how the decision on change is applied affecting the way a capability is realized and capabilities' interrelationships. Regarding the delivery element in the meta-model, it is a change function, at least one decision leads to it, and as an association class, describes the transition between capability configurations.

Behavior element (Goal 4): Another abstract meta-element which is meant to depict every possible process, service or activity that is involved in the realization of the capability. A behavior element is part of one or more capability configurations.

State (complies with [16]): The notion of state has been explored in earlier research in relation to capability and change. The attribute potentiality has two possible values, that is, enabled or disabled. In the meta-model the state class is a generalization for capability and change states.

Capability state (complies with [16]): A specialization of the state class, is associated to one or more capabilities. The purpose attribute reflects if the capability is meant to fulfil a goal or avoid a problem.

Change state (complies with [16]): A specialization of the state class, this element includes as attributes the dimensions of change that have been introduced in [16], which are scope, control, frequency, stride, desire, intention and tempo, specified for every state, which means that the attributes always need to have a value.

5   Case Study: Improving a Public Healthcare Capability

RH is an organization whose responsibility is healthcare provision in a Swedish county. One of its capabilities is providing healthcare advice via phone to residents and visitors of the county. This capability is delivered by specially trained nurses, who are supported by various information sources incorporated in specialized software. The capability is known as 1177, named after the 4-digit number used for contacting the nurses. 1177's goal is to filter the cases and provide advice to the ones that are not in urgent need of a physician's attention, so that the workload of other health providing organizations is reduced.

1177 is owned by RH but several public and private organizations are collaborating by providing resources for it, a fact which results in a complex capability configuration.

Any proposed change to the capabilities of RH requires detailed analysis in order to identify what will be affected and how. There are proposed changes that will have an effect not only on how the capability is delivered but also on the interaction with collaborating organizations, for example by requiring different contractual agreements.

The driving forces behind the changes are coming both via top-down and bottom up motivations, the former as political interventions, pushing for quality improvement and cost reduction, and the latter as employee and partner proposals. Furthermore, technological developments like video calls, provide an opportunity for capability updates.

The incoming changes need to be analyzed and the meta-model should support the analysis by including all the needed information. One specific change request has been selected in order to demonstrate the meta-model's efficiency for this task. It concerns an improvement in the guidance support that enables the nurses that respond to the calls to guide a caller directly to a health provider through an assessment of their symptoms.

5.1   Change Case: Guidance Support Improvement

Every call is handled using a Guidance support system, whose ownership, development and usage are nationwide. The caller is asked to state existing symptoms which are registered by the nurse and the system responds by presenting possible sub-symptoms, that the caller confirms or rejects in order to distinguish the state and emergency of the case. There is a wide spectrum of responses depending on the emergency level, from advising on self-treatment to calling an ambulance or suggesting a healthcare provider. This is possible using an integrated healthcare provider catalogue. This catalogue is developed and maintained by a collaborating private provider, in contrast with the guidance support system.

A proposed improvement concerns the association of each provider in the catalogue with a list of symptoms that the provider can handle. This change will make it possible for a caller to be guided directly to a provider having, in the meantime, avoided the need to reach a diagnosis of the case. There are several benefits involved from the implementation of this change. First of all, the caller is guided to a provider with the optimal expertise. Additionally, the capability gains increased efficiency, reducing the required cost and effort. Furthermore, it improves the usage of human resources, having the physicians handle the cases that are most relevant to their expertise. A group of expert physicians is currently working on mapping healthcare providers to symptoms, in order to facilitate the development of a web system for direct use and an .xml file that could be compatible for usage in other systems.

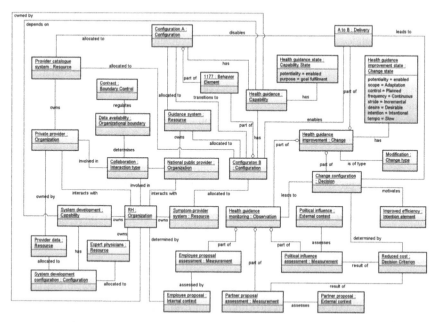

Fig. 2. An instance of the meta-model for a capability modification case.

In practice, the change concerns the modification of a capability, which translates to a different configuration according to our approach. The case has been modeled as an instantiated version of our meta-model, which results in an object diagram, as shown in Fig. 2. The Health Guidance capability has a goal-fulfilment purpose and is enabled, as depicted through the association with the Health guidance state object of the Capability state class. The Capability object is also associated to an instance of the Organization class to depict its ownership by RH. The Change object, named Health guidance improvement, has an enabled state, and it is characterized through its attributes as a planned, continuous, incremental, desirable, intentional, and slow adaptation. Its type is Modification and consists of three objects, the Health guidance monitoring Observation object, the Change configuration Decision object, and the A to B Delivery object. Observation leads to Decision and then to Delivery. Observation consists of three measurement objects which depict the assessment of three context factors, Employee proposals, Partner proposals and Political influence, which are all included as objects and associated to the respective measurement objects. The first factor concerns internal context, and is associated to the RH object, while the other two are external context factors. The external factor objects are also resulting in a Reduced cost Criterion which determines the Decision object. This is also motivated by Improved efficiency, which is an Intention element object. Additional associations of the capability object are connecting it with two configuration objects, namely Configuration A and B. The former is the one enabled before the change and the latter is the one enabled after the change. This is captured in the Delivery object, which is associated to both Configuration objects to depict the transition. The delivery of change disables Configuration A and enables configuration B. The difference between the two configurations is depicted through their allocated resources. Configuration A is only associated to the Guidance system and Provider catalogue system, while B is also associated to the Symptom – provider system. An 1177 Behavior element object is associated to both configurations. It is interesting to note that the Provider catalogue and Guidance system are associated to the Private provider and National public provider respectively, so as to represent ownership. This means that while RH owns the capability, the two collaborating organizations own involved resources. Especially when it comes to the symptom – provider system, the object, which is part of Configuration B, is owned by RH along with the System development capability, on which Health guidance depends, and the Expert physicians used to develop it. However, the Provider catalogue system and the Provider data are owned by Private provider, so the Collaboration Interaction type object is not enough to represent the case. A Data availability Organizational boundary and a Contract Boundary control object complement the required information for this part of the diagram.

6   Discussion

This study is a part of an ongoing work, hence, the development of the presented meta-model artifact will evolve in the following design-evaluation cycles. DSR guidelines are also stating that artifact development is almost always an iterative step [13]. What an iterative process implies is the identification of weaknesses and strengths in the artifact, which can be translated to opportunities for improvement. Since a meta-model is an essential method component, the current version of the meta-model contributes towards establishing the foundation for the development of a method specially designed for managing capability change, by (i) capturing the relevant information according to the elicited goals and (ii) decomposing change into the previously elicited functions that it consists of, and, (iii) depicting the transition during change implementation.

Regarding the efficiency of the meta-model in capturing the needed information and depicting the aspects of capability change, the demonstration using the RH case suggests that all the required factors have been taken into consideration and the information structure seems adequate for the particular case. The set of goals elicited in our previous work have been fulfilled, even though the case was not optimal for details in goals like the elicitation of context, because to a certain degree, the elicitation had already been performed by the stakeholders and interviewees, in terms of recognizing the political, employee and partner influence on the Health guidance capability. Therefore, any future application of the meta-model should favor the selection of a case, where the need and reasons for change are not obvious, so that the meta-model's possible deficiencies will be indicated.

The main concern that has risen from the application in this study is the complexity of the produced models, which is a result of the meta-model's structure, and seems to produce visually cluttered models. During the instantiation of the meta-model to an object diagram, the complexity of the object diagram exceeded our initial expectations and what can intuitively be seen as practical for the purpose of communicating with domain experts. For this reason, several pieces of information have been omitted in order to reduce the complexity of the result, in terms of a less cluttered model. For example, many resources involved in the configurations of the capability are missing because their role in the undergoing change was deemed of lower priority. For example, the specialized nurses that perform the guidance, the telephone system and the journal system are not affecting the change project. Yet, omitting pieces of information is not feasible in every case, and this should be addressed in the meta-model.

During the development of the meta-model the decision to develop a single unified meta-model that would encompass all aspects of change already indicated a high level of complexity. For this reason, certain aspects of capability change were slightly neglected, which means that a higher level of abstraction was applied, a fact that resulted in more generic meta-elements, for example, Intention element and Behavior element. However, it is not a coincidence, that all the generic meta-elements reflect aspects that could be decomposed into entire models. For example, decomposing Intention, Behavior or Context elements may require the integration of a goal, process [18] or context model [29] respectively. Among the elements that were included in the meta-model, the point of emphasis that stands out as the epicenter of change is the Configuration class and its recursive association that depicts transitions between configurations. Any further decomposition of this part will only promote the initial goal, to model capability change. Nevertheless, decomposing goals and processes may be useful, yet, it is not the main focus point of this project.

This raises the question of employing the technique of slicing meta-models [20], which means that the meta-model is split according to specific viewpoints. On one hand, pre-existing common viewpoints like goals, processes and context can be integrated using existing compatible approaches, to save significant time and effort. On the other hand, within this project, new viewpoints can also be elaborated, i.e. capability, observation, decision, delivery and ownership. This is a possible future step that is worth exploring before deciding to finalize the artifact.

7   Conclusion

In this study a meta-model has been presented that will act as a basis for the development of a method for modeling and analyzing capability change. Being a DSR project, its nature is iterative, therefore, several iterations are expected before the artifact is finalized. Therefore, the introduction of the meta-model was succeeded by an application of the artifact on a real case for demonstrative reasons. This application provided opportunities for improvement, especially in the area of complexity, including the possibility to introduce viewpoints in a later version of the model.

The next step in our project is to validate the meta-model via interviews with experienced decision-makers. This activity will provide additional insights towards the finalization of the artifact. In parallel, the initial experience of this study will be taken into consideration, in order to explore the implementation of viewpoints in the next stage of method development.

Acknowledgment. We would like to express our gratitude to the employees of RH who took their time in letting us interview them to identify and describe the presented case.

References

1. Proper, H.A., Winter, R., Aier, S., de Kinderen, S. (eds.): Architectural Coordination of Enterprise Transformation. Springer, Cham (2017). https://doi.org/10.1007/978-3-319-69584-6

2. Burnes, B.: Managing Change. Pearson, Harlow, England (2014)

3. Zimmermann, N.: Dynamics of Drivers of Organizational Change. Gabler, Wiesbaden (2011). https://doi.org/10.1007/978-3-8349-6811-1

4. Burke, W.W.: Organization Change: Theory and Practice. Sage Publications, Thousand Oaks (2017)

5. van Gils, B., Proper, H.A.: Enterprise modelling in the age of digital transformation. In: Buchmann, R.A., Karagiannis, D., Kirikova, M. (eds.) PoEM 2018. LNBIP, vol. 335, pp. 257–273. Springer, Cham (2018). https://doi.org/10.1007/978-3-030-02302-7_16

6. Hoverstadt, P., Loh, L.: Patterns of strategy. Routledge, Taylor & Francis Group, London, New York (2017)

7. Loucopoulos, P., Stratigaki, C., Danesh, M.H., Bravos, G., Anagnostopoulos, D., Dimitrakopoulos, G.: Enterprise capability modeling: concepts, method, and application. In: 2015 International Conference on Enterprise Systems (ES), pp. 66–77. IEEE, Basel (2015)

8. Sandkuhl, K., Stirna, J. (eds.): Capability Management in Digital Enterprises. Springer, Cham (2018). https://doi.org/10.1007/978-3-319-90424-5

9. Loucopoulos, P., Kavakli, E.: Capability oriented enterprise knowledge modeling: the CODEK approach. In: Karagiannis, D., Mayr, H.C., Mylopoulos, J. (eds.) Domain-Specific Conceptual Modeling, pp. 197–215. Springer, Cham (2016). https://doi.org/10.1007/978-3-319-39417-6_9

10. Persson, A., Stirna, J.: An explorative study into the influence of business goals on the practical use of enterprise modelling methods and tools. In: Harindranath, G. et al. (eds.) New Perspectives on Information Systems Development, pp. 275–287 Springer, Boston (2002). https://doi.org/10.1007/978-1-4615-0595-2_22

11. Pearlson, K.E., Saunders, C.S., Galletta, D.F.: Managing and Using Information Systems: a Strategic Approach. Wiley, Hoboken (2020)

12. Hevner, A., Chatterjee, S.: Design Research in Information Systems. Springer, Boston (2010). https://doi.org/10.1007/978-1-4419-5653-8

13. Johannesson, P., Perjons, E.: An Introduction to Design Science. Springer, Cham (2014). https://doi.org/10.1007/978-3-319-10632-8

14. Koutsopoulos, G., Henkel, M., Stirna, J.: Dynamic adaptation of capabilities: exploring meta-model diversity. In: Reinhartz-Berger, I., Zdravkovic, J., Gulden, J., Schmidt, R. (eds.) BPMDS/EMMSAD -2019. LNBIP, vol. 352, pp. 181–195. Springer, Cham (2019). https://doi.org/10.1007/978-3-030-20618-5_13

15. Koutsopoulos, G., Henkel, M., Stirna, J.: Requirements for observing, deciding, and delivering capability change. In: Gordijn, J., Guédria, W., Proper, H.A. (eds.) PoEM 2019. LNBIP, vol. 369, pp. 20–35. Springer, Cham (2019). https://doi.org/10.1007/978-3-030-35151-9_2

16. Koutsopoulos, G., Henkel, M., Stirna, J.: Modeling the dichotomies of organizational change: a state-based capability typology. In: Feltus, C., Johannesson, P., Proper, H.A. (eds.) Proceedings of the PoEM 2019 Forum, pp. 26–39. CEUR-WS.org, Luxembourg (2020)

17. Maes, G., Van Hootegem, G.: Toward a dynamic description of the attributes of organizational change. In: Research in Organizational Change and Development, pp. 191–231. Emerald Group Publishing Limited (2011)
18. Sandkuhl, K., Stirna, J., Persson, A., Wißotzki, M.: Enterprise Modeling: Tackling Business Challenges with the 4EM Method. Springer, Heidelberg (2014). https://doi.org/10.1007/978-3-662-43725-4
19. Frank, U.: Enterprise modelling: The next steps. Enterp. Model. Inf. Syst. Architect. (EMISAJ) **9**, 22–37 (2014)
20. Bork, D., Karagiannis, D., Pittl, B.: How are metamodels specified in practice? Empirical insights and recommendations. Presented at the 24th Americas Conference on Information Systems, AMCIS 2018, New Orleans, LA, USA, 16 August 2018
21. Koutsopoulos, G.: Modeling organizational potentials using the dynamic nature of capabilities. In: Joint Proceedings of the BIR 2018 Short Papers, Workshops and Doctoral Consortium, pp. 387–398. CEUR-WS.org, Stockholm (2018)
22. Ulrich, W., Rosen, M.: The business capability map: the "Rosetta stone" of business/IT alignment. Cutter Consort. Enterp. Archit. **14**(2) (2011)
23. España, S., et al.: Strategies for capability modelling: analysis based on initial experiences. In: Persson, A., Stirna, J. (eds.) CAiSE 2015. LNBIP, vol. 215, pp. 40–52. Springer, Cham (2015). https://doi.org/10.1007/978-3-319-19243-7_4
24. Karagiannis, D., Bork, D., Utz, W.: Metamodels as a conceptual structure: some semantical and syntactical operations. In: Bergener, K., Räckers, M., Stein, A. (eds.) The Art of Structuring, pp. 75–86. Springer, Cham (2019). https://doi.org/10.1007/978-3-030-06234-7_8
25. Object Management Group (OMG): OMG® Unified Modeling Language®. https://www.omg.org/spec/UML/2.5.1/PDF (2017)
26. Bork, D., Karagiannis, D., Pittl, B.: A survey of modeling language specification techniques. Inf. Syst. **87**, 101425 (2020). https://doi.org/10.1016/j.is.2019.101425
27. Kurpjuweit, S., Winter, R.: Viewpoint-based meta model engineering. In: Reichert, M., Strecker, S., Turowski, K. (eds.) Enterprise Modelling and Information Systems Architectures: Concepts and Applications, pp. 143–161. Ges. für Informatik, Bonn (2007)
28. Kilpinen, M.S.: The emergence of change at the systems engineering and software design interface (2008)
29. Koç, H., Sandkuhl, K.: Context modelling in capability management. In: Sandkuhl, K., Stirna, J. (eds.) Capability Management in Digital Enterprises, pp. 117–138. Springer, Cham (2018). https://doi.org/10.1007/978-3-319-90424-5_7
30. Lynch, R.L.: Strategic Management. Pearson Education, Harlow, New York (2018)
31. Henkel, M., Koutsopoulos, G., Bider, I., Perjons, E.: Using the fractal enterprise model for inter-organizational business processes. In: Joint Proceedings of the ER Forum and Poster & Demos Session 2019, pp. 56–69. CEUR-WS.org, Salvador (2019)

Supporting Early Phases of Digital Twin Development with Enterprise Modeling and Capability Management: Requirements from Two Industrial Cases

Kurt Sandkuhl[1] and Janis Stirna[2(✉)]

[1] University of Rostock, Rostock, Germany
kurt.sandkuhl@uni-rostock.de
[2] Department of Computer and Systems Sciences, Stockholm University, Stockholm, Sweden
js@dsv.su.se

Abstract. Industry 4.0 is a concept that has attracted much research and development over the last decade. At its core is the need to connect physical devices with their digital representations which essentially means establishing a digital twin. Currently, the technological development of digital twins has gathered much attention while the organizational and business aspects are less investigated. In response, the suitability of enterprise modeling and capability management for the purpose of developing and management of business-driven digital twins has been analyzed. A number of requirements from literature are summarized and two industrial cases have been analyzed for the purpose of investigating how the digital twin initiatives emerge and what forces drive the start of their implementation projects. The findings are discussed with respect to how Enterprise Modeling and the Capability-Driven Development method are able to support the business motivation, design and runtime management of digital twins.

Keywords: Capability management · Digital twins · Digital transformation

1 Introduction

In manufacturing industries, industry 4.0 and digital transformation are interrelated fields that both motivate the development of digital twins. *Industry 4.0* is a concept attracting much research and development over the last decade, including reference models [1], applications [2], standards [3] and supporting methods [4]. A core idea of Industry 4.0 is to connect physical devices (e.g., manufacturing systems and the objects they produce), digital components (e.g. ERP or MES systems) and human actors along production processes for the sake of seamless integration and continuous monitoring and control [5]. *Digital twins* (DT) support this core idea and can be defined as "a dynamic virtual representation of a physical object or system across its lifecycle, using real-time data to enable understanding, learning and reasoning" [6]. *Digital transformation*, in general, denotes adopting digital technologies, such as industry 4.0 related technologies or DTs, in the digitalization of an organization's business model and its operations (cf. Sect. 2.3).

© Springer Nature Switzerland AG 2020
S. Nurcan et al. (Eds.): BPMDS 2020/EMMSAD 2020, LNBIP 387, pp. 284–299, 2020.
https://doi.org/10.1007/978-3-030-49418-6_19

Several researchers emphasize the importance of industry 4.0 for digital transformation [21] or, vice versa, that digital transformation motivates the implementation of industry 4.0 [20]. However, DTs as an element of digital transformation or digital transformation as driver for DT development are not included in the aforementioned work. A literature analysis (see Sect. 5) confirmed that digital twin research predominantly focuses on technological questions of DT design and operations. So far, organizational and business model related aspects of DTs are only sparsely covered in research which motivated this paper. In response to this, the paper's objective is *to investigate how DT solutions are integrated into organizational structures and business models of manufacturing enterprises, and what motivates the development of DT from a digital transformation perspective.*

Enterprise Modeling (EM) is a versatile approach and is able to tackle various organizational design problems by means of multi-perspective conceptual modeling. EM captures organizational knowledge about the motivation and business requirements for designing IS [7]. Hence it has the potential of capturing and representing the organizational motivation for DT design. A key aspect of operating and managing DTs is to configure and adjust them according to the situational changes in operations. Capability Management, and in particular Capability Driven Development (CDD), has been proven applicable for managing information systems (IS) in changing context [10]. E.g., CDD supports generation of monitoring dashboards from models that include context elements, measurable properties, KPIs as well as rule-based based adjustments based on context data. In concrete terms, the goal of this paper is *to analyze the suitability of EM and capability management for the purpose of supporting the development and management of DTs from an organizational perspective.* We have chosen the 4EM and CDD methods for the purpose of this study because they have already established integration mechanisms between themselves and with other modeling languages.

The rest of the paper is structured as follows. Section 2 gives background to EM, CDD, and digital transformation. Section 3 describes our research approach. Section 4 presents two case studies. Section 5 summarizes the main requirements for developing Industry 4.0 solutions found in literature. Section 6 discusses the requirements from Sects. 4 and 5 with respect to CDD. Section 7 discusses an example of a capability model for the purpose of DT development. Section 8 provides concluding remarks.

2 Background

2.1 Enterprise Modeling and 4EM

EM is the process of creating an enterprise model that captures all the enterprise's aspects or perspectives that are required for a given modeling purpose. An enterprise model consists of a set of interlinked sub-models, each of them focusing on a specific perspective, like, processes, goals, concepts, actors, rules, IS components.

4EM [7] is a representative of the Scandinavian strand of EM methods. At its core is participatory stakeholder involvement and the modeling process is usually organized in the form of facilitated workshops. 4EM shares many underlying principles of the, so called, multi-perspective, approaches that recommend analyzing organizational problems from various perspectives, e.g. AKM [12] and MEMO [11]. 4EM consists of six interconnected sub-model types for modeling a specific aspect or perspective of the enterprise – Goals Model, Business Rules Model, Concepts Model, Business Process Model, Actors and Resources Model, as well as Technical Components and Requirements Model. 4EM also supports integration with other modeling languages and methods by allowing to define new inter-model relationships between the 4EM components and components of the modeling language to be integrated.

2.2 Capability Driven Development

In [10] the concept of *capability thinking* and a method to capability management are introduced. It is an organizational mindset that puts capabilities in focus of the business model and IS development. Capability thinking emphasizes that capabilities are not self-emergent, instead they should be planned, implemented, controlled, and adjusted. In doing so they need to be addressed from the perspectives of (1) vision (e.g. goals and KPIs), (2) enterprise designs such as processes and IS architectures, (3) situation context incl. measurable properties, as well (4) best practices such as process variants and patterns for dealing with context changes. Capability as a concept allows reasoning about these four aspects of the business in an integrated way because enterprises need to know how to realize the business vision and designs as well as what needs to be changed depending on real-life situations. The definition of *capability is the ability and capacity that enables an enterprise to achieve a business goal in a certain context* [10]. Successful implementation of capability thinking will lead to *capability management* as a systematic way to plan, design, develop, deploy, operate, and adjust capabilities.

CDD is a method supporting the four perspectives of capability thinking. CDD consists of a number of method components each focusing on a specific task of the capability cycle, such as Capability Design, Context Modeling, Patterns and Variability Modeling, Capability Adjustment Algorithm Specification, as well as method extensions for dealing with certain business challenges such as supporting business process outsourcing and managing service configuration with the support of open data [17].

2.3 Digital Transformation

In scientific literature, digital transformation often is discussed in the general context of digitalization and considered the most complex digitalization phase [13]. Its focus is on the disruptive social and economic consequences which, due to the potential of digital technologies to substantially change markets, lead to new technological application potentials and the resulting changes in economic structures, qualification requirements for employees and working life in general. [14] proposes to distinguish between transformation of the value proposition and the value creation when analysing and planning digital transformation. These two "dimensions" can be divided into different steps of digitalization which form the prerequisite for the next step. In [15] we have proposed the steps for the dimensions of operations and product digitization.

In the operations dimension, the steps are (1) replacing paper documents with digital representations, (2) end-to-end automated processing of this digital representation within a process and (3) integration of relevant processes within the enterprise and with partners. On the product dimension, the departure point for digitization are physical products without built-in information or communication technology. Digitization steps are (1) to enhance the product/service by providing complementary services (maintenance information, service catalogs) without actually changing it, (2) to extend functionality and value proposition of products by integration of sensors and actuators, and (3) redefinition of the product or service which leads to a completely new value proposition. A completed digital transformation requires all three steps in both dimensions.

3   Research Approach

This study is part of a research program aiming to provide methodological and tool support for organizations in dynamic contexts, e.g., supporting the process of digital transformation and capability management. It follows the five stages of Design Science research [16], namely, problem explication, requirements definition, design and development of the design artifact, demonstration, as well as evaluation. This study concerns the first two steps for the design artifact supporting DT design and management from an organizational perspective. This part of our research started from the following research question which is based on the motivation presented in Sect. 1: *RQ: In the context of digital transformation, how are digital twin initiatives emerging and what are the driving forces for starting implementation projects?*

The research method used for working on this research question is a combination of literature study and descriptive case study. Based on the research question, we identified industrial cases of digital transformation suitable for studying the origin of DT developments, i.e. we performed qualitative case studies in order to obtain relevant and original data (see Sect. 4). Qualitative case study is an approach to research that facilitates exploration of a phenomenon within its context using a variety of data sources. This ensures that the subject under consideration is explored from a variety of perspectives which allows for multiple facets of the phenomenon to be revealed and understood. Within the case studies, we used three different perspectives, which at the same time represent sources of data: we analyzed documents about business models, products, manufacturing process of the companies; we performed workshops targeting digital transformation and DTs as part thereof; and we interviewed domain experts. Yin [18] differentiates case studies explanatory, exploratory and descriptive. The case studies in Sect. 4 are considered descriptive, as they describe the phenomenon of initiating DT development and the real-life context in which it occurs.

Based on the results of the case studies, primarily case study requirements to DT development, we selected research areas with relevant work for these requirements and analyzed the literature in these areas. The purpose of the analysis was to find existing approaches and methods for modeling DT and how they are integrated into the business. This work limits the focus on DTs in manufacturing, although they can also be used in other application fields. To summarize,

- The case studies explore whether business models and organizational context are really relevant from industrial perspective. We focus on the early phases of DT realization, i.e. decision making and specification,
- A literature study explores whether existing research work covers modeling approaches for business models and organizational context of DT.

4   Industrial Case Studies

4.1   Case Study A: Producer of Pumps

Company A is a medium-sized manufacturer of different kinds of pumps and pumping technologies, e.g. swimming pool pumps, sewage pumps, industrial pumps for heavy environments or ship pumps. Company A is well-established on the international market with a market share of more than 50% in some segments. Although its business is stable and developing well, the management decided to explore new service opportunities and business models applying digital technologies. More concretely, the idea of the company's product management is to integrate sensors into pumps and transmit the information to the back-office by using a datalink. This idea can be classified as converting the pumps into smart connected products or Internet-of-Things (IoT) devices.

The opportunity for data collection at company A emerged when the it agreed to start a study on digital transformation options. The study so far had two workshops at the company's headquarter and several interviews. The first workshop was directed to the management with a focus on clarifying general steps of digital transformation, possible procedures and aspects of the enterprise to be considered. The second workshop was directed towards identifying concrete digital transformation options and potential ways of implementation. For our research question, the second workshop and the preparatory interviews were the most relevant and will be in focus of the analysis.

One purpose of the preparatory interviews for the second workshop was to understand the current situation of IoT and sensor integration into the company's products. The key expert here was the research and development manager. Before the interview, guidelines consisting of a list of questions and aspects to explore were prepared. The interview took 30 min and was conducted by one researcher; notes were taken. As a preparation of the digital transformation workshop, the participants were selected to include all relevant departments of company A (product development, production, marketing, sales & distribution, and services) and members of top and middle management. All eight participants were informed in beforehand about the purpose of the workshop and importance of their participation. The workshop included the collection and clustering of new product and services ideas from the participants, joint definition of priorities, and development of a business model prototype for the top three product/service ideas. The workshop was documented in photo documentation of collected ideas and clusters, written documentation of the business model prototypes. Notes were taken to capture additional information regarding ideas and the business model.

The product manager stated as one of the motivations for the workshop: "Our datalink device is nearly ready. It captures data and puts them into our own cloud. So far, we only capture data about malfunction or energy consumption that is anyhow visible on the pump's display. But we do not have a good idea, how to do business with this data. And we probably need more sensors."

Among the top innovation ideas were (a) smart pumps and (b) pumping as a service, which the workshop participants both related to the topic of digital twins. When discussing the smart pump, the sales representative explained: "We think that our bigger customers want to have control if our pumps do what they are supposed to do in their installations. Some of them call it the digital twin. This would help us to sell pumps to them. We have to use or develop sensors that deliver this kind of information."

Pumping as a service aims at selling the functionality of the pump instead of the pump as physical device which would lead to a service agreement where the company is paid for pumped cubic meters or hours of pumping. One of the participants remarked to this idea: "For this, we need full control what is happening with the pump. So, we need something a bit like a digital twin, but for our internal purposes."

When developing the business model prototype for pumping as a service, most of the discussion time was spent on organizational issues within the company: "where does all the information from our pumps arrive, how do we make sense out of it and how do we organize the reaction?" For the smart pumps, the discussion was more about "how do we integrate our pumps in the DT system of our customer and what kind of sensors do we need?" Furthermore, the development department mentioned "We would need to know what technical basis our customers use for their DTs and what interfaces we have to provide. But most of our customers have no real answers to these questions. Sometimes we get the impression that they simply don't know."

4.2 Case Study B: Tool Produces for Automotive Industry

Company B is a subsidiary of a major automotive manufacturer responsible for producing tools for the metal parts of chassis production, such as roofs, doors, side panels, etc. These tools, called (press) forms, are developed individually for each car model variant in an iterative process of casting, milling and/or welding, and polishing. Active components, such as cutters, hydraulic springs or punchers are integrated into the actual form. Putting the forms into operation in a press shop requires a try-out phase to fine-tune the forms' precision. Company B is doing the largest share of its business with the automotive manufacturer. It also serves other automotive and truck suppliers. Due to its unique specialization on forms for a specific metal, company B is well-positioned in the market. However, its management aims to increase efficiency and flexibility in the business model to be prepared for possible future market changes.

This case study emerged when company B decided to investigate radical digital innovation focusing on disruptive ways of working or technologies instead of gradual optimization or increase in efficiency. A workshop was planned to investigate the potential for radical innovation concerning the possibilities for drastic and seemingly unrealistic changes, like, reduction of production time for forms to 10% of the current value, no setup time of the production system or internal logistics requiring no staff.

Preparation and execution of the workshop was similar to what was described for the first case study: the selected participants represented all relevant departments of the company (design, production, logistics, procurement, human resources, economics, service and customer care), mostly represented by the head of the unit or senior experts. All ten participants were informed beforehand about purpose of the workshop, the need to think "out-of-the-box" and the importance of their participation. The workshop included the collection and clustering of radical transformation of products and of operations, joint clustering and definition of priorities. Based on the priorities, an initial evaluation of the top three options for radical transformation of products and the top three transformations in operations was done. The content of the workshop was documented in photo documentation of collected ideas and clusters, written documentation of the evaluation results, and notes. The workshop was conducted by two researchers: one facilitator and one note taker. In this paper analyzes the documented content.

For radical transformation of internal operations, one of the clusters identified was named "digital twin of the own factory". The primary intention was to always have a real-time status of all resource in the own production system including facilities, parts and staff. For the radical transformation of the products, one of the clusters was the DT of each individual form on the customers' site. It is expected that a fully digitalized and automated press shop would need full control and real-time monitoring of the complete production flow and all components of the press shop. In this regard, the workshop participants discussed how to set up the cooperation with press manufacturers and logistics companies to discuss standards for the DT.

4.3   Case Study Analysis

The case study requirements (CSR) are derived from analysis of the two case studies and are presented in the following with a short motivation from the cases.

CSR1: DTs have to support the goals and business models of the company.

Both companies did not have any ongoing DT activity before the start of the digital transformation initiative. Once the workshops explicated ideas for service and business models that demand DT-like functionality, DTs were seriously considered and finally selected for implementation. In both cases, the primary goal is not to implement DT per se but to provide services or create a platform which can be facilitated by DTs.

CSR2: DTs are part of operations in an enterprise – either to support manufacturing execution in the own or the client's production, or to facilitate value-added services on the customer side, like, e.g. predictive/preventive maintenance.

The concept of DT and envisioned functionality appeared in the use cases in different shapes: a) the DTs of the company's products installed at the clients' sites for the purpose of offering services depending on (real-time) data supply and monitoring (e.g., pumping-as-a-service requires monitoring of the pumps installed at the clients' industrial facility), b) the DT for the control of a facility possibly integrating various components (e.g. the DT of the manufacturing facility of company B or the DT of a ship which has a pump of company A installed), and c) the combination of a) and b), i.e. the company's product monitored in a client's facility. E.g., the form of company B with remote monitoring for purposes of preventive maintenance and local monitoring for optimizing production in the press shop. Options a) and b) require different information to be aggregated, displayed, and monitored.

CSR3: What aspect of reality has to be represented in a DT depends on the organizational integration and the intended business model of the company.

CSR1 sates that DTs must be supporting a company's business model. When implementing business models, this means that the digital twin has to provide the information about status or operations of the product required for the value creation underlying the business model. E.g. in case A, pumping-as-a-service requires to capture the performance of a pump to be able to invoice the provided hours or pumped volume, the energy consumption of the pump, and the status of lubricants to avoid problems in the service.

CSR4: Identification of features and parameters that have to be visible in the DT can be supported by developing business model prototypes and investigating organizational integration.

In both case studies, the options for new DT-based services were subject to an initial feasibility study. This study started from the definition of what service has to be provided for the customer, what information and functionality are required for the services (i.e., specification of features and parameters) and how this information is processed and used in the enterprise to deliver the service (i.e. the organizational processes).

CSR5: Component developers request a better methodical and technical integration of DTs (platform) development and component development.

In particular in case B, the case study company made clear that the development of a smart form would require collaboration with the manufacturer of the press for implementing the vision of a smart press shop. In case A, a similar request emerged when discussing the integration of pumps in complex systems, like, e.g. a cruising ship. Both cases showed the need for technical agreements (interfaces and platforms) and methodical agreements with the digital twin provider.

CSR6: Business models and organizational processes are subject to continuous improvement and so are DT features and parameters.

During development of business model prototypes, in both cases a kind of roadmap for stepwise implementing and extending services and business model was discussed, and the actual prototype intended to cover only the first stage. An expectation was expressed that the first stage would have to be extended based on the feedback of the customer and lessons learned from operations. With respect to modeling support, our recommendation is to explicitly model organizational context and business models as preparation of the DT design.

5 Requirements for Digital Twin Design from Literature

DTs are usually designed and operated in the context of industry 4.0. In the field of production systems, there is a substantial amount of work on DTs. In the context of this paper, the intersection of digital transformation and DT as industry 4.0 solution is most relevant. Mittal et al. [20] investigated what manufacturing small and medium-sized enterprises (SME) need to successfully adopt industry 4.0. As a result, 16 specific requirements for SME were identified including smart manufacturing solutions for specialized products, which includes DTs. Schumacher et al. [21] proposed a maturity model for assessing Industry 4.0 readiness and identify nine dimensions of maturity and 62 maturity items in their Industry 4.0 Maturity Model. The maturity items include technology and product related aspects, like digitalization of products, product integration into other systems, and DTs. Considering the objective of this research our primary focus is on supporting the fit of the DT to the organization's needs in the industry 4.0 program, which, as discussed previously, can be supported by modeling. There have been several investigations of the needs for modeling support for industry 4.0. Hermann et al. [9] present four main principles of industry 4.0, namely:

- *Interconnection* supporting various aspects of communication between actors, such as human to human, human to machine, and machine to machine.
- *Information transparency* requires supporting the identification and linking of various data types and sources, e.g. sensor data, process execution data, and factory designs, which in essence leads to DTs. A part of this task is the creation and monitoring the surrounding environment and situational properties related to the factory, i.e. the application context needs to be modelled and monitored. Some of the context information might also be needed in advance which requires using the means of predictive data analytics. All data needs to be presented to participants in the industry 4.0 design, depending on the criticality and relevance.
- *Decentralized decisions*. The design should be able to combine local as well as global information to support decentralized and autonomous decision making.
- *Technical assistance*. The decentralized decision making needs to be supported by assistance IS that are able to aggregate and visualize content in various formats suitable for different application contexts.

Wortmann et al. [8] report on a systematic literature review and in terms of the expected benefits for modeling for industry 4.0 puts forward the following: reducing time (development time, time-to-market), reducing costs (of development, integration, configuration), improving sustainability, and improving international competitiveness. This is in line of what are the general intentions of allying development methods and tools. In the context of industry 4.0 modeling addresses cyber aspects, physical aspects, or cyber-physical aspects of which the latter is the least researched and for which the least number of contributions have been elaborated. Wortmann et al. indicate that the current trends include methods for modeling digital representation, failure handling, human factors, information management, integration, process, product, configuration validation and verification, as well as visualization. The areas of product modeling, validation and verification, and information management attracting the most attention right now. Human factors and visualization are addressed by considerably fewer contributions. However, this study focused mostly on methods that have proven useful for IS design and development, and these methods do not support a holistic view on design that integrates organizational and human aspects with the more common IS aspects.

The analysis of the current state of modeling for the purpose of designing industry 4.0 solutions, including DTs, calls for a number of areas of advancements, as follows. Concerning *modeling and model management*:

– Support for integrated multi-perspective views on all aspects of, such as, business and organizational, IS architecture, implementation, and operation at runtime.
– Integration of different artifact kinds such as models, 3D drawings. In this regard, Wortmann et al. call for the integration of models in the engineering, deployment process, and operation processes. To achieve alignment, the integration should start with the business design and requirements for the engineering process.
– Supporting design models with runtime data and, consequently, extracting models that can be used in later design iterations from runtime data. Using runtime data for the purpose of assessing the performance of designs, especially reusable designs that are applied in several operational installations.

Concerning *adaptation and adjustment:*

– Support for adaptation and adjustment of the solution according to changing business goals and requirements as well as application context.
– The solution should have built-in means for runtime adaptations that do not require re-design and re-deployment.

Concerning *continuous lifecycle management:*

– Supporting visualizations of runtime data in design models, e.g. by specifying what data should be presented and in what format. Management dashboards and presentation views can be generated from models.
– Support of the management of the complete lifecycle including design and runtime.

With respect to the latter, [8] discuss the possibility of adopting the DevOps principles for developing industry 4.0 solutions. The proposed vision for such a lifecycle is similar to the CDD process [10], discussed in Sect. 6.

6   Analysis

6.1   Discussing the Requirements from Literature and Case Studies

First, we will discuss the requirements from Sect. 5 and how the three main topics of (1) modeling and model management, (2) adaptation and adjustment; and (3) continuous lifecycle management, can be addressed by EM and CDD. This will be followed by a discussion of the case study requirements.

Modeling and model management. It calls for multi-perspective views to integrate various aspects and artefacts of the organizational design and align them with the DT design. Multi-perspective EM methods, such as 4EM, are suitable for supporting this. The organizational aspects need to be linked with capabilities and DT designs. A part of this task would be modeling the context information that affects the operation of the DT. Since DTs are operated continuously the runtime data allows the assessment and improvement of the design models. E.g. the Context Modeling component supports the design by officering a set of measurable context elements that are already available in the context platform. CDD includes a component for Reuse of Capability Designs supported by a pattern repository that captures pattern performance data over time [19]. This information is valuable for new as well as for improving the existing designs.

Adaptation and adjustment. DTs need to be operated continuously, in various situations, and according to various business models. It can also be expected that these change under the lifetime of a DT. In this respect EM can be used for capturing the business dimensions of change, and CDD components for Capability Design and Context Modeling are to be used for capturing changes in the application context. Components for Reuse of Capability Designs and for Runtime Adjustments can be used to specify automatic adjustments or reconfigurations of the solutions including the DTs.

Continuous lifecycle management pertain to two key aspects. First, visualization of operational and contextual data at runtime and then using this data and information to create new business models and DT designs as well as to change the existing ones. Part of the CDD method is generation of capability monitoring applications from capability design models and context models. Similarly, a monitoring dashboard for DTs can be generated from capability models, because it allows specifying KPIs and context elements together with their calculation from measurable properties that can be assembled from various data sources – internal application data as well as external environment data. Concerning the second aspect, the lifecycle support, CDD is focusing on capability design and context-based adjustment of IS. To include DT designs in capability designs would need having a more explicit integration with EM as well as dedicated tasks for designing the functionality of DTs. This would imply that the DT is designed together with the capability as a solution to a business goal. Such an approach would contribute to ensuring that the DT fits the business design. The CDD method is also supported by a tool environment which would be needed to monitor context and runtime data, calculate KPI values, and, if necessary, to trigger adjustment algorithms.

The requirements elicited in the case studies are to a large extend addressing similar issues to the requirements from literature. Table 1 summarizes the CDD support.

The requirements from literature and the case studies point to the need for the extension of the DT design with the aspects of business motivation and lifecycle management. The following modeling artifacts and practices contribute to this purpose:

– Enterprise models to capture the business models. Later they can be linked with the DT design models repressing the technical details of the DT.
– Capability design models to represent the more detailed designs of the DT.

Table 1. Requirements from case studies supported by the CDD method components

CSRs	CDD method components				
	Enterprise Modeling	Capability Design	Context Modeling	Reuse of Capability Designs	Runtime Del. Adjustments
CSR1	Captures the business motivation	DT design linked to the requiring parts of the enterprise model		Captures reusable solutions, e.g. DT capabilities	
CSR2	Captures the business motivation	Links design to the business motivation	Context monitoring with model driven dashboards		Specify operational adjustments of DTs
CSR3	Captures the business model	Links the capability driven DT to the business model	Model the context data for monitoring	Supports management of reusable components	
CSR4	Captures the business motivation	Capability driven DT and allows model driven	Context monitoring with model driven dashboards		
CSR5				Management of reusable artifacts, incl. their performance	
CSR6	Captures the business motivation	Capability-based development of DT functionality	Modeling of the DT usage context, generation of dashboards		Context driven adjustment at runtime

- Context models to show the dependence on local and global data in the environment as well as to adjustments of the DTs and their monitoring dashboards.
- The capability design models and the enterprise models need to be linked to establish the business motivation and fit of the DT.
- Capability designs and context models should be used for generating dashboards for DT management. Key data types that have the potential of being useful here are context data, KPI, historical data about performance of reusable components.
- The models used need to be reasonably open and extendable in order to be able to incorporate additional perspectives of modeling.

6.2 Supporting the Continuous Way of Working

Concerning requirements CSR5 and CSR6, they can be supported by the CDD's method components as discussed in the previous section, but they also call for the establishment of a new way of working. It needs to support the core tasks of development and management of efficient DTs, such as, capturing the business motivation, design of the DT, and delivery and operation of the DT. The CDD process, which shares similarities with the DevOps principle of continuous development and operation, has the potential of being adapted for this purpose. Wortmann et al. [8] also call for this kind of approach to DT development and operation. The case study requirements suggest that to make the DTs more fitting to the business model, explicit focus should be on the issues such as business goals, processes, and integration with the IS architecture. These are issues suitable for EM. Figure 1 proposes a DT development and management lifecycle that incorporates three sub-cycles – EM, DT Design, and Delivery and Operation. The internal steps and tasks in the sub-cycles follow the established procedures in [7] for EM and in [10] for Design and Operation. The following artifacts support the transition between the sub-cycles (grey arrows in Fig. 1):

- EM provides explicated knowledge about the business motivation for the DT in the form of enterprise models.
- Capability design provides (1) capability based digital twin design that are executable in the sense that they are integrated with the physical twins, and (2) generates the monitoring applications for digital twin management from the context model.
- The delivery and operation sub-cycle provides data types (e.g. context element types, measurable properties, KPIs) of available data used at runtime of the digital twin. This allows extending the existing designs as well as selecting existing and obtainable data in new designs. The Design provides best practices and reusable components on which the EM sub-cycle can base new business developments.

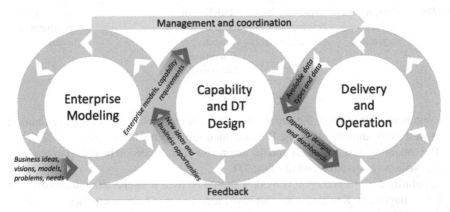

Fig. 1. An overview of the envisioned capability-driven cycle of management digital twins.

7 Feasibility Demonstration

Figure 2 illustrates the feasibility of the CDD use with a fragment of a capability model consisting of goals, capabilities, and context modeling elements. The digital transformation workshop at company A identified an option to develop a pump-as-a-service product. When prioritizing the options, this option was top rated and, hence, converted into Goal 1 to develop pumping-as-a-service. It was refined into three sub-goals aiming at low maintenance pumps (1.1), possibility for real-time monitoring (1.2) and development of a preventive maintenance service (1.3). KPIs were set for all three sub-goals. The goal model is shown on the right side of Fig. 2 and follows the 4EM notation.

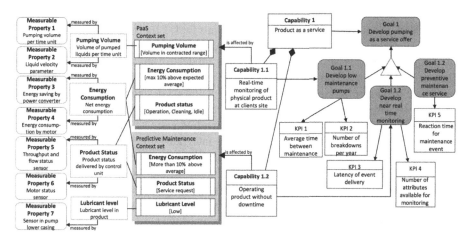

Fig. 2. A capability model for operating product as a service.

From a capability perspective, pump-as-a-service can be considered in more general terms as product-as-a-service capability if company A wants to offer other physical products as a service. The core sub-capabilities of product-as-a-service are real-time monitoring a product at the client site (which motivates the digital twin) and a reliable product without downtimes. The capabilities are visible in the center of the model.

The left side shows the context elements and the measurable properties on which they are based, in which context sets they are included, and their relation to capabilities. These context elements are calculated from the measurable properties and monitored once the capability is implemented. This also specifies the data to be provided by the DT. An example for a context element is the total energy consumption of the pump measured by the energy consumption of the motor and the energy recuperation achieved by the installed power converter. This context element is required for providing the product as a service (as part of the cost structure) and also for evaluating when to trigger preventive maintenance. From this model the CDD Environment would be able to generate a monitoring dashboard for Capability 1.2. It would display energy consumption, product status, and lubricant level as runtime properties of the application for operational monitoring. For a more strategic view on the capability fulfillment of KPI3 and KPI4 also need to be monitored. For brevity reasons, context and KPI calculations as well as the operational processes linked to the capabilities are not shown in the model.

8 Concluding Remarks and Future Work

The starting point for our work was the analysis of two industrial cases on how digital twin initiatives emerge and what the driving forces for starting implementation projects are. An observation from both cases is that digital transformation and development of new business model options are a motivation and driving force of DT implementation. Both case studies resulted from the need of companies to explore innovative products or services based on digital technologies, embedded into their operational processes and structures. DTs are considered as a way of integrating innovative products/services into the operational context, which leads to requirements for DT functionality and implementation. In summary, we see clear support for our conjecture that DT have to be integrated into the organizational structures and business models of manufacturing enterprises. Furthermore, we analyzed requirements for DT development from literature. Requirements pose a number of issues concerning a model-based design and management with a particularly strong emphasis on establishing a good fit between the business issues and DT-based solutions. This is an area to which EM and CDD have the potential of contributing. In this regard we have proposed an integrated lifecycle and discussed how capability-based DT designs could be used. The initial feasibility demonstration gives reason to the assumption that this approach is promising and should be pursued.

Concerning future work, we plan to investigate to what extent existing technically motivated DT implementations are used for new services or products and cause digital transformation in the enterprise and how the design of the DT features can be included in the capability design. We also aim to establish a development environment for the proposed way of working by integrating components of the CDD Environment with the modeling support by the ADOxx tool.

References

1. IIRA: Technology Working Group Industrial Internet Consortium, IIC Architecture Task Group: The Industrial Internet Reference Architecture v1.8 (2017)
2. Strange, R., Zucchella, A.: Industry 4.0, global value chains and international business. Multinational Bus. Rev. **25**(4) (2017)
3. International Electrotechnical Commission: IEC PAS 63088:2017. Smart Manufacturing - Reference Architecture Model Industry 4.0 (RAMI4.0) (2017)
4. Nardello, M., Han, S., Møller, C., Gøtze, J.: Automated Modeling with Abstraction for Enterprise Architecture (AMA4EA): Business Process Model Automation in an Industry 4.0 Laboratory, CSIMQ, no. 19 (2019)
5. Sniderman, B., Mahto, M., Cotteleer, M.: Industry 4.0 and Manufacturing Ecosystems: Exploring the World of Connected Enterprises. Deloitte University Press (2016)
6. Bolton, R., et al.: Customer experience challenges: bringing together digital, physical and social realms. J. Serv. Manag. **29**(5) (2018)
7. Sandkuhl, K., Stirna, J., Persson, A., Wißotzki, M.: Enterprise Modeling. Tackling Business Challenges with the 4EM Method. Springer, Heidelberg (2014). https://doi.org/10.1007/978-3-662-43725-4

8. Wortmann, A., Barais, O., Combemale, B., et al.: Modeling languages in Industry 4.0: an extended systematic mapping study. Softw. Syst. Model. **19**, 67–94 (2020)
9. Hermann, M., Pentek, T., Otto, B.: Design principles for Industrie 4.0 scenarios. In: Proceedings of the HICSS 2016. IEEE (2016)
10. Sandkuhl, K., Stirna, J. (eds.): Capability Management in Digital Enterprises. Springer, Cham (2018). https://doi.org/10.1007/978-3-319-90424-5
11. Frank, U.: Multi-perspective enterprise modeling: foundational concepts, prospects and future research challenges. Softw. Syst. Model. **13**(3), 941–962 (2012)
12. Lillehagen, F., Krogstie, J.: Active Knowledge Modeling of Enterprises. Springer, Heidelberg (2018). https://doi.org/10.1007/978-3-540-79416-5
13. Hirsch-Kreinsen, H., ten Hompel, M.: Digitalisierung industrieller Arbeit: Entwicklungsper-spektiven und Gestaltungsansätze. In: Handbuch Industrie 4.0 Bd.3 (2017)
14. Berman, S.J., Bell, R.: Digital transformation: creating new business models where digital meets physical. In: IBM Institute for Business Value (2011)
15. Sandkuhl, K., Shilov, N., Smirnov, A.: Facilitating digital transformation by multi-aspect ontologies: approach and application steps. IJSM (2020)
16. Johannesson, P., Perjons, E.: An Introduction to Design Science. Springer, Cham (2014). https://doi.org/10.1007/978-3-319-10632-8
17. Kampars, J., Zdravkovic, J., Stirna, J., Grabis, J.: Extending organizational capabilities with open data to support sustainable and dynamic business ecosystems. Softw. Syst. Model (2019). https://doi.org/10.1007/s10270-019-00756-7
18. Yin, R.K.: Case Study Research: Design and Methods. SAGE Publications, Thousand Oaks (2002)
19. Kampars, J., Stirna, J.: A repository for pattern governance supporting capability driven development. In: CEUR Workshop Proceedings, pp. 1–12 (2017)
20. Mittal, S., Khan, M.A., Romero, D., Wuest, T.: A critical review of smart manufacturing & Industry 4.0 maturity models: implications for small and medium-sized enterprises (SMEs). J. Manufact. Syst. **49**, 194–214 (2018)
21. Schumacher, A., Erol, S., Sihn, W.: A maturity model for assessing Industry 4.0 readiness and maturity of manufacturing enterprises. Procedia Cirp **52**(1), 161–166 (2016)

Integrated On-demand Modeling
for Configuration of Trusted ICT Supply Chains

Jānis Grabis(⊠)

Department of Management Information Technology, Riga Technical University,
Kalku 1, Riga, Latvia
grabis@rtu.lv

Abstract. Digital enterprises and their networks increasingly rely on advanced decision-making capabilities, however, development of decision-making models requires significant effort and is often performed independently of other digitalization activities. Additionally, dynamic nature of many decision-making problems requires rapid ramp-up of decision-making capabilities. To addresses these challenges, this position paper proposes to elaborate a method for integrated on-demand decision modeling. The method combines mathematical programming and data analytics models to create case specific models on the basis of generic decision-making models. The integrated model and its data supply pipelines are configured using enterprise models allowing for consistent and rapid model deployment. The integrated model is intended for the trusted ICT supply chain configuration problem though it can be used for solving various types of decision-making problems. The main expected results are formulation of the new type decision-making model and the method for on-demand configuration of such models.

Keywords: On-demand modeling · Integrated modeling · ICT supply chain

1 Introduction

Digital enterprises increasingly rely on smart and intelligent decision-making based on non-trivial computations and complex algorithms (Carlsson 2018). **Decision-making** is perceived as a selection of business process execution alternatives (e.g., accept or decline a customer request in Customer Relationships Management system) or finding values of quantitative decision variables (i.e., how many products to order in Warehouse management System). It is assumed that decisions are made using a kind of algorithm or model referred as to decision-making model and the process of creating and using the model is referred as to decision-modelling. There are different types of decision-making problems, for example, capacity planning, supplier selection, fraud detection. Decision-making models have been developed for these typical decision-making problems, however these models still need to be adapted for specific use cases.

Decision-modelling often is time consuming and complex endeavor while dynamic operations increasingly require decision-making capabilities provided on short notice for solving short life-cycle decision-making problems (Halpern 2015), for example,

© Springer Nature Switzerland AG 2020
S. Nurcan et al. (Eds.): BPMDS 2020/EMMSAD 2020, LNBIP 387, pp. 300–307, 2020.
https://doi.org/10.1007/978-3-030-49418-6_20

selection of the delivery mode in hyperconnected systems (Sallez et al. 2016). That creates a need for on-demand decision-modelling (ODDM) allowing for quick model development, deployment and execution for a particular short-life cycle application case.

It is proposed that ODDM models can be developed by integrating various modelling paradigms. In particular, mathematical programming models are prescriptive models allowing to generate the optimal solution for the decision-making problem though requiring significant development expertise and effort. Data analytical models (e.g., regression, deep neural networks) on the other hand have predictive capabilities and given their structure and data can be estimated on-demand. Therefore, we propose to create ODDM models as integrated models or iODDM. On-demand models are envisioned to have multiple applications. The proposed research will focus specifically on configuration of Information and Communication Technology (ICT) supply chains (SC) what is a topical problem in practice (Kshetri and Voas 2019).

Challenges associated with intelligent applications and on-demand decision modelling can be summarized as follows:

1. Digital enterprises require rapidly deployable advanced decision-making models;
2. Models are still developed independently and their integration with other systems is done in an ad-hoc manner;
3. Data analytics models are more suitable for on-demand decision-making (e.g., non-parametric models) though some of data analytics models lack explanatory capabilities;
4. Model development is time consuming and performed on the case-to-case basis;
5. Many applications such as SC configuration are context dependent and require application case specific data structures.

To address these challenges, the goal of the proposed research is to enable development of on-demand decision-making models for configuration of trusted ICT SCs by integrating three modeling paradigms - enterprise modelling, mathematical programming and big data analysis. Enterprise models represent the decision-making problem in the enterprise context to facilitate integration, mathematical programming models capture underlying structure of the decision-modeling problem and big data analysis or data analytical models account for case specific variations in data structures and content. Expected scientific contributions are: 1) formulation of the general iODDM model and a new type of SC configuration model; 2) method for development of iODDM models as a part of decision-making information systems; 3) extension of enterprise modelling to support representation of trusted SC modelling aspects; and 4) big data processing pipeline for decision-modelling data supply.

2 Related Work

Integrated on-demand modeling and configuration of trusted ICT SC are two key areas of innovation of this proposal. Integrated and hybrid modelling is often used to attain benefits brought by different modelling paradigms (Chandra and Grabis 2016a). Complexity of current decision-making models also requires an appropriate development and execution environment (Chen and Zhang 2014).

Models are typically integrated using a staged approach when one model serves as an input to another model (Chandra and Grabis 2016b). Optimization models are often combined with simulation models (Amaran et al. 2016). However, simultaneous running of mathematical programming and data analytical models is rarely considered. Kuo et al. (2015) provide one example where data analytical models feed mathematical programming models in real-time. The proposal's authors have made early attempts to integrate mathematical programming models and data analysis models (Grabis et al. 2012) though that is done without generalizing the integration approach. Ning and You (2019) point out that further development of integrated models requires better closed-loop feedback mechanisms. From the computational perspective, specification of decision-making components using domain specific languages allows development of reusable components pluggable in different enterprise applications (Brodsky et al. 2015). Wei and Ma (2014) integrate product configuration, production planning and production execution on the basis of the ERP system. Decision Model and Notation allows representing decision-making logics in business processes (Hasic et al. 2018). However, these technologies are often restricted to specific types of decision-models and do not cover the full-cycle of integrated modelling, especially, integration with enterprise modelling or on-demand modelling data provisioning. There is an increasing interest in modelling as a service though practical applications are mainly restricted to descriptive models (e.g., Schuff et al. 2018).

Mathematical and simulation models mainly have been used in SC configuration (Chandra and Grabis 2016b) and qualitative and descriptive techniques have been used to evaluate SC risks (Sigler et al. 2017). Patrignani and Kavathatzopoulos (2018) point out that complexity of ICT systems pose new challenges not addressed by the existing methods. Baryannis et al. (2019) conclude that artificial intelligence could help to address these concerns though comprehensive methods are yet to be developed.

The proposed research will extend the state of the art by elaborating a new type of integrated decision-making models, which fuse mathematical programming and data analytics in a generalized manner and are configurable according to enterprise models. The model when tailored to the trusted ICT SC configuration problem will be provide a novel solution to configuration of this type of SC using mathematical programming for typical SC configuration decisions and data analytics for risk and trustworthiness evaluation.

3 Model Formulation

A digital enterprise (or network of enterprises) face a decision-making problem (e.g., SC configuration). A generic decision-making model is available to solve this problem. The generic decision-making model needs to be tailored for a specific use case. The proposed method streamlines the tailoring process. Application of the method is supported by the decision support information system. Figure 1 shows the conceptual landscape of ODDM. The decision making problem is formally defined using enterprise modelling, which will be extended to cover needs specific to iODDM. The case specific model addressing the decision-making problem is developed as an iODDM consisting of the generic model and the data analytical model. It is configured according to the enterprise model to rise level of abstraction and improve integration with the decision support information system. The generic model captures core aspects of decision making and is formulated as a mathematical programming model while the data analytical model provides case specific customization using models fitted for the specific case.

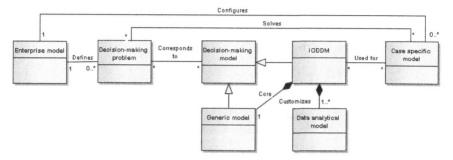

Fig. 1. Conceptual landscape of ODDM.

The integrated model combines enterprise modeling, mathematical programming and data analytics. Mathematical programming is used to represent the core part of the decision-making problem and data analytics is used to represent the case specific part of the decision-making problem. For instance, in the case of SC configuration, the mathematical programming model represents cost optimization and data analytical models are incorporated to represent influence of trust related aspects such supplier reputation, risk of delays and impact of shock events.

Figure 2 shows an initial proposal for the integrated SC configuration model. The SC configuration model deals with selection of suitable SC nodes, establishing connections among the nodes and allocating SC activities to the nodes and connections. In the case of ICT SCs, one needs to ensure that all components used in end-products and services meet security and reliability standards and requirements and SC can deliver products as promised withstanding various shock events. The core part of the model is a mathematical programming model. $\mathbf{X, Y,}$ and $\mathbf{V}$ are matrices representing decision variables concerning node selection, definition of connections and activity allocation, respectively. The vector $\mathbf{c}$ represents cost parameters associated with nodes, connections and activities as indicated by their indices (e.g., costs of operating a SC node). Vectors $\mathbf{a_i}$ and $\mathbf{b_i}$ are parameters used to specify constraints. The generic model is augmented by a customizable part. That includes customization of the objective function by adding a term $\mathbf{v'P}$, where $\mathbf{P}$ is a vector of penalties for not meeting case specific goals and $\mathbf{v}$ is a vector of weights indicating a relative importance of each goal. A corresponding set of constraints 4th item in Fig. 2 is also added to the model. These constraints represent relationships among target values of KPI and values estimated by the model. $\mathbf{kpi}^T$ are target values set by decision-makers and $\mathbf{KPI}^C$ is a KPI value estimated using the model. The penalty term in the objective function and the KPI constraint are added according to the enterprise model. Additionally, SC trustworthiness factor $\mathbf{R}$ is added to the objective and a constraint is added (3rd item in Fig. 2). The trustworthiness factor is a combination of security and trust factors characterizing the SC and it is evaluated using data analytical models. Various types of data analytical models could be used ranging from linear regression model to neural networks. The model can be estimated on-demand and represents security and reliability concerns relevant to particular case.

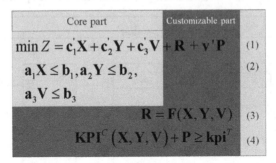

Fig. 2. The initial proposal of iODDM model.

The specific features to ICT SCs are representation of complex product structure, combination of virtual and physical aspects, and domain specific performance and quality attributes such as data security, performance and reliability attributes and licensing.

The enterprise model provides means for business analysts to configure iODDM. It represents the case specific goals and their KPI as well as restricts a number of plausible scenarios. For instance, configuration of SC for a new product has fewer constrains on decision variables than changing one of the nodes of the existing SC. The decision-making information system provides data needed for estimation and operation of data analytical models in a speedy and scalable manner.

It is important to note that data analytical models are an integral part of the model rather than just input data providers as it is a case in traditional multi-stage modeling. Results of the data analytical modeling are recalculated in every model solving iteration. Depending on the type of analytical models used traditional or non-parametric (e.g., genetic algorithms) will be used to solve the model.

4 Modeling Process

The iODDM model should be available for decision-making within a short time period measured from couple of minutes to one week. The method supports all steps of model development and includes three main stages: 1) Model development; 2) on-demand configuration; and 3) model execution and adaptation (Fig. 3). The model development stage concerns creation of the iODDM for the decision-making problem. Enterprise modeling techniques are used to specify modeling goals, constraints and data entities characteristic for the decision-making problem. The mathematical programming model is also formulated and it is linked with the enterprise model. The data entities represent data requirements for decision-making purposes. Usage of data analytical models is represented in an abstract form.

Whenever a need arises for an on-demand modeling, the model developed is configured in the second stage of the method. The enterprise model is changed to represent

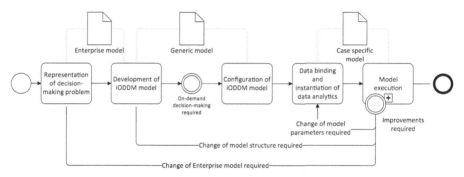

Fig. 3. Overview of the iODDM method.

case specific objectives and constraints and these changes are represented in the decision-making model by means of transformations. Case specific data sources are bound to the data requirements. That includes specification of data transformation procedures. It is important to note that both data streams and batch data can be used as data sources. The abstract data analytical models are instantiated using the case specific data and are made ready for usage in the optimization model.

The model execution stage concerns actual usage of the models. Two main challenges addressed during this stage are monitoring of data sources and scalability what is supported by the modeling platform. Additionally, adaptation of the modeling parameters also could be performed.

5   Tool Support

Development and execution of iODDM models is supported by the appropriate technological solution what is essential to deal with usability, scalability and reliability requirements of the iODDM method. The architecture of this decision-making information system or ODDM platform is given in Fig. 4.

It consists of the following key components:

- ODDM core - the central element of the architecture. It provides a web-based user interface that is used for iODDM model authoring and deployment. After models have been deployed and run various model related performance dashboards can be monitored in ODDM user interface. ODDM core also takes care of the infrastructure management and configuration of the remaining components of the ODDM architecture.
- Data ingest - used for ingesting data into the ODDM stream processor. Data ingestion in Fig. 4 is marked with #1. Typical data sources are open data, internet of things and other types of data streams. The intelligent application itself can serve as a data source (e.g. passing in streams of log files or transactions).
- Stream processor - used for processing ingested data streams (#2), which serve as the input for the iODDM model, and executing the model itself. Stream processor also aggregates the input data up to the defined level of granularity and persists it in the

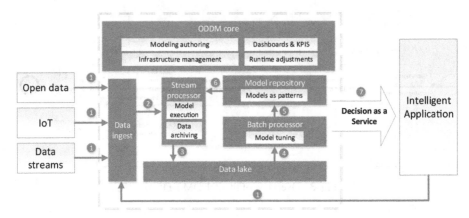

Fig. 4. Architecture of the ODDM platform.

data lake (#3). During the model execution, Runtime adjustments are triggered to pass decision-modeling results to consumers, e.g., supply chain (#7).

- Batch processor - provides batch processing of the archived data from the data lake (#4) and fine tuning of model parameters which are then saved in the model repository (#5). Various machine learning approaches are applied based on the available input data and model specifics.
- Model repository - provides storage of the integrated on-demand decision-making models in a form of reusable patterns that are then used by the Stream processor (#6). The repository also accumulates models' usage performance data. Model performance is measured under specific contextual situation (defined by the input data) and Stream processor is able to switch to a more appropriate alternative model if the context would change.
- Data lake - a distributed, horizontally scalable persistent data store that integrates with the Stream processor (#3) and batch data processor (#4).

6   Conclusion

The paper describes an idea of creating iODDM models what includes both the modeling approach and tool support to enable complex computations required. The immediate steps of further research are development of case specific models and generalization of the observations made.

The proposed approach has a number of potential risks. That includes proving utility of using enterprise models to configure analytical models, data availability and stability of mathematical models with data modeling augmented constraints. Additionally, the proposed method relays having sufficient level of similarity among the case specific models and reusability of modeling components.

References

Amaran, S., Sahinidis, N.V., Sharda, B., Bury, S.J.: Simulation optimization: a review of algorithms and applications). Ann. Oper. Res. **240**(1), 351–380 (2016)

Brodsky, A., Krishnamoorthy, M., Menasce, D.A., Shao, G., Rachuri, S.: Toward smart manufacturing using decision analytics. In: Proceedings of 2014 IEEE International Conference on Big Data, p. 967 (2015)

Baryannis, G., Validi, S., Dani, S., Antoniou, G.: Supply chain risk management and artificial intelligence: state of the art and future research directions. Int. J. Prod. Res. **57**(7), 2179–2202 (2019)

Carlsson, C.: Decision analytics-Key to digitalisation. Inf. Sci. **460**, 424–438 (2018)

Chandra, C., Grabis, J.: Reconfigurable supply chains: an integrated framework. In: Chandra, C., Grabis, J. (eds.) SC Configuration, pp. 69–86. Springer, Heidelberg (2016a). https://doi.org/10.1007/978-1-4939-3557-4_4

Chandra, C., Grabis, J.: Simulation modeling and hybrid approaches. In: Chandra, C., Grabis, J. (eds.) SC Configuration, pp. 173–197. Springer, Heidelberg (2016b). https://doi.org/10.1007/978-1-4939-3557-4_9

Chen, C.L.P., Zhang, C.-Y.: Data-intensive applications, challenges, techniques and technologies: a survey on big data. Inf. Sci. **275**, 314–347 (2014)

Grabis, J., Chandra, C., Kampars, J.: Use of distributed data sources in facility location. Comput. Ind. Eng. **63**(4), 855–863 (2012)

Halpern, F.: Next-generation analytics and platforms for business success: tDWI research report (2015). www.tdwi.org

Hasić, F., De Smedt, J., Vanthienen, J.: Augmenting processes with decision intelligence: principles for integrated modelling. Decis. Support Syst. **107**, 1–12 (2018)

Kshetri, N., Voas, J.: Supply Chain Trust. IT Prof. **21**(2), 6–10 (2019)

Kuo, Y., Leung, J.M.Y., Meng, H.M., Tsoi, K.K.F.: A real-time decision support tool for disaster response: a mathematical programming approach. In: Proceedings - 2015 IEEE International Congress on Big Data, BigData Congress 2015, p. 639 (2015)

Ning, C., You, F.: Optimization under uncertainty in the era of big data and deep learning: when machine learning meets mathematical programming. Comput. Chem. Eng. **125**, 434–448 (2019)

Patrignani, N., Kavathatzopoulos, I.: On the complex relationship between ICT systems and the planet. In: Kreps, D., Ess, C., Leenen, L., Kimppa, K. (eds.) HCC13 2018, vol. 537, pp. 181–187. Springer, Heidelberg (2018). https://doi.org/10.1007/978-3-319-99605-9_13

Sallez, Y., Pan, S., Montreui, B., et al.: On the activeness of intelligent Physical Internet containers. Comput. Ind. **81**, 96–104 (2016)

Schuff, D., Corral, K., St. Louis, R.D., Schymik, G.: Enabling self-service BI: a methodology and a case study for a model management warehouse. Inf. Syst. Front. **20**(2), 275–288 (2018)

Sigler, K., Shoemaker, D., Kohnke, A.: Supply Chain Risk Management: Applying Secure Acquisition Principles to Ensure a Trusted Technology Product. CRC Press, Auburn Hills (2017)

Wei, J., Ma, Y.-S.: Design of a feature-based order acceptance and scheduling module in an ERP system. Comput. Ind. **65**(1), 64–78 (2014)

Software-Related Modeling
(EMMSAD 2020)

A Modeling Method for Systematic Architecture Reconstruction of Microservice-Based Software Systems

Florian Rademacher[1]([envelope]) [iD], Sabine Sachweh[1], and Albert Zündorf[2]

[1] IDiAL Institute, University of Applied Sciences and Arts Dortmund,
Otto-Hahn-Straße 27, 44227 Dortmund, Germany
`{florian.rademacher,sabine.sachweh}@fh-dortmund.de`
[2] Department of Computer Science and Electrical Engineering, University of Kassel,
Wilhelmshöher Allee 73, 34121 Kassel, Germany
`zuendorf@uni-kassel.de`

Abstract. Microservice Architecture (MSA) is an approach to architecting service-based software systems, which aims for decreasing service coupling to enable independent service development and deployment. Consequently, the adoption of MSA is expected to particularly benefit the scalability, maintainability, and reliability of monolithic systems. However, MSA adoption also increases architectural complexity in service design, implementation, and operation. As a result, Software Architecture Reconstruction (SAR) of microservice architectures is aggravated. This paper presents a modeling method that systematizes SAR of microservice architectures with the goal to facilitate its execution. The method yields reconstruction models for certain architecture viewpoints in MSA to enable efficient architecture analysis. We validate the method's applicability by means of a case study architecture and the assessment of its risk in technical debt using derived reconstruction models.

Keywords: Microservice architecture · Software Architecture Reconstruction · Model-driven engineering · Modeling languages

1 Introduction

Microservice Architecture (MSA) is a novel approach to architecting service-based software systems that puts a strong emphasis on *service-specific independence* [11]. MSA promotes to (i) tailor services to exactly one, distinct capability; (ii) shift responsibilities in a service's design, development, and deployment to a single team composed of members with heterogeneous professional skills; and (iii) keep services executable, testable, and deployable in isolation [10,11].

MSA is expected to benefit quality attributes like scalability, maintainability, and reliability [11]. Thus, it is frequently used to refactor monolithic systems for which these quality attributes decreased critically [16].

© Springer Nature Switzerland AG 2020
S. Nurcan et al. (Eds.): BPMDS 2020/EMMSAD 2020, LNBIP 387, pp. 311–326, 2020.
https://doi.org/10.1007/978-3-030-49418-6_21

However, MSA adoption increases architectural complexity significantly. For example, MSA architects and developers need to make sure that microservices do not become too fine-grained to lower network load [4]. Additionally, MSA allows for choosing different technologies per technical concern and microservice, which can increase learning curves for developers and the risk for technical debt [15]. Moreover, MSA requires a sophisticated operation infrastructure to enable independent service deployment and DevOps practices [17], as well as the provisioning of components for, e.g., service discovery and monitoring [2].

The different degrees in complexity aggravate *software architecture reconstruction* (SAR) [3] of MSA-based software systems [1]. While SAR is key to architecture verification, conformance checking, and trade-off analysis [3], research on SAR of microservice architectures is still formative [1,6].

In this paper, we present a modeling method that systematizes SAR of microservice architectures with the goal to guide its structured execution. The method builds upon our previous research on model-driven MSA engineering, in which we developed a set of modeling languages for the specification of microservice architectures [12,13] based on *architecture viewpoints* [3]. Our modeling method exploits these languages to capture reconstructed architecture information in *reconstruction models*. They aim to facilitate architecture analysis in the context of MSA. We validate the applicability of our SAR modeling method by means of a case study microservice architecture and the assessment of its risk in technical debt [14] leveraging the derived reconstruction models.

The remainder of the paper is organized as follows. Section 2 presents background information on SAR and our languages for model-driven MSA engineering. Section 3 introduces our method for systematic SAR of microservice architectures. In Sect. 4, we apply the method to a case study architecture and assess its risk in technical debt using the reconstruction models. Section 5 discusses our approach. Section 6 presents related work and Sect. 7 concludes the paper.

2   Background

This section presents background information on SAR and an overview of our modeling languages for viewpoint-based, model-driven MSA engineering.

2.1   Software Architecture Reconstruction

SAR is an iterative reverse engineering process that derives a representation of a software architecture from artifacts like documentation or source code [3]. It aims to document architecture implementations, which lack thorough documentation, and enable subsequent architecture analysis. SAR consists of four phases [3]:

1. *Raw view extraction*: Gathers architecture information from architecture-related artifacts. Each set of artifact-specific information can be considered a *view* that represents certain architecture elements and their relations [3].
2. *Database construction*: Transforms views into a canonical representation and stores them in a structured form like a database.

3. *View fusion and manipulation*: Combines views to improve accuracy of reconstructed information. For instance, a domain view may be associated with a component view to document runtime processing of domain data.
4. *Architecture analysis*: Aims for answering hypotheses about architecture implementations from reconstructed architecture information.

2.2 Viewpoint-Based Modeling of Microservice Architectures

In our previous works, we developed a set of modeling languages for model-driven MSA engineering [12,13]. Each language focuses on an architecture viewpoint in MSA and thus addresses the concerns of certain MSA stakeholder groups [3]. In the following, we provide an overview of our modeling languages per viewpoint.

Domain Viewpoint. This viewpoint addresses the concerns of domain experts and service developers in MSA engineering. Its Domain Data Modeling Language [13] enables both stakeholder groups to collaboratively construct *domain models* and augment them with patterns from Domain-driven Design (DDD) [7,11].

Technology Viewpoint. This viewpoint focuses on service developers and operators. Its Technology Modeling Language [12] allows for constructing *technology models* that prescribe available technologies for microservice implementation and operation. In addition, generic *technology aspects* may be modeled to augment, e.g., microservices with technology-specific access means and configuration.

The viewpoint also comprises the Technology Mapping Language. *Mapping models* extend domain and service models with technology information.

Service Viewpoint. The viewpoint's Service Modeling Language [13] targets the Dev perspective in DevOps-based MSA teams [10]. It enables service developers to construct *service models* that specify microservices, interfaces, and endpoints.

Operation Viewpoint. The Operation Modeling Language [13] targets the Ops perspective [10]. It enables service operators to construct *operation models* that describe service deployment and infrastructure for, e.g., service discovery and monitoring [2].

The modeling languages integrate an import mechanism to connect viewpoints' models and create coherent architecture descriptions. For example, service models may import domain models to relate domain concepts with microservices. Moreover, operation models may import service models to express service deployment and infrastructure usage.

3   A Modeling Method for Systematic Reconstruction of Microservice Architecture

It is the goal of our modeling method to systematize SAR of microservice architectures. To this end, we explore the application of our viewpoint-based languages (cf. Subsect. 2.2), which were originally developed to enable model-driven MSA engineering [13], for realizing the SAR process described in Subsect. 2.1.

Figure 1 shows our SAR modeling method in a UML activity diagram. The sequence of its six activities follows the relationships between MSA viewpoints (cf. Subsect. 2.2). Each activity targets certain phases of the SAR process (cf. Subsect. 2.1) and is described in the following subsections together with example reconstruction models expressed in corresponding modeling languages.

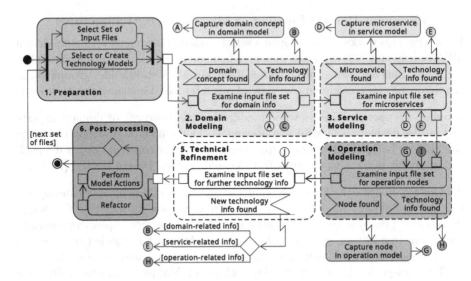

Fig. 1. Definition of our SAR modeling method in a UML activity diagram.

3.1   Activity 1: Preparation

Each instance of the SAR modeling method starts with the Preparation activity (cf. Fig. 1). In its first action, a set of input files, from which the examined microservice architecture shall be reconstructed, is selected. Such files may contain, e.g., documentation, source code, build scripts, or configuration values [1].

In the second action, technology models (cf. Subsect. 2.2) are selected or created. In case the technologies employed by the examined architecture are known, already existing technology models, e.g., constructed in previous method instances, may be reused. If no such models exist or the technology stack is unknown, empty technology models are created. A reasonable default is the creation of three technology models for domain-, service-, and operation-related technologies to be discovered (cf. Subsects. 3.2 to 3.4).

The Preparation activity contributes to Phase 1 of the SAR process as they identify the sources to extract architecture information from (cf. Subsect. 2.1).

3.2   Activity 2: Domain Modeling

This activity examines the selected input file set for domain concepts (cf. Fig. 1). In object-oriented programming languages like Java, domain concepts may be realized by POJOs[1], i.e., classes that implement concepts of the application domain independent of external frameworks. Discovered domain concepts are captured in reconstruction domain models via our Domain Data Modeling Language (cf. Subsect. 2.2). Listing 1 shows a reconstruction domain model excerpt.

Listing 1. Excerpt of a reconstruction domain model (cf. Subsect. 2.2).

```
1  // Reconstruction domain model "customerCore.data"
2  context customer { structure Address <valueObject> {
3      string streetAddress, string postalCode, string city } }
```

The reconstruction domain model excerpt captures a reconstructed domain concept called **Address** as a structure with three string fields, i.e., **streetAddress**, **postalCode**, and **city**. The structure carries the semantics of a DDD Value Object [7]. Value Objects are typically immutable and lack a domain-specific identity. Hence, they may act as value containers for data exchange.

The **Address** structure belongs to the **customer** Bounded Context. In DDD, a Bounded Context is a means to cluster domain concepts and constrain their scope [7]. Bounded Contexts are crucial to MSA, since each microservice should be responsible for exactly one context [11]. Thus, when the input file set of an instance of our SAR modeling method (cf. Subsect. 3.1) belongs to a single service, the Domain Modeling activity should yield a domain model with only one context. In case the input files concern several services, ambiguous assignment of discovered domain concepts to contexts hints at wrong service tailoring.

During the examination of input files for domain concepts, technology-related information, e.g., for mapping concept instances to database tables, may be discovered. In this case, our modeling method delegates to a *technology modeling sub-activity* via activity edge connector "B" (cf. Fig. 1). It handles the occurrence of technology-related information in domain concepts and is shown in Fig. 2.

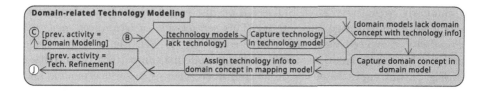

Fig. 2. Domain-related technology modeling sub-activity

Starting at connector "B", the sub-activity checks if the discovered technology information was already captured in a technology model. Otherwise, it is added to a suitable existing technology model (cf. Subsect. 3.6) or to the domain-related technology model created in Activity 1 (cf. Subsect. 3.1). Next, the domain concept itself is captured in a domain model if it was not yet, which may happen, e.g., for Java code where annotations like @Table from the Java Persistence

---

[1] https://www.martinfowler.com/bliki/POJO.html.

API (JPA)[2] are placed before class definitions. Finally, the discovered technology information is assigned to the captured domain concept within a mapping model (cf. Subsect. 2.2). Listing 2 shows a reconstruction domain-related technology model and mapping model derived during the Domain Modeling SAR activity.

Listing 2. Reconstruction domain-related technology model and reconstruction mapping model (cf. Subsect. 2.2).

```
1  // Reconstruction domain-related technology model "domainTech.technology"
2  technology domainTech {service aspects{ aspect Table for types { string name; } }}
3  // Reconstruction mapping model "customerCore.mapping"
4  import technology from "domainTech.technology" as domainTech
5  @technology(domainTech)
6  type customer::Address { aspects { domainTech::_aspects.Table("addresses"); } }
```

Line 2 specifies an aspect in a technology model [12]. The aspect reflects the discovered @Table annotation. The mapping model in Lines 4 to 6 imports the technology model and assigns the aspect to the Address data structure (cf. Listing 1) to prescribe address storage in a database table called "addresses".

The Domain Modeling activity and its successor Activities 3 to 5 (cf. Subsects. 3.3 to 3.5) cover SAR Phases 2 and 3 (cf. Subsect. 2.1). Discovered architecture information is transformed into canonical forms, i.e., models (Phase 2), which are then combined via imports to reflect architectural relations (Phase 3).

3.3 Activity 3: Service Modeling

The Service Modeling activity (cf. Fig. 1) examines the input file set for microservices and related information, which are then to be captured in service models (cf. Subsect. 2.2). In Java-based microservice architectures such information may be found, e.g., in classes that employ annotations for web-based data binding like @RestController and @GetMapping from the Spring[3] framework. Docker Compose[4] and build scripts also support microservice identification [1].

Similarly to Activity 2 (cf. Subsect. 3.2), discovered technology information is handled in a dedicated sub-activity. This *service-related technology modeling sub-activity* is entered via activity edge connector "E" (cf. Fig. 1). It proceeds analogously to the domain-related technology modeling sub-activity of Activity 2 (cf. Fig. 2), but captures newly discovered microservices in service models and returns to the current method instance via edge connector "F" (cf. Fig. 1).

Listing 3 shows reconstruction models that result during the Service Modeling activity, i.e., a service-related technology model, a service model, and a mapping model (cf. Subsect. 2.2).

---

[2] https://jakarta.ee/specifications/platform/8/apidocs/javax/persistence/Table.html.

[3] https://spring.io.

[4] https://docs.docker.com/compose.

Listing 3. A reconstruction service-related technology model, a reconstruction service model, and a reconstruction mapping model (cf. Subsect. 2.2).

```
1   // Reconstruction service-related technology model "serviceTech.technology"
2   technology serviceTech {
3     protocols { sync http data formats json; }
4     service aspects { aspect PutMapping for operations; } }
5   // Reconstruction service model "customerCore.services"
6   import datatypes from "customerCore.data" as domainData
7   functional microservice com.example.CustomerCore { interface management {
8     changeAddress(sync id : long, sync address : domainData::customer.Address); } }
9   // Reconstruction mapping model "customerCore.mapping"
10  import technology from "serviceTech.technology" as serviceTech
11  import microservices from "customerCore.services" as services
12  @technology(serviceTech)
13  services::com.example.CustomerCore {
14    protocols { sync: serviceTech::_protocols.http }
15    endpoints { serviceTech::_protocols.http: "/customers"; }
16    operation management.changeAddress {
17      aspects { serviceTech::_aspects.PutMapping; } } }
```

The technology model in Lines 2 to 4 comprises discovered protocols and technology aspects [12]. Line 3 captures the HTTP protocol and JSON data format. Line 4 defines the PutMapping aspect for the eponymous Spring annotation. Lines 6 to 8 show a service model, which imports the domain model in Listing 1 to refer to the Address domain concept. Lines 7 to 8 capture the discovered CustomerCore service. Its management interface clusters the changeAddress operation, whose address parameter is typed with the Address concept.

Lines 10 to 17 of Listing 3 show a mapping model. According to the examined input files, it specifies that the CustomerCore service (i) uses the HTTP protocol from the service-related technology model (Line 14); (ii) has an HTTP endpoint in the form of a URI path (Line 15); and (iii) enables invocation of the changeAddress operation via Spring's @PutMapping annotation (Lines 16 and 17).

3.4   Activity 4: Operation Modeling

This activity captures discovered operation nodes (cf. Fig. 1) in reconstruction operation models (cf. Subsect. 2.2). Operation nodes may represent *containers* for service deployment [10] or provide infrastructure capabilities to the examined architecture [2]. From the input file set, containers and infrastructure nodes may be discovered in Dockerfiles[5], or Docker Compose or build files [1], respectively.

The Operation Modeling activity invokes a sub-activity when operation-related technology is discovered (cf. activity edge connector "H" in Fig. 1). The sub-activity proceeds analogously to the domain-related technology modeling sub-activity (cf. Fig. 2), but captures newly discovered operation nodes in operation models. It returns to a method instance via connector "I" (cf. Fig. 1).

Listing 4 shows reconstruction models derived during the execution of the Operation Modeling SAR activity.

---

[5] https://docs.docker.com/engine/reference/builder/.

Listing 4. Reconstruction operation-related technology model and reconstruction operation model (cf. Subsect. 2.2).

```
1   // Reconstruction operation-related technology model "operationTech.technology"
2   technology operationTech {
3       protocols { sync http data formats json; }
4       deployment technologies {
5           Docker { operation environments = "openjdk:8-jre" default; } }
6       operation aspects {
7           aspect Dockerfile<singleval> for containers {
8               selector(technology = Docker); string contents <mandatory>; } } }
9   // Reconstruction operation model "customerCore.operation"
10  import microservices from "customerCore.services" as customerServices
11  import technology from "operationTech.technology" as opTech
12  @technology(opTech)
13  container CC_Container deployment technology opTech::_deployment.Docker
14      deploys customerServices::com.example.CustomerCore {
15          aspects { opTech::_aspects.Dockerfile("FROM openjdk:8-jre AS build ..."); 
                }
16          default values { basic endpoints {
17              opTech::_protocols.http: "http://localhost:8110"; } } }
```

Lines 2 to 8 of Listing 4 capture discovered technology information in an operation-related technology model. Line 3 specifies the HTTP protocol with the JSON format. Lines 4 to 5 model the discovered deployment technology Docker[6]. Its default operation environment (Line 5) corresponds to the Docker image discovered as being used to execute microservices. Lines 6 to 8 define the `Dockerfile` aspect. It can be used in combination with the Docker deployment technology to capture reconstructed Dockerfile contents in operation models.

Lines 10 to 17 of Listing 4 show a reconstruction operation model for the `CustomerCore` microservice. The service's reconstruction model (cf. Listing 3) is imported in Line 10. The `CC_Container` uses the Docker deployment technology (Line 13) from the operation-related technology model to deploy the service (Line 14). In Line 15, the `Dockerfile` aspect captures discovered Dockerfile contents, and Lines 16 and 17 determine a discovered container endpoint.

3.5   Activity 5: Technical Refinement

This activity focuses on discovering technology information (cf. Fig. 1), which was yet not captured in Activities 2 to 4 (cf. Subsects. 3.2 to 3.4). For example, the Spring framework allows for keeping microservice configuration separate from source code in distinct configuration files. Thus, these files may not have been examined in Activity 3 and are hence explicitly targeted by the Technical Refinement activity. In the event of discovering a yet not reconstructed technology information, the technology modeling sub-activity corresponding to the type of the new information is invoked via activity edge connectors "B", "E", or "H" (cf. Fig. 1 and the descriptions of the sub-activities in Subsects. 3.2 to 3.4).

The Technical Refinement SAR activity focuses on extending previously captured reconstruction models. Thus, it specifically targets Phase 3 of the SAR process (cf. Subsect. 2.1), i.e., the manipulation of derived architecture models.

---

[6] https://www.docker.com.

3.6   Activity 6: Post-processing

The Post-processing activity comprises two SAR actions (cf. Fig. 1). The Refactor action is concerned with refactoring reconstruction models and thus contributes to SAR Phase 3 (cf. Subsect. 2.1). For example, when conducting Activities 2 and 3 (cf. Subsects. 3.2 and 3.3) it is convenient to collect all discovered Bounded Contexts and their domain concepts, as well as all discovered microservices, in a single domain and a single service model, respectively. However, when adopting DDD in MSA engineering, domain and service models should be aligned to Bounded Contexts [11]. That is, a domain model should specify a single context and a related service model should only comprise microservices being responsible for concepts from that context (cf. Listings 1 and 3). Another Refactor task is to derive reusable technology models from domain-, service-, and operation-related technology models (cf. Subsect. 3.1). For instance, both service- and operation-related technology models in Listings 3 and 4 define the HTTP protocol. Both protocol specifications may therefore be merged into a technology model dedicated to clustering protocol specifications only.

The Post-processing activity concludes with executing actions, e.g., for architecture verification, conformance checking, or trade-off analysis [3], on reconstruction models. Hence, it covers Phase 4 of the SAR process (cf. Subsect. 2.1). Subsection 4.2 illustrates the processing of reconstruction models to assess indicators for the risk in technical debt of reconstructed microservice architectures.

4   Validation

In the following, we validate the applicability of our SAR modeling method (cf. Sect. 3) on a case study microservice architecture (cf. Subsect. 4.1). Moreover, we illustrate the usage of the reconstruction models in the Post-processing activity of our method (cf. Subsect. 3.6) on the example of assessing certain indicators for the risk in technical debt of the reconstructed architecture (cf. Subsect. 4.2).

4.1   Executing the Modeling Method on a Case Study Architecture

We validated the applicability of our SAR modeling method with a case study microservice architecture called "Lakeside Mutual" (LM)[7]. LM realizes an application for a fictitious insurance company. For the validation of our modeling method, we focused on LM's backend microservices, because they implement LM's domain concepts and business logic. Table 1 describes the capabilities of the examined microservices according to their documentation on GitHub (See footnote 7).

The following paragraphs summarize, per activity (cf. Sect. 3), the results from executing our SAR modeling method on the LM architecture. To enable reproducibility, we provide a comprehensive validation package on GitHub[8]. It includes the examined source code and the derived reconstruction models.

---

[7] https://github.com/Microservice-API-Patterns/LakesideMutual.
[8] https://github.com/SeelabFhdo/emmsad2020.

Table 1. Overview of the backend microservices of the LM case study architecture.

#	Service name	Capabilities
1	Customer Core	Manages LM customer data. The service provides REST endpoints [8] to interact with Services 2, 3, and 4
2	Customer Management Backend	Enables employees of LM's customer service to interact with customers
3	Customer Self-Service Backend	Allows customers for registering to an LM web portal, change their address, and view their insurance policy
4	Policy Management Backend	Provides management functionalities to LM employees regarding customers' insurance policies

Activity 1: Preparation. We used the files in the source code folders of LM, which correspond to the examined microservices (cf. Table 1), and the files on the top-level folder hierarchy of LM's repository (See footnote 7), e.g., "docker-compose.yml", as input file set. Together, the set comprised 160 files with 8858 lines of code (LOC). Moreover, we created empty technology models for Activities 2, 3, and 4 (cf. Subsect. 3.1), because we were not aware of the technologies employed by LM.

Activity 2: Domain Modeling. We created a reconstruction domain model with a Bounded Context for each LM backend microservice (cf. Subsect. 3.2 and Table 1). The domain concepts in the contexts were reconstructed from Java classes found in the corresponding services' source code folders. Whenever recognizable from their classes, DDD information were added to domain concepts. For example, classes that represent Data Transfer Objects (DTOs) [5] were modeled as DDD Value Objects, since in MSA they are used to prescribe data exchange [13]. In total, we reconstructed 99 domain concepts from the input files.

We also discovered that LM uses JPA for database mapping of domain concepts and Spring for DTO serialization. Hence, technology aspects were created in the domain-related technology model (cf. Subsect. 3.2). They reflect, e.g., JPA's @Table annotation and Spring's @ResourceParam[9] annotation. Aspects were then assigned to domain concepts in mapping models (cf. Listing 2).

Activity 3: Service Modeling. We created a reconstruction service model for each examined microservice (cf. Subsect. 3.3 and Table 1). Microservice elements were reconstructed from Java classes that employed Spring annotations for web controllers and mapping of HTTP methods (cf. Subsect. 3.3). For all four services, we discovered 13 interfaces with 39 operations.

Based on the Spring annotations for HTTP mapping, we reconstructed 16 operations with an explicit REST endpoint (cf. Listing 3). The annotations

---

[9] https://docs.spring.io/spring-hateoas/docs/0.25.3.BUILD-SNAPSHOT/api.

were captured in the service-related technology model and assigned to modeled microservices via mapping models (cf. Listing 3).

Activity 4: Operation Modeling. This activity discovered that each microservice source code folder of LM exhibits a Dockerfile (cf. Subsect. 3.4). Hence, we created a reconstruction operation model for each LM backend service (cf. Table 1) and specified a Docker container for each reconstructed microservice (cf. Listing 4). To capture Dockerfiles' contents, we modeled a dedicated `Dockerfile` technology aspect. From the source code of Service 4, we also reconstructed an ActiveMQ[10] broker as infrastructure node and the AMQP[11] protocol, which was added to the operation-related technology model (cf. Subsect. 3.4).

Activity 5: Technical Refinement. In this activity, we reconstructed information from yet unconsidered input files (cf. Subsect. 3.5). For example, from Spring-related configuration files like "application.properties" we extracted information about URIs and ports of microservice containers (cf. Listing 4). Moreover, LM's "docker-compose.yml" file provided us with information about service interactions. As a result, we extended the reconstruction models of Services 2, 3, and 4 (cf. Table 1) to *require* Service 1 for their operation. For this purpose, our Service Modeling Language defines the `required microservices` statement [13].

Activity 6: Post-processing. We refactored the domain-, service-, and operation-related technology models created during Activities 2 to 4 (cf. Subsect. 3.6). To this end, we first merged all three models and removed duplicate information. Next, we split the merged technology model into six models, each dedicated to a certain technology. For example, the "java" technology model only clusters Java- and Spring-related information, while the "activemq" and "docker" technology models only focus on the eponymous technologies. The refactored technology models can thus be reused in future instances of the SAR modeling method.

Next, we processed the reconstruction models for assessing certain indicators of LM's architecture concerning its risk in technical debt (cf. Subsect. 4.2).

4.2   Post-processing Example: Technical Debt Assessment

Toledo et al. discovered indicators for MSA-specific *architectural technical debt* (ATD), which can be examined by analyzing service communication characteristics [14]. We illustrate the processing of reconstruction models derived by our SAR modeling method (cf. Subsect. 4.1) to assess these indicators and thus a part of LM's risk in technical debt. The following paragraphs describe, per ATD type [14], our findings from processing LM's reconstruction models.

---

[10] https://activemq.apache.org.
[11] https://www.amqp.org.

Too Many Point-to-Point (PtP) Connections. PtP connections between microservices are identifiable from reconstruction models by two characteristics. First, an infrastructure node realizes a *communication layer* [14] used only by a small subset of services. Second, services not using the node require other services. LM defines a communication layer with an ActiveMQ node used by Service 4 only (cf. Activity 4 in Subsect. 4.1). It is thus likely that Services 2 to 4, which require Service 1 (cf. Activity 5 in Subsect. 4.1), interact with it via PtP connections.

Business Logic Inside Communication Layer. Reconstruction domain and mapping models may indicate this ATD type. For instance, the Domain Data Modeling Language (cf. Subsect. 2.2) allows for declaring function signatures in data structures. Thus, functions conveying the semantics of data format conversions hint at this ATD type [14]. These functions usually take a single input parameter typed by a Value Object that reflects a DTO (cf. Activity 2 in Subsect. 4.1) and return an instance of another data structure within the Bounded Context of the function. Moreover, this ATD type is also indicated by protocol assignments in mapping models (cf. Listing 3). Microservices, that convert requests for use by other services, exhibit endpoints, whose protocols differ from the majority of services in the same Bounded Context. Our analysis of the reconstruction models showed that LM does not exhibit conversion domain functions or microservices.

No Standardized Communication Model. This ATD type is identifiable from reconstruction domain models (cf. Subsect. 3.2). They capture *business-related communication models* [14]. For example, data structures, which cannot be unambiguously assigned to a single Bounded Context, violate the principle of a *canonical domain model* [14]. We did not find such violations for LM.

Reconstruction domain models also allow for efficient analysis of the consistency of *shared domain concepts* [11]. For instance, the domain models of Services 2 to 4 (cf. Table 1) all specify the Value Object `CustomerProfileDto` as a DTO for the `CustomerProfileEntity` of Service 1. LM thus exhibits the risk that the Value Objects evolve differently from the Entity [7], although they are meant to be shareable representations of it. Our analysis of the three versions of `CustomerProfileDto` showed, however, that they all exhibit the same structure. Hence, they could be refactored into a single shared domain model.

Weak Source Code and Knowledge Management. Our SAR modeling method does not directly support in assessing this ATD type. However, reconstruction models provide a well-defined means for documenting views on microservice architectures (cf. Subsect. 2.1). Consequently, they can accompany *centralized MSA documentation* [14] as they capture architecture knowledge in a concise format.

Different Middleware Technologies for Service Communication. Reconstruction technology and mapping models facilitate identification of this ATD type, because they capture discovered communication technologies and their usage (cf. Listing 3). LM employs different means for synchronous and asynchronous communication, i.e., REST and ActiveMQ (cf. Activities 3 and 4 in Subsect. 4.1). We consider LM's risk in this ATD type to only be slightly increased, as in MSA it is common to employ at most one protocol for each communication kind [11].

However, our analysis of reconstruction mapping models showed that more REST operations are invokable via an HTTP method (26) than explicit REST endpoints were specified (16). Such inconsistencies in services' communication specifications are likely to cause communication failures at runtime.

5   Discussion

For the validation of our SAR modeling method (cf. Sect. 4), we executed it manually on the input file set. We then ensured the correctness of the reconstruction models by comparing them with LM's documentation and double-checking their consistency with LM's source code. Consequently, we perceive our method to be basically applicable on microservice architectures. Nonetheless, a current threat to validity is the increased error-proneness given the manual execution of the method. However, this weakness may be mitigated by employing automated source code analysis techniques, particularly in SAR Activities 2 to 4 (cf. Subsects. 3.2 to 3.4). For example, in case of Java-based microservice architectures, class bodies and employed annotations, as well as Dockerfiles in general, represent valuable analysis targets (cf. Sect. 4).

The input file set selected in Activity 1 of our SAR modeling method (cf. Subsect. 3.1) depends on the availability of artifacts in the targeted microservice architecture. For instance, due to the structure of the case study architecture, the input file set for the method's validation mainly consisted of Java files (cf. Sect. 4). Hence, the reconstruction effort was relatively high, because all LOC needed to be examined. However, source code files that reflect domain concepts or service implementations may also be replaced, e.g., by concise models of database structures or API documentation. Like the SAR process (cf. Subsect. 2.1), our modeling method does not constrain input file types.

In its current form, the SAR modeling method directly aligns its activities to the viewpoints being addressed by our languages for model-driven MSA engineering and their relationships (cf. Fig. 1 and Subsect. 2.2). As a result, the method does not take the perspective of stakeholders like business analysts or project managers into account, yet. To this end, the set of SAR activities would need to be extended with modeling approaches tailored to stakeholders, who do not directly participate in software engineering in the context of MSA. Further research is necessary to identify the concerns of these stakeholders and derive corresponding SAR activities.

Since our method anticipates reconstruction of technology information, the degree of abstraction in reconstruction models may be comparatively close to that of source code. However, due to the usage of mapping models, reconstruction domain and service models are basically technology-agnostic (cf. Subsects. 3.2 and 3.3). Thus, the execution of sub-activities, which capture technology information, may be omitted in Activities 2 and 3, depending on the goal of the conducted SAR process (cf. Subsect. 2.1) and technology information being irrelevant to its achievement.

6   Related Work

Alshuqayran et al. [1] conduct an empirical study on eight open source microservice architectures to derive a metamodel for SAR in MSA. They also analyze a set of heterogeneous input files that contain, e.g., Java source code, build scripts, and configuration files (cf. Sects. 3 and 4). The derived metamodel is similar to the ones of our Service and Operation Modeling Languages [13]. However, it does not support the reconstruction of domain concepts. Furthermore, technologies like `Asynchronous Message Bus` are fixed metamodel concepts, while with our Technology Modeling Language [12] they can flexibly be integrated in reconstruction models as they occur in input files. In addition, Alshuqayran et al. do not present a concrete syntax for their metamodel, nor do they specify its systematic usage in a SAR process like our modeling method.

MicroART [9] is a tool for reconstructing microservice architectures. It extracts service-related information, e.g., services' names, ports, and developers from source code repositories. Moreover, it performs a runtime analysis of log files in order to determine containers, network interfaces, and service interaction relationships. From the gathered information, MicroART instantiates a model from a specifically designed metamodel. Like our approach, MicroART is model-based. On the contrary, it does not consider the Domain, Operation, and Technology viewpoints (cf. Subsect. 2.2) when gathering architecture information. Furthermore, a systematic method and concrete syntax for facilitating architecture analyses is not presented.

Zdun et al. introduce an approach towards assessing MSA conformance [18]. Therefore, existing microservice architectures are reconstructed leveraging a formal model with MSA-specific component and connector types. MSA conformance of reconstructed architectures is then assessed via metrics and constraints defined by the relationships between these types. Like for our SAR modeling method, reconstructed formal models also need to be derived manually from existing architecture implementations. However, no modeling language with MSA-specific abstractions is employed to facilitate the creation of the formal models. Moreover, a systematic reconstruction method is not presented and domain-specific information is not considered.

7   Conclusion and Future Work

In this paper, we presented a modeling method for systematic Software Architecture Reconstruction (SAR) of software systems based on Microservice Architecture (MSA). The method employs a set of modeling languages for model-driven MSA engineering to capture reconstructed information in viewpoint-specific architecture models. Consequently, method instances yield domain, technology, service, and operation reconstruction models for examined microservice architectures. These models aim to facilitate architecture analysis in the context of MSA. We validated our SAR modeling method with a case study microservice architecture and showed the applicability of derived reconstruction models on the example of assessing certain indicators of the case study's risk in technical debt.

In future works, we plan to investigate the extension of our SAR modeling method with automation capabilities. First, the derivation of the reconstruction models may be facilitated by automated source code analysis. Second, postprocessing of reconstruction models would benefit from static model analysis in order to automatically gather metrics like the diversity of communication technologies, their usage by microservices, or the existence of duplicate domain concepts. Moreover, we are currently working on a code generator to produce source code and configuration files from reconstruction models. With the generator, architecture design and refactoring based on reconstruction models would become feasible, because architecture models and architecture implementation could be automatically kept consistent.

References

1. Alshuqayran, N., Ali, N., Evans, R.: Towards micro service architecture recovery: an empirical study. In: 2018 IEEE International Conference on Software Architecture (ICSA), pp. 47–56 (2018)
2. Balalaie, A., Heydarnoori, A., Jamshidi, P.: Microservices architecture enables devops: migration to a cloud-native architecture. IEEE Softw. **33**(3), 42–52 (2016)
3. Bass, L., Clements, P., Kazman, R.: Software Architecture in Practice, 3rd edn. Addison-Wesley, Boston (2013)
4. Bogner, J., Fritzsch, J., Wagner, S., Zimmermann, A.: Microservices in industry: insights into technologies, characteristics, and software quality. In: 2019 IEEE International Conference on Software Architecture Companion (ICSA-C), pp. 187–195 (2019)
5. Daigneau, R.: Service Design Patterns. Addison-Wesley, Boston (2012)
6. Di Francesco, P., Malavolta, I., Lago, P.: Research on architecting microservices: trends, focus, and potential for industrial adoption. In: 2017 IEEE International Conference on Software Architecture (ICSA), pp. 21–30. IEEE (2017)
7. Evans, E.: Domain-Driven Design. Addison-Wesley, Boston (2004)
8. Fielding, R.: Representational state transfer. Ph.D. thesis (2000)
9. Granchelli, G., Cardarelli, M., Francesco, P.D., Malavolta, I., Iovino, L., Salle, A.D.: Towards recovering the software architecture of microservice-based systems. In: 2017 IEEE International Conference on Software Architecture Workshops (ICSAW), pp. 46–53 (2017)
10. Nadareishvili, I., Mitra, R., Mclarty, M., Amundsen, M.: Microservice Architecture. O'Reilly Media, Sebastopol (2016)
11. Newman, S.: Building Microservices. O'Reilly Media, Sebastopol (2015)
12. Rademacher, F., Sachweh, S., Zündorf, A.: Aspect-oriented modeling of technology heterogeneity in microservice architecture. In: 2019 IEEE International Conference on Software Architecture (ICSA), pp. 21–30. IEEE (2019)

13. Rademacher, F., Sorgalla, J., Wizenty, P., Sachweh, S., Zündorf, A.: Graphical and textual model-driven microservice development. In: Bucchiarone, A., et al. (eds.) Microservices, pp. 147–179. Springer, Cham (2020). https://doi.org/10.1007/978-3-030-31646-4_7
14. Soares de Toledo, S., Martini, A., Przybyszewska, A., Sjøberg, D.I.K.: Architectural technical debt in microservices: a case study in a large company. In: 2019 IEEE/ACM International Conference on Technical Debt (TechDebt), pp. 78–87. IEEE (2019)
15. Taibi, D., Lenarduzzi, V.: On the definition of microservice bad smells. IEEE Softw. 35(3), 56–62 (2018)
16. Taibi, D., Lenarduzzi, V., Pahl, C.: Processes, motivations, and issues for migrating to microservices architectures: an empirical investigation. IEEE Cloud Comput. 5, 22–32 (2017)
17. Taibi, D., Lenarduzzi, V., Pahl, C.: Continuous architecting with microservices and DevOps: a systematic mapping study. In: Muñoz, V.M., Ferguson, D., Helfert, M., Pahl, C. (eds.) CLOSER 2018. CCIS, vol. 1073, pp. 126–151. Springer, Cham (2019). https://doi.org/10.1007/978-3-030-29193-8_7
18. Zdun, U., Navarro, E., Leymann, F.: Ensuring and assessing architecture conformance to microservice decomposition patterns. In: Maximilien, M., Vallecillo, A., Wang, J., Oriol, M. (eds.) ICSOC 2017. LNCS, vol. 10601, pp. 411–429. Springer, Cham (2017). https://doi.org/10.1007/978-3-319-69035-3_29

Can We Design Software as We Talk?
A Research Idea

Marcela Ruiz$^{(\boxtimes)}$ (iD) and Björn Hasselman

Institute of Applied Information Technology, Zurich University of Applied Sciences,
Winterthur, Switzerland
`marcela.ruiz@zhaw.ch, hassebjo@students.zhaw.ch`

Abstract. In the context of digital transformation, speeding up the time-to-market of high-quality software products is a big challenge. **Main challenges.** Software quality correlates with the success of requirements engineering (RE) sessions. RE sessions demand software analysts to collect all relevant material usually specified on written notes, flip charts, pictures, etc. Afterwards comprehensible requirements need to be specified for software implementation and testing. These activities are mostly performed manually, which causes process delays and software quality attributes like reliability, usability, comprehensibility, etc., are diminished causing software devaluation. **Innovative aspects.** This research idea paper proposes a framework for automating the tasks of requirements specification. The proposed framework involves computational mechanisms to enable the automatic generation of software design while requirements are discussed. The innovative aspect of this research comes from digitally transforming the software development life cycle (SDLC) where requirements are generated "on the fly" and virtual reality systems are in place. **Potential to make change.** The proposed framework has the potential to renovate the role of software analysts, which can experience substantial reduction of manual tasks, more efficient communication, dedication to more analytical tasks, and assurance of software quality from conception phases. This research idea paper introduces the framework for automating the task of requirements specification, and report our progress. We conclude the paper by outlining lessons learnt and future lines of work.

Keywords: Requirements engineering · Digital transformation · Software development life cycle · User stories generation

1 Introduction

Living in a digital era, service providers are challenged to offer services to their customers through a wide spectrum of channels. This constant introduction of new devices and technology challenges organisations to provide rapid

This research project is supported by ZHAW Digital and the Digitalisation Initiative of Zürich Universities DIZH.

S. Nurcan et al. (Eds.): BPMDS 2020/EMMSAD 2020, LNBIP 387, pp. 327–334, 2020.
https://doi.org/10.1007/978-3-030-49418-6_22

improvements of their IT infrastructure, while ensuring the highest user experience possible. Digital transformation stimulates the adaptation of existent business models and the creation of new ones; while society adapts to new ways to interact with services. Software systems are omnipresent in digital transformation process; making software quality of crucial value to ensure successful digital transformation [1].

Software quality correlates with the success of requirements engineering (RE) sessions [2], which makes RE a crucial phase of the software development life cycle (SDLC) [3]. The agile movement have proposed user stories as a minimal but complete language for the specification of software requirements [4]. This language has been proven to be successful and widely adopted by software developers [5]. software requirements are collected during RE sessions in the shape of pictures, flip chart notes, documentation etc. Later on, relevant information is digitalised in order to specify a set of comprehensible user stories to be used during development phases. Digitalisation of discussed requirements demands extra effort that has to be undertaken by software analysts [6]. All this complexity is magnified if we consider that software development is not usually taking place in the same geographical location. Big companies make use of software providers located in different continents. Teleworking is posing big challenges at the moment to ensuring collaborative requirements engineering [7].

The main objective of our research endeavour is *to reduce the time-to-market of software products by automating the task of requirements specification while requirements are discussed*. In this research idea paper, we introduce a framework for automating the task of requirements specification (see Fig. 1). We conceive a requirements engineering room where participants discuss requirements that are automatically specified in the shape of user stories, and transformed into software prototypes. In this room, we incorporate virtual reality tools like double robots for embodiment of remote participants, and interactive boards with collaborative tools as they have demonstrated to facilitate access and real-time edition of discussed requirements [8]. By implementing the proposed framework in practical settings, it is expected that SDLC goes through a process of digital transformation where software analysts are going to experience a significant reduction of manual tasks. User stories will be generated on the fly during the session, and virtual reality systems will allow efficient communication. Software analysts get empowered by focusing on meaningful tasks like analysing created user stories and prioritization. Software quality is then assured from the first release. The framework components are still under design and evaluation phases. Particularly, this paper reports our first steps towards automating the specification of user stories "on the fly" during RE elicitation sessions. We discuss the design and illustrate the use of the DEEP LEARNING CLASSIFIER and ONTOLOGY CRAWLER components presented in Fig. 1. Setting up of the requirements engineering room and software prototype generation are considered part of our short term research plans.

Paper Organisation: After reviewing related work in Sect. 2, we introduce our advances on providing automatic specification of user stores in Sect. 3. We summarise the design of two components: a deep learning classifier in Sect. 3.1, and an ontology crawler in

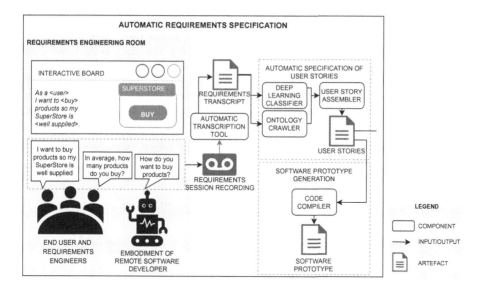

Fig. 1. Framework for automating the task of requirements specification

Sect. 3.2. Finally, we conclude our idea research paper by discussing lessons learnt and future lines of work in Sect. 4.

2   Related Work

In the field of requirements engineering there are several related work that approach the challenge of automate requirements specifications from different angles. We analyse these approaches based on: (a) requirements source: audio recordings/transcripts from requirements meetings, tweets, bug reports, user stories, existing documentation, domain repository; (b) generated requirements specification in the shape of: meeting minutes, knowledge extraction, tweets classification, relevant topics, remedied user stories, meeting summaries, and user stories; (c) Existing validation or evaluation: laboratory demonstration, comparative experiment; (d) Existence or not of tool support; and (e) Whether or has been applied in practice.

Some works focus on supporting software requirements specification by generating meeting minutes. For instance, Kaiya et al. [9] proposes a tool to support requirement elicitation meetings by recording the sessions and providing an assistant tool to manage the recordings and mark the important points via hypertext. Authors conclude that further collaboration mechanisms need to be incorporated to facilitate real-time edition of requirements and knowledge share. Murray et al. [10] developed a natural language processing approach to summarize emails and conversations in general, more projects involving textual sources appeared. Especially in the field of machine learning were multiple techniques developed to extract requirements engineering relevant information from different written origins [4,11–14].

Rodeghero et al. [13] proposed a machine learning classification algorithm trained to recognise user stories' information [15]. As a conclusion of this study, the authors found out that information about software functionality and requirements rationale can be identified by means of classification algorithms. Nevertheless, no information about the role can be automatically extracted. Another tool assisted approach to dynamic requirement elicitation was introduced by Abad et al. [14]. The tool extracts relevant snippets and simultaneously uses a third-party API to recognize tone and intentions of statements' providers.

We have taken the aforementioned research works as a reference to cover the gaps in terms of providing complete user stories from spoken software requirements during elicitation sessions (see last row in Table 1).

Table 1. Summary of related research for automatic generation of software requirements.

Ref	Requirements source	Generated requirements specification	Validation or evaluation	Tool support?	Applied in practice?
[9]	Audio recordings from requirements meetings	Meeting minutes, meeting summaries	Comparative experiment	Management tool	Yes
[13]	Audio transcripts from requirements meetings	Partial user stories (functions and rationale)	Comparative experiment	Machine Learning classifier	No
[14]	Audio transcripts from requirements meetings, existing documentation, domain repository	Relevant topics	Expert analysis	ELICA tool	Case study
[11]	Tweets	Tweets classification	Comparative experiment	ALERTme tool	Tested using Twitter
[4]	User stories	Remedied user stories	Supervised learning	AQUSA tool	Tested in University lab
[12]	Bug reports	Meeting summaries	Comparative experiment	Machine Learning classifier	No
Ours	Audio transcripts from requirements meetings	Complete user stories (roles, functions and rationales)	Laboratory demonstration	Yes	No

3   Automatic Specification of User Stories

Our goal is to elicit complete user stories including information related to "Role, Function and Rationale". Based on the research work presented in Rodeghero et al. [13], we propose to classify software functionality in terms of functional and non-funcional requirements; as well as identify requirements' rationale from requirement elicitation sessions. Our research strategy is summarised in Fig. 2. In short, our research idea is to build a deep learning algorithm that can be further trained by providing labeled requirements elicitation sessions. For identifying missing roles, we propose to make use of existing ontologies that provide information related to typical roles belonging to the context in which software elicitation sessions take place.

In this paper, we summarise the deep learning classifier (see Sect. 3.1) and the ontology crawler components (see Sect. 3.2). For implementation purposes We chose the Java language as it guarantees portability and its popularity results in maintained and tested frameworks we can use. It has a sophisticated deep learning framework available in DL4J[1] and the Java OWL API[2] for handling Ontology files. The components will later provide the data to be used by the user story assembler component (out of scope of this paper).

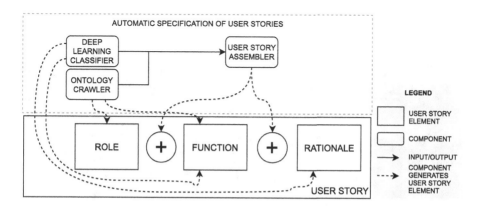

Fig. 2. Research strategy for automatic generation of user stories

3.1 Deep Learning Classifier Component

We propose a deep learning classifier based on the work proposed by [13]. We used deep learning specifically, because our intention is to imitating the classification process that has been done by using machine learning. In this way we can further compare performance values in subsequent experiments.

A **turn** is an established unit of analysis in natural language processing as opposed to using single sentences. It describes, when a person speaks in a conversation in between other speakers. To represent a turn in a learnable format, we use word embeddings provided by the model described in the work of Pennington et al. "GloVe: Global Vectors for Word Representation" [17]. Here, words will be represented as multidimensional, real-value vectors. In a three-dimensional space, similar words would lie 'closer' together than those, that semantically differ. Different, pre-trained word embedding models are available . The available representation dimensions depend on the vectors but range from 50 to 300. They also differ in terms of topic and number of tokens.

---

[1] https://deeplearning4j.org/.
[2] http://owlcs.github.io/owlapi/.

For our initial development process, we used the smallest set; the "Wikipedia 2014 + Gigawords", which consists of 6 billion tokens and a representation of 50 dimensions.

The implementation of the deep learning classifier is available in our public GitHub repository at https://github.com/lmruizcar/requirements_classifier. An example of classification is presented in Fig. 3. The model in its current state performs about as well as random guessing since we need data for training purposes. As it has been mentioned by [16], the lack of data from requirements elicitation sessions is an obstacle in this type of investigations. Our model differentiates between three labels: None (0), Non-Functional (1) and Functional (2). A caveat of this deep learning approach is, that it only cares indirectly for the fact that turns can be both; labelled 1 and 2. Whereas [13] built multiple binary classifiers which each analysed the turn, our approach uses a SoftMax layer for which the output is interpret able as probabilities. A turn that falls into both categories, would have probabilities around 0.5 for both labels which can be interpreted individually, but is not represented in the standard evaluation method of machine learning classifiers.

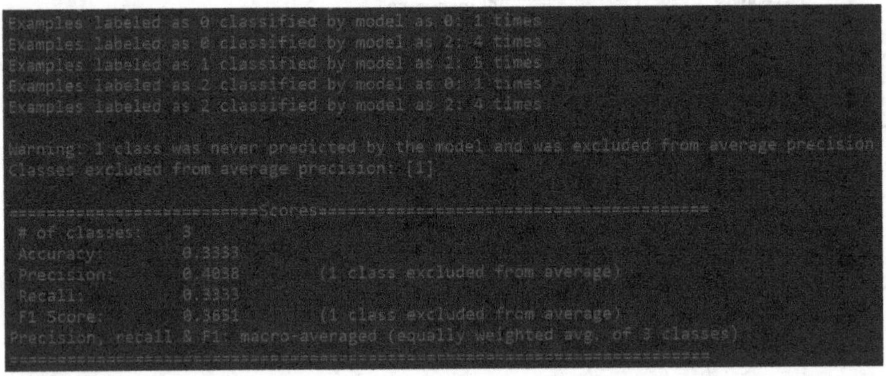

Fig. 3. Results from running the deep learning classifier component

3.2   Ontology Crawler Component

Rodeghero et al. stated, that in conversations in requirement elicitation meetings "only 0.5% discussed role" [13]. Which is why they concluded that it is not feasible to extract role information from transcripts. For a complete user story, this role information is crucial. An established practice in information science is the use of ontologies to organize data and reduce complexity. We propose the ontology crawler component. The ontology crawler searches an ontology for defined entities and their restrictions to identify possible roles in the required context. As input, it takes an ontology from a file formatted in Web Ontology Language format. As output, it generates a list of foundational user stories, which consist of a role, an action and an object. For this, we have implemented a prototype based on Java OWL API. The prototype is available on our GitHub public repository at https://github.com/lmruizcar/ontology_crawler.

Figure 4 exemplifies the generation of foundational user stories for the SmallShop Case. A product manager needs to be able to add products to the shop and remove it, e.g., if they are not in stock anymore. The customers that use the shop want to buy

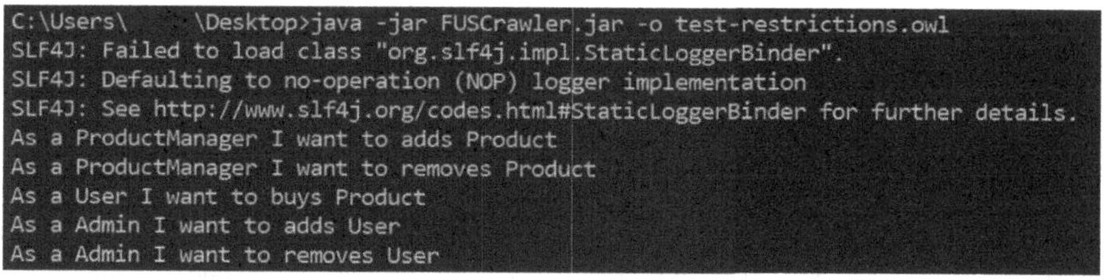

```
C:\Users\        \Desktop>java -jar FUSCrawler.jar -o test-restrictions.owl
SLF4J: Failed to load class "org.slf4j.impl.StaticLoggerBinder".
SLF4J: Defaulting to no-operation (NOP) logger implementation
SLF4J: See http://www.slf4j.org/codes.html#StaticLoggerBinder for further details.
As a ProductManager I want to adds Product
As a ProductManager I want to removes Product
As a User I want to buys Product
As a Admin I want to adds User
As a Admin I want to removes User
```

Fig. 4. Example of executing the ontology crawler component in the context of the SmallShop case

products. And for returning customers it is good practice to store relevant information like the shipping address in a user account.

4   Lessons Learnt and Future Work

The current paper presents a research idea for automating the process of requirements specification. We propose a framework consisting of a requirements engineering room, and components to support the automatic generation of user stories and software prototype generation. This paper presents results from the implementation of the components for automatic generation of user stories while requirements are discussed. Our efforts lead to the development of prototypes for a deep learning classifier and ontology crawler. Initial results are promising and proves the feasibility of the proposed research idea. Prototypes are made available on our public GitHub repository to motivate further research in the field.

For the near future, we plan to keep evolving the prototype for user stories assembler component. In this way, we can obtain full user stories from elicitation sessions. For our framework to mature and being implemented in practical settings, we envision to build a flexible environment to support the plug-and-play of components that conform the framework. In this way, we can incorporate alternative components while ensuring a proper interoperability. In addition to evaluating the extent to which our solution improves user stories' generation in terms of efficiency, we plan to evaluate the intention to use and usability of the framework from the perspective of requirements engineers. For our long term plans, we plan to investigate the quality of software engineering recordings to further adjust and improve our framework.

References

1. Gebhart, M., Giessler, P., Abeck, S.: Challenges of the digital transformation in software engineering. In: The Eleventh International Conference on Software Engineering Advances (ICSEA) (2016)
2. Mund, J., Femmer, H., Mendez, D., Eckhardt, J.: Does quality of requirements specifications matter? Combined results of two empirical studies (2017). https://arxiv.org/pdf/1702.07656.pdf
3. Chakraborty, A., Baowaly, M., Arefin, A., Bahar, A.: The role of requirement engineering in software development life cycle. J. Emerg. Trends Comput. Inf. Sci. **3**, 723–729 (2012)

4. Dalpiaz, F., Brinkkemper, S.: Agile requirements engineering with user stories. In: 26th International Requirements Engineering Conference (RE), Banff, AB, Canada (2018)

5. Wagenaar, G., Overbeek, S., Lucassen, G., Brinkkemper, S., Schneider, K.: Working software over comprehensive documentation - rationales of agile teams for artefacts usage. J. Softw. Eng. Res. Dev. **6**, 7 (2018). https://doi.org/10.1186/s40411-018-0051-7

6. Wüest, D., Seyff, N., Glinz, M.: FlexiSketch: a lightweight sketching and meta-modeling approach for end-users. Softw. Syst. Model. **18**(2), 1513–1541 (2017). https://doi.org/10.1007/s10270-017-0623-8

7. Damian, D., Zowghi, D.: RE challenges in multi-site software development organizations. Requir. Eng. J. **8**, 149–160 (2003). https://doi.org/10.1007/s00766-003-0173-1

8. Wüest, D., Seyff, N., Glinz, M.: Sketching and notation creation with FlexiSketch team: evaluating a new means for collaborative requirements elicitation. In: 23rd International Requirements Engineering Conference (RE), Ottawa (2015)

9. Kaiya, H., Saeki, M., Ochimizu, K.: Design of a hyper media tool to support requirements elicitation meetings. In: Proceedings Seventh International Workshop on Computer-Aided Software Engineering (1995)

10. Murray, G., Carenini, G.: Summarizing spoken and written conversations. In: Conference on Empirical Methods in Natural Language Processing, PA, USA, Stroudsburg (2008)

11. Guzman, E., Ibrahim, M., Glinz, M.: A little bird told me: mining tweets for requirements and software evolution. In: 25th International Requirements Engineering Conference (RE) (2017)

12. Rastkar, S., Murphy, G.C., Murray, G.: Summarizing software artifacts: a case study of bug reports. In: Proceedings of the 32nd International Conference on Software Engineering, NY, USA, New York, vol. 1 (2010)

13. Rodeghero, P., Jiang, S., Armaly, A., McMillan, C.: Detecting user story information in developer-client conversations to generate extractive summaries. In: 39th International Conference on Software Engineering (ICSE) (2017)

14. Abad, Z.S.H., Gervasi, V., Zowghi, D., Barker, K.: ELICA: an automated tool for dynamic extraction of requirements relevant information. In: International Workshop on Artificial Intelligence for Requirements Engineering (AIRE) (2018)

15. Krasniqi, R., Jiang, S., McMillan, C.: TraceLab components for generating extractive summaries of user stories. In: International Conference on Software Maintenance and Evolution (ICSME) (2017)

16. Rodeghero, P.: Behavior-informed algorithms for automatic documentation generation. In: International Conference on Software Maintenance and Evolution (ICSME) (2017)

17. Pennington, J., Socher, R., Manning, C.: Glove: global vectors for word representation. In: Conference on Empirical Methods in Natural Language Processing (EMNLP), Doha, Qatar (2014)

Non-Functional Requirements Orienting the Development of Socially Responsible Software

Luiz Marcio Cysneiros[1] and Julio Cesar Sampaio do Prado Leite[2(✉)]

[1] School of Information Technology, York University, Toronto, ON, Canada
cysneiro@yorku.ca
[2] Departamento de Informática, PUC-Rio, Rio de Janeiro, Brazil
julio@inf.puc-rio.br

Abstract. Nowadays, software is ubiquitous and present in almost everything we buy and use. Artificial intelligence (AI) is becoming prevalent in software products. The use of AI entices consumer inquisitiveness, promising software products that can make our lives easier, productive, and in some mission-critical applications safer. Similar reasoning can be applied to systems exploring Internet of Things, cloud services, and mobile technologies. However, there is a trust deficit when it comes to accepting AI as well as the other above-mentioned features, as a reliable technology platform. This paper argues that the more critical the domain is, the less consumers seem to trust software to make decisions on their behalf or even to be used. Aspects such as safety, privacy, and ethics challenges the perception of trustworthy computing. In the past two decades, several works have suggested that Corporate Social Responsibility (CSR) may play an essential role in creating a trust paradigm between customers and businesses promoting loyalty, customer retention and thus enhancing customer trust and increasing corporate profit. We believe that the software industry will need soon rather than later to encourage trust in their embedded software. A promising approach lies in adapting principles associated with CSR to guide the software development processes. Such an approach could help to achieve two goals: Deliver trustworthy software and, if desired, deliver socially responsible software. We believe that Non-Functional Requirements (NFR) will play a crucial role in this endeavor. This paper highlights a first approach to establishing a basic set of NFRs that should always be carefully considered when developing software, as to aim socially responsible software.

Keywords: Socially responsible software · Non-Functional Requirements · Trust · Transparency · Ethics

1 Introduction

Today, software is embedded in almost everything we buy or use daily in our lives. In recent years, AI has been increasingly used to deliver solutions in many different commercial and regulatory domains, from personal assistance devices such as Alexa[1]

---

[1] https://developer.amazon.com/en-US/alexa.

© Springer Nature Switzerland AG 2020
S. Nurcan et al. (Eds.): BPMDS 2020/EMMSAD 2020, LNBIP 387, pp. 335–342, 2020.
https://doi.org/10.1007/978-3-030-49418-6_23

to face recognition technologies used by law enforcement agencies. However, the use of AI raises doubts in the mind of consumers regarding how much we can trust AI[2] to make decisions on our behalf. The lack of trust seems to be more prevalent in mission-critical systems where personal safety is in the care of the machine. Kolm shows [1] that 70% of Canadians are comfortable with AI scheduling appointments, but only 39% feel comfortable with AI piloting autonomous vehicles. Therefore, we believe that the software development process needs to address ways to assure consumers they can trust the software embedded in the products they are buying and/or using.

Applications utilizing concepts related to Internet of Things, cloud services, and mobile technologies will raise similar concerns aggravated with the expectation of privacy and safety, triggering ethical questions that will directly impact how much customers can trust their devices. Although there are works [2, 3] tackling trust related to machine learning and decision support systems, they look at trust in a single dimension and do not capture the consequences of trust from a social perspective.

Our work aims to consider trust of AI-based software from a citizen's viewpoint, using the metaphor of Corporate Social Responsibility (CSR)[3]. In the past two decades, many works have pointed out that CSR goes a long way in promoting positive outcomes such as loyalty, repeat business, and purchase intention [4, 5]. Furthermore, CSR efforts may also positively impact the market value of companies that are perceived to be committed to social responsibility [6]. One important aspect of CSR is that its adoption reduces information asymmetry [7], and as such, it brings out transparency. It is to note the tangling effect of CSR in the broader concept of Corporate/Company Reputation [30].

One of the main reasons for consumers to value CSR is because it promotes intrinsic trust in the company. One way of looking at trust is to measure how much a consumer thinks a company can be deemed reliable in situations entailing risk to the consumer. One critical factor is how much consumers believe the company's actions and behaviors have the consumers' interest and welfare in mind [9].

This work builds an initial argumentation of why using CSR knowledge does help software engineers develop trustful Software. The benefits of using CSR concepts would be twofold i) Develop trustworthy systems that would help to retain customers and to increase market share ii) Use this trustworthy as the basis for developing a socially responsible system that is likely to be in high demand in the near future.

In this idea paper, we present the foundation for our ongoing work. We are tackling what we believe will be the core requirements to deliver trustworthy software. We associate these requirements with the perspective of society, in general, to be able to opt for socially responsible software together with the goal of repetitive business and improving market share. We hope to inspire other researchers to explore similar paths.

---

[2] https://www.nytimes.com/2020/01/18/technology/clearview-privacy-facial-recognition.html.

[3] The Business Domain debates over the similitudes/differences among the acronyms CS (Corporate Sustainability) and CSR. We side with those that consider CS and CSR as synonyms.

2   Method

We carried out a brief literature review starting with the CSR domain to investigate the qualitative properties used in their experience to promote corporate social responsibility that could be adapted to the software domain. We used keyword searches such as (csr AND trust), (corporate social responsibility AND Trust) from 2015 to 2019. We recovered 112 publications. After removing duplicated references, snowballing, and examining the abstracts, we reviewed 22 references. Our choice was based on the linkage of CSR and Trust.

We elicited knowledge from these references to create a matrix with the most often mentioned *properties* expected to be present in companies adopting the CSR approach. Following, we analyzed which of those *properties* should be implemented in company's Information Systems, in general, to contribute to a trustworthy and socially responsible environment. Using an NFR (Non-Functional Requirements) perspective [21], we found three NFRs: **Trust**, **Ethics,** and **Transparency** in these *properties*. Using earlier knowledge [22, 27], we searched for NFRs which may interact either positively or negatively with these three NFRs, and we elicited **Privacy**, **Safety,** and **Security**.

Our aim was not to build software to support CSR adoption by companies. We studied the CSR approach as a basis to propose which would be the critical qualitative *properties* to develop trustworthy Information Systems software, based on the company's goal. As such, these qualities would stand as essential NFRs to develop software to support the delivery of socially responsible Information Systems either as a goal by its own or as part of the adoption of CSR. At the same time, companies that are interested on a stricter approach to CSR will also have a solid base to start from.

3   Results

As pointed out by Vlachos et al. [10] and others, trust is central for companies to be perceived as socially responsible. By the same token, we set trust as the primary NFR to be satisfied, i.e., satisfied within acceptable limits. Our reasoning follows the idea that safety-critical systems and any software using AI as well as advanced forms of technology such as internet of things and cloud systems, will inherently trigger fear in many customers who are forced to relinquish their safety to a machine or to face unwanted misuse of their behaviors and preferences and sometimes both

In corporate domains, trust would come when providers demonstrate ethical behavior enforced in their software. Bowen illustrates such a scenario for safety-critical systems [11]. In order to promote trust, software engineers need to take a bottom-up approach in developing domain-specific knowledge of elements that build the foundations of trust.

Trust is also frequently linked to the concept of ethics. Consumers tend to trust companies that they perceive as ethically sound [12]. Nevertheless, consumers also identify and believe that companies are following moral standards if they are transparent in the way they do business [6]. The ISO 26000 standard points out how businesses and organizations should handle ethical and transparent concerns to act responsibly [13]. We believe that a similar perspective could be applied to software development in general.

Ethics helps to promote trust [5, 14], together with the understanding that safety-critical systems need to demonstrate ethical behavior to be accepted by consumers.

However, Ethics is not a straightforward concept that can be easily applied. It is a human compass that shifts with the sand of time. Researchers studying the self-driving car domain have pointed out many ethical dilemmas that need to be addressed [15]. Furthermore, ethical decisions made either by the software or its users choosing an ethical scenario may entail legal implications [15]. The first step to building ethics into a machine is to recognize that all models will have their faults and limitations. There can be no single software architecture which proclaims to be the benchmark of moral goodness. Since human interest cannot always be satisfied due to inherent conflicts, ethics will likely be aggressively contested in the court of law between those who seek to exploit AI technology in the public domain and those who wish to confine it to a controlled environment. Insurance companies will likely use such types of arguments in many cases when AI making decisions are involved. Software developers should be prepared to counter-argument any accusations or even better, be pro-active, and not give space to them.

Even for systems that are more benign in terms of damage, such as Alexa, ethical behavior can become a fundamental requirement for retaining customers, since its use may threaten privacy. Another critical requirement is privacy. Customers are re-discovering the importance of privacy [16], and states are enacting privacy laws, as the General Data Protection Regulation (GDPR). There have been many breaches of privacy such as the Samsung voice-recognition being activated by default in smart television models to Alexa capturing conversations and sending them to a repository [17].

Additionally, safety will play an essential role in many different domains. Software, AI based, will demand safety to be mandatory. Smart homes, for example, can bring threats to safety if not extensively analyzed when dealing with heating systems. It also should avoid exposing residents to external monitoring. Huang et al. survey points out most essential qualities to be satisfied [18] as to attain safety.

Systems like smart home administration can attract consumers with their convenience features, together with the expectations of saving money on things such as energy control. However, they may open the door for hackers to exploit vulnerabilities and misuse information. A recent study carried out in England shows the industry providing smart home solutions has not yet offered consumers with enough evidence they can trust that their home solutions will comply with the security and privacy standards they expect [19]. Poorly managing security and privacy can expose vendors to *legal disputes*, which is the price to pay by not observing social responsibility.

We advocate that software engineers should start investigating how to operationalize[4] Ethics, Safety, Security, and Privacy requirements. They can either carry out literature reviews to identify possible operationalizations for each NFR or use existing knowledge bases that capture knowledge that can be reused [20]. One of our goals for future work is to produce or improve existing knowledge bases representing them in the form of Softgoal Interdependencies Goals (SIG) catalogues [21], for example, those proposed by Zinovatna for Privacy and Transparency together [22]. There is empirical evidence that the use of SIG catalogues helps to obtain an improved set of NFRs [20, 23, 24].

---

[4] Recent work [31] brings an operationalization perspective on how to use goal models to define systems considering privacy, security and trust.

All the NFRs mentioned above alone will not be enough to promote trust in software. Trust will only be achieved if the software is transparent enough to demonstrate its qualities to consumers and illustrate that the software is acting accordingly to what consumers expect from it. In fact, Bachmann

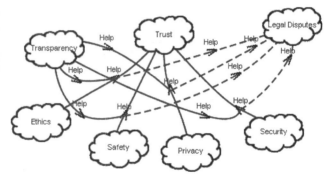

Fig. 1. A SIG with the Key NFRs for responsible software

et al. [25] point out that transparency is one of the critical issues for companies to recover from a situation that led to a lack of trust by consumers. Furthermore, no matter how well-designed software is, there will always be scenarios where failures, accidents, and damages will be inevitable. In these cases, transparent software can help to determine responsibilities and deal with liabilities and civil and criminal implications. Software Transparency implies that software will supply transparency not only of the data it has used and manipulated but also on the *process of development* behind this software. Leite and Cappelli provides a catalogue of transparency with a set of possible solutions to build transparent software [28]. Cysneiros et al. point out that transparency may play an essential role in the acceptance and willingness to buy and use self-driving cars. It also illustrates how legal disputes are an important requirement in the self-driving car domain, suggesting that transparency may play an important role in *legal disputes* [27].

Hence, we believe that *legal disputes* will certainly also be a requirement that will often be necessary to be tackled in a pro-active manner delivering systems that make use of AI, IofT, or cloud computing. Systems may have to embed ethical choices to guide the reasoning behind decisions made by the software. Injuries, damages, or even deaths resulting from these choices may result in both civil and criminal procedures [15]. On the other hand, in many cases manufacturers will be able to allow users to set their own scenario for ethical and safety decisions which could shift the liability away from software companies but may result in lower sales sparking fear in consumers to accept the risk without totally understanding, or more importantly, trusting how this feature would work. Systems that connect to several devices may be exposed to mal-function due to failures that can go from problems in communication to the lack of appropriate procedures to deal with mal-functions. This can also lead to *legal disputes*, and once again, systems prepared to be transparent can mitigate the consequences of legal actions.

Summarizing, it is our understanding that to support a socially responsible software development that can stimulate citizens/consumers to trust software embedded artifacts that they will be using or buying, we must develop the software with a close look at Ethics, Safety, Security and Privacy. These four NFRs should promote trust when the software is developed, and they must be transparent enough to demonstrate to consumers that the software will meet their expectations for these four NFRs. Each of these NFRs, when managed with Transparency, may have a positive impact on *legal disputes* that may arise due to suspect software behavior. In Fig. 1, a SIG maps the interactions among Softgoals (NFRs) [21]; so Ethics, Safety, Privacy, and Security contribute positively (*Help*) for Trust, but it needs Transparency to allow the contribution to be effective in mitigating *legal disputes*. We certainly acknowledge that other NFRs will also play a relevant role in distinct types of applications, like Reliability, for instance. Nevertheless, we believe the NFRs illustrated in Fig. 1 is the anchor we need to carefully elicit and model operationalizations for developing software, that people can trust.

4   Conclusion

Society has been changing and evolving at a fast pace. Ubiquitous computing, massive social connection, and growing use of AI/ML (Machine Learning) quite often linked to IofT concepts have been pushing software development to a new paradigm. In a recent paper [8] Agrawal et al. stated: "Machine Learning models are software artifacts derived from data". More then ever, we can not afford to build software targeting one single scenario of use. New software may have immense social impact with legal implications. We need to move our practice to embrace this new scenario where we must build software that is trustworthy and can be accountable for behaving in a socially responsible way.

Our contribution relies on eliciting, from social sciences, basic qualities for socially responsible software to be represented as SIG catalogues, anchored on the NFR Framework [21]. We will be developing catalogues to capture as many as possible solutions (operationalizations) to each NFR illustrated in Fig. 1. We aim to research systematic ways to search and find satisficing solutions to each of the above NFRs and integrate these solutions into a software reuse processes, taking in consideration how each possible solution will impact other NFRs. We will revisit and extend existing catalogues such as Leite's transparency [28] and Zinovatna's privacy and transparency [22], as well as exploring existing operationalizations, such as [31]. We will also focus on better understanding the implications of ethical concepts in the development of software and how it would impact trust as well as its legal ramifications. That will lead to investigate personal and group values that are closely related to ethics aspects [29].

At the core of our research, trust is the primary goal to be achieved. If consumers can trust your company and, by extension, your products (software), they tend to become loyal to your brand and refer your products to acquaintances, which in a social network era can translate into benefits, avoiding *legal disputes*.

References

1. Kolm, J.: How comfortable are Canadians with AI? strategy. http://strategyonline.ca/2017/12/14/how-comfortable-are-canadians-with-ai/. Accessed 13 Nov 2018
2. Bussone, A., Stumpf, S., O'Sullivan, D.: The role of explanations on trust and reliance in clinical decision support systems. In: Proceedings - 2015 IEEE International Conference on Healthcare Informatics, ICHI 2015, pp. 160–169. Institute of Electrical and Electronics Engineers Inc. (2015). https://doi.org/10.1109/ICHI.2015.26
3. Ribeiro, M.T., Singh, S., Guestrin, C.: "Why should i trust you?" Explaining the predictions of any classifier. In: Proceedings of the ACM SIGKDD International Conference on Knowledge Discovery and Data Mining, pp. 1135–1144. Association for Computing Machinery, New York (2016). https://doi.org/10.1145/2939672.2939778

 4. Chaudhuri, A., Holbrook, M.B.: The chain of effects from brand trust and brand affect to brand performance: the role of brand loyalty. J. Mark. **65**, 81–93 (2001). https://doi.org/10.1509/jmkg.65.2.81.18255

 5. Park, E., Kim, K.J., Kwon, S.J.: Corporate social responsibility as a determinant of consumer loyalty: an examination of ethical standard, satisfaction, and trust. J. Bus. Res. **76**, 8–13 (2017). https://doi.org/10.1016/J.JBUSRES.2017.02.017

 6. Kang, J., Hustvedt, G.: Building Trust Between Consumers and Corporations: The Role of Consumer Perceptions of Transparency and Social Responsibility. https://doi.org/10.1007/s10551-013-1916-7

 7. Cui, J., Jo, H., Na, H.: Does corporate social responsibility affect information asymmetry? J. Bus. Ethics **148**, 549–572 (2018). https://doi.org/10.1007/s10551-015-3003-8

 8. Agrawal, A., et al.: Cloudy with high chance of DBMS: a 10-year prediction for Enterprise-Grade ML (2019)

 9. Delgado-Ballester, E., Munuera-Aleman, J.L., Yague-Guillen, M.J.: Development and validation of a brand trust scale. Int. J. Mark. Res. **45**, 35–56 (2003)

10. Vlachos, P.A., Tsamakos, A., Vrechopoulos, A.P., Avramidis, P.K.: Corporate social responsibility: attributions, loyalty, and the mediating role of trust. J. Acad. Mark. Sci. **37**, 170–180 (2009). https://doi.org/10.1007/s11747-008-0117-x

11. Bowen, J.: The ethics of safety-critical systems. Commun. ACM **43**, 91–97 (2000). https://doi.org/10.1145/332051.332078

12. Pivato, S., Misani, N., Tencati, A.: The impact of corporate social responsibility on consumer trust: the case of organic food. Bus. Ethics A Eur. Rev. **17**, 3–12 (2007). https://doi.org/10.1111/j.1467-8608.2008.00515.x

13. ISO - ISO 26000 Social responsibility. https://www.iso.org/iso-26000-social-responsibility.html. Accessed 22 Oct 2019

14. Bews, N.F., Rossouw, G.J.: A role for business ethics in facilitating trustworthiness. J. Bus. Ethics **39**, 377–390 (2002). https://doi.org/10.1023/A:1019700704414

15. Lin, P.: Why ethics matters for autonomous cars. In: Maurer, M., Gerdes, J., Lenz, B., Winner, H. (eds.) Autonomes Fahren, pp. 69–85. Springer, Heidelberg (2015). https://doi.org/10.1007/978-3-662-45854-9_4

16. Buck, C., Stadler, F., Suckau, K., Eymann, T.: Privacy as a part of the preference structure of users app buying decision. In: Proceedings of the Wirtschaftsinformatik 2017 (2017)

17. Thierer, A.D.: The internet of things and wearable technology: addressing privacy and security concerns without derailing innovation. SSRN **21** (2014). https://doi.org/10.2139/ssrn.2494382

18. Huang, F., Wang, Y., Wang, Y., Zong, P.: What software quality characteristics most concern safety-critical domains? In: 2018 IEEE International Conference on Software Quality, Reliability and Security Companion (QRS-C), pp. 635–636. IEEE (2018). https://doi.org/10.1109/QRS-C.2018.00111

19. Wilson, C., Hargreaves, T., Hauxwell-Baldwin, R.: Benefits and risks of smart home technologies. Energy Policy **103**, 72–83 (2017). https://doi.org/10.1016/J.ENPOL.2016.12.047

20. Veleda, R., Cysneiros, L.M.: Towards an ontology-based approach for eliciting possible solutions to non-functional requirements. In: Giorgini, P., Weber, B. (eds.) CAiSE 2019. LNCS, vol. 11483, pp. 145–161. Springer, Cham (2019). https://doi.org/10.1007/978-3-030-21290-2_10

21. Chung, L., Nixon, B.A., Yu, E., Mylopoulos, J.: Non-Functional Requirements in Software Engineering. Springer, Boston (1999). https://doi.org/10.1007/978-1-4615-5269-7

22. Zinovatna, O., Cysneiros, L.M.: Reusing knowledge on delivering privacy and transparency together. In: 2015 IEEE Fifth International Workshop on Requirements Patterns (RePa), pp. 17–24 (2015). https://doi.org/10.1109/RePa.2015.7407733

23. de Gramatica, M., Labunets, K., Massacci, F., Paci, F., Tedeschi, A.: The role of catalogues of threats and security controls in security risk assessment: an empirical study with ATM professionals. In: Fricker, S., Schneider, K. (eds.) REFSQ 2015. LNCS, vol. 9013, pp. 98–114. Springer, Cham (2015). https://doi.org/10.1007/978-3-319-16101-3_7
24. Cardoso, E., Almeida, J.P., Guizzardi, R.S., Guizzardi, G.: A method for eliciting goals for business process models based on non-functional requirements catalogues. In: Frameworks for Developing Efficient Information Systems: Models, Theory, and Practice: Models, Theory, and Practice, pp. 226–242 (2013)
25. Bachmann, R., Gillespie, N., Priem, R.: Repairing trust in organizations and institutions: toward a conceptual framework. Organ. Stud. **36**, 1123–1142 (2015). https://doi.org/10.1177/0170840615599334
26. Cysneiros, L.M., Yu, E.: Non-functional requirements elicitation. In: do Prado Leite, J.C.S., Doorn, J.H. (eds.) Perspectives on Software Requirements. SECS, vol. 753, pp. 115–138. Springer, Boston (2004). https://doi.org/10.1007/978-1-4615-0465-8_6
27. Cysneiros, L.M., Raffi, M., Sampaio do Prado Leite, J.C.: Software transparency as a key requirement for self-driving cars. In: 2018 IEEE 26th International Requirements Engineering Conference (RE), pp. 382–387. IEEE (2018). https://doi.org/10.1109/RE.2018.00-21
28. do Prado Leite, J.C.S., Cappelli, C.: Software transparency. Bus. Inf. Syst. Eng. **2**, 127–139 (2010). https://doi.org/10.1007/s12599-010-0102-z
29. Angela Ferrario, M., Simm, W., Forshaw, S., Gradinar, A., Tavares Smith, M., Smith, I.: Values-first SE: research principles in practice. https://doi.org/10.1145/2889160.2889219
30. Shim, K., Yang, S.: The effect of bad reputation: the occurrence of crisis, corporate social responsibility, and perceptions of hypocrisy and attitudes toward a company. Public Relat. Rev. **42**(1), 68–78 (2016)
31. Salnitri, M., Angelopoulos, K., Pavlidis, M., et al.: Modelling the interplay of security, privacy and trust in sociotechnical systems: a computer-aided design approach. Softw. Syst. Model. **19**, 467–491 (2020). https://doi.org/10.1007/s10270-019-00744-x

Domain-Specific Modeling (EMMSAD 2020)

A Journey to BSO: Evaluating Earlier and More Recent Ideas of Mario Bunge as a Foundation for Information Systems and Software Development

Roman Lukyanenko[✉]

HEC Montreal, Montreal, QC, Canada
`roman.lukyanenko@hec.ca`

Abstract. A prominent theoretical foundation for IT analysis, design and development is general ontology - a branch of philosophy which studies what exists in reality. A widely used general ontology is BWW (Bunge-Wand-Weber) – based on ideas of the philosopher and physicist Mario Bunge, synthesized by Wand and Weber. It is regarded as a major contribution to conceptual modeling, database design, data collection design and information quality, as well as theory of IT. At the same time, the ontology was founded on an early subset of Bunge's philosophy and Bunge's ideas have evolved since then. An important question, therefore, is: do the more recent ideas expressed by Bunge call for a new ontology? In this paper we conduct an analysis of research by Bunge aiming at addressing this question. We compare the constructs of BWW with what we call Bunge's Systemist Ontology (BSO) – a new ontology based on broader and more recent ideas developed by Bunge. Informed by this comparison we offer suggestions for ontology studies as well as future applications of Bunge in conceptual modeling and other areas of IT.

Keywords: Ontology · Upper-level ontology · Bunge · Bunge-Wand-Weber ontology · Bunge's Systemist Ontology · Conceptual modeling · IT development

1 Introduction

With the increased reliance on information technology (IT), grows the importance of building IT based on solid foundations [1, 2]. Historically, one of the most prolific and effective references for IT analysis, design and development has been *ontology*. In this paper we focus on *general ontology* – a branch of philosophy which studies what exists in reality (and what reality is) [3, 4] – rather than a *domain ontology* – a description (often formal) of constructs in a particular domain (e.g., ontology of Software Defects, Errors and Failures, see [5] or ontology of research validity [6]) [7].

A general (also known as foundational or upper level) ontology offers IT development theoretically grounded (i.e., based on established knowledge from other disciplines as psychology or physics), consistent, formalized and rigorous meaning for the basic notions of what exists in reality and thus in a domain of IT. As such, ontological studies are

© Springer Nature Switzerland AG 2020
S. Nurcan et al. (Eds.): BPMDS 2020/EMMSAD 2020, LNBIP 387, pp. 345–358, 2020.
https://doi.org/10.1007/978-3-030-49418-6_24

now widely embraced by the IT community. Applications of ontologies are especially prolific in research on semantic web (which aims to move beyond syntactic matches to deeper interoperability), and conceptual data and process modeling (which develops representations of application domains and user requirements), but have also been used in knowledge management, artificial intelligence, interface design, data collection processes, database schema integration, analysis of software performance, information quality, among others [4, 8–14]. Empirical benefits of adopting a particular domain ontology (e.g., in the design of conceptual modeling grammars or improving quality of data produced by an IT) have been documented [8, 15–19].

Considering the demonstrable benefits of general ontologies, research has proposed a number of general ontologies to be used for IT analysis, design and development, such as Unified Foundational Ontology (UFO) [20], social ontology of Searle [21], General Formal Ontology [22], DOLCE [23]. A prominent ontology is BWW (Bunge-Wand-Weber) – based on ideas of the philosopher and physicist Mario Bunge (1919-Feb 2020), synthesized by Wand and Weber [24, 25].

The BWW is widely regarded as major contribution to theory and practice of IT and conceptual modeling, at it has been informing theoretical, empirical and design works across a wide range of disciplines [26, 27]. At the same time, the ontology has been criticized e.g., [28], especially on grounds related to the assumptions underlying the ontology rooted in philosophical beliefs of Bunge.

Notable, BWW was developed on a subset of Bunge's ontology [29, 30] which is now over 40 years old (i.e., 1977 and 79). In the 40 years since the publication of the two primary sources of BWW [29, 30], Bunge published over 100 books and 300 papers [31], in which his ideas were further expanded, refined, and sometimes, altered. Several question, therefore, arise:

Research Questions (RQs): is there a need for a revision to the original BWW? Are statements such as "Bunge believes the world is made of things" justified in light of more recent publications? Should this be a minor, or a major revision? Does it result in an expansion of BWW e.g., [32], or do the ideas expressed (since 1979) by Bunge call for a completely new ontology?

In this paper we provide results of a first phase of the project aiming at addressing these questions. In this phase we compare key constructs of BWW with what we coin **Bunge's Systemist Ontology** (BSO) – a more recent set of ideas developed by Bunge since the volumes which formed basis for BWW. Informed by this analysis we offer suggestions for future research on both development of ontology as well as use of Bunge in conceptual modeling and other areas of IT.

2   Background: Bunge-Wand Weber Ontology

In a recent essay, Yair Wand and Ron Weber offer a first-hand account [26] of what motivated them to pursue their program of grounding information systems (IS) research in foundational ontology and how they developed a set of theories (e.g., theory of ontological expressiveness, representation model, good-decomposition model) based on what became known as Bunge-Wand-Weber ontology. Although they consulted other sources, the primary foundation of BWW are two seminal manuscripts on ontology by Bunge [29, 30], part of his eight volume *Treatise on Basic Philosophy*.

Briefly, following philosophy of Bunge, BWW [24, 25] argues that the world is made of *things* – substantial individuals – which possess properties; things may compose forming composite things, interact with one another, leading to acquisition of new or loss of existing properties, resulting in events; sets of things from systems. Properties are not directly accessible to human observers, resulting in the notion of attributes; attributes which humans ascribe to things may or may not be accurate or complete representations of the underlying properties. In sum, the key constructs from Bunge which have been adopted into BWW are: thing, property, attributes, functional schema, state, law, state space, event, history, coupling, system, class, kind, and their derivatives (e.g., lawful state space) i.e., see Table 1, p. 222 [33] and [34].

The BWW ontology and the theories, models and methods derived from it, have been used widely in conceptual, empirical and design work in information systems, conceptual modeling, software engineering and other areas [26], making it among the most important developments in the area of ontology in disciplines of IT [35].

Despite the prolific use of BWW (for most recent reviews, see [35, 36]) the ontology has been criticized for its narrow physicalist focus, lack of attention to social and psychological phenomena, as well as postulates which may be problematic for modeling certain type of domain rules (e.g., BWW proscribed optional properties, denied independent existence of properties, and properties of properties) [4, 21, 28, 37].

Despite the many debates centered on BWW, a generally overlooked issue is that the original ontology is based on select references from Bunge. Although there have some attempts at expanding BWW to incorporate other ideas of Bunge [32], these were still narrow in scope and did not see widespread adoption compared with BWW.

The basis for BWW have been two, albeit seminal and focused on ontology, manuscripts by Bunge. However, as Bunge frequently noted, ontology is inseparable from other beliefs, such as on how to obtain knowledge in the world [38]. Indeed, the *Treatise* contained many additional beliefs, including on matters of semantics, epistemology, methodology, ethics, technology, among others.

Additionally, in the over 40 years since the publication of the 1977 and 79 volumes (and even since the last book of the *Treatise* - on ethics [39]), Bunge published over 400 manuscripts, in which his ideas were further expanded, refined, and sometimes, altered[1]. Some of these more recent ideas were of great potential relevance to IT, as they directly dealt with issues of information technology e.g., [41].

Considering the broad and profound impact BWW had on the disciplines of IT, such as conceptual modeling, an important question to ask is: Can we further IT research and practice by incorporating these, more recent views and beliefs of Mario Bunge? In order to answer this question, it is first incumbent to assess the extent to which the original basis for BWW and the more recent thinking agree and diverge.

---

[1] An example of a reversal is Bunge's admiration for Marxism-Leninism (an extensive set of beliefs transcending the general public's most familiar ideas about politics and economy). It was Bunge's first major philosophical doctrine, according to his own confessions but over the years he distanced himself and then ended up being a vehement critic of Marxist-Leninist "ontology and politics" [31, p. vii], [40].

3 Constructing Bunge's Systemist Ontology

The task of understanding the differences between Bunge's ideas enshrined in BWW and his other, and more recent thinking, meets a challenge: the ideas which formed BWW were carefully distilled, while the more recent thinking was not. Although based on two volumes, BWW was founded on a self-contained *Treatise on Basic Philosophy* which developed and present ideas systematically and with great internal consistency: beginning with semantics [42], then ontology [29], followed by epistemology [43], methodology [43] and ethics [39]. In contrast, the more recent thinking of Bunge (e.g., since the *Treatise*) has not been assembled into a dedicated, self-contained single compendium. Rather is a collection of over 400 essays, papers and books (e.g., [38, 41, 44–46]), which require dedicated synthesis[2].

To answer the RQs of the paper, we engaged in a comprehensive and systematic effort to catalog and present these beliefs, a project which was done over a period of five years (2015–2020), covering up to the last known publication by late Bunge.

The procedure was conducted in the following steps: First, we began to assemble a library of publications by Bunge and conducted a scoping survey of the writing to gain a preliminary idea of the extend of alternations and expansions compared with the *Treatise*. Second, half-way into the process, the author contacted Mario Bunge, who kindly agreed to meet and provided a general overview of his earlier and most recent thinking and answered numerous clarifying questions. Third, we reviewed all pertinent publications using *GoogleScholar* and [31] as the sources[3]. Fourth, we followed the logical path outlined in the *Treatise* (i.e., ontology, epistemology, methodology and ethics) and re-iterated and explained by Bunge in other sources e.g., [38] to catalog the ideas beginning with basic assumptions about reality, followed by the problem of knowledge of reality and then the application and use of the knowledge by society (e.g., in policy-making, science and daily life). Fifth, we began synthesizing the ideas, favoring the most recent publications e.g., [45, 46] as the primary signal and referencing earlier publications e.g., [38], Bunge's own memoirs [40], and authoritative studies on Bunge [31], for clarification or expansion of ideas, when needed[4].

The result is a systematic synthesis of Bunge's publications aimed at distilling and presenting a single, coherent and consistent set of beliefs with the aim of using these ideas in the context of IT. As mentioned, Bunge kindly clarified some of the ideas of his ontology and also shared a copy of his most recent and (as of February 2020) unpublished manuscript. However, all claims made here are justified either through direct references to published works by Bunge or are explicitly noted as author's own inferences, and derivations. To report the findings, we analyze the constructs of BWW presented in see Table 1, p. 222 [33] compared with what we refer to as **Bunge's Systemist Ontology**

---

[2] For example, although Bunge has made a stronger emphasis toward *systems*, his recent writing is still rich in references to *things*, including in the same texts where he talks about systems being primary existents and preferable to notion of things (e.g., [45, p. 174]).

[3] https://scholar.google.com/citations?user=7MmcYgEAAAAJ&hl=en&oi=ao.

[4] For example, whereas Bunge describe systems in [44, p. 270] (among many other sources), to find more detailed discussion of properties of systems, one can consult, for example, [38, pp. 10–19].

(BSO) which as we argue later is a new ontology. Bunge uses multiple labels to describe his set of beliefs (e.g., "emergentist materialism" [47], "hylorealism" [38, p. 27]), but the most frequently used appears to be "systemism" [30, 46, 48].

4 Bunge's Systemist Ontology Vs Foundations of BWW

The BSO claims *reality* is all that we know to exist and distinguishes five "kinds" or "levels" of *reality*, including physical, chemical, biological, social and technical [44, p. 25]. These levels may have different actual or perceptible to human properties or events, but all are ultimately grounded in the underlying physical level.

The BWW ontology postulated that *reality* is made of *things*, which have properties [29, pp. 26–29]. Things are "substantial individuals", which could be *composed* of other individuals or be *simple* [34, p. 126]. A set of things forms a *system* [30, p. 6].

Although the notion of system exists in BWW, through the passage of time, BSO has been adopting a new postulate that under some interpretation inverts the relationship between things and systems. In BSO, Bunge believes the world is made of *systems:* "everything is a system or a component of a system" [46, p. 23]. Thus, Bunge argues, "every *thing* is either a system or a component of such", "every construct is a component of at least one conceptual system", "every symbol is a component of at least one symbolic system" [44, p. 266]. A thing is a type of system (although this view is not consistent through Bunge's recent wring).

By drawing upon recent advances in physics, especially particle physics that Bunge followed closely e.g., [49], Bunge [45] explains (p. 174, emphasis added):

> The word 'system' is more neutral than 'thing', which in most cases denotes a system endowed with mass an perhaps tactually perceptible; we find it natural to speak of a force or field as a system, but we would be reluctant to call it a thing. By calling all existents "concrete systems" we tacitly commit ourselves *in tune with a growing suspicion in all scientific quarters* - that there are no simple, structureless entities.

Systemism doesn't suggest things no longer exist, but for Bunge it appears more productive to think about the basic elements of the world as systems, rather than things. Yet, it is notable that he has not fully committed himself to this thinking as he admits a possibility of atomic things (i.e., "non-systems") [48, p. 148]:

> Only particle physicists study non-systems, such as quarks, electrons, and photons. But they know that all such simple things are parts of systems or will eventually be absorbed by some system.

Yet, as conceptual modeling and many other areas of IT do not engage with quarks, electrons, and protons (perhaps the progress in quantum computing may change this in the future), effectively these disciplines may disregard the caveat in [48, p. 148] and treat all existents of interest as systems. Thus, we can conclude that in BSO, the world is made of systems.

For Bunge, systmism holds numerous advantages, as it conceptually lies in between individualism (which under-represents internal structures of a system, its relationship with outer environment, its levels of composition and emergence) and holism (which is not interested in the components and specificity of subsystems). For Bunge, systemism represents the best of these two ideas, without sacrificing the benefits of each [48]. This is how Agazzi, a friend and close associate of Bunge, summarizes his views, which he debated with Bunge extensively over the years [50, p. 224]:

> [Bunge] explicitly presents his position (which he calls "systemism") as intermediate between two erroneous extremes, "atomism" and "holism". The weakness of atomism resides in that it ignores the relevance of properties and especially relations, without which it is impossible to distinguish a single "aggregate" from a "system". The weakness of holism resides (according to Bunge) in its pretension that the knowledge of the whole must precede and make possible the knowledge of the parts. Systemism avoids both mistakes by recognizing that the whole "results" from the correlation of its parts and at the same time has influence on their functioning.

Bunge believes, systems are always composed of components or parts [46, p. 23]. However, it is not clear what the construct of "part" or "component" mean – we have not seen their definition in Bunge's writings. A way to avoid this problem is to recognize, one again, that in the domains of interest to IT, parts or components of systems are systems themselves. This is an important realization, as it liberates the field of IT from the need to resolve the fundamental ontological status of the "component" or "system part".

Over the years, Bunge developed and expanded his ontology of systems. Thus, in the *Treatise*, Bunge postulated that any system should have "a definite composition, a different environment, and a different structure. The composition of the system is the set of its components; the environment, the set of items with which it is connected; and the structure, the relations among its components as well as among these and the environment" [30, p. 4].

In later writings, this initial idea was developed into a CESM model, which in addition to the composition, environment, and structure (present in BWW), added "mechanism" [48]. Mechanism is defined as "characteristic processes, that make [the system] what it is and the peculiar ways it changes" [38, p. 126]. To illustrate, Bunge provides an example of a traditional nuclear family [38, p. 127]:

> Its components are the parents and the children; the relevant environment is the immediate physical environment, the neighbourhood, and the workplace; the structure is made up of such biological and psychological bonds as love, sharing, and relations with others; and the mechanism consists essentially of domestic chores, marital encounters of various kinds, and child rearing. If the central mechanism breaks down, so does the system as a whole.

Adopting BSO in the context of IT allows to potentially remove the notion of a thing from the ontology, simply replacing it with the system construct. The inversion of the relationship between things and systems, and the potential obviation of the need for *things* in BSO, represents a major change, as the construct of thing has been a founding one for BWW and has been the conceptual foundation for many studies which adopted BWW [19, 51].

However, as effectively, *things* in the social and technical levels of early Bunge were effectively systems [30], this change can be easily accommodated by much of prior work which used BWW with a mere replacement of a label.

As systems replace things, this results in a reduction of complexity of BWW ontology that dealt with the relationship between things and systems (e.g., obviating the need for constructs such as "composite thing" or "properties of things"). For example, BWW defines *internal event* as "an event that arises in a thing, subsystem, or system" [33, p. 222]. This definition can simply state that an internal event is an event that arises in a system. However, note, an ontology that uses systems as its fundamental ontological primitive, would probably borrow other constructs related to systems, which are beyond the BWW (e.g., CESM).

As in BWW, BSO continues to uphold the beliefs about the relationship between systems and properties. Systems have properties. Properties do not exist outside of systems [45, p. 175]: "Property-less entities would be unknowable, hence the hypothesis of their existence is untestable; and disembodied properties and relations are unknown." As in BWW, properties according to BSO do not exist in themselves: "However, ... can be material only derivatively, that is, by virtue of the materiality of the things involved: there are neither properties nor relations in themselves, except by abstraction." [38, p. 11].

Notions of classes and kinds are used in BSO, but somewhat differently compared with BWW. In BWW, classes are sets of things sharing "a common property", whereas *kinds* are sets of things which share "two or more" property [33, p. 223]). Systems with "one of more" common properties in BSO [44, p. 111], form *classes* and those with properties which are interrelated, form *kinds* [38, p. 13].

The greater emphasis on systems carries other implications, as this new postulate is propagated throughout most of Bunge's recent beliefs. According to BSO, some but not all (an important caveat cf. BWW) systems undergo change, resulting in emergence (addition of new) or submergence (loss of old) of properties. To account for this, BSO continues to use the construct of *state*. Bunge [45, p. 171] defines a state as "the list of the properties of the thing at that time" – a definition nearly identical to that in BWW [29, p. 125]. A state can describe multiple properties (at the same moment in time) [38]. A given system has the properties of its subsystems, as well as its own, termed emergent properties (and idea unchanged since BWW), but now gaining greater focus in BSO, as a key implication of systemism.

Whereas per BWW, Bunge applies the notion of a state to all things [29, p. 123], in BSO, Bunge [38] makes an important distinction between systems which undergo change and those do not. In BWW, a set of postulates deal with changes of states (i.e., events) and how the properties which make up the states are perceived by humans (i.e., attributes) [29]. However, for BSO these constructs do not apply to all systems.

Bunge distinguishes two kinds of system: *conceptual* and *concrete* [44, p. 270]. A *conceptual* (or formal) system is a system all the components of which are conceptual (e.g., propositions, classifications, and hypothetico-deductive systems-i.e., theories).

This is contrasted with *concrete* (or *material*) systems which are made of concrete components (i.e., subsystems, such as atoms, organisms, and societies), meaning that these components may undergo change.[5]

What distinguishes concrete and conceptual systems is the essential property of *mutability* – a key element of BSO - which *only concrete systems possess*: "mutability is the one property shared by all concrete things, whether natural or artificial, physical or chemical, biological or social, perceptible or imperceptible" [38, p. 10]. Bunge thus explains that changes in systems may only occur if the systems are concrete [38, p. 11]:

heat propagation, metabolism, and ideation qualify as material since they are processes in material things. By contrast, logical consistency, commutativity, and differentiability can only be predicated of mathematical objects.

Concrete systems change in the virtue of energy transfer. For Bunge, "the technical word for 'changeability' is energy" [38, p. 12], such that:

To repeat, energy is not just a property among many. Energy is the universal property, the universal par excellence.

We thus obtain a more formal definition of a *concrete system* in BSO as a system that has energy [38, p. 12].

The BSO dedicates considerable time to the notion of energy, as it underlies Bunge's thinking about (new to BWW) constructs of *causality, trigger* and *chance*. He analyzes these notions relative to different kinds of energy, including mechanical, thermal, kinetic, potential, electric, magnetic, gravitational, chemical (e.g., in [38]). Thus, per BSO, when systems interact, they transfer energy from one to another. This leads to change in states of things, as they acquire or lose their properties. This produces events and processes. Energy when paired with *artificial code* may transmit *information* (new to BWW constructs, and of special relevance to the field of IT).

The consequence of re-definition of systems as either energy-bearing or not, makes another major change compared with BWW. Thus, while in BWW an event has been understood as a "change in state of a thing" [33, p. 222], in BSO, event in understood in terms of energy, thus being only applicable to *concrete systems*[6]. Bunge views event as an energy-involving construct [38, p. 91]:

Event C in thing A causes event E in thing B if and only if the occurrence of C generates an energy transfer from A to B resulting in the occurrence of E.

Multiple events form *processes* (a new construct for BWW): defined as "a sequence, ordered in time, of events and such that every member of the sequence takes part in the determination of the succeeding member" [45, p. 172].

---

[5] Bunge [44, p. 270] also distinguishes a *symbolic* (or *semiotic*) system as a type of a concrete system some components of which stand for or represent other objects (e.g., languages, computer diskettes, and diagrams).

[6] This may potentially resolve the criticisms levied against Bunge's ontology by as being too physicalist [21, 28] - original ideas of Bunge captured in BWW without explicit qualification have indeed been casted by BSO as belonging to only material reality.

The demarcation between events applicable to concrete vs conceptual systems, affects the definition of the notion of *law*, which is applicable to concrete systems only. Laws are stable patterns which hold "independently of human knowledge or will" [44, p. 27]. In BSO, *conceptual systems* do not obey laws, but rather obey *rules of logic* [38, p. 19] – a new concept for BWW.

The BSO then draws a very close connection between ontology and epistemology, a connection which is not as evident in BWW. BSO's epistemology is vast and extensive and connects his ontology to other philosophical beliefs differently compared to BWW. Whereas in BWW, the connection is made via the constructs of attributes (i.e., properties as seen by people and model things), in BSO the connection is again, via systems.

For BSO, an event or a process as it appears to some human subject is termed *phenomenon* [45, p. 173] (new to BWW construct). It is an occurrence registered by the sensory apparatus of humans or other animals triggered by a change or a serious of changes in the state of a concrete system. For example, the rising of the sun or inauguration of the president calls a complex chain of events in the attentive, perceptive, cognitive and other biological and mental processes of the people who experience these events (either directly or via a signal, such as radio, Internet or television). Phenomena are always "in the intersection of the external world with the cognitive subject" [45, p. 173].

Events, processes, phenomena, and concrete systems are instances of the mental concept of *fact* – i.e., they lie "in the extension of the concept of fact" [45, p. 174]. Facts are kinds of *objects* – "whatever is or may become a subject of thought or action" [45, p. 174] i.e., "known or assumed - with some ground - to belong to reality" [45, p. 171]. Thus, through the notions of facts, BSO connects the fundamental ideas about the composition of reality to the mental world of humans.

As Bunge stresses, what can be observed as phenomena is a small fraction of the facts constituting the object of an investigation; "the observable facts or phenomena are documents suggesting or confirming the existence of more interesting facts behind" [45, p. 177]. Facts are iceberg-like: they are mostly submerged under the surface of immediate experience and, furthermore, the phenomena are often quite different from the concrete systems they are based on. Consider for example the difference between the visual sensations caused by aurora borealis and the actual chemical, magnetic, and other physical processes involved in the unraveling of this concrete system.

Thus, the "submerged" portion of facts must be hypothesized and, in order to test such hypotheses, definite relations between the unobserved and the observed must be added, by which the observed can count as evidence for or against the existence of the hypothetical unseen, and the unseen can explain what can be seen. These relations are represented by hypotheses and theories [45, p. 177].

It is a subject of centennial debates in philosophy whether human observers have access to more than just phenomena. The position of the *phenomenalism* holds that only direct sensations and experiences are knowable [52]. In contrast, various strands of *realism* generally believe that reality beyond sensations can be known [53]. This can be accomplished with the aid of experimentation, theory testing, imagination and logical inference. Bunge per BWW and BSO is a proponent of the latter [45]. For Bunge [45], the pragmatic benefit of realism is that it encourages thinking and action beyond sensations and encourages an active stance toward reality.

There is no "end" of the BSO per se (recall, BSO is not published in a self-contained treatise), as Bunge continuously stresses the interdependency between ontology and other beliefs, thus we draw a demarcation based on constructs in BWW [33]. We note, Wand and Weber engaged with other ideas of Bunge, as did other scholars e.g., [32, 54], and acknowledged the existence of other constructs and more recent set of beliefs. As they note, Bunge "has written extensively about social phenomena using constructs based upon his ontology (e.g., Bunge, 1998)" [26, p. 6]. Yet, much of IT community adopted the views of Bunge stemming from BWW, making this an important benchmark comparison.

5 Discussion and Implications

The Bunge-Wand-Weber ontology has been a seminal ontology having demonstrable and broad impact on various disciplines of IT. It has been proven effective at guiding conceptual, empirical and design research. The success of BWW motivates our efforts to examine the extent to which we could benefit from more recent ideas and beliefs of Mario Bunge. Based on our analysis above, we can draw the following conclusions and suggest several implications for future studies.

Frist, it is evident that more recent thinking by Bunge remains partially consistent with BWW. In particular, BSO continues to adhere to the tenets of scientific realism and grounds thinking into interpretation of the state-of-the-art knowledge in physics and other disciplines. Many ideas in BSO have not changed compared to BWW; these include the denial of the existence of properties (with known implications for conceptual modeling research, such as the problem of optional properties or properties of properties [15, 55–57]), emergence, lack of direct human access to reality (i.e., to the properties of systems), notions of state, event, and change.

Second, many of the changes introduced by BSO could be handled by appropriate qualifications or more precise specifications of the already existing notions (e.g., that concrete systems undergo change via energy transfer, but conceptual systems do not). The notion of *things* and their properties is still present, as some systems can be viewed as individual objects.

Thus, there is an important continuity between BSO and BWW - a continuity which is critical in assessing the status of impressive theoretical, conceptual and design research that stemmed from the ideas of Wand and Weber. Hence, BSO could still be used to posit that classes "tyrannize" instances [51] or that optional properties should be proscribed (although, in BSO, for concrete systems only, as conceptual systems do not follow the same principles as concrete ones).

On the other hand, BSO suggests a new way of thinking about reality, which is while somewhat compatible with the ideas in BWW, *creates significant new openings for future research.*

A more central role of systems carries profound implications beyond a mere potential for simplification of an ontology. In contrast to the emphasis on *unique things* BSO points a researcher and practitioner (e.g., in the context of conceptual modeling) to the importance of representing structure, relationship between systems, emergence, different levels, and interactions among sub-systems. In BSO, Bunge clearly wishes to balance his views between the value an individual-focused perspective may bring vs a perspective which is more sensitive to the whole. There have been many studies, including a number of recent ones, which followed early Bunge and emphasized the primacy of individuals (e.g., in the logical database design, conceptual modeling grammars, information quality, design collection processes, e.g., [19, 51, 58–60]). Bunge extensively talks about the limitations of the individual-focused perspective and suggests that a more balanced approach may be more fruitful, an approach which BSO appears to support better [44, 48].

Furthermore, BSO more than BWW enmeshed ontological issues with matters of epistemology, methodology, technology and ethics. It has provisions for social, mental and technological reality (including constructs such as *social facts*, *concepts*, *hypotheses*). These ideas stand to lessen many concerns raised earlier about Bunge related to the physicalist focus of his ontology. Furthermore, several studies used BWW to reason about notions of *information* and *information quality* [12, 19]. However, BSO explicitly contains some of these constructs, and shows a path from the ontological primitive of a system to the notion of *information*, for example. Indeed, Bunge made a concerted effort to incorporate advances in modern information technology [41]. Thus, adopting BSO for future studies promises a more direct grounding of many important concepts of modern society into ideas of Bunge. In short, BSO stands to broadly enrich conceptual modeling and other IT related topics with many new ideas.

Considering the differences between earlier and more recent thinking of Bunge, we respond affirmatively to our research question and propose **Bunge's Systemist Ontology** or BSO, as a new ontology, and a new addition to the theoretical toolbox of IT.

6   Conclusion

Mario Bunge made a profound mark on the field of conceptual modeling, software engineering, information quality, database design. Much of this influence has been via BWW ontology – an incredibly valuable body of knowledge which popularized Bunge in the field of IT and became the foundation for numerous studies on design and use of information technologies. Even researchers who disagreed with aspects of BWW and Bunge's ontology, benefited from these ideas greatly, as BWW provided a key benchmark and inspired to pursue ontological studies in IT [4, 20, 21].

The significance and success of BWW motivated us to seek new ways Bunge's extensive thinking can be leveraged in the design and use of IT. As we showed in our work, BSO contains ideas that although somewhat compatible with BWW, are also quite different, raising new prospects and opening new possibilities.

The new BSO emerges as a complex and extensive set of beliefs. In this paper, we began to expose its basic tenets and assumptions. However, this work is by no means complete. Our key objective was to establish BSO as a new ontology. Much work remains to study BSO in its own right (including its benefits and limitations for applications in IT), formalizing it into a finite set of postulates (as Wand and Weber did for BWW), and seeking out areas of IT practice which could benefit from the application of these ideas. In short, we call on researchers to consider adopting BSO as a promising new ontology.

References

1. Guerreiro, S., van Kervel, S.J., Babkin, E.: Towards devising an architectural framework for enterprise operating systems. In: ICSOFT, pp. 578–585 (2013)
2. Henderson-Sellers, B.: Why philosophize; why not just model? In: Johannesson, P., Lee, M.L., Liddle, S.W., Opdahl, A.L., López, Ó.P. (eds.) ER 2015. LNCS, vol. 9381, pp. 3–17. Springer, Cham (2015). https://doi.org/10.1007/978-3-319-25264-3_1
3. Gonzalez-Perez, C.: How ontologies can help in software engineering. In: Cunha, J., Fernandes, J.P., Lämmel, R., Saraiva, J., Zaytsev, V. (eds.) GTTSE 2015. LNCS, vol. 10223, pp. 26–44. Springer, Cham (2017). https://doi.org/10.1007/978-3-319-60074-1_2
4. Guizzardi, G.: Ontological foundations for structural conceptual models. Telematics Instituut Fundamental Research Series, Enschede, The Netherlands (2005)
5. Duarte, B.B., Falbo, R.A., Guizzardi, G., Guizzardi, R.S.S., Souza, V.E.S.: Towards an ontology of software defects, errors and failures. In: Trujillo, J.C., et al. (eds.) ER 2018. LNCS, vol. 11157, pp. 349–362. Springer, Cham (2018). https://doi.org/10.1007/978-3-030-00847-5_25
6. Lukyanenko, R., Larsen, K.R., Parsons, J., Gefen, D., Mueller, R.M.: Toward creating a general ontology for research validity. In: International Conference on Conceptual Modeling, Salvador, Brazil, pp. 133–137 (2019)
7. McDaniel, M., Storey, V.C.: Evaluating domain ontologies: clarification, classification, and challenges. ACM Comput. Surv. 53(1), 1–40 (2019)
8. Verdonck, M., Gailly, F., Pergl, R., Guizzardi, G., Martins, B., Pastor, O.: Comparing traditional conceptual modeling with ontology-driven conceptual modeling: an empirical study. Inf. Syst. 81, 92–103 (2019)
9. Recker, J., Rosemann, M., Krogstie, J.: Ontology-versus pattern-based evaluation of process modeling languages: a comparison. Commun. Assoc. Inf. Syst. 20(1), 48 (2007)
10. Martínez Ferrandis, A.M., Pastor López, O., Guizzardi, G.: Applying the principles of an ontology-based approach to a conceptual schema of human genome. In: Ng, W., Storey, V.C., Trujillo, J.C. (eds.) ER 2013. LNCS, vol. 8217, pp. 471–478. Springer, Heidelberg (2013). https://doi.org/10.1007/978-3-642-41924-9_40
11. Pastor, Ó., España, S., González, A.: An ontological-based approach to analyze software production methods. In: Kaschek, R., Kop, C., Steinberger, C., Fliedl, G. (eds.) UNISCON 2008. LNBIP, vol. 5, pp. 258–270. Springer, Heidelberg (2008). https://doi.org/10.1007/978-3-540-78942-0_26
12. Wand, Y., Wang, R.Y.: Anchoring data quality dimensions in ontological foundations. Commun. ACM 39(11), 86–95 (1996)
13. Reinhartz-Berger, I., Itzik, N., Wand, Y.: Analyzing variability of software product lines using semantic and ontological considerations. In: Jarke, M., et al. (eds.) CAiSE 2014. LNCS, vol. 8484, pp. 150–164. Springer, Cham (2014). https://doi.org/10.1007/978-3-319-07881-6_11
14. Guarino, N.: Formal ontology, conceptual analysis and knowledge representation. Int. J. Hum. Comput. Stud. 43(5–6), 625–640 (1995)
15. Bodart, F., Patel, A., Sim, M., Weber, R.: Should optional properties be used in conceptual modelling? A theory and three empirical tests. Inf. Syst. Res. 12(4), 384–405 (2001)
16. Burton-Jones, A., Weber, R.: Building conceptual modeling on the foundation of ontology. In: Computing Handbook: Information Systems and Information Technology, pp. 15.1–15.24. CRC Press, Boca Raton (2014)
17. Bera, P., Burton-Jones, A., Wand, Y.: Research note—how semantics and pragmatics interact in understanding conceptual models. Inf. Syst. Res. 25(2), 401–419 (2014)
18. Recker, J., Rosemann, M., Green, P., Indulska, M.: Do ontological deficiencies in modeling grammars matter? MIS Q. 35(1), 57–79 (2011)

19. Lukyanenko, R., Parsons, J., Wiersma, Y.: The IQ of the crowd: understanding and improving information quality in structured user-generated content. Inf. Syst. Res. **25**(4), 669–689 (2014)
20. Guizzardi, G., Wagner, G., Almeida, J.P.A., Guizzardi, R.S.: Towards ontological foundations for conceptual modeling: the unified foundational ontology (UFO) story. Appl. Ontol. **10**(3–4), 259–271 (2015)
21. March, S.T., Allen, G.N.: Toward a social ontology for conceptual modeling. In: Communications of the AIS, vol. 34 (2014)
22. Herre, H.: General formal ontology (GFO): a foundational ontology for conceptual modelling. In: Poli, R., Healy, M., Kameas, A. (eds.) Theory and Applications of Ontology: Computer Applications, pp. 297–345. Springer, Heidelberg (2010). https://doi.org/10.1007/978-90-481-8847-5_14
23. Gangemi, A., Guarino, N., Masolo, C., Oltramari, A., Schneider, L.: Sweetening ontologies with DOLCE. In: Gómez-Pérez, A., Benjamins, V.R. (eds.) EKAW 2002. LNCS (LNAI), vol. 2473, pp. 166–181. Springer, Heidelberg (2002). https://doi.org/10.1007/3-540-45810-7_18
24. Wand, Y., Weber, R.: Toward a theory of the deep structure of information systems. In: International Conference on Information Systems, Copenhagen, Denmark, pp. 61–71 (1990)
25. Wand, Y., Weber, R.: An ontological analysis of some fundamental information systems concepts. In: Proceedings of the Ninth International Conference on Information Systems, vol. 1988, pp. 213–226 (1988)
26. Wand, Y., Weber, R.: Thirty years later: some reflections on ontological analysis in conceptual modeling. J. Database Manag. (JDM) **28**(1), 1–17 (2017)
27. Burton-Jones, A., Recker, J., Indulska, M., Green, P., Weber, R.: Assessing representation theory with a framework for pursuing success and failure. MIS Q. **41**(4), 1307–1333 (2017)
28. Wyssusek, B.: On ontological foundations of conceptual modelling. Scand. J. Inf. Syst. **18**(1), 63–80 (2006)
29. Bunge, M.A.: Treatise on Basic Philosophy: Ontology I: The Furniture of The World. Reidel, Boston (1977)
30. Bunge, M.A.: Treatise on Basic Philosophy: Ontology II: A World of Systems. Reidel Publishing Company, Boston (1979)
31. Bunge, M.A., et al.: Mario Bunge: A Centenary Festschrift. Springer, Cham (2019). https://doi.org/10.1007/978-3-030-16673-1
32. Rosemann, M., Wyssusek, B.: Enhancing the expressiveness of the Bunge-Wand-Weber ontology. In: AMCIS 2005 Proceedings, pp. 1–8 (2005)
33. Wand, Y., Weber, R.: On the ontological expressiveness of information systems analysis and design grammars. Inf. Syst. J. **3**(4), 217–237 (1993)
34. Wand, Y., Weber, R.: Mario Bunge's ontology as a formal foundation for information systems concepts. In: Weingartner, P., Dorn, G. (eds.) Rodopi, pp. 123–150 (1990)
35. Jabbari, M., Lukyanenko, R., Recker, J., Samuel, B., Castellanos, A.: Conceptual modeling research: revisiting and updating Wand and Weber's 2002 research agenda. In: AIS SIGSAND, pp. 1–12 (2018)
36. Saghafi, A., Wand, Y.: Conceptual models? A meta-analysis of empirical work. In: Hawaii International Conference on System Sciences, Big Island, HI, pp. 1–15 (2014)
37. Veres, C., Mansson, G.: Psychological foundations for concept modeling. In: Blackwell, A.F., Marriott, K., Shimojima, A. (eds.) Diagrams 2004. LNCS (LNAI), vol. 2980, pp. 26–28. Springer, Heidelberg (2004). https://doi.org/10.1007/978-3-540-25931-2_5
38. Bunge, M.A.: Chasing reality: strife over realism. University of Toronto Press, Toronto (2006)
39. Bunge, M.A.: Treatise on Basic Philosophy: Ethics: The Good and The Right. Springer, Amsterdam (1989). https://doi.org/10.1007/978-94-009-2601-1
40. Bunge, M.A.: Between Two Worlds: Memoirs of a Philosopher-Scientist. Springer, Heidelberg (2016). https://doi.org/10.1007/978-3-319-29251-9

41. Bunge, M.A.: The dark side of technological progress. In: Sassower, R., Laor, N. (eds.) The Impact of Critical Rationalism, pp. 109–113. Springer, Cham (2019). https://doi.org/10.1007/978-3-319-90826-7_10

42. Bunge, M.A.: Treatise on Basic Philosophy: Semantics I: Sense and Reference. Springer, Amsterdam (1974). https://doi.org/10.1007/978-94-010-9920-2

43. Bunge, M.A.: Treatise on Basic Philosophy: Volume 6: Epistemology & Methodology II: Understanding the World. Reidel, Boston (1983)

44. Bunge, M.A.: Finding Philosophy in Social Science. Yale University Press, New Haven (1996)

45. Bunge, M.A.: Philosophy of Science: Volume 2, From Explanation to Justification. Routledge, New York (2017)

46. Bunge, M.A.: Systems everywhere. In: Cybernetics and Applied Systems, pp. 23–41. CRC Press, London (2018)

47. Bunge, M.A.: Emergence and Convergence: Qualitative Novelty and the Unity of Knowledge. University of Toronto Press, Toronto (2003)

48. Bunge, M.A.: Systemism: the alternative to individualism and holism. J. Soc. Econ. **2**(29), 147–157 (2000)

49. Bunge, M.A.: Gravitational waves and spacetime. Found. Sci. **23**(2), 399–403 (2018). https://doi.org/10.1007/s10699-017-9526-y

50. Agazzi, E.: Systemic thinking. In: Matthews, M.R. (ed.) Mario Bunge: A Centenary Festschrift, pp. 219–240. Springer, Cham (2019). https://doi.org/10.1007/978-3-030-16673-1_13

51. Parsons, J., Wand, Y.: Emancipating instances from the tyranny of classes in information modeling. ACM Trans. Database Syst. **25**(2), 228–268 (2000)

52. Hirst, R.J.: The Problems of Perception. Routledge, London (2002)

53. Hempel, C.G.: Philosophy of Natural Science. Pearson, London (1966)

54. Milton, S.K.: Ontological foundations of representational information systems. Scand. J. Inf. Syst. **19**(1), 5 (2007)

55. Bodart, F., Weber, R.: Optional properties versus subtyping in conceptual modeling: a theory and empirical test. In: International Conference on Information Systems (1996)

56. Burton-Jones, A., Weber, R.: Properties do not have properties: investigating a questionable conceptual modeling practice. In: Annual Symposium on Research in Systems Analysis and Design (2003)

57. Gemino, A., Wand, Y.: Complexity and clarity in conceptual modeling: comparison of mandatory and optional properties. Data Knowl. Eng. **55**(3), 301–326 (2005)

58. Lukyanenko, R., Parsons, J., Wiersma, Y.F., Wachinger, G., Huber, B., Meldt, R.: Representing crowd knowledge: guidelines for conceptual modeling of user-generated content. J. Assoc. Inf. Syst. **18**(4), 297–339 (2017)

59. Lukyanenko, R., Parsons, J., Samuel, B.M.: Representing instances: the case for reengineering conceptual modeling grammars. Eur. J. Inf. Syst. **28**(1), 68–90 (2019). https://doi.org/10.1080/0960085X.2018.1488567

60. Samuel, B.M., Khatri, V., Ramesh, V.: Exploring the effects of extensional versus intentional representations on domain understanding. MIS Q. **42**(4), 1187–1209 (2018)

A New DEMO Modelling Tool that Facilitates Model Transformations

Thomas Gray[1], Dominik Bork[2] (iD), and Marné De Vries[1 (✉)] (iD)

[1] Department of Industrial and Systems Engineering,
University of Pretoria, Pretoria, South Africa
{Thomas.Gray,Marne.DeVries}@up.ac.za
[2] Faculty of Computer Science, University of Vienna, Vienna, Austria
Dominik.Bork@univie.ac.at

Abstract. The age of digitization requires rapid design and re-design of enterprises. Rapid changes can be realized using conceptual modelling. The *design and engineering methodology for organizations* (DEMO) is an established modelling method for representing the organization domain of an enterprise. However, heterogeneity in enterprise design stakeholders generally demand for transformations between conceptual modelling languages. Specifically, in the case of DEMO, a transformation into business process modelling and notation (BPMN) models is desirable to account to both, the semantic sound foundation of the DEMO models, and the wide adoption of the de-facto industry standard BPMN. Model transformation can only be efficiently applied if tool support is available. Our research starts with a state-of-the-art analysis, comparing existing DEMO modelling tools. Using a design science research approach, our main contribution is the development of a DEMO modelling tool on the ADOxx platform. One of the main features of our tool is that it addresses stakeholder heterogeneity by enabling transformation of a DEMO organization construction diagram (OCD) into a BPMN collaboration diagram. A demonstration case shows the feasibility of our newly developed tool.

Keywords: DEMO · BPMN · ADOxx · Model transformation · Model consistency · Modelling tool

1 Introduction

The age of digitization requires rapid design and re-design of enterprises. In addition, the agile design paradigm embraces the use of multiple modelling languages to represent design knowledge. Unfortunately, this paradigm also has challenges regarding inconsistencies between model types that represent knowledge from the same knowledge domain. Modelling researchers should ensure to create models, languages, and methods that can be adapted to changing requirements in the future [1, p. 3].

Domain-specific languages are created to provide insight and understanding within a particular domain context and stakeholder group [2]. As an example, the *design and engineering methodology for organizations* (DEMO) provides models that represent the organization domain of an enterprise [3]. DEMO offers a unique design perspective, since

© Springer Nature Switzerland AG 2020
S. Nurcan et al. (Eds.): BPMDS 2020/EMMSAD 2020, LNBIP 387, pp. 359–374, 2020.
https://doi.org/10.1007/978-3-030-49418-6_25

its *four aspect models* have the ability to represent *organization design domain* knowledge in a concise and consistent way, removing technological realization and implementation details [3]. One of DEMO's aspect models, the construction model, incorporates an *organization construction diagram* (OCD) that provides a concise representation of enterprise operations. Managers value the OCD, since it becomes a blueprint that enables discussions on enterprise (re-)design and strategic alignment [3, 4]. Recker et al. [5] and Van Nuffel et al. [6] indicated that unguided use of the *Business Process Modeling Notation* (BPMN) constructs often leads to inconsistent models. It is thus our goal to combine the strengths of DEMO and BPMN by proposing a model transformation and modelling tool support.

Due to its characteristics of being consistent and concise, various authors experimented with transformations between modelling languages, as discussed in the remaining paragraph. De Kinderen, Gaaloul and Proper [7] indicated that "ArchiMate lacks specificity on how to model different perspectives *in-depth*" while [8, 9] add that ArchiMate lacks in expressing value exchange. As a solution to these deficiencies, [7] conducted a study to map concepts from DEMO to concepts contained within the business layer of the ArchiMate meta-model with the purpose of modelling the essential aspects of an enterprise first in DEMO, followed by a transformation into an ArchiMate model, adding technological realization and implementation details. Based on the work of Ceatano et al. [10] and Heller [11], Mraz et al. [12] presented transformation specifications to generate BPMN models from DEMO models. Yet, the specifications did not consider the complexity of hierarchical structures in DEMO models. In addition, their transformation specifications were not supported by tooling to automate DEMO-BPMN transformations.

This study starts with an evaluation of existing DEMO modelling tools. We conclude that existing modelling tools do not support all of DEMO's four *aspect models*. In addition, the tools do not facilitate transformations to other languages, such as BPMN. The main objective of this article is to address stakeholder heterogeneity by developing a DEMO modelling tool on the ADOxx platform. We demonstrate one of the main features of our tool, namely to transform a DEMO organization construction diagram (OCD) into a corresponding BPMN collaboration diagram.

The article is structured as follows. Section 2 provides background on multi-view modelling, as well as the existing knowledge on DEMO concepts that are explained via a demonstration case. Using design science research, as presented in Sect. 3, we present the requirements for a new DEMO tool in Sect. 4 and the DEMO constructional components that form part of the OMiLAB ecosystem, in Sect. 5. We also demonstrate the key functionality of the new DEMO tool, i.e. semi-automatic OCD-BPMN transformations for one out of four identified transformation scenarios. Section 6 ends with conclusions and suggestions for future research.

2 Background

Model-based development (MBD) approaches suggest separation of concerns, using multiple views, to manage the complexity of modern software systems [13]. Yet, one of the challenges of multi-view modelling is the lack of consistency management [14].

Bork [15] emphasised the need to develop consistent and concise conceptual models for domain-specific languages. Prior to developing tool support and model transformation, language specifications should at least consider to provide syntax, semantics, and notation for the different viewpoints [16].

Mulder [17] also acknowledged the need to validate the existing DEMO specification language (DEMOSL) prior to developing tool support. Using the meta-model definition presented by [18], metamodels should be sufficiently *complete* to describe all *set of models* (i.e. multiple viewpoints) that are allowed, rejecting models that are not valid. In addition, the metamodel should enable partial *transformation* of the model (e.g. from ontological to implementation level). With respect to the DEMO metamodels, Mulder [17] already suggested improvements regarding the multiple viewpoints evident in four aspect models. Since our first version of the DEMO-ADOxx tool only includes the construction model (CM), we elaborate within the next section on the updated metamodel for the CM.

2.1 DEMO Models and Metamodels

DEMO uses four linguistically based *aspect models* to represent the ontological model of the *organisation domain* of the enterprise, namely the *construction model* (CM), *process model* (PM), *action model* (AM), and *fact model* (FM) that exclude technology implementation details [19]. Each model is represented by different diagrams and tables, as illustrated in Fig. 1.

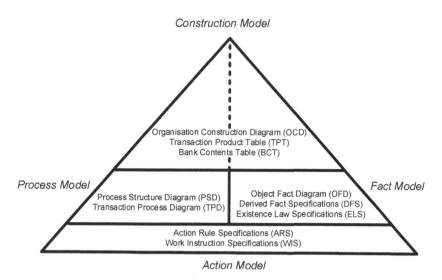

Fig. 1. DEMO aspect models with diagram types and tables, based on [19] and [20]

The ontological model is based on a key discovery that forms the basis of the aspect models, namely the identification of a *complete transaction pattern* that involves two *actor roles*, a *production act* (and fact), and *multiple coordination acts* (and facts) that are performed in a particular order [19]. Although it is possible to identify three different *sorts* of a transaction kind (TK), i.e. *original, informational* and *documental*, the four aspect models primarily focus on the *original* sort. A TK can also be classified as an *elementary* TK when it is executed by only one actor role, or an *aggregate* TK (ATK) when it is executed by multiple actor roles. Also, an *actor role* can be classified as either an *elementary actor role* (EAR) when s/he executes one TK and a *composite actor role* (CAR) when s/he is the executor of more than one TK [19, 20].

The concepts that were discussed so far, as well as the relationships between concepts, are described via a metamodel presented in [19]. Mulder [17] identified several inconsistencies with regards to the CM, addressing the issues in [21]. Figure 2 presents an updated metamodel that incorporates the extensions suggested by Mulder [21]. Note that the *Scope of Interest* (SoI) is not modelled as a separate concept, since Mulder [21] argues that the SoI is equivalent to the CAR. The relationships and cardinalities in Fig. 2 signify modelling constraints when a modeller composes a CM. The constraints should also be incorporated in the modelling tool. As an example, a single relationship exists between *Transaction Kind* (TK) and *Aggregate Transaction Kind* (ATK) in Fig. 2. The relationship can be interpreted in a *forward direction* as: "One TK is contained in zero or many ATKs". The relationship interpretation of the *reverse direction* is: "One ATK contains one or many TKs".

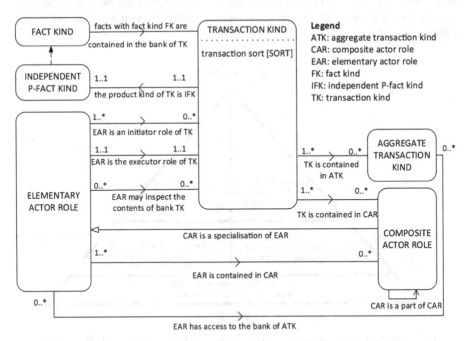

Fig. 2. DEMO construction model metamodel Version 3.7 [19] with extensions of [21]

2.2   The Demonstration Case

The demonstration case had to include the necessary complexity to ensure that a modeler would be able to construct a TPT (illustrated in Fig. 3) and an OCD (illustrated in Fig. 4) with all the relationships and cardinalities depicted in Fig. 2. Selecting a fictitious college as the universe of discourse, *some operations of the college* regarding the presentation of a new project-based module at the college, are incorporated, listed as *transaction kinds* in Fig. 3.

transaction ID	transaction kind	product ID	product kind
(T01)	supervisor allocation	(P01)	Supervisor-allocation is started
(T02)	project sponsoring	(P02)	the sponsorship of Project is done
(T03)	ip clearance	(P03)	the ip-clearance for Project is obtained
(T04)	module revision	(P04)	the revision of Module is done
(T05)	project control	(P05)	the project-control for Period is done
(T06)	internal project sponsoring	(P06)	the internal sponsorship of Project is done
(T07)	project involvement	(P07)	Project-involvement is started

Fig. 3. The TPT for a college, based on [19]

The reader is referred to [19] for a comprehensive introduction to the OCD and legend for concepts included in Fig. 2 and Fig. 4. In our demonstrating OCD, portrayed in Fig. 4, we assume that we only include TKs that are of the *original transaction sort,* in accordance with the guidelines presented by Dietz [20] to focus on the essential TKs. Based on the concepts declared in [19], we use **bold** style to indicate the type of construct and *italics* when referring to an instance of the construct (see Fig. 4).

Scope of Interest (SoI) indicates that the modeler analyses a particular scope of operations, namely *some operations at a college*. Given the SoI, Fig. 4 indicates that three **environmental actor roles** are defined, see the grey-shaded constructs *student,* *project sponsor* and *HR of project sponsor* that form part of the environment. Within the SoI, multiple **transaction kinds (TKs)** are linked to different types of **actor roles** via **initiation links** or **executor links**. As an example, *supervisor allocation (T01)* is a **TK** that is initiated (via an **initiation link**) by the **environmental actor role** *student (CA01)*. In accordance with [20], the *student (CA01)* is by default also regarded to be a **composite actor role** "of which one does not know (or want to know) the details". Since *T01* is linked to an **environmental actor role**, it is also called a **border transaction kind**. *T01* is executed (via the **executor link**) by the **elementary actor role** named *supervisor allocator (A01)*.

All the other actor roles in Fig. 4 within the **SoI** are **elementary actor roles**, since each of them is only responsible for executing one **transaction kind**. A special case of is where an **elementary actor role** is both the **initiator** and **executor** of a **transaction kind**, also called a **self-activating actor role**. Figure 4 exemplifies the **self-activating actor role** with *module reviser (A04)* and *project controller (A05)*. Since **actor roles** need to use facts created and stored in transaction banks, an **information link** is used to indicate access to facts. As an example, Fig. 4 indicates that *project controller (A05)* has an **information link** to **transaction kind** *module revision (T04)*, indicating that the *project controller (A05)* uses facts in the transaction bank of *module revision (T04)*. It is also possible that **actor roles** within the **SoI** need to use facts that are created via **transaction kinds** that are outside the **SoI**. As an example, Fig. 4 indicates that **actor roles** within the **SoI** (called, *some operations at a college*) need to use facts that are created outside the SoI and stored in the transaction banks of **aggregate transaction kinds,** namely *person facts* of *AT01, college facts* of *AT02, accreditation facts* of *AT03, timetable facts* of *AT04* and *student enrollment facts* of *AT05*. According to Fig. 4, the *student enrollment facts* of **aggregate transaction kind** *AT05* are not accessed by any **actor roles**, which should be possible (according to the meta-model depicted in Fig. 2).

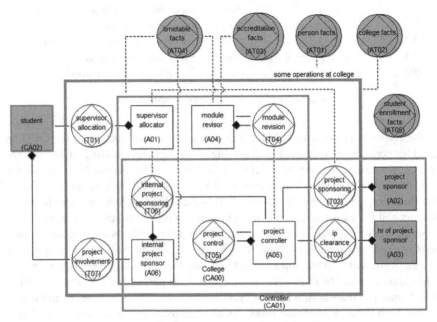

Fig. 4. The OCD for a college, based on [19]

Even though Fig. 4 only includes **elementary actor roles** within the **SoI**, it is possible to consolidate **elementary actor roles** within a **composite actor role**, where a composite actor role "is a network of transaction kinds and (elementary) actor roles" [20]. Figure 4 illustrates two **composite actor roles** within the **SoI,** namely *College (CA0)* and *Controller (CA01)*. Both *CA00* and *CA01* encapsulate a number of transaction kinds and elementary actor roles.

3   Research Method

Applying *design science research* (DSR), we developed the DEMO-ADOxx modelling tool. According to Gregor & Hevner's [22] knowledge contribution framework, the modelling tool can be considered as an improvement, since the tool will be used for solving a known problem. Referring to the DSR steps of Peffers et al. [23], this article addresses the *five steps* of the DSR cycle in the following way:

Identify a Problem: In Sect. 4.1 we present minimal requirements for a useful DEMO modelling tool. Based on the requirements, we assess in Sect. 4.2 that existing DEMO modelling tools are inadequate.

Define Objectives of the Solution: In Sects. 4.3 and 4.4 we specify a new DEMO-ADOxx tool to address the requirements. We highlight that the DEMO-ADOxx tool only supports one of the four aspect models, namely the CM. Furthermore, the tool only incorporates two of the three CM representations, namely the OCD and TPT.

Design and Development: In accordance with the specification, we developed a DEMO-ADOxx tool, whose constructional components are presented in Sect. 5.

Demonstration: In accordance with the demonstration case, discussed in Sect. 2.2, we demonstrate the tool, highlighting its key feature, i.e. the transformation of a user-selected transaction kind of an OCD into a corresponding BPMN diagram.

Evaluation: Evaluation was restricted to internal testing, using the DEMO-ADOxx tool to model a more extensive case (than the demonstration case in Sect. 2.2). Individual test scenarios were created to validate each of the relationships and cardinalities illustrated in Fig. 2. The study excluded further evaluation, but Sect. 6 provides suggestions on further evaluating and extending the DEMO-ADOxx tool.

4   Requirements Elicitation and DEMO Tool Specification

A number of tools exist that support, to a limited extent, the creation of DEMO models. Before we compare these tools, the next section presents three categories of tool requirements from the perspective of a DEMO modeller.

4.1   DEMO Requirements

During the development of new software application systems, the analyst needs to consider three main categories of requirements, namely functional requirements, non-functional requirements, and design constraints [24]. In terms of the DEMO modelling tool, *functional requirements* regard the inputs, outputs, functions and features that are needed [24] (see R1 to R3 below). The *non-functional requirements* (see R4 and R5 below) incorporate the qualities of a system, such as performance, cost, security, and usability. The *design constraints* pose restrictions on the design of the system to meet technical, business, or contractual obligations. Next, we present initial requirements for a DEMO tool, structured according to the first two categories. The purpose is to compare and evaluate the existing DEMO tools in terms of the following *minimum requirements* defined from the perspective of a lecturer teaching DEMO:

- R1: The DEMO tool should be *comprehensive* in supporting all of the DEMO aspect models, namely the CM, PM, AM and FM (refer to Fig. 1).
- R2: The DEMO tool should support the most recent published language specification, i.e. *DEMOSL 3.7* (see [19]) and the extensions that have been published (see [21]). The tool should be ready to accommodate future upgrades of the DEMO language.
- R3: The DEMO tool should facilitate *model transformations* to other modelling languages such as BPMN.
- R4: The DEMO tool should be available at *low cost*, especially for educational purposes.
- R5: The DEMO tool should be *usable*, i.e. user-friendly.

We used Nassar's *usability* requirements [25] to perform initial usability tests on some of the available DEMO tools:

- U1 Consistency: The system needs to be consistent in its actions, so that the modeller can get used to the system without constantly having to adapt to a new way of doing things. Consistency should apply to the way icons and commands are displayed and used.
- U2 User Control: The system should offer the user control in the way the model is built and run. This could include cancelling/pausing operations, undoing or redoing steps. The modeller should be able to foresee or undo errors.
- U3 Ease of learning: The system should be easy to learn for a new modeller. This is achieved by avoiding icons, layouts and terms that are unfamiliar to the modeller.
- U4 Flexibility: The system is expected to offer different ways to accomplish the same task so that the user experiences maximum freedom. Examples include shortcut keys, different icon options or even layout customisation.
- U5 Error Management: The system is expected to have built-in counter-measures to prevent mistakes by displaying error messages, warning icons or simply preventing incorrect placement of model elements.
- U6 Reduction of Excess: The system should avoid displaying unnecessary information or adding unnecessary functionality to the tool. The program should be functional and easy to understand.
- U7 Visibility of System Status: The user of the system should be aware of the status of the system at all times. For example, if a command does not occur instantaneously, then the system should inform the user of the delay.

4.2   Evaluating Existing DEMO Tools

In this section, we provide an overview of the existing tools, starting with a list presented in [26], adding Abacus and our ADOxx tool. In a first phase, we evaluated existing tools in terms of requirements R1 to R4 (see Table 1) using the following methods in order of preference: (1) experimenting with the tools that were available; (2) contacting the tool owners for information about their tools; and (3) using the tool evaluation results of Mulder [26]. During a second phase, we tested the usability (R5) of four tools that were openly available (see Table 2).

Table 1. Evaluation results for functional and meta-model requirements

Requirement No ->	R1				R2	R3	R4	Legend	
Aspect model	CM	PM	AM	FM				●	Fully supports
Aris	●	○	○	○	○	○	◐		
CaseWise modeler	●	●	○	●	○	○	?	◐	Partially supports
Connexio knowledge system	●	○	●	●	○	○	○		
DemoWorld	●	●	○	●	○	○	◐	○	Does not support
EC-Mod	●	◐	○	○	○	○	○		
Plena	●	●	◐	◐	★	○	◐	★	Does not support, but
ModelWorld	●	●	○	●	○	○	●		vision for future
uSoft studio	●	○	○	○	○	○	?		
Visio	●	○	○	●	○	○	◐	?	Level of support is unclear
Xemod	●	●	○	●	○	○	○		
Abacus	●	◐	○	○	○	○	◐		
DEMO-ADOxx	●	○	○	○	●	●	●		

Table 2. Evaluation of usability requirements

	U1	U2	U3	U4	U5	U6	U7
Abacus	●	●	●	●	●	●	●
ModelWorld	●	○	●	○	●	●	○
Plena	●	●	◐	●	●	◐	●
DEMO-ADOxx	●	●	●	◐	●	●	●

Phase 1 Evaluation: In Table 1, we present evaluation results of existing DEMO tools with respect to R1 to R4, indicating the extent to which a specific tool meets a requirement, as explained in the legend of Table 1. R1, R2 and R4 were evaluated by Mulder [26] already. In his study he found that only Plena (of the studied tools) complies with R1 (i.e. support all four DEMO aspect models), none of the tools comply with R2 (i.e. supports the DEMOSL 3.7 specification language with extensions), and only ModelWorld complies with R4 (i.e. is available free of charge for academics and students).

Our ADOxx tool does not comply with R1, since the initial focus of the tool is to support the CM. For R2, the ADOxx tool supports DEMOSL 3.7 and the extensions. For R3 only the ADOxx tool supports transformations from DEMO models to other model types. Regarding R4, the ADOxx tool is free of cost for education purposes.

Phase 2 Evaluation: We had access to three of the existing DEMO modelling tools listed in Table 1, namely Abacus, ModelWorld and Plena. Using Nassar's *usability* requirements [25] listed in Sect. 4.1, we evaluated each of the three tools, also adding the DEMO-ADOxx tool, to gain some insights regarding their usability. The results are summarised in Table 2, indicating that three of the tools have usability *drawbacks*:

- *Modelworld* scored very low on U2 (User Control), U4 (Flexibility) and U7 (Visibility on System Status). Regarding U2 and U4, the modeller is unable to cancel any steps, undo any actions or navigate forwards and backwards. Basic keyboard shortcuts are not available to the user, such as the delete key. With reference to U7, ModelWorld offers no indication regarding the status of the system.
- *Plena* scored low on U3 (Ease of Learning), and U6 (Reduction of Excess). Plena is initially a challenge to use as it needs to be installed separately from Enterprise Architect and then imported as a plugin. Since Plena is a plugin to Enterprise Architect, some functionality is not applicable to DEMO.
- *DEMO-ADOxx* scored low on U4 (Flexibility), since the tool deviates from the standard drag-and-drop behaviour of other modelling tools. For this tool, a modeller needs to "left-click" on the construct in the template, dropping the construct by "left-clicking" within the modelling area on the right. It is possible to reason that the drag-and-drop behaviour is merely a behaviour-preference of one modeller and that *other modellers* will not highlight this as a usability deficiency.

The purpose of the evaluation was to provide an overview of the existing DEMO modelling tools to establish whether a new DEMO tool was needed. Even though existing tools are available, our main concern is that existing tools do not address requirements R2, R3 and R4. The new DEMO-ADOxx tool has been developed as a main deliverable for this study to address these three requirements. In terms of R1, the next section motivates the decision to initially set the scope to the DEMO CM.

4.3 DEMO Tool Specifications for the OCD and TPT

A qualitative analysis on DEMO aspect models, indicate that the CM, detailed by the PM, are useful for assigning responsibilities and duties to individuals [4]. The AM and FM "are necessary if you are going to develop or select applications" [4]. Since the conceptual knowledge embedded in the PM is similar to the BPMN collaboration diagram [12] and BPMN is widely adopted by industry [27, 28], the initial DEMO-ADOxx tool focuses on the CM. We exclude the PM, since the PM logic can be also represented by the industry-accepted notation BPMN. Our tool ensures consistent OCD-derived BPMN collaboration diagrams that incorporate the logic embedded in the *DEMO standard transaction pattern* as defined in [19].

We incorporated recent specifications regarding the OCD and TPT, as stated in [19] and [21], as well as BPMN 2.0 [29] for the first version of the DEMO-ADOxx tool. All of the existence rules, shown in Fig. 2 were implemented, except for one. The rule "facts with fact kind FK are contained in the bank of TK", indicated on Fig. 2, has not been incorporated in the DEMO-ADOxx tool, since it relates to the *bank contents table* (BCT), and the BCT relates to concepts that are used as part of the FM.

4.4 OCD-BPMN Transformations Specification

We identified four transformation scenarios that should be addressed by the DEMO tool. The specifications are excluded for the purpose of this article. Although the ADOxx-DEMO tool incorporates all four scenarios, we only include the *second scenario*, since this scenario already includes complexity of parent-and-part TKs. Referring back to the OCD depicted in Fig. 4, the four scenarios are as follows:

- *Scenario 1: Customer-initiated TK with no parts.* For this scenario, an **actor role** that is outside the **scope-of-interest**, initiates a **TK**. Also, the **TK** does not have any parts, i.e., the **executor** of the **TK**, is **not initiating** other **TKs**. Referring to Fig. 4, the TK labelled *T01* (*supervisor allocation*) is an example of this scenario. *T01* is initiated by the **actor role** *student*. The **executor** of *T01* is the *supervisor allocator.* Yet, the *supervisor allocator* does not initiate any other TKs as parts.
- *Scenario 2: TK is part of another TK.* For this scenario, the selected **TK** forms part of another **TK**. Referring to Fig. 4 the TK labelled *T07* (*project involvement*) is **initiated** by an **actor role** *A06* (*internal project sponsor*). Since the *internal project sponsor* is both the **executor** of *T06* (*internal project sponsoring*) and the **initiator** of *T07* (*project involvement*), *T07* is a part of *T06*.
- *Scenario 3: TK is self-initiating.* For this scenario, the selected **TK** is **initiated** and **executed** by the same **actor role**. Referring to Fig. 4, the TK labelled *T04* (*module revision*) is **initiated** and **executed** by *A04* (*module reviser*).
- *Scenario 4: TK has one or more parts.* For this scenario, the selected **TK** has one or more parts, i.e. the **actor role** that **executes** the **TK**, is also **initiating** one or more other **TKs**. Referring to Fig. 4 the TK labelled *T5* (*project control*) is executed by **actor role** *A05* (*project controller*). The same **actor role** *A05* (*project controller*) also **initiates** multiple other **TKs**, namely *T02* (*project sponsoring*), *T03* (*IP clearance*), and *T06* (*internal project sponsoring*).

5   Demonstration of the DEMO-ADOxx Tool in Use

The ADOxx platform, part the Open Models Laboratory (OMiLAB) digital ecosystem, is designed to support conceptualization and operationalization of conceptual modelling methods [30]. ADOxx allows a developer to create new modelling tools, or to extend existing ones to cater for any number of user requirements and customizations. The DEMO-ADOxx tool is realized as an OMiLAB project which enables free download[1].

---

[1] DEMO-ADOxx download: https://austria.omilab.org/psm/content/demo, last accessed: 09.04.2020.

5.1 Modelling and Validation Features

Figure 5 illustrates two main tool sections: (1) *Explorer* section - models (created before) are listed far left; and (2) *Modelling* section - OCD constructs are selected by "left-clicking" on the construct in the template, dropping the construct by "left-clicking" within the modelling area on the right. The relationships can be created either from dragging and dropping, or by using the *model assistant* which allows one to create a relationship directly from an existing construct in the model.

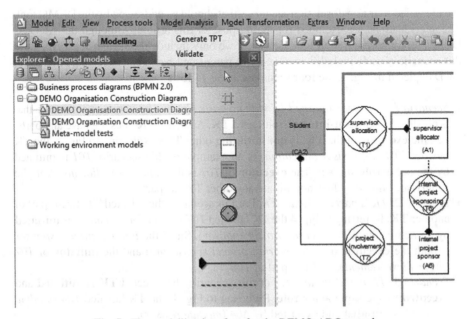

Fig. 5. The modelling interface for the DEMO-ADOxx tool

At the top of the screen are the menu options depicted. We implemented a *Model Analysis* menu that provides the option to either generate a TPT such as the one in Fig. 3, or to validate a model.

The *Validation* feature implemented each of the existence rules (relationships and cardinalities) presented in Fig. 2, except for one, as indicated before in Sect. 4.3. Figure 6 illustrates a validation table that communicates to the modeller: (1) The nature of a mistake in the model; and (2) The model constructs involved.

Based on the demonstration case discussed in Sect. 2.2, we used the new tool to generate an OCD (see Fig. 4) as well as a TPT (see Fig. 3) by utilizing the implemented semi-automatic model transformations of the DEMO-ADOxx tool.

5.2 Transformation Features

Selecting the *Model Transformation* menu option, the modeller can select one of the transaction kinds in the current OCD model. In our example the modeller selected *T07*

Description	Elements involved
Relationship with CAR needs to be more specific:	College
Actor role does not execute transaction kind:	supervisor allocator
No product kind defined	supervisor allocation
No product kind defined	project involvement

Fig. 6. Validation feature of the DEMO-ADOxx tool

(project involvement) that represents a *Scenario 2* transformation. The modeller also needs to specify the detail of interaction between parent-and-part TK's. In addition, cardinalities that exist between relevant parent-part structures, have to be specified by the modeller. As an example, Fig. 4 indicates that T07 is initiated by A06 (*internal project sponsor*). Yet, A06 is also the executor of T06 (*internal project sponsoring*). Therefore, T06 can only be requested when a T07 has made some progress through the sequence of coordination acts associated with the universal transaction pattern.

As indicated in Fig. 7, the modeller needs to indicate how T07 (project involvement) is initiated as a-part-of-T06 (internal project sponsoring), i.e. which one of the four basic coordination facts for T06 (requested, promised, stated or accepted) is a prerequisite for initiating T07. In addition, the modeller needs to indicate the cardinalities involved between one instance of the parent (T06) that generates a number of instances of the part (T07). For our demonstration (see Fig. 7), the modeller indicated that an instance of T06 has to be *stated* before T07 is *requested*. Also, one instance of T06 initiates zero-to-many (0..*) instances of T07. Since the transaction-progress of the parts may also regulate the transaction-progress of the parent, the modeller also has to indicate how the zero-to-many (0..*) part-instances (T06 instances) should all be *accepted* before the parent instance (T07 instance) can be *accepted*.

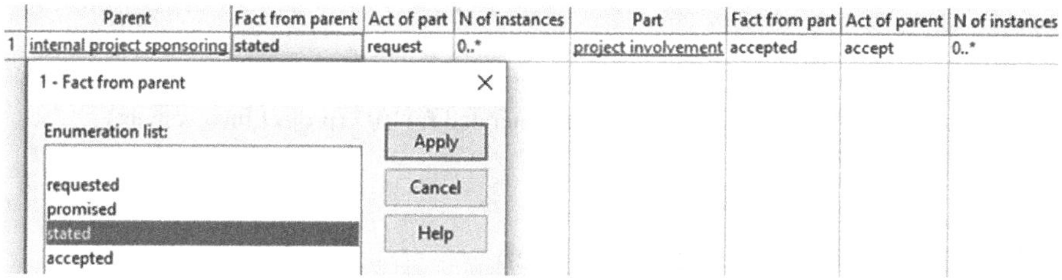

	Parent	Fact from parent	Act of part	N of instances	Part	Fact from part	Act of parent	N of instances
1	internal project sponsoring	stated	request	0..*	project involvement	accepted	accept	0..*

1 - Fact from parent   ✕

Enumeration list: Apply

requested   Cancel
promised
stated   Help
accepted

Fig. 7. User-interface to specify cardinalities for parent-part structures

Based on the modeller selections illustrated in Fig. 7, the DEMO-ADOxx tool automatically generates the corresponding BPMN collaboration diagram (see Fig. 8). The BPMN diagram (Fig. 8) presents the initiating actor role (*internal project sponsor*) as a BPMN pool and the executing actor role (*student*) as a BPMN pool. In accordance with transformation specifications (not detailed in this article), transaction pattern detail for the *standard pattern*, is depicted via BPMN concepts.

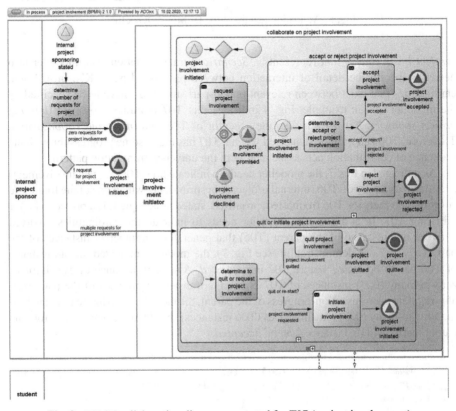

Fig. 8. BPMN collaboration diagram generated for T07 (project involvement)

6   Conclusions and Future Research

Our research indicated that existing DEMO modelling tools do not meet the minimum requirements. One of the key requirements is that the modelling tool needs to allow for model transformations, specifically transformations from a DEMO OCD to a BPMN collaboration diagram.

We have used two sets of specifications, (1) recent DEMO specifications from [19] and [21], and (2) OCD-BPMN transformation specifications, to develop a new DEMO-ADOxx tool to demonstrate the modelling and validation features, as well as the OCD-BPMN transformation feature.

The meta-model provided a good baseline for the DEMO-ADOxx tool. Yet, we accept that the meta-model will change in the future and these changes need to be accommodated by our tool in future. We still wait for feedback on the OCD-DEMO transformation specifications that will require further work on the DEMO-ADOxx tool. Realizing the tool as an open source project within the OMiLAB ensures that a community can take over future tool enhancements.

The demonstration case was useful in presenting the key features of the new DEMO-ADOxx tool. In terms of the *usability* requirements, additional evaluation is required. For future work, DEMO modellers will be involved during usability tests to inform further tool enhancements. In addition, a new version of DEMOSL will be released during 2020 and need to be incorporated within the DEMO-ADOxx tool.

References

1. Frank, U., Strecker, S., Fettke, P., Vom Brocke, J., Becker, J., Sinz, E.J.: The research field: modelling business information systems. Bus. Inf. Syst. Eng. **6**(1), 1–5 (2014). https://doi.org/10.1007/s12599-013-0301-5
2. Karagiannis, D., Mayr, H.C., Mylopoulos, J.: Domain-specific Conceptual Modeling: Concepts, Methods and Tools. Springer, Switzerland (2016). https://doi.org/10.1007/978-3-319-39417-6
3. Dietz, J.L.G.: Enterprise Ontology. Springer, Berlin (2006). https://doi.org/10.1007/3-540-33149-2
4. Décosse, C., Molnar, W.A., Proper, H.A.: What does DEMO do? A qualitative analysis about DEMO in practice: founders, modellers and beneficiaries. In: Aveiro, D., Tribolet, J., Gouveia, D. (eds.) EEWC 2014. LNBIP, vol. 174, pp. 16–30. Springer, Cham (2014). https://doi.org/10.1007/978-3-319-06505-2_2
5. Recker, J., Indulska, M., Rosemann, M., Green, P.: How good is BPMN really? Insights from theory and practice. In: Ljungberg, J., Andersson, M. (eds.) Proceedings 14th European Conference on Information Systems, ECIS, pp. 1582–1593 (2006)
6. Van Nuffel, D., Mulder, H., Van Kervel, S.: Enhancing the formal foundations of BPMN by enterprise ontology. In: Albani, A., Barjis, J., Dietz, J.L.G. (eds.) CIAO!/EOMAS -2009. LNBIP, vol. 34, pp. 115–129. Springer, Heidelberg (2009). https://doi.org/10.1007/978-3-642-01915-9_9
7. de Kinderen, S., Gaaloul, K., Proper, H.A.: On transforming DEMO models to ArchiMate. In: Bider, I., et al. (eds.) BPMDS/EMMSAD -2012. LNBIP, vol. 113, pp. 270–284. Springer, Heidelberg (2012). https://doi.org/10.1007/978-3-642-31072-0_19
8. Pijpers, V., Gordijn, G., Akkermans, H.: E3alignment: exploring inter-organizational alignment in networked value constellations. Int. J. Comput. Sci. Appl. **6**(5), 59–88 (2009)
9. Ettema, R., Dietz, J.L.G.: ArchiMate and DEMO – mates to date? In: Albani, A., Barjis, J., Dietz, J.L.G. (eds.) CIAO!/EOMAS -2009. LNBIP, vol. 34, pp. 172–186. Springer, Heidelberg (2009). https://doi.org/10.1007/978-3-642-01915-9_13
10. Caetano, A., Assis, A., Tribolet, J.: Using DEMO to analyse the consistency of business process models. In: Moller, C., Chaudhry, S. (eds.) Advances in Enterprise Information Systems II, pp. 133–146. Taylor & Francis Group, London (2012)
11. Heller, S.: Usage of DEMO methods for BPMN models creation. Czech Technical University in Prague (2016)
12. Mráz, O., Náplava, P., Pergl, R., Skotnica, M.: Converting DEMO PSI transaction pattern into BPMN: a complete method. In: Aveiro, D., Pergl, R., Guizzardi, G., Almeida, J.P., Magalhães,

R., Lekkerkerk, H. (eds.) EEWC 2017. LNBIP, vol. 284, pp. 85–98. Springer, Cham (2017). https://doi.org/10.1007/978-3-319-57955-9_7

13. France, R., Rumpe, B.: Model-based development. Softw. Syst. Model. **7**(1), 1–2 (2008)

14. Cicchetti, A., Ciccozzi, F., Pierantonio, A.: Multi-view approaches for software and system modelling: a systematic literature review. Softw. Syst. Model. **18**(6), 3207–3233 (2019). https://doi.org/10.1007/s10270-018-00713-w

15. Bork, D.: A development method for conceptual design of multi-view modeling tools with an emphasis on consistency requirements. University of Bamberg (2016)

16. Grundy, J., Hosking, J., Li, K.N., Ali, N.M., Huh, J., Li, R.L.: Generating domain-specific visual language tools from abstract visual specifications. IEEE Trans. Softw. Eng. **39**(4), 487–515 (2013)

17. Mulder, M.A.T.: Validating the DEMO specification language. In: Aveiro, D., Guizzardi, G., Guerreiro, S., Guédria, W. (eds.) EEWC 2018. LNBIP, vol. 334, pp. 131–143. Springer, Cham (2019). https://doi.org/10.1007/978-3-030-06097-8_8

18. Aßmann, U., Zschaler, S., Wagner, G.: Ontologies, meta-models, and the model driven paradigm. In: Calero, C., Ruiz, F., Piattini, M. (eds.) Ontologies for Software Engineering and Software Technology, pp. 249–273. Springer, Heidelberg (2006). https://doi.org/10.1007/3-540-34518-3_9

19. Dietz, J.L.G., Mulder, M.A.T.: DEMOSL-3: demo specification language version 3.7. SAPIO (2017)

20. Perinforma, A.P.C.: The Essence of Organisation, 3rd ed. Sapio (2017). www.sapio.nl

21. Mulder, M.A.T.: Towards a complete metamodel for DEMO CM. In: Debruyne, C., Panetto, H., Guédria, W., Bollen, P., Ciuciu, I., Meersman, R. (eds.) OTM 2018. LNCS, vol. 11231, pp. 97–106. Springer, Cham (2019). https://doi.org/10.1007/978-3-030-11683-5_10

22. Gregor, S., Hevner, A.: Positioning and presenting design science research for maximum impact. MIS Q. **37**(2), 337–355 (2013)

23. Peffers, K., Tuunanen, T., Rothenberger, M., Chatterjee, S.: A design science research methodology for information systems research. J. MIS **24**(3), 45–77 (2008)

24. Leffingwell, D.: Agile Software Requirements: Lean Requirements Practices for Teams, Programs, and the Enterprise. Addison-Wesley, New Jersey (2011)

25. Nassar, V.: Common criteria for usability review. Work **41**(Suppl 1), 1053–1057 (2012)

26. Mulder, M.A.T.: Enabling the automatic verification and exchange of DEMO models. Ph.D. thesis (n.d.)

27. Grigorova, K., Mironov, K.: Comparison of business process modeling standards. Int. J. Eng. Sci. Manag. Res. **1**(3), 1–8 (2014)

28. Recker, J., Wohed, P., Rosemann, M.: Representation theory versus workflow patterns – the case of BPMN. In: Embley, David W., Olivé, A., Ram, S. (eds.) ER 2006. LNCS, vol. 4215, pp. 68–83. Springer, Heidelberg (2006). https://doi.org/10.1007/11901181_7

29. Object Management Group: Business process model & notation. https://www.omg.org/bpmn/. Accessed 30 May 2019

30. Bork, D., Buchmann, R.A., Karagiannis, D., Lee, M., Miron, E.-T.: An open platform for modeling method conceptualisation: the OMiLAB digital ecosystem. Commun. AIS **44**(32), 673–697 (2019)

Reference Method for the Development of Domain Action Recognition Classifiers: The Case of Medical Consultations

Sabine Molenaar[✉], Laura Schiphorst, Metehan Doyran, Albert Ali Salah, Fabiano Dalpiaz, and Sjaak Brinkkemper

Department of Information and Computing Sciences,
Utrecht University, Utrecht, The Netherlands
{s.molenaar,l.a.f.schiphorst,m.doyran,a.a.salah,
f.dalpiaz,s.brinkkemper}@uu.nl

Abstract. Advances in human action recognition and interaction recognition enable the reliable execution of action classification tasks through machine learning algorithms. However, no systematic approach for developing such classifiers exists and since actions vary between domains, appropriate and usable datasets are uncommon. In this paper, we propose a reference method that assists non-experts in building classifiers for domain action recognition. To demonstrate feasibility, we instantiate it in a case study in the medical domain that concerns the recognition of basic actions of general practitioners. The developed classifier is effective, as it shows a prediction accuracy of 75.6% for the medical action classification task and of more than 90% for three related classification tasks. The study shows that the method can be applied to a specific activity context and that the resulting classifier has an acceptable prediction accuracy. In the future, fine-tuning of the method parameters will endorse the applicability to other domains.

Keywords: Human action recognition · Interaction recognition · Reference method · Method engineering · Machine learning · Domain action recognition classifier · Computer vision

1 Introduction

Machine Learning (ML) and Artificial Intelligence (AI) have been introduced to many different industries and fields of research to automate many tasks, including the recognition and classification of human actions. Large, context-specific datasets are needed to train, validate and test the classifiers, but not every available dataset can be used for every purpose [24]. When a specific classification task needs to be executed, chances are that no relevant dataset exists.

We focus on human action recognition: the classification problem of "*labeling videos containing human motion with action classes*" [20]. Thanks to the advancements in action recognition, researchers are now able to analyze more

© Springer Nature Switzerland AG 2020
S. Nurcan et al. (Eds.): BPMDS 2020/EMMSAD 2020, LNBIP 387, pp. 375–391, 2020.
https://doi.org/10.1007/978-3-030-49418-6_26

complex tasks such as human-human interaction recognition, which considers actions between two or more subjects, rather than the movement of a single subject. Additional challenges exist regarding (i) how to distinguish multiple subjects, (ii) subjects who (partially) block each other, and (iii) the lack of large datasets for the different contexts [24]. For this kind of classifier, no systematic method exists for their development, training, and validation.

To overcome this gap, we introduce a reference method for the development of classifiers for actions and interactions in a particular domain, including a sub-process for the creation of a suitable dataset: the DARC-method. Our aim is to increase the maturity of action recognition processes through the proposal of a reference method that can be used by people who have limited expertise in ML, such as information systems engineers. Besides providing an easy-to-follow process, our method provides links to literature in the field that a user may want to check to customize the method for the specific case at hand.

We describe our research method in Sect. 2 and discuss related work in Sect. 3. We present the reference method in Sect. 4. We demonstrate its feasibility in Sect. 5, by applying it to healthcare through the use of videos that record domain actions. Finally, in Sect. 6, we discuss validity threats, present our conclusions, and outline future work.

2   Research Method

Techniques, methods and processes for data analysis and ML already exist, but are not tailored to the specific purpose of developing domain action recognition classifiers[1]. Typically, ML literature assumes the reader has some knowledge or experience with ML. While they tend to have an implicit method, they predominantly explain how certain algorithms can be implemented and domain understanding is assumed when a case study is described. Therefore, we use an assembly-based method engineering approach, resulting in the following research question: *"How can a reference method be assembled for the development of domain action recognition classifiers?"*

Ralyté *et al.* [21] distinguish three main activities in their assembly-based process model: (i) specify method requirements, (ii) select method chunks and (iii) assemble chunks. In our case, the method requirements are as follows. First, the method should provide guidance to practitioners in information systems, rather than ML experts. Second, we focus only on action recognition classifiers. Third, we are concerned with classifiers for a given domain: the method should cover the entire process from domain understanding to deploying the classifier. However, the method should be domain-independent, i.e., applicable to any domain in which action recognition is used.

The reference method aims to provide a structured overview of the activities and deliverables and consistent terminology [27]. We hope our method mitigates the risk of introducing errors throughout the process. Also, since all activities

---

[1] Throughout this paper, 'action recognition' stands for both action and interaction recognition.

and deliverables have been predefined, there is a lower chance of accidentally omitting any steps. Following the method should also aid auditing whether the classifier was developed correctly and solves the problem at hand. The generic activities in the method are extracted from existing processes and frameworks, see Sect. 3. More detailed activities and the concepts are extracted from literature on this topic and assembled and described in Sect. 4.

3   Related Works

To the best of our knowledge, no systematic approach exists that describes the development of action recognition classifiers from problem statement to deployment. Thus, we start from data science frameworks and assemble a reference method for building effective classifiers for action recognition. We compare three processes: the Common Task Framework (CTF) [6], the Knowledge Discovery in Databases (KDD) [7] process, and the CRoss Industry Standard Process for Data Mining (CRISP-DM) [28].

CTF is meant for predictive modeling, making it suitable for classifier development. However, it only includes three main elements according to Donoho [6]: (i) a publicly available training dataset with feature measurements and labels, (ii) competitors that infer class prediction rules from the data and (iii) a referee that receives the predictions compares them to the test data and returns the prediction accuracy. This framework, however, requires an existing dataset. In addition, competing teams are needed to conduct the common task, which may not be readily available and/or willing to participate.

The KDD process describes the following steps: data selection, preprocessing, transformation, data mining and interpretation/evaluation. The process was designed for use in the data mining field [7]. KDD differentiates itself by focusing on the entire knowledge discovery process. Unfortunately, the process does not start with a specific problem that needs to be solved. Moreover, it does not address deployment of the process in another system, since the result of the process is knowledge that can be used.

Thirdly, CRISP-DM is selected, since it was designed for projects with large amounts of data and achieving specific business-related objectives. The CRISP-DM process model prescribes six phases [28]:

1. Business understanding: involves understanding the business requirements and objectives and formulating a data mining problem from this knowledge;
2. Data understanding: includes data collection, familiarization and data quality assessment;
3. Data preparation: focuses on converting the raw data into a usable dataset through cleaning and attribute selection among others;
4. Modeling: selection and use of modeling techniques, determining parameters for optimal results;
5. Evaluation: evaluate whether the selected techniques sufficiently address the initial problems and objectives;

6. Deployment: presenting the results in such a way that the customer can use them, for instance by writing a report.

The application to specific domains requires the classifier to be trained for each domain, which requires the method to be able to handle large amounts of data. Furthermore, the classifier should be deployed in the domain context or system so that it can be used for prediction tasks by the stakeholder(s). Therefore, the CRISP-DM process is used as a starting point, as it fits best the requirements for the reference method.

4   Reference Method for Domain Action Recognition Classifiers

The reference method for the development of Domain Action Recognition Classifiers (DARC-method) is visualized in a Process Deliverable Diagram (PDD) in Fig. 1. A PDD describes a method in a process side on the left based on UML activity diagrams, and the resulting (indicated with dashed arrows) concepts and deliverables on the right based on UML class diagrams. Open concepts are described via aggregation relationships in the PDD, while the elaboration of closed activities and concepts has to be obtained elsewhere [26]. Based on the CRISP-DM process model, the reference method consists of six consecutive phases with adapted names and purposes:

1. **Domain understanding:** documentation related to the domain needs to be gathered, in particular the actions the classifier should recognize. Also, the relevance and correctness of these actions should be discussed with domain professionals;
2. **Dataset creation:** if no datasets containing the relevant domain actions exist, it is necessary to create one (if a suitable dataset is available, this phase can be skipped);
3. **Dataset preparation:** videos in the dataset need to be prepared before they can be utilized for classifier training, testing and validation;
4. **Classifier modeling:** the classifier is modeled, the feature sets are created and the experimental protocol is determined;
5. **Classifier training:** the classifier is trained using the main part of the dataset, then validated using another part of the dataset, parameters are changed in an attempt to improve the performance (paying attention to avoiding overfitting) and finally the classifier is tested using the remaining data;
6. **Deployment:** once the classifier achieves good results, it needs to be deployed in the domain system, which changes per domain, and feedback from domain users can be taken into account for further development and/or improvement.

Firstly, in the **domain understanding** phase, information related to the domain is gathered. The CRISP-DM process model describes tasks such as 'business objectives' and 'determine data mining goals' [28]. In the context of action

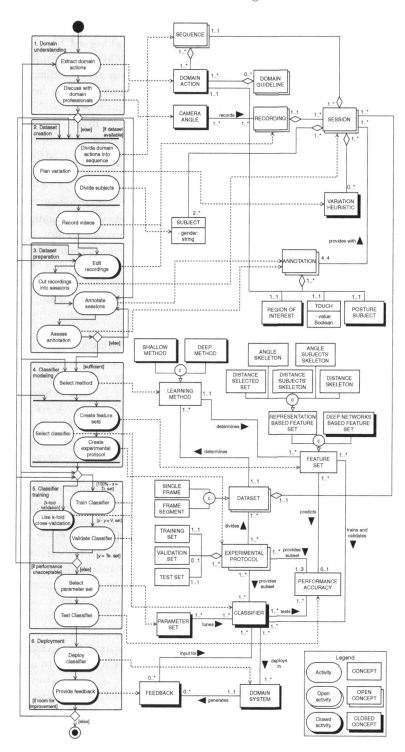

Fig. 1. Reference method for Domain Action Recognition Classifier (DARC) development.

recognition, these tasks can be translated to determining the domain objective: what action recognition problem or need should be addressed by the classifier? For the latter, the prediction goals can be determined, for example which actions the classifier should be able to classify. Domain actions that need to be recognized need to be identified, for instance by extracting them from available domain guideline repositories. In addition, domain professionals should give insight into which actions are performed most frequently, in which order they are performed and which camera angles might be needed to be able to record all actions to avoid occlusion. Intra-class variation and inter-class variation should be included in the actions, since subjects perform actions slightly differently every time and some actions may seem very similar to others and be classified incorrectly as a result. These variations should also include fluctuating duration, referred to as temporal variation [20]. Supporting variation is becoming easier: recent publicly available datasets for action recognition often include hundreds of actions, and datasets have become more realistic in terms of their settings [20]. However, **dataset creation** is needed if datasets containing actions related to a specific domain are not readily available, which is often the case [24].

Based on knowledge gathered in the first phase, the domain actions can be divided into sequences. For instance, actions that are nearly always performed together will be recorded in sequence, along with variations and combinations of other actions. Previously developed algorithms have, at times, been trained on segmented videos, meaning that the annotations have clear boundaries. In case of real-time action recognition, such boundaries are less evident. The classifier should be able to detect when an action starts and ends, also referred to as action spotting [4], and then classify said action. Therefore, the videos, with or without sequences, should not exclusively include actions [20].

In addition, to mitigate the risk of the classifier focusing on specific, irrelevant features, dataset variation (i.e. videos) is needed. Variation can be introduced by using different locations, clothing, camera angles, hairstyles, etc. Also, different subjects should be used to ensure that the classifiers are not trained to recognize actions performed by men and not by women or vice versa. The collection of these types of variation are referred to as *variation heuristics*. In addition, multiple subjects need to be distinguished. The subjects may occlude each other, which is why multiple camera angles should be used to decrease the risk of occlusion [19]. The setting (fore- and back-ground) plays an important role in dataset creation too. Lighting conditions and additional movement in the recordings can affect the accuracy of the classifier. It is, however, ill-advised to create a 'clean' and static environment, since this is not comparable to the real-world context [20]. Variations in location may be desirable. When variation plans have been made, subjects have been divided and actions and sequences have been determined, the videos can be recorded. The minimal amount of data is difficult to ascertain, since this may vary between classification tasks, but more is nearly always better. Finally, statistical sparsity is a valid dataset quality concern. Even large datasets may be lacking in their inclusion of varied scenarios [8].

In the data preparation phase, the CRISP-DM model prescribes data cleaning and formatting. To prepare for supervised learning, the instances (actions) in the data should be labeled [13]. So, after recording, the videos should be prepared for training in the **dataset preparation** phase. If multiple cameras were used, the videos should be edited, such that they have the same dimensions and are uniform in terms of brightness, frame rate, etc. This is done to ensure that the variations in formatting do not affect the predictions. Besides, data augmentation can be applied during the editing activity, which means adding noisy versions of existing data to increase the size of the dataset. The augmentation approach depends on the data. For instance, when working with imagery, it is possible to mirror the existing images to create additional data. Alternatively, 3D synthesis can be utilized to generate synthetic data from real data, also with the intent of increasing the volume of data [25]. Then, recordings need to be cut into different sessions, since recordings can span over multiple sessions (to save time while recording). Subsequently, they can be annotated (supplied with the correct labels), so that the ground truth is available for training the classifier.

For the annotation, we distinguish four different labels: posture of the subject, region of interest, domain action and touch. Since the former three should be defined for a specific domain, they have not been extended with specific options. According to Moeslund *et al.* [16], concepts like action, activity and behavior are sometimes considered synonyms. In this method, however, we adopt their action taxonomy: (i) action primitives, which are atomic entities that comprise an action, (ii) actions, a set of action primitives that are needed to perform the particular action and (iii) activities, a collection of actions that describe a larger event. For example, 'playing tennis' is an activity, that contains action such as 'serve' and 'return ball', in which the latter consists of action primitives like 'forehand', 'run right' and 'jump' [16]. Preferably, the quality of the annotations is assessed. As an example, Mathias *et al.* [15] illustrated that re-annotating data with strict and consistent rules, as well as adding 'ignore' tags to unrealistically difficult samples, can have a significant impact on the assessment of classifiers. Incorrect annotations counted as errors created an artificial slope on the assessment curves and biased the results. Multiple labels for individual items, also referred to as repeated labeling, was also proven to be valuable [23].

Subsequently, in the **classifier modeling** phase, a learning method is selected. Kong and Fu distinguish two types of methods: *shallow* and *deep*. Action recognition predominantly makes use of deep methods, with shallow methods being better suitable when small amounts of training data are available [12]. Herath *et al.* divide action recognition in two similar categories, namely representation-based solutions and deep networks-based solutions [10]. For the former, some sort of representation, e.g., keypoints, silhouettes, 2D/3D models, are required in order to train, validate and test the classifier. If a deep method is selected, there are three different options: (i) if a large, labeled dataset is available, it is possible to perform end-to-end training of a deep neural net, (ii) if the dataset has some labeled data, data augmentation or transfer learning can be applied, i.e., employing large datasets to train deep networks and then using intermediate layer representations as deep features for a different classification task [24] and (iii) if there is little labeled data available, active learning can be applied to select and annotate additional, relevant data to increase the size of the dataset [17].

Feature sets need to be extracted in order to recognize actions. Herath *et al.* distinguish between methods that are based on handcrafted features and those that use deep learning based techniques [10]. The former are referred to as representation-based feature sets in the method. An example of a spatial feature set is provided in Fig. 1, which includes distance between the keypoints within the person for all subjects, distance between keypoints of one subject and another, among others. Deep network solutions, on the other hand, implicitly extract features from the input data, which means they cannot be determined a-priori and are therefore not specified in the method. In addition, one or multiple classifiers need to be selected for the classification task. Multiple classification methods (e.g., Naive Bayes, Random Forest, k-Nearest Neighbor) can be trained to see which one yields the best results. Given that not every classifier may be appropriate for every classification task or dataset and classifier selection may be influenced by the available time and computing power, no classifiers are prescribed in the method.

To validate and test the classifier, we either rely on standard techniques or use k-fold cross-validation. In case of the former, the dataset is divided into subsets to be used for training, validation and testing the classifiers, these subsets are used in the training phase. To avoid overfitting on a specific angle (if multiple cameras are used), subsets should be created based on actions, rather than individual sessions. Overfitting can be described as the risk of "*memorizing various peculiarities of the training data rather than finding a general predictive rule*" [5]. If this occurs, the classifier might perform well on training data and less so on unseen data. Alternatively, k-fold cross-validation splits a single dataset into a training set (known data) and test set (unknown data) k times. For instance, if $k = 3$, the classifier is trained and tested on three different training and test sets, which are derived by slicing the dataset in different ways.

Furthermore, the dataset can be fed to the classifier using single frames or frame segments. Some domain actions may appear similar or nearly identical when single frames are considered, but can be distinguished when multiple frames are shown. Therefore, the classifier can be provided with multiple frames at once, for instance 30. If within those 30 frames 20 are identified as a specific action, all 30 frames will receive that label. The length of the sliding window (or skip length) refers to the number of frames the window moves through time (temporal direction) before a new segment is started [2].

The **classifier training** phase uses the subsets specified in the experimental protocol and the created feature sets to train, validate and test. The classifiers are trained and validated using several parameter sets. If parameters are only optimized for the training data, there is a risk of overfitting [5]. In case of limited data availability, training starts from a classifier trained for a similar, related task (i.e. transfer learning). Alternatively, using k-fold cross-validation, training and testing are conducted k times. After training and validation is completed using all selected parameter sets, the parameter set that yields the best performance is selected for testing the classifiers. No specific parameter sets are described, since these may vary between domains. It should be noted that the subsets of the dataset should under no circumstances overlap. However, it is possible to join the training and validation sets for a final round of training before reporting results on the test set. In some cases, dataset creation and classifier training are performed iteratively, until a certain accuracy level is reached. If the accuracy level on the validation set is unacceptable, there are four options: (i) re-train the classifier using k-fold cross-validation, for example, (ii) creating different feature sets and/or selecting a different classifier, (iii) editing or augmenting the recordings in order to increase the size of the dataset or creating synthetic data and (iv) creating additional data from scratch.

If the classifier is sufficiently accurate, it can be used in its intended domain during the **deployment** phase. If not, the classifier should not be considered for deployment. Instead, an attempt can be made to identify more appropriate feature sets or a better suiting classifier. Context systems are systems used in the specific domain. The results of the classifiers might need to be included in an existing system, for instance. Finally, end-users of the classifier might want or need to provide feedback on its performance. If users notice that one specific action is often classified as another, additional data and training might be needed. This is in accordance with the monitoring and maintenance plan task included in the CRISP-DM process [28]. Since feedback cannot be predicted beforehand, it is assumed all phases in the process can be affected.

5   Case Study: Medical Consultations

The DARC-method was applied to a case study within the context of the Care2Report research program regarding the automated reporting of medical consultations [14]. The purpose of the case study is twofold: (i) to assess the feasibility of the method by demonstrating how the activities and deliverables can be applied, and (ii) to evaluate the effectiveness, by reporting on the prediction accuracy of the resulting classifier.

The method was applied to the healthcare domain, since General Practitioners (GPs) generally experience a high workload. A classifier that is able to recognize medical actions performed in a GP's office can support the administrative work of GPs, not by diagnosing disease or by detecting anomalies, but by serving the medical reporting of the consultation. The classifier and its results are also discussed in [22].

1. Domain understanding. In the Netherlands, GPs make use of clinical guidelines and standards developed by the Nederlands Huisartsen Genootschap[2] (transl. Dutch General Practitioners Society). First, all medical actions that occur in the clinical guidelines were extracted. Then, a selection was made based

---

[2] https://www.nhg.org/nhg-standaarden.

on the instruments available for this study and whether the actions are of a sensitive nature. For the former, actions such as performing an ECG were excluded, since we did not possess such instruments. For the latter, actions that require subjects to (partially) undress were excluded to preserve the privacy of subjects participating in the recordings. The following medical actions were included in the dataset, in decreasing occurrence order in the guidelines [22]: Blood pressure measurement (BPM), Palpation abdomen (PaA), Percussion abdomen (PeA), Auscultation lungs (AL), Auscultation heart (AH), and Auscultation abdomen (AA).

In addition, there is a 'no action' class, in case no action is occurring in a segment of the video. We also distinguish the following classes: 'sitting upright', 'laying down' and 'laying down with knees bent' (posture of patient), whether the GP touches the patient or not (distance to patient) and 'arm', 'chest', 'upper back' and 'abdomen' (region of interest). Actions, however, are not always performed in isolation, but may be part of a sequence. In discussion with medical professionals, and taking into account the guidelines, the most frequently occurring combinations and order within those combinations were used most often, with some slight variation to mitigate overtraining on specific sequences. Using the previously mentioned taxonomy [16], we distinguish the following examples: (i) 'pressing with the hand' and 'releasing pressure of the hand' as action primitives, (ii) 'palpation of the abdomen' as action and (iii) 'physical examination' or 'medical consultation' as activity.

2. Dataset creation. The videos [22] were recorded with four subjects (three female, one male), who all played the roles of both GP and patient. Since GPs examine one patient at a time, exactly two subjects appear in all videos. In 68% of the videos, both subject were female, in 15% only the GP was female and in 17% only the patient was female. In addition, they all changed clothes, hair and jewelry. The GP is required to wear their hair up, but the patient can have any hairstyle. The same is true for jewelry, since GPs are not allowed to wear any jewelry while patients are. It should also be noted that, in the Netherlands, GPs rarely wear white coats, which is why the GP role also changed clothing throughout the recordings. Glasses were worn by both GP and patients. During examinations, the patient is either sitting upright, laying down flat or laying down with their knees bent. The GP performed actions from either side of the patient and there is variation within actions. For instance, when listening to the lungs, sometimes they started on the right and sometimes on the left. Stethoscopes were used during recordings, both a red and black one to introduce variation. Finally, three cameras from three different angles were used, which is visualized in [22].

Since the GP (subject A) only performs medical actions using their hands, the lower half of their body is not of importance and can be hidden behind the examination table or gurney. The GP may have to move around to perform the appropriate medical actions, which is why three cameras were used. By placing them in different positions and thus acquiring three different angles, the chances of occlusion are reduced. A total of 451 videos were recorded, 73.6% of which included a single action (those videos contained frames without any action as well), the rest contained sequences [22].

3. Dataset preparation. All recordings were cut into sessions, 192 in total [22], which were then annotated, meaning they were provided with the right labels. The online annotation tool ELAN [9] was used, since it allows for annotating multiple videos concurrently. An example of how part of a video is annotated is: 'sitting upright' (posture subject), 'arm' (region of interest), 'true' (touch) and 'BPM' (domain action).

4. Classifier modeling. In this case a representation-based solution was used, due to the small amount of data and since the human body structure and its movements are the focus of the classifier [10]. Either keypoints (also referred to as skeleton joints) can be extracted or images or videos can be used as input for the classifier [11]. Since distances between the subjects are important, to recognize interaction, and actions can be defined using distances and angles, keypoints are used. Information such as colors and background is present in images and videos, but is not required to recognize domain actions. Keypoints are used to extract a skeletal representation from the subjects in the videos. These representations can also be used to reduce the dimensionality of the dataset, by determining the minimum and maximum values of the feature set, as well as the average and variance, of multiple frames. This results in improved computational efficiency and accuracy [3].

Fig. 2. 2D skeleton generated by Open-Pose with patient laying down.

Fig. 3. 2D skeleton generated by Open-Pose with patient sitting up. (Color figure online)

OpenPose was applied to all sessions to extract keypoints, since it is publicly available and able to recognize multiple subjects [1]. Examples of 2D skeletons generated by Openpose are depicted in Figs. 2 and 3. Note that in Fig. 2 the GP's face is blurred for privacy reasons. These keypoints are then utilized to create mathematical representations of the subjects and to determine the distances between skeleton joints and angles that each line between two neighbor joints makes with the horizontal axis of each camera viewpoint [29,30]. We calculate angles differently from previous literature, where they use angles of two lines between three neighbor joints. Our approach on computing angles allows us to embed the body orientation of each subject both relative to camera viewpoint and therefore to each other as well. The 2D joint coordinates (Eq. 1) are determined in order to calculate the angles and distances:

$$J_c = J_c(J) = (J_x, J_y) \qquad (1)$$

We use J for joint and J_c for 2D joint coordinate where J_x and J_y represent the x and y axis, respectively. Secondly, the angle between a line of two neighbor joints and the horizontal axis (Eq. 2) is calculated as follows [18]:

$$LL_a = LL_a(L_{J_1 \to J_2}, L_h) = arctan(\frac{J_{1_x} - J_{2_x}}{J_{1_y} - J_{2_y}}) \qquad (2)$$

LL_a, $L_{J_1 \to J_2}$, L_h represent line-line angle, line between two joints, and horizontal line, respectively. Finally, the (Euclidean) distance between two or more joints of one subject and the distances between the joints of two or more subjects are determined (Eq. 3) using the following equation:

$$JJ_d = JJ_d(J_1, J_2) = \overrightarrow{||J_1 J_2||} = \sqrt{(J_{1_x} - J_{2_x})^2 + (J_{1_y} - J_{2_y})^2} \qquad (3)$$

In Fig. 3 an example of how Eq. 3 is calculated can be seen. The distance between the right hand of the GP (in yellow) and the back of the patient (in red) can be used to determine whether the GP is touching the patient and which medical action (in this case AL) is being performed. The calculation of angles and distances was done as defined in Eqs. 1, 2 and 3.

Considering the medical actions, experiments were conducted using five different feature sets, to determine which set(s) offered the most valuable information. The following sets of features were included in experimentation:

Feature set 1: Pre-selected group of features: (i) angle between the neck and mid-hip of both subjects, (ii) distances between both hands of subject A and a specific body part (i.e. chest, abdomen, arm, left hand and right hand) of subject B and vice versa;

Feature set 2: Distances between all keypoints within subjects;

Feature set 3: Angles of keypoints relative to other keypoints within subjects;

Feature set 4: Distances between both hands of subject A and the upper body of subject B and vice versa;

Feature set 5: Angle of the hands of subject A relative to the upper body of subject B and vice versa.

Note that in these feature sets, the upper body is considered to range from the head to the lower abdomen (right above the keypoints of the hips).

5. Classifier training. We selected Random Forest (RF) to be used in the medical action recognition. Some experimentation was done with both k-Nearest Neighbors and Decision Trees, but results are left out for the sake of brevity. The classifiers were trained using 60% of the dataset (i.e. sessions). Then, 20% of the remaining 40% was used to validate the classifier. Based on the validation results, the parameter set with the highest accuracy was selected. Finally, the last 20% was used to test the classifiers. For all three subsets, the training set contained 60% of the sessions, distributed evenly over available angles. The RF classifier was trained, validated and tested on the aforementioned feature sets, as well as combinations of the sets, resulting in a predication accuracy of 0.697. An example of distance parameters that were used to classify the medical actions is shown in Fig. 4. Note that these distance parameters were fixed, but the decision tree was not, due to the nature of RF classifiers.

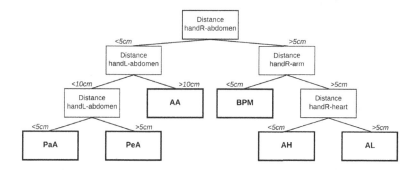

Fig. 4. Example of distance parameters in a decision tree.

At first, single frames were used to recognize actions. However, some medical actions are quite similar when comparing individual frames rather than a segment of a video, because they are performed on the same region of interest. For instance, during palpation of the abdomen, both hands are pressed on the abdomen, while during percussion one hand is not released from the abdomen, while the other is. Therefore, percussion is easily confused with palpation. The same is true for auscultation of the lungs and heart. In case of the heart, only the area of the chest around the heart is covered, while in case of the lungs the entire chest is examined. The two are more difficult to distinguish when only individual frames are considered. When taking into account frame segments of videos as opposed to single frames, the accuracy of the classifier increases by 0.059, using 120 frames and a sliding window of 20 frames, to 0.756.

The use of segments increased the accuracy of the classifier when distinguishing palpation and percussion of the abdomen and auscultation of the lungs and heart. Confusion matrices illustrating the prediction accuracy of the best performing feature set using both individual frames and segments of the classifier are shown in Figs. 5 and 6, respectively. While the prediction accuracy does not increase for all individual actions, the average prediction accuracy does. The

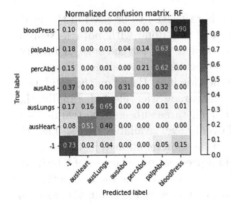
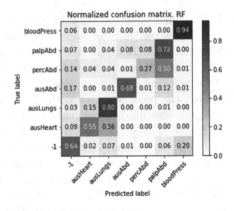

Fig. 5. Confusion matrix of feature set with best test accuracy (sets 3–5) of RF classifier.

Fig. 6. Confusion matrix of best performing segment (120, 20) for RF (feature sets 3–5).

prediction accuracy of the other annotations, i.e. posture of patient, distance to patient and region of interest are 0.996, 0.910 and 0.908, respectively, using feature sets 3, 4 and 5 and frame segments of 30 frames with a sliding window of 15 frames. In [22] we report on the results of a 4-fold cross-validation.

6. Deployment. The Care2Report (C2R) system, first presented by Maas *et al.* [14], strives for fully automated medical reporting. Currently, the system is able to generate medical reports adhering to clinical guidelines by using audio of a consultation as input. However, the consultation with a patient often includes a physical examination as well, which requires video for analysis. The recorded medical actions need to be identified automatically, for which the described classifier can be used. The goal for the C2R system is recognition of medical actions performed by GPs in real-time, so that its results complement the report generated from the audio input. Therefore, the deployment context of the classifier is a GP's office. In addition, it will have to interact with the electronic medical record in the C2R system, but this is left to future work.

6   Discussion

In this paper, we presented the DARC-method, a reference method for developing classifiers for domain action recognition, based on existing methods and techniques. We then applied the method to a case study and reported on the prediction accuracy of the developed classifier.

Validity Threats. Firstly, the DARC-method was only applied to a single case and a single domain; it may need customization when applied to other domains. Secondly, the method was applied by people with some experience with both

ML and classifiers and the specific domain it was used for. Additionally, we were unable to conduct the deployment phase as of yet, meaning this part was never tested in a real-world situation and cannot be described in detail. Given that there are additional steps to developing the classifier, there is a risk of introducing errors throughout the process [24]. Finally, others less familiar with the subject matter and process may have a more difficult time applying the method to their own case and/or domain. However, the method is based on existing and validated techniques, which should improve its external validity.

Conclusion. Our research question *"how can a reference method be assembled for the development of domain action recognition classifiers?"* was answered by designing a reference method using a method assembly approach, combining existing methods and techniques. We expect the method to provide assistance, in line with the first requirement, when developing a classifier, by providing a step-wise process, related literature and consistent terminology. In accordance with the second requirement, the method is tailored to action recognition learning methods and relies on video input. Also, the DARC-method introduces algorithmic restrictions by defining a standard set of representation-based features. The domain understanding and deployment phases support the third requirement. The developed classifier proves that the reference method can be applied to a case in the medical domain. Thanks to the method, the decisions made for each activity in the process were reported in a structured manner. The classifier was trained to perform four different classification tasks: identifying medical actions, the posture of the patient, the distance of the GP to the patient and the region of interest. The prediction accuracy of the tasks are 75.6%, 99.6%, 91.0% and 90.8% respectively.

Future Work. In order to evaluate the effectiveness of the method an experiment using students as test subjects will be conducted. Students with little to no experience with action recognition will be divided into an experimental and a control group. The former will make use of the method, while the latter will use no method. The effectiveness of the method can then be assessed by comparing the efficiency, number of errors and quality of the resulting work of both groups. Next steps include the classifier being trained using different datasets for additional contexts and purposes. For instance, the method and its resulting classifier can be applied to the orthopedics specialization. Thanks to the use of imagery, we should be able record a patient's range of movement over a period of time and analyze the data. Placing the method in a broader perspective, classifiers can be developed and trained for use in other contexts, such as police reporting. Furthermore, the deployment of the trained classifier in the automated reporting system C2R should be investigated to evaluate the final phase of the method.

References

1. Cao, Z., Hidalgo, G., Simon, T., Wei, S.E., Sheikh, Y.: OpenPose: real-time multi-person 2D pose estimation using part affinity fields. arXiv preprint arXiv:1812.08008 (2018)
2. Colleoni, E., Moccia, S., Du, X., De Momi, E., Stoyanov, D.: Deep learning based robotic tool detection and articulation estimation with spatio-temporal layers. IEEE Robot. Autom. Lett. **4**(3), 2714–2721 (2019)
3. Cunningham, P.: Dimension reduction. In: Cord, M., Cunningham, P. (eds.) Machine Learning Techniques for Multimedia. COGTECH, pp. 91–112. Springer, Heidelberg (2008). https://doi.org/10.1007/978-3-540-75171-7_4
4. Derpanis, K.G., Sizintsev, M., Cannons, K., Wildes, R.P.: Efficient action spotting based on a spacetime oriented structure representation. In: Proceedings of the CVPR, pp. 1990–1997. IEEE (2010)
5. Dietterich, T.: Overfitting and undercomputing in machine learning. ACM Comput. Surv. (CSUR) **27**(3), 326–327 (1995)
6. Donoho, D.: 50 years of data science. J. Comput. Graph. Stat. **26**(4), 745–766 (2017)
7. Fayyad, U., Piatetsky-Shapiro, G., Smyth, P.: The KDD process for extracting useful knowledge from volumes of data. Commun. ACM **39**(11), 27–34 (1996)
8. Gudivada, V., Apon, A., Ding, J.: Data quality considerations for big data and machine learning: going beyond data cleaning and transformations. Int. J. Adv. Softw. **10**(1), 1–20 (2017)
9. Hellwig, B.: EUDICO linguistic annotator (ELAN) version 1.4-manual. Last updated (2003)
10. Herath, S., Harandi, M., Porikli, F.: Going deeper into action recognition: a survey. Image Vis. Comput. **60**, 4–21 (2017)
11. Jordan, M.I., Mitchell, T.M.: Machine learning: trends, perspectives, and prospects. Science **349**(6245), 255–260 (2015)
12. Kong, Y., Fu, Y.: Human action recognition and prediction: a survey. arXiv preprint arXiv:1806.11230 (2018)
13. Kotsiantis, S.B., Zaharakis, I., Pintelas, P.: Supervised machine learning: a review of classification techniques. Emerg. Artif. Intell. Appl. Comput. Eng. **160**, 3–24 (2007)
14. Maas, L., et al.: The Care2Report system: automated medical reporting as an integrated solution to reduce administrative burden in healthcare. In: Proceedings of the 53rd HICSS (2020)
15. Mathias, M., Benenson, R., Pedersoli, M., Van Gool, L.: Face detection without bells and whistles. In: Fleet, D., Pajdla, T., Schiele, B., Tuytelaars, T. (eds.) ECCV 2014. LNCS, vol. 8692, pp. 720–735. Springer, Cham (2014). https://doi.org/10.1007/978-3-319-10593-2_47
16. Moeslund, T.B., Hilton, A., Krüger, V.: A survey of advances in vision-based human motion capture and analysis. Comput. Vis. Image Underst. **104**(2–3), 90–126 (2006)
17. Nath, T., Mathis, A., Chen, A.C., Patel, A., Bethge, M., Mathis, M.W.: Using DeepLabCut for 3D markerless pose estimation across species and behaviors. Nat. Protoc. **14**(7), 2152–2176 (2019)

18. Noori, F.M., Wallace, B., Uddin, M.Z., Torresen, J.: A robust human activity recognition approach using OpenPose, motion features, and deep recurrent neural network. In: Felsberg, M., Forssén, P.-E., Sintorn, I.-M., Unger, J. (eds.) SCIA 2019. LNCS, vol. 11482, pp. 299–310. Springer, Cham (2019). https://doi.org/10.1007/978-3-030-20205-7_25

19. Park, S., Trivedi, M.M.: Understanding human interactions with track and body synergies (TBS) captured from multiple views. Comput. Vis. Image Underst. **111**(1), 2–20 (2008)

20. Poppe, R.: A survey on vision-based human action recognition. Image Vis. Comput. **28**(6), 976–990 (2010)

21. Ralyté, J., Deneckère, R., Rolland, C.: Towards a generic model for situational method engineering. In: International Conference on Advanced Information Systems Engineering, pp. 95–110 (2003)

22. Schiphorst, L., Doyran, M., Salah, A.A., Molenaar, S., Brinkkemper, S.: Video2report: a video database for automatic reporting of medical consultancy sessions. In: 15th IEEE International Conference on Automatic Face and Gesture Recognition, Buenos Aires (2020)

23. Sheng, V.S., Provost, F., Ipeirotis, P.G.: Get another label? Improving data quality and data mining using multiple, noisy labelers. In: Proceedings of the 14th ACM SIGKDD International Conference on Knowledge Discovery and Data Mining, pp. 614–622 (2008)

24. Stergiou, A., Poppe, R.: Analyzing human-human interactions: a survey. Comput. Vis. Image Underst. **188**, 102799 (2019)

25. Varol, G., et al.: Learning from synthetic humans. In: Proceedings of the CVPR, pp. 109–117 (2017)

26. van de Weerd, I., Brinkkemper, S.: Meta-modeling for situational analysis and design methods. In: Handbook of Research on Modern Systems Analysis and Design Technologies and Applications, pp. 35–54. IGI Global (2009)

27. van de Weerd, I., de Weerd, S., Brinkkemper, S.: Developing a reference method for game production by method comparison. In: Ralyté, J., Brinkkemper, S., Henderson-Sellers, B. (eds.) Situational Method Engineering: Fundamentals and Experiences. ITIFIP, vol. 244, pp. 313–327. Springer, Boston, MA (2007). https://doi.org/10.1007/978-0-387-73947-2_24

28. Wirth, R., Hipp, J.: CRISP-DM: towards a standard process model for data mining. In: Proceedings of the 4th International Conference on the Practical Applications of Knowledge Discovery and Data Mining, pp. 29–39 (2000)

29. Yun, K., Honorio, J., Chattopadhyay, D., Berg, T.L., Samaras, D.: Two-person interaction detection using body-pose features and multiple instance learning. In: Proceedings of the CVPRW (2012)

30. Zhang, S., Liu, X., Xiao, J.: On geometric features for skeleton-based action recognition using multilayer LSTM networks. In: Proceedings of the WACV, pp. 148–157. IEEE (2017)

Evaluation-Related Research
(EMMSAD 2020)

An Evaluation of the Intuitiveness of the PGA Modeling Language Notation

Ben Roelens[1,2]([envelope])[iD] and Dominik Bork[3][iD]

[1] Faculty of Management, Science and Technology,
Open University, Heerlen, The Netherlands
`ben.roelens@ou.nl`
[2] Faculty of Economics and Business Administration,
Ghent University, Ghent, Belgium
[3] Faculty of Computer Science, University of Vienna,
Waehringer Street 29, 1090 Vienna, Austria
`dominik.bork@univie.ac.at`

Abstract. The Process-Goal Alignment (PGA) modeling method is a domain-specific modeling language that aims to achieve strategic fit of the business strategy with the internal infrastructure and processes. To ensure the acceptance and correct understanding of PGA models by business-oriented end-users, an intuitively understandable notation is of paramount importance. However, the current PGA notation was not formally tested up to now. In the paper at hand, we apply an evaluation technique for testing the intuitiveness of domain-specific modeling languages to bridge that research gap. Based on an analysis of the tasks, we propose improvements to six elements of the initial PGA notation. Our research contributes a comprehensive description of the empirical modeling language evaluation, which enables the reproducibility of the evaluation procedure by the conceptual modeling community.

Keywords: Conceptual modeling · Intuitiveness · Modeling notation · Process-goal alignment method

1 Introduction

The design of Domain-Specific Modeling Languages (DSMLs) is gaining popularity in the Conceptual Modeling field [9]. DSMLs are specifically designed for a specific purpose (e.g., to analyze and communicate about a problem) in a particular domain [6]. In comparison to General Purpose Modeling Languages (e.g., UML or ER), DSMLs reduce the complexity of the modeling effort by using concepts that are familiar to the intended end-users and by hiding complex model constraints in the tailored meta-model [6].

The Process-Goal Alignment (PGA) modeling method is a specific DSML, which has the purpose to achieve strategic fit in the business architecture [15]. Strategic fit is an important architectural concern for organizations, as it requires

© Springer Nature Switzerland AG 2020
S. Nurcan et al. (Eds.): BPMDS 2020/EMMSAD 2020, LNBIP 387, pp. 395–410, 2020.
https://doi.org/10.1007/978-3-030-49418-6_27

to align the business strategy with the internal infrastructure and processes [7]. This enables companies to adequately react on opportunities and threats in its external environment. The design of the PGA modeling method is the result of different iterations of Action Design Research [17], which allowed the gradual refinement of its syntax, semantics, and modeling procedure [15].

One of the design requirements of the PGA method is a clear communication of the organizational strategy to ensure its understanding by business-oriented experts [15]. These experts are not applying the method themselves, but are guided by a modeler, who collects the necessary information and constructs the PGA models. Therefore, ensuring that PGA models can be intuitively understood by business-oriented end-users is of paramount importance to reduce the cognitive load for them. This will foster the use of the models to identify possible organizational improvements. To realize this, the PGA notation was initially guided by the principle of semantic transparency. This principle imposes that the graphical notation of a modeling language element suggests its meaning [10]. However, the intuitiveness of the PGA notation was not tested yet.

This research gap can be solved by an evaluation technique for testing the intuitiveness of DSMLs [3]. The technique comprises a set of tasks which are divided into three phases: (i) *term association*, (ii) *notation association*, and (iii) *case study*. These tasks were conducted by Master students of Ghent University to test the intuitiveness of the PGA notation. Based on an analysis of the results, improvements to the initial notation are proposed.

The paper is structured as follows. Section 2 reviews foundational literature about conceptual modeling, modeling language notations, and the PGA modeling method. Afterwards, Sect. 3 describes how the evaluation technique and the data analysis were performed. In Sect. 4, the results of the analysis are presented, which leads to the proposal of an improved PGA notation in Sect. 5. The paper ends with a reflection and concluding remarks in Sect. 6.

2   Foundations

2.1   Conceptual Modeling

Conceptual modeling concerns the application of abstraction to reduce the complexity of a certain domain for a specific stakeholder purpose. Originally, conceptual modeling was targeting to support human beings for the purposes of a common understanding and communication [11]. In recent years, the scope of the discipline has exceeded this pure representative means toward using the created models as a formalized knowledge base that enables automated processing. Modeling methods are the core of conceptual modeling [8], which consist of: a *modeling language*, a *modeling procedure*, and *mechanisms & algorithms*. The modeling language encompasses its syntax, semantics, and notation. The syntax defines the grammar of the language, which includes the available concepts and the allowed relationships between them. Semantics refers to the meaning, whereas notation is the visual representation of the language concepts.

2.2   Modeling Language Notation

Information processing can be divided into two steps [12]: *Perceptual Processing (seeing)* which is fast and automatic, and *Cognitive Processing (understanding)* which is slow and resource-intensive. Conceptual models should aim for *computational offloading*, i.e., replacing some cognitive tasks by perceptual ones. Moody states that *"Designing cognitively effective visual notations can [..] be seen as a problem of optimizing them for processing by the human mind"* [10, p. 761].

"The extent to which diagrams exploit perceptual processing largely explains differences in their effectiveness" [10, p. 761]. When analyzing the perceptual processing quality of a visual notation, one needs to consider *semantic transparency* [10]. Semantic transparency is defined as *"the extent to which a novice reader can infer the meaning of a symbol from its appearance alone"* [10, p. 765]. In literature, semantic transparency is often considered synonymous to an intuitive understanding. A notation with a high semantic transparency enables users to infer the meaning of a symbol/model from their working and/or long-term memory. Semantic transparency therefore *"plays a crucial role in [...] acceptance"* of modeling languages [5, p. 123].

2.3   PGA Modeling Method

PGA has been introduced in [14] and further developed in [15] as a project within the Open Models Laboratory (OMiLAB) [2]. A tool prototype has been realized with the ADOxx meta-modeling platform [1]. To achieve strategic fit in the business architecture, PGA aims at the development of a business architecture heat map following a modeling procedure that consists of three activities: (i) developing a prioritized business architecture hierarchy, (ii) executing the performance measurement, and (iii) performing the strategic fit improvement analysis.

The first step aims to model the creation of value throughout a hierarchical structure of business architecture elements. Based on Strategic Management frameworks, the PGA meta-model incorporates the following elements (i.e., capitalized in the remainder of the text): Activity, Process, Competence, Value Proposition, Financial Structure, Internal Goal, Customer Goal, and Financial Goal. To design an intuitive notation for business-oriented end-users, icons were used to represent these elements. An overview of the initial PGA notation is found in Table 4. Afterwards, valueStream relations are added between these elements to show the hierarchical value structure. Each valueStream relation is prioritized by using the AHP mechanism (i.e., based on pairwise comparisons) [16] and a color coding with accompanying line texture is used to differentiate between a high (i.e., solid red color), medium (i.e., dashed orange color), or low priority (i.e., dotted green color) w.r.t. their strategic Importance.

The performance measurement mechanism is applied to each business architecture element to identify an appropriate performance indicator, set a performance target and an allowed deviation percentage, and to analyze the actual outcome for each indicator. This enables the differentiation between an excellent, expected, or bad Performance for each element. Following existing heat mapping techniques, bad Performance is visualized by using a solid red, expected Performance by a dashed orange, and excellent Performance by a dotted green color.

The first two activities result in a business architecture heat map (see Fig. 1 for an example[1]), which can be further analyzed during the strategic fit improvement analysis. The main objective of this analysis is to identify operational changes that could potentially improve the value creation throughout the business architecture to result in a better realization of the strategic objectives. To support this, a critical path can be identified starting from a Goal with a bad Performance (e.g., Improve short-term solvency in Fig. 1) as a chain of valueStream relations that have a high or medium Importance and that connect business architecture elements on downstream hierarchical levels of which the Performance can be improved (e.g., Increase current assets, Sale additional products, Operational excellence, and Baking) [15]. A critical path ends at the

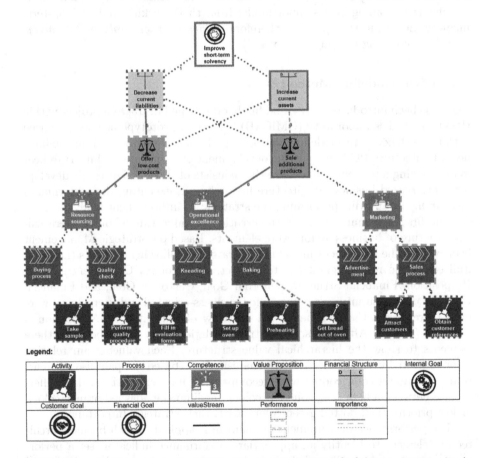

Fig. 1. Example of a business architecture heat map in PGA [14] (Color figure online)

---

[1] The labels were manually adapted to improve readability on a limited space.

Activity or Process level of the business architecture (e.g., Preheating), which leads to concrete changes that can be applied to the organizational processes.

3   Methodology

3.1   Evaluation Technique

In this paper, we applied the evaluation technique of [3] to test the intuitiveness of the PGA notation by the intended end-users[2]. The participants were given 60 min to complete the evaluation questions. This evaluation comprised a set of tasks, which were clustered in three core phases surrounded by an initiation and a conclusion phase (see Fig. 2).

Fig. 2. Procedure of the evaluation technique [3]

Initiation Phase. Participants were briefly introduced to the relevant domain (i.e., strategic fit in the business architecture) and the building blocks of the PGA modeling method without showing any visual aspects like language concepts or sample models. Besides this, some information about the participants was collected. This information comprised demographic aspects (i.e., gender, age) as well as questions regarding the experience of the participant with modeling languages. An informed consent was used to provide the necessary information about voluntary participation to the user study and the anonymous processing of the collected data.

Phase 1 – Term Association. Participants were provided terms that refer to names of PGA modeling language concepts. Each participant then individually drafted one or more graphical representations that he/she deems as the most intuitive for the element. Participants received a blank paper with a list of the terms and they were asked to use a variation of colors to perform this task.

Phase 2 – Notation Association. Afterwards, samples of the current PGA notation were presented and participants were asked to record up to three intuitive associations that pop out when looking at them. Notably, the notations were presented without any hint of e.g., the name or the semantics of this concept. Furthermore, the concepts forming part of the term association were different to the ones of the notation association to omit hampering intuitiveness. In order to enable a full coverage of the PGA notation, we decided

---

[2] The evaluation forms can be found via: https://doi.org/10.13140/RG.2.2.27473. 48489.

to divide the participants into two groups. Group A had half of the concepts as part of the term association and the other half as part of the notation association. For group B, the order of the phases was the same, but the concepts were divided oppositely between the two tasks.

Phase 3 – Case Study. This task included comprehension questions targeting an example of a business architecture heat map (see Fig. 1). The legend is added here for clarification but was not provided to the respondents. Each question was oriented towards the identification of particular meta-model elements in the model, e.g., how many elements have a good performance, which type of element is supported by Operational excellence, etc.

Concluding Phase. As a last step, participants were asked to provide qualitative feedback and improvement suggestions about the current PGA notation.

3.2 Data Analysis

Phase 1 – Term Association. For the analysis, one needs to deconstruct the participants' graphical representations according to different visual variables [10], such as color, shape, icons, texture, or any other visual aspect that pops out. As not all respondents used the full range of visual variables, their relative frequency per meta-model element is analyzed. For example, 75% of the shapes used to depict an Activity is a (rounded) rectangle (see Table 1).

Phase 2 – Notation Association. The percentage of participants that provided a matching association with the name of the meta-model element is calculated. Besides, the relative rank of this percentage is interesting to analyze, as it is an indicator of the extent to which the PGA element is outperformed by other meta-model constructs. This would show that there is a problem with the perceptual discriminability as the different symbols are not clearly distinguishable from each other in the current notation [10].

Phase 3 – Case Study. Comprehension questions can be answered based on the available information in the sample model. Therefore, it is possible to analyze the given responses and calculate the percentage of participants that provided a correct answer to a certain comprehension question.

All participant responses were digitized and stored in a shared cloud infrastructure. All authors started a pretest for analyzing the results with only a few responses. Afterwards, the gained experience was exchanged to streamline the structure of the analysis, e.g., the visual variables to be applied during the classification of the term associations. Next, the authors independently analyzed all responses, after which the analysis was condensed toward a harmonized result.

4   Evaluation Results

4.1   Participants

The participants were students following a Master level class on IT Management at the Faculty of Economics and Business Administration of Ghent University.

In total, 139 students participated in the user study. The participants were randomly assigned to two different groups (see Sect. 3.1), resulting in 70 participants for group A and 69 for group B. Their average age was 22 years and 41% of them were female. Although the participants were not familiar with the PGA method, 86% had some prior modeling knowledge about ER modeling, 90% about business process modeling, and 34% about ArchiMate.

4.2   Analysis of the Term Association Phase

Table 1 shows the deconstruction of the participants' graphical representations according to different visual variables. The relevant variables that were used by participants include *color*, *shape*, *icons*, and *text*. In this respect, icons are symbols that perceptually resemble the concepts they represent [10], while shape refers to geometric figures (e.g., square, line). Due to limited space, Table 1 only covers the most used visual variables (i.e., a cumulative frequency of at least 50% if the individual absolute frequency is at least two).

During the term association analysis, some interesting insights are obtained. First, it is observed that the participants dominantly used a blue color to design a graphical representation for a given meta-model element. To efficiently handle a large group of 139 respondents, they were asked to bring a variety of colors. However, we see that the majority of the participants only used one color to draft a notation. This unexpected result is a limitation in the set-up of the evaluation technique.

Concerning shape, some recurring proposals can be seen such as a rectangle, triangle, ellipse, or arrow. The origin of these proposals can be explained by the modeling experience of the participants, which are familiar with ER and business process modeling. Although the intuitiveness of such shapes is quite limited, participants added to them corresponding icons to further shape the meaning of the concepts (e.g., thinking balloon, dollar/euro sign, bull's-eye, graph, exclamation mark, etc.). These icons seem to provide an important instrument for participants to design an intuitive notation.

In line with the principle of Dual Coding [10], participants used text to complement the proposed graphics, which enabled them to depict the meaning of an element both visually and verbally. In most cases, the text is equal to the first letter of the meta-model element (e.g., C for Competence) or its complete name (e.g., Activity). In other cases, text refers to the content of a meta-model element. This is the case for Financial structure, which is a representation of the cost and revenue structure (e.g., as coded by C & R) that is implemented by an organization.

Finally, *number* and *graphical position* were used for specific meta-model elements. More specifically, participants employed spatial enclosure to represent activities as a subset of the overarching process. In this case, we see a dominant proposal of three rectangles connected by arrows. Graphical position is also proposed for the representation of a valueStream. In this case, participants use a hierarchy of arrows to depict the value creation throughout the business architecture.

Table 1. Results of the term association task

PGA concept	Color	Shape	Icons	Text
Activity	1. Blue (71%)	1. (Rounded) rectangle (75%)	1. Person (18%)	1. Activity (46%) 2. A (23%)
Process	1. Blue (75%)	1. Arrow (28%) 2. Rectangle (28%)	–	1. Act. nr. (71%)
Competence	1. Blue (76%)	1. Rectangle (31%) 2. Triangle (23%)	1. Thinking balloon (21%) 2. Person (14%) 3. Light bulb (14%) 4. Brain (10%)	1. C (57%)
Value Proposition	1. Blue (78%)	1. Ellipse (27%) 2. Rectangle (24%)	1. Dollar/Euro (29%) 2. + sign (10%) 3. Light bulb (10%) 4. People (6%)	1. V (27%) 2. VP (27%)
Financial Structure	1. Blue (63%)	1. Ellipse (35%) 2. Rectangle (33%)	1. Dollar/Euro (80%)	1. Cost & revenues (40%) 2. C & R (20%)
Internal Goal	1. Blue (67%)	1. Ellipse (54%)	1. Bull's-eye/arrow (64%)	1. I (29%) 2. x (21%)
Customer Goal	1. Blue (65%)	1. Ellipse (34%) 2. Cloud (16%)	1. Bull's-eye/arrow (48%) 2. Person (33%)	1. C (44%) 2. Customer (goal) (22%)
Financial Goal	1. Blue (65%)	1. Ellipse (30%) 2. Rectangle (30%)	1. Dollar/Euro (67%)	–
valueStream	1. Blue (73%)	1. Arrow (69%)	1. Dollar/Euro (47%) 2. Stream (18%)	1. V (67%)
Performance	1. Blue (72%)	1. Rectangle (32%) 2. Ellipse (21%)	1. Graph (18%) 2. V checkbox (18%) 3. Muscle (13%) 4. Trophy (10%)	–
Importance	1. Blue (66%)	1. Rectangle (26%) 2. Triangle (26%)	1. Exclamation mark (75%)	–

4.3   Analysis of the Notation Association Phase

Table 2 shows the results of the notation association task. For each element, the percentage of participants giving a matching association and the relative rank of this association is listed. Important to note here is that the visualization of the valueStream relation (i.e., a non-directed line, see Table 4), was not explicitly tested as the meaning of this relation only becomes clear when included in a hierarchical business architecture heat map.

The percentage of correct associations ranges between 0% and 36.23%. The PGA concepts Activity (24.29% - rank 1), Process (36.23% - rank 1), Financial Structure (12.75% - rank 3), and Financial Goal (20.29% - rank 2) perform the best as we analyze both the percentage and the relative rank of the correct associations. The notation of the other elements is less intuitive, as the percentages are below 5%. Moreover, some of them are outperformed by other meta-model elements. More specifically, the Competence notation (i.e., a stage icon) is con-

Table 2. Results of the notation association task

PGA concept	Percentage of correct associations	Relative rank of correct association
Activity	24.29%	1
Process	36.23%	1
Competence	2.90%	8
Value Proposition	2.83%	9
Financial Structure	12.75%	3
Internal Goal	4.90%	5
Customer Goal	0%	–
Financial Goal	20.29%	2
Performance	0%	–
Importance	0%	–

fused with Performance by 52.17% of the participants and the icon of Internal Goal (i.e., a cogwheel) is associated with a Process by 35.29% of the participants.

4.4 Analysis of the Case Study Phase

In Table 3, the results of the case study are given. To keep this example manageable for participants in the given time, only one type of Goal (i.e., Financial Goal) was included in the sample model. This is the reason why no results are available for Customer and Internal Goal in Table 3. Although all questions were oriented towards the identification of meta-model elements, partially correct answers could also be identified. These include naming elements at the instance level (e.g., Take sample instead of Activity) or using close synonyms for the meta-model element (i.e., Task as a synonym for Activity). Besides, there was not a question that directly targeted the identification of a valueStream, but problems with the intuitiveness of this relation can be derived from incorrect answers to the questions about the Activity and Value Proposition concept. More specifically, some incorrect answers indicate that the valueStream relation was interpreted in the wrong direction.

Although the mean score of complete correct answers for this task is 41.32%, Table 3 shows that the meaning of the Value Proposition (i.e., 5.04% correct answers) and Importance (i.e., 5.76% correct answers) notation cannot easily be derived from the business architecture heat map. Even if partially correct answers are included, these elements are the two least performing of all PGA concepts with total scores of 21.59% for Value Proposition and 14.39% for Importance. Besides, there seems to be a problem with the intuitiveness of the valueStream notation, which was read in the wrong direction in the Activity and Value Proposition question by respectively 18.71% and 27.34% of the participants. As one can notice, the scores for Financial Structure and Financial Goal are the same,

Table 3. Results of the case study task

PGA concept	Percentage of correct answers	Partially correct/incorrect answers
Activity	23.02%	Synonym (task): 9.35%
		Instance level elements: 15.83%
Process	74.10%	
Competence	42.45%	
Value Proposition	5.04%	Instance level elements: 16.55%
Financial Structure	57.55%	
Financial Goal	57.55%	
valueStream	–	Incorrect question activity: 18.71%
		Incorrect question value proposition: 27.34%
Performance	81.29%	
Importance	5.76%	Partial answer: 8.63%

as the identification of these meta-model elements was included in one question during the case study task.

4.5   Analysis of the Concluding Phase

During the conclusion phase, we obtained 104 remarks from 58 unique participants (i.e., a response rate of 41.73%). Of the responses, 45 could be specifically traced back to the PGA meta-model, distributed among the aspects color and line style (24 remarks), Importance (12 remarks), valueStream (5 remarks), and Activity (4 remarks). As can be seen in Table 4, color and line style refer both to Performance and Importance in the PGA meta-model. We provide illustrative feedback in the following.

- Color & line style: "Using colors is a good idea, it gives a nice and quick overview."
  "The meaning of the different colors & line styles is not clear."
- Importance: "It is not clear what the numbers next to the relations mean."
- valueStream: "It is difficult to see where certain value streams go to."
- Activity: "The model would improve if the total process of how the organization operates was represented."

5   Towards an Improved PGA Notation

We conclude the design cycle by proposing directions for improving the PGA notation. This proposal is based on the combined evaluation results discussed previously. In particular, we distinguish between (i) no change is required and

(ii) the suggestion of a new notation. In the first case, no change is required as the results confirm the intuitiveness of the initial notation. In the latter, we use (some of) the suggestions of the participants to propose a new notation. For some elements, this also includes changes aimed at the homogenization of the notations of all PGA elements.

For the PGA elements Activity, Process, Financial Structure, Financial Goal, and Performance, we propose to preserve the initial notation based on the analysis of the results. The notation association, case study, and qualitative feedback confirm the intuitiveness of these elements. Moreover, the suggested notations of the term association phase only include generic shapes (i.e., rectangle and ellipse) with no or recurring icons (i.e., dollar/euro sign). Following these suggestions would have a negative impact on the perceptual discriminability between Activity and Process on the one hand, and Financial Structure and Financial Goal on the other hand. Besides, we understand the qualitative feedback about the lack of a complete process description in the PGA models. However, this is a deliberate design choice of the modeling method as the main purpose of the business architecture heat maps is to achieve alignment between the different layers. Therefore, it is not always needed to offer a complete view on the business architecture, as this may hamper the understanding of the models [15]. Performance is an exception in the analysis, as it combines a low score for the notation association (i.e., 0%) with a score of 81.29% for the case study. This can be explained by the fact that Performance is implemented as an attribute to the other PGA meta-model elements. Consequently, the meaning of the color coding only becomes intuitive when implemented in a complete business architecture heat map (see Fig. 1). Qualitative feedback further confirmed that the use of color enables to give a nice and quick overview of alignment opportunities in the business architecture.

The main argument to propose a new notation for Competence is the confusion that the initial one causes for end-users. Indeed, during the notation association phase, it became clear that people naturally attach the meaning of Performance to the visualization. Based on the suggestions of the participants during the term association task, we propose a combination of a person and light bulb icon as the new notation (see Table 4). This notation should refer to the cognitive abilities that are associated with the definition of a Competence as the internal knowledge, skills and abilities of an organization.

A new notation for Value Proposition is also proposed in Table 4, as the initial notation was one of the least performing PGA elements during the notation association (i.e., 2.83%) and case study (i.e., 5.04%) tasks. However, the suggested icons by participants do not show a clear preference as they are closely related to financial elements (i.e., dollar/euro or + sign) or cognitive abilities (i.e., light bulb). Therefore, the new notation is a gift that is exchanged between two hands. We believe this provides a more intuitive notation for the products and services that are exchanged between a company and its customers. This proposal is in line with the notation of a Value Proposition in the Business Model Canvas (i.e., a gift icon) [13].

Table 4. Suggested improvements to the current PGA notation

PGA concept	Initial notation	Suggestion by Participants	Suggested new notation
Activity		Blue (rounded) rectangle	No change is required
Process		Three blue rectangles, connected by arrows	No change is required
Competence		Blue rectangle/triangle with a thinking cloud, person or light bulb icon	
Value Proposition		Blue ellipse/rectangle with a euro/dollar icon	
Financial Structure		Blue ellipse/rectangle with a euro/dollar icon	No change is required
Internal Goal		Blue ellipse with a bull's-eye/arrow icon and text I	
Customer Goal		Blue ellipse with a bull's-eye/arrow and person icon and text C	
Financial Goal		Blue ellipse/rectangle with a bull's-eye/arrow and euro/dollar icon	No change is required
valueStream	—	Blue arrow in a hierarchical structure	
Performance		Blue rectangle with a graph or V checkbox icon	No change is required
Importance		Blue rectangle with an exclamation mark icon	

The notation of an Internal Goal needed improvement as respondents confused it with processes during the notation association phase. As the current PGA notation already includes a bull's-eye to represent the goal aspect, the analysis of the term association task did not provide further concrete suggestions. To stress the internal characteristic of the term, it was decided to graphically enclose cog wheel icons (i.e., the initial notation) inside a factory icon (see Table 4).

A similar argument can be provided for the new notation of a Customer Goal. This element scored low (i.e., 0%) in the notation association task, which clearly shows that the intuitiveness of the current notation needs improvement. Based on the suggestions of the term association phase, it was decided to clearly represent the customer by a person icon in the new notation. To stress the meaning of a customer, the person is shaking hands with another person, holding a briefcase (see Table 4).

Problems with the understanding of the valueStream relation became apparent during the case study, in which a large part of the participants applied it in the wrong direction. Furthermore, some of the qualitative feedback confirms that the direction of the valueStream is not clear. In line with the term association task, this issue is solved by using an arrow in the newly proposed PGA notation. This arrow points towards the element in business architecture heat map, of which the value creation is supported by an element on the downstream hierarchical level.

A last change that is proposed concerns the Importance element. In the initial notation, this attribute was visualized by a colored valueStream accompanied by a certain texture. Furthermore, we added a number (i.e., showing its relative importance) to this visualization as a form of dual coding. However, the results of the different evaluation tasks showed that this notation was poorly understood by participants. This was also confirmed by the qualitative feedback about the confusing color coding and numbers of the valueStream relations. A first improvement could be identified based on the term association phase, of which the results show that an exclamation mark is an intuitive way of representing Importance. We combine this suggestion by replacing the color coding by a different thickness of the valueStream relations. As a result, a valueStream with a high Importance will be depicted by a thick arrow, combined with three exclamation marks. The thickness and number of exclamation marks decreases for a valueStream with a medium or low Importance (see Table 4).

6   Reflection and Concluding Remarks

This paper describes the execution of an evaluation technique [3] to test the intuitiveness of the initial PGA notation [15]. This evaluation was needed to validate the communication potential of PGA and to improve the understanding and acceptance of the resulting models by business-oriented end-users. The evaluation tasks were performed by 139 Master's students of Ghent University with an elaborate economical background and basic modeling experience. The analysis of these tasks and the qualitative feedback led to the proposal of an alternative notation for six of the 11 elements of the PGA modeling method.

This research is not free from threats to validity [18]. To preserve **construct validity**, it is important to ensure that the executed tasks are suited to evaluate the intuitiveness of a DSML. Therefore, we applied an existing evaluation technique, for which the origin of the tasks is rigorously substantiated [3]. With respect to **internal validity**, external factors that influence the results need to be avoided. In this respect, participants were chosen with the same educational background (i.e., Master's students in Business Engineering and Business Administration). Besides this, the participants had similar foreknowledge in conceptual modeling and received a collective introduction to PGA. Furthermore, participation was voluntarily and no compensation was provided. Finally, we used two different randomly assigned groups and divided the PGA concepts between the term association and notation association tasks to mitigate an allocation bias. In this way, we made sure that the terms given during the first task did not influence the associations of the notation association phase. The choice of participants also affects the **external validity** or generalizability of the results. The students have a strong economic orientation which enabled us to obtain a group of respondents with knowledge and skills that can act as a proxy for business-oriented stakeholders. These stakeholders are the targeted end-users of the PGA modeling method. Nevertheless, the choice for students is an inherent limitation and further research is needed to replicate the evaluation technique with business practitioners. **Reliability** reflects the degree to which the results could be reproduced by the modeling community. To ensure this, the procedure that was used to apply the evaluation technique and the URL of the evaluation questionnaires can be found in Sect. 3.1. Finally, we added the details about the analysis of the different evaluation tasks in Sect. 3.2.

Future research is needed for the evaluation of the proposed improvements. This includes an experiment, in which the intuitiveness of the initial and newly proposed notation is compared. Such an experiment could be based on recall and comprehension questions, which compare the effectiveness and efficiency of interpreting both versions of the PGA notation [4]. Nevertheless, more research is needed to set-up a rigorous experimental design. In this respect, we are currently implementing the new version of the notation to become part of a future version of the PGA modeling tool. The new tool shall be made available through the PGA project space within the OMiLAB[3] of the Open Models Laboratory [2].

On a separate research stream, we will investigate possibilities of automating the applied evaluation technique [3]. In this respect, we aim to set up a web-environment that automatically generates the evaluation sheets once the concepts and sample notations are uploaded. Moreover, it shall provide a WYSIWYG web editor for drawing notations and storing them. To support the analysis of the collected data, this system shall use OpenCV or similar technologies to automatically analyze the created proposals for new notations. Besides this,

---

[3] PGA project space within OMiLAB [online], https://austria.omilab.org/psm/content/PGA/info, last accessed: 04.03.2020.

enabling text analysis could be useful for the results of the notation association task as well as implementing statistical analysis of the responses and the
automated generation of evaluation reports. Ultimately, the web-environment
will increase the possibilities of testing a modeling language comprehensively,
as it enables an efficient set-up, execution, and analysis of the evaluation. Consequently, it will mitigate issues related to the paper-and-pen evaluation of a
tool-based modeling language.

References

1. ADOxx.org: ADOxx Metamodelling Platform (2020). https://www.adoxx.org/
   live/home. Accessed 15 Jan 2020
2. Bork, D., Buchmann, R.A., Karagiannis, D., Lee, M., Miron, E.T.: An open platform for modeling method conceptualization: the OMiLAB digital ecosystem. Commun. Assoc. Inf. Syst. **44**, 673–697 (2019)
3. Bork, D., Schrüffer, C., Karagiannis, D.: Intuitive understanding of domain-specific
   modeling languages: proposition and application of an evaluation technique. In:
   Laender, A.H.F., Pernici, B., Lim, E.-P., de Oliveira, J.P.M. (eds.) ER 2019. LNCS,
   vol. 11788, pp. 311–319. Springer, Cham (2019). https://doi.org/10.1007/978-3-
   030-33223-5_26
4. Burton-Jones, A., Wand, Y., Weber, R.: Guidelines for empirical evaluations of
   conceptual modeling grammars. J. Assoc. Inf. Syst. **10**(6), 495–532 (2009)
5. El Kouhen, A., Gherbi, A., Dumoulin, C., Khendek, F.: On the semantic transparency of visual notations: experiments with UML. In: Fischer, J., Scheidgen,
   M., Schieferdecker, I., Reed, R. (eds.) SDL 2015. LNCS, vol. 9369, pp. 122–137.
   Springer, Cham (2015). https://doi.org/10.1007/978-3-319-24912-4_10
6. Frank, U.: Domain-specific modeling languages: requirements analysis and design
   guidelines. In: Reinhartz-Berger, I., Sturm, A., Clark, T., Cohen, S., Bettin, J.
   (eds.) Domain Engineering, pp. 133–157. Springer, Heidelberg (2013). https://doi.
   org/10.1007/978-3-642-36654-3_6
7. Henderson, J., Venkatraman, N.: Strategic alignment: leveraging information technology for transforming organizations. IBM Syst. J. **38**(2–3), 472–484 (1999)
8. Karagiannis, D., Kühn, H.: Metamodelling platforms. In: Bauknecht, K., Tjoa,
   A.M., Quirchmayr, G. (eds.) EC-Web 2002. LNCS, vol. 2455, pp. 182–182.
   Springer, Heidelberg (2002). https://doi.org/10.1007/3-540-45705-4_19
9. Karagiannis, D., Mayr, H.C., Mylopoulos, J.: Domain-Specific Conceptual Modeling - Concepts, Methods and Tools. Springer, Cham (2016). https://doi.org/10.
   1007/978-3-319-39417-6
10. Moody, D.: The "physics" of notations: toward a scientific basis for constructing
    visual notations in software engineering. IEEE Trans. Softw. Eng. **35**(6), 756–779
    (2009)
11. Mylopoulos, J.: Conceptual Modelling and Telos. Conceptual Modelling,
    Databases, and CASE: an Integrated View of Information System Development,
    pp. pp. 49–68. Wiley, New York (1992)
12. Newell, A., Simon, H.A.: Human Problem Solving, vol. 104. Prentice-Hall, Engle-
    wood Cliffs (1972)
13. Osterwalder, A., Pigneur, Y., Tucci, C.: Business Model Generation: A Handbook
    for Visionaries, Game Changers, and Challengers. Wiley, Hoboken (2010)

14. Roelens, B., Poels, G.: The creation of business architecture heat maps to support strategy-aligned organizational decisions. In: 8th European Conference on IS Management and Evaluation (ECIME), pp. 388–392. Acad. Conferences Ltd. (2014)

15. Roelens, B., Steenacker, W., Poels, G.: Realizing strategic fit within the business architecture: the design of a process-goal alignment modeling and analysis technique. Softw. Syst. Model. **18**(1), 631–662 (2019)

16. Saaty, T.: How to make a decision: the analytic hierarchy process. Eur. J. Oper. Res. **48**(1), 9–26 (1990)

17. Sein, M., Henfridsson, O., Purao, S., Rossi, M., Lindgren, R.: Action design research. MIS Q. **35**(1), 37–56 (2011)

18. Wohlin, C., Runeson, P., Höst, M., Ohlsson, M.C., Regnell, B., Wesslén, A.: Experimentation in Software Engineering. Springer, Heidelberg (2012). https://doi.org/10.1007/978-3-642-29044-2

Does Enterprise Architecture Support Customer Experience Improvement? Towards a Conceptualization in Digital Transformation Context

Mouaad Hafsi[✉] and Saïd Assar[✉] (ORCID)

LITEM, Univ Evry, IMT-BS, Université Paris-Saclay, 91025 Evry, France
{mouaad.hafsi,said.assar}@imt-bs.eu

Abstract. Customer Experience (CE) is often presented as a competitive battle-field in the new digital context. However, it is defined so broadly, so holistically, that companies find it challenging to improve it through well-defined projects with an impact analysis of the different changes that could be brought about. Enterprise Architecture Management (EAM) is supposed to be a suitable means to support the management of such transformation projects. However, the depth and disruptive nature of these changes raise multiple questions concerning the adequacy of EAM for Customer Experience Improvement (CEI). In current corporate practice, there seems to be no regular application of EAM as a central support service for CEI in the digital context. In this paper, we explore how EAM can support CEI and examine how digitalization transforms the customer experience. We further identify the required information inputs for these transformations. Based on this foundation, we identify content elements that EAM can provide by analyzing EAM meta-models. Comparing the requirements by CEI projects and the supply by EAM shows that EAM, in general, provides valuable inputs for organizational issues and roles but shows weaknesses when it comes to information about trends, contextual and environmental information.

Keywords: Digital transformation · Customer Experience Improvement · Enterprise Architecture Management · Enterprise Models · ArchiMate

1 Introduction

Digital transformation (DT) is proliferating in organizations around the world [1b]. Increasingly demanding customers are pushing digital competition to its edges [8]. Many organizations operating in the products and services marketing, involving direct interactions with customers, invest considerably in digital transformation [1b, 2b]. One of the main reasons for these investments is the ability of DT to improve customer experience [3b, 4b, 8, 9b]. Banks are, for example, among the first industries engaging DT projects [36]. Changing consumer habits and the new competitive environment, are forcing banks to urgently deal with their customer process so as not to be left behind in a rapidly fluctuating market. Customers expect financial services to be available 24 h a day, seven

© Springer Nature Switzerland AG 2020
S. Nurcan et al. (Eds.): BPMDS 2020/EMMSAD 2020, LNBIP 387, pp. 411–427, 2020.
https://doi.org/10.1007/978-3-030-49418-6_28

days a week, and as user-friendly as social networks or messaging solutions that they use every day [4b, 5b, 6b].

Thus, customer experience is seen as the new competitive field of marketing. The consulting firm Gartner pointed out that 57% of customers stopped buying from a company because a competitor offered a better experience [37], and that 67% of customers are willing to pay more for better customer experience. However, digital projects concerning improving customer experience often remain at the starting point [36, 37]. This is due to the complexity of implementing this transformation; indeed, it is a complex process impacting several areas and components of the organization [4b, 8b]. It involves managing the volatile behavior of customers, understanding their complex data [7b, 16b, 17b, 18b, 19b], carrying out numerous optimizations of customer processes [14b], transforming business models [6b, 13b, 14b], integrating various digital technologies [6b, 7b, 8b] and adapting to changing business conditions [8b, 12b, 14b].

This implementation is even more complex since organizations do not start from a blank page to design their customer experiences. Many have already established customers, processes, and assets that require reorientation to carry out strategies specific to the customer experience [5b]. Drawing on our expertise in digital transformation consulting, managers suffer from the absence of tools helping to define a reachable target while considering their existing environment. Consultants often tend to start their analyzes from a blank sheet and to design ideal transformative customer experiences almost independent of the real context that the company operates.

Among the techniques that appeared in recent years to support such transformations, Enterprise Architecture (EA) and EA Management (EAM) seem to be essential [1, 4, 5]. While EA describes the fundamental structures of an organization, EAM is believed to support transformations management by guiding the necessary coordination efforts [3] and providing information for strategy development [4, 5, 7]. It also provides Enterprise Models (EM) to various stakeholders in transformation projects and enhances communication by establishing shared and mutual understandings [5]. Likewise, EAM can guide decision processes and contributes to better design choices that align with the operational and strategic goals of the transformation endeavor [6, 10, 11, 16, 17].

Nevertheless, and according to our consulting experience, EAM is not commonly applied. It is rarely perceived as a support service for digital projects, especially projects concerning experience client improvement. There is a tendency to consider EAM as a discipline mostly about IT and located in the IT departments [23]. Customer Experience Improvement (CEI) projects are, however, more profound and broader than an IT transformation and could impact commercial processes and business models [8, 9, 5b, 10b].

We tend to consider that there is a severe gap between the information offered by EAM and the managers' demands in digital transformation projects. Architects seem not to know how to support CEI project managers, and these managers are not aware of how EAM might support their effort [23]. For this paper, we try to provide the first step towards a better understanding of EAM support for CEI in a digital transformation context. This leads to the research question:

- RQ: Does EAM support ECI projects in a digital transformation context?

  - RQ1a: How digitalization transforms customer experience?
  - RQ1b: And what are the necessary information needs to these transformations?

- RQ2: What are the content elements that Enterprise Models can provide to cover these necessary information needs?

In order to answer the question, we proceed as follows. We first introduce related work and go on with illustrating our research approach. We present the results and provide a discussion. We close with a summary and implications.

2 Related Work

2.1 Digital Transformation for a Better Customer Experience

Digital transformation operates a radical change in the organization structure, processes, functions and business models [5b, 8b, 9b, 10b]. Companies adopt digital technologies to mainly improve business performance [1b, 7b]. Digital transformation promises many benefits: enhancing organizational processes [7b, 9b, 10b, 12, 38]; improving value propositions to the customer [3b, 5b, 13]; rising the services quality [12b, 13b]; reducing the products and services costs [2b, 14]; innovating new products and services [3b, 15]; increasing customer loyalty and revenues [5b, 13–15]; and finally, improving the customer experience [5b, 8b, 9b, 10b, 12b].

The study by [8] summarizes DT impacts in three main areas: customer experience, operational processes, and business model. Each of these three areas is divided into three sub-elements. The customer experience is divided into customer understanding, growth, and customer touchpoints. What is interesting is that, traditionally, the customer experience has only been seen from different points of contact [5b]. Westerman et al. in [8] draw a broader picture by adding elements around sales rationalization and marketing processes improvement, as well as new digital capabilities to understand customers and their volatile behaviors.

Numerous studies have examined the implementation of projects for improving the customer experience in organizations [1b]. For example, assessing target strategies and policies around the customer experience [8b], examining engagement processes [16b], or analyzing the critical factors to reshape the customer value proposition [11b, 14b]. These studies tend to focus mainly on defining what customer experience is about and its ecosystem in the company. Few attempts have been made to develop a comprehensive approach helping managers to understand the impact of CEI projects on the organization ecosystems, considering the new context of digital transformation.

2.2 Enterprise Architecture as a Support Tool to Manage Digital Transformation

Many research studies have stated that EAM can address partial problems within DT from a management point of view. In [15], the authors consider EAM as a governing tool that helps mastering the alignment of portfolios of transformation steps. They also claim potential capacities in different fields, such as strategic direction, gap analysis, strategic planning, and operational planning. In [17], the focus is on the strategic change process and how EAM can support it. The author sees that the strategic fit with the market environment and business-IT alignment can be, presumably, supported by EAM. Moreover, EAM can help in preparing the change by standardizing and modularizing parts of the enterprise.

Over the years, studies have associated several benefits with EAM. These are generally indirect, large-scale, and perceived over a long period, which generally makes it difficult to calculate an exact return on investment (ROI) [35]. However, in the occasional cases where the ROI has been calculated, the results seem remarkable [35]. Among these benefits, we highlight: increasing flexibility, integration and interoperability [7, 15, 17, 19–22]; better alignment of IT with business [1, 3, 10, 11, 15, 17, 19, 22]; IT costs reduction [1, 3, 15, 17]; improved risk management, situational awareness and decision-making [3, 9, 16, 21]; better results from strategic business initiatives [10, 11, 21, 38].

Other recent studies (e.g. [21, 22]) examine the evolution of modeling languages and techniques to make them better adapted to the new age of digital transformation. They assume that during enterprise transformations, companies need shared understanding and agreement on topics such as the overall strategy of the enterprise, the existent processes, as well as the future vision of the top management. However, when enterprise modeling languages were developed, the digital transformation challenges were not yet that noticeable. At that time, the focus was more on consolidation and optimization [38, 39]. As such, it is logical to expect that the existing languages may require some updates concerning new element content to be truly ready for modeling the digital transformation impacts on the organization ecosystem [23].

To conclude, many studies focus on how EAM can support transformations management from an EAM point of view (e.g. [10, 15–18]). However, the demand perspective of CEI projects in a digital transformation context is not available in the current discussion. Thus, we will investigate which information inputs the demand side needs and if current EAM can provide them.

3   Research Approach

To answer our research questions, we proceeded in three steps (Fig. 1):

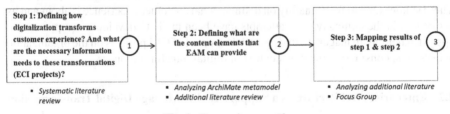

Fig. 1. Research approach

3.1 Step 1: Defining How Digitalization Transforms Customer Experience and What Are the Necessary Information Needs to These Transformations

In order to assess if CEI projects can be supported by EAM, we conduct a systematic literature review, following [24] and [25] protocol, to identify how digitalization affects CE and what are the information needed to succeed these transformations (c.f. Fig. 2).

Research Identification
For this paper we investigated the research question RQ described in the introduction.

Search Strategy
We developed the terms related to the research questions; the aim is identifying synonyms for these terms by leading several tests. We used the Boolean operators (OR, AND) for connecting the founded terms. We used strings for automated search: ("digital transformation" OR "digitalization") AND ("customer experience" OR "consumer experience" OR "client experience"). We conducted the search of articles by using Scopus database. The search started on 25 of January 2020.

Study Selection
We have included papers that respect the following criteria: a) written in English; b) published in a scientific journal; c) it deals with digital transformation; d) documents which weren't accessible were excluded, as well as, master and doctoral theses, proceedings or conference articles, working papers and textbooks. This choice of journal articles respects the position of [26], who claims *"academics and practitioners a like use journals most often for acquiring information and disseminating new findings and represent the highest level of research"*.

Quality Assessment
Based on the works of [27–29], we assessed the rigor and relevance of the selected articles. We used criteria's such as clear description of the context in which the research was carried out, precise statement of research aims, high level of rigor in conducting the data collection and analysis, relevance of the findings and the extent to which the study is valuable for research or practice. The assessment was conducted by both authors and

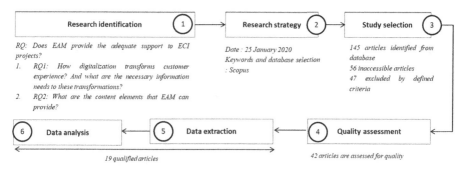

Fig. 2. Steps of systematic literature review

each paper was given a quality score. At the end of this process, we had qualified 19 articles to be analyzed for the data extraction step. These articles are numbered 1b, 2b, etc. and appear separately in an online appendix [1].

Data Extraction
We extracted data from the qualified articles and categorized it according to the model proposed by [8]. The authors of this work have defined three blocks of digital transformation impact on the customer experience (*Customer understanding, Top Line Growth, and Customer Touch point*). Thus, from each paper, we extracted the data requirements that were considered necessary to carry out these transformations and categorized them according to the three proposed blocks.

Data Synthesis and Analysis
The extracted data is classified according to the three blocks mentioned previously [8] and analyzed in terms of content and semantics. Our analysis allowed us to rename the three proposed group of transformations (*Understanding Customer, Enabling selling activities, Managing Customer touch points*), and also to add a new group (*Integrating Digital capabilities*) to take into account all data extracted and new items that emerged.

3.2 Step 2: Defining What Are the Content Elements that EAM Can Provide by Analyzing ArchiMate Meta-Model

In a second step, we analyze and then conceptualize the information inputs that EAM can provide to the CEI projects. We relied for our work on the content meta-model of ArchiMate 3.0. ArchiMate is a mature industry standard that, on the one hand, is maintained by companies and research partners; on the other hand, it is often used as a foundation for many corporate EAM frameworks [29]. ArchiMate provides a conceptual macro overview of the information that EAM can provide and thus allows for a more generic discussion. Again, we ensured reliability and validity by comparing the identified content elements with other meta-models like TOGAF [2], GERAM [30], Zachman [31], DODAF [32] and IEEE [33].

3.3 Step 3: Mapping Results of Steps 1 and 2 Using Focus Group Technique

After identifying the needed information inputs of ECI projects and the available information outputs of EAM, we mapped both in a third step. Major challenges were the different languages apparent in both disciplines that inhibited a straightforward one-to-one mapping. Hence, at start, we based our first mapping test on the meta-model specification and additional literature. Then we proceeded for a Focus Group [34] where we presented our pre-filled mapping to six enterprise architects from a French bank who use and master ArchiMate as a meta-model in their daily modeling activities (Table 1).

We collected feedback on our initial mapping by explaining our choices based on literature. Then, the architects tried to analyze for each ECI information need, the content that ArchiMate meta-model could provide in terms of concepts, based on concrete

---

[1] Available online at ResearchGate: https://doi.org/10.13140/RG.2.2.33596.18560.

examples of their modeling activities. The focus group process took almost two weeks. Three meetings (2 to 3 h for each one) were held to introduce and work on Mapping. The process can be summarized as follows:

Table 1. Profiles of the enterprise architects in the focus group

Enterprise architect	Experience in EA	Expertise level
FTX	10 years	Expert – had worked in other banks before
FAR	9 years	Expert – had worked in other banks before
MHI	6 years	TOGAF certified – has worked in other banks before
CTR	12 years	ArchiMate expert – has worked in other banks before
YLE	3 years	Confirmed
AZE	11 years	Expert & TOGAF certified

First, we discussed the initial results of our first literature-based mapping. One of the co-authors led this stage. He was invited to share ideas from the literature concerning ArchiMate modeling. This first meeting was more like an open discussion and discussed the advantages and limitations of ArchiMate in the banking context.

Second, the architects realized out the mapping by relying on transformation projects related to CEI. We asked each architect to define, alone, a mapping; and then we discussed the outputs to agree on a common mapping, which was adopted by all participants at the end of this meeting. The final mapping is accomplished through a collegial reconciliation of the individual results, which did not differ much at the base.

In the last step the final mapping is presented by one of the co-authors to reflect collegially on the limits of the ArchiMate modeling. This is formulated in the "Discussion" section of this paper.

4   Results

4.1   Required Information for Customer Experience Improvement

Based on [8] work and our data analysis, we have identified four major groups of how digitalization transforms customer experience and the information needed to these transformations:

A)   **Understanding Customer:** Companies are exploring social media to comprehend customer satisfaction. Depending on that, they launched special products, based on their customer context. In addition, companies are learning more about customer feeling and habits, it helps companies to promote their brands more effectively through digital media. Companies are also building new online communities to collect feedbacks, to advise and build loyalty with clients (Table 2).

Table 2. "Understanding Customer" and required information.

Information needs	Description restitution	References
Social knowledge	*To know company's client through social networks, so that to collect informal information on the attitude of the client and their preferences*	[4b, 9b, 12b, 13b, 19b]
Value proposition	*Companies offer personalized products with a clear added value in the customer's context*	[2b, 3b, 5b, 7b, 8b, 11b, 13b, 19b]
Feedback	*Organizations collect customer feedback to use it in product creation and to master loyalty management*	[1b, 2b, 3b, 4b, 8b, 15b, 17b, 19b]
Satisfaction measurement	*Companies must continuously measure customer satisfaction to satisfy their changing needs and habits*	[6b, 5b, 15b, 16b, 19b]
Information confidentiality	*To protect their customers, companies must control the information collected from them and trace its lifecycle in the company without abusing its use*	[1b, 5b, 11b]
Customer context	*The company uses the history of its relationship with the client to understand his context, it also uses social networks to fuel this understanding*	[1b, 2b, 3b, 4b, 6b, 7b, 18b, 19b]
Customer journey	*The company must trace all the customers' commercial activities in order to understand their habits and preferences*	[1b, 4b, 5b, 7b, 8b, 13b, 18b, 19b]
Customer feelings	*The company is interested in the feelings at a moment T of a customer, the change of its feelings feeds the personalization of the products for these customers*	[1b, 2b, 12b, 17b, 18b]
Trends	*The company is also interested in modes and trends in the customer consumption, these trends are classified by age groups or by social categorization*	[1b, 5b, 11b]

B) **Enabling selling activities:** Companies evolve their business models by proposing new digital strategies. They use technology to enhance sales conversations and self-interactions and introduce mobile tools to help salespeople and customers engage in analytics-based exploration. They simplify their processes through digitalization and seek to make the customer's life more comfortable. They also develop integrated multi-channel experiences to make customer's purchases more efficient (Table 3).

Table 3. "Enabling selling activities" and required information.

Information requirements	Description restitution	References
Business network	*The company needs to collaborate with other market players to cover all the services that their customers need, the company needs to know more about these market players*	[1b, 2b, 4b, 19b]
Digital strategy	*The company is evolving its strategy by considering new digital products and by changing the way it interacts with its customers*	[1b, 2b, 3b, 4b, 5b, 7b, 8b, 10b, 12b, 19b]
Business model	*The business model also evolves and carries the digital strategy of the company*	[1b, 4b, 13b, 18b]
Process	*The company must know its processes because the change takes place first on the internal processes*	[1b, 4b, 5b, 7b, 8b, 10b, 13b, 18b, 19b]
Sales history	*The company needs to draw more information on the products which are well bought or not, and to rely on data analytics to predict the change in the commercial conditions of the market*	[1b, 2b, 3b, 4b, 15b, 17b, 19b]
Performance measurement	*The company sets up indicators to measure its commercial performance*	[3b, 16b, 17b, 18b, 19b]

C) **Managing Customer Touch Points:** Companies that provide multiple channels to the customer, are experiencing new approaches to provide an integrated experience. In retail and financial services in particular, firms are focusing on integrated multichannel activity. However, multichannel services require implementing change

Table 4. "Managing Customer touch points" and required information.

Information requirements	Description restitution	References
Organizational structure	*Organization must master the composition of their current organizational structure and how it evolves*	[4b, 9b, 12b, 13b, 19b]
Self service	*The company offers increasingly services where the customer realizes the whole sales process alone or in interaction with machines*	[1b, 4b, 5b, 7b, 8b, 10b, 13b, 18b, 19b]
Cross channel	*The company allows customers to move from one channel to another while preserving the same elements of the customer's context*	[1b, 5b, 8b, 11b, 12b, 18b]
Process	*The company evolves the operational processes to take into consideration the new distribution channels*	[1b, 5b, 7b, 8b, 10b, 13b, 14b, 18b, 19b]
Customer accessibility	*The company allows the customer to manage accessibility to all distribution channels*	[12b]

across customer experience and operational processes; for examples, many retailers now offer home shopping with the option to receive products by mail or in a store (Table 4).

D) **Integrating Digital Capabilities:** Digital capabilities are fundamental components for transforming customer experience. While top management and existing IT departments are leading digital initiatives across companies, they hire new digital skills around Big Data, real time communication, etc. During the 'Data Analysis' phase, we introduced this group to classify all the information input that the company needs to know about the digital capabilities it has, and how to integrate and reuse them for other transformation needs (Table 5).

4.2 EAM Outputs

ArchiMate is an Enterprise Architecture modeling language, a visual language with a set of default iconography for describing, analyzing, and communicating many concerns of Enterprise Architectures as they change over time. The ArchiMate standard provides a set of entities and relationships with their corresponding iconography for the representation of Architecture Descriptions [29, 40].

Table 5. "Integrating Digital capabilities" and necessary Information needs

Information requirements	Description restitution	References
Digital capabilities	*The company is using more and more new technologies to improve operational performance and their commercial activities*	[1b, 4b, 17b, 18b, 19b]
Integration	*The company is asking questions about its ability to integrate new technologies into its information system, and to be agile in absorbing new changes in existing processes*	[3b, 16b, 17b, 18b, 19b]
Skills	*The company needs to know if its employees use and master new technologies, e.g., Big Data, real time communication, etc.*	[1b, 5b, 8b, 11b, 12b, 18b]

In this part, we illustrate, which information EAM can provide by following the basic structure of the ArchiMate 3.0 content meta-model [29]. This meta-model contains general elements that are connected in a one-to-one manner. The other elements are differentiated into business, data, application and technology architecture.

4.3   Mapping EAM Inputs with CEI Needed Information

Based on step 1 and step 2, we analyzed for each CEI information need the extent to which it can be provided by ArchiMate meta-model. During this analysis, it became

Table 6. Major input of CEI projects supported by EAM

Major support by EAM		
Digital capabilities	Process	Business model
Self service	Interaction	Digital strategy
Customer journey	Organizational structure	Cross channel
Value proposition	Performance measurement	Customer accessibility

Table 7. Minor input of CEI projects supported by EAM

Minor support by EAM		
Business network	Customer context	Social knowledge
Customer feedbacks	Satisfaction measurement	Trends
Customer feelings skills	Information confidentiality sales history	Integration

CEI needs \ EAM Inputs	Active structure			Behavior						Passive element	Motivation element									Strategy element		
	Internal element	Collaboration	Interface	Internal behavior	Process	Function	Interaction	Service	Event	Passive element	Meaning	Driver	Assessment	Goal	Outcome	Principle	Requirement	Constraint	Value	Capability	Resource	Course of action
Social knowledge																						
Customer journey	X			X	X	X	X	X	X	X	X	X	X	X	X	X	X	X	X	X	X	X
Customer feeling																						
Satisfaction measurement																						
Feedback																						
Customer Context																						
Value proposition											X	X	X	X	X	X	X	X	X			
Information Confidentiality																		X				
Trends																						

Fig. 3. Results for 'Understanding Customer' information mapping

CEI needs \ EAM Inputs	Active structure			Behavior						Passive element	Motivation element									Strategy element		
	Internal element	Collaboration	Interface	Internal behavior	Process	Function	Interaction	Service	Event	Passive element	Meaning	Driver	Assessment	Goal	Outcome	Principle	Requirement	Constraint	Value	Capability	Resource	Course of action
Business network																						
Digital strategy											X	X	X	X	X	X	X	X	X	X	X	X
Process	X			X	X	X	X	X	X		X	X	X	X	X	X	X	X	X	X	X	X
Performance Measurement					X	X	X	X					X		X							
Seles history																						
Business Model	X	X	X	X	X					X	X	X	X	X	X	X	X	X	X	X	X	

Fig. 4. Results for 'Enabling selling activities' information mapping

apparent that some CEI needed information can be (almost) fully provided by EAM, and some, almost not. We rated this on a five-point scale ranging from one "ECI needs almost not supported by EAM" to five "full support". In Figs. 3, 4, 5, 6, we provide the mapping results.

CEI needs \ EAM Inputs	Active structure			Behavior						Passive element	Motivation element									Strategy element		
	Internal element	Collaboration	Interface	Internal behavior	Process	Function	Interaction	Service	Event	Passive element	Meaning	Driver	Assessment	Goal	Outcome	Principle	Requirement	Constraint	Value	Capability	Resource	Course of action
Organizational structure	X			X	X	X	X	X	X	X										X	X	X
Self service				X	X	X	X	X	X											X		
Cross channel				X	X	X	X	X	X													
Process	X			X	X	X	X	X	X	X	X	X	X	X	X	X	X	X	X	X	X	X
Customer Accessibility				X	X	X	X	X	X													

Fig. 5. Results for 'Managing Customer touch points' information mapping

CEI needs \ EAM Inputs	Active structure			Behavior						Passive element	Motivation element									Strategy element		
	Internal element	Collaboration	Interface	Internal behavior	Process	Function	Interaction	Service	Event	Passive element	Meaning	Driver	Assessment	Goal	Outcome	Principle	Requirement	Constraint	Value	Capability	Resource	Course of action
Digital Capabilities	X			X	X	X		X		X										X	X	
Integration		X	X																			
Skills																				X	X	

Fig. 6. Results for 'Integrating digital capabilities' information mapping

In Tables 6 and 7, we summarize the findings of the mapping process, focusing on the information needs for CEI that can be well supported (rated five during the analysis) by EAM and those that can be less supported (rated one or two during the analysis).

Our mapping process reveals some meta-model elements that are more important for CEI support than others are. Especially knowledge about processes is needed for almost transformation groups that we have identified. Sometimes they are directly requested, sometimes in combination with the general EAM elements like goals.

5 Discussion

The findings show that, from a modeling point of view, EAM has the potential to support CEI projects. Our results further show that there are some information elements that EAM can easily deliver since the relevant information source exists explicitly and is maintained frequently (e.g., process, goals, or roles). Other information inputs require more analysis and interpretation by the architects to be a valuable input to the requesting CEI projects (e.g., digital strategy, business model). CEI required elements of information that are well supported by EAM, have some common characteristics:

A) They do not focus on individuals but cover an overall perspective (e.g., goals, structures of the enterprise). Activities that take a social and a narrower focus would be better documented by other disciplines like human-focused management or psychology (e.g., customer ideologies, trends, etc.).

B) The information has a strong focus on the internal perspective of the enterprise; they are about the organizational processes, structures, etc. Thus, data that needs to be collected outside the company like context, business networks, market trends, customer satisfaction or feeling, etc. are not included in the current EAM practice. Such external information is explicitly hard to collect for EAM (because of limitations in the meta-model), and thus, should be instead piloted by other disciplines like marketing departments or special projects that sense for such needed information. We also claim that EAM does not offer enough elements to describe the context of customers and their feedback because organizations are not used to putting them at the heart of project design. With the emergence of collaborative and agile innovation methods in companies, the EAM must adapt their meta-models to consider customer trends and their feedback before the completion of projects.

C) EAM mostly supports digital projects that are based on explicit and formal requirements. Inputs that are related to society, trends (socially informed knowledge, market information), or predictive analysis are usually not supported. EAM also does not address the confidentiality of customer information through modeling.

6 Conclusion

In this paper, we discussed how EAM could support CEI projects in terms of modeling using ArchiMate. We contributed first with a detailed literature survey to identify the digitalization impact on customer experience. Our systematic literature identifies four major groups of how digitalization transforms customer experience: *Understanding Customer, Enabling selling activities, Managing Customer Touch Points,* and *Integrating digital technologies.* Then, we have defined the information inputs required for these transformations to understand what CEI is comprised of, and to provide a solid foundation for further research in the customer experience and digital transformation area. The results show that, in general, EAM is suited to support customer experience projects in a digital transformation context. Such transformations have a strong focus on the internal perspective of the enterprise that is based on formal requirements (e.g., organizational structure). Nevertheless, EAM lacks support when it comes to activities that require inputs from the environment (e.g., trends, customer needs, customer satisfaction, etc.) or society, trends, or predictive aspects.

This work has some limitations. First, our SLR is limited to a single database and we chose to use only the journal articles that we had access to. Second, the ArchiMate meta-model reflects the information that Enterprise Modeling can provide but do not integrate specific potentials that EAM as an overall framework could additionally cover (e.g., architecture principles, best practices, etc.). We dealt with this limitation by conducting several iterations during the Focus Group and by including additional EAM literature during the mapping procedure. Third, we carried out the Focus Group with only banking experts; nevertheless, we tend to believe that this work could be generalized in other industrial fields because the customer experience has been impacted by digitalization in the same way for all retailers (banks and others). We intend to ensure this in our future work. Moreover, as future work, we intend to focus on the Enterprise Architecture Support to other shapes of digital transformations.

References[2]

1. Ross, J.W., Weill, P., Robertson, D.: Enterprise Architecture as Strategy: Creating a Foundation for Business Execution. Harvard Business Press, Brighton (2006)
2. TOG, The Open Group: TOGAF Version 9.1. The Open Group, Berkshire, UK (2011)
3. Rouse, W.B.: A theory of enterprise transformation. Syst. Eng. **8**(4), 279–295 (2005)
4. Tamm, T., Seddon, P.B., Shanks, G., Reynolds, P.: How does enterprise architecture add value to organisations. Commun. AIS **28**(1), 141–168 (2011)
5. Abraham, R., Aier, S., Labusch, N.: Enterprise architecture as a means for coordination – an empirical study on actual and potential practice. In: The 7th Mediterranean Conference on Information Systems, Paper 33. AIS Electronic Library (2012)
6. Asfaw, T., Bada, A., Allario, F.: Enablers and challenges in using enterprise architecture concepts to drive transformation: perspectives from private organizations and federal government agencies. J. Enterpr. Architect. **5**(3), 18–28 (2009)
7. Greefhorst, D., Proper, E.: Architecture Principles – The Cornerstones of Enterprise Architecture. Springer, Heidelberg (2011). https://doi.org/10.1007/978-3-642-20279-7
8. Westerman, G., Calméjane, C., Bonnet, D., Ferraris, P., McAfee, A.: Digital Transformation: A Roadmap for Billion-Dollar Organizations. MIT Center for Digital Business and Capgemini Consulting (2011)
9. Pittl, B., Bork, D.: Modeling digital enterprise ecosystems with ArchiMate: a mobility provision case study. ICServ 2017. LNCS, vol. 10371, pp. 178–189. Springer, Cham (2017). https://doi.org/10.1007/978-3-319-61240-9_17
10. Lankhorst, M.: Enterprise Architecture at Work: Modelling, Communication and Analysis, 2nd edn. Springer, Heidelberg (2009)
11. Winter, R., Townson, S., Labusch, N., Noack, J.: Enterprise architecture and transformation: the differences and the synergy potential of enterprise architecture and business transformation management. In: Uhl, A., Gollenia, L.A. (eds.) Business Transformation Essentials: Case Studies and Articles, pp. 219–231. Routledge (2013)
12. Stolterman, E., Fors, A.C.: Information technology and the good life. In: Kaplan, B., Truex, D.P., Wastell, D., Wood-Harper, A.T., DeGross, J.I. (eds.) Information Systems Research. IIFIP, vol. 143, pp. 687–692. Springer, Boston, MA (2004). https://doi.org/10.1007/1-4020-8095-6_45
13. Fitzgerald, M., Kruschwitz, N., Bonnet, D., Welch, M.: Embracing digital technology: a new strategic imperative. MIT Sloan Management Review, Research Report (2013)
14. Martin, A.: Digital Literacy for the Third Age: Sustaining Identity in an Uncertain World. eLearning Papers, no. 12, p. 1 (2009)

---

[2] The references of the 19 articles selected for the Systematic Literature Review can be found in the online appendix at ResearchGate: https://doi.org/10.13140/RG.2.2.33596.18560.

15. Harmsen, F., Proper, H.A.E., Kok, N.: Informed governance of enterprise transformations. In: Proper, E., Harmsen, F., Dietz, Jan L.G. (eds.) PRET 2009. LNBIP, vol. 28, pp. 155–180. Springer, Heidelberg (2009). https://doi.org/10.1007/978-3-642-01859-6_9

16. Boh, W.F., Yellin, D.: Using enterprise architecture standards in managing information technology. J. Manag. Inf. Syst. **23**(3), 163–207 (2007)

17. Radeke, F.: Toward understanding enterprise architecture management's role in strategic change: antecedents, processes, outcomes. In: Wirtschaftinformatik, Paper 62, Zuerich (2011)

18. Pulkkinen, M., Naumenko, A., Luostarinen, K.: Managing information security in a business network of machinery maintenance services business - enterprise architecture as a coordination tool. J. Syst. Softw. **80**(10), 1607–1620 (2007)

19. Foorthuis, R., Van Steenbergen, M., Mushkudiani, N., Bruls, W., Brinkkemper, S., Bos, R.: On course, but not there yet: enterprise architecture conformance and benefits in systems development. In International Conference on IS (ICIS), Paper 110 (2010)

20. Lange, M., Mendling, J., Recker, J.: Realizing benefits from enterprise architecture: a measurement model. In 20th European Conference on IS (ECIS), Paper 10 (2012)

21. van Gils, B., Proper, H.A.: Enterprise modelling in the age of digital transformation. In: Buchmann, R.A., Karagiannis, D., Kirikova, M. (eds.) PoEM 2018. LNBIP, vol. 335, pp. 257–273. Springer, Cham (2018). https://doi.org/10.1007/978-3-030-02302-7_16

22. Fayoumi, A.: Toward an adaptive enterprise modelling platform. In: Buchmann, R.A., Karagiannis, D., Kirikova, M. (eds.) PoEM 2018. LNBIP, vol. 335, pp. 362–371. Springer, Cham (2018). https://doi.org/10.1007/978-3-030-02302-7_23

23. Winter, R., Labusch, N.: Towards a conceptualization of architectural support for enterprise transformation. In: ECIS 2013. AIS Library (2013)

24. Kitchenham, B.: Guidelines for performing systematic literature reviews in software. Technical Report EBSE-2007-01, UK, Keele University and University of Durham (2007)

25. Okoli, C.: A guide to conducting a standalone systematic literature review. Commun. AIS **37** (2015). https://doi.org/10.17705/1CAIS.03743

26. Ngai, E.W.T., Wat, F.K.T.: A literature review and classification of electronic commerce research. Inf. Manag. **39**(5), 415–429 (2002)

27. Nguyen-Duc, A., Cruzes, D.S., Conradi, R.: The impact of global dispersion on coordination, team performance and software quality: a systematic literature review. Inf. Softw. Technol. **57**, 277–294 (2015)

28. Hauge, O., Ayala, C., Conradi, R.: Adoption of open source software in software intensive organizations – a systematic literature review. Inf. Softw. Technol. **52**(11), 1133–1154 (2010)

29. The Open Group: ArchiMate® 2.0 Specification. The Open Group, Berkshire, UK (2017)

30. Bernus, P., Noran, O.: A metamodel for enterprise architecture. In: Bernus, P., Doumeingts, G., Fox, M. (eds.) EAI2N 2010. IAICT, vol. 326, pp. 56–65. Springer, Heidelberg (2010). https://doi.org/10.1007/978-3-642-15509-3_6

31. Chen, Z., Pooley, R.: Requirement analysis for enterprise IS – developing an ontological metamodel for Zackman framework. In: ICIS Proceedings, Paper 182. AIS Electronic Library (2009)

32. DoD, Department of Defense: DoD Architecture Framework Version 2.02 (2012). https://dodcio.defense.gov/Library/DoD-Architecture-Framework/dodaf20_dm2/. Accessed 05 Feb 2020

33. IEEE: IEEE Recommended Practice for Architectural Description of Software Intensive Systems (IEEE Std 1471-2000), New York, NY (2000)

34. Rabiee, F.: Focus-group interview and data analysis. Proc. Nutr. Soc. **63**, 655–660 (2004)

35. Rico, D.F.: Optimizing the ROI of enterprise architecture using real options. In: End User Computing Challenges and Technologies: Emerging Tools and Applications, Information Science Reference, Hershey, PA (2007)

36. Forrester: Banking of the future: how banks will use digital capabilities to remain competitive (2019). https://www.forrester.com/webinar/Banking+Of+The+Future+How+Banks+Will+Use+Digital+Capabilities+To+Remain+Competitive/-/E-WEB19183. Accessed 05 Feb 2020
37. Gartner: Hype Cycle for Digital Banking Transformation (2019). https://www.gartner.com/en/documents/3955840/hype-cycle-for-digital-banking-transformation-2019. Accessed 05 Feb 2020
38. Hafsi, M., Assar, S.: Does enterprise architecture support digital transformation endeavors? Questionning the old concepts in light of new findings. In: Proceedings Mediterranean Conference on Information Systems (MCIS) (2019)
39. Hafsi, M., Asaar, S.; What enterprise architecture can bring for digital transformation: an exploratory study. In: IEEE 18th Conference on Business Informatics (2016)
40. Hafsi, M., Assar, S.: Managing strategy in digital transformation context: an exploratory analysis of enterprise architecture management support. In: IEEE 21st Conference on Business Informatics (2019)

A Formal Basis for Business Model Evaluation with Linguistic Summaries
(Work-in-Progress Paper)

Rick Gilsing, Anna Wilbik$^{(\boxtimes)}$, Paul Grefen, Oktay Turetken, and Baris Ozkan

Eindhoven University of Technology, Eindhoven, The Netherlands
{R.A.M.Gilsing,A.M.Wilbik,P.W.P.J.Grefen,O.Turetken,
B.Ozkan}@tue.nl

Abstract. Given its essential role in understanding, explaining and structuring digital innovation, we see the increased prevalence of the business model concept as a unit of analysis in IS research. In contemporary, fast-paced markets, business models are volatile in nature and should be continuously innovated to accommodate new customer needs and technology developments. Business model innovation can be considered as an iterative process to guide business models from ideation towards implementation, in which the proper evaluation of business model prototypes is essential. For this evaluation, we need normative guidance, tools and rules to understand the relative performance of a new business model design. In the early design phases, this implies dealing with high levels of uncertainty. A few techniques and methods have been proposed for this purpose, but these lack the formal basis required for systematical application and development of automated evaluation tools. As a novel approach, we have earlier proposed the application of linguistic summarization to support early-phase, soft-quantitative business model evaluation. In this paper, we focus on a structural formalization of this approach as the basis for the development of well-defined user guidelines and automated evaluation tools. In doing so, we bridge the existing gap between qualitative and quantitative business model evaluation. We demonstrate the formalization by means of a running case inspired by a real-world project in the highly dynamic urban mobility domain.

Keywords: Business models · Business model evaluation · Linguistic summarization · Formal model

1 Introduction

Factors such as digitization, globalization and rapid technology change cause evolution of contemporary markets at an accelerated pace [1, 2]. Although these factors provide organizations promising opportunities with respect to digital innovation and customer engagement, organizations increasingly are forced to adapt their current business logic to enable the adoption of new IT developments and the adherence to shifting customer needs. It is therefore not surprising that we see the increased prevalence of the *business model* concept in IS research [1, 3]. A business model describes the logic of how value

© Springer Nature Switzerland AG 2020
S. Nurcan et al. (Eds.): BPMDS 2020/EMMSAD 2020, LNBIP 387, pp. 428–442, 2020.
https://doi.org/10.1007/978-3-030-49418-6_29

is created and captured, the internal and external resources used to enable value creation and the organizational and technical architecture deployed to support the business model [4, 5]. Business models bridge the gap between business strategy [6] and operational business process models [7] as they concretize strategy and provide the context for the underlying process models. As such, given their pivotal role in business conceptualization and their descriptive and explanatory power, they are often used as a unit of analysis to understand the impact of IT or digital innovation and to structure its implementation [1, 8].

The adaptation or *innovation* of business models to accommodate or integrate digital innovation is a complex, non-linear design process and requires several iterative design and evaluation tasks [9]. Normative guidance, technological rules and methodological support can aid both research and practitioners in understanding or conducting business model innovation [10]. Although tools and methods have been proposed in research to support or guide business model design [11–13], limited support is present, particularly from an engineering or methodological perspective, for the *evaluation* of business models [1, 14]. This issue is even more apparent for the early phases of business model innovation, for which business model design decisions often are high-level in nature and uncertain [15, 16], resulting in difficulties with respect to quantifying or even merely assessing the potential risks and outcomes as a part of business model evaluation. As a result, qualitative evaluation approaches are advocated to support early-phase business model innovation [17]. Although qualitative techniques such as focus groups or expert judgment are frequently used [18], these techniques are informal and lack structure to be systematically applied. On the other hand, we see the use of performance criteria or metrics as a more formalized approach to qualitative business model evaluation [19, 20]. However, these techniques lack methodological guidance on how these should be catered to the specific characteristics of business model designs, and they often require quantitative support to be effectively used.

As a novel technique, we have proposed the use of linguistic summarization as a means to derive and specify 'soft' key performance indicators (SKPIs) that describe performance characteristics of specific business model designs [21]. These SKPIs are expressed in soft-quantitative terms, which makes them suitable to support early business model evaluation, when 'hard' quantitative data on a business model is not yet available. So far, the technique has been proposed in an informal way. To support systematic application and the development of tooling towards business model evaluation, we make the next step in this paper: we focus on the formalization of the approach, linking formal specification of business models and formal specification of the type of linguistic summaries that we use (*intentional linguistic summaries*). On this basis, we show how the formal model is a basis for the development of support for our approach. Accordingly, the research question for this paper is as follows:

"How can the application of linguistic summarization to support soft-quantitative business model evaluation be formalized and how can this formalization be applied?"

The answer to this question helps bridging the currently existing gap between the fully qualitative evaluation business models (which relies heavily on intuition of designers) and the fully quantitative evaluation of business models (which requires far more data than is typically available in the early stages of business model design). Bridging this gap is of interest to both the business model research community and the design and use of business models in business practice.

The remainder of this research-in-progress paper is structured as follows. In Sect. 2, we discuss the research background on business models, business model evaluation and linguistic summarization. Section 3 introduces the running example that we use for the remainder of this paper to illustrate the application of linguistic summarization. Section 4 details the formalization to our approach. We illustrate how formalization supports the practical application of our method in Sect. 5 through ILSs with respect to the running case. Section 6 concludes the paper, expressing the avenues for future work and the outlook of our research.

2 Related Work

In this section, we describe related work in three fields of research that form the basis for our work: business model design, business model evaluation and linguistic summaries.

Business Model Design. Business models are increasingly used in IS research as a means to explore how digital innovations or IT-enabled innovations may impact the current business logic [1, 11]. Given its pivotal role between business strategy and operational models [7], the concept of business model often serves as a bridge to support business-IT alignment. Many componentizations have been proposed to structure the business model construct [22]. For instance, from an IS perspective, Hedman and Kalling [3] componentize business models into levels related to the market or environment, the offerings of the business model, the architectural structure and the resource deployed. Through detailing each level, organizations obtain a better understanding of what business logic is followed, how resources can be integrated or deployed and how this may influence or support customer offerings.

Several tools have been proposed to guide the design of business models. For instance, Osterwalder and Pigneur [11] propose the widely popular Business Model Canvas (BMC), which represents a graphical template consisting of nine building blocks that address various elements of business model design. The BMC takes an organization-centric, resource-based perspective and focuses explicitly on customer-supplier interactions and relationships. However, we see that as organizations increasingly transition towards service-orientation and collaborative networks [23–25], tooling towards networked, service-dominant business model design is proposed. For instance, Zolnowski et al. [26] propose the Service Business Model Canvas, which adapts the original BMC to accommodate the modelling of service business. Similarly, Grefen [27] and Turetken et al. [12] describe and evaluate the Service-Dominant Business Model Radar (SDBM/R), which through its circular template accommodates an explicitly networked perspective of business model design.

Business Model Evaluation. Business model evaluation is an essential activity to support design decision making either to reduce uncertainty and risk with respect to a business model design, to motivate the continuation of business model innovation or to support the selection of a specific design configuration or alternative [15]. Business model evaluation is argued to positively influence business model innovation [28]. Although some tools exist with respect to business model evaluation, either qualitatively-oriented [20, 29] or quantitatively-oriented [13, 30, 31], limited normative guidance has been investigated for structuring business model evaluation, especially in the context of business model innovation [1, 32]. Simmert et al. [14] propose a process-oriented, multi-step evaluation approach to support business model improvement. Although it provides initial structure towards business model evaluation, the techniques used for evaluation (focus groups and quality criteria) are informal and hence provide limited support for detailed structure of application.

Linguistic Summaries. Linguistic summaries (LS) are statements with a specific format (template or protoform) that are used to describe data in brief natural language constructs and that can be automatically generated [33]. LS allow to more easily comprehend a set of data [34]. Linguistic data summaries are quantified propositions with two protoforms (or templates): a simple protoform, Q y's are P, exemplified by "*most cars are new*" and an extended protoform, Q $R y$'s are P, exemplified by "*most fast cars are new*". Q is the linguistic quantifier, e.g. *most*. P is the summarizer, an attribute together with a linguistic value, e.g. *new car*. R is an optional qualifier, another attribute together with a linguistic value, which narrows down the scope of universe, e.g., *fast car*. *Intentional linguistic summaries* (ILSs) [21] are quantified statements with the same structure as linguistic summaries: Q y's are P and Q $R y$'s are P. The main difference is that ILSs are not created from existing data, but capture intentions that the stakeholders want to be true. In other words, they specify desired constraints over future data. We use this construct to specify constraints over future effects of business models.

3   Running Example

We demonstrate the application of linguistic summarization to support business model evaluation by means of an illustrative case study. The case concerns a business model design that emerged from the urban mobility business domain as the result of a workshop with industry practitioners. The business model design was generated as an initial solution to address challenges of increased traffic problems in the city of Amsterdam at days when large public events (such as pop concerts or soccer matches) are organized in the city [35]. As a result of these large events, which often start around peak hours, a significant inflow of traffic users (event visitors that travel by car) is generated in this period, causing many severe traffic jams. Therefore, the city explored together with partners such as parking providers, event providers and road authority a collaborative solution aimed at decreasing the negative traffic effects of these large events.

The solution that emerged from the workshop constituted a service platform that enables event visitors to use their event ticket to receive free parking tickets at predetermined arrival times. Receiving free parking tickets encourages event visitors to arrive at the specified time, as parking is expensive in Amsterdam. The arrival times consequently can be set in such a way that it balances the load to the road infrastructure. To offer the

solution, the resources of partners such as platform providers, municipality, road authority, parking provider and event location and event providers were integrated. To further
stimulate the financial viability of the collaboration, retailers were involved as they may
significantly benefit from event visitors arriving early in the city. The SDBM/R technique was used as the tool for business model design [12, 27, 36]. The resulting business
model design to accommodate the solution is presented in Fig. 1. In this business model
radar (which we label TJFERC), we see the central value (*value-in-use*) of the business
model in the center of the radar and the involved customer (Large City) as one of the
eight involved business *parties* (the actors in the network) – each having one 'slice'
of the radar, labeled in the outer ring. Apart from the customer, the *orchestrator* party
(Mobility Broker) and six other parties are present. A party can be a *core party* (i.e.,
essential for the functioning of the business model and operation of the offered service)
or an *enriching party* (i.e., bringing non-essential added value). The three rings around
the central value detail for each party (from the center outwards) the value that each
party contributes to the central value-in-use (its *actor value proposition*), the activities
it has to perform to create this value (*value coproduction activities*), and its *costs* and
benefits (both financial and non-financial). Note that each business model only has a
single *value-in-use*, which is construed from the set of actor value propositions. As a
consequence, to generate a different value-in-use, a different set of value propositions
would be needed (which in turn results in a different business model design).

Fig. 1. Business model design draft to address event induced traffic challenges in the inner-city.

To support the evaluation of the business model design, we generate ILSs per party of
the business model. ILSs represent operationalized, strategic preferences or summaries
per party that are specifically catered to the business model design. As such, each business

model design, depending on its contents, may result in different ILSs. The ILSs serve as the basis for communicating under what conditions a party is willing to participate in the business model. By assessing whether the ILSs can be achieved, the viability of the business model can be evaluated [21]. The ILSs are presented in a pre-specified structure (named *protoforms*), as usual in research into linguistic summarization [34]. Although the ILSs are initially soft-quantitative in nature, the structure of the summaries allows the ILSs consequently to be further quantified through concrete membership functions of the linguistic summaries [33, 34]. We will demonstrate the ILSs for this example in Sect. 5.

4 Groundwork for the Formal Approach

In this section, we describe the groundwork for the formalization of our approach. We do this by formalizing the two main elements of the approach: business model radars (SDBM/R) and intentional linguistic summaries (ILS). In Sect. 5, we integrate these two formalizations to become the 'formal spine' of our business model evaluation approach.

4.1 Formalizing the SDBM/R Concept

To formalize the SDBM/R concept (which we call *business model radar* or *BMR* from now on for easy readability), we identify that this concept has an overall structure that is independent from the number of involved parties, and a structure per party. Hence, we provide the formalization in two steps: the radar and the parties.

A *business model radar* (BMR) is a business model specification with the following formal type and constraint:

$$BMR = \langle name: L, value: ViU, cust: P, orch: P, parts: \{\langle part: P, core: BOOL \rangle\} \rangle$$
$$parts \neq \emptyset$$

Here, *name* is the name of the business model from the set of *labels L*, *value* is the value in use of the business model from the set of *values-in-use ViU*, *cust* is the *customer* from the set of *parties P*, *orch* is the *orchestrator party* from *P*, and *parts* is the set of *other parties* of type $\{\langle P, BOOL \rangle\}$, i.e., a set of pairs of parties and an indication whether a party is a *core party* in the business model. The structure states that exactly one customer party is present and exactly one orchestrator party. The additional constraint specifies that at least one other party must be present – this to make it a true networked business model and not a dyadic relation.

A BMR instance *b* therefore has the following format:

$$b = \langle l, viu, p_1, p_2, \{\langle p_3, b_3 \rangle, \cdots, \langle p_n, b_n \rangle\} \rangle \, n \geq 3$$

A *party* is the specification of a role in a business model radar with the following type:

$$P = \langle name: L, avalp: \{AVP\}, acopa: \{ACA\}, aben: \{AB\}, acost: \{AC\} \rangle$$
$$avalp, acopa, aben, acost \neq \emptyset$$

The set *avalp* contains the set of *actor value propositions* of a party (a party can have more than one actor value proposition), *acopa* the set of *actor coproduction activities* (a party can have more than one activity), *aben* the set of *actor benefits*, and *accost* the set of *actor costs*. All of the four sets need to be non-empty for a business model to be viable: each actor needs to contribute to the central value-in-use, each actor needs to perform at least one activity to generate this contribution, and each actor needs to have both benefits (its reason to participate in the business model) and costs (not to be a 'free rider' to the other parties).

The above shows that this simple formalization already provides a nice set of correctness criteria for business models specified in the SDBM/R technique, which can be automatically checked. These criteria are of a syntactical nature though and specify nothing about the intended business effects of the business model. To enable this, we use intentional linguistic summaries.

4.2 Formalizing the ILS Concept

To use it in the business model context, we operationalize the concept of intentional linguistic summary (ILS) into the concept of *intentional soft quantified statement* (ISQS). In general, an ISQS specifies a desired characteristic of a set of objects of a specific type in a universe of discourse (UoD) in soft quantified terms. We first discuss the overall formal structure of the ISQS concept. Then, we detail each of its components.

The set of ISQS QS has the following type (following the structure of a protoform of linguistic summaries [33]):

$$QS = \langle quant: QF, obj: \{OB\}, oqual: \{OQ\}, ochar: \{OC\}\rangle$$

Here, *quant* is a *soft quantifier* of type QF, *obj* is the set of *quantified objects* of type OB, *oqual* is the set of *object qualifications (features)* of type OQ, and *ochar* is the set of *object characteristics (features)* of type OC. Object qualification *oqual* can be a feature describing all objects in a UoD.

An ISQS instance *qs* therefore has the following format:

$$qs = \langle qf, ob, oq, oc\rangle$$

In the above specification, QF is the enumerated set of *soft quantifiers*, which state the intended fraction of the set of quantified objects. Usually relational quantifiers are used (i.e., describing the proportion within the set), like *most*, indicating *above 50%*. Seldom, absolute quantifiers (i.e., referring to the absolute object count) are used, e.g., *around 5*, *more than 7*. An often used set of soft quantifiers is the following, and we will use it in our work for soft quantification of business models:

$$QF_{ou} = \{ALL, ALMOST ALL, MANY, SOME, FEW, ALMOST NONE, NONE\}$$

We use only a part of the expressiveness of the linguistic summaries model to stay pragmatic. Therefore, we define the elements of QF_{ou} to have a fuzzy ordinal relation denoted with the fuzzy comparison operator $\succ$:

$$ALL \succ ALMOST ALL \succ MANY \succ SOME \succ FEW \succ ALMOST NONE \succ NONE$$

The elements of *QF* indicate the *desired proportion* of a set, modelled using a fuzzy set. An *actual proportion* of a subset may therefore satisfy two adjacent soft quantifiers, where adjacent is defined by the fuzzy ordinal relation specified above.

The set of *quantified objects OB* is the powerset of objects in the UoD over which we want to state soft quantifications:

$$OB = \{\{O \in UoD\}\}$$

Consequently, a *set of quantified objects ob* is a set of elements in the UoD:

$$ob = \{o \in UoD\}$$

A *feature* of an object is a tuple of type *F* that contains the feature label and the set of linguistic value labels:

$$F = \langle featureLabel: FL, \{linguisticValue: LV\}\rangle$$

For instance

$$f = \langle "color", \{"red", "blue", "green", "black", "yellow"\}\rangle$$

Linguistic value labels can be made precise and represented as fuzzy sets, with $\mathbb{M}$ as the membership function:

$$\mathbb{M}: OB \times FL \times LV \rightarrow [0, 1]$$

The membership functions do not have to be defined for intentional soft quantified statements at the early design stage, allowing the linguistic value labels to have more intuitive definition and meaning and be made more precise in later design stages.

The set of features of an object is given by the function *ofeat* that takes an object:

$$ofeat: UoD \rightarrow \{F\}$$

Every feature is associated to an enumerated set of possible values. In principle, a feature can possibly have multiple values with different membership values – but we abstract from them. For example, we take object $c \in Cars$:

$$ofeat(c) = \{\langle "color", "red"\rangle \langle "speed", "fast"\rangle\langle "class", "luxury"\rangle\}$$

The set of *object qualifications OQ* consists of pairs of a feature label and a linguistic value. More complex situations are allowed, where multiple feature labels and linguistic values can be combined with conjunctions. For pragmatic reasons, we focus only on the simple case in this work.

$$OQ: FL \times LV$$

We have a function *oqmem* which for the sets of objects in the *UoD* and a feature combined with a linguistic value identifies subsets of the *UoD* of which the elements have the same type, plus a feature label and a feature value:

$$oqmem: OB \times FL \times LV \rightarrow OB$$

An *object qualification oq* is applied to a set of qualified objects to constrain this set to a subset under consideration.

The last element in the ISQS structure is the set of *object characteristics OC. OC* contains pairs of a feature label and a linguistic value, similar to *OQ*. In general case, more complex expressions of feature labels and linguistics values are possible, but for reasons of pragmatism, this is beyond scope of the current formalization.

$$OC\text{: }FL \times LV$$

OC is intended predicate over *QF* objects resulting from *oqmem*.

With the above formalism, we can precisely describe an ISQS in a structured way that is fit for tooling. To make things easier to interpret for humans, we can obviously generate a textual representation of an ISQS, using the natural language format that is typical for linguistic summaries. An ISQS instance $qs_1 = \langle qf, ob, oq, oc \rangle$ can for example be:

$$qs_1 = \langle MANY, Cars, \langle color, red \rangle, \langle speed, fast \rangle \rangle$$

This can be textually represented as "MANY red cars ARE fast". A simplified ISQS instance $qs_2 = \langle qf, ob, oq, oc \rangle$ can for example be:

$$qs_2 = \langle SOME, Cars, \langle any\ F, all\ V \rangle, \langle speed, fast \rangle \rangle$$

In this case <any F, all V> is a feature describing all objects in a *UoD*. This can be textually represented as "SOME cars ARE fast".

5   Integration for Business Model Evaluation

In this section we discuss how we combine the formalisms of business model radars and intentional linguistic summaries into an integrated formalism for the specification of soft-quantified characteristics of business models. We also show illustrative examples for the BMR example presented in Sect. 3.

To generate intentional linguistic summaries for specifying intentions of business models, we use ISQS templates that represent typical characteristics of business models. The templates presented in this paper are important representatives of this class, but the presented set is certainly not yet complete. For instance, we wish to expand this set such that it covers all elements of the business model design. Moreover, we aim to explore what operation elements per ISQS suit best under what conditions. As this paper presents work in progress, we aim to construct a complete set and test this in the real-world practice of business model design and evaluation.

Given a BMR instance *b* (following the structure introduced in the previous section):

$$b = \langle l, viu, p_1, p_2, \{\langle p_3, b_3 \rangle, \cdots, \langle p_n, b_n \rangle\} \rangle$$

we want to specify ISQS instances over this BMR instance and create a soft-quantified BMR with the following type (which combines the two formalizations of the previous section):

$$SQBMR = \langle bmr\text{: }BMR, sq\text{: }\{QS\} \rangle$$

So in short, an instance s of the type $SQBMR$ is a soft-quantified business model radar, i.e., the next step after drafting a non-quantified BMR in the ideation process of creating new business models. The set of soft quantifications sq attached to a business model b contains a number of ISQSs that describe the desired soft-quantified behavior of b when it will be executed in practice.

This formalization allows the precise specification of the nature of these ISQSs to obtain a structured soft-quantification and to reason about the set of ISQSs. To do so, the ISQSs are organized in categories that we describe in the subsections below in detail: the customer with its value-in-use, its benefits and its costs, and the core parties with characteristics that vary by the nature of the party. As the orchestrator essentially also represents a core party, we can use the same templates for this role. For now, we do not include characteristics of enriching (non-core) parties in the set of ISQSs for business model evaluation, as these parties are not essential for the operation of the business model. After we have described the categories of ISQSs, we present an initial discussion on the soft-quantified intentional validity of business models.

5.1 Customer

From a customer-oriented perspective, we create a set of ISQS templates that describe the most important aspects of a business model for evaluation from the customer perspective, i.e., the value-in-use, the benefits and the costs. Note that based on this template the respective stakeholder (in this case the customer) can select the objects that are most appropriate to express its strategic goals or motivation to participate.

Value-in-Use. We create a soft quantification over the value-in-use for the set of customers of a business model, stating that the majority of customers indeed receives this value-in-use:

$$qs_0 = \langle qf, p_1, \langle any\ F, all\ V \rangle, f(viu) \rangle$$
$$with\ qf \in \{ALL, ALMOST\ ALL, MOST\}$$

Note that the value $\langle any\ F, all\ V \rangle$ for the object qualification function means that all objects are included. $f(viu)$ is a linguistic label for a feature of the value-in-use.

For the running example of Sect. 3, the value-in-use is *traffic-jam free event rich city*. A feature of this value-in-use is the amount of traffic jams and their classification. Traffic jams can be characterized by, e.g. three linguistic labels into three classes: heavy, medium and small. In this case, the ISQS can be as follows:

$$qs_0 = \langle MOST, large\ city, \langle any\ F, all\ V \rangle, \langle few\ traffic - jams, heavy \rangle \rangle$$

which can be transformed to textual format for easy reading:

qs_0: Most large cities have few heavy traffic-jams caused by the events.

where *most* is the quantifier (qf), *large city* is the customer (p_1), and *few traffic-jams caused by the event* is the feature label for the value-in-use, and *heavy* is its linguistic label.

Benefits. We create a soft quantification over the benefits for the customer, stating that desired benefits occur often:

$$qs_{1a} = \langle qf, p_1, \langle any\ F, all\ V \rangle, f(p_1.aben) \rangle$$
$$with\ qf \in \{ALL, ALMOST\ ALL, MOST\}$$

For the running example we use the above template to create the following ISQSs describing the benefits of the customer (large city):

$$qs_{1a} = \langle MOST, large\ city, \langle any\ F, all\ V \rangle, \langle less\ traffic - jam, heavy \rangle \rangle$$
$$qs_{1a'} = \langle MOST, large\ city, \langle any\ F, all\ V \rangle, \langle more\ events, big \rangle \rangle$$
$$qs_{1a''} = \langle MOST, large\ city, \langle any\ F, all\ V \rangle, \langle image\ of\ city, positive \rangle \rangle$$

Those ISQSs can be represented in textual form as:

qs_{1a}:   *Most large cities have less heavy traffic jams.*
$qs_{1a'}$:   *Most large cities have more big events.*
$qs_{1a''}$:   *Most large cities have positive image of the city.*

Costs. We make a soft quantification over the costs for the customer, stating that unacceptable costs do not occur often:

$$qs_{1b} = \langle qf, p_1, \langle any\ F, all\ V \rangle, f(p_1.acost) \rangle$$
$$with\ qf \in \{NONE, ALMOST\ NONE, FEW\}$$

For the running example this can be the following ISQS

$$qs_{1b} = \langle NONE, large\ city, \langle any\ F, all\ V \rangle, \langle monthly\ subsidy, large \rangle \rangle$$

and in textual format:

qs_{1b}: *None of the large cities is paying a large monthly subsidy.*

Through use of the template, a customer consequently is able to translate strategic motives into concrete, business model specific conditions to participate, which can be used for evaluative purposes.

5.2   Core Parties

The core parties are essential for the functioning of a business model. Consequently, we make soft quantifications over the costs/benefits for each core party, stating that an acceptable cost/benefit ratio occurs often:

$$qs_k = \langle qf, p_k, oq, f(p_k.aben, p_k.acost) \rangle\ for\ 3 \le k \le n\ if\ b_k$$
$$with\ qf \in \{ALL, ALMOST\ ALL, MOST\}$$

For the running example we have created a set of example statements. For the parking provider an ISQS is:

$$qs_{k1} = \langle \begin{array}{c} MOST, \ parking \ provider, \langle any \ F, all \ V \rangle, \\ \langle parking \ planning, significantly \ improved \rangle \end{array} \rangle,$$

or in a textual format:

qs_{k1}: *Most parking providers have significantly improved planning on most events.*

The retailer is mostly focused on the financial aspect, therefore a good ISQS is:

qs_{k2}: *All retailers make an acceptable profit on most events.*

For the visitor the concert experience and memories are the most important, leading us to the following ISQS:

qs_{k3}: *Most visitors have a very high concert satisfaction.*

For the event organizers and the event location providers the focus is also on customer satisfaction:

qs_{k4}: *All event organizers (location providers) have a high customer satisfaction on most events.*

Again, each stakeholder can change the set of objects of the introduced templates to generate ISQSs that express its strategic motives or goals. Please note that in the summaries presented above, the focus is on the stakeholder, e.g., the summaries describe the retailers, visitors and event organizers. A different set of summaries can be obtained, if we put the operation, in this case an event, in the focus of linguistic summaries. Currently we are working on normative guidance towards what level of the operation should be used as focus of the linguistic summaries, given the preferences of stakeholders and the context of the BMR.

Given all the above ingredients for the formal representation of example from Sect. 3, we can specify the soft-quantified business model:

$$sqbm_{tjferc} = \langle TJFERC, \{qs_0, qs_{1a}, qs_{1a'}, qs_{1a''}, qs_{1b}, qs_{k1}, qs_{k2}, qs_{k3}, qs_{k4}\} \rangle$$

5.3   Soft-Quantified Intentional Validity of Business Models

Once an initial business model design is generated, the ISQSs can be compared amongst stakeholders or domain experts who can judge whether these statements are acceptable and achievable. This can be used using the linguistic value scale <*not feasible, rather not feasible, not sure, rather feasible, feasible*>.

To allow for automated reasoning about the validity of soft-quantified business models, we can formalize this as well. Formally, a business model is intentionally valid from a soft-quantified perspective if all ISQSs for that BMR are above the fuzzy 'truth value' $T \in \mathbb{M}$, where T can be chosen depending on the 'strictness' of business model evaluation:

$$FValid(b) \Leftrightarrow ((Truth(qs_o) > T) \wedge (Truth(qs_{1a}) > T) \wedge (Truth(qs_{1b}) > T)$$
$$\wedge (Truth(qs_3) > T) \wedge \cdots \wedge (Truth(qs_n) > T))$$

If we define *FValid* in terms of a complete SQBMR instance *sqb*, we get:

$$FValid(sqb) \Leftrightarrow (\forall s \in sqb.sq)(Truth(s))$$

If for example, all the statements we have generated are evaluated as at least "rather feasible", the model is judged to be valid for all stakeholders. For instance, if by means of collaborative discussions, all stakeholders determine that the linguistic summary "*all retailers makes an acceptable profit on most events*" is rather feasible, the business model design for the retailer is considered feasible. If all generated linguistic summaries are feasible, the business model design can progress to the next phase (integration), in which the design is further concretized and quantified in a more traditional way.

6   Conclusions and Outlook

As markets evolve at an accelerated pace, we see that contemporary organizations increasingly are required to adapt their business logic in order to adhere to shifting customer needs and to support new business activities through the inclusion of digital innovations. The consequently increased prevalence of the business model concept as a unit of analysis to support IT implementation and to understand its impact or implications for business strategy [3, 8] calls for structured approaches for business model evaluation. To assess the market potential of business models in early design stages, existing strictly qualitative approaches for evaluation need to be complemented with approaches that bridge the gap towards traditional, strictly quantitative approaches (e.g., from business economics).

To bridge this gap, we have focused in this paper on the formalization of the application of linguistic summarization as a method to support business model evaluation. Linguistic summarization facilitates users to derive ILSs, which capture the strategic preferences or KPIs of stakeholders without a need to specify or quantify these KPIs to a large extent. The formalization builds upon the groundwork that we have established in Wilbik et al. [21] which elaborates on how the method is used. The formalization consisted of two parts, namely formalizing a business model representation (to which we used the SDBM/R [12]) and formalizing the generation of ILSs [21] in ISQS format. We have integrated and combined these formalizations to illustrate how, in a systematic way, ILSs can be generated on the basis of a service-dominant business model design. We demonstrate the formalization by means of a set of examples and show how these may contribute towards support for business model evaluation.

As an outlook to the approach presented in this paper, we aim to further develop the set of ISQSs that can be developed per application. This includes finalizing the set of ISQS templates that can be generated, such that all business model elements can be expressed by means of ISQSs, as well as providing rules with respect to the generation of ISQSs. Currently, an almost infinite set of ISQSs can be generated per party in a business model, which may inhibit the usability and interpretability of the outcomes. Therefore, we will assess which ISQS templates should be generated under which circumstances, or how the strategic preferences of a stakeholder can be captured through a limited set of ISQSs. Moreover, we also aim to validate our method further to understand the initial usability, usefulness and ease-of-use of the proposed method.

Future research will build upon this formalization. One promising approach is to use the formalization as a basis for developing automated tooling for business model evaluation. The formalisms presented in this paper can rather straightforwardly be translated into a data model and a rule base for such a tool. A second approach is the development of a directive on how different evaluation methods can be formalized to accommodate business model evaluation.

References

1. Veit, D., et al.: Business models. Bus. Inf. Syst. Eng. **6**(1), 45–53 (2014)
2. Gambardella, A., Mcgahan, A.: Business-model innovation: general purpose technologies and their implications for industry structure. Long Range Plann. **43**, 262–271 (2010)
3. Hedman, J., Kalling, T.: The business model concept: theoretical underpinnings and empirical illustrations. Eur. J. Inf. Syst. **12**(1), 49–59 (2003)
4. Al-Debei, M., Avison, D.: Developing a unified framework of the business model concept. Eur. J. Inf. Syst. **19**(3), 359–376 (2010)
5. Zott, C., Amit, R.: Business model design: an activity system perspective. Long Range Plann. **43**(2–3), 216–226 (2010)
6. Shafer, S., Smith, J., Linder, J.: The power of business models. Bus. Horiz. **48**, 199–207 (2005)
7. Al-Debei, M., El-Haddadeh, R., Avison, D.: Defining the business model in the new world of digital business. In: AMCIS 2008 Proceedings (2008)
8. Teece, D.: Business models, business strategy and innovation. Long Range Plann. **43**, 172–194 (2010)
9. Sosna, M., Trevinyo-Rodriguez, R., Velamuri, S.: Business model innovation through trial-and-error learning: the naturhouse case. Long Range Plann. **43**(2–3), 383–407 (2010)
10. Bucherer, E., Eisert, U., Gassmann, O.: Towards systematic business model innovation: lessons from product innovation management. Creat. Innov. Manag. **21**(2), 183–198 (2012)
11. Osterwalder, A., Pigneur, Y.: Business Model Generation: A Handbook for Visionaries, Game Changers, and Challengers. Wiley, Hoboken (2010)
12. Turetken, O., Grefen, P., Gilsing, R., Adali, O.: Service-dominant business model design for digital innovation in smart mobility. Bus. Inf. Syst. Eng. **61**(1), 9–29 (2019)
13. Gordijn, J., Akkermans, H.: Designing and evaluating E-business models. IEEE Intell. Syst. Appl. **16**(4), 11–17 (2001)
14. Simmert, B., Ebel, P., Peters, C., Bittner, E., Leimeister, J.: Conquering the challenge of continuous business model improvement. Bus. Inf. Syst. Eng. **61**(4), 451–468 (2019)
15. McGrath, R.: Business models: a discovery driven approach. Long Range Plann. **43**(2–3), 247–261 (2010)
16. Zott, C., Amit, R.: Business model innovation: toward a process perspective, pp. 395–406 (2015)

17. Tesch, J., Brillinger, A.: The evaluation aspect of digital business model innovation: a literature review on tools and methodologies. In: 25th European Conference on Information Systems, pp. 2250–2268 (2017)
18. Bocken, N.M.P., Antikainen, M.: Circular business model experimentation: concept and approaches. In: Dao, D., Howlett, R.J., Setchi, R., Vlacic, L. (eds.) KES-SDM 2018. SIST, vol. 130, pp. 239–250. Springer, Cham (2019). https://doi.org/10.1007/978-3-030-04290-5_25
19. Heikkila, M., Bouwman, H., Heikkila, J., Solaimani, S., Janssen, W.: Business model metrics: an open repository. Inf. Syst. E-bus. Manag. **14**(2), 337–366 (2016)
20. Diaz-Diaz, R., Muñoz, L., Pérez-González, D.: The business model evaluation tool for smart cities: application to SmartSantander use cases. Energies **10**(3), 262 (2017)
21. Wilbik, A., Gilsing, R., Grefen, P., Turetken, O., Ozkan, B.: Intentional linguistic summaries for collaborative business model radars. In: WCCI (2020)
22. DaSilva, C., Trkman, P.: Business model: what it is and what it is not. Long Range Plann. **47**(6), 379–389 (2014)
23. Kindström, D.: Towards a service-based business model – key aspects for future competitive advantage. Eur. Manag. J. **28**(6), 479–490 (2010)
24. Gebauer, H., Fleisch, E., Friedli, T.: Overcoming the service paradox in manufacturing companies. Eur. Manag. J. **23**(1), 14–26 (2005)
25. Grefen, P., Turetken, O.: Achieving business process agility through service engineering in extended business networks. In: BPTrends (2018)
26. Zolnowski, A., Weiß, C., Böhmann, T.: Representing service business models with the service business model canvas - the case of a mobile payment service in the retail industry. In: 47th Hawaii International Conference on System Science, pp. 718–727 (2014)
27. Grefen, P.: Service-Dominant Business Engineering with BASE/X: Business Modeling Handbook. Amazon CreateSpace (2015)
28. Schrauder, S., Kock, A., Baccarella, C., Voigt, K.: Takin' care of business models: the impact of business model evaluation on front-end success. J. Prod. Innov. Manag. **35**(3), 410–426 (2018)
29. Mateu, J., March-Chorda, I.: Searching for better business models assessment methods. Manag. Decis. **54**(10), 2433–2446 (2016)
30. Moellers, T., Von der Burg, L., Bansemir, B., Pretzl, M., Gassmann, O.: System dynamics for corporate business model innovation. Electron. Mark. **29**, 387–406 (2019). https://doi.org/10.1007/s12525-019-00329-y
31. Daas, D., Hurkmans, T., Overbeek, S., Bouwman, H.: Developing a decision support system for business model design. Electron. Mark. **23**, 251–265 (2013). https://doi.org/10.1007/s12525-012-0115-1
32. Schoormann, T., Kaufhold, A., Behrens, D., Knackstedt, R.: Towards a typology of approaches for sustainability-oriented business model evaluation. In: Abramowicz, W., Paschke, A. (eds.) BIS 2018. LNBIP, vol. 320, pp. 58–70. Springer, Cham (2018). https://doi.org/10.1007/978-3-319-93931-5_5
33. Yager, R.R.: A new approach to the summarization of data. Inf. Sci. **28**(1), 69–86 (1982)
34. Kacprzyk, J., Zadrożny, S.: Linguistic database summaries and their protoforms: towards natural language based knowledge discovery tools. Inf. Sci. **173**(4), 281–304 (2005)
35. Grefen, P., Turetken, O., Traganos, K., den Hollander, A., Eshuis, R.: Creating agility in traffic management by collaborative service-dominant business engineering. In: Camarinha-Matos, L.M., Bénaben, F., Picard, W. (eds.) PRO-VE 2015. IAICT, vol. 463, pp. 100–109. Springer, Cham (2015). https://doi.org/10.1007/978-3-319-24141-8_9
36. Gilsing, R., Turetken, O., Adali, O.E., Grefen, P.: A reference model for the design of service-dominant business models in the smart mobility domain. In: International Conference on Information Systems (2018)

Author Index

Printed in the United States
By Bookmasters